BUSINESS STATISTICS

HARCOURT BRACE COLLEGE OUTLINE SERIES

BUSINESS STATISTICS

Lawrence L. Lapin

San Jose State University

Harcourt Brace College Publishers

Fort Worth Philadelphia San Diego
New York Orlando Austin San Antonio
Toronto Montreal London Sydney Tokyo

Printed in the United States of America

Library of Congress Cataloging in Publication Data

Lapin, Lawrence L.
Business statistics.

(Harcourt Brace Jovanovich college outline series) (Books for professionals)
Includes index.
1. Commercial statistics. I. Title. II. Series. III. Series: Books for professionals.
HF1017.L36 1984   519.5′024658   84-6690

ISBN 0-15-601553-6

First edition

PREFACE

You are aware of how important statistics is in the business world. Whether you are a student, own your own business, or hold a responsible position in some organization, a better knowledge of statistics will enhance your ability to succeed. This is because quantitative skills are nearly as important for good business communication as speaking and writing—and statistics is one of the keys to acquiring these skills.

If you have never had a course in statistics, this book can help you learn what it is all about. If you once took a statistics course in school, you will find this book a valuable, self-contained refresher course. If you are a student, you will find that this book provides essential supplementary material for digesting statistics as you take the course at a college or university.

You will find several features of this book especially valuable. Every concept and procedure is richly illustrated by examples that are incorporated into the text discussions. A complete *Summary* appears at the end of each chapter to help you review all important concepts and expressions. Following the *Summary* is a *Raise Your Grades* section, consisting of a series of conceptual questions designed to reinforce what you have read. These are followed by a *Rapid Review* section, consisting of a series of short problems having multiple-choice answers. Each problem refers you to the place in the text where that procedure is discussed; thus, you can check your answers at any time.

Most of this book is devoted to the *Solved Problems*. This is the last section of each chapter and consists of problems that are intended to help you develop and apply your statistical skills. Each problem set starts easy, with problems becoming a little harder and more complicated along the way. You will find the solutions very complete as they work step-by-step toward the correct answers. All problems have been carefully developed to illustrate relevant business applications.

There are other attractive features of this book. It is written in an outline form for quick and easy assimilation of technical material. It is loaded with graphs, charts, and figures that clearly illustrate important concepts and problems. A symbolic glossary located at the back of the book explains every symbol used. Finally, this book contains two examinations to help you verify your statistical skills.

This book assumes no mathematical background other than a course in algebra. Algebra is necessary so that you will be able to use symbolic expressions for computing various quantities. A basic knowledge of statistics does not require that you actually solve algebra problems, however, and the statistical problems are confined largely to plugging numbers into equations. You learn which values go where and what equations to use. To help you, each important expression appears in the text discussion where it is introduced and is repeated again in the *Summary*.

I wish to thank the many people who made this book possible. Special thanks go to Susan Clark, who molded the text and the solved problems into their present form. I also wish to acknowledge the efforts of Janet Anaya, who proofread the manuscript, verifying it for technical accuracy, and who checked all problems and examples for accuracy.

LAWRENCE L. LAPIN

CONTENTS

CHAPTER 1 **Statistics: Purpose and Evaluation** 1

1-1: The Meaning and Role of Statistics 1

1-2: The Nature of Statistical Data 2

1-3: The Use of Samples 2

1-4: Selecting the Sample 3

1-5: Selecting Statistical Procedures 5

1-6: Describing Statistical Data 5

CHAPTER 2 **Summary Statistical Measures** **24**

2-1: The Arithmetic Mean 24

2-2: The Median and the Mode 25

2-3: The Range, Variance, and Standard Deviation 27

2-4: The Proportion 30

2-5: Other Common Statistical Measures 30

CHAPTER 3 **Probability: Fundamental Concepts** **38**

3-1: The Language of Probability: Basic Terms 38

3-2: Compound Events and Event Relationships 42

3-3: Probabilities for Compound Events 46

CHAPTER 4 **Probability: Applications and Extension** **60**

4-1: Probabilities Computed Under Given Conditions 60

4-2: The Joint Probability Table 62

4-3: The General Multiplication Law 63

4-4: Probability Trees and Sampling 64

CHAPTER 5 **Special Topics in Probability** **84**

5-1: Counting Methods for Finding Probabilities 84

5-2: Revising Probabilities Using Bayes' Theorem 90

CHAPTER 6   **Probability Distributions, Expected Value, and Sampling**   **104**

6-1: Probability Distributions   104

6-2: Expected Value and Variance   106

6-3: Sampling Distribution of the Mean   108

CHAPTER 7   **Binomial Probabilities: The Sampling Distribution of the Proportion**   **121**

7-1: The Binomial Distribution   121

7-2: Important Properties of the Binomial Distribution   124

7-3: Sampling Distribution of the Proportion   128

CHAPTER 8   **The Normal Distribution**   **138**

8-1: The Normal Curve   138

8-2: Finding Areas Under the Normal Curve   140

8-3: The Sampling Distribution of the Mean: Central Limit Theorem   145

8-4: The Sampling Distribution of the Proportion: The Normal Approximation   147

MIDTERM EXAMINATION   **162**

CHAPTER 9   **Statistical Estimation**   **164**

9-1: Estimators and Estimates   164

9-2: Interval Estimates of the Mean   165

9-3: Small Sample Statistics: Student t Distribution   168

9-4: Interval Estimates of the Proportion   170

CHAPTER 10   **Statistical Testing**   **180**

10-1: Basic Concepts: Hypothesis Testing with the Mean   180

10-2: Standard Procedure for Testing the Mean—Large Sample Sizes   185

10-3: Small Sample Test of the Mean   189

10-4: Testing with the Proportion   190

CHAPTER 11   **Regression and Correlation**   **202**

11-1: Regression Analysis   202

11-2: Correlation Analysis   206

11-3: Multiple Regression Analysis   208

CHAPTER 12   **Time-Series Analysis**   229
    12-1: The Basic Time-Series
              Model   229
    12-2: Analysis of Trend   230
    12-3: Forecasting Using Seasonal
              Indexes   234
    12-4: Cyclical and Irregular
              Fluctuation   235
    12-5: Exponential Smoothing   235

CHAPTER 13   **Index Numbers**   247
    13-1: Aggregate Price Indexes   247
    13-2: Deflating Time Series   249

CHAPTER 14   **Two-Sample Investigations**   256
    14-1: Comparing Two Means
              Using Large Samples   256
    14-2: Comparing Two Means
              Using Small Samples   260
    14-3: Comparing Two
              Proportions   263
    14-4: Comparisons Using
              Non-parametric Statistics   264

CHAPTER 15   **Chi-Square Applications**   286
    15-1: The Chi-Square Test for
              Independence   286
    15-2: Testing for the Equality of
              Several Proportions   289
    15-3: Estimating the Variance
              and Standard Deviation   290
    15-4: Testing the Variance   291

CHAPTER 16   **Analysis of Variance**   307
    16-1: Testing for the Equality of
              Several Means   307
    16-2: Two-Way Analysis of
              Variance   311

FINAL EXAMINATION   326

SYMBOLIC GLOSSARY   329

APPENDIX A   **Areas Under the Standard
              Normal Curve**   333

APPENDIX B   **Student *t* Distribution**   334

APPENDIX C   **Chi-Square Distribution**   335

APPENDIX D   **F Distribution**   336

INDEX   338

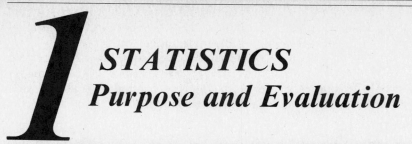

1 STATISTICS
Purpose and Evaluation

THIS CHAPTER IS ABOUT

- ☑ **The Meaning and Role of Statistics**
- ☑ **The Nature of Statistical Data**
- ☑ **The Use of Samples**
- ☑ **Selecting the Sample**
- ☑ **Selecting Statistical Procedures**
- ☑ **Describing Statistical Data**

Some knowledge of statistics is almost essential for today's college or university student—regardless of your major. Schools of business integrate statistics throughout their courses, applying it to an extent rarely encountered in other disciplines. Even those persons no longer working on degrees will find that a solid foundation in statistics enhances their careers and better equips them to cope with the modern world—both on and off the job.

This book treats statistics as a field of study, much like accounting, marketing, and economics. But it is much more than an academic subject, such as history or algebra. Statistics plays a fundamental role in evaluating numerical information. Some think that statistics approaches the importance of language itself. In today's world those who are uninformed about statistics are to a great extent "educationally handicapped."

1-1. The Meaning and Role of Statistics

When hearing the word *statistics*, you probably get visions of masses of numbers and tables, perhaps even a stack of computer printouts. Indeed, the term *statistics* is used to describe almost any collection of data. However, books on the subject use a more refined working definition of statistics.

A. The working definition of statistics differs from the popular conception.

In its modern sense, **statistics** is the use of numerical evidence in making decisions. Besides data, statistics includes all methods and procedures that are useful in translating numerical facts into action. Statistics must also include the concepts and theory needed to explain and justify that underlying methodology.

The connection with decision making distinguishes statistics from more passive number-based activities, such as preparing a payroll, balancing your checkbook, or bookkeeping. The main distinction between the working definition of statistics and its popular usage is its form; singular versus plural. Statistics (singular) is a subject of study; statistics (plural) are numerical facts.

B. There are several types of statistics.

Even if you've never studied the subject, there is one broad area of statistics with which you are probably familiar. This is called **descriptive statistics**, which is largely concerned with sorting and simplifying data and with making graphical displays. Unless you have had some formal training, you are probably unfamiliar with **inferential statistics**, which involves drawing conclusions based on incomplete sample evidence. Although you will start by working with descriptive statistics, much of this book is concerned with inferential statistics. The latter is essential when making decisions under uncertainty.

There are, in addition, two other areas of statistics that you will study. **Deductive statistics** uses probability to establish how likely it is that you will get a particular sample result from a known population. This process is reversed when you use **inductive statistics** to generalize about the unknown population from the known sample.

1-2. The Nature of Statistical Data

The single data point, or **observation**, is the basic element of statistics. An observation may be a numerical value, such as a family's income, a person's height, or a loan's annual percentage rate. It might also be an attribute, such as a person's occupation or marital status, an industrial category (e.g., textiles, banking, publishing), or a brand preference.

A. A collection of observations may be either a population or a sample.

A complete collection of observations—one that includes every data point in a certain grouping—is a statistical **population**. However, it is seldom possible to observe all data points of a population. For instance, it would be difficult to establish the population of earnings of all CPA's in the United States. But a partial collection of observations from this grouping could be readily established. Such an incomplete set of observations constitutes a statistical **sample**.

It is important to understand that the population (or the sample) consists *only* of the observations. It is the *incomes* of CPA's, not the persons themselves, that constitute the population just discussed. The individuals are the **elementary units** and can give rise to a variety of different populations, such as years of education, size of firm, or years in practice. Elementary units need not be people; they can be *things*, such as investments or computer runs or lightbulbs. Thus, you might be concerned with the following populations: rates of return from investments of a particular kind, the processing times of computer runs, or the lifetimes of a brand of lightbulbs.

B. Statistical groupings may be classified by the type of observation.

When the observations are numerical values, the population or sample is a **quantitative** one. Attribute observations form **qualitative** populations and samples. You will use parallel but distinct statistical procedures in evaluating quantitative versus qualitative data.

1-3. The Use of Samples

Sample observations are ordinarily the only ones available. For a variety of reasons it is rare to make a complete enumeration, or **census**, of population data. Economic considerations usually dictate how many observations can be made. Seldom is there enough money available to observe an entire population.

A. There are several noneconomic reasons for sampling.

A sample may be *more timely*, because it can be collected more quickly. Taking a census of a very large population can take so long that any results would be obtained too late to use them in choosing an action. For example, television program ratings are based on sample data; they usually reflect the viewing selections in only a few hundred homes. This is because networks must make their programming decisions within a few days of a program's appearance. Even if a polling agency could ignore the enormous cost, and even if it were practical, it would take months, even years, to conduct a nationwide census of one night's TV selections.

A sample may thus be necessary because of a *large population*. Some populations, like the TV viewing audience, could be fully observed, but not within a reasonable time frame. Other populations are theoretically infinite, and so could never be fully observed. Consider the quality of items leaving a production line that will continue to operate indefinitely.

Some populations involve elementary units that may be impossible to observe. These comprise a *partly inaccessible population*, for which a census is impossible. A vivid illustration is provided by airplane crashes. Since accident investigators can't find the wreckage of some aircraft, they can only observe the accessible portion of the population of crash causes. These data constitute a sample.

Another very compelling reason for sampling is that the very act of observation might ruin the elementary units. Such *destructive observations* are encountered in quality testing, where the lifetime of a lightbulb can only be determined after the bulb has burned out. Likewise, a marketing research interview can seriously bias a subject's future perspective regarding a product.

B. A sample might not accurately reflect its population.

There is one glaring disadvantage of using samples. *There are no guarantees that a sample will be typical of the population or accurate in portraying it.* Statisticians are concerned with **sampling error**, or the difference between the sample and the population that is due to the particular elementary units selected for observation. Statistical procedures are designed to minimize sampling error or to keep it within acceptable limits.

One way to control sampling error is to avoid **sampling bias**, the tendency to favor particular elementary units over the rest in making observations. Sampling bias might occur whenever the convenient or "easy to get" observations prevail. Underrepresentation by the units that are difficult to observe may lead to the **bias of nonresponse**. Imagine a convenience food manufacturer who collects opinions only during the day from persons who happen to be at home; such a procedure practically excludes working people—the major consumers of convenience foods—from such a sample.

Nonsampling error, which arises from inaccuracies in the observation process itself, can be equally serious. Good statistical procedure requires attention to the details of measurement and data gathering and processing. Studies based on persons' answers to questions are ripe grounds for nonsampling error. Keep in mind that people may shade the truth for a variety of psychological reasons. A glaring example is **prestige bias**, where subjects give untruthful responses to impress the interviewer.

1-4. Selecting the Sample

How should the sample be selected? This will be your first statistical procedure.

A. There are several different types of samples.

Statisticians categorize samples in three ways. One grouping is the **convenience sample**, in which only the more convenient elementary units are observed. A senator's mail provides a convenience sample of constituent opinions. Similarly, the political views of your friends provide a convenience sample that might influence some of your own opinions. The advantages of such samples are obvious. You should be aware, however, of the tremendous potential for sampling bias. For instance, an outspoken and well-organized group may conduct a letter-writing campaign on behalf of an issue not favored by the majority of the senator's constituents.

A second type, the **judgment sample**, is frequently used in business. Such a collection of observations arises when the investigator tries to select units that give a "representative sample." The stocks comprising the Dow-Jones Industrial Average are a judgment sample of the New York Stock Exchange listings. So are those items included in the "market basket" used to compute the Consumer Price Index. Such samples have an important role to play, but they could be fraught with sampling error and bias.

The lion's share of statistical procedures is based on the **random sample**, wherein all elementary units have an equal chance of being selected for observation. Only random samples are free from sampling bias, although some sampling error may be unavoidable. But with random samples the potential for error can be quantified using probabilities.

B. Random numbers are used to select a random sample.

Faced with the prospect of selecting a random sample of person's ages, you could write each subject's name down on a slip of paper, place the slips in a hat and mix thoroughly, and then draw names one at a time until you reach the quota. You would then obtain the age of each selected person.

You must agree that such a lottery would be cumbersome. And a large population might require a very big hat indeed! Furthermore, your findings could be challenged solely because of the selection procedure. (The 1970 Draft Lottery was nearly invalidated because of faulty mixing.)

Statisticians achieve the same type of lottery result with no controversy and a lot less fuss. Each sample is selected according to a list of **random numbers**. These are originally generated by an electromechanical device in such a way that each integer has an equal chance of being the next number. The sample selection begins after all elementary units have been given an identification number. The sample units are those whose identification numbers match the random numbers on the investigator's list.

To illustrate, consider the names of the symphony conductors listed in Figure 1-1. Each name has been assigned a two-digit identification number. Following is a list of a random sample involving 10 names:

12651	Cantelli	**74**146	Sanderling
81769	Serafin	**90**759	Svetlanov
36737	Kletzki	**55**683	Newman
82861	Silvestri	**79**686	Schmidt-Isserstedt
21325	Frühbeck de Burgos	**70**333	Rodzinski

The random numbers listed alongside each name were read from an existing table of random numbers. The first two digits were used to establish matching names. Since the source table gives five-digit values, the other three places were ignored.

Figure 1-1

00. Abbado	25. Golschmann	50. Mehta	75. Santini
01. André	26. Hannikainen	51. Mitropoulos	76. Sargent
02. Anosov	27. Hollingsworth	52. Monteux	77. Scherchen
03. Ansermet	28. Horenstein	53. Morel	78. Schippers
04. Argenta	29. Horvat	54. Mravinsky	**79.** Schmidt Isserstedt
05. Barbirolli	30. Jacquillat	**55.** Newman	80. Sejna
06. Beecham	31. Jorda	56. Ormandy	**81.** Serafin
07. Bernstein	32. Karajan	57. Ozawa	**82.** Silvestri
08. Black	33. Kempe	58. Patanè	83. Skrowaczewski
09. Bloomfield	34. Kertesz	59. Pedrotti	84. Slatkin
10. Bonynge	35. Klemperer	60. Perlea	85. Smetáček
11. Boult	**36.** Kletzki	61. Prêtre	86. Solti
12. Cantelli	37. Klima	62. Previn	87. Stein
13. Cluytens	38. Kondrashin	63. Previtali	88. Steinberg
14. Dorati	39. Kostelanetz	64. Prohaska	89. Stokowski
15. Dragon	40. Koussevitzky	65. Reiner	**90.** Svetlanov
16. Erede	41. Krips	66. Reinhardt	91. Swarowsky
17. Ferencsik	42. Kubelik	67. Rekai	92. Szell
18. Fiedler	43. Lane	68. Rignold	93. Toscanini
19. Fistoulari	44. Leinsdorf	69. Ristenpart	94. Van Otterloo
20. Fricsay	45. Maag	**70.** Rodzinski	95. Van Remoortel
21. Frühbeck de Burgos	46. Maazel	71. Rosenthal	96. Vogel
22. Furtwängler	47. Mackerras	72. Rowicki	97. Von Matacic
23. Gamba	48. Markevitch	73. Rozhdestvensky	98. Walter
24. Giulini	49. Martin	**74.** Sanderling	99. Watanabee

A very good source of random numbers is the RAND Corporation book, *A Million Random Digits with 100,000 Normal Deviates*. In reading such a list, you ordinarily select the starting point at random. You skip any random number having a value already encountered or having no matching identification. There is no other reason for passing over a random number. Although the values might repeat, you should never use a random number from one spot more than once.

• Most statistics books will have a table of random numbers listed in the back.

C. There are several types of random samples.

A random sample where each remaining elementary unit has an equal chance of being selected each time is called a **simple random sample**. The random sample of conductors' names is of this type.

For ease of selection, an investigator might decide to use instead a **systematic random sample**, picking the first code number at random and then proceeding to take every 10th (50th, 100th, etc.) unit thereafter. Although some obscure bias may influence such a procedure, the sample obtained is ordinarily treated the same as a simple random sample.

There may be compelling reasons to deviate from the simple random sample. A statistician might want to guarantee that various population segments, or **strata**, are included in the final sample. To this end she would achieve a **stratified sample** by taking separate simple random samples from each segment. A stratified sample might be used by an auditor who wants to select journal entries so that all size categories are guaranteed to be included in the observations.

Economic considerations often lead to another deviation from a simple random sample. This is the **cluster sample**. The statistician achieves such a sample by first identifying a few **clusters** or small contiguous groupings of elementary units. He then chooses some of these clusters at random and selects all of the elementary units in each chosen cluster for observation. Cluster samples are often used in marketing research and political polling. In assessing the attitudes of a city's apartment dwellers, it is far less costly to use the opinions of all residents in a few apartment complexes than it is to interview randomly selected individuals from all over the city.

- Both the stratified sample and the cluster sample are prone to sampling bias.
- The statistical procedures described in the remainder of this book are based on the simple random sample.

1-5. Selecting Statistical Procedures

Much of the statistical art is concerned with the selection of procedure. In this book you will encounter a variety of methods. The primary focus of the beginning chapters will be investigations involving a single population and one simple random sample. Later you will encounter procedures involving *several* populations. Then you will see how to use the known values from one or more populations to predict an unknown value from yet another population. For example, you will learn how to use sample data to predict a student's college GPA using the known high-school GPA and SAT score (Chapter 11).

A very broad area of statistical investigation is the comparison of two populations. A personnel director might want to determine if a new training technique improves job performance more than the current procedure. Or a designer might need to know whether an "improved" product in fact is more reliable or has a longer lifetime than the present one. Or a purchasing manager may need to determine whether a new supplier will provide better quality than the source now used. The sample from the existing population is sometimes referred to as the **control group**. The observations representing the proposed population constitute the **experimental group**.

You will encounter two basic approaches for selecting the samples. You should find it easiest to select the units by **independent sampling**, so that no information about the other population influences which sample units are selected.

You might instead achieve greater information from fewer data points by using **matched-pairs sampling**. Here, you pair units from the two populations in advance and perform a **controlled experiment** by placing one partner into the control group and the other into the experimental group. For example, you could evaluate two training programs by comparing the performance of similar partners or "near twins" who each learn by one of the methods. Matched-pairs sampling is ordinarily more expensive than independent sampling.

1-6. Describing Statistical Data

In order to be able to communicate the results of a sampling study, you must first reduce the data to a useful form. Consider the following table, which gives the ages of a sample of 100 statistics students. What do you think is important to know in describing this group to someone?

Age (years)

20.9	33.4	18.7	24.2	22.1	18.9	21.9	20.5	21.9	37.3
57.2	25.3	24.6	29.0	26.3	19.1	48.7	23.5	23.1	28.6
21.3	22.4	22.3	20.0	30.3	31.7	34.3	28.5	36.1	32.6
33.7	19.6	18.7	24.3	27.1	20.7	22.2	19.2	26.5	27.4
22.8	51.3	44.4	22.9	20.6	32.8	27.3	23.5	23.8	22.4
18.1	23.9	20.8	41.5	20.4	21.3	19.3	24.2	22.3	23.1
22.9	21.3	29.7	25.6	33.7	24.2	24.5	21.2	21.5	25.8
21.5	21.5	27.0	19.9	29.2	25.3	26.4	22.7	27.9	22.0
23.3	28.1	24.8	19.6	23.7	26.3	30.1	29.7	24.8	24.7
23.5	22.9	26.0	25.2	23.6	21.0	30.9	21.7	28.3	22.1

A. The frequency distribution provides some organization to the sample data.

A statistical investigation might begin by establishing some kind of pattern from the masses of unorganized **raw data**. This is usually achieved by grouping the observations. With quantitative data the groupings take the form of **class intervals**. In this illustration, each interval is two years wide, so that each age falls into one of the intervals: 18.0–under 20.0, 20.0–under 22.0, and so on. Keeping a running tally of the number of observations falling into each category, you can construct the following table.

Age	Tally	Number of persons (Class frequency)
18.0–under 20.0	⦀⦀ ⦀⦀	10
20.0–under 22.0	⦀⦀ ⦀⦀ ⦀⦀ ⦀⦀⦀	18
22.0–under 24.0	⦀⦀ ⦀⦀ ⦀⦀ ⦀⦀ ⦀⦀⦀	23
24.0–under 26.0	⦀⦀ ⦀⦀ ⦀⦀⦀⦀	14
26.0–under 28.0	⦀⦀ ⦀⦀	10
28.0–under 30.0	⦀⦀ ⦀⦀⦀	8
30.0–under 32.0	⦀⦀⦀⦀	4
32.0–under 34.0	⦀⦀	5
34.0–under 36.0	⦀	1
36.0–under 38.0	⦀⦀	2
38.0–under 58.0	⦀⦀	5
	Total	100

This table provides the **sample frequency distribution**. If all the *population* observations were made, they might be similarly arranged. Details of the **population frequency distribution** are generally unknown, although you may glean some essential characteristics from the sample.

Ordinarily, class intervals are of the same width. But beginning and ending intervals may be wider because of the scarcity of large or small values. The last interval, 38.0–under 58.0, is 20 years wide.

B. Frequency distributions provide convenient graphical displays.

You can graph sample frequency distributions in two useful ways. The most common is the **histogram**. Figure 1-2 shows the histogram for the ages of the statistics students. The horizontal axis represents the observed quantity (age), and the vertical axis represents the **class frequency**, or number of observations in each category. The standard-sized class intervals are each represented by a bar whose height is equal to the class frequency. The bar for the last intervals is 10 times the standard width, and it therefore has a height that is 1/10 of its class frequency of 5: $5/10 = 1/2$.

Some investigators prefer to use the **frequency polygon**, shown for the same data in Figure 1-3. Each class interval is represented by a dot positioned above the interval's midpoint at a height equal to the class frequency. The first dot falls at $(18.0 + 20.0)/2 = 19.0$ years, the second at $(20.0 + 22.0)/2 = 21.0$ years, and so on. The last dot lies above the midpoint $(38.0 + 58.0)/2 = 48.0$ for the extra-wide final interval; its height is 1/2, as before. The dots are then connected, with beginning and ending line segments connecting the horizontal axis at half of the standard interval width below the lowest limit and above the highest.

Figure 1-2

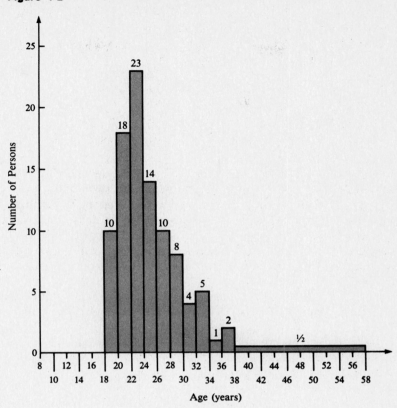

Figure 1-3

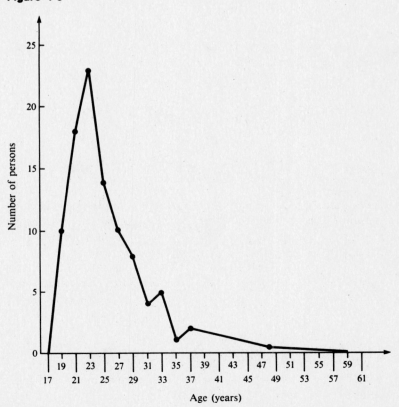

C. Frequency distributions also apply to qualitative observations.

When the sample observations are qualitative, you treat each category like a class interval. The following sample frequency distribution applies to the majors of a sample of 100 business majors at a university.

Major	Frequency
Accounting	17
Finance	4
Management	38
Marketing	27
Human resources	14
Total	100

D. Relative and cumulative frequency distributions are sometimes useful.

You find **relative frequency** for a class interval or category by dividing the number of observations by the total sample size. When using sample data, you can ordinarily make meaningful comparisons by using relative frequencies rather than class frequencies. For example, you are told that 13 first-year CPA's earned between $30,000 and $40,000, while 23 first-year sales persons had similar incomes. Can you conclude that sales provides a better income than accounting?

Now you are told that the CPA incomes were based on a sample of 57 persons, while the sample size for the salespersons was 133. The relative frequencies are as follows:

$$\frac{13}{57} = .23 \text{ for CPA's} \quad \text{and} \quad \frac{23}{133} = .17 \text{ for salespersons}$$

According to the sample data, which group had the greatest concentration of higher incomes?

The following table provides the **relative frequency distribution** for the student ages given earlier.

Age	Class frequency	Relative frequency
18.0–under 20.0	10	10/100 = .10
20.0–under 22.0	18	.18
22.0–under 24.0	23	.23
24.0–under 26.0	14	.14
26.0–under 28.0	10	.10
28.0–under 30.0	8	.08
30.0–under 32.0	4	.04
32.0–under 34.0	5	.05
34.0–under 36.0	1	.01
36.0–under 38.0	2	.02
38.0–under 58.0	5	.05
Totals	100	1.00

Notice that the relative frequencies sum to 1.00. If the sample is an accurate representation of the population of the ages of all statistics students, then .10 is the proportion of the population that is from 26.0 to 28.0 years old. If the population consists of 345,000 members, then there are .10(345,000) = 34,500 students in that age class.

You might be more interested in establishing the number of students who are in or below a particular age group. To do this, you first find the **cumulative frequency**. This value, used only with numerical data, is the sum of the class frequencies for an interval and all lower ones. For the statistics student ages, the cumulative frequency for the interval 26.0–under 28.0 is the sum

$$10 + 18 + 23 + 14 + 10 = 75$$

An even more useful description of the sample data is the **cumulative relative frequency**, which you find either by dividing the cumulative frequency by the number of observations or by summing the corresponding relative frequencies. For the interval 26.0–under 28.0, the cumulative relative frequency is

$$\frac{75}{100} = .75 \qquad \text{or} \qquad .10 + .18 + .23 + .14 + .10 = .75$$

Thus, .75 or 75% of the students are under the age of 28.0 years.

A complete listing of cumulative relative frequencies provides the **cumulative frequency distribution**. For the statistics student ages, the table on page 10 applies.

Figure 1-4

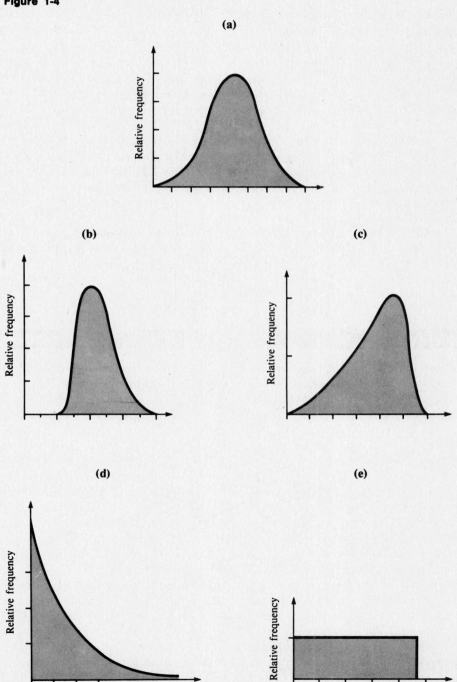

Age	Cumulative relative frequency
18.0–under 20.0	.10
20.0–under 22.0	.28
22.0–under 24.0	.51
24.0–under 26.0	.65
26.0–under 28.0	.75
28.0–under 30.0	.83
30.0–under 32.0	.87
32.0–under 34.0	.92
34.0–under 36.0	.93
36.0–under 38.0	.95
38.0–under 58.0	1.00

E. Populations are categorized by their frequency distributions, which are represented by frequency curves of various shapes.

Although complete population data are usually not obtained, the underlying **shape** of a population frequency distribution may be represented by a **frequency curve**. Some examples of frequency curves are shown in Figure 1-4. Such curves are idealizations of the histogram or frequency polygon obtained when the population values are divided into a great many narrow class intervals. The relative frequency is ordinarily used for the vertical axis.

The "bell-shaped" curve in Figure 1-4(a) applies to a population having a **normal distribution**. Such a curve is often appropriate for distributions of physical measurements. The frequency curve in (b) represents a **positively skewed distribution**, often encountered with financial data where there is practically no upper limit. The **negatively skewed distribution** shown in Figure 1-4(c) is representative of populations having a definite upper limit on the size of values.

Curve (d) in Figure 1-4 applies to an **exponential distribution**, where zero is the absolute lower limit and there is no theoretical upper limit. Lifetimes of electrical components often fit this shape. In (e) a **uniform distribution** applies. All values over the possible range occur with the same frequency. This distribution might be used to represent the values obtained from a random-number generator.

SUMMARY

Though in popular usage statistics are masses of numbers, to investigators, students, and practicioners, *statistics* is the use of numerical evidence in making decisions. Two broad areas of statistics are *descriptive* and *inferential* statistics. The first is concerned with presenting and summarizing data, the latter with making generalizations using partial data. Two other areas involve *deductive* statistics, which employs probability, and *inductive* statistics, which is used to make inferences.

Statistical data may be quantitative or qualitative. The basic building block is the *observation*, a measurement or classification made up of an *elementary unit*. A complete collection of possible observations is called a *population*. Ordinarily, only a limited number of observations are actually made; these constitute a *sample*.

There are several compelling reasons for sampling. The usual reason is that a sample is less expensive than a complete enumeration or *census* of the population. Samples are also more timely and more desirable when the population is large or not totally accessible. The use of samples is mandatory when the observation itself is destructive.

Although there are no guarantees that a sample will be typical or accurate, good statistical procedures control *sampling error*—the difference between the population and the sample that is due to the particular units selected for observation. You can control sampling error by eliminating *sampling bias*, thereby giving all units the same chance of being selected. You can avoid *nonsampling error* by eliminating inaccuracies in the observation process itself.

There are three broad categories of samples: the *convenience sample*, where the easiest observations are made; the *judgment sample*, where particular sample units are chosen to "guarantee" a representative sample; and the *random sample*, where all elementary units have an equal chance of being observed and included in the sample. Only the random sample is free from sampling bias, but it still may involve some unavoidable sampling error.

The most common type of random sample is the *simple random sample*, which allows an equal chance that any particular unit will·be observed. The sample units are often chosen using a list of *random numbers*. A *systematic random sample* uses a single random number to establish a sequential starting point. A *stratified sample* guarantees inclusion of units from various *strata*. A *cluster sample* involves the complete enumeration of a few randomly selected *clusters*.

Most statistical methodology assumes that simple random samples will be used. Although one population and sample is the usual case, some statistical investigations involve multiple populations. One common investigation compares a *control group* to an *experimental group*. Often the two samples are selected independently. An efficient alternative is the *controlled experiment*, which uses *matched-pairs sampling*.

A first step in organizing the *raw data* obtained from a statistical investigation is to establish the *frequency distribution*. All observations are classified by category or size. Numerical values are placed into *class intervals*. The number of observations in a particular group is the *class frequency*. Two graphical displays are commonly obtained from sample data. One is the *histogram*, a chart having a bar for each class; each bar is as tall as the number of observations found for that group. A similar picture is provided by the *frequency polygon*, which is applicable only when the data are quantitative.

Comparisons are best made using *relative frequencies* instead of the original tallies. A complete collection of these constitutes the *relative frequency distribution*. Another useful set of values applicable to quantitative observations are the *cumulative frequencies*. Even more helpful are the *cumulative relative frequencies*, which collectively provide a table called the *cumulative frequency distribution*.

Frequency distributions are not ordinarily known for populations, since a census is not usually taken. Nevertheless, the form of the underlying distribution may be known. Populations are often represented by familiar *frequency curves*, such as the bell-shaped normal curve.

RAISE YOUR GRADES

Can you explain...?

☑ the difference between a sample and a population
☑ why sampling might be necessary
☑ how you could generate your own list of random numbers
☑ what distinguishes a collection of elementary units from the population
☑ why both descriptive and inferential statistics might be needed in an investigation

Do you know...?

☑ the various reasons for sampling
☑ where to start when using a table of random numbers
☑ the advantages of cluster sampling
☑ the difference between a systematic and a stratified sample
☑ the difference between sampling error and sampling bias

RAPID REVIEW

1. Which one of the following is not a legitimate reason for sampling?   [Section 1-3A]

    (a) economy   **(c)** avoidance of nonsampling error
    (b) timeliness   **(d)** destructive observations

2. The following are populations of the student body in a particular university system: ages, majors, sexes, names, incomes, and heights. Which are the qualitative populations? [Section 1-2B]

   (a) ages, incomes, heights   (c) majors, incomes
   (b) sexes, ages   (d) majors, sexes

3. The relative frequency of accounting majors in a business school having 600 students is .15. What is the frequency or number of accounting majors? [Section 1-6D]

   (a) 150   (b) 9   (c) 15   (d) 90

4. For a certain population of 11,000 student ages, the class interval 60–under 65 has a cumulative frequency of 11,000, and another, 55–under 60, has a cumulative frequency of 10,879. What is the relative frequency of observations between 60 and 65? [Section 1-6D]

   (a) 11   (b) .011   (c) 121   (d) .10879

5. A government agency has classified all firms employing 10 or more persons into 40 categories (cannery, consulting, electronics, manufacturing, etc.). Which one of the following statements is meaningless? [Section 1-6D]

   (a) The relative frequency of electronics firms is .03.
   (b) The frequency of retail food stores is 9,853.
   (c) The cumulative frequency of manufacturing establishments is .32.
   (d) The total number of firms is 113,727.

6. Nonsampling error [Section 1-3B] may occur in
   (a) a simple random sample.
   (b) a census.
   (c) either of the above.
   (d) none of the above.

7. The bias of nonresponse [Section 1-3B] may be minimized by
   (a) more accurate observations.
   (b) improved interview technique.
   (c) either of the above.
   (d) none of the above.

8. A researcher investigating a population of a few hundred people needs to obtain a simple random sample of product preferences. Which procedure could *not* be used? [Section 1-4B]
   (a) Conducting a physical lottery using capsules containing the names of all persons in the population.
   (b) Assigning a number to each person and then selecting a sample using random numbers.
   (c) Dialing randomly chosen telephone numbers of persons in the group and interviewing only those who answer.

9. Statisticians regard a population census [Section 1-3A] as
   (a) usually unnecessary.
   (b) often a waste of resources.
   (c) both of the above.
   (d) none of the above.

10. Which one of the following doesn't involve sampling error? [Section 1-3B]
    (a) census
    (b) stratified sample
    (c) simple random sample
    (d) cluster sample

Answers

1. (c)   2. (d)   3. (d)   4. (b)   5. (c)
6. (c)   7. (d)   8. (c)   9. (c)   10. (a)

SOLVED PROBLEMS

PROBLEM 1-1   Use the first two digits of the following random numbers to select a simple random sample of symphony conductors from those listed in Figure 1-1.

03478	82378
67301	68113
44366	51235
12879	94572
33478	29683

List the names selected.

Solution: Matching the first two digits of the random numbers to the numbers in the list, you select the following names.

03. Ansermet	82. Silvestri
67. Rekai	68. Rignold
44. Leinsdorf	51. Mitropoulos
12. Cantelli	94. Van Otterloo
33. Kempe	29. Horvat

PROBLEM 1-2   List the names for a systematic random sample of ten symphony conductors chosen from those in Figure 1-1. Assume that the first selection is Leonard Bernstein, and that every tenth name is included.

Solution: The following names apply.

07. Bernstein	57. Ozawa
17. Ferencsik	67. Rekai
27. Hollingsworth	77. Scherchen
37. Klima	87. Stein
47. Mackerras	97. Von Matacic

PROBLEM 1-3   Suppose that each successive ten names in Figure 1-1 makes up a stratum. Renumber the names in each stratum, starting with 0 and ending with 9, maintaining the original alphabetical sequence. Then select a stratified sample that contains one conductor from each group. Use the following random numbers in selecting the random sample.

$$2, 3, 3, 6, 4, 9, 7, 6, 5, 0$$

Solution: The following names apply.

2 Anosov	9 Pedrotti
3 Cluytens	7 Rekai
3 Gamba	6 Sargent
6 Kletzki	5 Smetáček
4 Leinsdorf	0 Svetlanov

PROBLEM 1-4   Treat each successive five names in Figure 1-1 as a cluster. Make up a cluster sample by selecting two clusters at random and including all units in each. Proceeding alphabetically, number each successive cluster from 00 to 19. Then use the random numbers 11 and 05 to select the sample. List the names obtained.

Solution: The following names apply.

55. Newman	25. Golschmann
56. Ormandy	26. Hannikainen
57. Ozawa	27. Hollingsworth
58. Patanè	28. Horenstein
59. Pedrotti	29. Horvat

PROBLEM 1-5 Consider the following population for the operating incomes of doughnut franchises.

Franchise number	Income	Franchise number	Income	Franchise number	Income	Franchise number	Income
01	$21,844	14	$10,694	27	$19,574	39	$14,249
02	8,914	15	17,801	28	7,987	40	21,347
03	16,026	16	5,993	29	15,949	41	9,980
04	5,964	17	13,961	30	5,763	42	17,936
05	11,971	18	3,843	31	13,427	43	7,681
06	19,921	19	11,513	32	21,068	44	15,339
07	9,598	20	19,160	33	36,429	45	22,975
08	17,250	21	14,693	34	8,141	46	7,848
09	7,257	22	7,020	35	19,745	47	20,563
10	6,833	23	13,942	36	8,632	48	6,121
11	9,651	24	13,754	37	11,884	49	9,089
12	6,519	25	9,512	38	2,337	50	7,773
13	17,246	26	12,472				

Use the following list of two-digit random numbers to select a sample of 10 incomes for further analysis. Start with the random numbers in the first row, and skip any random number equal to a value already used or which doesn't match a franchise number. List the sample observations.

97	78	17	40	30	23	80	32	94	31
20	91	46	75	29	15	31	82	44	77

Solution: You obtain the following sample observations.

Franchise number	Income
17	$13,961
40	21,347
30	5,763
23	13,942
32	21,068
31	13,427
20	19,160
46	7,848
29	15,949
15	17,801

PROBLEM 1-6 Figure 1-5 is a map of a hypothetical city, Dullsville. The homes have been arbitrarily placed into "census tracts," each representing a contiguous neighborhood. Figure 1-6 provides household codes, addresses, and income data.

Matching the following random numbers with household codes, select a simple random sample of 10 household incomes.

34	01	17	73	93	05	54	89	42	29

Solution: You select the following sample.

Household	Income
34	$ 7,088
01	15,772
17	12,225
73	15,876
93	22,115
05	7,644
54	24,665
89	13,665
42	21,119
29	4,675

Figure 1-5

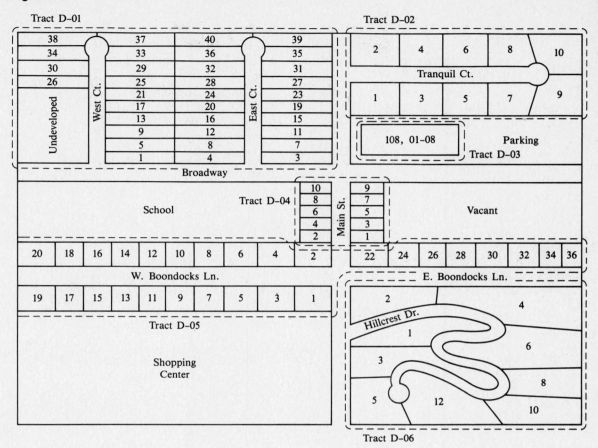

Figure 1-6

Household	Address	Income	Household	Address	Income
	East Boondocks Lane		22	14	8,553
01	22	$15,772	23	15	11,863
02	24	14,667	24	16	13,119
03	26	21,539	25	17	12,225
04	28	11,814	26	18	10,887
05	30	7,644	27	19	11,008
06	32	12,888	28	20	11,080
07	34	11,119		*Main Street*	
08	36	10,024	29	1	4,675
	West Boondocks Lane		30	2	6,778
09	1	9,836	31	3	5,558
10	2	8,448	32	4	8,905
11	3	10,887	33	5	5,731
12	4	13,464	34	6	7,088
13	5	11,118	35	7	6,775
14	6	12,747	36	8	9,222
15	7	10,777	37	9	9,776
16	8	9,007	38	10	5,783
17	9	12,225	39	108-01	14,453
18	10	12,345	40	108-02	10,113
19	11	10,554	41	108-03	8,985
20	12	13,098	42	108-04	21,119
21	13	10,567	43	108-05	16,668

Figure 1-6 (*cont.*)

Household	Address	Income	Household	Address	Income
	Main Street		72	32	18,444
44	108-06	10,560	73	35	15,876
45	108-07	14,554	74	36	16,123
46	108-08	11,800	75	39	20,001
	Tranquil Court		76	40	18,888
47	1	24,776		*Hillcrest Drive*	
48	2	26,123	77	1	57,845
49	3	30,001	78	2	28,553
50	4	$28,888	79	3	42,735
51	5	28,998	80	4	60,600
52	6	23,556	81	5	38,887
53	7	27,956	82	6	71,775
54	8	24,665	83	8	31,119
55	9	29,545	84	10	40,000
56	10	26,997	85	12	56,337
	East Court			*West Court*	
57	3	18,998	86	1	12,223
58	4	13,556	87	5	10,678
59	7	17,956	88	9	14,556
60	8	14,665	89	13	13,665
61	11	19,545	90	17	15,997
62	12	16,997	91	21	14,555
63	15	15,305	92	25	16,554
64	16	15,555	93	26	22,115
65	19	16,885	94	29	19,997
66	20	17,554	95	30	17,666
67	23	21,115	96	33	16,002
68	24	20,997	97	34	16,155
69	27	16,666	98	37	17,444
70	28	17,002	99	38	16,876
71	31	15,155			

PROBLEM 1-7 You are to take a cluster sample of Dullsville family incomes.

(a) Treating each census tract in Figure 1-5 as a cluster, select two clusters by matching the first applicable random numbers in the following sequence to the appropriate census tract identity codes.

2 6 8 6 3 8 7 4

(b) List the household codes, addresses, and incomes for the sample.

Solution:
(a) The census tracts are D-02 and D-06.
(b) The following sample observations apply. The sample includes all homes on Tranquil Court and Hillcrest Drive.

Household	Address	Income
47	1 Tranquil Ct.	$24,776
48	2 Tranquil Ct.	26,123
49	3 Tranquil Ct.	30,001
50	4 Tranquil Ct.	28,888
51	5 Tranquil Ct.	28,998
52	6 Tranquil Ct.	23,556
53	7 Tranquil Ct.	27,956
54	8 Tranquil Ct.	24,665
55	9 Tranquil Ct.	29,545
56	10 Tranquil Ct.	26,997

Household	Address	Income
77	1 Hillcrest Dr.	57,845
78	2 Hillcrest Dr.	28,553
79	3 Hillcrest Dr.	42,735
80	4 Hillcrest Dr.	60,600
81	5 Hillcrest Dr.	38,887
82	6 Hillcrest Dr.	71,775
83	8 Hillcrest Dr.	31,119
84	10 Hillcrest Dr.	40,000
85	12 Hillcrest Dr.	56,337

PROBLEM 1-8 Select a stratified sample containing two household incomes from each Dullsville census tract shown on the map in Figure 1-5, based on street address or apartment number. Use the following random numbers, proceeding across the rows and starting at the top left entry. Be sure to skip those random numbers that don't apply to an address, and never return to an earlier entry. Start with tract D-01, and select each census tract's incomes in turn.

56	04	57	55	85	34	01	17	73	93	05	54	89	42	29	57
69	43	10	77	97	78	17	40	30	23	80	32	94	31	20	91
46	75	29	15	31	82	44	77	32	42	11	09	14	61	19	00
12	05	63	29	23	33	05	49	29	48	21	90	01	58	07	03
24	25	47	16	41	14	61	12	55	86	88	02	39	44	57	56

Solution: The following addresses and incomes apply.

Address	Income
4 East Ct.	$13,556
34 West Ct.	16,155
1 Tranquil Ct.	24,776
5 Tranquil Ct.	28,998
108-5 Main St.	16,668
108-1 Main St.	14,453
7 Main St.	6,775
3 Main St.	5,558
24 E. Boondocks Ln.	14,667
16 W. Boondocks Ln.	13,119
12 Hillcrest Dr.	56,337
2 Hillcrest Dr.	28,553

PROBLEM 1-9 Suppose that a canvass has been made of Dullsville household incomes but that the census data aren't yet known. As a convenience sample, the incomes of residents of the apartment house (108 Main Street in Figure 1-5) are considered. No family member in unit 02 was home, and the tenant in 05 slammed the door on the canvasser. The remaining family incomes were obtained. List the sample.

Solution: The following sample is obtained.

Address	Income
108-01 Main St.	$14,453
108-03	8,985
108-04	21,119
108-06	10,560
108-07	14,554
108-08	11,800

PROBLEM 1-10 Select a judgment sample of Dullsville household incomes by choosing from each census tract the household(s) with the lowest identity number(s). All tracts are to be represented by one household, except for the largest ones (D-01 and D-05), which are to be represented by three households each. List the sample obtained.

Solution: You obtain the following sample.

Census tract	Household	Income
D-01	57	$18,998
D-01	58	13,556
D-01	59	17,956
D-02	47	24,776
D-03	39	14,453
D-04	29	4,675
D-05	01	15,772
D-05	02	14,667
D-05	03	21,539
D-06	77	57,845

PROBLEM 1-11 The following data represent the gasoline mileages, in miles per gallon, achieved by a random sample of 34 cars.

Miles per gallon

14.6	12.4	14.4	14.5	17.4	18.3	14.4
10.0	14.8	11.0	16.0	11.3	12.4	16.1
10.5	15.7	15.2	15.1	10.0	10.4	11.3
12.0	10.9	14.6	11.4	16.2	13.1	13.8
11.9	14.4	16.4	14.0	18.6	10.7	

(a) Use two-year-wide class intervals, starting with 9.0–under 11.0 and ending with 17.0–under 19.0, to determine the sample frequency distribution.

(b) Construct a histogram for the frequency distribution found in **(a)**. Use the following graph, making sure to label the axes.

(c) Construct the frequency polygon for the frequency distribution found in **(a)**.

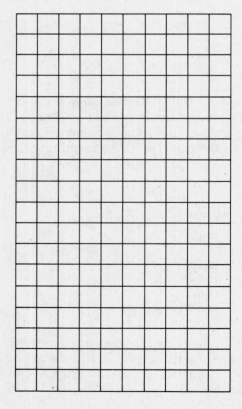

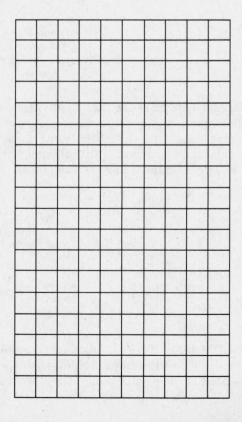

Solution:

(a) You find the following sample frequency distribution by counting the number of cars that have gasoline mileages in each of the class intervals.

Miles per gallon	Tally	Number of cars
9.0–under 11	⫻	6
11.0–under 13	⫻ ⫼	8
13.0–under 15	⫻ ⫻	10
15.0–under 17	⫻ ⫼	7
17.0–under 19	⫼	3
	Total	34

(b) See Figure 1-7.
(c) See Figure 1-8.

Figure 1-7

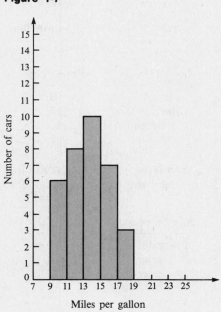

Figure 1-8

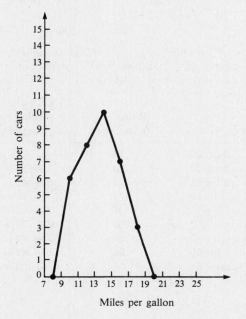

PROBLEM 1-12   The following data represent the marital status of the heads of households for a sample of welfare recipients.

File no.	Status	File no.	Status	File no.	Status	File no.	Status
00357	M	06315	D	10586	S	16627	M
01112	M	07448	D	10794	S	17051	M
01267	D	07496	S	10813	M	17834	M
01448	S	08523	S	10915	D	18215	D
02536	D	09117	M	17317	W	19006	M
02699	S	09856	W	12225	D	19853	D
03419	M	10013	M	12806	M	20017	W
03212	W	10074	M	13115	W	20556	W
04896	W	10176	M	14083	S	20562	S
05517	M	10324	D	14118	D	21010	M

Code: S—Single   D—Divorced   M—Married   W—Widowed

Determine the simple frequency distribution for marital status.

Solution: Counting the total number of recipients who fall into each category of marital status, you get

Marital status	Frequency
Single	8
Married	15
Divorced	10
Widowed	7

PROBLEM 1-13   The following frequency distribution applies to ages. Determine for each class interval the relative frequency and the cumulative relative frequency.

Age (in years)	Class frequency
20–under 25	18
25–under 30	23
30–under 35	15
35–under 40	13
40–under 45	7
45–under 50	6
50–under 55	5
55–under 60	5
60–under 65	8
Total	100

Solution: You find relative frequencies by dividing each class frequency by the sample size, 100. You then find the cumulative relative frequencies by adding each relative frequency to the cumulative value for the preceding interval. The initial cumulative relative frequency is .18. The following apply.

Age (in years)	Relative frequency	Cumulative relative frequency
20–under 25	.18	.18
25–under 30	.23	.23 + .18 = .41
30–under 35	.15	.15 + .41 = .56
35–under 40	.13	.13 + .56 = .69
40–under 45	.07	.07 + .69 = .76
45–under 50	.06	.06 + .76 = .82
50–under 55	.05	.05 + .82 = .87
55–under 60	.05	.05 + .87 = .92
60–under 65	.08	.08 + .92 = 1.00
Total	1.00	

PROBLEM 1-14 The following table lists the average rates of return achieved from buying and holding each of a sample of 34 stocks over the period 1966–1970.

Stock	Average annual percentage rate of return	Stock	Average annual percentage rate of return
Abacus Fund	13.3	McDonnell Douglas	8.2
American Motors	− 2.1	Monarch Machine Tool	16.6
Baltimore Gas and Electric	7.1	National Steel Corporation	10.3
Campbell Red Lake	21.7	Northwestern Steel Wire	34.4
Chemway Corporation	20.7	Owens-Illinois, Inc.	2.2
Consolidated Foods	19.1	Penn Fruit Company	3.1
Distiller Corp.—Seagrams	18.7	Quaker Oats Company	30.0
Evans Products	32.0	Revere Copper and Brass	7.6
First Charter Financial	52.1	St. Joseph Light and Power	4.9
General Cable Corporation	6.0	Simmons Company	24.3
Gimbel Brothers	19.1	Southwestern Publishing Service	9.8
Helme Products	8.5	Sunshine Mining Company	22.8
Indianapolis Power and Light	4.2	Timken Company	3.8
International Rectifier	−13.9	Union Carbide Corporation	0.0
Kayser-Roth Corporation	4.5	Vendo Company	− 4.3
Leesona Corporation	6.1	Welbit Corporation	27.8
R. H. Macy and Company	15.5	Youngstown Steel Door	6.3

(a) Starting with the category −15.0–under −5.0, construct a frequency distribution using class intervals with widths of 10%.

(b) Plot the histogram for the frequency distribution in (a).

Solution:

(a) Counting the number of stocks in each class interval, you get

Average annual percentage rate of return	Number of stocks
−15.0–under −5.0	1
−5.0–under 5.0	9
5.0–under 15.0	10
15.0–under 25.0	9
25.0–under 35.0	4
35.0–under 45.0	0
45.0–under 55.0	1
Total	34

(b) See Figure 1-9.

PROBLEM 1-15 Consider again the stock data given in the table in Problem 1-14.

    (a) Construct the sample frequency distribution using 5 class intervals with widths of 15%, starting with the interval −20.0–under −5.0.

    (b) Plot the histogram for the frequency distribution of **(a)**.

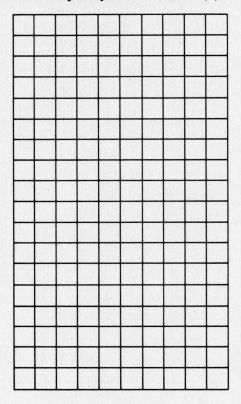

Solution:

(a) Counting the number of stocks in each class interval, you get

Average annual percentage rate of return	Number of stocks
−20.0–under −5.0	1
−5.0–under 10.0	17
10.0–under 25.0	11
25.0–under 40.0	4
40.0–under 55.0	1
Total	34

(b) See Figure 1-10.

Figure 1-9

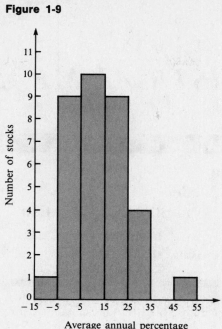

Average annual percentage
rate of return

Figure 1-10

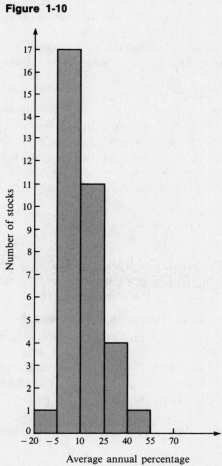

Average annual percentage
rate of return

2 SUMMARY STATISTICAL MEASURES

THIS CHAPTER IS ABOUT

- ☑ **The Arithmetic Mean**
- ☑ **The Median and the Mode**
- ☑ **The Range, Variance, and Standard Deviation**
- ☑ **The Proportion**
- ☑ **Other Common Statistical Measures**

The frequency distribution arranges statistical data into a meaningful pattern, but that is just the starting point in a statistical investigation. You will ordinarily want to determine **summary measures**, which are numbers that reveal a variety of properties of the observations.

Summary measures may correspond either to populations or samples. Computed values based on census data are referred to as **population parameters**. Populations aren't usually censused, however, and the true value of the parameter is ordinarily an unknown quantity. Much of statistics is concerned with estimating population parameters from sample data. A summary value computed from sample data is a **sample statistic**.

2-1. The Arithmetic Mean

A very useful type of statistical summary for quantitative data identifies the center of the population or sample. Such a quantity is referred to as a **measure of central tendency**. The most common of these is the **arithmetic mean**, which is computed by adding together the observed values and dividing by the number of observations included. For example, consider the times (in seconds) that 5 successive customers waited in a bank line: 15, 124, 28, 0, 47. You calculate the mean by adding these values and dividing the sum by the number of persons (5):

$$\frac{15 + 124 + 28 + 0 + 47}{5} = 42.8$$

Thus the mean waiting time is 42.8 seconds. If the 5 customer waiting times constitute a sample from a population, then the value 42.8 is the **sample mean**. Should the 5 values constitute a complete population, then 42.8 would be the **population mean**.

A. It is convenient to use a symbolic expression to represent the mean.

You calculate the arithmetic mean in the same way for any group of raw data. You will find it convenient to express the calculations symbolically. It is conventional to use the letter X to represent an observed value. To distinguish the individual observations, the numbers 1, 2, 3,... are used as *subscripts*. The symbol X_1 represents the first observed value; X_2, the second; X_3, the third; and so on. The special symbol $\bar{X}$, called "X bar," represents the sample mean.

Now you see how to calculate the sample mean from the following expression.

Sample mean
$$\bar{X} = \frac{X_1 + X_2 + \cdots + X_n}{n}$$

In the waiting-time illustration, the **sample size** is $n = 5$, and the observed values are $X_1 = 15$, $X_2 = 124$, $X_3 = 28$, $X_4 = 0$, and $X_5 = 47$.

A similar calculation applies for the population mean, which is represented by the symbol μ (the lowercase Greek *mu*).

- Keep in mind that μ isn't ordinarily computed because complete population data aren't usually available.

You can write the numerator of the sample mean equation more concisely by using a *summation sign*. Thus, you will ordinarily see the sample mean represented by the following equivalent expression.

$$\bar{X} = \frac{\sum X}{n}$$

The term $\sum X$ simply indicates that you add up all the X terms.

B. You may compute the mean from grouped data.

You may wish to compute the sample mean using a statistical investigation for which you have only the summarized, instead of the raw, data. Often the summarized data are in the form of a frequency distribution. You can use that distribution table to compute an *approximate* value for $\bar{X}$. The following expression applies

Sample mean using grouped data $\bar{X} = \frac{\sum fX}{n}$

An illustration of this procedure uses the following frequency distribution for a sample of 100 gasoline mileages experienced by drivers of medium-sized cars in the city.

Class interval mileage	Number of cars f	Class interval midpoint X	fX
14.0–under 16.0	9	15	135
16.0–under 18.0	13	17	221
18.0–under 20.0	24	19	456
20.0–under 22.0	38	21	798
22.0–under 24.0	16	23	368
Totals	100		1978

A **midpoint**, denoted by X, represents each class interval. You find the midpoints by averaging the limits of each interval. For example, for the first interval, $(14.0 + 16.0)/2 = 15$. Then you multiply each midpoint by its class frequency, represented by the letter f. Finally, divide the sum of these products by the sample size, n, to find the sample mean:

$$\bar{X} = \frac{1978}{100} = 19.78$$

C. Extreme values may greatly affect the level of the mean.

Although it is perhaps the most popular measure of central tendency, the arithmetic mean has one serious drawback. It is greatly affected by extremely large or small values. Imagine what the mean income of your friends would be if you added a billionaire to the group.

2-2. The Median and the Mode

There are other measures of central tendency that you might use in place of the mean.

A. The sample median isn't unduly influenced by extremes.

In some sampling applications the preferred summary is the **sample median**, which is the middle value identified after sorting all observations by increasing value. Rearranging the waiting times from before, you can see that the median is 28:

0   15   **28**   47   124

If a sixth time of 71 seconds was added to the list, you would obtain the median by averaging the middle two values from the sequence 0, 15, 28, 47, 71, 124:

$$\text{Median} = \frac{28 + 47}{2} = 37.5$$

The median is often used to summarize the center of data when the frequency distribution is skewed. For example, the mean income of attorneys would be heavily influenced by the top earners who command huge fees. The median, however, would be pretty much the same regardless of the earnings of those rare superstars. It is a more "democratic" measure of central tendency than the mean, giving equal position weight to each observation.

B. The mode locates the peak frequency.

Less used than the median is another measure of central tendency, the **sample mode**, which is the most frequently occurring value. For example, consider the number of children in a random sample of 100 families. There might be 15 families with no children, 34 with 1 child, 37 with 2 children, and 14 with 3 or more children. The sample mode is 2 children.

When the sample data are grouped in a frequency distribution, the mode is approximated by the midpoint of the class interval having the greatest frequency. For the gasoline mileages on page 25, the sample mode is the midpoint of the interval 20.0–under 22.0, or 21.0 miles per gallon.

C. The central tendency measures are helpful in describing population distributions.

When computed from census data, the median and the mode are population parameters. Although their true values are not ordinarily known exactly, the population mean, median, and mode are still conceptually helpful in describing the frequency distributions. Figure 2-1 shows the frequency curves for three important cases. When the distribution is symmetrical, as in (a), all three parameters coincide at the same value. The curve in (b) represents a positively skewed distribution; notice that the mean has the greatest value, the mode takes the smallest, and the median falls in between. The reverse alignment applies for the negatively skewed distribution in (c).

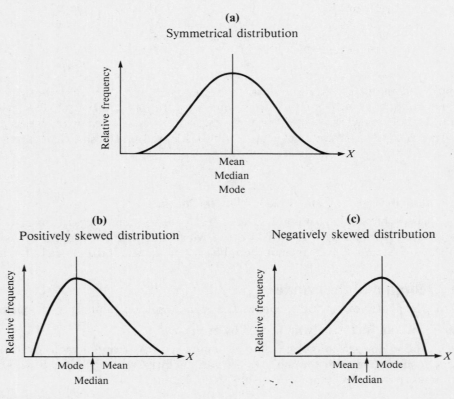

(a)
Symmetrical distribution

(b)
Positively skewed distribution

(c)
Negatively skewed distribution

Figure 2-1

You will sometimes encounter a frequency curve belonging to a **bimodal distribution**, illustrated in Figure 2-2. Notice the double-humped shape, reflective of two modes. You can expect such a distribution when two nonhomogeneous groups are combined into a single population. A good example is provided in (a), where the heights of women and men have been grouped together. Should the men outnumber the women, a curve like that in (b) might apply. Statisticians will ordinarily split the two groups in a bimodal population into two separate populations.

Figure 2-2

(a)

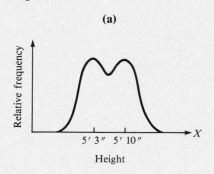

(b)

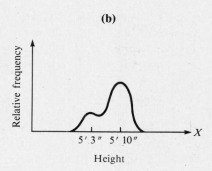

2-3. The Range, Variance, and Standard Deviation

Measures of central tendency are one type of summary measure. A second type are measures of **variability**, or the extent to which observed values differ from each other.

A. The range is the simplest measure of variability.

The easiest measure of variability to compute is the **range**. It is found by subtracting the smallest observation from the greatest.

Sample range   Sample range = Greatest value − smallest value

You ordinarily compute the range for sample data only. For the waiting times of the 5 bank customers, the following applies:

$$\text{Range} = 124 - 0 = 124$$

Although there are a few limited applications where the range is favored, statistical investigators prefer other measures of variability. One objection to the range is that it tends to become larger as the sample size is increased. Another fault is that the sample range will usually be smaller than its population counterpart. Even more than the mean, the range is unduly influenced by extreme values.

B. The variance has many desirable properties.

Two important measures of variability are based on the **deviation**, or the difference between an observed value and the mean. Deviations computed from sample data are represented symbolically as $X - \bar{X}$, while for population data you will see $X - \mu$ instead.

To illustrate, suppose that the number of employees at the 5 largest office buildings in a particular city are 314, 325, 348, 402, and 411. The mean value is

$$\frac{314 + 325 + 348 + 402 + 411}{5} = 360$$

The deviations from the mean are

$$314 - 360 = -46$$
$$325 - 360 = -35$$
$$348 - 360 = -12$$
$$402 - 360 = 42$$
$$411 - 360 = 51$$

These deviations must be combined into a single summary value to be useful. There wouldn't be much point in adding them together: The positive and negative values cancel each other, and you would obtain zero for any set of data.

Instead, you square the deviations and then obtain the average squared deviation:

$$\frac{(-46)^2 + (-35)^2 + (-12)^2 + 42^2 + 51^2}{5} = \frac{2,116 + 1,225 + 144 + 1,764 + 2,601}{5}$$

$$= \frac{7,850}{5} = 1,570$$

The resulting value is called the **variance**; it may be calculated from either sample or population data. When all of the population data are available, this procedure provides the **population variance**, denoted by σ^2. (The symbol σ is the lowercase Greek *sigma*, and you read σ^2 as "sigma squared.") You use the following expression to calculate the population variance.

$$\sigma^2 = \frac{\sum(X - \mu)^2}{N}$$

Here, you sum the squared deviations from the population mean and then divide by the **population size** N.

As with μ, you don't ordinarily calculate the value of σ^2 because you don't usually observe the entire population. Instead, you compute the **sample variance**, denoted as s^2, by averaging the squares of deviations from the *sample* mean. To find the sample variance, you use the expression for the population variance replacing μ with $\bar{X}$ and using n in place of N.

Sample variance
$$s^2 = \frac{\sum(X - \bar{X})^2}{n - 1}$$

For technical reasons, the divisor is $n - 1$, not n itself. That slight modification improves the quality of s^2 as an estimator of σ^2.

As an illustration, consider again the sample of waiting times for the 5 bank customers.

$$s^2 = \frac{(15 - 42.8)^2 + (124 - 42.8)^2 + (28 - 42.8)^2 + (0 - 42.8)^2 + (47 - 42.8)^2}{5 - 1}$$

$$= \frac{9,434.80}{4} = 2,358.7$$

C. The standard deviation is easier to use than the variance.

The value $s^2 = 2,358.7$ summarizes the variability in customer waiting times. Unfortunately, most persons find it hard to relate to s^2 because it is in *squared* units (here, seconds squared). You will find it easier to substitute the square root,

$$s = \sqrt{s^2} = \sqrt{2,358.7} = 48.6$$

The square root of the variance is the **standard deviation**. It is denoted either as s when computed from sample data or as σ when applicable to the entire population. You ordinarily compute the sample standard deviation in a single step using either one of the following expressions, which are mathematically equivalent.

Sample standard deviation

$$s = \sqrt{\frac{\sum(X - \bar{X})^2}{n - 1}} \qquad \text{or} \qquad s = \sqrt{\frac{\sum X^2 - n\bar{X}^2}{n - 1}}$$

EXAMPLE 2-1: FIRST-YEAR EARNINGS OF MARKETING AND ACCOUNTING MAJORS

A university placement director collected sample data giving first-year earnings of marketing and accounting majors. The following calculations apply to the 12 marketing majors.

Earnings (in thousands of dollars) X	Deviation $(X - \bar{X})$	Squared deviation $(X - \bar{X})^2$
18.5	− .4	.16
12.0	−6.9	47.61
17.0	−1.9	3.61
22.5	3.6	12.96
31.4	12.5	156.25
10.2	−8.7	75.69
25.6	6.7	44.89
19.2	.3	.09
17.6	−1.3	1.69
17.3	−1.6	2.56
22.2	3.3	10.89
13.3	−5.6	31.36
226.8		387.76

The sample mean and standard deviation for marketing majors are

$$\bar{X} = \frac{226.8}{12} = 18.9 \qquad s = \sqrt{\frac{387.76}{12 - 1}} = 5.94$$

A sample of size $n = 9$ applies to the earnings of accounting majors. The following data and calculations apply. (Here the sample standard deviation is computed using the second expression.)

Earnings (in thousands of dollars) X	X^2
18.5	342.25
20.1	404.01
19.4	376.36
17.3	299.29
21.0	441.00
20.5	420.25
20.2	408.04
19.0	361.00
18.6	345.96
174.6	3,398.16

The sample mean and standard deviation for accounting majors are

$$\bar{X} = \frac{174.6}{9} = 19.4 \qquad s = \sqrt{\frac{3,398.16 - 9(19.4)^2}{9 - 1}} = 1.17$$

Notice that the sample earnings for the accounting majors involve the higher mean. However, the sample standard deviation of earnings for marketing majors is substantially greater, reflecting higher variability in that sample. (This might be explained by a substantial number of commission sales positions held by the persons in that sample group.)

D. The standard deviation and the mean provide a great deal of information.

The frequency of population values lying within any particular interval can be determined for many distributions from knowledge of the mean and standard deviation alone. For instance, should the normal distribution apply, then it has been established that about 68% of the observations fall within the region $\mu \pm 1\sigma$. Furthermore, about 95.5% of the population lie within $\mu \pm 2\sigma$, and 99.7% fall within $\mu \pm 3\sigma$.

The normal curve is described mathematically in terms of only two parameters, μ and σ. Thus, for populations having that frequency curve, you can obtain a detailed description of the complete frequency distribution simply by knowing the mean and the standard deviation. You will encounter a thorough discussion of this concept in Chapter 8.

2-4. The Proportion

The key summary measure for qualitative data is the **proportion** of observations falling into a particular category. As with the earlier measures, the proportion may be either a population parameter or a sample statistic. The **population proportion** is denoted by π (the lowercase Greek *pi*). The **sample proportion** is denoted by the letter P. You won't ordinarily compute the value of π, owing to lack of complete data. You compute the sample proportion from the following expression.

Sample proportion
$$P = \frac{\text{Number of observations in category}}{\text{Sample size}}$$

A proportion is a value between 0 and 1.

The sample proportion expresses the relative frequency for the occurrence of a particular category. In a sample containing $n = 500$ persons, 200 of which are men and 300 women, the sample proportion of women is $P = 300/500 = .60$. If a machine has produced a sample of $n = 100$ parts, 5 of which are defective, then the sample proportion defective is $P = 5/100 = .05$. The same machine might actually produce defective items at a consistently higher rate than experienced in the sample, so that the population of defective parts could be a different value, such as $\pi = .06$.

2-5. Other Common Statistical Measures

Another broad category of statistical measures expresses frequency information for quantitative populations. The most common is the **percentile**, which is that value below which a stated percentage of the observations lie. For example, an instructor might find that 32 out of 40 students earned less than 150 points on a final examination. The percentage of such scores is $(32/40) \times 100 = 80$, and 150 points is the 80th percentile. If 165 points is the 90th percentile, then 90% of the 40 test scores—$(.90 \times 40 = 36$ of them)—fell below 165.

Another way of conveying the same information is in terms of the **fractile**, which is that point below which a stated fraction of the values lie. Thus, 150 points is the .80-fractile, while 165 is the .90-fractile.

Earlier in this chapter you encountered one percentile in another context. *The median is the same quantity as the 50th percentile or the .50-fractile.*

A. Quartiles are those percentiles dividing the data into four equal-sized groupings.

There are three special percentiles. These are the **quartiles**, which divide the data into four groups of equal size. The **first quartile** is the same as the 25th percentile and the .25-fractile. The **second quartile** is the 50th percentile, while the **third quartile** equals the 75th percentile. (There is no need for a "fourth" quartile.)

EXAMPLE 2-2: YOUR CLASS STANDING

When you graduate, your school might classify your relative percentile position in terms of your grade point average (GPA). The following data apply to a particular class having exactly 800 graduates.

GPA	Percentile
3.9	99
3.7	95
3.5	90
3.1	75
2.5	50
2.3	25

The first quartile is 2.3; 25% of the graduates, or $.25 \times 800 = 200$ students, earned a grade point average lower than 2.3. The second quartile is 2.5, the 50th percentile; $.50 \times 800 = 400$ students earned GPA's of less than 2.5. The third quartile (also the 75th percentile) is 3.1; $.75 \times 800 = 600$ earned GPA's below 3.1. There are 200 GPA's in each of the following groups: below the first quartile (2.3); at or above the first quartile but below the second (2.5); at or above the second quartile but below the third (3.1); and at or above the third quartile.

B. The interquartile range is a useful summary measure.

The difference between the third and first quartiles is the **interquartile range**. This encompasses the middle 50% of the data values. In the preceding example, the interquartile range is $3.1 - 2.3 = .8$ grade points. You can use this quantity to summarize the amount of variability in the underlying sample or population.

EXAMPLE 2-3: DOCTORS' INCOMES VS. TEACHERS' SALARIES

You are told that the population of earnings of doctors in Kent County has a first quartile of $55,000 and a third quartile of $135,000, so that the interquartile range is

$$\$135,000 - 55,000 = \$80,000$$

The salaries of teachers in the same county have a first quartile of $13,500 and a third quartile of $22,000. The interquartile range is

$$\$22,000 - 13,500 = \$8,500$$

This means that the earnings of doctors is nearly 10 times as varied as teachers' salaries.

SUMMARY

Statistical data are ordinarily evaluated in terms of *summary measures*. When applicable to all possible population observations, these are referred to as *population parameters*. Summary values, however, are usually computed from sample data only, and the resulting quantities are called *sample statistics*.

With quantitative data the *sample mean* $\bar{X}$ is the common measure of *central tendency*. It can be used to estimate the value of the *population mean* μ. You compute the sample mean using the expression

$$\bar{X} = \frac{\sum X}{n}$$

or, for grouped data,

$$\bar{X} = \frac{\sum fX}{n}$$

There are also two other measures of central tendency. The *sample median* is the point dividing the data into two groups of equal size. The *sample mode* is the most frequently occurring value. All three measures of central tendency are helpful in describing frequency distributions, and the mode is important in explaining a *bimodal distribution*, which arises when nonhomogeneous units are observed.

In addition to identifying the center of a sample or a population, statisticians are concerned with measuring its *variability*, or the extent to which the observed values differ from one another. The simplest measure of variability is the *range*, which expresses the difference between the greatest and the smallest observation values. Since the range provides limited information, statisticians prefer to use the *variance* as the basic measure of variability. You find the variance by computing for each observation its *deviation* from the mean, then squaring those deviations and finding their average. You won't ordinarily compute the *population variance*, represented by the symbol σ^2. Instead, you will find the *sample variance*, which is denoted by s^2:

$$s^2 = \frac{\sum (X - \bar{X})^2}{n - 1}$$

You will find it more convenient to work with the *standard deviation*, s or σ, obtained by taking the square root of the appropriate variance.

The population mean and standard deviation provide useful summaries of the underlying frequency distribution. For normally distributed populations, the values for μ and σ completely specify the characteristics of the frequency curve.

Qualitative populations are summarized by a single parameter, the *population proportion*, denoted by π. This quantity is estimated by the *sample proportion P*, which is equal to the number of observations having a particular characteristic divided by the sample size.

Quantitative data are sometimes summarized in terms of *percentiles* and *fractiles*. Such a number is the point below which a stated percentage or proportion of the observations lie. There are three special percentiles, the *quartiles*, which divide the observations into groups of successive size, each containing 25% of the data points. The *interquartile range* is the useful summary measure that encompasses the middle 50% of values; it equals the difference between the third and first quartiles.

RAISE YOUR GRADES

Can you explain...?

☑ the difference between central tendency and variability
☑ why a bimodal distribution occurs
☑ why the median equals the second quartile
☑ why the mean can be distorted by extremes
☑ why some knowledge of variability is useful

Do you know...?

☑ how to find the standard deviation from the variance
☑ for which type of frequency distribution the mean lies above the median
☑ what information must be available before the population mean can be known exactly
☑ how to find a 90th percentile
☑ under what circumstance the mean, median, and mode all lie at a common value

RAPID REVIEW

1. The following sample data give the price-earnings ratio for various shares of stock.

30	25	7	15	8
18	11	12	14	21

Compute the sample mean.   [Section 2-1A]

2. Following are the test scores of 5 randomly chosen statistics students.

80	70	60	90	100

Compute (**a**) the sample variance and (**b**) the sample standard deviation.
[Sections 2-3B, C]

3. The following sample data apply.

2	3	4	3	4	5	6	7	8	0
9	6	4	2	1	3	4	5	6	7

Find the following.   [Sections 2-1, 2]

(**a**) mean   (**b**) median   (**c**) mode

4. At a particular business school, all MBA's must have taken the GMAT. The following data apply.

GMAT	Percentile
490	25th
550	50th
575	75th
610	90th
640	95th
705	99th

Find the following. [Section 2-5]

(a) first quartile   (c) third quartile
(b) second quartile   (d) interquartile range

5. The following sample values were calculated for the waiting times (in minutes) experienced by customers checking out of five different supermarkets. Indicate whether each population is negatively skewed, symmetrical, or positively skewed. [Section 2-2C]

	(a)	(b)	(c)	(d)	(e)
Mean	5	12	20	14	12
Median	7	12	19	10	13
Mode	8	12	18	9	14

6. The following frequency distribution applies for the ages of patients in a rest home.

Age	Number of patients
60–under 70	15
70–under 80	20
80–under 90	5
	40

Determine approximate values for the following:
(a) sample mean   [Section 2-1B]
(b) mode   [Section 2-2B]

7. A population is positively skewed when which one of the following is true?   [Section 2-2C]

(a) Its mean is less than its median.
(b) Its mean is less than its mode.
(c) Its median is less than its mode.
(d) Its mean is greater than its median.

8. For a symmetrical population, which one of the following is untrue?   [Section 2-2C]

(a) median = mode
(b) mean = median
(c) median = second quartile
(d) first quartile = third quartile

9. Which one of the following is *not* a measure of central tendency?   [Sections 2-2A, 2-5]

(a) second quartile   (c) 50th percentile
(b) median   (d) third quartile

10. The range of a sample of temperatures is 73°. The highest temperature is 98°. What is the lowest temperature?   [Section 2-3A]

(a) 25°   (b) 0°   (c) 85.5°   (d) 73°

Answers
1. 16.1
2. (a) 250   (b) 15.81
3. (a) 4.45   (b) 4   (c) 4
4. (a) 490   (b) 550   (c) 575   (d) 85

5. (a) negatively skewed   (d) positively skewed
   (b) symmetrical   (e) negatively skewed
   (c) positively skewed
6. (a) 72.5   (b) 75
7. (d)   8. (d)   9. (d)   10. (a)

SOLVED PROBLEMS

PROBLEM 2-1   A sample of SAT scores is comprised of the following values: 364, 555, 645, 446, 590. Determine the value of the sample mean.

Solution: Find the sample mean $\bar{X}$ by adding the values together and dividing by the total number of values.

$$\bar{X} = \frac{364 + 555 + 645 + 446 + 590}{5} = \frac{2,600}{5} = 520$$

PROBLEM 2-2   Following is the frequency distribution for the annual earnings of a sample of MBA's. Calculate the approximate level of the sample mean.

Earnings	Number of MBA's
$15,000–under 25,000	3
25,000–under 35,000	4
35,000–under 45,000	11
45,000–under 55,000	14
55,000–under 65,000	21
65,000–under 75,000	16
75,000–under 85,000	14
85,000–under 95,000	9
95,000–under 105,000	8
	100

Solution: To find the appropriate sample mean, use the expression $\bar{X} = \sum fX/n$. For each category, X is equal to the midpoint.

Earnings	Midpoint X	Frequency f	fX
$15,000–under 25,000	$20,000	3	$ 60,000
25,000–under 35,000	30,000	4	120,000
35,000–under 45,000	40,000	11	440,000
45,000–under 55,000	50,000	14	700,000
55,000–under 65,000	60,000	21	1,260,000
65,000–under 75,000	70,000	16	1,120,000
75,000–under 85,000	80,000	14	1,120,000
85,000–under 95,000	90,000	9	810,000
95,000–under 105,000	100,000	8	800,000
		$n = 100$	$6,430,000

Thus,

$$\bar{X} = \frac{6,430,000}{100} = 64,300$$

PROBLEM 2-3   The students in a statistics class received the following scores on an examination:

84   77   67   94   90   93   81   56   89   77   88   74   76
28   80   58   66   77   89   81   78   77   72   94   93   79

(a) Determine the median.
(b) Determine the mode.
(c) A make-up test score of 76 points is added to the above group. Determine the new median.

Solution:
(a) You must first arrange the scores by increasing value:

$$28 \quad 56 \quad 58 \quad 66 \quad 67 \quad 72 \quad 74 \quad 76 \quad 77 \quad 77 \quad 77 \quad 77 \quad 78$$
$$79 \quad 80 \quad 81 \quad 81 \quad 84 \quad 88 \quad 89 \quad 89 \quad 90 \quad 93 \quad 93 \quad 94 \quad 94$$

Since there is an even number of scores—26—the median is the average of the middle two:

$$\text{Median} = \frac{78 + 79}{2} = 78.5$$

(b) The mode is the most frequently occurring score:

$$\text{Mode} = 77$$

(c) If you insert 76 into the list for (a), the middle value of the 27 scores (an odd number of observations) becomes 78. Thus,

$$\text{Median} = 78$$

PROBLEM 2-4 The following numbers of dependents have been obtained from a sample of withholding statements on file in a personnel office.

$$4 \quad 2 \quad 4 \quad 1 \quad 0 \quad 3 \quad 3 \quad 2 \quad 2 \quad 1$$

Find the values of the following:

(a) sample range
(b) sample mean
(c) sample variance
(d) sample standard deviation

Solution: (a) The sample range is the largest value minus the smallest value:

$$\text{Sample range} = 4 - 0 = 4$$

(b) $\bar{X} = \dfrac{4 + 2 + 4 + 1 + 0 + 3 + 3 + 2 + 2 + 1}{10} = \dfrac{22}{10} = 2.2$

(c) To find the sample variance, first subtract the sample mean from each value and square the resulting value. Then sum the squared deviations.

X	$(X - \bar{X})$	$(X - \bar{X})^2$
4	1.8	3.24
2	$-.2$	.04
4	1.8	3.24
1	-1.2	1.44
0	-2.2	4.84
3	.8	.64
3	.8	.64
2	$-.2$	.04
2	$-.2$	.04
1	-1.2	1.44
		15.60

Now, divide the total squared deviations by $(n - 1)$.

$$s^2 = \frac{15.60}{10 - 1} = 1.73$$

(d) The sample standard deviation is equal to the square root of the sample variance.

$$s = \sqrt{1.73} = 1.32$$

PROBLEM 2-5   Using the marital status data in Problem 1-12 (page 20), determine the sample proportion for

(a) single   (b) married   (c) divorced   (d) widowed

Solution: Dividing the number of sample units in each category by the sample size of 40, the following sample proportions are obtained.

(a) $P = 8/40 = .2$ (c) $P = 10/40 = .25$
(b) $P = 15/40 = .375$ (d) $P = 7/40 = .175$

PROBLEM 2-6   The following sample examination scores were obtained from a class.

$$\begin{array}{cccccccccccccc} 94 & 81 & 74 & 66 & 87 & 83 & 77 & 59 & 26 & 77 & 79 & 67 & 86 \\ 78 & 79 & 93 & 94 & 77 & 80 & 81 & 94 & 80 & 78 & 58 & 78 & 72 \end{array}$$

Compute (a) the sample mean and (b) the sample standard deviation.

Solution: (a) The sample size is $n = 26$. Summing the observations and dividing by n, you get

$$\bar{X} = \frac{1{,}998}{26} = 76.846$$

(b) The sum of the squares of the examination scores is 158,480.

$$s = \sqrt{\frac{\sum X^2 - n\bar{X}^2}{n-1}} = \sqrt{\frac{158{,}480 - 26(76.846)^2}{26-1}} = \sqrt{197.68} = 14.06$$

PROBLEM 2-7   The concentrations of pollutants obtained in air samples have the following cumulative frequency distribution.

Concentration (in parts/million)	Cumulative relative frequency
0–under 1	.05
1–under 2	.12
2–under 3	.25
3–under 4	.37
4–under 5	.50
5–under 6	.67
6–under 7	.75
7–under 8	.84
8–under 9	.89
9–under 10	.90
10–under 11	.95
11–under 12	.98
12–under 13	1.00

Determine the following:

(a) .90 fractile   (d) 3rd quartile
(b) 37th percentile   (e) interquartile range
(c) 1st quartile   (f) median

Solution: First, match each value to the appropriate cumulative relative frequency. For instance, for (c) the first quartile equals a cumulative relative frequency of .25. Then determine the value *below which* the corresponding concentration falls. Thus, a concentration of 2–under 3 falls below 3 ppm.
(a) 10 ppm.   (d) 7 ppm
(b) 4 ppm   (e) 7 ppm − 3 ppm = 4 ppm
(c) 3 ppm   (f) 5 ppm

PROBLEM 2-8   For each of the following sets of sample data, determine (*1*) the mean, (*2*) the median, and (*3*) the mode.

(a)	(b)	(c)	(d)
90	12	$200,000	6
87	14	8,000	5
86	18	9,000	6
86	19	15,000	5
86	21	16,000	6
79	21	57,000	7
78	24	31,000	8
78	27	2,000	7
77	29	8,000	8
58	32	10,000	

Solution:

	(a)	(b)	(c)	(d)
(*1*) Mean	805/10	217/10	$356,000/10	58/9
	= 80.5	= 21.7	= $35,600	= 6.44
(*2*) Median	82.5	21	$12,500	6
(*3*) Mode	86	21	$8,000	6

3 PROBABILITY
Fundamental Concepts

THIS CHAPTER IS ABOUT

☑ **The Language of Probability: Basic Terms**
☑ **Compound Events and Event Relationships**
☑ **Probabilities for Compound Events**

A **probability** is a numerical value that measures the uncertainty that a particular event will occur. The probability for an event ordinarily represents *the proportion of times under identical circumstances that the event can be expected to occur*. For example, if you repeatedly toss a fair coin, heads will turn up about half the time. Thus, the probability is 1/2 that the coin will land head-side-up.

3-1. The Language of Probability: Basic Terms

A. Events are the uncertain outcomes of random experiments.

Statisticians refer to an uncertain outcome as an **event**. There are two common outcomes associated with a coin toss: the two events "head" and "tail." An event is the result of a **random experiment**. For example, the event "head" is the result of a coin toss, which is the random experiment. Tomorrow's weather, your statistics class, an oil wildcatter's drilling venture, and the introduction of a new product are all random experiments.

- The first step you must take in any probability evaluation is to identify the relevant events of the random experiment in detail.

1. **Elementary events:** The simplest possible outcomes of a random experiment are called **elementary events**. Imagine a deck of 52 playing cards. You thoroughly shuffle the cards; then you cut the deck and remove the top card. Each card that you can draw is an elementary event. Since there are 52 cards in a deck, there will be 52 elementary events, as shown in Figure 3-1.

2. **Sample space:** The complete collection of elementary events is called the **sample space**. Although often pictured, like the sample space in Figure 3-1, a sample space for drawing one card can also be represented as a list:

$$\text{Sample space} = \{\heartsuit K, \heartsuit Q, \ldots, \heartsuit 3, \heartsuit 2, \heartsuit A, \diamondsuit K, \ldots, \spadesuit A\}$$

For a coin toss the sample space can be listed as

$$\text{Sample space} = \{\text{head, tail}\}$$

Note: A random experiment can result in many different elementary events. You must decide what you're looking for. If you're interested in the *side showing*, a coin toss has just the two elementary events "head" and "tail." But suppose you're interested instead in the *number of times a coin spins* before it comes to rest. The coin may not spin at all, or it may keep spinning for a very long time. Therefore, the sample space of the coin toss would have all the integers as elementary events:

$$\text{Sample space} = \{0, 1, 2, 3, 4, \ldots\}$$

Figure 3-1

	Hearts	Diamonds	Clubs	Spades
King	♡ K •	◇ K •	♣ K •	♠ K •
Queen	♡ Q •	◇ Q •	♣ Q •	♠ Q •
Jack	♡ J •	◇ J •	♣ J •	♠ J •
10	♡ 10 •	◇ 10 •	♣ 10 •	♠ 10 •
9	♡ 9 •	◇ 9 •	♣ 9 •	♠ 9 •
8	♡ 8 •	◇ 8 •	♣ 8 •	♠ 8 •
7	♡ 7 •	◇ 7 •	♣ 7 •	♠ 7 •
6	♡ 6 •	◇ 6 •	♣ 6 •	♠ 6 •
5	♡ 5 •	◇ 5 •	♣ 5 •	♠ 5 •
4	♡ 4 •	◇ 4 •	♣ 4 •	♠ 4 •
3	♡ 3 •	◇ 3 •	♣ 3 •	♠ 3 •
Deuce	♡ 2 •	◇ 2 •	♣ 2 •	♠ 2 •
Ace	♡ A •	◇ A •	♣ A •	♠ A •

Sample space

EXAMPLE 3-1: TOSSING THREE COINS

Charlie Brown has a penny, a nickel, and a dime, all of which he plans to toss at the same time. Since all three coins will land at the same time—making one outcome—each outcome, or elementary event, is a different combination of the sides of the coins that will be showing. To impress his friends, Charlie Brown lists the *sample space*—all these combinations (Figure 3-2). In this listing, H stands for a head, T for a tail, and the subscripts p, n, and d for the respective coins. Thus, if Charlie Brown tosses his three coins and gets heads with the penny and the nickel and a tail with the dime, he would represent this event as $H_p H_n T_d$.

Figure 3-2

Penny — Nickel — Dime

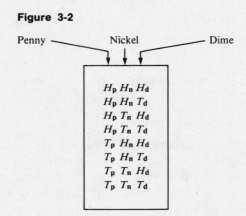

$$H_p\,H_n\,H_d$$
$$H_p\,H_n\,T_d$$
$$H_p\,T_n\,H_d$$
$$H_p\,T_n\,T_d$$
$$T_p\,H_n\,H_d$$
$$T_p\,H_n\,T_d$$
$$T_p\,T_n\,H_d$$
$$T_p\,T_n\,T_d$$

---

3. **Composite events and event sets:** In finding probabilities you will ordinarily be interested in more complex outcomes than individual elementary events. You can represent such results conveniently as *groupings* of elementary events, or **composite events**:

Composite event		Elementary events in event set
King	=	$\{♡K, ◇K, ♣K, ♠K\}$
Heart	=	$\{♡K, ♡Q, ♡J, ♡10, ♡9, ♡8, ♡7, ♡6, ♡5, ♡4, ♡3, ♡2, ♡A\}$
Dime is a head	=	$\{H_pH_nH_d, H_pT_nH_d, T_pH_nH_d, T_pT_nH_d\}$

Each *composite event will occur if any one of its elementary events occurs*. The collections of elementary events given on the right are partial listings of the elementary events of the whole sample space (e.g., all 52 playing cards of a deck). Such collections are called **event sets**.

An event set may contain a single element, as with

$$\text{Queen of hearts} = \{\heartsuit Q\}$$

or (as in Example 3-1)

$$\text{All heads} = \{H_p H_n H_d\}$$

When an event set contains no elements, the outcome is an **impossible event**:

$$\text{Impossible event} = \{\ \}$$

(The empty braces indicate that there are no elements in the set.) Such an event set is called a **null set** and is denoted by $\varnothing$. An example of an impossible event is "queen" when all of the face cards have been removed from the deck.

B. Some events have probabilities that are long-run frequencies.

The probability for an event may be defined as the **long-run frequency** at which the event will occur in a series of identical random experiments.

1. Some probabilities can be found by the count-and-divide method: When the elementary events are *equally likely*, a probability (Pr) can be found by counting and dividing:

$$\Pr[\text{event}] = \frac{\text{Number of elementary events in the event set}}{\text{Total number of equally likely elementary events}}$$

You can apply the count-and-divide method to the examples you've just been studying:

$$\Pr[\text{head}] = \frac{1}{2} \quad \text{(single coin)}$$

$$\Pr[\text{king}] = \frac{4}{52} = \frac{1}{13}$$

$$\Pr[\text{heart}] = \frac{13}{52} = \frac{1}{4}$$

$$\Pr[\text{dime is a head}] = \frac{4}{8} = \frac{1}{2} \quad \text{(three coins)}$$

EXAMPLE 3-2: CATEGORIES FOR SCHOLARSHIP STUDENTS

The business students who hold scholarships at State University are represented by a biological symbol in Figure 3-3. You'll select one student from this group at random, so Figure 3-3 represents the sample space. To find the probability that the student you select will be a woman, count the number of women and divide by the number of students. There are 32 women out of 72 scholarship students. Thus,

$$\Pr[\text{woman}] = \frac{32}{72}$$

Similarly, there are 16 accounting majors, so the probability that the selected student's major is accounting is

$$\Pr[\text{accounting}] = \frac{16}{72}$$

And, there are 30 graduate students, so that

$$\Pr[\text{graduate}] = \frac{30}{72}$$

Figure 3-3

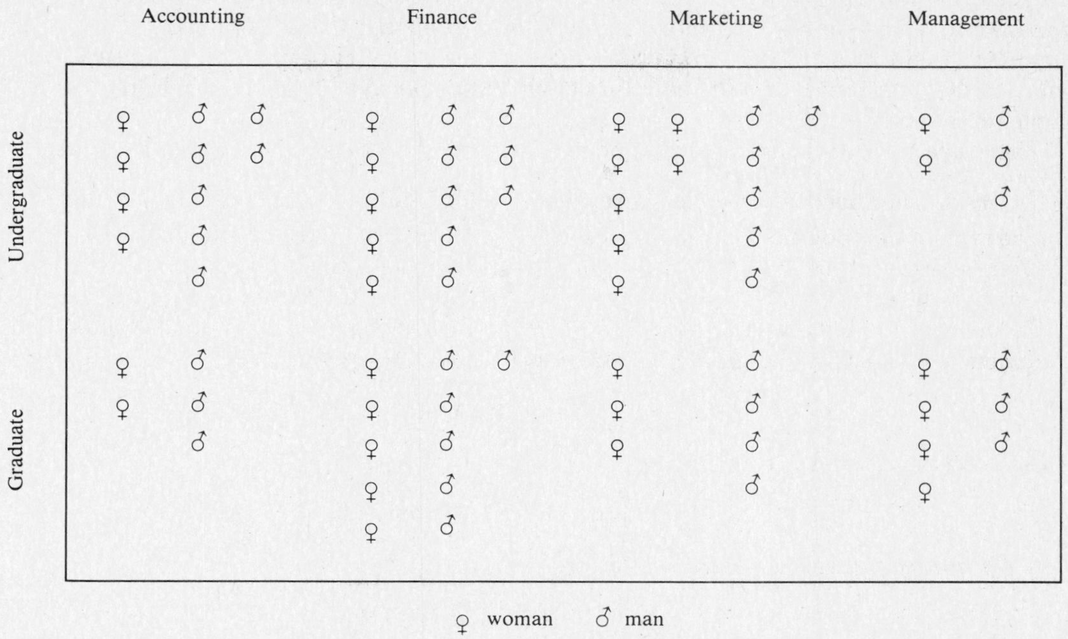

| | Accounting | Finance | Marketing | Management |

♀ woman   ♂ man

Note: The count-and-divide method applies only if the elementary events are *equally likely*.

What if, for example, a lopsided coin is tossed? The probability for an event in such a random experiment is still a long-run frequency, but it can only be *estimated* from the actual results experienced by repeating the experiment many times.

EXAMPLE 3-3: DEFECTIVE ITEMS IN A PRODUCTION PROCESS

A quality control inspector removes 100 widgets from production and finds that 14 are defective. If you assume that the production process will behave identically in the future, the probability that any particular widget is defective is *estimated* to be 14/100, or .14.

2. **Probabilities are fractions:** An event's probability must always be a fraction or decimal between 0 and 1. You can see this by looking at two extreme probabilities. Since an **impossible event** *never* occurs,

$$Pr[\text{impossible event}] = 0$$

Similarly, a **certain event** (e.g., "the selected card has a suit") will *always* occur:

$$Pr[\text{certain event}] = 1$$

All other probabilities will lie between these two extremes.

3. **Objective probabilities:** All probability values considered so far apply to *repeatable* random experiments. Quantities obtained from repeatable experiments are called **objective probabilities**.

C. **Subjective probabilities apply to experiments that cannot be repeated.**

Many important uncertain business events arise from nonrepeatable circumstances. Consider next year's sales of a product, the yearly high of the Dow-Jones Industrials, or your final grade in statistics. Any probabilities given to such events must be based solely on *judgment*. Since people often disagree on the values, these numbers are called **subjective probabilities**. (Subjective probabilities will always be provided in problems you are asked to solve.)

3-2. Compound Events and Event Relationships

It is sometimes helpful to treat an uncertain outcome as a **compound event** that can be expressed in terms of two or more **component events**. One reason for this is that the component event probabilities are often given values or are easier to calculate first. You can then use these given or easily calculated values to arrive at the probability for a more complex outcome.

There are several types of compound events.

A. Unions are obtained by grouping several events together.

One type of compound event is created by the **union** of the sets of two or more component events. This type is illustrated in Figure 3-4, where the compound event "face card" is the union of the component events "king," "queen," and "jack." *The union of several sets is a set having as its elements the elements of those sets being joined.* You can conveniently summarize this by the logical connective *or*:

$$\text{Face card} = \text{King } or \text{ Queen } or \text{ Jack}$$

You can use the symbol $\cup$ instead:

$$\text{Face card} = \text{King } \cup \text{ Queen } \cup \text{ Jack}$$

● Whenever you see $\cup$, think of it as *or*.

Figure 3-4

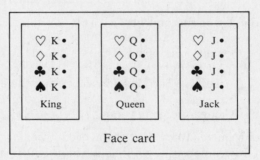

Face card = King *or* Queen *or* Jack

B. Intersections are joint events.

Another type of compound event is created by the **intersection** of the sets of two or more component events. Figure 3-5 shows the intersection of the two events "dime is a head" and "all coins show the same side." The result is an event set having the single elementary event

Figure 3-5

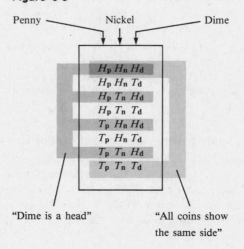

"Dime is a head"   "All coins show the same side"

$H_p H_n H_d$. *The intersection of several sets is a set having as its elements just those elements common to all the sets*. You can represent this relationship by the logical connective *and*:

"Dime is a head" *and* "All coins show same side" = $\{H_p H_n H_d\}$

You can use the symbol ∩ instead:

"Dime is a head" ∩ "All coins show same side" = $\{H_p H_n H_d\}$

* Whenever you see ∩, think of it as *and*.

A compound event formed by the intersection of several component events is often referred to as a **joint event**.

Note: Try not to confuse union and intersection. Refer to Figure 3-6, which illustrates the random selection of a scholarship student with the characteristics "finance major" and "undergraduate." These two characteristics are the component events. Any student included in the shaded areas is an elementary event in the *union* of the two component events, "undergraduate *or* finance major," and in finding probabilities each elementary event is counted just once. The *intersection* of the two component events, "undergraduate *and* finance major," is represented by the darker area, which includes only those students defined by *both* event sets.

Figure 3-6

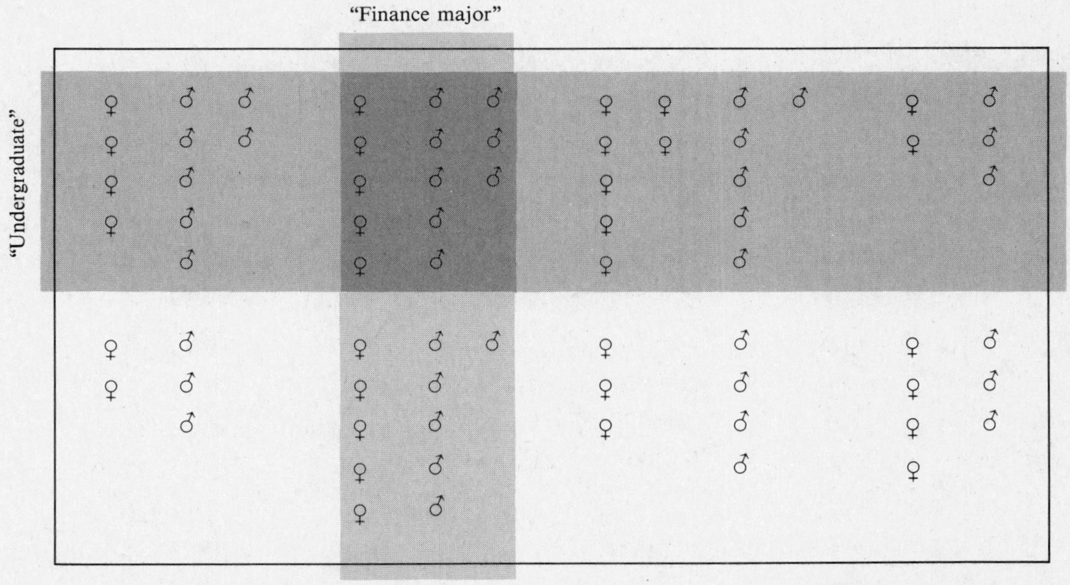

A commonly encountered case is shown in Figure 3-7 for the student selection events "woman" and "finance major." The event set for the intersection of these two component events (represented by the darker area) lies totally *within* that of "finance major." Here the elements of "woman *and* finance major" constitute a **subset** of the event set "finance major."

C. Mutually exclusive events arise when it is impossible for more than one of them to occur.

Two events A and B are **mutually exclusive** if the occurrence of one precludes the other, so that A *and* B is impossible. For example, in drawing only one playing card, you can't get both the events "king" and "queen." These events are mutually exclusive because a card has only one denomination:

$$\Pr[\text{king } and \text{ queen}] = 0$$

The intersection of mutually exclusive events is an empty set ($\{\ \}$ or $\varnothing$), as illustrated in Figure 3-8 for "finance major" and "management major." (State University does not allow double majors.)

Figure 3-7

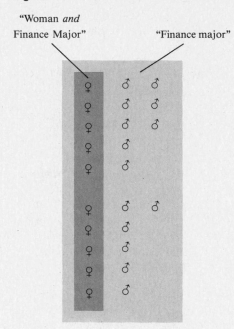

"Woman *and*
Finance Major"   "Finance major"

Figure 3-8

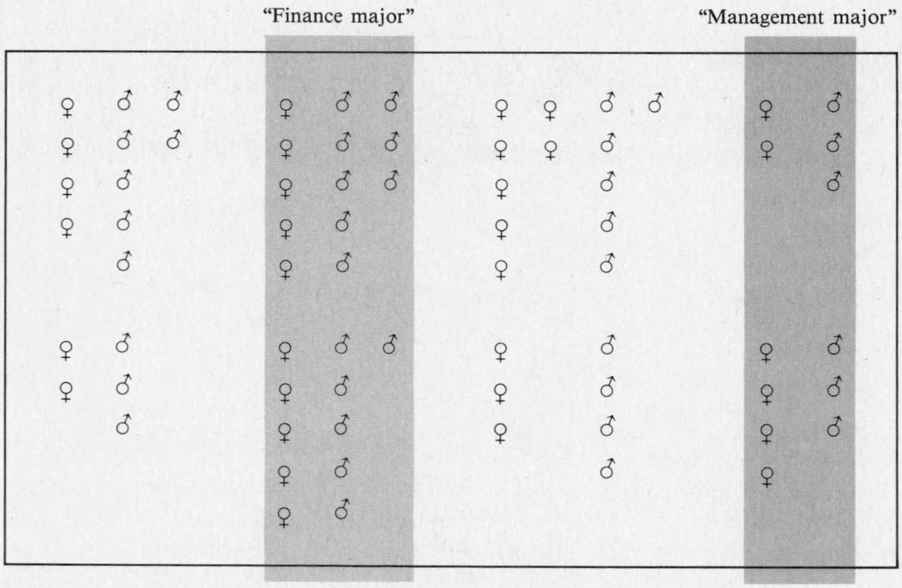

"Finance major"   "Management major"

"Finance major *and* Management major" = {   }

D. Collectively exhaustive events include the whole sample space.

Events that include the entire sample space are **collectively exhaustive**. When considered as separate events, the four possible majors for the selected scholarship student are collectively exhaustive, since every student is included:

"accounting major"   "marketing major"

"finance major   "management major"

Although this group of events is also mutually exclusive, this need not be true for a group of collectively exhaustive events. Consider the events

"woman"   "undergraduate"   "man"

These events are collectively exhaustive because they include all the students, but they are not mutually exclusive because the undergraduates also belong to the groups "woman" and "man."

The union of collectively exhaustive events is a certain event and has a probability of 1. For example,

$$Pr[\text{woman } or \text{ undergraduate } or \text{ man}] = 1$$

E. Complementary events are opposites.

When a pair of events are both mutually exclusive and collectively exhaustive they are **complementary events**, or *opposites*. Looking at Figure 3-9, you can see that the student selection events "undergraduate" and "graduate" are complementary.

Figure 3-9

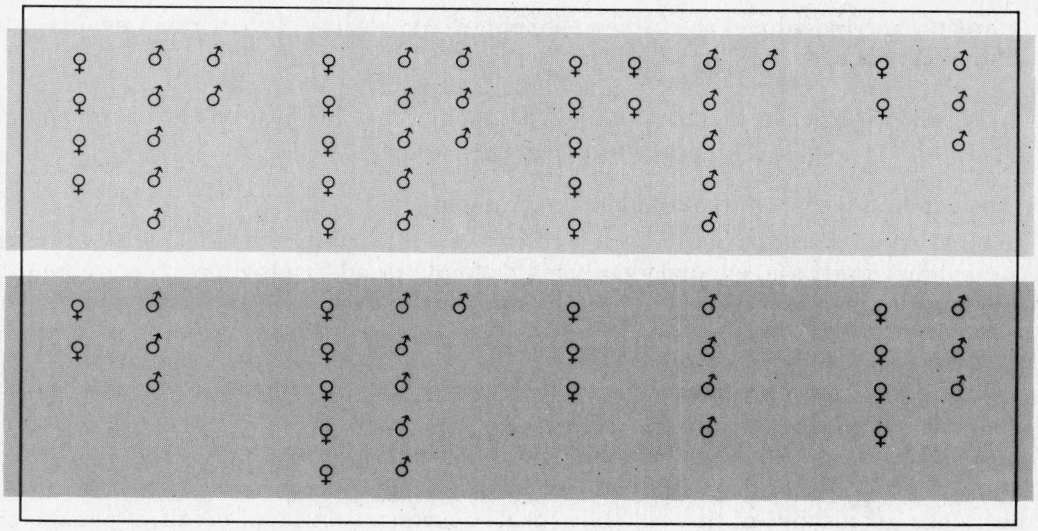

F. Events may be independent or dependent.

Two events A and B are **statistically independent** if the probability for A will be the same value when B occurs, when B does not occur, or when nothing is known about the occurrence of B. In tossing three coins (look back at Example 3-1), the events H_p and H_n are statistically independent because the showing side obtained with one coin will not be influenced in any way by the showing side for the other. Each individual event has a probability of 1/2 regardless of whether or not the other occurs.

Such is not the case for the experiment of randomly selecting a person from the business scholarship students at State University. Consider the events "graduate" and "woman." The probability for "woman" does not have the same value when the event "graduate" occurs as when some other event, such as "all students" occurs:

$$Pr[\text{woman}] = \frac{32}{72} = .444 \qquad \text{(all students considered)}$$

$$Pr[\text{woman}] = \frac{14}{30} = .467 \qquad \text{(graduate students considered)}$$

Thus, the events "graduate" and "woman" are **dependent**.

Our concern is with a *statistical* dependence or independence between two events. These are special relationships that can be established by comparing probabilities under various conditions. Statistical independence is concerned with event *frequencies* rather than cause-and-effect or timing. (Do you think two possible mutually exclusive events can ever be independent? The answer is no, since the probability of either one of them is zero if the other is known to occur.)

3-3. Probabilities for Compound Events

A. The count-and-divide method sometimes provides probabilities for compound events.

Consider the event sets "finance major" and "undergraduate" shown in Figure 3-6 for a randomly selected scholarship student. The probability that the chosen person is either a finance major or an undergraduate is found by counting the elementary events in the union of the two event sets (53) and then dividing by the size of the sample space (72):

$$\Pr[\text{finance major } or \text{ undergraduate}] = \frac{53}{72}$$

Similarly, the **joint probability**—the probability for a joint event, or intersection—that the selected student is *both* a finance major and an undergraduate is

$$\Pr[\text{finance major } and \text{ undergraduate}] = \frac{13}{72}$$

Here, the intersection of the two component event sets has 13 elementary events out of the entire sample space of 72.

The count-and-divide method can only be used when each elementary event is equally likely and the number of them is known. Other methods can be used to find compound event probabilities from known probabilities for the components.

B. The addition law provides probabilities for unions.

When two or more mutually exclusive events are combined by means of union (*or*), the probability for the compound event may be found by adding together the probabilities for the component events. This is the **addition law for mutually exclusive events**:

$$\Pr[A \text{ } or \text{ } B \text{ } or \text{ } C] = \Pr[A] + \Pr[B] + \Pr[C]$$

EXAMPLE 3-4: REASONS FOR DENIAL OF CREDIT

The credit manager for the Hide-Away Safe Co. has several reasons for denying credit to buyers: (*1*) low income, (*2*) poor repayment history, (*3*) high debts, and (*4*) no collateral. Records of past transactions list just one of these as the primary reason for denial of credit. If you assume that past frequencies will apply in the future, you have the following probabilities that the next credit application will be rejected for each primary reason:

$$\Pr[\text{low income}] = .15$$
$$\Pr[\text{poor repayment}] = .20$$
$$\Pr[\text{high debts}] = .25$$
$$\Pr[\text{no collateral}] = .40$$

Reasons (*3*) and (*4*) apply to what are called "balance sheet deficiencies." To find the probability that a balance sheet deficiency will be the reason for the next credit denial, you can apply the addition law:

$$\Pr[\text{balance sheet}] = \Pr[\text{high debts } or \text{ no collateral}]$$
$$= \Pr[\text{high debts}] + \Pr[\text{no collateral}]$$
$$= .25 + .40 = .65$$

---

1. **The addition law and collectively exhaustive events:** If a collection of events is collectively exhaustive as well as mutually exclusive, then their union will be a certainty, so that

$$\Pr[A \text{ } or \text{ } B \text{ } or \text{ } C] = \Pr[A] + \Pr[B] + \Pr[C] = 1$$

EXAMPLE 3-5: THE NUMBER OF SAMPLE DEFECTIVES

Soft-Where-House takes a sample of its program diskettes every hour to determine the quality of its final product. If only 10% of the diskettes are defective, then the following probabilities apply for the number of defectives in a sample of 5 diskettes.

Number defective	Probability
0	.5905
1	.3280
2	.0729
3	.0081
4	.0005
5	.0000
	1.0000

The events for "number defective" are mutually exclusive and collectively exhaustive, and their probabilities add up to 1.

2. **Complementary events have an important relationship:** When two events are complementary (opposite), their probabilities add up to 1. Thus,

$$Pr[A] = 1 - Pr[\text{not } A]$$

This is helpful when you want to know an event's probability, but the probability of its complementary event is easier to find. If you want to find the probability of "at least 1" defective diskette (Example 3-5), you can use the addition law and add together the probabilities for "exactly 1," "exactly 2," etc. But you can find the answer faster if you recognize that "at least 1" is the opposite of "exactly 0." Example 3-5 gives the probability for "0 defective" as .5905, so that

$$Pr[\text{at least 1 defective}] = 1 - Pr[\text{exactly 0 defective}]$$
$$= 1 - .5905 = .4095$$

3. **The general addition law does not require mutually exclusive components:** When the component events are *not* mutually exclusive, you should use the **general addition law**:

$$Pr[A \text{ or } B] = Pr[A] + Pr[B] - Pr[A \text{ and } B]$$

For example, consider the selection of playing cards that are either "heart" or "queen." (The event sets for these outcomes are given in Figure 3-10.) You can use the general addition law to find

$$Pr[\text{queen } or \text{ heart}] = Pr[\text{queen}] + Pr[\text{heart}] - Pr[\text{queen } and \text{ heart}]$$
$$= \frac{4}{52} + \frac{13}{52} - \frac{1}{52} = \frac{16}{52}$$

Since the events "queen" and "heart" are not mutually exclusive (both include the queen of hearts as a possible elementary event), it is necessary to subtract the joint probability for "queen *and* heart." This way the event "queen of hearts" is not counted twice.

Figure 3-10

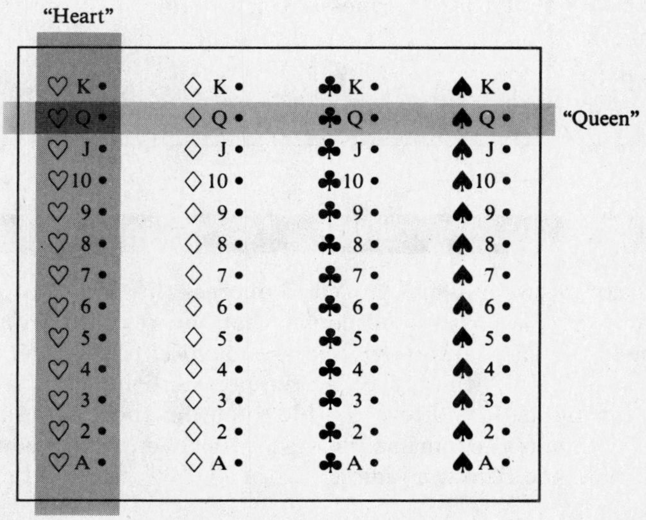

C.   The multiplication law provides joint probabilities.

If you want to find the probability that two or more events occur jointly (i.e., intersect), you will sometimes find it convenient to use the **multiplication law for independent events**:

$$\Pr[A \ and \ B] = \Pr[A] \times \Pr[B]$$

To illustrate, consider once more the events "queen" and "heart." The joint probability for these independent events can be found from the multiplication law:

$$\Pr[\text{queen } and \text{ heart}] = \Pr[\text{queen}] \times \Pr[\text{heart}]$$

$$= \frac{4}{52} \times \frac{13}{52} = \frac{1}{52}$$

The multiplication law is not usually applied when the answer may be obtained more easily by counting and dividing. (There is 1 "queen *and* heart" out of a total of 52 cards.) In the following example the multiplication law is essential to finding the answer.

EXAMPLE 3-6: BUSY COMPUTER TELEPORTS

Giant Enterprises has a central computer connected to district offices in a telecommunications network. At any given moment there is a 20% chance that all teleports are busy and incoming messages must be placed on hold. Messages are sent out infrequently by any particular office, so that the teleports at successive inquiries have *independent* status, much like two coin tosses.

We will let B_1 represent the event that an office's first message of the day encounters a busy signal, B_2 likewise for the second message, etc. For any individual query the probabilities for a busy signal are $\Pr[B_1] = .20$ and $\Pr[B_2] = .20$. The joint probability that the first two messages encounter busy signals is

$$\Pr[B_1 \ and \ B_2] = \Pr[B_1] \times \Pr[B_2]$$
$$= .20 \times .20 = .04$$

The multiplication law applies to the joint occurrence of any number of independent component events. Thus, the joint probability that the first three queries encounter a busy computer system is

$$\Pr[B_1 \ and \ B_2 \ and \ B_3] = \Pr[B_1] \times \Pr[B_2] \times \Pr[B_3]$$
$$= .20 \times .20 \times .20 = .008$$

and the joint probability that five successive busy signals will be encountered is

$$(.20)^5 = .00032$$

The probability that the first query reaches the computer directly (D_1) is

$$\Pr[D_1] = 1 - \Pr[B_1] = 1 - .20 = .80$$

Thus, the joint probability that the first message is connected directly and the two after encounter a busy signal is

$$\Pr[D_1 \ and \ B_2 \ and \ B_3] = \Pr[D_1] \times \Pr[B_2] \times \Pr[B_3]$$
$$= .80 \times .20 \times .20 = .032$$

SUMMARY

A probability is a fraction between 0 and 1 used to express the degree of uncertainty that an *event* will occur. Events are the possible outcomes that can result from *random experiments*. Some random experiments are repeatable, giving rise to *objective probabilities*—which may be viewed as *long-run frequencies*. Although objective probabilities can be estimated from the results of repeated experiments, it is often possible to obtain them using the *count-and-divide method*. Nonrepeatable random experiments result in events for which only *subjective probabilities* can be established through judgment.

The simplest outcomes of a random experiment are called *elementary events*. A complete collection of these constitutes the *sample space*. When grouped, these elements form *composite events*, and it can be helpful to represent these in terms of *event sets*. A *certain event* encompasses the entire sample space and has a probability of 1. An *impossible event* has an empty, or *null*, event set and a probability of 0.

Compound events involve a grouping of one or more *component events* (each of which can be formed from one or more elementary events). Compound events may be classified in terms of how the components are to be combined. One type of compound event is formed by the *union* (*or*, $\cup$) of the components' event sets. Such an event will be the outcome whenever ANY ONE of the components occurs. The second type of component event is formed by the *intersection* (*and*, $\cap$) of the components' event sets. The resulting outcome is called a *joint event* and can happen only if ALL the components occur. The probability for a joint event is called a *joint probability*.

Although probabilities for compound events can sometimes be found using the count-and-divide method, it can be easier to figure them from the probabilities for the component events, when these values are known. Two laws apply: the *addition law* (for unions) and the *multiplication law* (for intersections). The simplest form of the addition law

$$\Pr[A \text{ or } B \text{ or } C] = \Pr[A] + \Pr[B] + \Pr[C]$$

presumes that the components are *mutually exclusive*, so that there can be no intersection. The general addition law

$$\Pr[A \text{ or } B] = \Pr[A] + \Pr[B] - \Pr[A \text{ and } B]$$

adjusts for any component events that may be counted twice because they aren't mutually exclusive. The multiplication law

$$\Pr[A \text{ and } B] = \Pr[A] \times \Pr[B]$$

assumes that events are *statistically independent*—i.e., the probability of any one component event remains the same regardless of the occurrence or nonoccurrence of the others.

A group of events may be *collectively exhaustive*, so that at least one of them must occur. The union of these events is certain. Events that are both collectively exhaustive and mutually exclusive have probabilities that sum to 1. Special cases are *complementary events* (opposites). It is always true that

$$\Pr[A] = 1 - \Pr[\text{not } A]$$

RAISE YOUR GRADES

Can you explain . . . ?

☑ the difference between statistically independent events and mutually exclusive events
☑ how to determine what outcomes to call elementary events
☑ how to use the count-and-divide method
☑ how joint events are related to intersection
☑ the ways to find objective probabilities

Do you know . . . ?

☑ the difference between an elementary event and a composite event
☑ the various ways to find an event's probability
☑ when to apply the two versions of the addition law
☑ the difference between union and intersection
☑ when to apply the addition law and when to use the multiplication law
☑ when objective probabilities apply and when subjective probabilities are appropriate instead

RAPID REVIEW

1. In each of the following situations events A and B are mutually exclusive. Use the addition law to find $\Pr[A\ or\ B]$.   [Section 3-3B]

	(a)	(b)	(c)	(d)
$\Pr[A]$	.2	.1	.5	.07
$\Pr[B]$	.4	.3	.2	.05

2. In each of the following situations events A and B are independent. Use the multiplication law to find $\Pr[A\ and\ B]$.   [Section 3-3C]

	(a)	(b)	(c)	(d)
$\Pr[A]$	.3	.2	.4	.15
$\Pr[B]$	.2	.8	.3	.2

3. The following audit results have been obtained.

	Company	Number of Account Balances: Incorrect	Number of Account Balances: Audited
(a)	W	12	80
(b)	X	2	100
(c)	Y	3	30
(d)	Z	5	40

   For each company find the probability that any particular account was found to be incorrect.   [Section 3-3A]

4. Which of the following is a collection of mutually exclusive events representing a randomly selected playing card?   [Section 3-2C]

   (a) king, queen, face
   (b) heart, diamond, black, red
   (c) 10, 7, jack
   (d) 10, red

5. Which of the following is a collection of collectively exhaustive events representing a randomly selected playing card?   [Section 3-2D]

   (a) club, spade, black, diamond
   (b) 7 of spades, spade, club, red
   (c) face, 7, 9, 10, jack
   (d) red, spade

6. A and B are complementary events. All but which one of the following statements must apply?   [Section 3-3B]

   (a) $\Pr[A] = \Pr[B]$
   (b) $\Pr[A\ or\ B] = 1$
   (c) $\Pr[A\ and\ B] = 0$
   (d) $\Pr[A] = 1 - \Pr[B]$

7. Which one of the following statements is always true?   [Section 3-3B]

   (a) $\Pr[A] = \Pr[\text{not } A]$
   (b) $\Pr[\text{not } A] = \Pr[A] - 1$
   (c) $\Pr[A] = \Pr[A] - \Pr[\text{not } A]$
   (d) $\Pr[A] = 1 - \Pr[\text{not } A]$

8. Which of the following statements is false?

   (a) Mutually exclusive events are statistically independent.   [Section 3-2F]
   (b) Complementary events have probabilities that sum to 1.   [Section 3-3B]
   (c) Complementary events are statistically dependent.   [Section 3-2F]
   (d) An experiment's elementary events are collectively exhaustive and mutually exclusive.   [Sections 3-2A, B]

9. A, B, and C are mutually exclusive and collectively exhaustive. None of these events is impossible. Which one of the following statements can be correct?   [Section 3-3C]

   (a) $\Pr[A] = 1 - \Pr[B]$
   (b) $\Pr[A] = 1/3;\ \Pr[B] = 1/2;\ \Pr[C] = 1/6$

(c) $\Pr[A] = 1/2$; $\Pr[B] = 1/2$; $\Pr[C] = 0$
(d) $\Pr[A \text{ or } B] = \Pr[C] = 1/3$

10. A joint probability might be found in all but which one of the following ways? [Sections 3-1B and 3-3A, C]

    (a) multiplying the component event probabilities together
    (b) dividing the number of events in the intersection by the total number of equally likely events in the sample space
    (c) adding the component event probabilities
    (d) finding the long-run frequency of times that the events in question occur simultaneously

Answers
1. (a) .6   (b) .4   (c) .7   (d) .12
2. (a) .06   (b) .16   (c) .12   (d) .03
3. (a) $12/80 = .15$ (b) $2/100 = .02$
    (c) $3/30 = .10$ (d) $5/40 = .125$
4. (c)   **5.** (b)   **6.** (a)   **7.** (d)   **8.** (a)   **9.** (b)   **10.** (c)

SOLVED PROBLEMS

PROBLEM 3-1 You are selecting cards at random from a shuffled deck and arguing with your friends over various probabilities. For each of the following composite events, (*1*) list the corresponding elementary events in the event set, and (*2*) express the probability as a fraction.

    (a) club   (c) face card   (e) black card
    (b) five   (d) numbered *and* even   (f) diamond *and* nonface

Solution: Refer to the sample space shown in Figure 3-1.
(a) (*1*) List each club, from king to ace:

$$\clubsuit K, \clubsuit Q, \clubsuit J, \clubsuit 10, \clubsuit 9, \clubsuit 8, \clubsuit 7, \clubsuit 6, \clubsuit 5, \clubsuit 4, \clubsuit 3, \clubsuit 2, \clubsuit A$$

    (*2*) Since the elementary events are equally likely, use the count-and-divide method. Count the number of clubs and divide by the number of cards in the deck. The probability that the selected card is a club is

$$\Pr[\text{club}] = \frac{13}{52} = \frac{1}{4}$$

(b) (*1*) $\heartsuit 5, \diamondsuit 5, \clubsuit 5, \spadesuit 5$
    (*2*) $\Pr[\text{five}] = 4/52 = 1/13$
(c) (*1*) $\heartsuit K, \heartsuit Q, \heartsuit J, \diamondsuit K, \diamondsuit Q, \diamondsuit J, \clubsuit K, \clubsuit Q, \clubsuit J, \spadesuit K, \spadesuit Q, \spadesuit J$
    (*2*) $\Pr[\text{face card}] = 12/52 = 3/13$
(d) (*1*) $\heartsuit 10, \heartsuit 8, \heartsuit 6, \heartsuit 4, \heartsuit 2, \diamondsuit 10, \diamondsuit 8, \diamondsuit 6, \diamondsuit 4, \diamondsuit 2,$
    $\clubsuit 10, \clubsuit 8, \clubsuit 6, \clubsuit 4, \clubsuit 2, \spadesuit 10, \spadesuit 8, \spadesuit 6, \spadesuit 4, \spadesuit 2$
    (*2*) $\Pr[\text{numbered } and \text{ even}] = 20/52 = 5/13$
(e) (*1*) $\clubsuit K, \clubsuit Q, \clubsuit J, \clubsuit 10, \clubsuit 9, \clubsuit 8, \clubsuit 7, \clubsuit 6, \clubsuit 5, \clubsuit 4, \clubsuit 3, \clubsuit 2, \clubsuit A,$
    $\spadesuit K, \spadesuit Q, \spadesuit J, \spadesuit 10, \spadesuit 9, \spadesuit 8, \spadesuit 7, \spadesuit 6, \spadesuit 5, \spadesuit 4, \spadesuit 3, \spadesuit 2, \spadesuit A$
    (*2*) $\Pr[\text{black card}] = 26/52 = 1/2$
(f) (*1*) $\diamondsuit 10, \diamondsuit 9, \diamondsuit 8, \diamondsuit 7, \diamondsuit 6, \diamondsuit 5, \diamondsuit 4, \diamondsuit 3, \diamondsuit 2, \diamondsuit A$
    (*2*) $\Pr[\text{diamond } and \text{ nonface}] = 10/52 = 5/26$

PROBLEM 3-2 You are going to toss a penny, a nickel, and a dime. For each of the following composite events, (*1*) list the corresponding elementary events, and (*2*) express the probability as a fraction.

    (a) nickel is a head   (d) all tails
    (b) exactly two heads   (e) penny and dime show different sides
    (c) exactly one head   (f) penny and dime show same side

Solution: Refer to the sample space shown in Figure 3-2.

(a) *(1)* List those outcomes where the nickel is a head:

$$H_p H_n H_d, H_p H_n T_d, T_p H_n H_d, T_p H_n T_d$$

(2) Using the count-and-divide method, divide the number of outcomes where the nickel is a head by the total number of possible outcomes:

$$\Pr[\text{nickel is a head}] = \frac{4}{8} = \frac{1}{2}$$

(b) *(1)* $H_n H_n T_d, H_p T_n H_d, T_p H_n H_d$
    (2) Pr[exactly two heads] = 3/8
(c) *(1)* $H_p T_n T_d, T_p H_n T_d, T_p T_n H_d$
    (2) Pr[exactly one head] = 3/8
(d) *(1)* $T_p T_n T_d$ *(2)* Pr[all tails] = 1/8
(e) *(1)* $H_p H_n T_d, H_p T_n T_d, T_p H_n H_d, T_p T_n H_d$
    (2) Pr[penny and dime show different sides] = 4/8 = 1/2
(f) *(1)* $H_p H_n H_d, H_p T_n H_d, T_p H_n T_d, T_p T_n T_d$
    (2) Pr[penny and dime show same side] = 4/8 = 1/2

PROBLEM 3-3 Consider the random experiment in Figure 3-3 for a student chosen at random. Express the probability that the selected student is

(a) a finance major

(b) a graduate *and* a woman

(c) a man *and* a marketing major

(d) either a man *or* a woman

(e) not an accounting major

(f) a graduate in marketing

Solution: In all cases the desired probability may be found by counting the number of applicable elementary events in Figure 3-3 and dividing by the size of the sample space.
(a) Pr[finance major] = 24/72 = 1/3
(b) Pr[graduate *and* woman] = 14/72 = 7/36
(c) Pr[man *and* marketing major] = 10/72 = 5/36
(d) Pr[either a man *or* a woman] = 72/72 = 1
(e) Pr[not an accounting major] = 56/72 = 7/9
(f) Pr[graduate in marketing] = 7/72

PROBLEM 3-4 The following table shows the number of panelists in each category of a consumer test group.

Occupation	Family Income			Total
	Low	Medium	High	
Homemaker	8	26	6	40
Blue-collar worker	16	40	14	70
White-collar worker	6	62	12	80
Professional	0	2	8	10
Total	30	130	40	200

One person is selected at random.

(a) Find the probability that the selected person is
  (1) a homemaker   *(3)* a white-collar worker
  (2) a blue-collar worker   *(4)* a professional
(b) Find the probability that the selected person's family income is *(1)* low; *(2)* medium; *(3)* high.
(c) Find the probability that the selected person is
  (1) a white-collar worker with a high income
  (2) a homemaker with a low income
  (3) a professional with a medium income

Solution: The count-and-divide method provides the desired probabilities. Divide the given number of persons in each category by the total number of panelists.

(a) (*1*) Pr[homemaker] = 40/200 = .20
    (*2*) Pr[blue-collar worker] = 70/200 = .35
    (*3*) Pr[white-collar worker] = 80/200 = .40
    (*4*) Pr[professional] = 10/200 = .05
(b) (*1*) Pr[low] = 30/200 = .15
    (*2*) Pr[medium] = 130/200 = .65
    (*3*) Pr[high] = 40/200 = .20
(c) (*1*) Pr[white-collar worker with high income] = 12/200 = .06
    (*2*) Pr[homemaker with low income] = 8/200 = .04
    (*3*) Pr[professional with medium income] = 2/200 = .01

PROBLEM 3-5 You are asked to toss a pair of six-sided dice, one red and one green. Each side of a die cube has a different number of dots, 1 through 6.

(a) List the possible sums of the number of dots on the two showing sides.
(b) For each possible sum, list the corresponding elementary events and determine the sum's probability. (Identify your elementary events using a convenient code, such as 2R-5G for 2 dots showing on the red die and 5 on the green.)

Solution:

	(a)	(b)
Sum	Applicable elementary events	Probability
2	1R-1G	1/36
3	1R-2G 2R-1G	2/36
4	1R-3G 3R-1G 2R-2G	3/36
5	1R-4G 4R-1G 2R-3G 3R-2G	4/36
6	1R-5G 5R-1G 2R-4G 4R-2G 3R-3G	5/36
7	1R-6G 6R-1G 2R-5G 5R-2G 3R-4G 4R-3G	6/36
8	2R-6G 6R-2G 3R-5G 5R-3G 4R-4G	5/36
9	3R-6G 6R-3G 4R-5G 5R-4G	4/36
10	4R-6G 6R-4G 5R-5G	3/36
11	5R-6G 6R-5G	2/36
12	6R-6G	1/36
		36/36

PROBLEM 3-6 The following data apply to the 10 employees of the Gotham City office of GizMo Corporation.

Name	Age	College graduate	Marital status	Previous experience
Ms. Brown	38	yes	married	no
Ms. Curlie	27	no	single	yes
Ms. Fish	32	yes	single	no
Mr. Gibbs	43	no	married	yes
Mr. Korngold	38	no	single	yes
Mr. Lake	45	no	married	yes
Mr. Morris	55	yes	single	no
Ms. O'Hara	43	no	single	no
Mr. Smith	39	yes	single	yes
Mr. Waters	35	no	married	yes

The file of one person is chosen at random. For each of the following characteristics, list (*1*) the elementary event (applicable names), and (*2*) the characteristic's probability.

(a) college graduate
(b) older than 35
(c) same age as another
(d) no previous experience
(e) married
(f) younger than 40

Solution:
(a) (*1*) List the name of each person who is a college graduate.

Ms. Brown, Ms. Fish, Mr. Morris, Mr. Smith

(*2*) Find the characteristic's probability by using the count-and-divide method. Divide the number of college graduates by the total number of employees.

$$\Pr[\text{college graduate}] = 4/10 = .4$$

(b) (*1*) Ms. Brown, Mr. Gibbs, Mr. Korngold, Mr. Lake, Mr. Morris, Ms. O'Hara, Mr. Smith
   (*2*) $\Pr[\text{older than 35}] = 7/10 = .7$
(c) (*1*) Ms. Brown, Mr. Korngold, Mr. Gibbs, Ms. O'Hara
   (*2*) $\Pr[\text{same age as another}] = 4/10 = .4$
(d) (*1*) Ms. Brown, Ms. Fish, Mr. Morris, Ms. O'Hara
   (*2*) $\Pr[\text{no previous experience}] = 4/10 = .4$
(e) (*1*) Ms. Brown, Mr. Gibbs, Mr. Lake, Mr. Waters
   (*2*) $\Pr[\text{married}] = 4/10 = .4$
(f) (*1*) Ms. Brown, Ms. Curlie, Ms. Fish, Mr. Korngold, Mr. Smith, Mr. Waters
   (*2*) $\Pr[\text{younger than 40}] = 6/10 = .6$

PROBLEM 3-7 You are again asked to toss a penny, a nickel, and a dime. List the elementary events in the following event sets:

(a) exactly one head *or* exactly two heads
(b) penny is a tail *or* nickel is a tail
(c) same side for penny and dime *or* dime is a head
(d) opposite side for penny and dime *or* penny is a tail

Solution: Refer to the sample space in Figure 3-2. Each event set is the union of the composite events and includes any elementary event that occurs in the set of either composite event. Any elementary event that occurs in both composite events' sets is listed only once.
(a) $H_pH_nT_d, H_pT_nH_d, H_pT_nT_d, T_pH_nH_d, T_pH_nT_d, T_pT_nH_d$
(b) $H_pT_nH_d, H_pT_nT_d, T_pH_nH_d, T_pH_nT_d, T_pT_nH_d, T_pT_nT_d$
(c) $H_pH_nH_d, H_pT_nH_d, T_pH_nH_d, T_pH_nT_d, T_pT_nH_d, T_pT_nT_d$
(d) $H_pH_nT_d, H_pT_nT_d, T_pH_nH_d, T_pH_nT_d, T_pT_nH_d, T_pT_nT_d$

PROBLEM 3-8 Once more, consider the results from tossing a penny, a nickel, and a dime. List the elementary events in the following event sets:

(a) exactly one head *and* penny is a tail
(b) at least one tail *and* dime is a head
(c) penny and nickel are opposites *and* at least two heads
(d) exactly two tails *and* nickel is a tail

Solution: Refer to the sample space in Figure 3-2. Each event set is the intersection of the composite events and includes any elementary event that occurs in the sets of both composite events.
(a) $T_pH_nT_d, T_pT_nH_d$
(b) $H_pT_nH_d, T_pH_nH_d, T_pT_nH_d$
(c) $H_pT_nH_d, T_pH_nH_d$
(d) $H_pT_nT_d, T_pT_nH_d$

PROBLEM 3-9 You are about to draw one card from a shuffled deck of playing cards. List the elementary events in the following event sets:

(a) ten *or* ace   (c) red two *or* black three
(b) diamond *or* ten   (d) black queen *or* red king *or* ace

Solution: Refer to the sample space in Figure 3-1. Since the event sets are a union, list the elementary events that occur in the set of either composite events. Any elementary event that occurs in both composite events' sets is listed only once.
(a) ♡10, ◇10, ♣10, ♠10, ♡A, ◇A, ♣A, ♠A
(b) ◇K, ◇Q, ◇J, ◇10, ◇9, ◇8, ◇7, ◇6, ◇5, ◇4, ◇3, ◇2, ◇A,
   ♡10, ♣10, ♠10
(c) ♡2, ◇2, ♣3, ♠3
(d) ♣Q, ♠Q, ♡K, ◇K, ♡A, ◇A, ♣A, ♠A

PROBLEM 3-10 Once more, you are going to draw a card from a shuffled deck. List the elementary events in the following event sets:

   (a) diamond *and* ten   (c) face card *and* diamond
   (b) black *and* club   (d) ten *and* ace

Solution: Refer to the sample space in Figure 3-1. Since the event sets are an intersection, list the elementary events that occur in the sets of both composite events.
(a) ◇10
(b) ♣K, ♣Q, ♣J, ♣10, ♣9, ♣8, ♣7, ♣6, ♣5, ♣4, ♣3, ♣2, ♣A
(c) ◇K, ◇Q, ◇J
(d) none

PROBLEM 3-11 For each of the following situations, indicate whether or not the events are mutually exclusive.

   (a) The toss of a six-sided die: even-valued result; 1-face; 2-face; 5-face
   (b) Thermometers are inspected and rejected if any of the following is found: poor calibration; inability to withstand extreme temperatures; not within specified size tolerances
   (c) A manager will reject a job applicant for any of the following reasons: slovenly appearance; too young; too old

Solution:
(a) The events are *not* mutually exclusive since 2-faces are even.
(b) The events are *not* mutually exclusive since more than one thing can be wrong at the same time.
(c) The events are *not* mutually exclusive since there can be more than one reason why a candidate is rejected. A person with a slovenly appearance can also be too young or too old.

PROBLEM 3-12 An inspector for Make-Wave Corporation is weighing a small shipment of 10 ballast buoys. Suppose that 8 are satisfactory (S) and 2 are overweight (O). Consider the events S_1, O_1 and S_2, O_2 for the characteristics of the first and second buoy weighed.

   (a) Calculate the probability of S_1.
   (b) Suppose the first buoy is satisfactory. Calculate the probability of S_2 (assuming that the first buoy is not weighed again).
   (c) Suppose instead that the first buoy is overweight. Calculate the probability of S_2.
   (d) Are the events S_1 and S_2 independent or dependent?

Solution:
(a) To find the probability of S_1, use the count-and-divide method.

$$\Pr[S_1] = \frac{8}{10}$$

(b) To find the probability of S_2, the number of satisfactory buoys remaining $(8 - 1)$ must be divided by the total number possible for selection $(10 - 1)$. The satisfactory first buoy can't be counted.

$$\Pr[S_2] = \frac{7}{9}$$

(c) Since the first buoy was unsatisfactory, there are still 8 satisfactory buoys remaining, but again there are only 9 possible buoys to select from.

$$\Pr[S_2] = \frac{8}{9}$$

(d) The events are *dependent* since a different value is obtained for S_2 when S_1 occurs than when it does not.

PROBLEM 3-13 Consider again one randomly selected playing card. Use the count-and-divide method to determine the probabilities for the following equally likely compound events.

   (a) club *or* king   (d) ace *or* red
   (b) 4 *or* 5 *or* 6   (e) ace *or* jack
   (c) club *or* heart   (f) heart *and* face card

(g) king *and* black   (i) even-numbered *and* spade

(h) black *and* face card   (j) (4 *or* 5) *and* diamond

Solution: Refer to the sample space in Figure 3-1. Where the compound events are unions, count the number of elementary events in each composite event and divide by the total number of events possible (52, the number of cards in the deck). Be sure to count only once any elementary event that occurs in both component events' sets. Where the compound events are intersections, count only those elementary events that occur in both of the composite events and divide by the total number of events possible.

(a) 16/52   (f) 3/52

(b) 12/52   (g) 2/52

(c) 26/52   (h) 6/52

(d) 28/52   (i) 5/52

(e) 8/52   (j) 2/52

PROBLEM 3-14   Refer to Problem 3-13. Now use the appropriate addition law to find the probabilities for the compound events listed in parts (a)–(e).

Solution: Refer to Figure 3-1. The count-and-divide method provides the probabilities for the component and joint events. You apply the addition law using those values.

(a) $13/52 + 4/52 - 1/52 = 16/52$ (general law)

(b) $4/52 + 4/52 + 4/52 = 12/52$ (law for mutually exclusive events)

(c) $13/52 + 13/52 = 26/52$ (law for mutually exclusive events)

(d) $4/52 + 26/52 - 2/52 = 28/52$ (general law)

(e) $4/52 + 4/52 = 8/52$ (law for mutually exclusive events)

PROBLEM 3-15   Refer to Problem 3-13. Apply the multiplication law for independent events to find the probabilities for the joint events listed in parts (f)–(j).

Solution: Refer to Figure 3-1. The count-and-divide method provides the probabilities for the component events. You apply the multiplication law using those values.

(f) $13/52 \times 12/52 = 1/4 \times 3/13 = 3/52$

(g) $4/52 \times 26/52 = 1/13 \times 1/2 = 1/26 = 2/52$

(h) $26/52 \times 12/52 = 1/2 \times 3/13 = 3/26 = 6/52$

(i) $20/52 \times 13/52 = 5/13 \times 1/4 = 5/52$

(j) $8/52 \times 13/52 = 2/13 \times 1/4 = 2/52$

PROBLEM 3-16   An accountant randomly selects 5 trial balances out of 10. Exactly 4 of the 10 are in error. The following probabilities apply for the number of selected accounts having incorrect balances.

Number of incorrect balances	Probability
0	1/42
1	10/42
2	20/42
3	10/42
4	1/42

Determine the probability that the selected number of incorrect balances is

(a) at least 2   (c) 1 or more   (e) less than 4

(b) at most 3   (d) greater than 2   (f) 4 or less

Solution: The probabilities are found by using the addition law for mutually exclusive events.

(a) Pr[at least 2] = Pr[2] + Pr[3] + Pr[4]

$$= 20/42 + 10/42 + 1/42 = 31/42$$

(b) Pr[at most 3] = Pr[0] + Pr[1] + Pr[2] + Pr[3]

$$= 1/42 + 10/42 + 20/42 + 10/42 = 41/42$$

(c) Pr[1 or more] = Pr[1] + Pr[2] + Pr[3] + Pr[4]

$$= 10/42 + 20/42 + 10/42 + 1/42 = 41/42$$

(d) Pr[greater than 2] = Pr[3] + Pr[4]

$$= 10/42 + 1/42 = 11/42$$

(e) Pr[less than 4] = Pr[0] + Pr[1] + Pr[2] + Pr[3]

$$= 1/42 + 10/42 + 20/42 + 10/42 = 41/42$$

(f) Pr[4 or less] = Pr[0] + Pr[1] + Pr[2] + Pr[3] + Pr[4]

$$= 1/42 + 10/42 + 20/42 + 10/42 + 1/42 = 42/42 = 1$$

PROBLEM 3-17 There is a .60 probability that each toss of a lopsided coin will result in a head. Find the following for the outcome of three tosses.

(a) Pr[three heads] **(c)** Pr[head first, tail second, head third]
(b) Pr[three tails] **(d)** Pr[tail first, head second, head third]

Solution: Since head and tail are complementary events,

$$Pr[tail] = 1 - .60 = .40$$

Now the multiplication law for independent events is used.
(a) .60 × .60 × .60 = .216
(b) .40 × .40 × .40 = .064
(c) .60 × .40 × .60 = .144
(d) .40 × .60 × .60 = .144

PROBLEM 3-18 Suppose that Giant Enterprises increases its computer facilities so that a busy signal is encountered only 10% of the time. Let B_1 denote that the first message gets a busy signal, D_1 that it goes through directly, and similarly for remaining messages. List all the joint events possible for the first three messages, and find the probabilities for these events.

Solution: Each B event has a probability of .10, so its complementary event, D, has a probability of .90. The joint probabilities are found using the multiplication law for independent events.

Joint event	Joint probability	
B_1 and B_2 and B_3	.10 × .10 × .10 =	.001
B_1 and B_2 and D_3	.10 × .10 × .90 =	.009
B_1 and D_2 and B_3	.10 × .90 × .10 =	.009
B_1 and D_2 and D_3	.10 × .90 × .90 =	.081
D_1 and B_2 and B_3	.90 × .10 × .10 =	.009
D_1 and B_2 and D_3	.90 × .10 × .90 =	.081
D_1 and D_2 and B_3	.90 × .90 × .10 =	.081
D_1 and D_2 and D_3	.90 × .90 × .90 =	$\dfrac{.729}{1.000}$

PROBLEM 3-19 Refer to your answers to Problem 3-18.
 (a) Determine the following for the number of busy signals encountered in the three messages:
   (1) Pr[exactly 0] *(3)* Pr[exactly 2]
   (2) Pr[exactly 1] *(4)* Pr[exactly 3]
 (b) Using your answers to part **(a)**, determine the following for the number of busy signals encountered in the three messages:
   (1) Pr[exactly 2 *or* exactly 3] *(3)* Pr[at least 1]
   (2) Pr[at most 2]   *(4)* Pr[at most 1]

Solution: The joint events from Problem 3-18 are treated as elementary events. The joint probabilities from Problem 3-18 are also used. When more than one of these probabilities is applicable, the addition law for mutually exclusive events provides the composite event probability.
(a) *(1)* Pr[exactly 0] = .729
   (2) Pr[exactly 1] = .081 + .081 + .081 = .243
   (3) Pr[exactly 2] = .009 + .009 + .009 = .027
   (4) Pr[exactly 3] = .001

(b) Apply the addition law for mutually exclusive events to obtain the respective component event probabilities. Use the composite event probabilities found in **(a)**.

(1) Pr[exactly 2] + Pr[exactly 3] = .027 + .001 = .028

(2) Pr[exactly 0] + Pr[exactly 1] + Pr[exactly 2] = .729 + .243 + .027 = .999

(3) 1 − Pr[exactly 0] = 1 − .729 = .271

  Also,

  Pr[exactly 1] + Pr[exactly 2] + Pr[exactly 3] = .243 + .027 + .001 = .271

(4) Pr[exactly 0] + Pr[exactly 1] = .729 + .243 = .972

PROBLEM 3-20 The following data pertain to employees of the Metropolis branch office of Kryptonite Corporation.

Name	Age	Sex	Salary	Marital status	Years of education	Years of service
Emily Brown	26	female	$150/week	single	12	2
Thomas Duncan	54	male	3/hour	single	8	1
David Eckhart	34	male	400/week	married	18	10
Thelda Hunt	48	female	3/hour	widowed	10	21
James Mohair	33	male	200/week	single	12	7
Irvin Odle	31	male	175/week	married	14	2
Stacy Parker	35	female	190/week	divorced	12	4
Norman Raab	27	male	4/hour	divorced	12	2
Tammy Salazar	28	female	200/week	married	15	1
Ted VanDorn	42	male	500/week	married	16	15

Determine the following for one person chosen at random from this group.

(a) Pr[older than 35]   **(c)** Pr[more than 12 years' education]

(b) Pr[paid hourly]   **(d)** Pr[more than 5 years' service]

Solution: Count the number of persons in each category, then divide by the total number of employees to find the desired probabilities.

  (a) 3/10   **(b)** 3/10   **(c)** 4/10   **(d)** 4/10

PROBLEM 3-21 The probability is .95 that a GizMo Corp. traveling sales representative will have no automobile accidents in a year. Assuming that accident experiences in successive years are independent events, find the probability that a particular driver **(a)** goes 5 straight years with no accident; **(b)** has at least 1 accident in 5 years.

Solution:

(a) The multiplication law for independent events applies.

$$(.95)^5 = .774$$

(b) This event is complementary to that found in **(a)**.

$$1 − .774 = .226$$

PROBLEM 3-22 The Centralia plant of DanDee Assemblers experiences power failures with a probability of .10 during any given month. Assuming that power events in successive months are independent, find the probability that there will be **(a)** no power failures during a 3-month span of time; **(b)** exactly 1 month involving a power failure during the next 4 months; **(c)** at least 1 power failure during the next 5 months.

Solution:

(a) The probability of no power failures is

$$1 − .10 = .90$$

Now the multiplication law for independent events applies.

$$.9^3 = .729$$

(b) First the multiplication law for independent events provides the probability for each applicable elementary event. The addition law for mutually exclusive events is then applied to those probabilities.

$$.9 \times .9 \times .9 \times .1 + .9 \times .9 \times .1 \times .9$$
$$+ .9 \times .1 \times .9 \times .9 + .1 \times .9 \times .9 \times .9 = .2916$$

(c) The complementary event is that there will be no power failures during the next 5 months. The multiplication law provides this event's probability.

$$.9^5 = .59049$$

Subtract this value from 1 to find the probability for at least one power failure in the next 5 months.

$$1 - .59049 = .40951$$

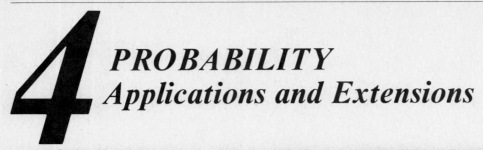

4 PROBABILITY
Applications and Extensions

THIS CHAPTER IS ABOUT

☑ **Probabilities Computed Under Given Conditions**
☑ **The Joint Probability Table**
☑ **The General Multiplication Law**
☑ **Probability Trees and Sampling**

In this chapter you'll learn about some important applications and extensions of probability.

4-1. Probabilities Computed Under Given Conditions

A. Conditional probabilities treat one event as given.

A probability value for an event computed under the assumption that some other event is going to occur is a **conditional probability**. The weather provides some examples. Consider the events "rain" and "cloudy," for which the following might be true:

$$Pr[\text{rain} \mid \text{cloudy}] = .70$$

This equation is read, "The probability that there will be rain *given* that it is cloudy is .70." The event "rain" is listed first, and .70 is the probability for this event. The second event, which appears after the vertical bar, is the **given event**, "cloudy." This event establishes the condition under which .70 applies. Given some other event, "rain" could have a different probability. For example,

$$Pr[\text{rain} \mid \text{low pressure}] = .30$$

In either case, the probability for rain is conditional because it assumes that another event—cloudy or low pressure—is going to occur. Should no conditions be stipulated for the weather, we might have the value

$$Pr[\text{rain}] = .20$$

which is an **unconditional probability**.

B. Conditional probabilities are often easier to compute than unconditional probabilities.

1. **Computation using the count-and-divide method:** The condition, or given event, eliminates extraneous possibilities that would need to be accounted for in establishing unconditional probabilities. For example consider a randomly selected playing card. You can see that

$$Pr[\text{jack} \mid \text{face card}] = \frac{4}{12} = \frac{1}{3}$$

since there are only 12 face cards and just 4 of these are jacks. The condition of "face card" effectively reduces the sample space to just 12 cards, and the count-and-divide method can then be applied to the smaller, or restricted, sample space. Without the condition, you would have to consider the entire sample space, so that

$$\Pr[\text{jack}] = \frac{4}{52} = \frac{1}{13}$$

As another example, consider the student selection experiment in Figure 3-6 (page 43). You can find the probability of "finance major given undergraduate" by observing that the condition "undergraduate" eliminates all graduate students. Therefore, the 42 students in the event set for "undergraduate" are the restricted sample space. Of those students, 13 are finance majors, so that

$$\Pr[\text{finance} \mid \text{undergraduate}] = \frac{13}{42}$$

2. **Computation using the conditional probability identity:** If the necessary probability values are known, you may find it helpful to use the **conditional probability identity**:

$$\Pr[A \mid B] = \frac{\Pr[A \text{ and } B]}{\Pr[B]}$$

This equation states that the conditional probability for an event can be found by dividing the joint probability for the two events (if it is known) by the unconditional probability for the given event (if that value is also known).

We can see from Figure 3-6 that

$$\Pr[\text{finance } and \text{ undergraduate}] = \frac{13}{72}$$

and that

$$\Pr[\text{undergraduate}] = \frac{42}{72}$$

Thus, the conditional probability for "finance" given "undergraduate" is

$$\Pr[\text{finance} \mid \text{undergraduate}] = \frac{\Pr[\text{finance } and \text{ undergraduate}]}{\Pr[\text{undergraduate}]}$$

$$= \frac{13/72}{42/72} = \frac{13}{42}$$

In this case, the conditional probability identity is a more roundabout method than counting and dividing to find the probability. However, the identity will often be useful when the count-and-divide method can't be used.

Note: The conditional probability identity only works when the probability values are available to plug into the formula.

EXAMPLE 4-1: SAMPLE DEFECTIVES

The receiving department of Soft-Where-House is sample-testing a small shipment of high-velocity recording heads. Suppose that out of the 10 heads in the shipment, 2 are defective (D) and the rest are satisfactory (S). (Of course, the inspector doesn't know this fact.) Two heads, represented by the subscripts 1 and 2, are randomly selected one at a time and tested just once.

You can see that

$$\Pr[D_1] = \frac{2}{10}$$

and given that the first head is defective, only 1 defective is among the 9 remaining heads, so that

$$\Pr[D_2 \mid D_1] = \frac{1}{9}$$

Should the first head instead be satisfactory, then 2 defectives are left in the remaining 9, and

$$Pr[D_2 \mid S_1] = \frac{2}{9}$$

You can't use the conditional probability identity here since you don't know the values for $Pr[D_1 \text{ and } D_2]$ or $Pr[S_1 \text{ and } D_2]$.

4-2. The Joint Probability Table

The following table shows the number of State University scholarship students classified in terms of sex (man, woman) and level (undergraduate, graduate).

Sex	Level		Total
	Undergraduate	Graduate	
Man	24	16	40
Woman	18	14	32
Total	42	30	72

A. Joint probabilities may be found for each cell.

By dividing the number of students in each category by the total number of students, you get the following **joint probability table**.

Sex	Level		Marginal probability
	Undergraduate (U)	Graduate (G)	
Man (M)	24/72	16/72	40/72
Woman (W)	18/72	14/72	32/72
Marginal probability	42/72	30/72	1

You can read the *joint probabilities* for various combinations of sex and level events directly from this table. For example, the probability that the selected student will be both a man and an undergraduate ($Pr[M \text{ and } U]$) is 24/72, and the probability for a woman graduate student ($Pr[W \text{ and } G]$) is 14/72.

B. Marginal probabilities relate to single events.

The values in the margins of the table are referred to as **marginal probabilities**. Each represents the probability for the event listed at the head of its row or column. Thus, $Pr[M] = 40/72$ and $Pr[U] = 42/72$ may be read directly from the table. Notice that each marginal probability is equal to the sum of the joint probabilities in its row or column.

C. Conditional probabilities may be computed using entries from the joint probability table.

Once you have found the entries in the joint probability table, you can figure various conditional probabilities. For example, the probability that a randomly selected scholarship student is a "man" given that he is a "graduate" is

$$Pr[M \mid G] = \frac{Pr[M \text{ and } G]}{Pr[G]} = \frac{16/72}{30/72} = \frac{16}{30} = .533$$

You may reverse the events to obtain the conditional probability for "graduate given man":

$$Pr[G \mid M] = \frac{Pr[M \text{ and } G]}{Pr[M]} = \frac{16/72}{40/72} = \frac{16}{40} = .400$$

Although the numerators in these two probability calculations are the same, different divisors apply in the two cases because the uncertain and given events are reversed.

D. A comparison of conditional and unconditional probabilities establishes whether two events are independent or dependent.

Remember from Chapter 3 that two events are *independent* if the probability for one is unaffected by the occurrence of the other.

1. *A* and *B* are *independent* events whenever

$$\Pr[A] = \Pr[A \mid B]$$

2. *A* and *B* are *dependent* events whenever

$$\Pr[A] \neq \Pr[A \mid B]$$

Note: To establish that two events are independent or dependent, you only need to compare the unconditional probability for one event to its conditional probability given the other event.

To better understand this point, think again of playing cards. The events "queen" and "heart" are independent, since

$$\Pr[\text{queen}] = \frac{4}{52} = \frac{1}{13} = \Pr[\text{queen} \mid \text{heart}]$$

And the events "queen" and "face card" are dependent, since

$$\Pr[\text{queen}] = \frac{4}{52} \neq \frac{1}{3} = \Pr[\text{queen} \mid \text{face card}]$$

4-3. The General Multiplication Law

The multiplication law that you used in Chapter 3 to find joint probabilities applies only to *independent* events. To determine joint probabilities when the components are dependent events, you must use the **general multiplication law**:

$$\Pr[A \text{ and } B] = \Pr[A] \times \Pr[B \mid A]$$

and

$$\Pr[A \text{ and } B] = \Pr[B] \times \Pr[A \mid B]$$

As you can see, these equations use both conditional and unconditional probabilities.

EXAMPLE 4-2: OIL WILDCATTING WITH SEISMIC SURVEY

The owner of The Petroleum Entrepeneurship has judged that there is a 30% chance of oil (*O*) beneath his leasehold on Fossil Ridges, with complementary chances that the site is dry (*D*). That is, the following unconditional probabilities apply:

$$\Pr[O] = .30 \quad \text{and} \quad \Pr[D] = 1 - .30 = .70$$

The wildcatter has the option of drilling now or ordering a seismic survey. Such a test is 90% reliable in predicting favorable (*F*) when there is actually oil, but only 70% reliable in providing an unfavorable (*U*) forecast when a site is dry. Stated more precisely,

$$\Pr[F \mid O] = .90 \quad \text{and} \quad \Pr[U \mid D] = .70$$

The general multiplication law may be used to establish the joint probability both that Fossil Ridges does indeed contain oil and that the seismic survey will be favorable:

$$\Pr[O \text{ and } F] = \Pr[O] \times \Pr[F \mid O]$$
$$= .30 \times .90 = .27$$

Similarly, the joint probability for a dry site and an unfavorable seismic survey is

$$\Pr[D \text{ and } U] = \Pr[D] \times \Pr[U \mid D]$$
$$= .70 \times .70 = .49$$

With this information, you can construct a joint probability table:

Geology	Survey Result		Marginal probability
	Favorable (F)	Unfavorable (U)	
Oil (O)	.27	.03	.30
Dry (D)	.21	.49	.70
Marginal probability	.48	.52	1.00

The joint probability for "oil" and "unfavorable," .03, is found by subtracting the joint probability for "oil" and "favorable,". 27, from the marginal probability for "oil," which is .30. The joint probability for "dry" and "favorable," .21, represents the difference between the marginal probability for "dry," .70, and the joint probability for "dry" and "unfavorable," .49. The marginal probabilities of .48 for a favorable seismic survey and .52 for an unfavorable one are found by summing the joint probabilities in each column.

4-4. Probability Trees and Sampling

Figure 4-1 shows the **probability tree diagram** for the random selection of three items from a production line from which 95% of the output is satisfactory. The quality of each observed item is an event, denoted by D for defective and G for good. The subscripts 1, 2, and 3 indicate which of the three items is being considered.

A. Events are represented by branches on the tree.

Each event is represented by a branch. The leftmost branch or **event fork** summarizes the first event, which is either D_1 or G_1. The probability values .05 and .95 are placed alongside the respective branches. Continuing off of each of these branches are two separate event forks, representing the quality events for the second item. Each of these second-stage branching points involves the same pair of events, D_2 and G_2. The quality events for successive items are assumed to be independent, so that the same probability values apply to the second forks as to the first, .05 for D_2 and .95 for G_2. There are four possible combinations for the quality of the first two items, and each of these culminates in a final branching point representing the events for the final item. Again, the probabilities are .05 for D_3 and .95 for G_3.

B. Each path of branches represents an elementary event.

Each path from the start to the end represents a different possible combination of qualities for the three selected items, and each of these combinations is an elementary event in the sampling experiment. The possible events are listed under "Sample Space" in Figure 4-1. The probability for any of these events is the product of the appropriate branch probabilities. For example, the topmost path involves all defective items, and by the multiplication law for independent events you find

$$Pr[D_1 \text{ and } D_2 \text{ and } D_3] = Pr[D_1] \times Pr[D_2] \times Pr[D_3]$$
$$= .05 \times .05 \times .05 = .000125$$

This value is the first joint probability and is placed alongside the elementary event $D_1 D_2 D_3$.

C. Probability trees also apply when successive events are dependent.

The situation is somewhat different if the sample item is taken from a fixed population of small size and the item is not replaced after each selection. Then the quality events for successive items are statistically dependent.

Figure 4-1

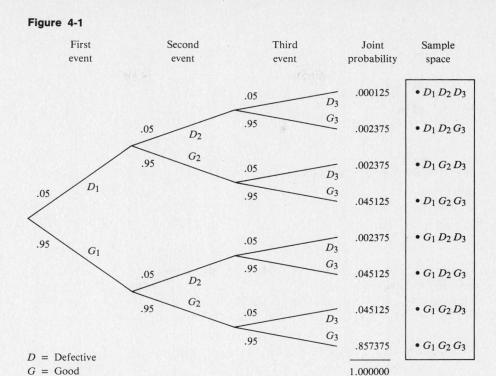

First event	Second event	Third event	Joint probability	Sample space
		.05 D_3	.000125	• $D_1 D_2 D_3$
	.05 D_2	.95 G_3	.002375	• $D_1 D_2 G_3$
	.95 G_2	.05 D_3	.002375	• $D_1 G_2 D_3$
.05 D_1		.95 G_3	.045125	• $D_1 G_2 G_3$
		.05 D_3	.002375	• $G_1 D_2 D_3$
.95 G_1	.05 D_2	.95 G_3	.045125	• $G_1 D_2 G_3$
	.95 G_2	.05 D_3	.045125	• $G_1 G_2 D_3$
		.95 G_3	.857375	• $G_1 G_2 G_3$

D = Defective
G = Good

1.000000

Figure 4-2

First event	Second event	Third event	Joint probability	Sample space
		3/98 D_3	.0000618	• $D_1 D_2 D_3$
	4/99 D_2	95/98 G_3	.0019584	• $D_1 D_2 G_3$
	95/99 G_2	4/98 D_3	.0019584	• $D_1 G_2 D_3$
5/100 D_1		94/98 G_3	.0460214	• $D_1 G_2 G_3$
		4/98 D_3	.0019584	• $G_1 D_2 D_3$
95/100 G_1	5/99 D_2	94/98 G_3	.0460214	• $G_1 D_2 G_3$
	94/99 G_2	5/98 D_3	.0460214	• $G_1 G_2 D_3$
		93/98 G_3	.8559988	• $G_1 G_2 G_3$

D = Defective
G = Good

1.0000000

Figure 4-2 shows a probability tree for a customer who receives a shipment of 100 items, 95 of which are assumed to be good and 5 bad. Different probabilities apply on the "good" and "defective" branches, depending on the quality of the items that have already been selected. Thus, for the second and third stages these values are *conditional probabilities*.

For instance, suppose the first sample item is defective, so that the value $\Pr[D_1] = 5/100$ appears alongside the D_1 branch. Because 1 defective item has been removed from the sample, there are only 4 defectives in the 99 remaining items. Thus, the branch probabilities for the second fork are

$$\Pr[D_2 \,|\, D_1] = \frac{4}{99} \qquad \text{and} \qquad \Pr[G_2 \,|\, D_1] = \frac{95}{99}$$

Suppose D_2 then occurs. This leaves 3 defectives in 98 items, so that the top third-stage fork involves the following conditional probabilities:

$$\Pr[D_3 \,|\, D_1 \text{ and } D_2] = \frac{3}{98} \qquad \text{and} \qquad \Pr[G_3 \,|\, D_1 \text{ and } D_2] = \frac{95}{98}$$

D.   The general multiplication law provides the joint probabilities for elementary events in a probability tree.

The general multiplication law can be expanded to apply to situations involving more than two component events. For instance,

$$\Pr[A \text{ and } B \text{ and } C] = \Pr[A] \times \Pr[B \,|\, A] \times \Pr[C \,|\, A \text{ and } B]$$

All terms except the first one are conditional probabilities, with the preceding events assumed as given events.

You can now use the general multiplication law to find the joint probability for each path of a probability tree. Using the numbers on the topmost path of Figure 4-2, you would obtain

$$\Pr[D_1 \text{ and } D_2 \text{ and } D_3] = \Pr[D_1] \times \Pr[D_2 \,|\, D_1] \times \Pr[D_3 \,|\, D_1 \text{ and } D_2]$$

$$= \left(\frac{5}{100}\right)\left(\frac{4}{99}\right)\left(\frac{3}{98}\right) = .0000618$$

SUMMARY

A *conditional probability* is a probability value that is computed for an event under the assumption that one or more other events will occur. These assumed events are referred to as conditions, or *given events*. Conditional probabilities can be easier to compute than *unconditional probabilities*, since the condition reduces the possible outcomes. When two events are *independent*, the unconditional probability for either event is the same as its conditional probability given the other event.

• If $\Pr[A] = \Pr[A \,|\, B]$, A and B are independent.

Should these probabilities differ, the events are *dependent*.

• If $\Pr[A] \neq \Pr[A \,|\, B]$, A and B are dependent.

The *joint probability table* relates two categories of events. The rows present a set of mutually exclusive and collectively exhaustive events for one category, and the columns present the same for the second category. Each cell of the table gives the joint probability for the events occurring in its row and column. The probability for each single event is equal to the total of the joint probabilities in its row or column. Each event's probability is written in one of the margins and is referred to as a *marginal probability*. The information from the joint probability table can be used to compute conditional probabilities using the *conditional probability identity*:

$$\Pr[A \,|\, B] = \frac{\Pr[A \text{ and } B]}{\Pr[B]}$$

The *general multiplication law* may be used to compute joint probabilities when the component events are dependent. When there are two components joined by *and*, the conditional probability for one event will be multiplied by the unconditional probability for the given event.

$$\Pr[A \text{ and } B] = \Pr[A] \times \Pr[B \,|\, A]$$

and

$$\Pr[A \text{ and } B] = \Pr[B] \times \Pr[A \,|\, B]$$

Often the only way you can compute joint probabilities with the available information is by applying the general multiplication law. This law is also useful in evaluating probability trees.

A *probability tree* is a diagram in which a series of uncertain events in a multiple-stage experiment are portrayed as branches. These branches for the possible events come together at a single point to form an *event fork*. Uncertain events are shown chronologically, with the earlier possibilities at the left. Each branch of the tree is given a probability for the respective event. The elementary events of the experiment are all the different possible combinations of outcomes, each represented on the tree by a different sequence of branches, or *path*. To compute the joint probability for an elementary event, use the multiplication law. The joint probability will be equal to the product of the branch probabilities on the path that corresponds.

RAISE YOUR GRADES

Can you explain ...?

☑ the difference between a conditional and an unconditional probability
☑ why the count-and-divide method might not be appropriate for finding probabilities in some situations
☑ why probability trees can be helpful in representing the outcomes of a sampling experiment
☑ how to construct a joint probability table

Do you know ...?

☑ when you can use the conditional probability identity
☑ the difference between conditional and marginal probabilities
☑ how to compute a joint probability for an elementary event from a probability tree
☑ how to construct a joint probability table when a complete listing of the sample space is unavailable

RAPID REVIEW

1. Use the general multiplication law to find $\Pr[A \text{ and } B]$ for the following situations. [Section 4-3]

	(a)	(b)	(c)	(d)
$\Pr[A]$	1/2	1/3	3/4	1/5
$\Pr[B \mid A]$	1/2	1/2	1/3	1/2

2. For each of the following situations, use the conditional probability identity to compute (1) $\Pr[A \mid B]$ and (2) $\Pr[B \mid A]$. [Section 4-1B]

	(a)	(b)	(c)	(d)
$\Pr[A \text{ and } B]$	.4	1/4	.5	1/3
$\Pr[A]$	.7	1/2	.6	3/4
$\Pr[B]$	.5	2/3	.7	1/2

3. A and B are independent. Which one of the following statements cannot be true? [Section 4-2D]

   (a) $\Pr[A] + \Pr[B] > 1$
   (b) $\Pr[A] = \Pr[B]$
   (c) $\Pr[A] = 1/2$; $\Pr[B] = 1/2$; $\Pr[A \text{ and } B] = 1/4$
   (d) $\Pr[A] = 1/2$; $\Pr[B] = 1/2$; $\Pr[A \text{ and } B] = 1/8$

4. Which one of the following statements is false regarding a joint probability table? [Section 4-2A, B]

   (a) The sum of all the joint probabilities is 1.
   (b) The entire set of marginal probabilities sums to 2.
   (c) No joint probability value of zero is allowed.
   (d) No joint probability can exceed either of its marginal probabilities.

5. Which of the following statements is false for a joint probability table?   [Section 4-2]

   (a) A joint probability can never be found by applying the multiplication law to the marginal probabilities.
   (b) A conditional probability may be found by dividing an appropriate joint probability by the probability for the given event.
   (c) The probabilities listed in the right margin sum to 1.
   (d) The product of any row marginal probability and its column counterpart might be equal to the corresponding joint probability.

6. The probability for "head" with a lopsided coin is .3. The probability that two successive tosses will each be heads is

   (a) .6;   (b) .90;   (c) .09;   (d) .25.   [Sections 3-3C and 4-4A]

7. A shipment contains 50 parts, 3 of which are defective. Two successive parts are removed at random without replacement. The probability that the second part is defective given that the first is satisfactory is

   (a) 3/50;   (b) 3/49;   (c) 2/49;   (d) 2/50.   [Section 4-1B]

8. A regular coin and a two-headed coin are tossed. The probability that both coins land head-side up is

   (a) 1/2;   (b) 1/4;   (c) 1;   (d) 3/4.   [Sections 3-3C and 4-4A]

9. Indicate which one of the following statements is true.   [Section 4-4]

   (a) Elementary events are always equally likely.
   (b) The probability values for branches of the same event type (e.g., G for good) must be identical when they apply to a single path on a probability tree.
   (c) The events applicable to a single branching point must be statistically independent.
   (d) The probabilities for the events in the same fork must sum to 1.

10. Which of the following statements is false?

   (a) When several events are not mutually exclusive, their probabilities may sum to a value greater than 1.
   (b) A conditional probability can be zero even when the given event is not impossible.
   (c) A conditional probability can never be greater than 1.
   (d) In a series of tosses of a fair coin it is impossible for the number of heads to exceed the number of tails.

Answers
1. (a) 1/4 (b) 1/6 (c) 1/4 (d) 1/10
2. (a) (*1*) 4/5 = .80 (*2*) 4/7 = .57
   (b) (*1*) 3/8 = .375 (*2*) 1/2 = .50
   (c) (*1*) 5/7 = .71 (*2*) 5/6 = .83
   (d) (*1*) 2/3 = .67 (*2*) 4/9 = .44
3. (d)   4. (c)   5. (a)   6. (c)   7. (b)   8. (a)   9. (d)   10 (d)

SOLVED PROBLEMS

PROBLEM 4-1   The following joint probability table represents the characteristics of a randomly selected employee.

Rank	College Education		Marginal probability
	Yes	No	
Management	.15	.05	
Classified	.10	.70	
Marginal probability			1.00

(a) Find the missing marginal probability values.
(b) Find the conditional probability that the selected person
   (1) is in management given that he or she had no college
   (2) is classified given that he or she went to college
   (3) went to college given that he or she is in management
   (4) had no college given that he or she is classified

Solution:
(a) The missing marginal probabilities are found by summing the joint probabilities in each row or column.

	College Education		Marginal probability
Rank	Yes	No	
Management	.15	.05	.20
Classified	.10	.70	.80
Marginal probability	.25	.75	1.00

(b) Using the conditional probability identity, you divide the joint probability for the two events by the marginal probability for the given event.

(1) Pr[management | no college] $= \dfrac{\text{Pr[management } and \text{ no college]}}{\text{Pr[no college]}} = \dfrac{.05}{.75} = .067$

(2) Pr[classified | college] $= .10/.25 = .40$

(3) Pr[college | management] $= .15/.20 = .75$

(4) Pr[no college | classified] $= .70/.80 = .875$

PROBLEM 4-2 Refer to Problem 3-4 (page 52). One panelist from the consumer test group is selected at random.

(a) Construct the joint probability table for occupation versus family income events.
(b) Find the following:
   (1) Pr[homemaker *and* high]   (3) Pr[blue-collar *and* low]
   (2) Pr[white-collar *and* low]   (4) Pr[professional *and* high]
(c) Find the following:
   (1) Pr[high | homemaker]   (3) Pr[blue-collar | low]
   (2) Pr[white-collar | high]   (4) Pr[professional | low]

Solution:
(a) You can obtain the entries for the joint probability table by using the data given in the table in Problem 3-4. Use the count-and-divide method, dividing the number of panelists in each category by the total number of panelists. For instance, the joint probability for "homemaker *and* low" is 8/200, or .04. You can find the marginal probabilities by counting and dividing or by summing the joint probabilities in each row and column.

	Family Income			Marginal probability
Occupation	Low	Medium	High	
Homemaker	.04	.13	.03	.20
Blue-collar	.08	.20	.07	.35
White-collar	.03	.31	.06	.40
Professional	0	.01	.04	.05
Marginal probability	.15	.65	.20	1.00

(b) You can find the desired values by reading directly from the table in part (a):
  (1) .03   (2) .03   (3) .08   (4) .04
(c) To find these conditional probabilities, use the conditional probability identity. Divide the joint probability for the two events by the marginal probability for the given event.

  (1) $\Pr[\text{high}\,|\,\text{homemaker}] = \dfrac{\Pr[\text{high } and \text{ homemaker}]}{\Pr[\text{homemaker}]} = .03/.20 = .15$

  (2) $\Pr[\text{white-collar}\,|\,\text{high}] = .06/.20 = .30$

  (3) $\Pr[\text{blue-collar}\,|\,\text{low}] = .08/.15 = .533$

  (4) $\Pr[\text{professional}\,|\,\text{low}] = 0/.15 = 0$

PROBLEM 4-3 The business faculty at Near Miss University are categorized in Figure 4-3. One instructor is chosen at random. Construct a joint probability table for sex versus employment status events.

Figure 4-3

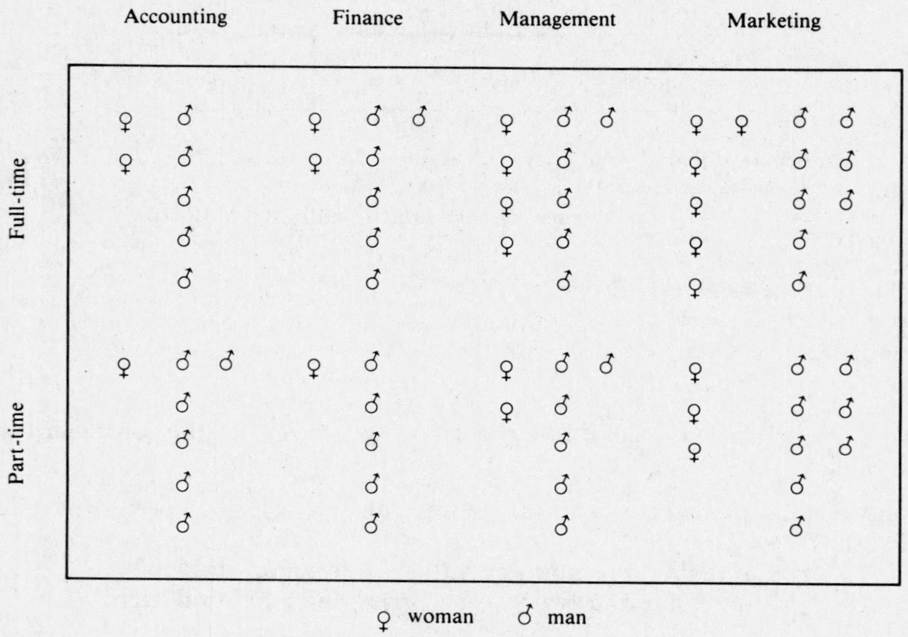

♀ woman   ♂ man

Solution: You can find the joint probabilities by counting the number of elementary events (instructors) in each category and dividing by the total number of events in the sample space. For instance, there are 25 full-time male instructors, and there are 71 instructors in the sample space. So the joint probability for "full-time *and* man" is 25/71. Find the marginal probabilities by counting and dividing or by summing the joint probabilities in each row and column.

Employment status	Sex		Marginal probability
	Man	Woman	
Full-time	25/71	14/71	39/71
Part-time	25/71	7/71	32/71
Marginal probability	50/71	21/71	1

PROBLEM 4-4 Repeat Problem 4-3 for discipline versus employment status events.

Solution: Again, find the joint probabilities by counting the number of elementary events in each category and dividing by the total number of events in the sample space. Find the marginal probabilities by counting and dividing or by summing the joint probabilities in each row and column.

Discipline	Employment status		Marginal probability
	Full-time	Part-time	
Accounting	7/71	7/71	14/71
Finance	8/71	6/71	14/71
Management	10/71	8/71	18/71
Marketing	14/71	11/71	25/71
Marginal probability	39/71	32/71	1

PROBLEM 4-5 A card is selected at random from a deck of playing cards. Find the following probabilities. (Count ace as a "1"—low and odd.)

   (a) Pr[heart | red]   **(d)** Pr[jack | face]
   (b) Pr[odd-numbered | below 6]   **(e)** Pr[below 6 | nonface]
   (c) Pr[club | black]   **(f)** Pr[above 3 | below 8]

Solution: Refer to the sample space in Figure 3-1 (page 39). To find each probability, first eliminate from the sample space those cards not permitted by the condition. Then using the count-and-divide method, divide the elementary events in the event set by the total number of events in the restricted sample space. For instance, to find Pr[heart | red], you first eliminate all the black cards from the sample space, because they are not permitted by the condition "red." You then divide the number of hearts (13) by the total number of cards remaining in the sample space (26).

(a) Pr[heart | red] = 13/26 = 1/2
(b) Pr[odd-numbered | below 6] = 12/20 = 3/5
(c) Pr[club | black] = 13/26 = 1/2
(d) Pr[jack | face] = 4/12 = 1/3
(e) Pr[below 6 | nonface] = 20/40 = 1/2
(f) Pr[above 3 | below 8] = 16/28 = 4/7

PROBLEM 4-6 Refer to the data given in Problem 3-6 (page 53). For the characteristics of a randomly chosen person, construct a joint probability table for sex versus marital status events.

Solution: The joint probabilities for the table are found by applying the count-and-divide method to the given data. For example, to find the probability for the event "man *and* married," divide the number of married male employees (3) by the total number of employees (10). Find the marginal probabilities by counting and dividing or by summing the joint probabilities in each row and column.

Sex	Marital status		Marginal probability
	Married	Unmarried	
Man	3/10	3/10	6/10
Woman	1/10	3/10	4/10
Marginal probability	4/10	6/10	1

PROBLEM 4-7 Again refer to the data given in Problem 3-6. For the characteristics of a randomly chosen person, construct a joint probability table for events pertaining to age (two categories: under 40, over 40) and previous experience.

Solution: The joint probabilities for the table are found by applying the count-and-divide method to the given data. For example, to find the probability for the event "under 40 *and* previous experience," divide the number of employees under 40 years of age with previous experience (4) by the total number of employees (10). Find the marginal probabilities by counting and dividing or by summing the joint probabilities in each row and column.

Age	Previous experience		Marginal probability
	Yes	No	
Under 40	4/10	2/10	6/10
Over 40	2/10	2/10	4/10
Marginal probability	6/10	4/10	1

PROBLEM 4-8 Matchless Garments test-markets its products with a consumer test panel provided by a consultant. Two panels, each made up of 100 persons, are available. Consider the characteristics of a person chosen at random from each group.

(a) Panel *A* is 50% men and 50% women; 70% of the panel members are married (the rest unmarried), and just as many men as women are married. Thus, any two sex and marital status events are *independent*. Construct a joint probability table by first finding the marginal probabilities and then using the multiplication law to obtain the joint probabilities, which in this case are the products of the two respective marginal probabilities.

(b) Panel *B* is also 50% men and 50% women, and 70% of the panel members are married. However, only 60% of the men are married, whereas 80% of the women are married. Thus, any two sex and marital status events are *dependent*. This means that the product of the respective marginal probabilities doesn't equal the corresponding joint probability, so the multiplication law can't be used to find the joint probabilities. Instead, construct the joint probability table using the count-and-divide method.

Solution:

(a) Since the marginal probabilities are the probabilities for each individual event, this information has been given. The probability for the event "man" is .50; for "woman," .50; for "married," .70; and for "unmarried," .30, or $(1 - .70)$. To find each joint probability, multiply the marginal probabilities for the two joint events. Thus, you obtain the joint probability for "man *and* married" by multiplying the marginal probability for "man"—.50—by that for "married"—.70.

Sex	Marital Status		Marginal probability
	Married	Unmarried	
Man	.35	.15	.50
Woman	.35	.15	.50
Marginal probability	.70	.30	1.00

(b) As in part (a), the marginal probabilities are given, so they need only be put in the table. Since 60% of the men are married, there are $.60 \times 50 = 30$ married men and the joint probability for "man" and "married" is $30/100 = .30$. Similarly, the joint probability for "woman" and "married" is $40/100 = .40$. You now find the remaining joint probabilities by subtracting the known joint probabilities from the marginal probabilities in their respective rows.

$$\text{Pr[man } and \text{ unmarried]} = .50 - .30 = .20$$
$$\text{Pr[woman } and \text{ unmarried]} = .50 - .40 = .10$$

Sex	Marital Status		Marginal probability
	Married	Unmarried	
Man	.30	.20	.50
Woman	.40	.10	.50
Marginal probability	.70	.30	1.00

PROBLEM 4-9 Dumpty-Humpty Disposal serves 100 industrial customers. Of these, 15 are delinquent (*D*) in paying their bills, and the rest are on time (*O*). An auditor randomly selects

3 accounts, one at a time without replacement. The subscripts 1, 2, and 3 denote the sequence in which the audited bills are selected.

(a) Find the following probabilities:
(*1*) $\Pr[D_1]$ (*3*) $\Pr[D_2 | D_1]$ (*5*) $\Pr[S_2 | D_1]$
(*2*) $\Pr[S_1]$ (*4*) $\Pr[D_2 | S_1]$ (*6*) $\Pr[S_2 | S_1]$

(b) Find the following probabilities:
(*1*) $\Pr[D_3 | D_1 \text{ and } D_2]$ (*5*) $\Pr[S_3 | D_1 \text{ and } D_2]$
(*2*) $\Pr[D_3 | D_1 \text{ and } S_2]$ (*6*) $\Pr[S_3 | D_1 \text{ and } S_2]$
(*3*) $\Pr[D_3 | S_1 \text{ and } D_2]$ (*7*) $\Pr[S_3 | S_1 \text{ and } D_2]$
(*4*) $\Pr[D_3 | S_1 \text{ and } S_2]$ (*8*) $\Pr[S_3 | S_1 \text{ and } S_2]$

Solution: You find the unconditional probabilities by dividing the number of accounts in the desired category by the total number of accounts. To find the conditional probabilities, you must remember to reduce the number of accounts in the category and/or the total number of accounts by the number of accounts that have already been selected. For instance, to find $\Pr[D_2 | D_1]$, you will have only 14 delinquent accounts because 1 has already been selected, and for the same reason you will have only 99 accounts total. Thus, the answer will be 14/99.

(a) (*1*) 15/100   (*3*) 14/99   (*5*) 85/99
  (*2*) 85/100   (*4*) 15/99   (*6*) 84/99
(b) (*1*) 13/98   (*4*) 15/98   (*7*) 84/98
  (*2*) 14/98   (*5*) 85/98   (*8*) 83/98
  (*3*) 14/98   (*6*) 84/98

PROBLEM 4-10   An oil wildcatter decides that the probability for striking gas (G) is .40. She orders a seismic survey that confirms (C) gas with a probability of .85 in known gas fields and denies (D) gas with a probability of .60 when there is no gas.

(a) Find (*1*) $\Pr[G \text{ and } C]$ and (*2*) $\Pr[\text{no } G \text{ and } D]$.
(b) Construct the joint probability table for geology and survey events.

Solution: You are given the following data:

$$\Pr[G] = .40 \qquad \Pr[C | G] = .85 \qquad \Pr[D | \text{no } G] = .60$$

Since the event "no G" is the complement of "G,"

$$\Pr[\text{no } G] = 1 - .40 = .60$$

(a) Applying the multiplication law to the given data provides the desired joint probabilities.
(*1*) $\Pr[G \text{ and } C] = \Pr[G] \times \Pr[C | G]$

$$= .40(.85) = .34$$

(*2*) $\Pr[\text{no } G \text{ and } D] = \Pr[\text{no } G] \times \Pr[D | \text{no } G]$

$$= .60(.60) = .36$$

(b) Since the joint probabilities in each row or column must sum to their respective marginal probabilities, you can find the joint probabilities for "G and D" and "no G and C" by subtracting the known joint probabilities from their respective marginal probabilities.

$$\Pr[G \text{ and } D] = .40 - .34 = .06$$
$$\Pr[\text{no } G \text{ and } C] = .60 - .36 = .24$$

You then find the remaining marginal probabilities by summing the joint probabilities in their respective columns.

	Survey Result		
Geology	Confirms (*C*)	Denies (*D*)	Marginal probability
Gas (*G*)	.34	.06	.40
No gas (no *G*)	.24	.36	.60
Marginal probability	.58	.42	1.00

PROBLEM 4-11 A State University business scholarship student is randomly selected. Figure 3-3 (page 41) summarizes the sample space. Let U and G denote level; M and W, sex; A, accounting major; and F, finance major.

(a) Find the following probabilities by applying the count-and-divide method to the elementary events given in Figure 3-3.

(1)	*(2)*	*(3)*	*(4)*	*(5)*	*(6)*
$\Pr[U]$	$\Pr[F]$	$\Pr[W]$	$\Pr[G]$	$\Pr[M]$	$\Pr[W]$
$\Pr[W\,|\,U]$	$\Pr[U\,|\,F]$	$\Pr[A\,|\,W]$	$\Pr[M\,|\,G]$	$\Pr[F\,|\,M]$	$\Pr[U\,|\,W]$

(b) Apply the multiplication law to each pair of probabilities in part (a) to find the following joint probabilities.

(1) $\Pr[U \text{ and } W]$ (3) $\Pr[W \text{ and } A]$ (5) $\Pr[M \text{ and } F]$

(2) $\Pr[F \text{ and } U]$ (4) $\Pr[G \text{ and } M]$ (6) $\Pr[W \text{ and } U]$

Solution:

(a) Use the count-and-divide method to find the specified probabilities.

(1) $\Pr[U] = 42/72$ $\Pr[W\,|\,U] = 18/42$

(2) $\Pr[F] = 24/72$ $\Pr[U\,|\,F] = 13/24$

(3) $\Pr[W] = 32/72$ $\Pr[A\,|\,W] = 6/32$

(4) $\Pr[G] = 30/72$ $\Pr[M\,|\,G] = 16/30$

(5) $\Pr[M] = 40/72$ $\Pr[F\,|\,M] = 14/40$

(6) $\Pr[W] = 32/72$ $\Pr[U\,|\,W] = 18/32$

(b) (1) $\Pr[U \text{ and } W] = \Pr[U] \times \Pr[W\,|\,U]$
$$= (42/72)(18/42) = 18/72$$

(2) $\Pr[F \text{ and } U] = \Pr[F] \times \Pr[U\,|\,F]$
$$= (24/72)(13/24) = 13/72$$

(3) $\Pr[W \text{ and } A] = \Pr[W] \times \Pr[A\,|\,W]$
$$= (32/72)(6/32) = 6/72$$

(4) $\Pr[G \text{ and } M] = \Pr[G] \times \Pr[M\,|\,G]$
$$= (30/72)(16/30) = 16/72$$

(5) $\Pr[M \text{ and } F] = \Pr[M] \times \Pr[F\,|\,M]$
$$= (40/72)(14/40) = 14/72$$

(6) $\Pr[W \text{ and } U] = \Pr[W] \times \Pr[U\,|\,W]$
$$= (32/72)(18/32) = 18/72$$

PROBLEM 4-12 A GizMo Corp. inspector randomly selects 3 widgets from a production line assumed to yield 90% satisfactory (S) and 10% unsatisfactory (U) output. You may assume successive quality events to be independent.

(a) Construct a probability tree diagram for this experiment, identify all the elementary events in the sample space, and compute the joint probability for each event.

(b) Find the probabilities for the following number of unsatisfactory items:

    (1) none   *(3)* exactly 2   *(5)* at least 1

    (2) exactly 1   *(4)* exactly 3   *(6)* at most 2

Solution:

(a) See Figure 4-4. Each event fork has a branch U, with a probability of .10, and a branch S, with a probability of .90. There are three stages of branching points, one for each widget chosen. The elementary events are all the possible paths of the tree, and the joint probabilities are found by multiplying the probabilities for successive quality events on each path.

(b) You find these probabilities by summing the probabilities for all the elementary events in the sample space with the required number of unsatisfactory events. For instance, the elementary events with "exactly 1" unsatisfactory item are $U_1 S_2 S_3$, $S_1 U_2 S_3$, and $S_1 S_2 U_3$. Therefore, $\Pr[\text{exactly 1}]$ is found by summing the probabilities for these three events.

(1) $\Pr[\text{none}] = .729$

(2) $\Pr[\text{exactly 1}] = .081 + .081 + .081 = .243$

(3) $\Pr[\text{exactly 2}] = .009 + .009 + .009 = .027$

(4) $\Pr[\text{exactly 3}] = .001$

(5) $\Pr[\text{at least 1}] = .243 + .027 + .001 = .271$

(6) $\Pr[\text{at most 2}] = .729 + .243 + .027 = .999$

Figure 4-4

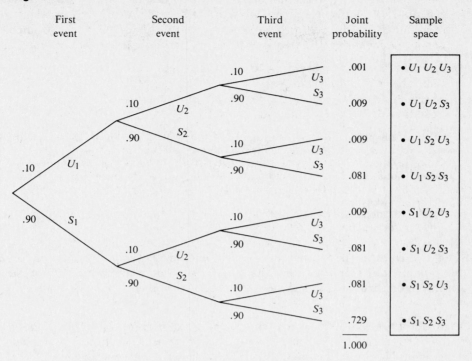

First event	Second event	Third event	Joint probability	Sample space

PROBLEM 4-13   Consider the characteristics for one employee of Kryptonite Corp. chosen at random from those listed in Problem 3-20 (page 58).

(a) Construct a joint probability table for sex versus marital status events.

(b) Determine the following:
  (1) Pr[widowed *or* divorced]   (3) Pr[male *or* single]
  (2) Pr[single *or* divorced]   (4) Pr[female *or* married]

Solution:

(a) Use the count-and-divide method to find the joint probabilities. Divide the number of events in each category by the total number of events. For instance, the probability for "single *and* male" is the number of single males (2) divided by the total number of employees (10). Find the marginal probabilities by counting and dividing or by summing the joint probabilities in each row and column.

Marital status	Sex		Marginal probability
	Male	Female	
Single	2/10	1/10	3/10
Married	3/10	1/10	4/10
Divorced	1/10	1/10	2/10
Widowed	0	1/10	1/10
Marginal probability	6/10	4/10	1

(b) Since you want to find the union of two events, use the addition law to obtain these probabilities. Be sure to determine if the events are dependent or independent, and then use the appropriate form of the addition law.

  (1) Pr[widowed *or* divorced] = 1/10 + 2/10 = 3/10
  (2) Pr[single *or* divorced] = 3/10 + 2/10 = 5/10 = 1/2
  (3) Pr[male *or* single] = 6/10 + 3/10 − 2/10 = 7/10
  (4) Pr[female *or* married] = 4/10 + 4/10 − 1/10 = 7/10

PROBLEM 4-14 Consider again the random selection of one Kryptonite Corp. employee from those listed in Problem 3-20. In each of the following cases find the unconditional probability of event (*1*). Then find the conditional probability of event (*1*) given event (*2*). Comparing each pair of values, indicate whether the two events are statistically independent or dependent.

(a) (*1*) age over 35　　(*2*) more than 10 years of service
(b) (*1*) female　　(*2*) hourly worker
(c) (*1*) married female　　(*2*) age under 30
(d) (*1*) more than 12 years of education　　(*2*) single

Solution: Find the probabilities by the count-and-divide method. In finding the unconditional probabilities, remember to divide only by those events not eliminated from the sample space by the condition. For example, in part (a) the condition "more than 10 years of service" reduces the sample size from 10 to 2. In all cases the conditional and unconditional probabilities differ, so the event pairs are dependent.

(a) (*1*) 3/10　　(*2*) 2/2 = 1　dependent
(b) (*1*) 4/10　　(*2*) 1/3　dependent
(c) (*1*) 1/10　　(*2*) 1/3　dependent
(d) (*1*) 4/10　　(*2*) 0　dependent

PROBLEM 4-15 DanDee Assemblers receives shipments of 50 widgets each from GizMo Corp. Suppose that a particular shipment contains exactly 90% satisfactory and 10% unsatisfactory widgets. A sample of three widgets is selected without replacement and the quality of each determined.

(a) Construct a probability tree diagram for this experiment, identify all the elementary events in the sample space, and compute the joint probability for each event.
(b) Find the probabilities for the following number of unsatisfactory items:
　　(*1*) none　　　(*4*) exactly 3
　　(*2*) exactly 1　(*5*) at least 1
　　(*3*) exactly 2　(*6*) at most 2

Solution:
(a) See Figure 4-5. The branch probabilities for each branch are found by dividing the number of possible widgets having at that point the applicable characteristic by the total remaining widgets. For example,

$$\Pr[U_2 \mid U_1] = 4/49$$

The joint probabilities for the elementary events are found using the general multiplication law.

Figure 4-5

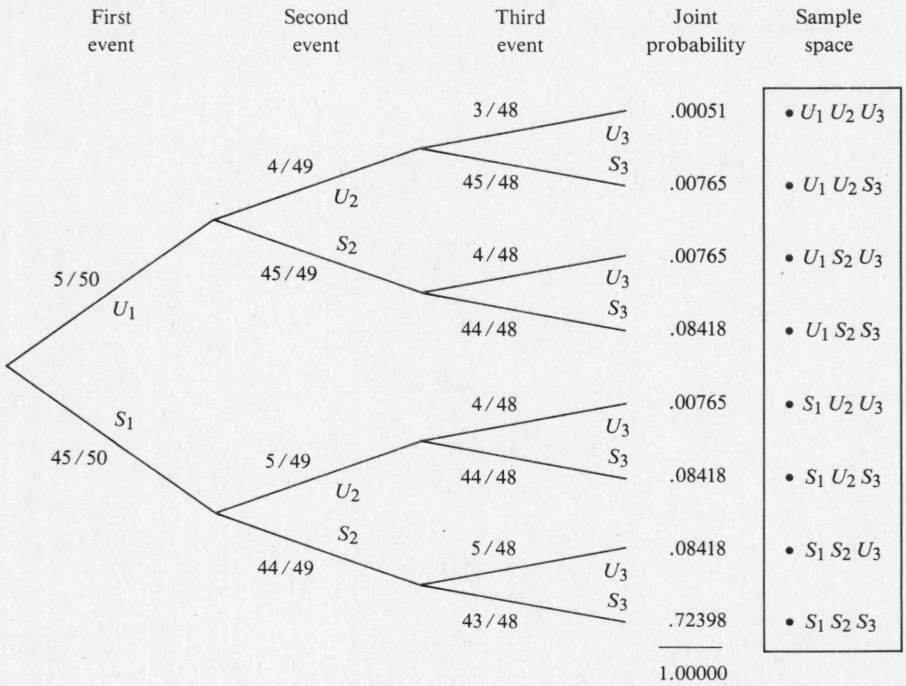

First event	Second event	Third event	Joint probability	Sample space
		3/48　U_3	.00051	• $U_1 U_2 U_3$
	4/49　U_2	45/48　S_3	.00765	• $U_1 U_2 S_3$
5/50　U_1	45/49　S_2	4/48　U_3	.00765	• $U_1 S_2 U_3$
		44/48　S_3	.08418	• $U_1 S_2 S_3$
45/50　S_1	5/49　U_2	4/48　U_3	.00765	• $S_1 U_2 U_3$
		44/48　S_3	.08418	• $S_1 U_2 S_3$
	44/49　S_2	5/48　U_3	.08418	• $S_1 S_2 U_3$
		43/48　S_3	.72398	• $S_1 S_2 S_3$

1.00000

(b) (*1*) Pr[none] = .72398
  (*2*) Pr[exactly 1] = .08418 + .08418 + .08418 = .25254
  (*3*) Pr[exactly 2] = .00765 + .00765 + .00765 = .02295
  (*4*) Pr[exactly 3] = .00051
  (*5*) Pr[at least 1] = .25254 + .02295 + .00051 = .27600
  (*6*) Pr[at most 2] = .72398 + .25254 + .02295 = .99947

PROBLEM 4-16 Bri-Dent toothpaste has a 20% market share. Thus, there is a 20% chance that a randomly selected user of toothpaste will be a buyer (*B*) of Bri-Dent. Suppose that 60% of Bri-Dent buyers remember (*R*) a funny commercial about the product, while only 10% of nonbuyers do.

  (a) Find the following: (*1*) Pr[*B*]; (*2*) Pr[not *B*]; (*3*) Pr[*R*|*B*]; (*4*) Pr[*R*|not *B*].
  (b) Construct the joint probability table for a person's buying category and memory regarding the commercial.
  (c) What percentage of all toothpaste users remember the commercial?

Solution:
(a) You are given the data for (*1*), (*3*), and (*4*). Since "not *B*" is complementary to "*B*", the answer to (*2*) is found by subtracting the probability for "*B*" from 1.
  (*1*) Pr[*B*] = .20
  (*2*) Pr[not *B*] = 1 − .20 = .80
  (*3*) Pr[*R*|*B*] = .60
  (*4*) Pr[*R*|not *B*] = .10

(b) You can find the joint probabilities for "*B and R*" and "not *B and R*" by applying the multiplication law.

$$\text{Pr}[B \text{ and } R] = \text{Pr}[B] \times \text{Pr}[R|B] = .20 \times .60 = .12$$
$$\text{Pr}[\text{not } B \text{ and } R] = \text{Pr}[\text{not } B] \times \text{Pr}[R|\text{not } B] = .80 \times .10 = .08$$

Since the joint probabilities in each row or column must sum to their respective marginal probabilities, you can find the joint probabilities for "*B and* not *R*" and "not *B and* not *R*" by subtracting the known joint probabilities from their respective marginal probabilities.

$$\text{Pr}[B \text{ and not } R] = .20 − .12 = .08$$
$$\text{Pr}[\text{not } B \text{ and not } R] = .80 − .08 = .72$$

You then find the remaining marginal probabilities by summing the joint probabilities in their respective columns.

Type of customer	Memory Events		Marginal probability
	R	Not *R*	
B	.12	.08	.20
Not *B*	.08	.72	.80
Marginal probability	.20	.80	1.00

(c) The probability of "*R*" includes all toothpaste users, whether or not they use Bri-Dent. Thus, since Pr[*R*] = .20, it follows that 20% of all toothpaste users remember the commercial.

PROBLEM 4-17 One GizMo Corp. employee is selected at random from those listed in Problem 3-6 (page 53). Let *M* and *W* stand for that person's sex; *C* and not *C*, his or her college background; and *E* and not *E*, his or her previous experience.

  (a) Find the following probabilities by applying the count-and-divide method to the elementary events given in Problem 3-6.

(*1*)	(*2*)	(*3*)	(*4*)	(*5*)	(*6*)
Pr[*M*]	Pr[*W*]	Pr[*E*]	Pr[not *E*]	Pr[*C*]	Pr[not *C*]
Pr[*E*|*M*]	Pr[*C*|*W*]	Pr[*M*|*E*]	Pr[*C*|not *E*]	Pr[*E*|*C*]	Pr[not *E*|not *C*]

(b) Apply the multiplication law to each pair of probabilities in part (a) to find the following joint probabilities.

(1) Pr[*M and E*]   (3) Pr[*E and M*]   (5) Pr[*C and E*]

(2) Pr[*W and C*]   (4) Pr[not *E and C*]   (6) Pr[not *C and* not *E*]

Solution:

(a) Use the count-and-divide method to find the specified probabilities.

(1) Pr[M] = 6/10   Pr[$E|M$] = 5/6

(2) Pr[W] = 4/10   Pr[$C|W$] = 2/4 = 1/2

(3) Pr[E] = 6/10   Pr[$M|E$] = 5/6

(4) Pr[not E] = 4/10   Pr[$C|$not E] = 3/4

(5) Pr[C] = 4/10   Pr[$E|C$] = 1/4

(6) Pr[not C] = 6/10   Pr[not $E|$not C] = 1/6

(b) (1) Pr[*M and E*] = Pr[M] × Pr[$E|M$]

$$= (6/10)(5/6) = 5/10$$

(2) Pr[*W and C*] = Pr[W] × Pr[$C|W$]

$$= (4/10)(2/4) = 2/10$$

(3) Pr[*E and M*] = Pr[E] × Pr[$M|E$]

$$= (6/10)(5/6) = 5/10$$

(4) Pr[not *E and C*] = Pr[not E] × Pr[$C|$not E]

$$= (4/10)(3/4) = 3/10$$

(5) Pr[*C and E*] = Pr[C] × Pr[$E|C$]

$$= (4/10)(1/4) = 1/10$$

(6) Pr[not *C and* not *E*] = Pr[not C] × Pr[not $E|$not C]

$$= (6/10)(1/6) = 1/10$$

PROBLEM 4-18 Consider the first three telecommunications queries by Giant Enterprises. Suppose that the system is busy (B) 20% of the time and that a direct connection (D) is achieved the rest. Assume that the status of the system at each query is independent of that for preceding messages.

Construct a probability tree diagram for the system status encountered by those three queries. Identify all elementary events, and compute the joint probability for each event.

Solution: See Figure 4-6. This solution follows the pattern of Problem 4-12.

Figure 4-6

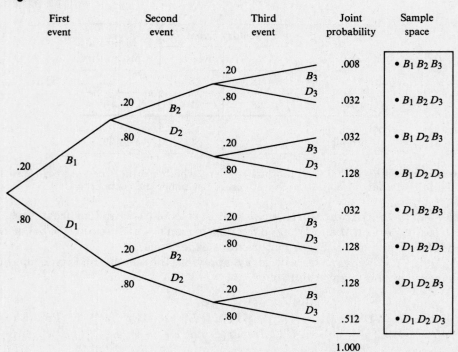

First event	Second event	Third event	Joint probability	Sample space
		.20 B_3	.008	• $B_1 B_2 B_3$
.20 B_2	.80 D_3	.032	• $B_1 B_2 D_3$
.80 D_2	.20 B_3	.032	• $B_1 D_2 B_3$
.20 B_1	.80 D_3	.128	• $B_1 D_2 D_3$
	.20 B_3	.032	• $D_1 B_2 B_3$
.80 D_1 .20 B_2	.80 D_3	.128	• $D_1 B_2 D_3$
.80 D_2 .20 B_3		.128	• $D_1 D_2 B_3$
	.80 D_3	.512	• $D_1 D_2 D_3$

1.000

PROBLEM 4-19   Callers to the Midget Motors switchboard encounter busy signals (*B*) 20% of the time. The remainder of the time calls are connected directly (*D*). Because of the slow rate at which calls are placed, the connection status of successive calls is dependent. Records show that half of all calls placed after a preceding call encountered a busy signal will also find the switchboard busy. But 90% of calls placed after the preceding call was directly connected will also be directly connected.

Construct a probability tree diagram for the system status encountered by the first three calls to the Midget Motors switchboard. Identify all elementary events, and compute the joint probability for each event.

Solution: See Figure 4-7.

Figure 4-7

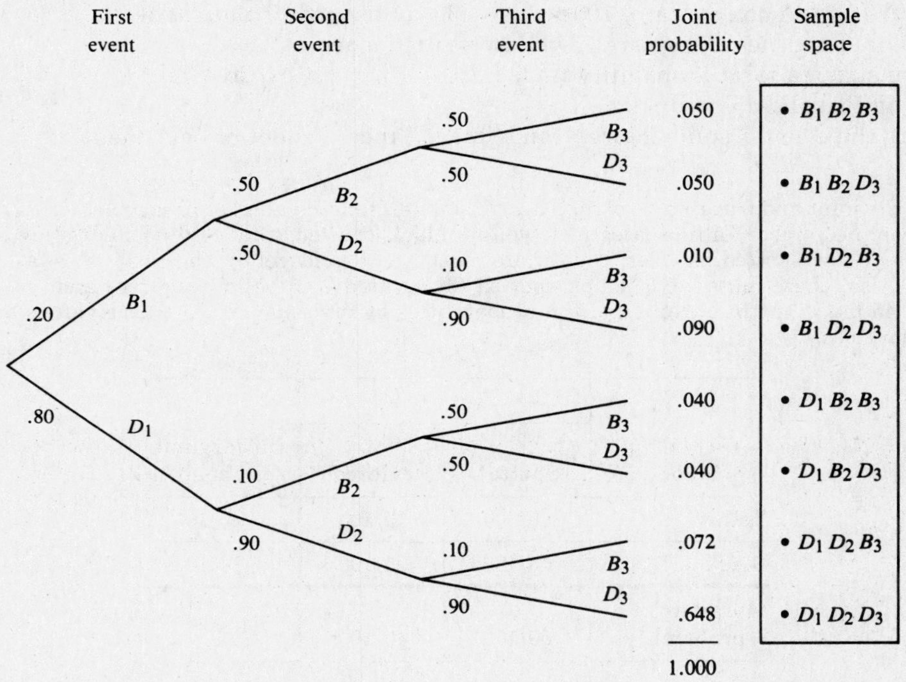

PROBLEM 4-20   One faculty member is chosen from those summarized in Figure 4-3 (page 70). All instructors have the same chance of being selected. Determine the following conditional probabilities.
   (a) Pr[accounting | woman]
   (b) Pr[finance | man]
   (c) Pr[management | man *and* full-time]
   (d) Pr[finance | woman *and* part-time]
   (e) Pr[full-time | woman]
   (f) Pr[full-time *and* finance | man]
   (g) Pr[man | accounting *or* finance]
   (h) Pr[part-time *and* accounting | man]

Solution: Find the probabilities by using the count-and-divide method. Divide the number of instructors in each category by the total number in the restricted sample space.
   (a) 3/21   (c) 6/25   (e) 14/21   (g) 22/28
   (b) 11/50   (d) 1/7   (f) 6/50   (h) 6/50

PROBLEM 4-21   Consider the faculty data in Figure 4-3. A lottery is held to select the membership of a university grievance panel. Three persons will be selected. Find the probability that
   (a) exactly 2 men will be chosen.
   (b) at least 1 woman will be chosen.
   (c) all will be from the finance department.
   (d) at least 1 part-time instructor will be chosen.

Solution: Use the count-and-divide method to find the event probabilities for each of the three selections. The selections are made without replacement, so the number of persons in a category and/or in the entire sample space will have to be adjusted after each selection. Thus, if the initial probability that a man will be chosen is 50/71, and if the first person chosen is a man, then the probability that the second person will be a man is 49/70. The multiplication law then provides the probabilities for the specified elementary events. Finally, apply the addition law or the property of complementary events, as needed.

(a) Pr[exactly 2 men] = $(50/71)(49/70)(21/69) + (50/71)(21/70)(49/69) + (21/71)(50/70)(49/69) = .450$

(b) Pr[at least 1 woman] = $1 - $ Pr[0 women]

$$= 1 - (50/71)(49/70)(48/69) = .657$$

(c) Pr[all finance] = $(14/71)(13/70)(12/69) = .0064$

(d) Pr[at least 1 part-timer] = $1 - $ Pr[no part-timer]

$$= 1 - (39/71)(38/70)(37/69) = .840$$

PROBLEM 4-22 A box contains 100 marbles, 30 yellow and 70 black. There are 60 spotted and 40 solid-colored marbles. There are 15 yellow spotted marbles.

   (a) Construct a joint probability table for color versus texture events.
   (b) Find Pr[solid-colored | black].
   (c) Are the events "solid-colored" and "black" independent or dependent?

Solution:

(a) To find the joint and marginal probabilities, first determine the number of marbles in each category. You are given the number for five categories (yellow, black, spotted, solid-colored, and yellow spotted). If there are 15 yellow spotted marbles, then there must be 15 solid yellow, because there are 30 yellow altogether. Also, there must be 45 black spotted (60 spotted − 15 yellow spotted) and 25 solid black (70 black − 45 black spotted). Now find the probabilities by dividing each of these values by the total number of marbles.

Color	Texture		
	Spotted	Solid colored	Marginal probability
Yellow	15/100	15/100	30/100
Black	45/100	25/100	70/100
Marginal probability	60/100	40/100	1

(b) Use the conditional probability identity.

$$\text{Pr[solid-colored | black]} = \frac{\text{Pr[solid-colored } and \text{ black]}}{\text{Pr[black]}} = \frac{25/100}{70/100} = \frac{25}{70} = \frac{5}{14} = .357$$

(c) The unconditional probability of "solid-colored" is $40/100 = .40$, which doesn't equal the conditional probability of "solid-colored" given "black." Therefore, solid-colored and black are statistically *dependent.*

PROBLEM 4-23 A banana inspector accepts only 10% of all bad shipments and rejects only 5% of the good ones. Overall, 90% of the shipments inspected are good.

   (a) Identify (*1*) Pr[accept | bad]; (*2*) Pr[reject | good]; (*3*) Pr[good].
   (b) Construct the joint probability table for shipment quality versus inspector action.
   (c) Determine the probability that the inspector will take the wrong action on the next shipment.

Solution:

(a) Find these probabilities directly from the given data.

$$\text{Pr[accept | bad]} = .10 \qquad \text{Pr[reject | good]} = .05$$
$$\text{Pr[good]} = .90$$

(b) The event "bad" is the complement of "good," so

$$\text{Pr[bad]} = 1 - \text{Pr[good]} = 1 - .90 = .10$$

Using the general multiplication law, find the joint probabilities "bad *and* accept" and "good *and* reject."

$$Pr[bad \; and \; accept] = Pr[bad] \times Pr[accept \,|\, bad]$$
$$= .10(.10) = .010$$
$$Pr[good \; and \; reject] = Pr[good] \times Pr[reject \,|\, good]$$
$$= .90(.05) = .045$$

Find the missing joint probabilities by subtracting the known joint probability in each row from its respective marginal probability.

$$Pr[good \; and \; accept] = .900 - .045 = .855$$
$$Pr[bad \; and \; reject] = .100 - .010 = .090$$

Now sum the joint probabilities in each column to find the missing marginal probabilities.

$$Pr[accept] = .855 + .010 = .865$$
$$Pr[reject] = .045 + .090 = .135$$

Shipment quality	Inspector Action		Marginal probability
	Accept	Reject	
Good	.855	.045	.900
Bad	.010	.090	.100
Marginal probability	.865	.135	1.000

(c) The inspector will take the wrong action if he either accepts bad shipments or rejects good shipments. Thus,

$$Pr[wrong \; action] = Pr[bad \; and \; accept] + Pr[good \; and \; reject]$$
$$= .010 + .045 = .055$$

PROBLEM 4-24 Consider the Kryptonite Corp. employees listed in Problem 3-20 (page 58). Two employees are selected by pulling names out of a hat. The first name picked is not placed back into the hat.

(a) Construct a probability tree diagram for this experiment, with the sex of the chosen employees as the events at each stage. Then identify the elementary events in the sample space, and compute the joint probability for each.

(b) Find the probability that the two selections will involve employees of the same sex.

Solution:
(a) See Figure 4-8. This solution follows the pattern of Problem 4-12.
(b) $Pr[same \; sex] = Pr[M_1 M_2] + Pr[F_1 F_2]$
$$= 30/90 + 12/90 = 42/90 = .467$$

Figure 4-8

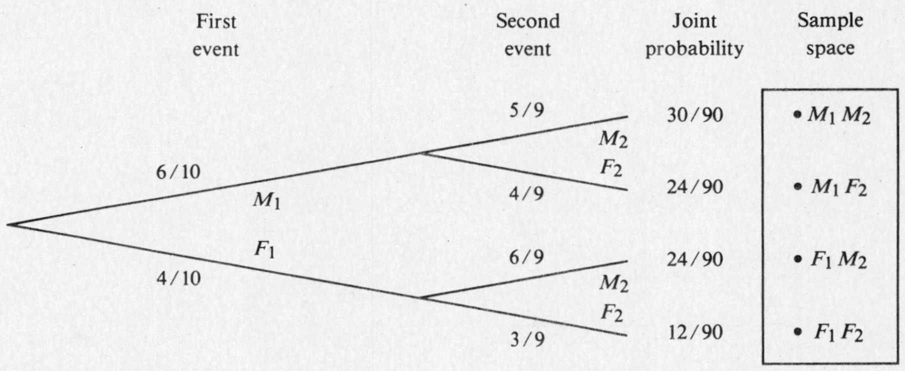

First event	Second event	Joint probability	Sample space
6/10 M_1	5/9 M_2	30/90	• $M_1 M_2$
	4/9 F_2	24/90	• $M_1 F_2$
4/10 F_1	6/9 M_2	24/90	• $F_1 M_2$
	3/9 F_2	12/90	• $F_1 F_2$

PROBLEM 4-25 The general manager of the Gotham City Hellcats is evaluating an employment screening test for the front-office clerical staff. During this experiment all new clerical employees are given the test. Seventy percent of them pass the test; the rest fail. At a later time it is determined whether the new clerks are satisfactory or unsatisfactory. Historically, 80% of all clerical hires have been found to be satisfactory, and 75% of the satisfactory clerks in the program have passed the screening test.

Consider the events applicable to a new clerk in the experiment.

(a) From the given information, provide the values of the following: (*1*) Pr[pass]; (*2*) Pr[satisfactory]; (*3*) Pr[pass | satisfactory].

(b) Use the answers in part (a) to find Pr[pass *and* satisfactory].

(c) Construct the joint probability table for test results versus employee performance events.

(d) Using your answers to part (c), determine the following conditional probabilities:

(*1*) Pr[fail | unsatisfactory]   (*5*) Pr[satisfactory | pass]

(*2*) Pr[fail | satisfactory]   (*6*) Pr[unsatisfactory | pass]

(*3*) Pr[pass | unsatisfactory]   (*7*) Pr[satisfactory | fail]

(*4*) Pr[unsatisfactory | fail]

(e) Using the above results, find

(*1*) the percentage of failing clerks who prove to be unsatisfactory employees;

(*2*) the percentage of passing clerks who prove to be satisfactory employees.

(f) Government guidelines are that a proper screening test must provide at least 20% for (*1*) in part (e) and at least 60% for (*2*). Does this test meet those guidelines?

Solution:

(a) The desired probabilities are given.

(*1*) Pr[pass] = .70

(*2*) Pr[satisfactory] = .80

(*3*) Pr[pass | satisfactory] = .75

(b) Use the general multiplication law to find this joint probability.

$$\text{Pr[pass \textit{and} satisfactory]} = \text{Pr[satisfactory]} \times \text{Pr[pass | satisfactory]} = .80 \times .75 = .60$$

(c) The event "fail" is the complement of "pass," and the event "unsatisfactory" is the complement of "satisfactory", so use the property of complementary events to find the missing marginal probabilities.

$$\text{Pr[fail]} = 1 - \text{Pr[pass]} = 1 - .70 = .30$$

and

$$\text{Pr[unsatisfactory]} = 1 - \text{Pr[satisfactory]} = 1 - .80 = .20$$

Now find two of the missing joint probabilities by subtracting the known joint probability in each row or column from its respective marginal probability.

$$\text{Pr[passing \textit{and} unsatisfactory]} = .70 - .60 = .10$$
$$\text{Pr[fail \textit{and} satisfactory]} = .80 - .60 = .20$$

You find the remaining joint probability by using either of the values just figured.

$$\text{Pr[fail \textit{and} unsatisfactory]} = .20 - .10 = .10$$

Test Results	Performance		Marginal probability
	Satisfactory	Unsatisfactory	
Pass	.60	.10	.70
Fail	.20	.10	.30
Marginal probability	.80	.20	1.00

(d) The following probabilities are computed by substituting the appropriate values from part **(c)** into the conditional probability identity.

(1) $\text{Pr[fail | unsatisfactory]} = \dfrac{\text{Pr[fail } and \text{ unsatisfactory]}}{\text{Pr[unsatisfactory]}} = \dfrac{.10}{.20} = .50$

(2) $.20/.80 = .25$ (5) $.60/.70 = .86$
(3) $.10/.20 = .50$ (6) $.10/.70 = .14$
(4) $.10/.30 = .33$ (7) $.20/.30 = .67$

(e) (1) This is the same as the answer to (4)—the probability of "unsatisfactory given fail"—or 33%.
 (2) This is the same as the answer to (5)—the probability of "satisfactory given pass"—or 86%.
(f) Yes

PROBLEM 4-26 Given the following probability data, answer the questions in parts **(a)** and **(b)**.

$$\text{Pr}[A] = \frac{1}{2} \qquad \text{Pr}[B] = \frac{1}{3} \qquad \text{Pr}[C] = \frac{1}{4}$$

$$\text{Pr}[A \text{ and } B] = \frac{1}{8} \qquad \text{Pr}[B|C] = \frac{1}{2} \qquad \text{Pr}[C|A] = \frac{1}{5}$$

$$\text{Pr}[A|B \text{ and } C] = \frac{2}{3} \qquad \text{Pr}[A \text{ or } B \text{ or } C] = \frac{17}{20}$$

(a) Determine the probabilities:
 (1) $\text{Pr}[A \text{ and } C]$ (6) $\text{Pr}[C|B]$
 (2) $\text{Pr}[B \text{ and } C]$ (7) $\text{Pr}[B \text{ and } C|A]$
 (3) $\text{Pr}[A \text{ and } B \text{ and } C]$ (8) $\text{Pr}[A \text{ or } B]$
 (4) $\text{Pr}[A|B]$ (9) $\text{Pr}[A \text{ or } C]$
 (5) $\text{Pr}[A|C]$ (10) $\text{Pr}[B \text{ or } C]$

(b) Answer the following:
 (1) Are any two of the events A, B, and C mutually exclusive?
 (2) Do A, B, and C form a collectively exhaustive collection of events?
 (3) Which event pairs are not statistically independent?

Solution:
(a) Apply the appropriate addition or multiplication law or conditional probability identity to the given data to find the desired probabilities.
 (1) $\text{Pr}[A \text{ and } C] = \text{Pr}[A] \times \text{Pr}[C|A] = (1/2)(1/5) = 1/10$
 (2) $\text{Pr}[B \text{ and } C] = \text{Pr}[C] \times \text{Pr}[B|C] = (1/4)(1/2) = 1/8$
 (3) $\text{Pr}[A \text{ and } B \text{ and } C] = \text{Pr}[A|B \text{ and } C] \times \text{Pr}[B \text{ and } C] = (2/3)(1/8) = 2/24 = 1/12$
 (4) $\text{Pr}[A|B] = \text{Pr}[A \text{ and } B]/\text{Pr}[B] = (1/8)/(1/3) = 3/8$
 (5) $\text{Pr}[A|C] = \text{Pr}[A \text{ and } C]/\text{Pr}[C] = (1/10)/(1/4) = 4/10 = 2/5$
 (6) $\text{Pr}[C|B] = \text{Pr}[C \text{ and } B]/\text{Pr}[B] = \text{Pr}[C] \times \text{Pr}[B|C]/\text{Pr}[B]$
   $= (1/4)(1/2)/(1/3) = 3/8$
 (7) $\text{Pr}[B \text{ and } C|A] = \text{Pr}[A \text{ and } (B \text{ and } C)]/\text{Pr}[A] = (1/12)/(1/2) = 1/6$
 (8) $\text{Pr}[A \text{ or } B] = \text{Pr}[A] + \text{Pr}[B] - \text{Pr}[A \text{ and } B] = 1/2 + 1/3 - 1/8 = 17/24$
 (9) $\text{Pr}[A \text{ or } C] = \text{Pr}[A] + \text{Pr}[C] - \text{Pr}[A \text{ and } C] = 1/2 + 1/4 - 1/10 = 13/20$
 (10) $\text{Pr}[B \text{ or } C] = \text{Pr}[B] + \text{Pr}[C] - \text{Pr}[B \text{ and } C] = 1/3 + 1/4 - 1/8 = 11/24$
(b) (1) No, since no joint probabilities are zero.
 (2) No, since $\text{Pr}[A \text{ or } B \text{ or } C]$ doesn't equal 1.
 (3) All pairs are statistically dependent, since
$$\text{Pr}[A] \neq \text{Pr}[A|B] \text{ or } \text{Pr}[A|C]$$
and
$$\text{Pr}[B] \neq \text{Pr}[B|A] \text{ or } \text{Pr}[B|C]$$
and
$$\text{Pr}[C] \neq \text{Pr}[C|A] \text{ or } \text{Pr}[C|B]$$

5 SPECIAL TOPICS IN PROBABILITY

THIS CHAPTER IS ABOUT

☑ **Counting Methods for Finding Probabilities**
☑ **Revising Probabilities Using Bayes' Theorem**

In this chapter you will study two special probability topics important to some business applications of statistics. One involves the streamlined counting methods used to compute probabilities when the number of possible events is huge. The second provides a procedure for revising probabilities in accordance with information found through sampling, testing, and similar experiments.

5-1. Counting Methods for Finding Probabilities

A. The principle of multiplication speeds up the count.

You can use the count-and-divide method even when there are so many possible elementary events that there wouldn't be enough sheets in a loose-leaf binder to completely list them. (For example, you will see later on in this chapter that there are over 3 million different sequences in which the first 10 letters of the alphabet can be written.) Rather than plod through such a listing, you can count large groups of elementary events by using the **principle of multiplication**, which is summarized as follows:

STEPS FOR COUNTING POSSIBILITIES
1. *Break the problem into successive stages.* You may conveniently think of each **stage as a** branching point on a probability tree diagram.
2. *Multiply together the number of possibilities at each stage to obtain the total number of possibilities.* In this way each path in your tree is counted.

Note: The tree is simply a convenient conceptual prop. You can ordinarily apply the principle of multiplication without actually drawing a tree.

To illustrate, consider a student who must pick 1 of 5 mathematics courses and 1 of 10 social science offerings for her electives. Altogether she has

$$5 \times 10 = 50$$

possible pairs of elective courses from which to choose.

EXAMPLE 5-1: THE NUMBER OF DIFFERENT STEREO SYSTEMS

Vick Trolla is about to purchase his first stereo system from Speak-EZ Sounds. He has limited himself to one item from each of the following possible choices:

5 receivers	10 speakers
3 turntables	4 tape decks
2 cartridges	3 earphones

Figure 5-1 shows a probability tree diagram that conveniently summarizes the possibilities by incorporating a branching point for each choice. By multiplying together the number of alternatives for each item, Vick finds the total number of different stereo systems he could buy:

$$5 \times 3 \times 2 \times 10 \times 4 \times 3 = 3,600$$

Each possible system would be represented on the tree by a different six-branch path. If all such paths were included in Figure 5-1, the resulting tree would be over 300 feet tall!

Figure 5-1

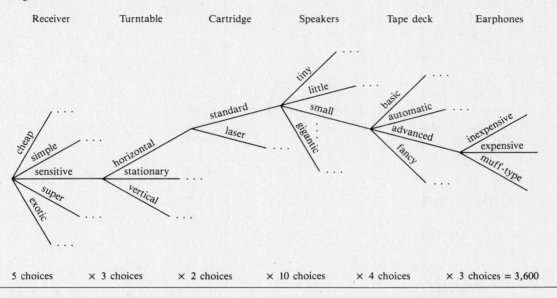

Receiver	Turntable	Cartridge	Speakers	Tape deck	Earphones

5 choices   × 3 choices   × 2 choices   × 10 choices   × 4 choices   × 3 choices = 3,600

B. Raise the number of possibilities to a power in counting with repeated trials.

Section 4-4 discussed the sample space for a series of repeated experiments and gave an illustration of sampling with replacement. The selection of each sample item in such experiments is referred to as a **trial**. An important class of random experiments involves a series of trials. We find the number of possible elementary events in the series' sample space by multiplying together the number of possible outcomes at each trial. For example, in 5 tosses of a coin, each of which involves just two possibilities (H or T), there are

$$2 \times 2 \times 2 \times 2 \times 2 = 32$$

possibilities for the entire series. Likewise, consider a quality control inspector who removes from a production line a sample of 6 items, each of which is classified into one of three categories: satisfactory, reworkable, or scrap. The number of possible sample outcomes is

$$3 \times 3 \times 3 \times 3 \times 3 \times 3 = 729$$

Notice that each product in these examples involves the same terms. Therefore, you may find it more convenient to express the two products in terms of powers:

$$2^5 = 32 \quad \text{and} \quad 3^6 = 729$$

In general, the number of possibilities from a series of n trials, each of which can result in the same k trial outcomes, is k raised to the power n. Consider the following:

Trial outcomes k	Number of trials n	Number of possibilities k^n
2	10	$2^{10} = 1,024$
5	2	$5^2 = 25$
2	5	$2^5 = 32$
10	3	$10^3 = 1,000$

EXAMPLE 5-2: TRUTH IN LABELING

Have you ever wondered how a food processor can actually claim that the net contents of a can of corn is say, 16 oz.? Even if any particular can is weighed with a very precise scale, it will be a little too heavy or too light. The processor's claim means that if the filling process is on target, exactly half the cans will be above the 16 oz. target (A) and the rest will be below (B).

Suppose a cannery inspector, to check the accuracy of the canning process, removes a sample of $n = 10$ cans and weighs their contents. Each can is classified in one of two ways ($k = 2$), and so altogether there are

$$2^{10} = 1,024$$

possible sample findings. The inspector's 10-can sample, with the cans listed in order of selection, might be as follows:

$$ABABBABBBA$$

Since any can is just as likely to be an A as a B, you can consider such a listing to be an elementary event for the sampling experiment. Each such elementary event is equally likely. Thus, you conclude the following for the inspector's sample:

$$\Pr[ABABBABBBA] = \frac{1}{1,024}$$

C.   A factorial product provides the number of ways to sequence items.

For some experiments you must count the number of **sequences** in which items might be arranged. Consider the different sequences in which you can arrange the first 10 letters of the alphabet. The principle of multiplication indicates that the number of possibilities is

$$10 \times 9 \times 8 \times 7 \times 6 \times 5 \times 4 \times 3 \times 2 \times 1 = 3,628,800$$

The terms of this equation reflect the fact that one letter is being selected at a time in stages, with one less possibility for each successive stage. Think of each letter as a branching point in a tree, with the number of branches at each stage equal to the number of letters that remain to be selected for that particular sequence position.

Mathematicians refer to the product of all successive integers (whole numbers) ending at 1 as a **factorial**. A factorial product is expressed symbolically as a number followed by an exclamation point. Note the following examples:

$$5! = 5 \times 4 \times 3 \times 2 \times 1 = 120$$
$$6! = 6 \times 5 \times 4 \times 3 \times 2 \times 1 = 6 \times 5! = 720$$
$$7! = 7 \times 6 \times 5 \times 4 \times 3 \times 2 \times 1 = 7 \times 6! = 5,040$$
$$20! = \text{approximately 2.4 billion billion}$$
$$100! = \text{approximately 9 followed by 157 zeros}$$

* The number of sequences of n objects is denoted as $n!$ By definition,

$$0! = 1$$

(There is only one way to sequence nothing.)

D.   A permutation is a sequence of objects when some may be missing.

You may be interested in counting the number of possibilities when not all available objects are selected. Consider again various possible groupings of the first 10 letters of the alphabet:

$$\text{ABC} \quad \text{ABHIJ} \quad \text{LADCJ} \quad \text{LKJHICDAB} \quad \text{A} \quad \text{BK} \quad \text{CDE} \quad \text{EDCA}$$

Each of these arrangements of letters is a permutation. A **permutation** is a collection of objects distinguished by which items are included and by their sequence. Thus, ABC and CBA are different permutations that happen to involve the same three letters. Although none of the groupings just listed includes all 10 letters, a permutation *can* include all objects. No item can appear more than once in a single permutation.

EXAMPLE 5-3: FIVE-CARD POKER HANDS

Imagine the various poker hands you can create by removing the top 5 cards from a shuffled deck of 52 playing cards. Listing the individual cards in order of their selection, each of the following hands may be viewed as a permutation:

$$\clubsuit K, \clubsuit 3, \clubsuit J, \clubsuit 7, \clubsuit 10$$

$$\diamondsuit 2, \spadesuit 3, \heartsuit 4, \heartsuit 5, \clubsuit 6$$

$$\spadesuit 5, \heartsuit 5, \clubsuit 7, \heartsuit 2, \diamondsuit 2$$

$$\heartsuit A, \heartsuit K, \heartsuit Q, \heartsuit J, \heartsuit 10$$

Notice that although the third hand involves two 5's and two 2's, each of these pairs is made up of two different cards. (The $\heartsuit 2$ cannot appear twice unless that particular card is replaced in the deck and reselected. A listing of any such outcome is not considered a permutation.) The top sequence is a club *flush*—all cards belonging to a common suit. The second hand is a *straight*—the cards can be arranged in a denominational sequence having no gaps. The last hand is a *royal flush* in hearts. The sequence in which a card gets selected is ordinarily unimportant in poker. If you consider just those cards in the heart royal flush, there are $5! = 120$ sequences in which they might be drawn.

1. **The number of permutations:** The number of possible permutations depends on the size of the original group and the number of items selected. It will be helpful to denote the number of permutations of size r from a group of n items ($r \leqslant n$) by the symbol P_r^n. You can find the number of possible permutations by using the following equation:

Number of permutations

$$P_r^n = n \times (n - 1) \times (n - 2) \times \cdots \times (n - r + 1)$$

Consider the following examples:

Group size n	Items selected r	Number of permutations P_r^n
7	4	$7 \times 6 \times 5 \times 4 = 840$
10	2	$10 \times 9 = 90$
5	5	$5 \times 4 \times 3 \times 2 \times 1 = 120$
52	5	$311{,}875{,}200$

2. **Factorials are helpful in computing the number of possible permutations.** If you multiply the equation for the number of permutations by $(n - r)!$ and then divide by $(n - r)!$, the original value is preserved. However, this results in the following more concise expression for the number of permutations.

Number of permutations

$$P_r^n = \frac{n \times (n - 1) \times (n - 2) \times \cdots \times (n - r + 1) \times (n - r)!}{(n - r)!} = \frac{n!}{(n - r)!}$$

EXAMPLE 5-4: COUNTING NAME ARRANGEMENTS

Consider the following six names:

Ann   Eve   Fay   Liz   May   Sue

Picking names one at a time from this group and applying the principle of multiplication, you may establish the number of permutations of four names from the six:

Choices of first name		Choices of second name		Choices of third name		Choices of fourth name		
6	$\times$	5	$\times$	4	$\times$	3	$=$	360

This result may also be found by working with factorials. Expressing the number of permutations for $n = 6$ names taken $r = 4$ at a time, you get

$$P_4^6 = \frac{6!}{(6-4)!} = \frac{6!}{2!} = \frac{720}{2} = 360$$

E. It is often easier to count possibilities in terms of combinations.

Accounting for possibilities in terms of permutations may be more detailed than necessary. It is sometimes satisfactory to ignore the sequence of items.

1. **The combination:** Any collection distinguishable only by which particular items are included (and not by their sequence) is a **combination**. A combination of the first 10 letters of the alphabet is the set of letters itself, ignoring their order of selection. All of the following sequences

    ABC   ACB   BAC   BCA   CAB   CBA

   are counted as a single combination. But since there are different letter sets in the following

    EFG   JFK   EIK   ADJ   BCL   EDJ

   each represents a different combination.

2. **The number of combinations:** As with permutations (where sequence counts), the number of combinations depends on the original group size and the number of items included. The expression C_r^n stands for the number of combinations of r items taken from n. The possible number of combinations can be found using the following expression:

   Number of combinations
   $$C_r^n = \frac{n!}{r!(n-r)!}$$

   As a further illustration, consider the number of combinations of $r = 4$ women's names taken from the $n = 6$ given in Example 5-4.

   $$C_4^6 = \frac{6!}{4!(6-4)!} = \frac{6!}{4!2!} = \frac{720}{24(2)} = 15$$

   Each one of these 15 possible combinations is listed below, with names arranged alphabetically.

Ann Eve Fay Liz	Ann Eve May Sue	Eve Fay Liz May
Ann Eve Fay May	Ann Fay Liz May	Eve Fay Liz Sue
Ann Eve Fay Sue	Ann Fay Liz Sue	Eve Fay May Sue
Ann Eve Liz May	Ann Fay May Sue	Eve Liz May Sue
Ann Eve Liz Sue	Ann Liz May Sue	Fay Liz May Sue

   Consider the following examples:

Group size n	Items selected r	Number of combinations C_r^n
5	3	10
8	5	56
12	7	792
20	5	15,504
100	50	about 100,000 trillion trillion

3. **Counting permutations starting with combinations:** Each of the 15 name combinations just listed could be sequenced in $4! = 24$ different ways, giving rise to the $24 \times 15 = 360$ permutations found earlier. More generally, the number of permutations may be obtained by multiplying the respective number of combinations by $r!$, while the number of combinations may be computed by dividing the corresponding number of permutations by $r!$. Thus,

   $$P_r^n = r! C_r^n \quad \text{and} \quad C_r^n = \frac{P_r^n}{r!}$$

4. **Computing probabilities using combinations:** Because there are always a smaller number of combinations than of permutations, combinations usually form the basis for probability calculations using the count-and-divide method.

EXAMPLE 5-5: CANNED CORN

Consider again the weight of cans of corn, discussed in Example 5-2. By counting combinations, you can establish various probabilities for the weight classifications of the 10 sample cans. To begin, represent each successive sample by a box:

1	2	3	4	5	6	7	8	9	10

Consider now the number of ways for getting exactly 3 cans that are above (*A*) 16 oz., with the rest below. This is the same as the number of ways to select 3 of the 10 boxes (which will then receive the letter *A*). One such result is

1	2	3	4	5	6	7	8	9	10
A				*A*		*A*			

Another is

1	2	3	4	5	6	7	8	9	10
		A	*A*					*A*	

Altogether, there are

$$C_3^{10} = \frac{10!}{3!(10-3)!} = \frac{10!}{3!7!} = \frac{3,628,800}{6(5,040)} = 120$$

ways to place the *A*'s. Since you determined in Example 5-2 that there are 1,024 possible elementary events, you can now use the count-and-divide method to determine the probability that there will be exactly 3 cans in the sample above 16 oz.:

$$\Pr[\text{exactly 3 } A\text{'s}] = \frac{120}{1,024} = .117$$

EXAMPLE 5-6: POKER–HAND PROBABILITIES

In most poker situations the *combination* of cards determines the winning hand. The number of combinations of $r = 5$ cards from $n = 52$ in the deck is

$$C_5^{52} = \frac{52!}{5!(52-5)!}$$

You can easily evaluate this fraction expressing the numerator and denominator as follows:

$$\frac{52!}{5!47!} = \frac{52 \times 51 \times 50 \times 49 \times 48 \times 47!}{5!47!}$$

By canceling the 47! terms, expanding 5! into its product form, and canceling again, you can reduce the final computation:

$$\frac{52 \times 51 \times 50 \times 49 \times 48}{5 \times 4 \times 3 \times 2 \times 1} = 52 \times 51 \times 5 \times 49 \times 4 = 2,598,960$$

This is the number of possible combinations of poker hands. It may be treated as the number of elementary events in the sample space generated by dealing the top five cards from a shuffled deck.

Probability of a straight: The number of 2–3–4–5–6 straights is 4^5, since each of the 5 denominations may belong to any one of 4 suits. Altogether there are 9 denominational categories for straights—2 through 6, 3 through 7, and so on (treating ace as high). The number of possible straights then is

$$9 \times 4^5 = 9,216$$

It follows that

$$\Pr[\text{straight}] = \frac{9,216}{2,598,960} = .00355$$

Probability of a flush: The number of flushes (5 cards, all of the same suit) in any one suit is the number of combinations of $r = 5$ cards selected from the $n = 13$ cards in that suit. There are 4 suit possibilities in getting a flush, so that the number of possible flushes is

$$4 \times C_5^{13} = 4 \times \frac{13!}{5!(13-5)!} = 4 \times 1,287 = 5,148$$

Thus,

$$\Pr[\text{flush}] = \frac{5,148}{2,598,960} = .00198$$

Since the flush is rarer, it will beat a straight.

5-2. Revising Probabilities Using Bayes' Theorem

You may find it valuable to apply the probability revision procedures originally proposed by the Reverend Thomas Bayes over 200 years ago. These involve changing an initial set of probability values in accordance with a particular experimental finding.

A. We begin with prior probabilities.

You often hear a weather forecast such as: "For tomorrow there is a 50% chance of rain." You might have even occasionally come up with your own chance percentage, or **prior probability**, for rain the next day. The adjective *prior* means that the probability value is temporary and might change, depending on what further information develops. There are two classes of prior probabilities.

1. **Subjective probabilities:** The value 50% for rain is a subjective probability [Section 3-1C], since another forecaster might disagree, believing perhaps that there is instead a 40% chance of rain. This subjectivity exists because the underlying random experiment (tomorrow's weather, in this case) is strictly nonrepeatable. Similar uncertainties are common in business. Consider one-shot events such as a new product's reception in the marketplace, a company's sales, or the state of the economy.

2. **Objective probabilities:** A prior probability can be an objective value, reflecting the long-run frequency at which the event would occur in repeated random experiments. Such probabilities are encountered in sampling experiments when the population has known frequencies for various characteristics.

B. Posterior probabilities reflect both prior judgment and experimental information.

If you decide there is a .50 prior probability for rain, you might go to bed planning to dress "for the weather" when you arise. But in the morning you might first look outside at the cloud cover. If it is solid and black, you might revise your probability for rain upward to a value like .90; if the clouds are patchy, you might instead reduce that probability to a number like .20, choosing to leave your umbrella at home. Such a revised value is called a **posterior probability**.

Posterior probabilities are *conditional* probabilities of the form

$$\Pr[\text{event} \mid \text{result}]$$

The given event is the **result** of an experiment (in the preceding, looking at the sky) upon which the revised probability is based. Thomas Bayes proposed a formal mechanism for finding posterior probabilities by merging prior judgment with empirical results. In doing this, you encounter a third type of probability.

C. Conditional result probabilities reflect the experiment's "batting averages" at predicting the future.

Suppose that for an entire year you keep records of a weather forecaster's predictions and the actual next day's weather. Assume that this weatherperson makes one of two forecasts: (*1*) rain likely and (*2*) rain unlikely. You may consider your viewing of the 11 P.M. TV weather broadcast as an experiment having those two *results*. Suppose that 60% of the days when rain actually occurred were preceded by an 11 P.M. forecast in which rain was predicted "likely." Suppose further that 80% of the days when no rain fell were preceded by an "unlikely" forecast. Assuming that this pattern continues into the future, the conditional probability is .60 that the forecast will be "likely" given that rain follows and .80 that it will be "unlikely" given that no rain follows. These numbers are referred to as **conditional result probabilities.** They provide a measure of the reliability of predictive information.

D. Thomas Bayes put it all together with a theorem.

Using the concepts of prior and conditional result probabilities, Bayes arrived at a theorem for determining posterior probabilities.

Bayes' Theorem

$$\Pr[E \mid R] = \frac{\Pr[E] \times \Pr[R \mid E]}{\Pr[E] \times \Pr[R \mid E] + \Pr[\text{not } E] \times \Pr[R \mid \text{not } E]}$$

Here E stands for "event" and R stands for "result." The prior probability for the main event of interest E is *specified in advance* as $\Pr[E]$, with $\Pr[\text{not } E] = 1 - \Pr[E]$. The conditional result probabilities must also be stipulated before making calculations.

You can apply Bayes' theorem to the weather illustration to find the posterior probability that it will rain (E) given a likely forecast (R). The prior probability is

$$\Pr[\text{rain}] = .50$$

and the conditional result probabilities are

$$\Pr[\text{likely} \mid \text{rain}] = .60$$
$$\Pr[\text{likely} \mid \text{no rain}] = 1 - \Pr[\text{unlikely} \mid \text{no rain}] = 1 - .80 = .20$$

Plugging these values into Bayes' theorem, you find

$$\Pr[\text{rain} \mid \text{likely}] = \frac{\Pr[\text{rain}] \times \Pr[\text{likely} \mid \text{rain}]}{\Pr[\text{rain}] \times \Pr[\text{likely} \mid \text{rain}] + \Pr[\text{no rain}] \times \Pr[\text{likely} \mid \text{no rain}]}$$

$$= \frac{.50(.60)}{.50(.60) + (1 - .50)(.20)} = \frac{.30}{.30 + .10} = .75$$

A similar calculation provides the posterior probability for rain (E) given an unlikely forecast (different R). The following conditional result probabilities apply:

$$\Pr[\text{unlikely} \mid \text{rain}] = 1 - .60 = .40$$
$$\Pr[\text{unlikely} \mid \text{no rain}] = .80$$

You find that

$$\Pr[\text{rain} \mid \text{unlikely}] = \frac{\Pr[\text{rain}] \times \Pr[\text{unlikely} \mid \text{rain}]}{\Pr[\text{rain}] \times \Pr[\text{unlikely} \mid \text{rain}] + \Pr[\text{no rain}] \times \Pr[\text{unlikely} \mid \text{no rain}]}$$

$$= \frac{.50(.40)}{.50(.40) + (1 - .50)(.80)} = \frac{.20}{.20 + .40} = .333$$

Notice how the posterior probability for rain *increases* to .75 from the prior level of .50 given a likely forecast. This is what we should expect with any reliable experimental result. Similarly the posterior probability for rain *decreases* from .50 to .33 given an unlikely forecast.

EXAMPLE 5-7: POSTERIOR PROBABILITIES FOR OIL USING A SEISMIC SURVEY

Based on 20 years of wildcatting experience, Lucky Luke assigns a prior probability of .20 for oil (*O*) beneath Crockpot Dome. Thus,

$$\Pr[O] = .20 \quad \text{and} \quad \Pr[\text{not } O] = 1 - .20 = .80$$

Luke has decided to order a seismic survey. A petroleum engineering consultant has rated this particular test as 90% reliable in confirming oil (*C*) when there is actually oil, but only 70% reliable in denying oil (*D*) when a site has no oil. These figures establish the conditional result probabilities:

$$\Pr[C \mid O] = .90 \quad \text{and} \quad \Pr[D \mid \text{not } O] = .70$$

Suppose that the seismic survey confirms the presence of oil. Luke's posterior probability for oil would then be

$$\Pr[O \mid C] = \frac{\Pr[O] \times \Pr[C \mid O]}{\Pr[O] \times \Pr[C \mid O] + \Pr[\text{not } O] \times \Pr[C \mid \text{not } O]}$$

$$= \frac{.20(.90)}{.20(.90) + .80(1 - .70)} = \frac{.18}{.18 + .24}$$

$$= .429$$

If you assume instead that the seismic survey denies any oil beneath Crockpot Dome, Luke's posterior probability for oil would be different:

$$\Pr[O \mid D] = \frac{\Pr[O] \times \Pr[D \mid O]}{\Pr[O] \times \Pr[D \mid O] + \Pr[\text{not } O] \times \Pr[D \mid \text{not } O]}$$

$$= \frac{.20(1 - .90)}{.20(1 - .90) + .80(.70)} = \frac{.02}{.02 + .56}$$

$$= .034$$

Notice how a positive experimental result raises the oil probability above its prior level, while a negative result lowers the oil probability below its initial value.

- Remember that a prior probability $\Pr[E]$ is a *given* value and is an *unconditional* probability.
- The posterior probability $\Pr[E \mid R]$ must be *computed*. This is a *conditional* probability.
- Don't confuse the posterior probability with the conditional result probabilities $\Pr[R \mid E]$ and $\Pr[R \mid \text{not } E]$. Here *E* and not *E* are the given events and are therefore listed last. Conditional result probabilities are *specified in advance*.

E. Posterior probabilities may be computed by first establishing the joint probability table.

The fraction used in expressing Bayes' theorem is really nothing more than a detailed rephrasing of the conditional probability identity (page 61):

$$\Pr[E \mid R] = \frac{\Pr[E \text{ and } R]}{\Pr[R]}$$

At times, rather than use Bayes' theorem, you might find it easier to first construct a joint probability table and then apply the above identity to find posterior probabilities.

To understand this, continue with the weather illustration. You can construct the following joint probability table using the data originally given.

Main event	Result (Forecast)		Marginal probability
	Likely	Unlikely	
Rain	.30	.20	.50
No rain	.10	.40	.50
Marginal probability	.40	.60	1.00

The marginal probabilities for "rain" and "no rain" were given as the prior probability values. You find the joint probability for "rain" and "likely" by using the general multiplication law (page 63):

$$Pr[\text{rain } and \text{ likely}] = Pr[\text{rain}] \times Pr[\text{likely} | \text{rain}]$$
$$= .50(.60) = .30$$

Subtracting this value from the marginal probability for the first row (.50), you get the second joint probability of .20. You can likewise find the joint probability for "no rain" and "unlikely":

$$Pr[\text{no rain } and \text{ unlikely}] = Pr[\text{no rain}] \times Pr[\text{unlikely} | \text{no rain}]$$
$$= .50(.80) = .40$$

Now you find the missing joint probability in the second row by subtracting .40 from the marginal probability for the row (.50). Finally, the marginal probabilities for the columns are found by adding together the joint probabilities in each column.

To find the posterior probability for rain given a likely weather forecast, you substitute the appropriate values into the identity directly from the joint probability table:

$$Pr[\text{rain} | \text{likely}] = \frac{Pr[\text{rain } and \text{ likely}]}{Pr[\text{likely}]} = \frac{.30}{.40} = .75$$

Likewise, the posterior probability for rain given an unlikely forecast is

$$Pr[\text{rain} | \text{unlikely}] = \frac{Pr[\text{rain } and \text{ unlikely}]}{Pr[\text{unlikely}]} = \frac{.20}{.60} = .333$$

SUMMARY

In counting possibilities the *principle of multiplication* allows you to break the process into stages. The total will be the product of the number of possibilities determined for each stage. This principle gives rise to three important calculations. First, the number of outcomes from a series of repeated *trials* is found by raising the number of possible trial outcomes (k) to the *power* of the number of trials (n), or k^n. The two other calculations involve the *factorial product*, formed by multiplying together a progression of successively smaller integers. One of these calculations is based on the number of *permutations* of items. A permutation is a subgrouping distinguishable by the particular items included and the order, or sequence, in which they occur. If you choose r items from a group of n items, the number of permutations P_r^n will be

$$P_r^n = \frac{n!}{(n-r)!}$$

The second calculation is based on the number of *combinations*, which are subgroupings differentiated only by the items themselves and not by the order in which the items are chosen. The number of combinations C_r^n of r items taken from a group of n items is

$$C_r^n = \frac{n!}{r!(n-r)!}$$

The possible number of combinations will always be smaller than that of permutations, so the use of combinations is preferred in applying the *count-and-divide* method for computing probabilities.

Bayes' theorem establishes the mechanism for revising probability values in accordance with a particular experimental result. The initial value is called the *prior probability*. Such values may be either objective (based on long-run frequency) or subjective (derived through judgment). The revised probability based on the particular experimental result is called the *posterior probability*. This is a conditional probability for the main event, with the result serving as the given event. Bayes' theorem

$$\Pr[E \mid R] = \frac{\Pr[E] \times \Pr[R \mid E]}{\Pr[E] \times \Pr[R \mid E] + \Pr[\text{not } E] \times \Pr[R \mid \text{not } E]}$$

merges prior knowledge regarding an event with an actual test result that provides a positive or negative prediction of the event. A set of *conditional result probabilities* for the test must be stipulated; these reflect the reliability of the experimental procedure.

RAISE YOUR GRADES

Can you explain ...?

☑ the difference between a permutation and a combination
☑ what a prior probability value is
☑ the difference between a posterior probability and a conditional result probability
☑ the difference between the multiplication law and the principle of multiplication
☑ why an event's posterior probability may be higher or lower than its prior probability.

Do you know ...?

☑ how to compute a posterior probability
☑ how to find the number of combinations if you know the number of permutations
☑ when to use a power and when to use a factorial
☑ the two different types of prior probabilities
☑ why for the same group sizes there are more permutations than combinations.

RAPID REVIEW

1. Evaluate each of the following quantities.   [Section 5-1B]

   (a) 2^6 **(b)** 5^5 **(c)** 4^3 **(d)** 10^5 **(e)** 3^4

2. Compute the following.   [Section 5-1C]

   (a) 5!   **(b)** 8!   **(c)** 9!   **(d)** 10!   **(e)** 11!

3. Determine the following quantities.   [Section 5-1D]

   (a) P_2^5 **(b)** P_4^7 **(c)** P_5^8 **(d)** P_8^{10} **(e)** P_7^{10}

4. Determine the following quantities.   [Section 5-1E]

   (a) C_2^{10} **(b)** C_4^8 **(c)** C_3^{52} **(d)** C_3^{13} **(e)** C_4^{100}

5. List all the permutations possible using the letters A, B, and C.   [Section 5-1D]

6. List all the combinations of size 3 from the first 5 letters of the alphabet.   [Section 5-1E]

7. The first 3 cards are dealt from the top of a shuffled deck of 26 playing cards that was made up from a complete deck by eliminating all cards belonging to the red suits.   [Section 5-1E]

   (a) How many hand combinations are possible?
   (b) How many possible hands involving face cards only can be dealt?
   (c) Determine the probability for getting a hand with all face cards.

8. The first 3 cards are dealt from the top of a shuffled deck of 40 playing cards that was made up from a complete deck by eliminating all face cards.   [Section 5-1E]

    (a) How many hand combinations are possible?
    (b) How many possible hands involving hearts only can be dealt?
    (c) Determine the probability for getting a hand with all hearts.

9. The following apply: $\Pr[E] = .1$; $\Pr[R\,|\,E] = .9$; $\Pr[R\,|\,\text{not } E] = .2$.   [Section 5-2D]

    (a) Find the posterior probability for E given R.
    (b) Find the posterior probability for E given not R.

10. The following apply: $\Pr[E] = .3$; $\Pr[R\,|\,E] = .8$; $\Pr[R\,|\,\text{not } E] = .3$.   [Section 5-2E]

    (a) Construct a joint probability table using E and not E versus R and not R.
    (b) Find the posterior probability for E given R.
    (c) Find the posterior probability for E given not R.

Answers

1. (a) 64   (b) 3,125   (c) 64   (d) 100,000   (e) 81
2. (a) 120   (b) 40,320   (c) 362,880   (d) 3,628,800   (e) 39,916,800
3. (a) 20   (b) 840   (c) 6,720   (d) 1,814,400   (e) 604,800
4. (a) 45   (b) 70   (c) 22,100   (d) 286   (e) 3,921,225
5. A   B   C   AB   BA   AC   CA   BC   CB   ABC   ACB   BAC   BCA
   CAB   CBA
6. ABC   ABD   ABE   ACD   ACE   ADE   BCD   BCE   BDE   CDE
7. (a) $C_3^{26} = 2,600$ (b) $C_3^6 = 20$ (c) $20/2,600$
8. (a) $C_3^{40} = 9,880$ (b) $C_3^{10} = 120$ (c) $120/9,880$
9. (a) .333
   (b) .014
10. (a)

Main event	Result		Marginal Probability
	R	Not R	
E	$.3 \times .8 = .24$	$.3 - .24 = .06$	.3
Not E	$.7 \times .3 = .21$	$.7 - .21 = .49$	.7
Marginal probability	.45	.55	1.00

   (b) $.24/.45 = .533$ (c) $.06/.55 = .109$

SOLVED PROBLEMS

PROBLEM 5-1   Freshmen at a certain college are required to take exactly one course from each of the following groupings:

Foreign language	Communications	Social science	Humanities
French	Speech	Economics	Art
German	English	Psychology	Philosophy
Italian		History	Music
Latin			Drama
Spanish			

How many different course combinations are possible in satisfying the requirement?

Solution: By the principle of multiplication, the total number of possibilities is the product of the choices in each grouping:

Choices of language		Choices of communications		Choices of social science		Choices of humanities		
5	×	2	×	3	×	4	=	120

PROBLEM 5-2 A *full house* in poker consists of 2 cards of one denomination and 3 cards of another. List each distinct combination of such hands involving 3 aces and 2 kings.

Solution: In creating such a list it is helpful to follow some sort of pattern, as is done here:

Heart	Diamond	Club	Spade	Heart	Diamond	Club	Spade
A, K	A, K	A		A	A,K		A, K
A, K	A, K		A	A	A	A, K	K
A, K	A	A, K		A	A	K	A, K
A, K	A	A	K	A	K	A, K	A
A, K	A	K	A	A	K	A	A, K
A, K	A		A, K	A		A, K	A, K
A, K	K	A	A	K	A, K	A	A
A, K		A, K	A	K	A	A, K	A
A, K		A	A, K	K	A	A	A, K
A	A, K	A, K			A, K	A, K	A
A	A, K	A	K		A, K	A	A, K
A	A, K	K	A		A	A, K	A, K

PROBLEM 5-3 Cal Culator is purchasing a personal computer system. He will select one each of the following: computer (4 choices), disk drive (5 brands), monitor (3 colors), modem (5 makes), and printer (10 choices). How many distinct system possibilities does Cal have to pick from?

Solution: By the principle of multiplication, the total number of possibilities is the product of the choices for each part of the system:

Choices of computer		Choices of disk drive		Choices of monitor		Choices of modem		Choices of printer		
4	×	5	×	3	×	5	×	10	=	3,000

PROBLEM 5-4 Consider all 5-card poker hands resulting in a 10-high straight consisting of black cards only. List all such combinations.

Solution: The combinations are distinguishable by which suit—clubs (C) or spades (S)—occurs for a specific denomination. The possibilities are shown in the following list:

Denomination					Denomination				
6	7	8	9	10	6	7	8	9	10
C	C	C	C	C	S	S	S	S	S
C	C	C	C	S	S	S	S	S	C
C	C	C	S	C	S	S	S	C	S
C	C	S	C	C	S	S	C	S	S
C	S	C	C	C	S	C	S	S	S
S	C	C	C	C	C	S	S	S	S
C	C	C	S	S	S	S	S	C	C
C	C	S	C	S	S	S	C	S	C
C	S	C	C	S	S	C	S	S	C
S	C	C	C	S	C	S	S	S	C
C	C	S	S	C	S	S	C	C	S
C	S	C	S	C	S	C	S	C	S
S	C	C	S	C	C	S	S	C	S
C	S	S	C	C	S	C	C	S	S
S	C	S	C	C	C	S	C	S	S
S	S	C	C	C	C	C	S	S	S

PROBLEM 5-5 Seven items are successively removed from a collection of 10 items. How many distinct possibilities are there when

(a) the order of selection matters?
(b) the order of selection doesn't matter?
(c) once removed, an item is replaced and allowed to be chosen later?

Solution:
(a) The number of possibilities equals the number of permutations of $r = 7$ items from $n = 10$:

$$P_7^{10} = \frac{10!}{(10-7)!} = \frac{10!}{3!} = \frac{10 \times 9 \times 8 \times 7 \times 6 \times 5 \times 4 \times 3!}{3!} = 604,800$$

(b) The number of possibilities equals the number of combinations of $r = 7$ items from $n = 10$:

$$C_7^{10} = \frac{10!}{7!(10-7)!} = \frac{10 \times 9 \times 8 \times 7!}{7!3!} = 120$$

(c) The number of possibilities equals the number of items (10) raised to the power of the number of trials (7): $10^7 = 10,000,000$.

PROBLEM 5-6 Nancy Wheeler is ordering a car. She must specify her choices for the following: model (3 choices), engine (3 sizes), body style (4 types), color (7 shades), and option package (10 choices). How many different cars must Nancy choose from?

Solution: By the principle of multiplication, the total number of possibilities is the product of each group of choices:

Choices of model		Choices of engine		Choices of body style		Choices of color		Choices of options	
3	×	3	×	4	×	7	×	10	= 2,520

PROBLEM 5-7 Determine the number of possible outcomes (distinguished by side obtained) when

(a) a coin is tossed 7 times.
(b) a die is rolled 5 times.
(c) a 4-sided pyramid is flipped 4 times.

Solution: In each case, the number of possible sides is raised to the power of the number of trials.
(a) $2^7 = 128$ (b) $6^5 = 7,776$ (c) $4^4 = 256$

PROBLEM 5-8 An oil wildcatter determines a prior probability for oil (O) of .2. A special rock-sample survey will be made. Historically, a positive (P) survey result has been obtained on 70% of sites where oil was found, while negative (N) survey results have occurred on 95% of the sites drilled and later found dry. Find the posterior probability for oil given

(a) a positive survey result.
(b) a negative survey result.

Solution: From the given data, you have the prior probability for oil,

$$\Pr[O] = .2.$$

and the conditional result probabilities,

$$\Pr[P \,|\, O] = .70 \quad \text{and} \quad \Pr[N \,|\, \text{not } O] = .95$$

(a) Substituting these probabilities or their complements into the Bayes' theorem expression, you have

$$\Pr[O \,|\, P] = \frac{\Pr[O] \times \Pr[P \,|\, O]}{\Pr[O] \times \Pr[P \,|\, O] + \Pr[\text{not } O] \times \Pr[P \,|\, \text{not } O]}$$

$$= \frac{.2(.70)}{.2(.70) + (1 - .2)(1 - .95)} = \frac{.14}{.14 + .04} = .778$$

(b) Likewise,

$$Pr[O|N] = \frac{Pr[O] \times Pr[N|O]}{Pr[O] \times Pr[N|O] + Pr[\text{not } O] \times Pr[N|\text{not } O]}$$

$$= \frac{.2(1 - .70)}{.2(1 - .70) + (1 - .2)(.95)} = \frac{.06}{.06 + .76} = .073$$

PROBLEM 5-9 Consider poker hands that involve a full house consisting of a pair and a triple of any two different denominations.

  (a) How many possibilities are there?
  (b) Find the probability for getting a full house.

Solution:
(a) Consider first the possibilities for the denominations. This is equal to the number of permutations of 2 values taken from the 13 possible denominations:

$$P_2^{13} = \frac{13!}{(13-2)!} = \frac{13 \times 12 \times 11!}{11!} = 13 \times 12 = 156$$

(We don't use combinations, since it does matter whether, for instance, the kings are included in the pair or in the triple instead.) Next, consider the particular cards that will make up the pair; this is equal to the number of combinations of 2 cards from the 4 suit possibilities:

$$C_2^4 = \frac{4!}{2!(4-2)!} = \frac{4 \times 3 \times 2!}{2 \times 1(2!)} = \frac{12}{2} = 6$$

Likewise, the number of triple possibilities is the number of combinations of 3 cards from 4:

$$C_3^4 = \frac{4!}{3!(4-3)!} = \frac{4 \times 3!}{3!(1!)} = 4$$

The number of possible full houses is thus:

$$P_2^{13}C_2^4C_3^4 = 156 \times 6 \times 4 = 3,744$$

(b) In Example 5-6 we saw that there are 2,598,960 equally likely poker-hand possibilities. By applying the count-and-divide method, you can find the probability for a full house:

$$Pr[\text{full house}] = \frac{3,744}{2,598,960} = .00144$$

(Note that a full house is rarer than both a flush and a straight, which is why a full house will beat either of those hands. Only a straight flush, a royal flush, or 4-of-a-kind beat a full house.)

PROBLEM 5-10 Suppose that a group of 5 students is selected at random from those represented in Figure 3-3 [page 41]. No student is chosen more than once, and their order of selection doesn't matter.

  (a) How many distinct outcomes are possible?
  (b) Suppose that the sample contains only graduate students.
    (1) How many such sample outcomes are possible?
    (2) What is the probability that such a result will occur?

Solution:
(a) There are $n = 72$ students from which $r = 5$ are chosen. The number of possibilities is

$$C_5^{72} = \frac{72!}{5!(72-5)!} = \frac{72 \times 71 \times 70 \times 69 \times 68 \times 67!}{5 \times 4 \times 3 \times 2 \times 1(67!)} = \frac{72 \times 71 \times 70 \times 69 \times 68}{120} = 13,991,544$$

(b) There are $n = 30$ graduate students from which $r = 5$ are taken.
  (1) The number of possibilities is

$$C_5^{30} = \frac{30!}{5!(30-5)!} = \frac{30 \times 29 \times 28 \times 27 \times 26 \times 25!}{5 \times 4 \times 3 \times 2 \times 1(25!)} = \frac{30 \times 29 \times 28 \times 27 \times 26}{120} = 142,506$$

  (2) Treating the outcomes in **(a)** as equally likely elementary events, the count-and-divide method provides:

$$Pr[\text{all graduates}] = \frac{142,506}{13,991,544} = .01$$

PROBLEM 5-11   One sack contains a crooked pair (C) of dice, one die having 3 dots on each face, the other having 4 dots on each face. A second sack contains an ordinary fair pair (F) of dice. One sack is chosen at random, and its dice are tossed.

(a) What is the prior probability that the crooked pair will be chosen?
(b) A 7-sum occurs. Find the posterior probability that the tossed dice are the crooked pair.

Solution:
(a) The two pairs are equally likely to be selected, so that

$$\Pr[C] = \frac{1}{2} \quad \text{and} \quad \Pr[F] = \frac{1}{2}$$

(b) The conditional result probabilities are computed as follows:

$$\Pr[7 \mid F] = \frac{6}{36} = \frac{1}{6}$$

[See the solution to Problem 3-5 on page 53.]

$$\Pr[7 \mid C] = 1$$

This probability for the crooked dice holds because 7 is the only possibility when they are tossed. Substituting the prior and conditional result probabilities into the expression for Bayes' theorem, you get

$$\Pr[C \mid 7] = \frac{\Pr[C] \times \Pr[7 \mid C]}{\Pr[C] \times \Pr[7 \mid C] + \Pr[F] \times \Pr[7 \mid F]}$$

$$= \frac{(1/2)(1)}{(1/2)(1) + (1/2)(1/6)} = \frac{1/2}{1/2 + 1/12} = .857$$

PROBLEM 5-12   A sample of 100 widgets is taken one at a time directly from production. Each item is classified as defective (D) or satisfactory (S). Answer the following, ignoring which particular items get selected.

(a) How many distinguishable quality outcomes are possible?
(b) Of the results counted in (a), how many involve
    (1) exactly 2 defectives?
    (2) exactly 5 defectives?
    (3) exactly 10 defectives?

Solution:
(a) One possible sample result, with the outcomes listed in the sequence obtained, might be

SSSSSDSSSSDSDSSSDSSSDSSSSSSSSSSSSSSSSSSSSSDSSSSSSSS
SSDSSSSSSSSSSSSSSSSSDSSSSSSSSSSSSDSSSSSSSSSSSSSSSSS

Altogether, there are 2^{100} possibilities.
(b) In each case, the number of possibilities equals the number of combinations of $n = 100$ sequence positions in which r number of Ds can be chosen.
(1) For $r = 2$, the number of possibilities is

$$C_2^{100} = \frac{100!}{2!(100 - 2)!} = \frac{100 \times 99 \times 98!}{2!98!} = \frac{100 \times 99}{2} = 4,950$$

(2) For $r = 5$, the number of possibilities is

$$C_5^{100} = \frac{100!}{5!(100 - 5)!} = \frac{100 \times 99 \times 98 \times 97 \times 96 \times 95!}{5!95!} = \frac{100 \times 99 \times 98 \times 97 \times 96}{120}$$

$$= 75,287,520$$

(3) For $r = 10$, the number of possibilities is

$$C_{10}^{100} = \frac{100!}{10!(100 - 10)!} = \frac{100 \times 99 \times 98 \times 97 \times 96 \times 95 \times 94 \times 93 \times 92 \times 91 \times 90!}{10!90!}$$

$$= \frac{100 \times 99 \times 98 \times 97 \times 96 \times 95 \times 94 \times 93 \times 92 \times 91}{10 \times 9 \times 8 \times 7 \times 6 \times 5 \times 4 \times 3 \times 2 \times 1} = 17,310,308,000,000 \,(\text{approx.})$$

PROBLEM 5-13 Consider poker hands involving 4-of-a-kind (same denomination).

(a) How many possible hands are there?
(b) Determine the probability for getting 4-of-a-kind.

Solution:
(a) There are 13 denominations in which the matching cards might occur. If you remove those 4 cards from the deck, there remain 48 possibilities for the fifth card. By the principle of multiplication, the number of possibilities is thus

$$13 \times 48 = 624$$

(b) Since you already know the number of equally likely poker hands (Example 5-6), the count-and-divide method provides

$$\Pr[\text{4-of-a-kind}] = \frac{624}{2,598,960} = .00024$$

(Note that this type of hand is even rarer than a flush, a straight, or a full house, which is why this hand will win over any of those.)

PROBLEM 5-14 Suppose that the situation in Problem 5-11 involves 2 sacks each having a crooked pair of dice (C) and 4 sacks each having a fair pair (F).

(a) What is the prior probability that the crooked pair will be chosen?
(b) A 3-4 combination occurs. Find the posterior probability that the tossed dice are the crooked pair.

Solution:
(a) There are 6 equally likely pairs, 2 of which are crooked, so that

$$\Pr[C] = \frac{2}{6} = \frac{1}{3}$$

and

$$\Pr[F] = \frac{4}{6} = \frac{2}{3}$$

(b) The conditional result probabilities are as follows:

$$\Pr[\text{3-4}\,|\,F] = \frac{2}{36} = \frac{1}{18}$$

[See the solution to Problem 3-5 on page 53.]

$$\Pr[\text{3-4}\,|\,C] = 1$$

This latter probability holds because 3-4 is the only possibility from tossing either crooked pair of dice. Substituting the prior and conditional result probabilities into the expression for Bayes' theorem, you find

$$\Pr[C\,|\,\text{3-4}] = \frac{\Pr[C] \times \Pr[\text{3-4}\,|\,C]}{\Pr[C] \times \Pr[\text{3-4}\,|\,C] + \Pr[F] \times \Pr[\text{3-4}\,|\,F]}$$

$$= \frac{(1/3)(1)}{(1/3)(1) + (2/3)(1/18)} = \frac{1/3}{1/3 + 1/27} = .90$$

PROBLEM 5-15 A phony card deck (P) contains 52 kings. This deck is placed into a sack with 4 standard decks (S) of 52 playing cards. One deck is selected at random.

(a) What is the prior probability that the phony deck is selected?
(b) A king is drawn at random from the selected deck. What is the posterior probability that the phony deck is selected?

Solution:
(a) There are 5 equally likely decks, one of which is phony, so that

$$\Pr[P] = \frac{1}{5} \quad \text{and} \quad \Pr[S] = \frac{4}{5}$$

(b) The conditional result probabilities are

$$\Pr[K \mid S] = \frac{1}{13} \quad \text{and} \quad \Pr[K \mid P] = 1$$

This probability for the phony deck holds because only one denomination is possible in drawing from it. Substituting the prior and conditional result probabilities into the expression for Bayes' theorem, you get

$$\Pr[P \mid K] = \frac{\Pr[P] \times \Pr[K \mid P]}{\Pr[P] \times \Pr[K \mid P] + \Pr[S] \times \Pr[K \mid S]}$$

$$= \frac{(1/5)(1)}{(1/5)(1) + (4/5)(1/13)} = \frac{1/5}{1/5 + 4/65} = .765$$

PROBLEM 5-16 An admissions committee must select students for an MBA program. Past data show that 70% of all admitted students complete (*C*) the degree program. It is also known that 50% of the graduating students scored above 500 (*A*) on the Graduate Management Admissions Test (GMAT), while only 20% of the dropouts (*D*) scored that well. Consider a newly matriculated MBA student.

    (a) What is the prior probability that she will complete the degree?
    (b) Given that she scores 575 on the GMAT, what is the posterior probability that she will complete her MBA?
    (c) Given that she scores 450 on the test, what is the posterior probability that she will graduate?

Solution:
(a) From the given data, $\Pr[C] = .70$.
(b) The conditional result probabilities are determined directly from the given information:

$$\Pr[A \mid C] = .50 \quad \text{and} \quad \Pr[A \mid D] = .20$$

Substituting the prior and conditional result probabilities into the expression for Bayes' theorem, you find

$$\Pr[C \mid A] = \frac{\Pr[C] \times \Pr[A \mid C]}{\Pr[C] \times \Pr[A \mid C] + \Pr[D] \times \Pr[A \mid D]}$$

$$= \frac{.70(.50)}{.70(.50) + (1 - .70)(.20)} = \frac{.35}{.35 + .06} = .854$$

(c) Again substituting the appropriate probability values into the expression for Bayes' theorem, you find

$$\Pr[C \mid \text{not } A] = \frac{\Pr[C] \times \Pr[\text{not } A \mid C]}{\Pr[C] \times \Pr[\text{not } A \mid C] + \Pr[D] \times \Pr[\text{not } A \mid D]}$$

$$= \frac{.70(1 - .50)}{.70(1 - .50) + (1 - .70)(1 - .20)} = \frac{.35}{.35 + .24} = .593$$

PROBLEM 5-17 Consider drawing the top 5 cards from a deck of 52 playing cards.

    (a) How many possible hands are there that involve *exactly* one pair (excluding three- or four-of-a-kind)?
    (b) Determine the probability for getting exactly one pair.

Solution:
(a) There are 13 denominations possible for the pair. Such a hand will contain 3 extra cards, each of a nonmatching denomination. The number of denomination possibilities for those extra cards is equal to the number of combinations of $r = 3$ from $n = 12$:

$$C_3^{12} = \frac{12!}{3!(12 - 3)!} = \frac{12 \times 11 \times 10 \times 9!}{3 \times 2 \times 1(9!)} = 220$$

The 2 cards that make up the pair are chosen from 4 suit possibilities, so that

$$C_2^4 = \frac{4!}{2!(4 - 2)!} = \frac{4 \times 3 \times 2!}{2 \times 1(2!)} = 6$$

There are $4^3 = 64$ suit possibilities for the extra cards. The number of exactly-one-pair hands is thus

$$13 \times C_3^{12} \times C_2^4 \times 4^3 = 13 \times 220 \times 6 \times 64 = 1{,}098{,}240$$

(b) Since the number of equally likely hands is known (Example 5-6), the count-and-divide method provides

$$\Pr[\text{exactly one pair}] = \frac{1{,}098{,}240}{2{,}598{,}960} = .423$$

PROBLEM 5-18   One student is selected at random from the sample space in Figure 3-3 [page 41].

(a) What is the prior probability that the student is a man (M)?
(b) Suppose that the student's major is known. What is the posterior probability that a man is chosen given that the student is a finance major (F)?

Solution:
(a) There are 40 men out of 72 students, so that $\Pr[M] = 40/72$.
(b) Here you can compute the posterior probability directly by counting and dividing the applicable elementary events in the sample space:

$$\Pr[M \mid F] = \frac{14}{24} = .583$$

(There is a moral here. Keep it simple. Just because there is a familiar way [Bayes' theorem] to compute posterior probabilities, that is no reason why you must use—or even can use—that method. Remember that above all else, a posterior probability is a conditional probability. Here the conditional probability may be computed directly.)

PROBLEM 5-19   A marketing researcher is evaluating the effectiveness of using brand recognition to forecast an individual's tendency to purchase a product. Suppose that Bri-Dent toothpaste has a 20% share of the market. Past study has shown that 95% of all persons who once bought Bri-Dent still recognize (R) the brand name, while only 20% of the nonbuyers recognize it. One new test subject is selected at random.

(a) What would be an appropriate prior probability that this person is a buyer (B) of Bri-Dent?
(b) Given that the subject recognizes the brand name, what is the posterior probability that she is a buyer?
(c) Given that the subject doesn't recognize the brand name, what is the posterior probability that she is a buyer?

Solution:
(a) The market share should be equal to the frequency at which buyers will be encountered. Thus, $\Pr[B] = .20$.
(b) You can determine the conditional result probabilities directly from the given information:

$$\Pr[R \mid B] = .95 \quad \text{and} \quad \Pr[R \mid \text{not } B] = .20$$

Substituting the appropriate probabilities into the expression for Bayes' theorem, you get

$$\Pr[B \mid R] = \frac{\Pr[B] \times \Pr[R \mid B]}{\Pr[B] \times \Pr[R \mid B] + \Pr[\text{not } B] \times \Pr[R \mid \text{not } B]}$$

$$= \frac{.20(.95)}{.20(.95) + (1 - .20)(.20)} = \frac{.19}{.19 + .16} = .543$$

(c) Again substituting the appropriate values into the expression for Bayes' theorem, you find

$$\Pr[B \mid \text{not } R] = \frac{\Pr[B] \times \Pr[\text{not } R \mid B]}{\Pr[B] \times \Pr[\text{not } R \mid B] + \Pr[\text{not } B] \times \Pr[\text{not } R \mid \text{not } B]}$$

$$= \frac{.20(1 - .95)}{.20(1 - .95) + (1 - .20)(1 - .20)} = \frac{.01}{.01 + .64} = .015$$

PROBLEM 5-20 A group contains 60 men and 40 women. Four names will be selected at random and without replacement for door prizes.

(a) How many different name combinations are possible?

(b) How many combinations of all female names are possible? What is the probability that women take all the door prizes?

Solution:

(a) The number of combinations is the number of ways of taking $r = 4$ items from $n = 100$:

$$C_4^{100} = \frac{100!}{4!(100-4)!} = \frac{100 \times 99 \times 98 \times 97 \times 96!}{4 \times 3 \times 2 \times 1(96!)} = \frac{100 \times 99 \times 98 \times 97}{24}$$

$$= 3,921,225$$

(b) The number of combinations is the number of ways of taking $r = 4$ items from $n = 40$:

$$C_4^{40} = \frac{40!}{4!(40-4)!} = \frac{40 \times 39 \times 38 \times 37 \times 36!}{4!(36!)} = \frac{40 \times 39 \times 38 \times 37}{24}$$

$$= 91,390$$

The desired probability is

$$\frac{91,390}{3,921,225} = .023$$

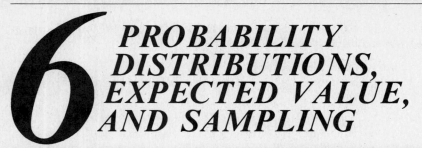

6 PROBABILITY DISTRIBUTIONS, EXPECTED VALUE, AND SAMPLING

THIS CHAPTER IS ABOUT

☑ **Probability Distributions**
☑ **Expected Value and Variance**
☑ **Sampling Distribution of the Mean**

Probability values express the frequency at which events occur. Probability theory thus provides a foundation for statistical methodology that uses random samples to draw conclusions about populations that can't be observed in their entirety. It tells us what values might be expected from a sample, and from random experiments in general.

6-1. Probability Distributions

You learned in Chapter 2 how to arrange raw data into a meaningful pattern useful for further evaluation. This is accomplished by constructing a frequency distribution. A similar distribution can be used to summarize the results of a random experiment, such as the sampling of accounts receivable by an auditor or the predicting of a new product's sales.

A. Random variables are uncertain quantities whose values are determined by chance.

A numerical value that may result from a future random experiment is unknown and should be considered a *variable*. The value actually achieved is subject to chance and is therefore determined *randomly*. For this reason any uncertain quantity arising from a random experiment is called a **random variable**.

A random variable must be a numerical quantity. There can be no random variable unless points, a cost, or some other number can be associated with the qualitative outcomes. Consider an inspection process where items are classified as defective or satisfactory; these are qualitative events. A useful random variable in such an experiment is the *number* of defectives obtained in a sample of inspected items.

B. Random variables have probability distributions.

Consider the number of customers arriving at a store checkout counter during a period of five minutes. The following probabilities might apply.

Number of customers	Probability
0	.3679
1	.3679
2	.1839
3	.0613
4	.0153
5	.0031
6	.0005
7	.0001

This table summarizes the **probability distribution** for the number-of-arrivals random variable. Usually summarized in a table, a probability distribution specifies the probability for each possible level of the random variable.

1. **Graphical representation:** Figure 6-1 shows how this probability distribution appears on a graph. The values for each possible variable level appear on the horizontal axis. The vertical axis provides the probability. For each variable level, a spike is drawn on the graph with a height equal to the appropriate probability.

Figure 6-1

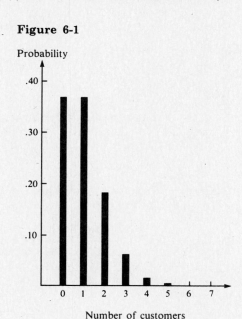

Number of customers

2. **Probability mass function:** Many random variables have probability distributions for which individual probabilities can be computed from a mathematical expression. Later you'll encounter illustrations of those expressions that are applicable to some common probability distributions. Such expressions are called **probability mass functions**.

3. **Discrete and continuous random variables:** Any random variable that can assume only integer (whole number) values is classified as **discrete**. An example is the number-of-arrivals random variable. But some variables, such as those involving physical measurements or time, might assume any value over a continuous range of possibilities. Those random variables are classified as **continuous**.

EXAMPLE 6-1: AMOUNT PAID FOR A PERSONAL COMPUTER

Quant Jacques wishes to buy a personal computer made by VBM (Very Big Machines). From past purchases, VBM has established the following breakdown for the percentage of times that a particular component is chosen for a system. (Costs are in parentheses.)

Computer and memory	Printer	Monitor
30%—250K (1500)	50%—Matrix (500)	60%—Monochrome (200)
70%—500K (2000)	50%—Daisy (1000)	40%—Color (400)

Assuming that Quant chooses the three components independently and that the probability for each choice agrees with the percentages given in the table, what is the probability distribution for his total system cost?

Begin by listing all the possible combinations. You can find the probability for each by using the multiplication law.

Computer and memory	Printer	Monitor	Cost	Probability
250K	Matrix	Monochrome	1,500 + 500 + 200 = 2,200	.3(.5)(.6) = .09
250K	Matrix	Color	1,500 + 500 + 400 = 2,400	.3(.5)(.4) = .06
250K	Daisy	Monochrome	1,500 + 1,000 + 200 = 2,700	.3(.5)(.6) = .09
250K	Daisy	Color	1,500 + 1,000 + 400 = 2,900	.3(.5)(.4) = .06
500K	Matrix	Monochrome	2,000 + 500 + 200 = 2,700	.7(.5)(.6) = .21
500K	Matrix	Color	2,000 + 500 + 400 = 2,900	.7(.5)(.4) = .14
500K	Daisy	Monochrome	2,000 + 1,000 + 200 = 3,200	.7(.5)(.6) = .21
500K	Daisy	Color	2,000 + 1,000 + 400 = 3,400	.7(.5)(.4) = .14

You now list the possible costs, applying the addition law as needed, to construct the probability distribution table:

Cost	Probability
$2,200	.09
2,400	.06
2,700	.09 + .21 = .30
2,900	.06 + .14 = .20
3,200	.21
3,400	.14
	1.00

- The possible values of a random variable are mutually exclusive and collectively exhaustive events. The probabilities in a complete listing must therefore sum to 1.

6-2. Expected Value and Variance

Just as the mean, standard deviation, and variance are used to describe raw data [Chapter 2], there are summary measures that are useful in analyzing random variable values.

A. The expected value is a measure of central tendency.

The most common summary measure is the **expected value**. You compute this quantity by taking a *weighted average* of the possible variable values; the respective probabilities serve as the weights.

To understand this, consider the number of dots on the showing face of a die cube that has been rolled. The probability distribution for this quantity is

Dots	Probability
1	1/6
2	1/6
3	1/6
4	1/6
5	1/6
6	1/6
	1

You find the expected number of dots by multiplying each possible value by its probability and summing the resulting products:

$$1\left(\frac{1}{6}\right) + 2\left(\frac{1}{6}\right) + 3\left(\frac{1}{6}\right) + 4\left(\frac{1}{6}\right) + 5\left(\frac{1}{6}\right) + 6\left(\frac{1}{6}\right) = \frac{21}{6} = 3.5$$

The quantity 3.5 expresses the *long-run average* number of dots that will be achieved after many rolls of a die cube.

The procedure for finding the expected value is summarized by the following mathematical expression:

Expected value $$E(X) = \sum x \Pr[X = x]$$

$E(X)$ is the symbol for expected value, with the random variable designated by an uppercase X. (Other letters, such as Y or Z, are often used in statistical applications.) Think of the lowercase x as a stand-in or *dummy variable* for all the possible levels of X considered individually. Thus, for the die cube illustration, if the value of the random variable is 3, then

$$\Pr[X = x] = \Pr[X = 3] = \frac{1}{6}$$

Since the expected value may be interpreted as a long-run average result, it measures central tendency. In Chapter 2 you learned that it is also important to know the degree of variability or dispersion in raw data. Summary measures exist that provide this information for random variables and their probability distributions.

B. The variance and standard deviation summarize dispersion.

Recall that for a collection of observed values, you find the *deviations* by subtracting the mean from each quantity. The mean of the *squared* deviations is called the **variance**, denoted either by σ^2 (for a population) or by s^2 (for a sample). You can find the variance of a random variable in a similar way.

Variance of a random variable

$$\sigma^2(X) = \sum [x - E(X)]^2 \Pr[X = x]$$

Like the two variances you encountered earlier, the variance of a random variable is the average of squared deviations about the center. As with $E(X)$, the probabilities serve as weights in computing the summary value.

To illustrate, consider again the number of dots on the showing face of a rolled die cube. The following computations apply. [Remember that in this case $E(X) = 3.5$.]

Number of dots x	Probability $\Pr[X = x]$	Deviation $[x - E(X)]$	Squared deviation $[x - E(X)]^2$	Weighted value $[x - E(X)]^2 \Pr[X = x]$
1	1/6	−2.5	6.25	6.25/6
2	1/6	−1.5	2.25	2.25/6
3	1/6	− .5	.25	.25/6
4	1/6	.5	.25	.25/6
5	1/6	1.5	2.25	2.25/6
6	1/6	2.5	6.25	6.25/6
	1			$\sigma^2(X) = 17.50/6 = 2.9167$

You have seen that the variance gives a distorted image of the amount of variability because of its size and units (the number of dots are *squared*). For this reason you ordinarily convert the variance to the **standard deviation** by taking its square root:

Standard deviation of a random variable

$$\sigma(X) = \sqrt{\sigma^2(X)}$$

For the die cube illustration, the standard deviation for the number of dots is

$$\sigma(X) = \sqrt{2.9167} = 1.708$$

C. Expected value is a useful concept in sampling.

You need to learn about probability because it will help you understand how to evaluate samples.

1. **Sample observation as a random variable:** Before the data are collected, quantitative observations are random variables. For example, the height of a man selected by lottery from all adult males in your town is a random variable, ordinarily represented by X. If several men are to be selected, each observed value is a distinct random variable. A succession of these might be designated as $X_1, X_2, X_3, \ldots$.

2. **Expected value and variance of an observed quantity:** You have used the symbols μ and σ to represent the mean and the standard deviation for any designated population. Consider a single observed value X for a randomly selected elementary event. When all population values are equally likely, the expected value of the observation is equal to the population mean, and its standard deviation is equal to the standard deviation of the population. That is,

$$E(X) = \mu \quad \text{and} \quad \sigma(X) = \sigma$$

EXAMPLE 6-2: AUDITING ACCOUNTS RECEIVABLE

Compu-Quik's accounts receivable balances constitute a population. One of these amounts is selected *at random*; you can denote this uncertain quantity as X. Historically, it has been established that the mean balance is $\mu = \$137.50$ and the standard deviation is $\sigma = \$15.20$. If these values presently apply, then the expected balance for the selected account is $E(X) = \$137.50$ and the standard deviation is $\sigma(X) = \$15.20$.

Of course, there may be no reason to assume that prior levels for μ and σ still apply.

If the actual values for μ and σ were known, there would be little purpose in collecting a sample, since most of the essential population information would already be known! But whatever μ and σ are—even unknown quantities—it is always true that $E(X) = \mu$ and $\sigma(X) = \sigma$.

6-3. Sampling Distribution of the Mean

Many statistical investigations are concerned with finding population means. Ordinarily you can't observe an entire population, and therefore you must base conclusions regarding μ on sample evidence. You use the *sample mean* $\bar{X}$ for this purpose. Before the data are collected, you treat $\bar{X}$ as a *random variable*. You should know how to establish probabilities for the various levels that $\bar{X}$ might assume.

A. The probability distribution of $\bar{X}$ is referred to as a sampling distribution.

In Chapter 2 you treated $\bar{X}$ as a computed sample statistic. *Before* the sample results are known, however, you must treat $\bar{X}$ like any other random variable. Statisticians use the specialized term **sampling distribution** when referring to the probability distribution for a sample statistic.

To help you understand the sampling distribution of $\bar{X}$, consider an illustration involving a tiny population. Keep in mind that *samples are not ordinarily taken from such a small population—especially when all of its essential properties are already known.* But a simple case does show the concepts involved.

A statistics class has five MBA students whose examination grades are as follows:

Name	Grade	Grade points
Ann	B	3
Bob	C	2
Cal	B	3
Don	A	4
Eve	C	2

As a review, establish to your own satisfaction that treating these grade point values as a population, you find the following mean and standard deviation:

$$\mu = 2.8 \quad \text{and} \quad \sigma = \sqrt{.56} = .7483$$

Two students will be selected at random. You will construct the sampling distribution for the mean number of grade points $\bar{X}$ achieved by the students in the sample.

For each combination of two students you can readily find the mean:

Possible mean $\bar{x}$	Applicable combinations	$\Pr[\bar{X} = \bar{x}]$
2.0	(Bob, Eve)	1/10
2.5	(Ann, Bob) (Ann, Eve) (Bob, Cal) (Cal, Eve)	4/10
3.0	(Ann, Cal) (Bob, Don) (Don, Eve)	3/10
3.5	(Ann, Don) (Cal, Don)	2/10
		1

This probability distribution is the sampling distribution of $\bar{X}$. The probabilities were found using the count-and-divide method, with each name combination being one of 10 equally likely elementary events.

B. The expected value and variance of $\bar{X}$ can be found.

Treating $\bar{X}$ just like any random variable, you have

$$E(\bar{X}) = \sum \bar{x} \Pr[\bar{X} = \bar{x}]$$

$$= 2.0\left(\frac{1}{10}\right) + 2.5\left(\frac{4}{10}\right) + 3.0\left(\frac{3}{10}\right) + 3.5\left(\frac{2}{10}\right) = 2.8$$

and

$$\sigma^2(\bar{X}) = \sum [\bar{x} - E(\bar{X})]^2 \Pr[\bar{X} = \bar{x}]$$

$$= (2.0 - 2.8)^2\left(\frac{1}{10}\right) + (2.5 - 2.8)^2\left(\frac{4}{10}\right) + (3.0 - 2.8)^2\left(\frac{3}{10}\right) + (3.5 - 2.8)^2\left(\frac{2}{10}\right)$$

$$= .21$$

so that

$$\sigma(\bar{X}) = \sqrt{.21} = .458$$

Notice that $E(\bar{X}) = 2.8$, which is the same value as the population mean, $\mu = 2.8$. This is true of all simple random samples, and it is summarized as follows:

Property of the sample mean $\qquad\qquad E(\bar{X}) = \mu$

C. The standard deviation of a sample statistic is called the standard error.

Partly because it is used so often and partly because (as you will see) it measures how precisely the computed sample value estimates its population counterpart, the standard deviation of $\bar{X}$ is called the **standard error of $\bar{X}$**. This quantity is used so frequently that a special symbol $\sigma_{\bar{x}}$ is reserved for it. The standard error of $\bar{X}$ is defined as follows:

$$\sigma_{\bar{x}} = \sigma(\bar{X})$$

You can compute the standard error of $\bar{X}$ directly from the population standard deviation and the sizes of the population (N) and sample (n) by using the following expression:

Standard error of $\bar{X}$ $\qquad\qquad \sigma_{\bar{x}} = \frac{\sigma}{\sqrt{n}} \sqrt{\frac{N - n}{N - 1}}$

You know that for the student grade point data,

$$\sigma_{\bar{X}} = \sigma(\bar{X}) = .458$$

To see that the expression for the standard error of $\bar{X}$ works, substitute $\sigma = .7483$, $N = 5$, and $n = 2$. You get

$$\sigma_{\bar{X}} = \frac{.7483}{\sqrt{2}} \sqrt{\frac{5-2}{5-1}} = .458$$

This is the same value you found by substituting individual $\bar{X}$'s and their probabilities into the variance expression and taking the square root.

- As a practical matter, you can find $\sigma_{\bar{X}}$ most easily by using the formula for the standard error of $\bar{X}$ instead of the more roundabout procedure.
- The expression for the standard error of $\bar{X}$ always works, even when the sampling distribution can't be fully specified.

EXAMPLE 6-3: DOG PATCH VERSUS METROPOLIS

Suppose you were to select $n = 100$ families at random from the community of Dog Patch (home of Li'l Abner). Assume that there are $N = 500$ families in the entire town. If the population standard deviation is known to be $\sigma = \$700$, what is the standard error of the sample mean family income?

The proper value is

$$\sigma_{\bar{X}} = \frac{\$700}{\sqrt{100}} \sqrt{\frac{500 - 100}{500 - 1}} = \$62.67$$

You then take a random sample of the same size from the residents of Metropolis (Superman's hometown). Assuming $N = 1,000,000$ and the same level for σ as before, you have

$$\sigma_{\bar{X}} = \frac{\$700}{\sqrt{100}} \sqrt{\frac{1,000,000 - 100}{1,000,000 - 1}} = \$70.00$$

Notice how close the two values are for $\sigma_{\bar{X}}$, even though the two population sizes differ drastically. This indicates that the means of successive samples (each involving 100 families) would exhibit similar variability—whether taken in Dog Patch or in Metropolis.

D. The finite population correction factor is needed only for small population sizes.

The term $\sqrt{(N - n)/(N - 1)}$ is called the **finite population correction factor**. When N is large in relation to n, this factor is close to 1, and its effect on $\sigma_{\bar{X}}$ is negligible. As a practical matter, the following approximation applies:

Standard error of $\bar{X}$ when population size is large

$$\sigma_{\bar{X}} = \frac{\sigma}{\sqrt{n}}$$

Applying this new expression for the standard error of $\bar{X}$ to Metropolis family incomes (Example 6-3), you get

$$\sigma_{\bar{X}} = \frac{\$700}{\sqrt{100}} = \$70.00$$

After rounding to the nearest penny, this is exactly the same result you found earlier using the finite population correction factor.

- Most of the time you will use the expression $\sigma/\sqrt{n}$ to determine $\sigma_{\bar{X}}$.

SUMMARY

An uncertain quantity whose value is subject to chance is a *random variable*. The set of possible variable values and their probabilities constitutes the *probability distribution* for the random variable. A probability distribution is sometimes graphed. *Discrete* random variables are those that assume integer values. A second type of random variable is the *continuous*, which may assume any value over a continuous range of possibilities.

Each random variable has a measure of central tendency, called its *expected value E(X)*. This quantity is found by taking a weighted average of the possible variable values, with their associated probabilities serving as weights:

$$E(X) = \sum x \Pr[X = x]$$

Two measures of dispersion, the *variance* $\sigma^2(X)$ and the *standard deviation* $\sigma(X)$, apply to any random variable.

$$\sigma^2(X) = \sum [x - E(X)]^2 \Pr[X = x]$$
$$\sigma(X) = \sqrt{\sigma^2(X)}$$

The standard deviation is the more useful of the two, because it doesn't distort the amount of variability. Expected value concepts apply to sampling, where each quantitative sample observation may be considered a random variable. The expected value and standard deviation for such an observation are equal to their population parameter counterparts.

Before sample data are collected, the values of the sample statistics are random variables. The probability distributions for these variables are called *sampling distributions*. The sample mean $\bar{X}$ is a very important statistic. Its sampling distribution may be derived from the known characteristics of the population. Even if the population details are sketchy, the expected value of $\bar{X}$ must always be equal to the population mean μ. The standard deviation of $\bar{X}$ may be derived using the values for n (sample size), N (population size), and σ (population standard deviation).

$$\sigma_{\bar{X}} = \frac{\sigma}{\sqrt{n}} \sqrt{\frac{N - n}{N - 1}}$$

The quantity $\sigma_{\bar{X}}$ is usually referred to as the *standard error of* $\bar{X}$. When the population size is large, the effect of N on the standard error may be ignored, and $\sigma_{\bar{X}}$ is equal to $\sigma/\sqrt{n}$.

RAISE YOUR GRADES

Can you explain...?

- ☑ what a long-run frequency is
- ☑ the difference between discrete and continuous random variables
- ☑ the difference between population mean and expected value
- ☑ why the expected value of $\bar{X}$ is equal to μ
- ☑ what distinguishes a sampling distribution from probability distributions in general
- ☑ why the standard error of $\bar{X}$ can be found even when you can't list all sample combinations giving rise to each possible level of $\bar{X}$

Do you know...?

- ☑ when to use the finite population correction factor
- ☑ why probability theory is a useful tool of statistical methodology
- ☑ what the standard error of a statistic measures

☑ the similarities between the population variance and the variance of the random variable associated with one sample observation

☑ why, when the same number of sample observations are taken from two populations having identical population standard deviations, the standard errors of $\bar{X}$ will be close in value—even when one population is considerably larger

RAPID REVIEW

1. The profit from a venture is equally likely to be −$10,000 or +$20,000. Find the expected profit. [Section 6-2A]

2. A random variable has the following probability distribution:

x	$\Pr[X = x]$
0	1/64
1	9/64
2	27/64
3	27/64

Compute **(a)** the expected value **(b)** the variance, and **(c)** the standard deviation. [Sections, 6-2A, C]

3. Determine the value for the standard error of $\bar{X}$ in each of the following situations.   [Section 6-3C]

(a)	**(b)**	**(c)**	**(d)**
$\sigma = 50$	$\sigma = 2.5$	$\sigma = 13$	$\sigma = 5$
$n = 100$	$n = 50$	$n = 169$	$n = 200$
$N = 500$	$N = 1,000$	$N = 500$	$N = 10,000$

4. An investor will buy one of the following stocks. The probability distributions for the respective rates of return are as follows:

(1) Stock A		(2) Stock B		(3) Stock C	
%	Prob.	%	Prob.	%	Prob.
8	.2	9	.6	7	.1
9	.4	10	.3	8	.1
10	.4	11	.1	9	.8

(a) Compute the expected rate of return for each stock.   [Section 6-2A]
(b) If she wishes to maximize the expected rate of return, which stock should the investor buy?

5. Following are the probability distributions for the rate of return on two investments. [Section 6-2B]

(1) Investment A		(2) Investment B	
%	Prob.	%	Prob.
−10	.1	−10	.3
0	.7	0	.3
10	.2	10	.4

Both random variables have expected values of 1%. A measure of risk is the variance in rate of return.

(a) Compute the variance in the rate of return for each random variable.
(b) Which investment is less risky?

6. Which one of the following statements is true   [Section 6-2C]?
    (a) The population standard deviation is the same value as the standard deviation of a future observed value for a randomly chosen unit.
    (b) The expected value of an observation is always equal to the population median.
    (c) The values of the variance and standard deviation of a random variable must always be different, since the latter is the square root of the former.
    (d) The sample standard deviation must be equal to the standard deviation of a random observation made of the parent population.

7. A sample of 4 persons is selected randomly from a very large population having a mean of 70 inches and a standard deviation of 3 inches. Ignoring the finite population correction factor, the standard error of the sample mean height is   [Section 6-3C]
    (a) 280 inches   (b) 1.5 inches   (c) 6 inches   (d) .75 inches

8. Samples of size $n = 100$ will be taken from four populations of size $N = 500$. Determine the standard error of $\bar{X}$ in each case, assuming the following population standard deviation.   [Section 6-3C]
    (a) $\sigma = \$12$ (b) $\sigma = 50''$ (c) $\sigma = .5\%$ (d) $\sigma = 5$ sec.

9. Successive samples of size n will be taken from a population of size $N = 1,000$ having a standard deviation of $\sigma = \$15$. Determine the standard error of $\bar{X}$ in each of the following cases.   [Section 6-3C]
    (a) $n = 25$ (b) $n = 50$ (c) $n = 100$ (d) $n = 200$

10. Samples of various sizes will be taken from populations of unlimited size. Determine the standard error of the sample mean for each of the following.   [Section 6-3D]

(a)	(b)	(c)	(d)
$\sigma = 5''$	$\sigma = 10$ lbs.	$\sigma = \$100$	$\sigma = 150\%$
$n = 100$	$n = 25$	$n = 64$	$n = 225$

Answers
1. $5,000
2. (a) 2.25 (b) .5625 (c) .75
3. (a) 4.48 (b) .345 (c) .814 (d) .35
4. (a) (1) 9.2 (2) 9.5 (3) 8.7
   (b) Stock *B*
5. (a) (1) 29 (2) 69
   (b) Investment *A*
6. (a)
7. (b)
8. (a) $1.07 (b) 4.48'' (c) .045% (d) .448 sec.
9. (a) $2.96 (b) $2.07 (c) $1.42 (d) $.95
10. (a) .5'' (b) 2 lbs. (c) $12.50 (d) 10%

SOLVED PROBLEMS

PROBLEM 6-1   A business student has assigned the following probabilities for final grades.

	A	B	C
Statistics	.2	.8	0
Finance	0	.4	.6
Accounting	.5	.5	0
Marketing	0	.2	.8

(a) List all possible elementary events for the student's grades. Assuming independence between courses, apply the multiplication law to determine the probability for each elementary event.

(b) Grade points are assigned as follows:

$$A = 4 \qquad B = 3 \qquad C = 2$$

Determine the student's total grade points for each elementary event identified in **(a)**. Then compute the grade point average (GPA) for each event. Finally, construct a table summarizing the probability distribution for GPA X.

Solution: **(a, b)** Arranging the possible combinations in order of increasing grade point totals, you obtain the following table. Find the probability for each elementary event by using the multiplication law for independent events. When several elementary events have the same point total, use the addition law to obtain the probability.

Total points	GPA x	Applicable grade combinations				$Pr[X = x]$
		Stat.	Fin.	Acctg.	Mktg.	
10	2.5	B	C	B	C	$.8 \times .6 \times .5 \times .8 = .1920$
11	2.75	A	C	B	C	$.2 \times .6 \times .5 \times .8 = .0480$
		B	B	B	C	$.8 \times .4 \times .5 \times .8 = .1280$
		B	C	B	B	$.8 \times .6 \times .5 \times .2 = .0480$
		B	C	A	C	$.8 \times .6 \times .5 \times .8 = .1920$
						$\overline{.4160}$
12	3	A	C	A	C	$.2 \times .6 \times .5 \times .8 = .0480$
		A	B	B	C	$.2 \times .4 \times .5 \times .8 = .0320$
		A	C	B	B	$.2 \times .6 \times .5 \times .2 = .0120$
		B	B	A	C	$.8 \times .4 \times .5 \times .8 = .1280$
		B	B	B	B	$.8 \times .4 \times .5 \times .2 = .0320$
		B	C	A	B	$.8 \times .6 \times .5 \times .2 = .0480$
						$\overline{.3000}$
13	3.25	B	B	A	B	$.8 \times .4 \times .5 \times .2 = .0320$
		A	B	A	C	$.2 \times .4 \times .5 \times .8 = .0320$
		A	B	B	B	$.2 \times .4 \times .5 \times .2 = .0080$
		A	C	A	B	$.2 \times .6 \times .5 \times .2 = .0120$
						$\overline{.0840}$
14	3.5	A	B	A	B	$.2 \times .4 \times .5 \times .2 = .0080$
						$\overline{1.0000}$

PROBLEM 6-2 The probability distribution for the number of telephone calls arriving at a particular switching device in any given millisecond is as follows:

x	$Pr[X = x]$
0	.37
1	.37
2	.18
3	.06
4	.02

Calculate the expected value, variance, and standard deviation of X.

Solution: Compute the expected value and variance as follows:

Number of calls x	Probability $Pr[X = x]$	Weighted value $x Pr[X = x]$	Deviation $[x - E(X)]$	Weighted squared deviation $[x - E(X)]^2 Pr[X = x]$
0	.37	0	−.99	.362637
1	.37	.37	.01	.000037
2	.18	.36	1.01	.183618
3	.06	.18	2.01	.242406
4	.02	.08	3.01	.181202
	$\overline{1.00}$	$E(X) = \overline{.99}$		$\sigma^2(X) = \overline{.969900}$

Find the standard deviation by taking the square root of the variance:

$$\sigma(X) = \sqrt{.969900} = .985$$

PROBLEM 6-3   The probability distribution for the number of unsatisfactory widgets in a random sample is as follows:

x	$\Pr[X = x]$
0	.35
1	.39
2	.19
3	.06
4	.01

Calculate the expected value, variance, and standard deviation of X.

Solution: Compute the expected value and variance as follows:

Number of unsatis. x	Probability $\Pr[X = x]$	Weighted value $x\Pr[X = x]$	Deviation $[x - E(X)]$	Weighted squared deviation $[x - E(X)]^2\Pr[X = x]$
0	.35	0	−.99	.343035
1	.39	.39	.01	.000039
2	.19	.38	1.01	.193819
3	.06	.18	2.01	.242406
4	.01	.04	3.01	.090601
	1.00	$E(X) = .99$		$\sigma^2(X) = .869900$

Find the standard deviation by taking the square root of the variance:

$$\sigma(X) = \sqrt{.869900} = .933$$

PROBLEM 6-4   Consider the probability distribution for arriving customers on page 104.

(a) Compute the expected value, variance, and standard deviation for this random variable.
(b) Comparing your answers to (a), what do you notice about the values for the summary measures obtained?

Solution:
(a) Compute the expected value and variance as follows:

Number of customers x	Probability $\Pr[X = x]$	Weighted value $x\Pr[X = x]$	Deviation $[x - E(X)]$	Weighted squared deviation $[x - E(X)]^2\Pr[X = x]$
0	.3679	0	−1.0000	.3679
1	.3679	.3679	0.0000	.0000
2	.1839	.3678	1.0000	.1839
3	.0613	.1839	2.0000	.2452
4	.0153	.0612	3.0000	.1377
5	.0031	.0155	4.0000	.0496
6	.0005	.0030	5.0000	.0125
7	.0001	.0007	6.0000	.0036
	1.0000	$E(X) = 1.0000$		$\sigma^2(X) = 1.0004$

Find the standard deviation by taking the square root of the variance:

$$\sigma(X) = \sqrt{1.0004} = 1.0002$$

(b) Except for rounding, all the summary measures are equal to 1. This particular distribution belongs to the Poisson family. For all random variables having a Poisson distribution, $E(X) = \sigma^2(X)$.

PROBLEM 6-5   Refer again to the probability distribution for arriving customers on page 104. Suppose that a congestion penalty of $2 arises for every customer over 3 who arrives within a five-minute period, while a congestion savings of $3 occurs whenever the number of arrivals falls below 2. Consider the net congestion payoff (reward − penalty) as a random variable. Construct a table of probabilities for this random variable.

Solution: Arrange each arrival possibility in terms of its net congestion payoff to get the following table. When more than one elementary event gives the same payoff, use the addition law to determine the probability.

Net payoff	Applicable numbers of customers	Probability	
$−8	7		.0001
−6	6		.0005
−4	5		.0031
−2	4		.0153
0	2, 3	.1839 + .0613 =	.2452
3	0, 1	.3679 + .3679 =	.7358
			1.0000

PROBLEM 6-6 Refer to the personal computer decision in Example 6-1. Suppose that the cost of the daisy printer is reduced to $700. Construct the new probability distribution table for total system cost.

Solution: The following outcomes are possible. Use the multiplication law to find the probability for each of these elementary events.

Computer and memory	Printer	Monitor	Cost	Probability
250K	Matrix	Monochrome	1,500 + 500 + 200 = 2,200	.3(.5)(.6) = .09
250K	Matrix	Color	1,500 + 500 + 400 = 2,400	.3(.5)(.4) = .06
250K	Daisy	Monochrome	1,500 + 700 + 200 = 2,400	.3(.5)(.6) = .09
250K	Daisy	Color	1,500 + 700 + 400 = 2,600	.3(.5)(.4) = .06
500K	Matrix	Monochrome	2,000 + 500 + 200 = 2,700	.7(.5)(.6) = .21
500K	Matrix	Color	2,000 + 500 + 400 = 2,900	.7(.5)(.4) = .14
500K	Daisy	Monochrome	2,000 + 700 + 200 = 2,900	.7(.5)(.6) = .21
500K	Daisy	Color	2,000 + 700 + 400 = 3,100	.7(.5)(.4) = .14

Now organize this information into a probability distribution table:

Cost		Probability
$2,200		.09
2,400	.06 + .09 =	.15
2,600		.06
2,700		.21
2,900	.14 + .21 =	.35
3,100		.14
		1.00

PROBLEM 6-7 Consider the *sum* of the dots on the showing sides when a pair of fair dice is rolled. [Refer to the solution to Problem 3-5 on page 53.] Compute for this random variable the expected value, variance, and standard deviation.

Solution: Compute the expected value and variance as follows:

Sum x	Probability Pr[X = x]	Weighted value xPr[X = x]	Deviation [x − E(X)]	Weighted squared deviation [x − E(X)]²Pr[X = x]
2	1/36	2/36	−5	25/36
3	2/36	6/36	−4	32/36
4	3/36	12/36	−3	27/36
5	4/36	20/36	−2	16/36
6	5/36	30/36	−1	5/36
7	6/36	42/36	0	0
8	5/36	40/36	+1	5/36
9	4/36	36/36	+2	16/36
10	3/36	30/36	+3	27/36
11	2/36	22/36	+4	32/36
12	1/36	12/36	+5	25/36
	1	E(X) = 252/36 = 7		σ²(X) = 210/36 = 5.833

Find the standard deviation by taking the square root of the variance:

$$\sigma(X) = \sqrt{5.833} = 2.42$$

PROBLEM 6-8 Consider once more the result from tossing a pair of fair dice. Construct the probability distribution table for the *range* (largest value minus smallest value) in the number of dots on the two showing sides.

Solution: It will help if you treat each elementary event in terms of a different color for each die. Grouping the events by the value for the range and listing the groups in order of increasing range value, you can construct the following table. Since all outcomes are equally likely, the count-and-divide method provides the probabilities.

Range	Applicable elementary events	Probability
0	1R-1G 2R-2G 3R-3G 4R-4G 5R-5G 6R-6G	6/36
1	2R-1G 1R-2G 3R-2G 2R-3G 4R-3G 3R-4G 5R-4G 4R-5G 6R-5G 5R-6G	10/36
2	3R-1G 1R-3G 4R-2G 2R-4G 5R-3G 3R-5G 6R-4G 4R-6G	8/36
3	4R-1G 1R-4G 5R-2G 2R-5G 6R-3G 3R-6G	6/36
4	5R-1G 1R-5G 6R-2G 2R-6G	4/36
5	6R-1G 1R-6G	2/36 ――― 1

PROBLEM 6-9 Refer once more to the personal computer decision in Example 6-1. Suppose that a third choice for a printer is allowed: the hybrid, at a cost of $1,200. The new probabilities are .3 (matrix), .5 (daisy), and .2 (hybrid). Suppose also that only the color monitor can be chosen. Construct the probability distribution table for the total system cost.

Solution: The following outcomes are possible. Use the multiplication law to find the probability for each of these elementary events.

Computer and memory	Printer	Monitor	Cost	Probability
250K	Matrix	Color	1,500 + 500 + 400 = 2,400	.3(.3) = .09
250K	Daisy	Color	1,500 + 1,000 + 400 = 2,900	.3(.5) = .15
250K	Hybrid	Color	1,500 + 1,200 + 400 = 3,100	.3(.2) = .06
500K	Matrix	Color	2,000 + 500 + 400 = 2,900	.7(.3) = .21
500K	Daisy	Color	2,000 + 1,000 + 400 = 3,400	.7(.5) = .35
500K	Hybrid	Color	2,000 + 1,200 + 400 = 3,600	.7(.2) = .14

Now organize this information into a probability distribution table:

Cost	Probability
$2,400	.09
2,900	.15 + .21 = .36
3,100	.06
3,400	.35
3,600	.14
	1.00

PROBLEM 6-10   Refer to the student grade point population on page 108. Construct a table of probabilities for the sampling distribution of the mean for *three* randomly chosen values.

Solution: A good way to figure out the elementary events is to determine the total points needed to get each possible mean. The lowest possible total for any combination is 7, which gives a mean of 2.33. One combination of names that gives a grade point total of 7 is (Ann, Bob, Eve) (3 + 2 + 2). Follow this procedure to figure out all the possible combinations. Next list these groups of possible sample outcomes in order of increasing mean value. Determine the probabilities by the count-and-divide method.

Possible mean $\bar{x}$	Applicable combinations	$\Pr[\bar{X} = \bar{x}]$
2.33	(Ann, Bob Eve) (Bob, Cal, Eve)	2/10
2.67	(Ann, Bob, Cal) (Ann, Cal, Eve) (Bob, Don, Eve)	3/10
3.00	(Ann, Bob, Don) (Ann, Don, Eve) (Bob, Cal, Don) (Cal, Don, Eve)	4/10
3.33	(Ann, Cal, Don)	1/10
		1

PROBLEM 6-11   The final examination scores for a population of six accounting students are as follows:

Student	Score	Student	Score
A.B.	70	K.L.	90
C.D.	80	O.P.	80
G.H.	60	S.T.	70

(a) Compute μ and σ for the population.
(b) For a sample of size 2, find $E(\bar{X})$ and $\sigma_{\bar{x}}$.

Solution:

(a)
$$\mu = \frac{70 + 80 + 60 + 90 + 80 + 70}{6} = 75$$

$$\sigma^2 = \frac{(70 - 75)^2 + (80 - 75)^2 + (60 - 75)^2 + (90 - 75)^2 + (80 - 75)^2 + (70 - 75)^2}{6}$$

$$= \frac{550}{6} = 91.67$$

Taking the square root of σ^2, you get

$$\sigma = \sqrt{91.67} = 9.6$$

(b)

$$E(\bar{X}) = \mu = 75$$

$$\sigma_{\bar{X}} = \frac{9.6}{\sqrt{2}} \sqrt{\frac{6-2}{6-1}} = 6.07$$

PROBLEM 6-12 Construct a table for the sampling distribution of $\bar{X}$ when $n = 2$ random observations are taken from the population in Problem 6-11.

Solution: Find the possible outcomes by determining which combinations of scores have the point totals needed to get each possible mean. The lowest point total is 130, for a mean of 65, and one combination that applies is (A.B., G.H.) (70 + 60). Listing these sample outcomes in order of increasing mean score, you obtain the following table. Determine the probabilities by the count-and-divide method.

$\bar{x}$	Possible combinations	$\Pr[\bar{X} = \bar{x}]$
65	(A.B., G.H.) (G.H., S.T.)	2/15
70	(A.B., S.T.) (C.D., G.H.) (G.H., O.P.)	3/15
75	(A.B., C.D.) (A.B., O.P.) (C.D., S.T.) (G.H., K.L.) (O.P., S.T.)	5/15
80	(A.B., K.L.) (C.D., O.P.) (K.L., S.T.)	3/15
85	(C.D., K.L.) (K.L., O.P.)	2/15
		1

PROBLEM 6-13 Construct a table for the sampling distribution of $\bar{X}$ when $n = 3$ random observations are taken from the population in Problem 6-11.

Solution: Find the possible outcomes by determining which combinations of scores have the point totals needed to get each possible mean. The lowest point total is 200, for a mean of 66.67, and the only combination that applies is (A.B., G.H., S.T.) (70 + 60 + 70). Listing these sample outcomes in order of increasing mean score, you obtain the following table. Determine the probabilities by the count-and-divide method.

$\bar{x}$	Possible combinations	$\Pr[\bar{X} = \bar{x}]$
66.67	(A.B., G.H., S.T.)	1/20
70.00	(A.B., C.D., G.H.) (A.B., G.H., O.P.) (C.D., G.H., S.T.) (G.H., O.P., S.T.)	4/20
73.33	(A.B., C.D., S.T.) (A.B., G.H., K.L.) (A.B., O.P, S.T.) (C.D., G.H., O.P.) (G.H., K.L., S.T.)	5/20
76.67	(A.B., C.D., O.P.) (A.B., K.L., S.T.) (C.D., G.H., K.L.) (C.D., O.P., S.T.) (G.H., K.L., O.P.)	5/20
80.00	(A.B., C.D., K.L.) (A.B., K.L., O.P.) (C.D., K.L., S.T.) (K.L., O.P., S.T.)	4/20
83.33	(C.D., K.L., O.P.)	1/20
		1

PROBLEM 6-14 Refer to the student grade point population on page 108. A random sample of $n = 2$ students is selected. Construct a table of sampling distributions for the following random variables:

    (a) the sample proportion of B's

    (b) the sample range (largest value minus smallest value)

Solution:

(a) Again follow the procedure for determining possible combinations, only here you will want to find those combinations that have the three possible proportions of B's: 0 (no student has a B), .5 (one of the two students has a B), and 1 (both students have a B). Listing these sample outcomes in order of increasing proportion, you get the following table. Determine the probabilities by the count-and-divide method.

Proportion	Applicable combinations	Probability
0	(Bob, Don) (Bob, Eve) (Don, Eve)	3/10
.5	(Ann, Bob) (Ann, Don) (Ann, Eve) (Bob, Cal) (Cal, Don) (Cal, Eve)	6/10
1.0	(Ann, Cal)	1/10
		1

(**b**) Follow the same procedure as in (**a**), except here you will group your sample outcomes according to whether the difference between their grade points is 0, 1, or 2.

Range	Applicable combinations	Probability
0	(Ann, Cal) (Bob, Eve)	2/10
1	(Ann, Bob) (Ann, Don) (Ann, Eve) (Bob, Cal) (Cal, Don) (Cal, Eve)	6/10
2	(Bob, Don) (Don, Eve)	2/10
		1

7 BINOMIAL PROBABILITIES
The Sampling Distribution of the Proportion

THIS CHAPTER IS ABOUT

- ☑ **The Binomial Distribution**
- ☑ **Important Properties of the Binomial Distribution**
- ☑ **Sampling Distribution of the Proportion**

You have seen that an uncertain quantity whose value is determined by chance is a random variable having a particular probability distribution. Sample observations taken of *quantitative* populations are important random variables. Especially useful in setting the groundwork for statistical evaluations is the sampling distribution of the sample mean. This chapter extends this foundation by focusing on random variables that are important in evaluating samples from *qualitative* populations.

Chapter 2 introduced a useful summary measure for data from qualitative populations—the *proportion* of observations falling into a particular category. In this chapter you will learn about the sampling distribution of the *sample proportion*.

Before explicitly considering the proportion, it is helpful to investigate a related random variable, the *number* of attributes of a particular kind. To set the stage, we will establish the *binomial distribution*, which applies to a wide class of situations that can be broken down into a series of *trials*.

7-1. The Binomial Distribution

Many important statistical applications involve considerations of two complementary attributes, such as satisfactory vs. defective, failure vs. success, or erroneous vs. correct. Because there are *two* types of outcomes to be accounted for, the adjective *binomial* ("two quantities") is a useful term. The number of attributes of a particular kind is a random variable often having a **binomial distribution**.

A. The binomial distribution applies to a Bernoulli process.

A binomial distribution provides the probabilities for the number of successes in a series of trials, each of which has only two possible outcomes. A situation where the binomial distribution applies is called a **Bernoulli process** (named after a pioneer mathematician). A Bernoulli process, which is epitomized by a coin toss, has three characteristics:

1. There are *two complementary outcomes* possible for each *trial* in the sequence. These are conveniently designated as **success** and **failure**. It doesn't matter which of the two outcomes gets labeled the success. (With coin experiments, each toss is a separate trial, and head is ordinarily treated as a success.)
2. The *trial success probability remains constant* throughout the process. (This requires that Pr[head] is always the same value, such as 1/2 or 2/3.)
3. *Successive trial outcomes are statistically independent.* (A head is therefore just as likely to follow an earlier head as a tail is.)

B. The binomial formula is used to compute probabilities.

Figure 7-1 shows the probability tree diagram for a particular Bernoulli process, the sequence of 5 tosses of a fair coin. Each successive toss or trial is represented as a different

Figure 7-1

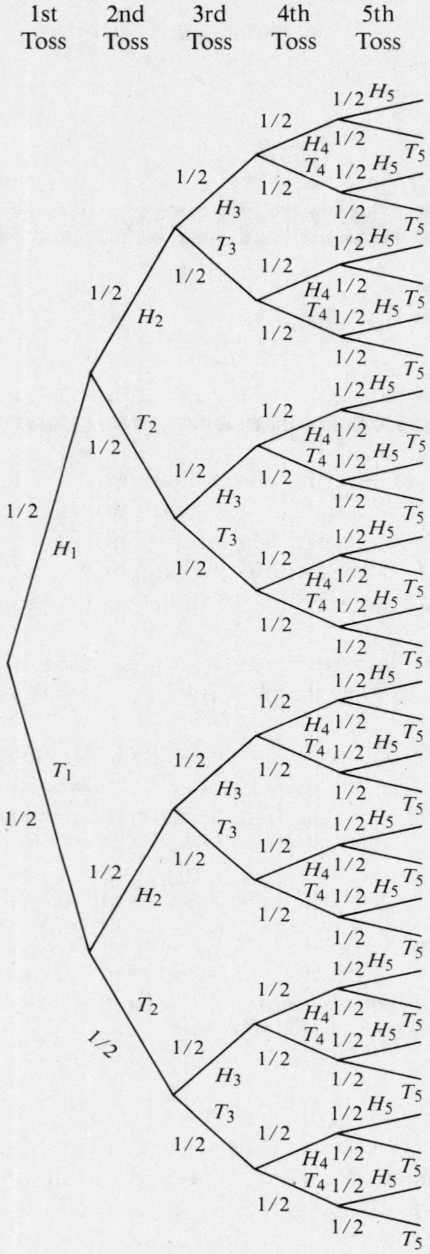

1st Toss	2nd Toss	3rd Toss	4th Toss	5th Toss	Sample Space	Probability	No. of heads	0	1	2	3	4	5
					$H_1\ H_2\ H_3\ H_4\ H_5$	1/32	5						*
					$H_1\ H_2\ H_3\ H_4\ T_5$	1/32	4					*	
					$H_1\ H_2\ H_3\ T_4\ H_5$	1/32	4					*	
					$H_1\ H_2\ H_3\ T_4\ T_5$	1/32	3				*		
					$H_1\ H_2\ T_3\ H_4\ H_5$	1/32	4					*	
					$H_1\ H_2\ T_3\ H_4\ T_5$	1/32	3				*		
					$H_1\ H_2\ T_3\ T_4\ H_5$	1/32	3				*		
					$H_1\ H_2\ T_3\ T_4\ T_5$	1/32	2			*			
					$H_1\ T_2\ H_3\ H_4\ H_5$	1/32	4					*	
					$H_1\ T_2\ H_3\ H_4\ T_5$	1/32	3				*		
					$H_1\ T_2\ H_3\ T_4\ H_5$	1/32	3				*		
					$H_1\ T_2\ H_3\ T_3\ T_5$	1/32	2			*			
					$H_1\ T_2\ T_3\ H_4\ H_5$	1/32	3				*		
					$H_1\ T_2\ T_3\ H_4\ T_5$	1/32	2			*			
					$H_1\ T_2\ T_3\ T_4\ H_5$	1/32	2			*			
					$H_1\ T_2\ T_3\ T_4\ T_5$	1/32	1		*				
					$T_1\ H_2\ H_3\ H_4\ H_5$	1/32	4					*	
					$T_1\ H_2\ H_3\ H_4\ T_5$	1/32	3				*		
					$T_1\ H_2\ H_3\ T_4\ H_5$	1/32	3				*		
					$T_1\ H_2\ H_3\ T_4\ T_5$	1/32	2			*			
					$T_1\ H_2\ T_3\ H_4\ H_5$	1/32	3				*		
					$T_1\ H_2\ T_3\ H_4\ T_5$	1/32	2			*			
					$T_1\ H_2\ T_3\ T_4\ H_5$	1/32	2			*			
					$T_1\ H_2\ T_3\ T_4\ T_5$	1/32	1		*				
					$T_1\ T_2\ H_3\ H_4\ H_5$	1/32	3				*		
					$T_1\ T_2\ H_3\ H_4\ T_5$	1/32	2			*			
					$T_1\ T_2\ H_3\ T_4\ H_5$	1/32	2			*			
					$T_1\ T_2\ H_3\ T_4\ T_5$	1/32	1		*				
					$T_1\ T_2\ T_3\ H_4\ H_5$	1/32	2			*			
					$T_1\ T_2\ T_3\ H_4\ T_5$	1/32	1		*				
					$T_1\ T_2\ T_3\ T_4\ H_5$	1/32	1		*				
					$T_1\ T_2\ T_3\ T_4\ T_5$	1/32	0	*					

Totals 32/32   1 5 10 10 5 1

stage, and a separate branching point is provided for every possible result from the earlier tosses.

Because Bernoulli processes are encountered so often under so many varied circumstances, there exists a special algebraic expression, called the **binomial formula**, for computing the probability that a specific number of successes will occur.

Binomial formula

$$\Pr[R = r] = \frac{n!}{r!(n - r)!}\,\pi^r(1 - \pi)^{n - r}$$

In this formula,

n = number of trials

R = number of successes obtained (the random variable)

$$r = \text{any one of the possible levels for } R$$
$$\pi = \text{Pr[success] for a single trial}$$

- π is the lowercase Greek *pi*. It is used just like a *p*. Here you may think of it as the first letter in the word *proportion*. (Since the coin whose trial outcomes are shown in Figure 7-1 is fair, the long-run proportion of heads is $\pi = 1/2$.)

Applying the binomial formula to the series of $n = 5$ coin tosses and using $\pi = \text{Pr[head]} = 1/2$, you can compute the probability for obtaining exactly $R = 2$ heads in the series:

$$\text{Pr}[R = 2] = \frac{5!}{2!(5-2)!}\left(\frac{1}{2}\right)^2\left(1 - \frac{1}{2}\right)^{5-2}$$

$$= \frac{5!}{2!3!}\left(\frac{1}{2}\right)^2\left(\frac{1}{2}\right)^3$$

$$= 10\left(\frac{1}{2}\right)^5 = \frac{10}{32} = .3125$$

C. Binomial probabilities can be explained using a tree diagram.

The tree in Figure 7-1 will help you understand why the binomial formula works. The first term of the formula, which involves factorials, is the number of combinations of 2 items from 5, $C_r^n = C_2^5 = 10$. This is the number of ways to designate which sequences will have 2 H's (*r* successes) in 5 tosses (*n* trials), the rest being T's (failures). You can verify that 10 paths in the tree involve exactly 2 heads.

Each path in the tree corresponds to an elementary event for the complete experiment. Remember that $\text{Pr[head]} = \pi = 1/2$ and $\text{Pr[tail]} = 1 - \pi = 1/2$, and that 2 heads and 3 tails make up each of the 2-head (*r*-success) elementary events. Therefore, by the multiplication law, each 2-head event has probability

$$\pi^r(1 - \pi)^{n-r} = \left(\frac{1}{2}\right)^2\left(\frac{1}{2}\right)^3 = \left(\frac{1}{2}\right)^5 = \frac{1}{32} = .03125$$

By the addition law, you can find the probability for exactly 2 heads (*r* successes) by adding together the probabilities for each of the 10 relevant elementary events. Or, since all the outcomes have the same probability, you can find the final probability by multiplying by $C_2^5 = 10$ (C_r^n), the number of elementary events. Thus,

$$10(.03125) = .3125$$

You can see that this is the same probability arrived at by using the binomial formula.

The following table shows the complete probability distribution for the number of heads R obtained in 5 tosses of a fair coin.

Possible number of heads r	$\text{Pr}[R = r]$
0	$\dfrac{5!}{0!5!}(1/2)^0(1/2)^5 = \ 1/32 = \ .03125$
1	$\dfrac{5!}{1!4!}(1/2)^1(1/2)^4 = \ 5/32 = \ .15625$
2	$\dfrac{5!}{2!3!}(1/2)^2(1/2)^3 = 10/32 = \ .31250$
3	$\dfrac{5!}{3!2!}(1/2)^3(1/2)^2 = 10/32 = \ .31250$
4	$\dfrac{5!}{4!1!}(1/2)^4(1/2)^1 = \ 5/32 = \ .15625$
5	$\dfrac{5!}{5!0!}(1/2)^5(1/2)^0 = \ 1/32 = \ .03125$
	$\overline{1.00000}$

- Some books use different symbols for the binomial formula. You may see the following:

$$\Pr[R = r] = \frac{n!}{r!(n - r)!} \, p^r(1 - p)^{n - r} = \frac{n!}{r!(n - r)!} \, p^r q^{n - r}$$

This is the same as our formula except that p appears in place of π, $1 - p$ or q is used instead of $1 - \pi$.

EXAMPLE 7-1: BRAND PREFERENCES—SKINNY SIP VS. TUMMY TRIM

A TipsiCola Bottling Company marketing researcher wishes to determine whether to recommend introduction of Skinny Sip, a new diet soda that will compete with HokeyCola's Tummy Trim. Her final action depends on how high a proportion of the millions of potential customers will prefer Skinny Sip over the other brand.

Some information is provided by the number of sample test subjects R who have been found to prefer Skinny Sip. The researcher is satisfied that the binomial distribution closely approximates the true probabilities for R. The probability that a randomly selected person will prefer the brand equals the true population proportion π. Although that quantity is unknown, the following value might apply:

$$\pi = \Pr[\text{a subject prefers Skinny Sip}] = .4$$

The researcher administered a taste test to $n = 20$ subjects. Although the numbers are large, the binomial formula can be used to establish the probability that 12 of those subjects prefer Skinny Dip:

$$\Pr[R = 12] = \frac{20!}{12!8!} \, (.4)^{12}(1 - .4)^8 = .0355$$

Of course the true value of π remains unknown. The actual sample resulted in 8 subjects preferring Skinny Sip. Consider how different levels of π affect the probability for getting that many or fewer positive responses. Using a probability table published by a statistician who originally applied the binomial formula with computer assistance, the researcher found the following:

Assumed value:	$\pi = .20$	$\pi = .30$	$\pi = .40$	$\pi = .50$	$\pi = .60$	$\pi = .70$
$\Pr[R \leqslant 8]$:	.9900	.8867	.5956	.2517	.0565	.0051

For $\pi = .50$ or higher, the probability is small that 8 or fewer positive responses would have been achieved. The researcher's sample evidence is consistent with a low level for π. Therefore, she doesn't recommend introducing Skinny Sip.

7-2. Important Properties of the Binomial Distribution

You should be aware of several important properties of the binomial distribution.

A. Binomial distributions apply to a family of random variables.

Two parameters, n and π, determine which specific binomial distribution applies. It is convenient to view all possible distributions as a *family*, members of which are distinguished by the levels for n and π. An infinite number of members exist. Consider varying one parameter while the other is held fixed.

1. **The role played by the trial success probability π:** Figure 7-2 shows the probability distributions for several levels of π when the number of trials is held fixed at $n = 5$. Notice that there is a skewed spike pattern except when $\pi = .5$. That symmetrical case applies to the series of coin tosses considered earlier. Notice also that complementary trial success probabilities, $\pi = .1$ and $\pi = .9$ or $\pi = .3$ and $\pi = .7$, have distributions that are mirror images.

2. **The effect of the number of trials n:** Figure 7-3 shows the binomial distributions for three levels of n when the trial success probability is fixed at $\pi = .2$. Notice how the spikes

Figure 7-2

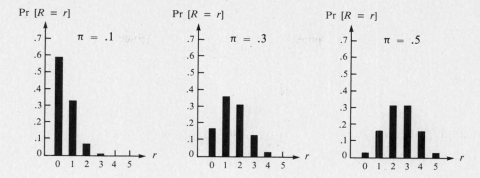

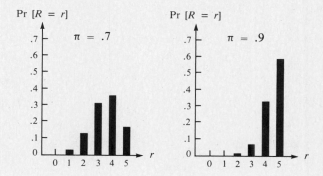

Figure 7-3

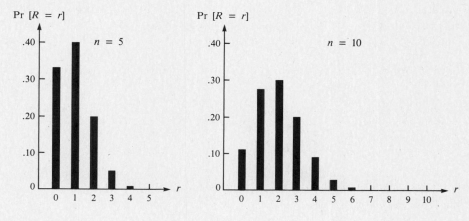

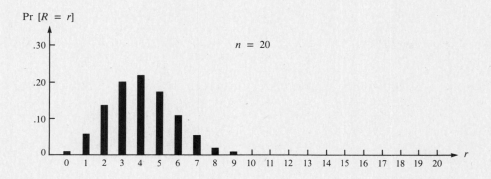

grow more numerous and become shorter as n increases. Notice also that the spike clusters take on progressively symmetrical patterns, becoming almost bell-shaped as n gets larger. This is an important feature that you'll learn more about in Chapter 8.

B. It is easy to compute the expected value and variance of a binomial random variable.

It's not necessary for you to use individual probabilities and take weighted averages to compute $E(R)$ or $\sigma^2(R)$. It has been mathematically established that the following apply:

$$E(R) = n\pi \qquad \text{and} \qquad \sigma^2(R) = n\pi(1 - \pi)$$

Returning to the coin-tossing illustration when $n = 5$ and $\pi = 1/2$, you have

$$E(R) = 5\left(\frac{1}{2}\right) = 2.5$$

so that you expect 2.5 heads whenever tossing a fair coin 5 times. That is, if you perform 5 tosses, repeating the experiment many times, you should come close to getting 2.5 heads for every 5 tosses.

Likewise, it is a fact that

$$\sigma^2(R) = 5\left(\frac{1}{2}\right)\left(1 - \frac{1}{2}\right) = 1.25$$

By taking the square root of this answer, you find that the standard deviation for the number of heads is

$$\sigma(R) = \sqrt{1.25} = 1.12$$

C. Composite binomial probabilities are useful.

When several levels of a random variable are lumped together, a **composite probability** results. There are three primary types of composite probabilities.

1. **Cumulative probability:** Often encountered is the **cumulative probability**, which represents events of the form $R \leqslant r$. You find this probability by adding together all individual probabilities for levels of the random variable at or below a stipulated value.

Consider once more 5 tosses of a fair coin. You can compute the cumulative probability for 3 heads or less by using the addition law with the individual probabilities found earlier:

$$\Pr[R \leqslant 3] = \Pr[R = 0] + \Pr[R = 1] + \Pr[R = 2] + \Pr[R = 3]$$
$$= .03125 + .15625 + .31250 + .31250$$
$$= .81250$$

It would be a great deal of work always to compute cumulative probabilities in this way. To ease this task, tables are available that provide cumulative binomial probabilities for many combinations of n and π.

The main advantage of cumulative probabilities is that they are more practical than individual probabilities. Investigators are usually interested in the probability that a random variable falls within some *range*, rather than exactly at a specific level.

2. **Interval probability:** A composite probability measuring the likelihood that a random variable falls within some range is an **interval probability**. You can obtain such a value by adding together the applicable individual probabilities. For example, you can find the probability for getting between 2 and 4 heads, inclusively:

$$\Pr[2 \leqslant R \leqslant 4] = \Pr[R = 2] + \Pr[R = 3] + \Pr[R = 4]$$
$$= .31250 + .31250 + .15625$$
$$= .78125$$

You can find an interval probability quickly by subtracting two cumulative probabilities, as shown in Example 7-2.

EXAMPLE 7-2: YELLOW GIANT'S OVERWEIGHT CANS

An inspector for Yellow Giant Corn will remove a random sample of 100 cans. He is interested in the number R of overweight cans found. The inspector assumes that 5% are overweight, so that $\pi = .05$ is the probability any particular can is overweight. He looks up the following cumulative probabilities from a table in the back of one of his statistics books:

r	$\Pr[R \leqslant r]$
0	.0059
1	.0371
2	.1183
3	.2578
4	.4360
5	.6160
6	.7660
7	.8720
8	.9369
9	.9718
10	.9885
11	.9957
12	.9985
⋮	⋮

From this he can find the probability that he will obtain between 5 and 10 overweight cans, inclusively.

$$\Pr[5 \leqslant R \leqslant 10] = \Pr[R \leqslant 10] - \Pr[R \leqslant 4]$$
$$= .9885 - .4360$$
$$= .5525$$

(He subtracts the cumulative probability for $R \leqslant 4$ since the desired event excludes anything below 5.)

3. **Upper-tail probabilities:** A final composite probability is the **upper-tail probability**, which represents events of the form $R \geqslant r$. The upper-tail probability is equal to the sum of the individual probabilities for levels of the random variable at or above the desired value. For example, consider the probability for at least 4 heads in 5 tosses of a fair coin:

$$\Pr[R \geqslant 4] = \Pr[R = 4] + \Pr[R = 5]$$
$$= .15625 + .03125$$
$$= .18750$$

Referring to Figure 7-2 where $\pi = .5$, you can see how such a probability gets its name. It represents the sum of the heights of those spikes located in the upper "tail" of the probability mass function.

You can find upper-tail probabilities by subtracting the complementary (opposite) cumulative probability from 1. Thus, the inspector in Example 7-2 found the probability that 9 or more cans would be overweight by subtracting the probability for 8 or less cans from 1:

$$\Pr[R \geqslant 9] = 1 - \Pr[R \leqslant 8]$$
$$= 1 - .9369$$
$$= .0631$$

Tables also exist that provide upper-tail binomial probabilities.

EXAMPLE 7-3: VBM'S LATE DELIVERIES

A marketing manager at VBM (Very Big Machines) wants to determine probabilities for the number of late deliveries to be experienced in the next 100 shipments of computer mainframes. Historically, 7% of all deliveries have been late. If that percentage still applies, then the manager can use the binomial distribution with $n = 100$ and $\pi = .07$.

The manager's statistics book provides tables for upper-tail probabilities only. Its entries for $n = 100$ and $\pi = .07$ are as follows:

r	$\Pr[R \geqslant r]$
0	1.0000
1	.9993
2	.9940
3	.9742
4	.9256
5	.8368
6	.7086
7	.5557
8	.4012
9	.2660
10	.1620
11	.0908
12	.0469
⋮	⋮

From this, the manager is able to determine the probability that between 5 and 10 late deliveries, inclusively, will be made:

$$\Pr[5 \leqslant R \leqslant 10] = Pr[R \geqslant 5] - Pr[R \geqslant 11]$$
$$= .8368 - .0908$$
$$= .7460$$

(He subtracts the upper-tail probability for $R \geqslant 11$ since the desired event excludes anything above 10.)

7-3. Sampling Distribution of the Proportion

So far you have considered the *number* of successes in n trials. As noted, statisticians are often interested instead in the *proportion* of successes. In sampling evaluations, the *sample proportion* P is widely used, partly because it makes comparisons of samples of different sizes easier. Under special conditions, you can use the binomial distribution as the sampling distribution of P.

A. The binomial distribution applies to the proportion of successes.

You can find the proportion of successes by dividing the number of successes by the number of trials:

$$P = \frac{R}{n}$$

You can find the probability that P assumes any level by using the probability for the corresponding value for R. Consider the following table, which partially lists the binomial probability distribution for the number of defectives and the proportion of defectives found in a batch of 100 items arriving from a production line yielding 10% defective, so that $\pi = .10$.

Number of defectives r	Proportion defective r/n	Probability $\Pr[R = r] = \Pr[P = r/n]$
0	0	.0000
1	.01	.0003
2	.02	.0016
3	.03	.0059
4	.04	.0159
5	.05	.0339
6	.06	.0596
7	.07	.0889
8	.08	.1148
9	.09	.1304
10	.10	.1319
⋮	⋮	⋮

B. Sampling situations aren't usually Bernoulli processes.

The major obstacle to using the binomial distribution is that in sampling, the assumption of independence between trial outcomes is usually violated. Consider a random sample taken from a population of fixed size *N*. Unless sampling is done *with replacement* (rarely the case), the proportion of the remaining population having a particular attribute will change as each successive unit is removed and observed. This makes every observation or trial outcome statistically dependent on the earlier findings. The Bernoulli process doesn't strictly apply, and the binomial formula doesn't provide the proper probability values.

C. The binomial distribution might serve as an approximation.

A probability distribution called the *hypergeometric*, which is related to the binomial, can provide exact probabilities when sampling *without replacement*. That distribution is very cumbersome to use, however. As long as the population size *N* is large in relation to the sample size *n*, the binomial distribution is a good approximation, since its values are very close to the hypergeometric.

D. The expected value and standard error of *P* may be computed.

Under either the binomial or the hypergeometric distribution, the expected value of *P* is π.

$$E(P) = \pi$$

Here π denotes the population proportion, which is a given value.

The variance of *P* differs somewhat. Recall that the square root of the variance equals the standard deviation, which is called the standard error when applied to a sample statistic. The following expression provides the standard error of *P* when the population size is small.

Standard error of *P* (small population size)

$$\sigma_P = \sqrt{\frac{\pi(1-\pi)}{n}} \sqrt{\frac{N-n}{N-1}}$$

You may recognize the second term as the *finite population correction factor* encountered in Chapter 6. Remember that this quantity can be ignored when *N* is large in relation to *n*. In those cases, we use the following expression.

Standard error of *P* (large population size)

$$\sigma_P = \sqrt{\frac{\pi(1-\pi)}{n}}$$

The levels of $E(P)$ and σ_P are useful in statistical procedures.

SUMMARY

The *binomial distribution* provides probabilities for the number of "successes" *R* in a series of repeated random experiments or trials with only two possible outcomes. These experiments where the binomial distribution applies are referred to as *Bernoulli processes*, and one example is a series of coin tosses. The requirements of a Bernoulli process are (1) there are just two complementary trial outcomes; (2) the probability of success must remain constant from trial to trial; and (3) successive trial outcomes must be statistically independent events.

Binomial probabilities are computed using an algebraic expression called the *binomial formula*. It is easy to see from a probability tree why the formula works. However, it is so computationally cumbersome that in actual practice, tables of binomial probabilities are used instead. These are usually provided for composite groupings of events, which can be of three types: *cumulative probabilities* (of the form $R \leqslant r$); *interval probabilities* ($r_1 \leqslant R \leqslant r_2$); and *upper-tail probabilities* ($R \geqslant r$).

There are two parameters that determine which particular member of the binomial distribution family applies. These are the trial success probability π and the number of trials *n*. Binomial distributions become progressively more skewed as π falls further above or below .5, the only level for that parameter for which the binomial distributions are symmetrical. As *n* gets larger, the graph of the mass functions has more numerous spikes, that tend progressively toward a bell-shaped pattern. The expected value and variance of *R*, the number of successes, may be computed directly from expressions involving *n* and π:

$$E(R) = n\pi \quad \text{and} \quad \sigma^2(R) = n\pi(1-\pi)$$

Perhaps the greatest importance of the binomial distribution is that it ordinarily represents the *sampling distribution of the sample proportion P*. That statistic is useful for investigations involving samples from qualitative populations. The binomial distribution usually only serves as an *approximation*, however, since random sampling typically violates the Bernoulli process assumptions of independence and constant trial success probability. That approximation is a good one if the population size N is large in relation to the sample size n.

The proportion of successes is the number of successes divided by the number of trials, $P = R/n$. The probability for any value r/n of P is equal to the probability for the same value of R. The expected value of P is π, and the standard error of P is computed by

$$\sigma_P = \sqrt{\frac{\pi(1 - \pi)}{n}}$$

The finite population factor is used when N is small.

RAISE YOUR GRADES

Can you explain...?

☑ the difference between a trial and a success
☑ the three assumptions required for a Bernoulli process
☑ why the binomial formula works
☑ why the same probabilities can be used for both R and P
☑ the difference between a cumulative probability and an upper-tail probability

Do you know...?

☑ that π is ordinarily an assumed value
☑ how to compute probabilities using the binomial formula
☑ under what circumstances the binomial distribution applies
☑ the role of the finite population correction factor in computing the standard error of P
☑ why a sample observation is analogous to a trial in a Bernoulli process

RAPID REVIEW

1. A fair coin is tossed 3 times. Determine the probability for each of the following numbers of heads.   [Section 7-1B]

   (a) 0   (b) 1   (c) 2   (d) 3

2. Which one of the following situations is a Bernoulli process?   [Section 7-1A]

   (a) A series of rolls of a perfect die cube, with success being an odd number of dots on the showing face.
   (b) Items are removed one at a time from a batch of fixed size and classified as defective or satisfactory.
   (c) Each finished item leaving production is classified as correct or incorrect in size, acceptable or unacceptable in weight, wide or narrow, and aligned or off-center.
   (d) Sample jars are removed from a production line and weighed. Each jar is classified as satisfactory or overweight. Whenever an overweight jar is found, all settings are readjusted.

3. A series of $n = 3$ Bernoulli trials is to be conducted. Compute the probability of exactly 2 successes for each of the following levels for the trial success probability.   [Section 7-1B]

   (a) $\pi = .05$ (b) $\pi = .10$ (c) $\pi = .20$ (d) $\pi = .40$

4. A series of n Bernoulli trials is to be conducted. Assuming that the trial success probability is $\pi = .10$, compute the probability of exactly 2 successes for each of the following numbers of trials. [Section 7-1B]

    (a) $n = 3$ (b) $n = 4$ (c) $n = 5$ (d) $n = 6$

5. A fair coin is tossed 3 times. Determine the cumulative probability that the number of heads is less than or equal to each of the following values. [Section 7-2C]

    (a) 0   (b) 1   (c) 2   (d) 3

6. The following cumulative probabilities apply for the number of heads R in 20 tosses of a fair coin.

r	$\Pr[R \leqslant r]$
8	.2517
9	.4119
10	.5881
11	.7483
12	.8684
13	.9423

Determine the following interval probabilities. [Section 7-2C]

    (a) $\Pr[9 \leqslant R \leqslant 13]$ (c) $\Pr[10 \leqslant R \leqslant 12]$
    (b) $\Pr[9 \leqslant R \leqslant 12]$ (d) $\Pr[9 \leqslant R \leqslant 11]$

7. The following upper-tail probabilities apply for the number of defectives R in a sample of $n = 100$ items removed from a production process where 10% of the total output is defective.

r	$\Pr[R \geqslant r]$
5	.9763
6	.9424
7	.8828
8	.7939
9	.6791
10	.5487

Determine the following interval probabilities. [Section 7-2C]

    (a) $\Pr[5 \leqslant R \leqslant 9]$ (c) $\Pr[5 \leqslant R \leqslant 7]$
    (b) $\Pr[6 \leqslant R \leqslant 8]$ (d) $\Pr[7 \leqslant R \leqslant 9]$

8. Determine for each of the following sample sizes n the standard error of the sample proportion defective P when the sample is removed randomly from a population of size $N = 500$ for which the proportion defective is $\pi = .01$. [Section 7-3D]

    (a) $n = 10$ (b) $n = 25$ (c) $n = 50$ (d) $n = 100$

9. Determine for each of the following population proportions π the standard error of the sample proportion defective P when a sample of size $n = 100$ is removed randomly from a population of size $N = 1,000$. [Section 7-3D]

    (a) $\pi = .01$ (b) $\pi = .05$ (c) $\pi = .10$ (d) $\pi = .20$

10. Determine for each of the following population sizes the standard error of the sample proportion defective P when a sample of size $n = 100$ is removed randomly from the population having proportion defective $\pi = .10$. [Section 7-3D]

    (a) $N = 500$ (b) $N = 1,000$ (c) $N = 2,000$ (d) $N = 5,000$

Answers
1. (a) $1/8 = .125$ (b) $3/8 = .375$ (c) $3/8 = .375$ (d) $1/8 = .125$
2. (a)
3. (a) .007125   (b) .027   (c) .096   (d) .288

4. (a) .027 (b) .0486 (c) .0729 (d) .098415
5. (a) .125 (b) .500 (c) .875 (d) 1.000
6. (a) .6906 (b) .6167 (c) .4565 (d) .4966
7. (a) .4276 (b) .2633 (c) .1824 (d) .3341
8. (a) .031 (b) .019 (c) .013 (d) .009
9. (a) .009 (b) .021 (c) .028 (d) .038
10. (a) .027 (b) .028 (c) .029 (d) .030

SOLVED PROBLEMS

PROBLEM 7-1 The proportion of consumers favoring a new product is $\pi = .70$. A random sample of $n = 5$ persons is selected. Use the binomial formula to determine the approximate probability that

  (a) exactly 5 favor it
  (b) none favor it
  (c) exactly 3 favor it

Solution: In each of the following, apply the binomial formula.

(a)
$$\Pr[R = 5] = \frac{5!}{5!0!}(.70)^5(1 - .70)^0 = 1(.70)^5(.30)^0 = (.70)^5 = .16807$$

(b)
$$\Pr[R = 0] = \frac{5!}{0!5!}(.70)^0(1 - .70)^5 = 1(.70)^0(.30)^5 = (.30)^5 = .00243$$

(c)
$$\Pr[R = 3] = \frac{5!}{3!2!}(.70)^3(1 - .70)^2 = 10(.70)^3(.30)^2 = .3087$$

PROBLEM 7-2 Twenty percent of the cars leaving an automobile assembly line have defective brakes. A random sample of $n = 4$ cars is chosen. Find the probability that the number of defective brake systems found is

  (a) 1 (b) 2 (c) 0

Solution: In each of the following, apply the binomial formula using $\pi = .20$.

(a)
$$\Pr[R = 1] = \frac{4!}{1!3!}(.20)^1(1 - .20)^3 = 4(.20)^1(.80)^3 = .4096$$

(b)
$$\Pr[R = 2] = \frac{4!}{2!2!}(.20)^2(1 - .20)^2 = 6(.20)^2(.80)^2 = .1536$$

(c)
$$\Pr[R = 0] = \frac{4!}{0!4!}(.20)^0(1 - .20)^4 = 1(.20)^0(.80)^4 = .4096$$

PROBLEM 7-3 The following binomial probabilities apply for the number of successes in $n = 10$ Bernoulli trials when the probability for success is $\pi = .49$.

r	$\Pr[R = r]$
0	.0012
1	.0114
2	.0495
3	.1267
4	.2130
5	.2456
6	.1966
7	.1080
8	.0389
9	.0083
10	.0008
	1.0000

Determine the table of cumulative probabilities.

Solution: You find the cumulative probabilities by adding each successive individual probability to the preceding cumulative probability.

r	$\Pr[R = r]$	$\Pr[R \leqslant r]$
0	.0012	.0012
1	.0114	.0012 + .0114 = .0126
2	.0495	.0126 + .0495 = .0621
3	.1267	.0621 + .1267 = .1888
4	.2130	.1888 + .2130 = .4018
5	.2456	.4018 + .2456 = .6474
6	.1966	.6474 + .1966 = .8440
7	.1080	.8440 + .1080 = .9520
8	.0389	.9520 + .0389 = .9909
9	.0083	.9909 + .0083 = .9992
10	.0008	.9992 + .0008 = 1.0000
	1.0000	

PROBLEM 7-4 Using the probability distribution given in Problem 7-3, determine the table of upper-tail probabilities.

Solution: You find the upper-tail probabilities by subtracting the preceding individual probability from the preceding upper-tail probability. The event $R \geqslant 0$ is certain, so that the first upper-tail probability is 1.0000.

r	$\Pr[R = r]$	$\Pr[R \geqslant r]$
0	.0012	1.0000
1	.0114	1.0000 − .0012 = .9988
2	.0495	.9988 − .0114 = .9874
3	.1267	.9874 − .0495 = .9379
4	.2130	.9379 − .1267 = .8112
5	.2456	.8112 − .2130 = .5982
6	.1966	.5982 − .2456 = .3526
7	.1080	.3526 − .1966 = .1560
8	.0389	.1560 − .1080 = .0480
9	.0083	.0480 − .0389 = .0091
10	.0008	.0091 − .0083 = .0008
	1.0000	

PROBLEM 7-5 Refer to the cumulative probabilities given in Example 7-2 for the number of overweight cans found in a sample of 100 taken from production when 5% of all cans are underweight ($\pi = .05$). Compute the probabilities for the following outcomes.

(a) $\Pr[4 \leqslant R \leqslant 10]$ (c) $\Pr[2 \leqslant R \leqslant 11]$
(b) $\Pr[7 \leqslant R \leqslant 9]$ (d) $\Pr[9 \leqslant R \leqslant 11]$

Solution: In each case you subtract the cumulative probability for the unwanted lower range from the cumulative probability for the upper limit.

(a) $\Pr[4 \leqslant R \leqslant 10] = \Pr[R \leqslant 10] - \Pr[R \leqslant 3] = .9885 - .2578 = .7307$

(b) $\Pr[7 \leqslant R \leqslant 9] = \Pr[R \leqslant 9] - \Pr[R \leqslant 6] = .9718 - .7660 = .2058$

(c) $\Pr[2 \leqslant R \leqslant 11] = \Pr[R \leqslant 11] - \Pr[R \leqslant 1] = .9957 - .0371 = .9586$

(d) $\Pr[9 \leqslant R \leqslant 11] = \Pr[R \leqslant 11] - \Pr[R \leqslant 8] = .9957 - .9369 = .0588$

PROBLEM 7-6 Refer to the upper-tail probabilities given in Example 7-3 for the number of late deliveries to be experienced in the next 100 shipments of computer mainframes, assuming that 7% of all deliveries have been late ($\pi = .07$). Compute the probabilities for the following outcomes.

(a) $\Pr[4 \leqslant R \leqslant 10]$ (c) $\Pr[2 \leqslant R \leqslant 11]$
(b) $\Pr[7 \leqslant R \leqslant 9]$ (d) $\Pr[9 \leqslant R \leqslant 11]$

Solution: In each case you subtract the probability for the unwanted upper tail from the upper-tail probability applicable for the lower limit.

(a) $$\Pr[4 \leqslant R \leqslant 10] = \Pr[R \geqslant 4] - \Pr[R \geqslant 11] = .9256 - .0908 = .8348$$

(b) $$\Pr[7 \leqslant R \leqslant 9] = \Pr[R \geqslant 7] - \Pr[R \geqslant 10] = .5557 - .1620 = .3937$$

(c) $$\Pr[2 \leqslant R \leqslant 11] = \Pr[R \geqslant 2] - \Pr[R \geqslant 12] = .9940 - .0469 = .9471$$

(d) $$\Pr[9 \leqslant R \leqslant 11] = \Pr[R \geqslant 9] - \Pr[R \geqslant 12] = .2660 - .0469 = .2191$$

PROBLEM 7-7 It is possible to use a table of cumulative probabilities to find individual binomial probability values. Refer to the table given in Example 7-2. Find the individual binomial probabilities for 0 through 12 overweight cans.

Solution: These probabilities are just like interval probabilities, except that the upper and lower limits are the same. Compute them by subtracting the cumulative probability for the unwanted lower range from the cumulative probability for the upper limit. For example,

$$\Pr[R = 4] = \Pr[R \leqslant 4] - \Pr[R \leqslant 3] = .4360 - .2578 = .1782$$

You construct the following table by subtracting from each cumulative probability the preceding one. Since it is impossible (and nonsensical) to achieve a negative number of successes, the events $R = 0$ and $R \leqslant 0$ are the same.

r	$\Pr[R \leqslant r]$	$\Pr[R = r]$
0	.0059	.0059
1	.0371	.0371 − .0059 = .0312
2	.1183	.1183 − .0371 = .0812
3	.2578	.2578 − .1183 = .1395
4	.4360	.4360 − .2578 = .1782
5	.6160	.6160 − .4360 = .1800
6	.7660	.7660 − .6160 = .1500
7	.8720	.8720 − .7660 = .1060
8	.9369	.9369 − .8720 = .0649
9	.9718	.9718 − .9369 = .0349
10	.9885	.9885 − .9718 = .0167
11	.9957	.9957 − .9885 = .0072
12	.9985	.9985 − .9957 = .0028

PROBLEM 7-8 It is possible to use a table of upper-tail probabilities to find individual binomial probability values. Refer to the table given in Example 7-3. Find the individual binomial probabilities for 0 through 11 late deliveries.

Solution: These probabilities are just like interval probabilities, except that the upper and lower limits are the same. Compute them by subtracting the probability for the unwanted upper tail from the upper-tail probability for the lower limit.

$$\Pr[R = 4] = \Pr[R \geqslant 4] - \Pr[R \geqslant 5] = .9256 - .8368 = .0888$$

You construct the following table by subtracting from each cumulative probability the one that follows. We can't compute the probability that $R = 12$, since the upper-tail probability beyond 12 successes isn't given.

r	$\Pr[R \geqslant r]$	$\Pr[R = r]$
0	1.0000	1.0000 − .9993 = .0007
1	.9993	.9993 − .9940 = .0053
2	.9940	.9940 − .9742 = .0198
3	.9742	.9742 − .9256 = .0486
4	.9256	.9256 − .8368 = .0888
5	.8368	.8368 − .7086 = .1282
6	.7086	.7086 − .5557 = .1529
7	.5557	.5557 − .4012 = .1545
8	.4012	.4012 − .2660 = .1352
9	.2660	.2660 − .1620 = .1040
10	.1620	.1620 − .0908 = .0712
11	.0908	.0908 − .0469 = .0439
12	.0469	

PROBLEM 7-9 A chemical flow-control device underfills 10% of all barrels. Find the probability that of any particular 5 barrels, the number underfilled will be

(a) exactly 3   (b) exactly 2   (c) zero   (d) at least 1

Solution: For (a)–(c), apply the binomial formula using $n = 5$ and $\pi = .10$.

(a)
$$\Pr[R = 3] = \frac{5!}{3!2!}(.10)^3(1 - .10)^2 = 10(.10)^3(.90)^2 = .0081$$

(b)
$$\Pr[R = 2] = \frac{5!}{2!3!}(.10)^2(1 - .10)^3 = 10(.10)^2(.90)^3 = .0729$$

(c)
$$\Pr[R = 0] = \frac{5!}{0!5!}(.10)^0(1 - .10)^5 = 1(.10)^0(.90)^5 = .59049$$

(d) To find Pr[at least 1], you can apply the binomial formula separately to find $\Pr[R = 1]$, $\Pr[R = 2]$, $\Pr[R = 3]$, $\Pr[R = 4]$, and $\Pr[R = 5]$. Then by the addition law,

$$\Pr[R \geqslant 1] = \Pr[R = 1] + \Pr[R = 2] + \Pr[R = 3] + \Pr[R = 4] + \Pr[R = 5]$$

However, it is easier to use the fact that "at least 1" and "none" are complementary events, so that using your answer from (c), you get

$$\Pr[R \geqslant 1] = 1 - \Pr[R = 0] = 1 - .59049 = .40951$$

PROBLEM 7-10 Construct a table of individual binomial probabilities (rounded to four places) when $n = 5$ and $\pi = .25$.

Solution: For each of the entries in the following table, you apply the binomial formula using $n = 5$ and $\pi = .25$.

r	$\Pr[R = r]$
0	$\dfrac{5!}{0!5!}(.25)^0(1 - .25)^5 = 1(.25)^0(.75)^5 = .2373$
1	$\dfrac{5!}{1!4!}(.25)^1(1 - .25)^4 = 5(.25)^1(.75)^4 = .3955$
2	$\dfrac{5!}{2!3!}(.25)^2(1 - .25)^3 = 10(.25)^2(.75)^3 = .2637$
3	$\dfrac{5!}{3!2!}(.25)^3(1 - .25)^2 = 10(.25)^3(.75)^2 = .0879$
4	$\dfrac{5!}{4!1!}(.25)^4(1 - .25)^1 = 5(.25)^4(.75)^1 = .0146$
5	$\dfrac{5!}{5!0!}(.25)^5(1 - .25)^0 = 1(.25)^5(.75)^0 = .0010$
	$\overline{1.0000}$

PROBLEM 7-11 Use your answer to Problem 7-10 to compute the following:

(a) the cumulative probabilities for each possible number of successes
(b) the upper-tail probabilities for each possible number of successes

Solution:
(a) Construct the following table by adding each successive individual probability to the preceding cumulative probability.

r	$\Pr[R = r]$	$\Pr[R \leqslant r]$
0	.2373	.2373
1	.3955	.2373 + .3955 = .6328
2	.2637	.6328 + .2637 = .8965
3	.0879	.8965 + .0879 = .9844
4	.0146	.9844 + .0146 = .9990
5	.0010	.9990 + .0010 = 1.0000
	$\overline{1.0000}$	

(b) Construct the following table by subtracting the preceding individual probability from the preceding upper-tail probability.

r	$\Pr[R = r]$	$\Pr[R \geqslant r]$
0	.2373	1.0000
1	.3955	$1.0000 - .2373 = .7627$
2	.2637	$.7627 - .3955 = .3672$
3	.0879	$.3672 - .2637 = .1035$
4	.0146	$.1035 - .0879 = .0156$
5	.0010	$.0156 - .0146 = .0010$
	1.0000	

PROBLEM 7-12   The proportion π of defective spindles wound on automatic fiber-processing systems is unknown. An inspector requests equipment adjustments whenever one or more spindles are found to be defective in a sample of $n = 100$. Determine the probability for adjustment assuming

(a) $\pi = .01$ (c) $\pi = .03$
(b) $\pi = .02$ (d) $\pi = .05$

Solution: In each case, adjustments will be made whenever at least one spindle is found to be defective. Therefore,

$$\Pr[\text{adjustment}] = \Pr[R \geqslant 1] = 1 - \Pr[R = 0]$$

$$= 1 - \frac{100!}{0!100!}\,\pi^0(1 - \pi)^{100}$$

$$= 1 - (1 - \pi)^{100}$$

With most hand-held calculators it is easy to raise a number to the power of 100. Even if your calculator doesn't have this capability, you can compute the answer by pushing the "square" button a few times:

$$(1 - \pi)^{100} = (1 - \pi)^4 \times (1 - \pi)^{32} \times (1 - \pi)^{64}$$
Hit the "square" button: 2 times   5 times   6 times

(a) $\Pr[\text{adjustment}] = 1 - (1 - .01)^{100} = 1 - (.96060 \times .72498 \times .52560)$
$$= 1 - .36604 = .63396$$

(b) $\Pr[\text{adjustment}] = 1 - (1 - .02)^{100} = 1 - (.92237 \times .52388 \times .27445)$
$$= 1 - .13262 = .86738$$

(c) $\Pr[\text{adjustment}] = 1 - (1 - .03)^{100} = 1 - (.88529 \times .37731 \times .14236)$
$$= 1 - .04755 = .95245$$

(d) $\Pr[\text{adjustment}] = 1 - (1 - .05)^{100} = 1 - (.81451 \times .19371 \times .03752)$
$$= 1 - .00592 = .99408$$

PROBLEM 7-13   An inspector accepts shipments of parts whenever 2 or fewer defectives are found in a sample of 10 items tested. Find **(a)** the expected number of defectives and **(b)** the approximate binomial probability for accepting a shipment when the proportion of defectives in the entire shipment is
   (1) $\pi = .01$ (2) $\pi = .05$ (3) $\pi = .10$ (4) $\pi = .20$

Solution:
(a) In each case, $E(R) = n\pi$
   (1) $10(.01) = .1$ (3) $10(.1) = 1.0$
   (2) $10(.05) = .5$ (4) $10(.2) = 2.0$
(b) In each of the following, use the binomial formula to evaluate the individual terms in the following equation:

$$\Pr[\text{accept}] = \Pr[R \leqslant 2] = \Pr[R = 0] + \Pr[R = 1] + \Pr[R = 2]$$

Then add the respective probabilities together.

(1) $\dfrac{10!}{0!10!}(.01)^0(1-.01)^{10} + \dfrac{10!}{1!9!}(.01)^1(1-.01)^9 + \dfrac{10!}{2!8!}(.01)^2(1-.01)^8 = .9044 + .0914 + .0042 = 1.0000$

(2) $\dfrac{10!}{0!10!}(.05)^0(1-.05)^{10} + \dfrac{10!}{1!9!}(.05)^1(1-.05)^9 + \dfrac{10!}{2!8!}(.05)^2(1-.05)^8 = .5987 + .3151 + .0746 = .9884$

(3) $\dfrac{10!}{0!10!}(.10)^0(1-.10)^{10} + \dfrac{10!}{1!9!}(.10)^1(1-.10)^9 + \dfrac{10!}{2!8!}(.10)^2(1-.10)^8 = .3487 + .3874 + .1937 = .9298$

(4) $\dfrac{10!}{0!10!}(.20)^0(1-.20)^{10} + \dfrac{10!}{1!9!}(.20)^1(1-.20)^9 + \dfrac{10!}{2!8!}(.20)^2(1-.20)^8 = .1074 + .2684 + .3020 = .6778$

 **THE NORMAL DISTRIBUTION**

THIS CHAPTER IS ABOUT

☑ **The Normal Curve**
☑ **Finding Areas Under the Normal Curve**
☑ **The Sampling Distribution of the Mean: Central Limit Theorem**
☑ **The Sampling Distribution of the Proportion: The Normal Approximation**

You first encountered the *normal curve* in Chapter 2. There you learned that this frequency curve provides a very good summary of the shape of the frequency distributions for a large class of populations, including IQ's, various physical measurements of people, and dimensions of many objects. You'll see that the normal curve also plays a fundamental role in characterizing the sampling distribution of the sample mean. This is a much more important application than the normal curve's purely descriptive role.

8-1. The Normal Curve

Figure 8-1 shows the essential features of a normal curve. It is "bell-shaped," with tails extending indefinitely above and below the center. These tails are a feature of the curves of populations for which extremely large or small values are rare. Since the frequency curve is symmetrical, the mean and median are identical. There is a single mode, which occurs at the same point as the mean and the median.

Figure 8-1

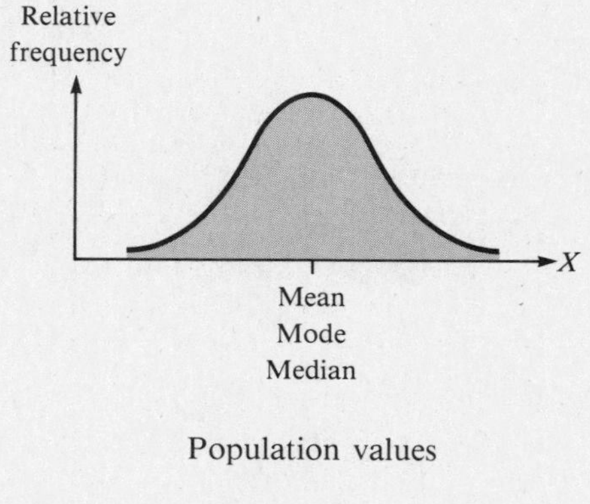

Relative
frequency

X

Mean
Mode
Median

Population values

A. A normal curve is specified by two parameters.

All normal curves belong to a common distribution family. Members are described by a mathematical expression involving two parameters. The parameter for the **location**, or center, of a normal curve is represented by μ, and the **scale**, or shape, of the curve is set by σ. Since the normal curve represents many populations, the same symbols and terms denote both these two parameters and the key population parameters. Thus *mean* refers both to the population's center and to the location parameter of the corresponding normal curve, and *standard deviation* is both a population's measure of dispersion and the scale parameter of its frequency curve.

Figure 8-2 shows three normal curves, each representing a different population. The curves are centered at their respective population means μ. Each has a different standard deviation σ. Note that the curve having the largest σ is short and spread out, while that with the smallest σ is tall and narrow.

Figure 8-2

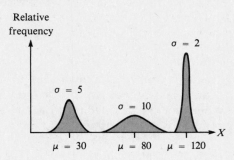

Population values

B. Areas under a normal curve provide the relative frequencies for various population values.

Many statistical procedures depend on the establishment of the *relative frequency* of various population values. These frequencies correspond to *areas* under the population frequency curve.

- For populations represented by normal curves, the area between the mean and any point depends only on how far that point falls above or below the mean. That distance is ordinarily expressed in standard deviations.

Figure 8-3 illustrates three important cases. These apply to all populations that have normal curves. Consider, for instance, the population of *men's heights* at Near Miss University, where the mean is $\mu = 5'9''$ (69") and the standard deviation is $\sigma = 2.5''$.

Figure 8-3

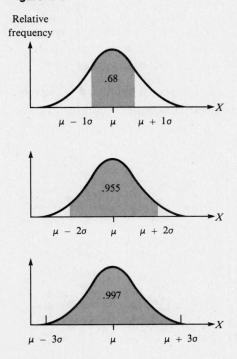

1. **About 68% of all population values lie within ±1σ of μ.** The area under any normal curve over the range $\mu \pm 1\sigma$ is .6826. This means that about 68% of Near Miss men are between $\mu - 1\sigma = 69'' - 1(2.5'')$ and $\mu + 1\sigma = 69'' + 1(2.5'') = 71.5''$ tall.

2. **Over 95% of all population values lie within μ ± 2σ.** The exact relative frequency is .9544 for values within two standard deviations of the mean. Slightly over 95% of the Near Miss men are between $69'' - 2(2.5'') = 64''$ and $69'' + 2(2.5'') = 74''$ tall.

3. **Exactly 99.73% of all population values lie within μ ± 3σ.** This means that nearly the entire male student body of Near Miss University is between $69'' - 3(2.5'') = 61.5''$ and $69'' + 3(2.5'') = 76.5''$ tall. Around one out of every thousand men (.1%) is shorter than 61.5'' tall, while about the same proportion are taller than 76.5''.

C. The normal distribution provides useful probabilities.

In addition to serving as a frequency curve for many populations, the normal curve provides probabilities for an important class of **continuous random variables** encountered in sampling investigations. Whenever the sampled population has a normal frequency curve, the observed value of a randomly selected unit is a random variable having a **normal distribution**.

Analogous to the probability mass function for discrete random variables, the probability distribution for a continuous random variable may be represented by a particular **probability density function**. When plotted on a graph, the probability density function for a normally distributed random variable is a normal curve, and **areas** under that curve provide probabilities.

Suppose that one Near Miss man is selected at random and measured. Let X denote his height. The probability that X falls into a particular range is identical to the corresponding area under the normal curve for the men's heights. For example,

$$\Pr[66.5'' \leqslant X \leqslant 71.5''] = .6826$$
$$\Pr[64.0'' \leqslant X \leqslant 74.0''] = .9544$$
$$\Pr[61.5'' \leqslant X \leqslant 76.5''] = .9973$$

8-2. Finding Areas Under the Normal Curve

If you want to know the relative frequency with which a range of population values occurs, you can find the area under the normal curve that is associated with that range. This area may lie above or below some point or perhaps between one point and another. The first step is to find out how many standard deviations separate the endpoints from the mean. You then search for the matching area in a table of normal curve areas. You will find these in the backs of most statistics books (see Table A in the Appendix to this outline).

A. The normal deviate expresses distance in standard deviations.

The distance between the mean and a point that lies a specific distance above the mean is referred to as a **normal deviate**. A normal deviate is expressed in standard deviation units. Traditionally the letter z is used to denote a normal deviate value. Letting the letter x represent any possible population value, you can compute a normal deviate using the following expression:

Normal deviate
$$z = \frac{x - \mu}{\sigma}$$

Levels for z will be negative when x lies below the mean.

To illustrate, if the mean is 25 and the standard deviation is 2, a population value of $x = 26.5$ will lie

$$z = \frac{26.5 - 25}{2} = .75$$

standard deviation units above the mean.

B. You can use one table to find areas under any normal curve.

Once you have found the normal deviate for a population value, you can turn to Table A in the Appendix to find the corresponding area. Following is a portion of Table A.

Normal deviate z	.00	.01	.02	.03	.04	.05	.06	.07
⋮				⋮				
.6	.2257	.2291	.2324	.2357	.2389	.2422	.2454	.2486
.7	.2580	.2612	.2642	.2673	.2704	**.2734**	.2764	.2794
.8	**.2881**	.2910	.2939	**.2967**	.2995	.3023	.3051	.3078
.9	.3159	.3186	.3212	.3238	.3264	.3289	.3315	.3340 ⋯
1.0	.3413	.3438	.3461	.3485	.3508	.3531	.3554	.3577
1.1	.3643	.3665	.3686	.3708	.3729	.3749	.3770	**.3790**
1.2	.3849	.3869	.3888	.3907	.3925	.3944	.3962	.3980
				⋮				

The first column lists values of z to the first decimal place. The second decimal place value is located at the head of one of the remaining ten columns. You find the area under the curve between the mean and z standard deviations at the intersection of the correct row and column. For example, when $z = .75$, you read the entry in the .7 row and the .05 column to find the area of .2734.

This table applies to all normal curves. For any x there is a matching z, computed from the expression for the normal deviate, and this z value is tabled. As another example, to establish the probability that a randomly chosen Near Miss man will be between $\mu = 69''$ and $x = 71''$ tall when $\sigma = 2.5''$, you must first compute the normal deviate:

$$z = \frac{71'' - 69''}{2.5''} = 0.80$$

You then find the tabled area in the .8 row and .00 column to be .2881. Thus

$$\Pr[69'' \leqslant X \leqslant 71''] = .2881$$

EXAMPLE 8-1: AIRLINE TICKETING TIME

An airline wants to find out how long it takes for a travel agent to complete an airplane ticket order from a remote computer terminal. Assume that the mean transaction time is $\mu = 150$ seconds, with a standard deviation of $\sigma = 30$ seconds. Also assume that the population of transaction times has a normal frequency curve. Find the probability that a future transaction will take between 150 and 175 seconds to complete.

It helps to draw the normal curve and identify the area you wish to find. The shaded area in Figure 8-4 represents the area between 150 and 175 seconds. This area is the same as the probability that the transaction time takes between 150 and 175 seconds.

Figure 8-4 Determining the area under a normal curve.

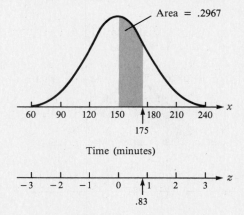

Since you know the values for x, μ, and σ, you can solve the expression for the normal deviate:

$$z = \frac{175 - 150}{30} = .83$$

Look up this value in Table A. Reading the entry in the .8 row and the .03 column, you find the area to be .2967. Thus, the probability that a future transaction will take between 150 and 175 seconds to complete is .2967.

C. You can use the normal curve table to find a variety of area types.

In Chapter 7 you encountered a variety of composite probabilities. You can use the normal curve table to establish any of these. You have already learned how to find an area between the mean and a point lying above the mean. Now consider the following cases, which are illustrated using the data from Example 8-1.

1. Area between the mean and some point lying below the mean.

To find the probability that the travel agent's ticket transaction time lies between 125 and 150 seconds, you must first calculate the normal deviate:

$$z = \frac{x - \mu}{\sigma} = \frac{125 - 150}{30} = -.83$$

Here z is negative because 125 lies below the mean. Since the normal curve is symmetrical about the mean, this area must be the same as it would be for a positive value of z of the same magnitude. The area for $z = -.83$ is .2967, just as it was for $z = .83$. It is therefore unnecessary to tabulate areas for negative values of z.

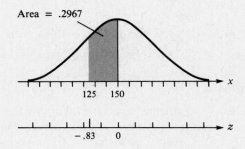

2. Area to the left of a value above the mean.

To find the probability that a ticket transaction will take 185 seconds or less, you must find the entire shaded area below 185. Since Table A considers only areas in the upper half of the normal curve, you must add the entire lower-half area of $1/2 = .5000$ to the area above the mean. Since $z = (185 - 150)/30 = 1.17$, the area above the mean is .3790. Thus the shaded area is the sum $.5000 + .3790 = .8790$.

3. Area in the upper tail.

To find the probability that the ticket order takes more than 195 seconds to complete, you must first determine the area between the mean and 195. The normal deviate is $z = (195 - 150)/30 = 1.50$. Table A provides the area .4332. Now you must subtract that value from the area in the upper half of the normal curve, $1/2 = .5000$, to arrive at the upper-tail area: $.5000 - .4332 = .0668$.

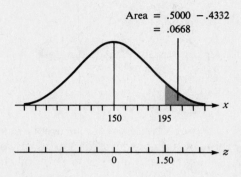

4. Area in the lower tail.

The probability that an order will take 90 seconds or less involves similar calculations. First, find the area between 90 and 150. Using $z = (90 - 150)/30 = -2.00$, you find the area of .4772 from Table A. Subtracting that value from .5 yields $.5000 - .4772 = .0228$.

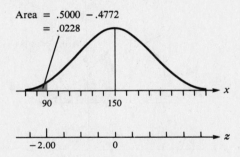

5. Area to the right of a value below the mean.

The probability that the time exceeds 85 seconds is equal to the area between 85 and the mean, added to the area in the upper half of the normal curve. The normal deviate is $z = (85 - 150)/30 = -2.17$, for which Table A provides .4850. The desired value is $.5000 + .4850 = .9850$.

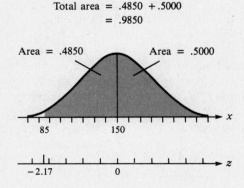

6. Area overlapping the mean.

Consider the probability that an order requires between 140 and 170 seconds to complete. This will equal the portion of the shaded area below the mean added to that above the mean. The respective normal deviates are $z = (140 - 150)/30 = -.33$ and $z = (170 - 150)/30 = .67$. Table A provides .1293 for the lower area and .2486 for the upper area. The combined area is $.1293 + .2486 = .3779$.

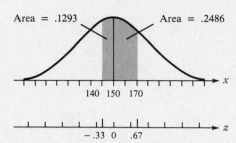

Total area = .1293 + .2486
= .3779

Area = .1293   Area = .2486

7. Area between two points, both lying on the same side of the mean.

To find the probability that the ticket order will require between 165 and 190 seconds, you must first find the areas between the mean and each of these values. The respective normal deviates are $z = (165 - 150)/30 = .50$ and $z = (190 - 150)/30 = 1.33$. The tabled areas for these values are .1915 and .4082. To get the desired area you must subtract the smaller area from the larger one: $.4082 - .1915 = .2167$. An analogous procedure applies when both points lie below the mean.

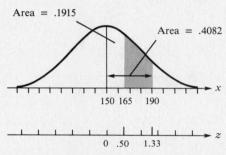

Area of shaded portion = .4082 − .1915
= .2167

Area = .1915

Area = .4082

- It is helpful if you first sketch the normal curve and shade in the area you wish to find.

D. Percentiles may be found directly by reversing the procedure for finding an area under the normal curve.

Recall from Chapter 2 that a *percentile* is that point below which some stipulated percentage of the population values will fall. For normally distributed populations, you may find percentiles by reading Table A in reverse. Suppose you want to find out how long the travel agent's ticket transaction took, knowing that the time is the 90th percentile. The area under the normal curve to the left of this point is .90, and so the area between the mean and that point is $.90 - .50 = .40$.

Searching through the body of Table A, you can see that the closest area to .40 is .3997. Since .3997 is in the $z = 1.2$ row and .08 column, the corresponding normal deviate is $z = 1.28$. The desired point is 1.28 standard deviations above the mean. Since $\sigma = 30$ seconds for the ticket transaction time, 1.28 standard deviations $= 1.28 \times 30 = 38.4$ seconds. Adding this to the mean of $\mu = 150$ seconds, you find that the 90th percentile is $150 + 38.4 = 188.4$ seconds.

To find any percentile, you first read Table A in reverse to establish that point's normal deviate z; you then apply the following expression:

Percentile for a normal population $x = \mu + z\sigma$

Note that below the 50th percentile, the lower-tail area is used to find z, which will then be negative.

EXAMPLE 8-2: DESIGNING WITHIN HUMAN LIMITATIONS

The hydraulic control foot-pedal of an aircraft must be designed so that 95% of pilots can actuate it during landings without becoming fatigued. Human factors engineers have established a frequency distribution for the amount of pressure that a seated person can continuously exert on a pedal for 5 minutes before the onset of fatigue. This population is approximately normally distributed, with a mean of $\mu = 25$ pounds and a standard deviation of $\sigma = 3.5$ pounds.

The foot force needed to actuate the hydraulic control can't be any greater than the 5th percentile of the pedal pressure population. To determine the maximum foot force, you must find the population value below which the normal curve area is .05.

Searching Table A, you find that the area closest to $.50 - .05 = .45$. Two areas, .4495 and .4505, are equally close to this value. Thus, the desired normal deviate falls somewhere between 1.64 and 1.65. It is common practice to err on the side of a smaller tail area, and so you would select 1.64. Since the 5th percentile lies below the 50th, the normal deviate is *negative*, so that $z = -1.64$. (The 5th percentile lies below the mean and is smaller, so that a distance of 1.64 standard deviations must be subtracted from the mean.) The 5th percentile is therefore

$$x = \mu + z\sigma = 25 - 1.64(3.5) = 19.26$$

This means that the pedal should need a force no greater than 19.26 pounds if 95% of pilots are to be able to operate it.

8-3. The Sampling Distribution of the Mean: Central Limit Theorem

You should recall from Chapter 6 that the *sampling distribution* of the sample mean $\bar{X}$ forms the basis for much statistical analysis. In many situations you can use the normal curve to find probabilities for $\bar{X}$.

A. The central limit theorem allows use of the normal curve to find probabilities for the sample mean.

Before the sample data are obtained, $\bar{X}$ is a random variable. Probabilities for it are specified by its sampling distribution. The **central limit theorem** of statistics allows you to use the normal distribution to determine these probabilities. This theorem states that for most populations being observed, the normal curve closely *approximates* the sampling distribution of $\bar{X}$. The normal approximation improves as the sample size n becomes larger— regardless of the shape of the population's frequency distribution. *The population itself need not be normally distributed.*

You can now appreciate why the normal curve is so important in statistics.

- Conclusions are often made regarding means. The computed level of $\bar{X}$ forms the basis for these.
- The normal curve tells what to expect regarding $\bar{X}$ and provides probabilities for various levels of that statistic.
- The $\bar{X}$ probabilities obtained from the normal curve are usually only approximate, their accuracy improving with larger sample sizes.

You don't even have to know the form of the population's frequency distribution (usually unknowable, since only sample observations will ever be made). Its frequency curve can be skewed, U-shaped, uniform, or of any other form. (The population variance must, however, be finite—a condition almost always met in practice.)

Should the population frequency curve itself be *normal*, further statistical theory stipulates that the sampling distribution of $\bar{X}$ is *exactly* normal, regardless of the level for n.

B. To apply the normal curve with $\bar{X}$, you must first determine the standard error.

Recall from Chapter 6 that $\bar{X}$ is a random variable having expected value μ. The means of repeated samples will cluster about μ. The standard error of $\bar{X}$ expresses how tight that clustering will be. When n sample observations are taken at random from a population of size N with standard deviation σ, you can find the standard error of $\bar{X}$ using the following expression.

Standard error of $\bar{X}$

$$\sigma_{\bar{X}} = \frac{\sigma}{\sqrt{n}} \sqrt{\frac{N-n}{N-1}}$$

To find the probability that $\bar{X}$ will fall between the population mean and some stipulated level $\bar{x}$, you may use $\sigma_{\bar{x}}$ in the following expression for the normal deviate of the sample mean.

Normal deviate of $\bar{X}$

$$z = \frac{\bar{x} - \mu}{\sigma_{\bar{X}}}$$

To illustrate, suppose you plan to take a sample of $n = 100$ account balances from a population of $N = 1,000$ charge accounts. You don't know μ, but you assume that it's unchanged from last month, when μ was \$138.50. You don't know σ either, but you assume the historical value of $\sigma = \$19.00$. The standard error of $\bar{X}$ is

$$\sigma_{\bar{x}} = \frac{\$19.00}{\sqrt{100}} \sqrt{\frac{1,000 - 100}{1,000 - 1}} = \$1.80$$

To find the probability that $\bar{X}$ falls somewhere between $\mu = \$138.50$ and $\bar{x} = \$140.00$, you must first establish the corresponding normal deviate:

$$z = \frac{\$140.00 - \$138.50}{\$1.80} = .83$$

From Table A the area for $z = .83$ is .2967. Thus you conclude that

$$\Pr[\$138.50 \leqslant \bar{X} \leqslant \$140.00] = .2967$$

When the population size is large relative to the sample size, you may ignore the finite population correction factor in computing $\sigma_{\bar{x}}$. In those cases, you can use the following simplified expression:

Standard error of $\bar{X}$ (large populations)

$$\sigma_{\bar{X}} = \frac{\sigma}{\sqrt{n}}$$

You continue to find normal deviates and probabilities as described in Section 8-2.

- A rule commonly used in statistics that this book will follow is to ignore the finite population correction factor whenever N is more than 10 times n.

C. Probabilities for the sample mean are affected in two major ways.

Both the population standard deviation σ and the sample size n have a significant effect on the standard error of the sample mean $\bar{X}$.

1. **Sample means tend to be closer to μ when σ is small.** $\sigma_{\bar{x}}$ is directly proportional to σ. Thus assuming that samples of the same size n are taken from two populations, $\sigma_{\bar{x}}$ will be smaller for the population having the smaller standard deviation. And the corresponding $\bar{X}$ normal curve will be narrower and taller, which makes it more likely that the computed value for $\bar{X}$ will fall near μ.

EXAMPLE 8-3: ESTIMATING MEAN INCOMES FOR SURGEONS AND TEACHERS

Suppose that you are asked to estimate the mean income of persons in various professions. You are to determine this by taking a random sample of persons from each group and finding the mean income $\bar{X}$.

Consider surgeons and teachers. You are interested in the population mean income μ for each group. These are unknowns, but the following "ballpark" guesses apply for the respective standard deviations:

Surgeons	Teachers
$\sigma = \$25,000$	$\sigma = \$2,000$

You will take samples of size $n = 100$ from each population. Since there are tens of thousands of surgeons and hundreds of thousands of teachers, the population size is large enough in both cases that you may ignore the finite population correction factor in computing the standard errors of $\bar{X}$:

Surgeons	Teachers
$\sigma_{\bar{X}} = \dfrac{\$25{,}000}{\sqrt{100}}$	$\sigma_{\bar{x}} = \dfrac{\$2{,}000}{\sqrt{100}}$
$= \$2{,}500$	$= \$200$

You now decide that you want to find the probability that $\bar{X}$ lies within $\pm\$500$ of the population mean of each group. Find the normal deviates, substituting 500 for $(\bar{x} - \mu)$ in the equation $z = (\bar{x} - \mu)/\sigma_{\bar{x}}$. Then read the areas from Table A. Since you wish to obtain a value that is both above and below the means ($\pm\$500$), you must multiply each tabled area by 2.

Surgeons	Teachers
$z = \dfrac{\$500}{\$2{,}500} = .20$	$z = \dfrac{\$500}{\$200} = 2.50$
$\Pr[-\$500 \leqslant \bar{X} - \mu \leqslant +\$500]$	$\Pr[-\$500 \leqslant \bar{X} - \mu \leqslant +\$500]$
$= 2(.0793) = .1586$	$= 2(.4938) = .9876$

Notice that there is a higher probability that $\bar{X}$ will be close to its target with teachers than with surgeons. This is because the smaller standard deviation for that more homogeneous income group provides a smaller standard error for $\bar{X}$.

---

2. **A larger sample size n raises the chance that $\bar{X}$ will be close to μ.** You can see that the square root of n appears in the denominator of the expression for $\sigma_{\bar{x}}$. Thus, $\sigma_{\bar{x}}$ is inversely proportional to n. An increasing n will reduce $\sigma_{\bar{x}}$, resulting in a taller, tighter normal curve for $\bar{X}$. The probability will then be greater that $\bar{X}$ will lie within some specified distance of μ.

EXAMPLE 8-4: PROBABILITY OF NOT MEETING THE MINIMUM LIFETIME

Idea Lightbulb Company replaces a seam control mechanism whenever a sample of test bulbs has a mean lifetime less than or equal to 450 hours. When the process is exactly on target, the mean lifetime of all bulbs μ is 500 hours. The lifetimes of individual bulbs have a standard deviation σ that is also 500 hours.

Present company policy calls for a test sample of $n = 25$ test bulbs, and a manager wants to determine the probability of unnecessarily replacing the control mechanism under this policy. The standard error of $\bar{X}$ is $\sigma_{\bar{x}} = 500/\sqrt{25} = 100$. The normal deviate for a possible level for the sample mean of 450 hours is $z = (450 - 500)/100 = -.50$. The tabled normal curve area between the mean and $z = .50$ is .1915. The probability of unnecessary replacement is thus

$$\Pr[\bar{X} \leqslant 450] = .5000 - .1915 = .3085 \qquad (\text{when } n = 25)$$

(Here you subtract the area between the mean and z from .5000, since you are interested in an area in the lower tail.)

This probability indicates a substantial chance of unnecessary repairs. The manager wants to see what effect increasing the sample size to $n = 400$ will have. The standard error of $\bar{X}$ now becomes $\sigma_{\bar{x}} = 500/\sqrt{400} = 25$, so that the normal deviate is $z = (450 - 500)/25 = -2.00$, giving a tabled area of .4772. If the company adopts this new policy, the probability for replacing the mechanism when it is functioning correctly will be

$$\Pr[\bar{X} \leqslant 450] = .5000 - .4772 = .0228 \qquad (\text{when } n = 400)$$

8-4. The Sampling Distribution of the Proportion: The Normal Approximation

The *population proportion* π plays a role in statistical investigations of qualitative populations that is analogous to the role of the mean with quantitative data. Like μ, π is ordinarily unknown, and it is often estimated by the *sample proportion* P. In Chapter 7 you saw that the binomial distribution may be an appropriate sampling distribution for P. But the binomial is computationally cumbersome, and tabled values exist for only the more common levels of n and π. Fortunately, the normal distribution often nicely approximates the sampling distribution for P.

A. The central limit theorem applies to a Bernoulli process.

In Chapter 7 you saw that coin tossing is one example of a *Bernoulli process*. Suppose that you assign points to the trial outcomes, with each success getting a 1 and each failure a 0. The outcome of any given trial, then, is a random variable having either of these two values. Let X_1 denote the first trial value, X_2 the second, and so on. Consider the mean of these,

$$\bar{X} = \frac{X_1 + X_2 + \cdots + X_n}{n}$$

This value $\bar{X}$ is the same as the proportion of successes P (because the sum of all the X's must equal the total number of successes, and P is that value divided by the number of trials n). When n is large, the *central limit theorem* states that $\bar{X}$, and hence P, has a sampling distribution closely approximated by the normal curve.

B. The normal approximation can provide adequate probabilities for *P*.

The normal curve that approximates the sampling distribution of P has its center at π and has a standard deviation equal to σ_P, the standard error of P. You may determine probabilities for P by computing the applicable normal deviates and finding the corresponding areas under the normal curve. If you let r/n represent any particular level of P, you can compute the normal deviate of P by using the following expression.

Normal deviate of the proportion $$z = \frac{(r + .5)/n - \pi}{\sigma_P}$$

Inclusion of .5 makes a **continuity correction**, which is necessary because you are using the *continuous* normal distribution to approximate the *discrete* binomial distribution. (For simplicity, some books ignore the continuity correction. You may also find p used in place of r/n to denote a possible level for P.)

Note: In computing z, don't make the mistake of dividing $(r + .5)$ by the quantity $(n - \pi)$. You must compute the quantity $(r + .5)/n$, and then subtract π.

In Chapter 7 you saw that there are two ways of computing σ_P, depending on whether the population size is large or small.

Standard error of P

(Large populations)	(Small populations)
$\sigma_P = \sqrt{\dfrac{\pi(1 - \pi)}{n}}$	$\sigma_P = \sqrt{\dfrac{\pi(1 - \pi)}{n}} \sqrt{\dfrac{N - n}{N - 1}}$

(As with the standard error of the sample mean $\bar{X}$, you can usually ignore the finite population correction factor when N is 10 or more times larger than n.)

To illustrate, suppose that you take a sample of $n = 100$ items at random from a shipment of $N = 500$. If you assume that the proportion defective in the entire shipment is $\pi = .10$, what is the probability that your sample proportion is less than or equal to 5/100 (r/n)?

The standard error of P is

$$\sigma_P = \sqrt{\frac{.10(1 - .10)}{100}} \sqrt{\frac{500 - 100}{500 - 1}} = .027$$

Computing the normal deviate, you get

$$z = \frac{(5 + .5)/100 - .10}{.027} = -1.67$$

The desired probability corresponds to a lower-tail area. The entry in Table A for $z = 1.67$ is .4525, which must be subtracted from .5.

$$\Pr[P \leqslant 5/100] = .5000 - .4525 = .0475 \quad \text{(approximately)}$$

C. There are restrictions in making the normal approximation with P.

You must exercise some care when making the normal approximation.

1. **Find the r, z, and area that matches.** To ensure that the proper normal curve area is found, you must compute the normal deviate for events of the orientation "$P \leqslant$". You should therefore convert the original form of the desired probability into an equivalent form.

Original form of desired probability	Equivalent form (used to find the area)
$\Pr[P \leqslant r/n]$	use original form
$\Pr[P > r/n]$	$1 - \Pr[P \leqslant r/n]$
$\Pr[P < r/n]$	$\Pr[P \leqslant (r-1)/n]$
$\Pr[P \geqslant r/n]$	$1 - \Pr[P \leqslant (r-1)/n]$
$\Pr[r_1/n \leqslant P \leqslant r_2/n]$	$\Pr[P \leqslant r_2/n] - \Pr[P \leqslant (r_1-1)/n]$

2. **Use the normal approximation only when n is large enough.** Various rules of thumb are used. Be sure you follow the one suggested in your statistics text.

EXAMPLE 8-5: WHEN TO REPLACE A RELAY SWITCH

Centralia Bell replaces its relay switches whenever the proportion of erroneous characters in a test transmission is greater than .0003. Each test involves $n = 10,000$ characters.

An error rate of $\pi = .0002$ is considered satisfactory. What is the probability that a satisfactory relay is replaced?

Since the population size is unlimited, you may ignore the finite population correction factor in computing the standard error of P:

$$\sigma_P = \sqrt{\frac{.0002(.9998)}{10,000}} = .00014$$

The normal deviate for a sample proportion of level $.0003 = 3/10,000$ is

$$z = \frac{(3 + .5)/10,000 - .0002}{.00014} = 1.07$$

Thus,

$$\Pr[\text{replacement}] = \Pr[P > 3/10,000] = 1 - \Pr[P \leqslant 3/10,000]$$
$$= 1 - [.5000 + .3577]$$
$$= .1423$$

About 14% of all tests involving satisfactory relays will involve unnecessary replacement.

The testing procedure also provides good protection against leaving an unsatisfactory relay switch in place. Suppose that the error rate π is instead a too high $\pi = .0004$. What is the probability that the unsatisfactory switch gets replaced?

The standard error of P is

$$\sigma_P = \sqrt{\frac{.0004(.9996)}{10,000}} = .00020$$

The normal deviate is

$$z = \frac{(3 + .5)/10,000 - .0004}{.00020} = -.25$$

which is negative and so lies in the lower tail of the normal curve. Thus,

$$\Pr[\text{replacement}] = \Pr[P > 3/10,000] = 1 - \Pr[P \leqslant 3/10,000]$$
$$= 1 - [.5000 - .0987]$$
$$= .5987$$

About 60% of all tests involving such grossly malfunctioning switches will result in replacement.

SUMMARY

The *normal distribution* is used to represent the frequency distributions of many populations that are often encountered—especially those resulting from physical measurements. The frequency curve of such a population is called a *normal curve*. Normal curves have a bell shape, are symmetrical, and have tails extending indefinitely above and below the center. Three measures of central tendency coincide at that point: the mean, the median, and the mode.

All normal curves belong to a common family, the members of which are distinguished by their *location* and *scale* parameters, the mean μ and standard deviation σ. The *area* under the normal curve between any two points provides the relative frequency for the population values in that range. That area is specified by the *normal deviate*, which is the distance (in units of standard deviations) separating each endpoint from the mean.

When a sample unit from a normally distributed population is observed at random, the possible value achieved is a random variable whose *probability density function* graphs as a normal curve. The probability that such a variable assumes a value in any particular range is equal to the matching area.

The key role played by the normal distribution in statistics is that it allows us to draw conclusions regarding the *sample mean* $\bar{X}$. According to the *central limit theorem*, $\bar{X}$ is a random variable whose sampling distribution can usually be represented by a normal curve. The mean of that normal distribution is the population mean itself, and its standard deviation is $\sigma_{\bar{x}} = \sigma/\sqrt{n}$ for large populations (but the quantity $\sigma/\sqrt{n}$ must be further multiplied by the finite population correction factor when N is small). The central limit theorem applies even when the population frequency curve isn't normal, although then the normal curve is only an *approximation* that improves as n increases. Before the sample data are available, the normal distribution provides probability values for any possible level of $\bar{X}$.

The normal distribution may also approximate the sampling distribution of the *sample proportion P*. This is advantageous primarily from a computational point of view, the normal distribution being easier to work with than the binomial. Care must be taken that n is large enough, and a *continuity correction* can be made to improve the accuracy of the approximation.

RAISE YOUR GRADES

Can you explain ...?

☑ what is meant by a frequency curve's location and scale
☑ why it is only necessary to table areas under half of the normal curve
☑ why you can use the same table to find areas under different normal curves
☑ what the central limit theorem allows statisticians to do regarding the sample mean
☑ why the total area under a normal curve must be equal to 1

Do you know...?

☑ when you can usually ignore the finite population correction factor
☑ the advantages of the normal approximation in finding probabilities for the sample proportion
☑ why, when it is taken literally, the normal distribution allows for no impossible values
☑ why the probability for getting a value lying at or below the mean must be the same for all normally distributed random variables

RAPID REVIEW

1. A standard normal random variable has a mean of 0 and a standard deviation of 1. Find the area between the mean and each of the following points.   [Section 8-2B]

   (a) 2.50   (b) .50   (c) 1.50   (d) 1.00

2. A normally distributed population has a mean of 100 and a standard deviation of 10. Find (*1*) the normal deviate that corresponds and (*2*) the probability for population values falling below the following points. [Section 8-2B]

    (a) 115   **(b)** 86   **(c)** 123   **(d)** 108

3. A normally distributed population has a mean of $\mu = 500$ and a standard deviation of $\sigma = 50$. Determine (*1*) the normal deviate that corresponds and (*2*) the relative frequency of population values lying above the following points. [Section 8-2C]

    (a) 420   **(b)** 475   **(c)** 520   **(d)** 625

4. Determine the normal deviate values z that best correspond to the following percentiles. [Section 8-2D]

    (a) 10th   **(b)** 25th   **(c)** 60th   **(d)** 90th

5. The women in a particular county have heights that are normally distributed with a mean of 5′ 6″ and a standard deviation of 2″. Determine (*1*) the normal deviate that corresponds and (*2*) the proportion of women whose heights are as follows. [Section 8-2C]

    (a) above 6′ 0″   **(b)** below 5′ 4″   **(c)** above 5′ 8″   **(d)** below 5′ 2″

6. The men in a region have heights that are normally distributed with a mean of 5′ 9″ and a standard deviation of 3″. Determine the height that establishes the following percentiles. [Section 8-2D]

    (a) 5th   **(b)** 30th   **(c)** 75th   **(d)** 99th

7. A sample of $n = 100$ is taken from a large population having a mean of $\mu = 450$ and a standard deviation of $\sigma = 60$. [Section 8-3B]

    (a) Find the standard error of $\bar{X}$.
    (b) Determine the probability that the sample mean will fall
        (*1*) below 440   (*2*) below 445   (*3*) above 442   (*4*) above 465

8. A random sample of 25 items from a shipment of $N = 200$ are weighed. The population mean is unknown, although the standard deviation is $\sigma = 1$ gram. [Section 8-3B]

    (a) Find the standard error of $\bar{X}$.
    (b) Determine the probability that the sample mean will fall within the following limits of the population mean.
        (*1*) $\pm.05$ gram   (*2*) $\pm.10$ gram   (*3*) $\pm.25$ gram   (*4*) $\pm.50$ gram

9. A fair coin is tossed 100 times. The normal approximation will provide probabilities for the proportion of heads. [Section 8-4B]

    (a) Compute the standard error of P.
    (b) Estimate the probability that the proportion of heads obtained will be
        (*1*) $\leqslant.42$ (*2*) $\leqslant.48$ (*3*) $\leqslant.53$ (*4*) $\leqslant.62$

10. A sample of $n = 100$ items is removed from a shipment of $N = 500$ having $\pi = .10$ defectives. [Section 8-4B]

    (a) Compute the standard error of P.
    (b) Use the normal approximation to determine the probability that the sample proportion defective will be
        (*1*) $\leqslant.05$ (*2*) $>.13$ (*3*) $<.07$ (*4*) $\geqslant.15$

Answers
1. **(a)** .4938 **(b)** .1915 **(c)** .4332 **(d)** .3413
2. **(a)** (*1*) 1.50 (*2*) .9332 **(c)** (*1*) 2.30 (*2*) .9893
   (b) (*1*) −1.40 (*2*) .0808 **(d)** (*1*) .80 (*2*) .7881
3. **(a)** (*1*) −1.60 (*2*) .9452 **(c)** (*1*) .40 (*2*) .3446
   (b) (*1*) −.50 (*2*) .6915 **(d)** (*1*) 2.50 (*2*) .0062
4. **(a)** −1.28 **(b)** −.67 **(c)** .25 **(d)** 1.28

5. (a) (*1*) 3.00 (*2*) .00135 **(c)** (*1*) 1.00 (*2*) .1587
  (b) (*1*) −1.00 (*2*) .1587 **(d)** (*1*) −2.00 (*2*) .0228
6. (a) 5′ 4.08″ **(b)** 5′ 7.44″ **(c)** 5′ 11.01″ **(d)** 6′ 3.99″
7. (a) 6.0 **(b)** (*1*) .0475 (*2*) .2033 (*3*) .9082 (*4*) .0062
8. (a) .188 **(b)** (*1*) .2128 (*2*) .4038 (*3*) .8164 (*4*) .9922
9. (a) .05 **(b)** (*1*) .0668 (*2*) .3821 (*3*) .7580 (*4*) .9938
10. (a) .0269 **(b)** (*1*) .0475 (*2*) .0968 (*3*) .0968 (*4*) .0475

SOLVED PROBLEMS

PROBLEM 8-1 Cash balance errors are approximately normally distributed with a mean of $0 and a standard deviation of $1.00. Determine the relative frequency for the following balance errors.

(a) less than $1.25	**(e)** between $1.50 and $1.75
(b) greater than −$.75	**(f)** between −$.50 and −$.25
(c) less than −$2.50	**(g)** less than −$2.80 or greater than $.65
(d) greater than $3.50	**(h)** less than $.65 or greater than $.75

Solution: Since the population mean is 0 and the standard deviation is 1, the stated levels of the random variable are already in the form of normal deviates. (Figuring the normal deviate, you would get $z = (x − 0)/1 = x$.) Then use Table A to find the area that corresponds to this z value. It will be helpful in each case to sketch a normal curve on scratch paper and identify the area that corresponds to the relative frequency of the error.

(a) The area corresponding to the relative frequency lies to the left of a value above the mean. Add the area between the mean and the error value, found from the z value, to the area below the mean (.5).

$$.5000 + .3944 = .8944$$

(b) The applicable area lies to the right of a value below the mean. Add the area between the mean and the error value to the area above the mean (.5).

$$.5000 + .2734 = .7734$$

(c) The applicable area lies in the lower tail. Subtract the area between the mean and the error value from the entire area below the mean.

$$.5000 − .4938 = .0062$$

(d) The applicable area lies in the upper tail. Subtract the area between the mean and the error value from the entire area above the mean.

$$.5000 − .49977 = .00023$$

(e) The applicable area lies between two values that are on the same side of the mean. Subtract the smaller area obtained from the larger one.

$$.4599 − .4332 = .0267$$

(f) You solve this just like (e).

$$.1915 − .0987 = .0928$$

(g) You want to find the total area that lies in the designated upper and lower tails. Subtract the areas that lie between the error values and the mean individually from .5, and then add the results together.

$$(.5000 − .4974) + (.5000 − .2422) = .2604$$

(h) Both error values lie above the mean, but for the smaller value you want to find the area that extends all the way to the left. Add the area between the smaller value and the mean to the area below the mean, and subtract the area between the larger value and the mean from the entire area above the mean. Then add the results together.

$$(.5000 + .2422) + (.5000 − .2734) = .9688$$

PROBLEM 8-2 Find the following percentiles for the cash balance errors described in Problem 8-1.

  (a) 10th   (b) 25th   (c) 85th   (d) 95th   (e) 99th

Solution: Reading Table A in reverse, you should find the area *closest* to the stated percentile decimal. Then read the matching z value. Remember that for decimal values below .50, the z will be negative, and you will be looking for areas closest to .50 minus the percentile decimal. For decimal values above .50, the z will be positive, and you will be looking for areas closest to the percentile decimal minus .50. Since the mean is 0 and the standard deviation 1, the z values obtained will also be the percentile values for the cash balance errors. (a) $-\$1.28$ (b) $-\$.67$ (c) \$1.04   (d) \$1.64   (e) \$2.33

PROBLEM 8-3 The heights of men attending Near Miss University form a normally distributed population with a mean of 69″ and a standard deviation of 2″. One man is selected at random. Find the probability that his height falls in the following ranges.

  (a) between 69″ and 70.5″   (e) 68″ or shorter
  (b) between 65″ and 69″   (f) taller than 65″
  (c) 72″ or taller   (g) between 69.5″ and 70″
  (d) taller than 72″   (h) between 67.6″ and 68.2″

Solution: In evaluating the probabilities you first find the normal deviate values for the end point(s) of the respective interval or tail. Then use Table A to find the area that corresponds to each z value, and use the procedures detailed in Problem 8-1 to find the desired probabilities. It will help if for each case you sketch a normal curve on scratch paper and identify the area that corresponds.

(a)
$$z = \frac{69 - 69}{2} = 0 \quad \text{and} \quad z = \frac{70.5 - 69}{2} = .75$$

$$\Pr[69 \leqslant X \leqslant 70.5] = .2734$$

(b)
$$z = \frac{65 - 69}{2} = -2.00 \quad \text{and} \quad z = \frac{69 - 69}{2} = 0$$

$$\Pr[65 \leqslant X \leqslant 69] = .4772$$

(c)
$$z = \frac{72 - 69}{2} = 1.50 \qquad \Pr[X \geqslant 72] = .5000 - .4332 = .0668$$

(d) See (c). $\Pr[X > 72] = .0668$

(e)
$$z = \frac{68 - 69}{2} = -.50 \qquad \Pr[X \leqslant 68] = .5000 - .1915 = .3085$$

(f)
$$z = \frac{65 - 69}{2} = -2.00 \qquad \Pr[X > 65] = .5000 + .4772 = .9772$$

(g)
$$z = \frac{69.5 - 69}{2} = .25 \quad \text{and} \quad z = \frac{70 - 69}{2} = .50$$

$$\Pr[69.5 \leqslant X \leqslant 70] = .1915 - .0987 = .0928$$

(h)
$$z = \frac{67.6 - 69}{2} = -.70 \quad \text{and} \quad z = \frac{68.2 - 69}{2} = -.40$$

$$\Pr[67.6 \leqslant X \leqslant 68.2] = .2580 - .1554 = .1026$$

PROBLEM 8-4 The wrist circumference of adult males is normally distributed with a mean of $\mu = 6.85''$ and a standard deviation of $\sigma = .40''$.

  (a) Find the probabilities for the following possible wrist sizes of a randomly chosen man.
       (*1*) less than 8.00″   (*3*) between 5.75″ and 6.75″
       (*2*) between 6.50″ and 7.50″   (*4*) greater than 7.00″
  (b) Find the following percentiles:
       (*1*) 5th   (*2*) 10th   (*3*) 75th   (*4*) 95th

Solution: You solve (a) as you did Problem 8-3. For (b) you proceed as for Problem 8-2, except that you must convert the normal deviates to the corresponding dimension value using the expression $x = \mu + z\sigma$.

(a) *(1)*
$$z = \frac{8.00 - 6.85}{.40} = 2.88 \qquad \Pr[X < 8.00] = .5000 + .4980 = .9980$$

(2)
$$z = \frac{6.50 - 6.85}{.40} = -.88 \quad \text{and} \quad z = \frac{7.50 - 6.85}{.40} = 1.63$$

$$\Pr[6.50 \leqslant X \leqslant 7.50] = .3106 + .4484 = .7590$$

(3)
$$z = \frac{5.75 - 6.85}{.40} = -2.75 \quad \text{and} \quad z = \frac{6.75 - 6.85}{.40} = -.25$$

$$\Pr[5.75 \leqslant X \leqslant 6.75] = .4970 - .0987 = .3983$$

(4)
$$z = \frac{7.00 - 6.85}{.40} = .38 \qquad \Pr[X > 7.00] = .5000 - .1480 = .3520$$

(b) *(1)* $z = -1.64 \qquad 6.85'' - 1.64(.40'') = 6.194''$
(2) $z = -1.28 \qquad 6.85'' - 1.28(.40'') = 6.338''$
(3) $z = .67 \qquad 6.85'' + .67(.40'') = 7.118''$
(4) $z = 1.64 \qquad 6.85'' + 1.64(.40'') = 7.506''$

PROBLEM 8-5 The hand length of adult males is normally distributed with a mean of $\mu = 7.49''$ and a standard deviation of $\sigma = .34''$.

(a) Find the probabilities for the following possible hand sizes of a randomly chosen man.
  (1) less than 7.00''   *(3)* between 7.80'' and 8.20''
  (2) between 6.75'' and 7.25''   *(4)* greater than 8.00''
(b) Find the following percentiles:
  (1) 1st   *(2)* 10th   *(3)* 90th   *(4)* 99th

Solution: This problem follows the same pattern as Problem 8-4.

(a) *(1)*
$$z = \frac{7.00 - 7.49}{.34} = -1.44 \qquad \Pr[X < 7.00] = .5000 - .4251 = .0749$$

(2)
$$z = \frac{6.75 - 7.49}{.34} = -2.18 \quad \text{and} \quad z = \frac{7.25 - 7.49}{.34} = -.71$$

$$\Pr[6.75 \leqslant X \leqslant 7.25] = .4854 - .2612 = .2242$$

(3)
$$z = \frac{7.80 - 7.49}{.34} = .91 \quad \text{and} \quad z = \frac{8.20 - 7.49}{.34} = 2.09$$

$$\Pr[7.80 \leqslant X \leqslant 8.20] = .4817 - .3186 = .1631$$

(4)
$$z = \frac{8.00 - 7.49}{.34} = 1.50 \qquad \Pr[X > 8.00] = .5000 - .4332 = .0668$$

(b) *(1)* $z = -2.33 \qquad 7.49'' - 2.33(.34'') = 6.698''$
(2) $z = -1.28 \qquad 7.49'' - 1.28(.34'') = 7.055''$
(3) $z = 1.28 \qquad 7.49'' + 1.28(.34'') = 7.925''$
(4) $z = 2.33 \qquad 7.49'' + 2.33(.34'') = 8.282''$

PROBLEM 8-6 A random sample of 100 Old Ivy men is chosen, and their heights are determined. Assume that the population mean is 69.5'' and the standard deviation is 3''.

(a) Determine the standard error of $\bar{X}$.
(b) Determine the probability that the mean height for the sample falls in the following ranges.
  (1) between 70'' and 70.3''   *(4)* less than 68''
  (2) less than 69.5''   *(5)* between 69.4'' and 70.3''
  (3) greater than 72''

Solution:
(a) Since the sample is taken from a very large population (all male students at Old Ivy), you don't use the finite population correction factor. Thus,

$$\sigma_{\bar{X}} = \frac{3''}{\sqrt{100}} = .3''$$

(b) *(1)*

$$z = \frac{70 - 69.5}{.3} = 1.67 \quad \text{and} \quad z = \frac{70.3 - 69.5}{.3} = 2.67$$

$$\Pr[70 \leqslant \bar{X} \leqslant 70.3] = .4962 - .4525 = .0437$$

(2)

$$z = \frac{69.5 - 69.5}{.3} = 0 \qquad \Pr[\bar{X} < 69.5] = .5000$$

(3)

$$z = \frac{72 - 69.5}{.3} = 8.33$$

This z is too large for Table A, so the area between the mean and 8.33 is approximately .5000. Thus,

$$\Pr[\bar{X} > 72] = .5000 - .5000 = .0000 \text{ (approximately)}$$

(4)

$$z = \frac{68 - 69.5}{.3} = -5.00$$

Again, this z is too large for Table A, so the area between the mean and -5.00 is approximately .5000. Thus,

$$\Pr[\bar{X} < 68] = .5000 - .5000 = .0000 \text{ (approximately)}$$

(5)

$$z = \frac{69.4 - 69.5}{.3} = -.33 \quad \text{and} \quad z = \frac{70.3 - 69.5}{.3} = 2.67$$

$$\Pr[69.4 \leqslant \bar{X} \leqslant 70.3] = .1293 + .4962 = .6255$$

PROBLEM 8-7 A paint maker is testing a solvent to determine the average drying time of the paint. The population of drying times for individual swatches has an unknown mean μ, and some value must be assumed for the standard deviation. A sample of $n = 25$ swatches will be tested to determine drying times. The underlying population is of unlimited size. Find the probability that the sample mean drying time deviates from the unknown μ by no more than 1 hour, assuming that the standard deviation has the following values:

   (a) $\sigma = 2$ **(b)** $\sigma = 4$ **(c)** $\sigma = 8$ **(d)** $\sigma = 16$

Solution: The population size is unlimited, so you compute the standard error of $\bar{X}$ from $\sigma_{\bar{X}} = \sigma/\sqrt{n}$. In solving for z, $(x - \mu)$ is ± 1, since the problem states that the sample mean isn't more than 1 hour larger or smaller than the unknown μ. Once you find the area that corresponds to the z value, you must multiply the areas by 2, since the same area lies both above and below the mean.

(a)
$$\sigma_{\bar{X}} = 2/\sqrt{25} = .4 \qquad z = \pm 1/.4 = \pm 2.50$$
$$\Pr[\bar{X} = \mu \pm 1] = 2(.4938) = .9876$$

(b)
$$\sigma_{\bar{X}} = 4/\sqrt{25} = .8 \qquad z = \pm 1/.8 = \pm 1.25$$
$$\Pr[\bar{X} = \mu \pm 1] = 2(.3944) = .7888$$

(c)
$$\sigma_{\bar{X}} = 8/\sqrt{25} = 1.60 \qquad z = \pm 1/1.60 = \pm .63$$
$$\Pr[\bar{X} = \mu \pm 1] = 2(.2357) = .4714$$

(d)
$$\sigma_{\bar{X}} = 16/\sqrt{25} = 3.2 \qquad z = \pm 1/3.2 = \pm .31$$
$$\Pr[\bar{X} = \mu \pm 1] = 2(.1217) = .2434$$

PROBLEM 8-8 The unemployment rates experienced by $N = 210$ medium-sized cities in one year have a mean of $\mu = 7\%$ and a standard deviation of $\sigma = 2\%$. A random sample of 25 of these cities is selected.

   (a) Determine the standard error of the sample mean.
   (b) Find the probability that the sample mean
      (1) exceeds 8%   (3) is between 6.5% and 7.5%
      (2) is smaller than 6.5%   (4) is between 6.0% and 6.5%

Solution:
(a) You must compute the standard error of the sample mean using the finite population correction factor, since $N = 210$ isn't 10 times larger than $n = 25$.

$$\sigma_{\bar{X}} = \frac{2}{\sqrt{25}} \sqrt{\frac{210 - 25}{210 - 1}} = .376$$

(b) (1) $z = \dfrac{8 - 7}{.376} = 2.66$ $\Pr[\bar{X} > 8] = .5000 - .4961 = .0039$

(2) $z = \dfrac{6.5 - 7}{.376} = -1.33$ $\Pr[\bar{X} < 6.5] = .5000 - .4082 = .0918$

(3) $z = \dfrac{6.5 - 7}{.376} = -1.33$ and $z = \dfrac{7.5 - 7}{.376} = 1.33$

$$\Pr[6.5 \leqslant \bar{X} \leqslant 7.5] = 2(.4082) = .8164$$

(4) $z = \dfrac{6.0 - 7}{.376} = -2.66$ and $z = \dfrac{6.5 - 7}{.376} = -1.33$

$$\Pr[6.0 \leqslant \bar{X} \leqslant 6.5] = .4961 - .4082 = .0879$$

PROBLEM 8-9 The mean μ and standard deviation σ for accountants' salaries is unknown. A sample of $n = 25$ is taken at random from a population of accountants, and the sample mean is computed. Assuming that the population is of large size, find the probability that $\bar{X}$ falls within $\mu \pm \$500$ when

    (a) $\sigma = \$1,500$ (b) $\sigma = \$2,000$ (c) $\sigma = \$2,500$

Solution: This problem follows the pattern of Problem 8-7.

(a) $\sigma_{\bar{X}} = \$1,500/\sqrt{25} = \$300$ $z = \pm\$500/\$300 = \pm1.67$

           $\Pr[\bar{X} = \mu \pm \$500] = 2(.4525) = .9050$

(b) $\sigma_{\bar{X}} = \$2,000/\sqrt{25} = \$400$ $z = \pm\$500/\$400 = \pm1.25$

           $\Pr[\bar{X} = \mu \pm \$500] = 2(.3944) = .7888$

(c) $\sigma_{\bar{X}} = \$2,500/\sqrt{25} = 500$ $z = \pm\$500/\$500 = \pm1.00$

           $\Pr[\bar{X} = \mu \pm \$500] = 2(.3413) = .6826$

PROBLEM 8-10 The time that each payroll waits to be processed at a data service bureau is assumed to have a positively skewed distribution. A sample of 25 waiting times is collected. Both the mean and the standard deviation for individual waiting times are equal to .5 day. A large population size is assumed. Determine the probability that the sample mean waiting time

    (a) doesn't exceed .6 day   (c) equals .5 $\pm$ .1 day
    (b) is greater than .7 day   (d) is between .3 and .7 day

Solution: First, compute the standard error of $\bar{X}$:

$$\sigma_{\bar{X}} = \frac{.5}{\sqrt{25}} = .1 \text{ day}$$

(a) $z = \dfrac{.6 - .5}{.1} = 1.00$ $\Pr[\bar{X} \leqslant .6] = .5000 + .3413 = .8413$

(b) $z = \dfrac{.7 - .5}{.1} = 2.00$ $\Pr[\bar{X} > .7] = .5000 - .4772 = .0228$

(c)
$$z = \frac{.6 - .5}{.1} = 1.00 \quad \text{and} \quad z = \frac{.4 - .5}{.1} = -1.00$$

$$\Pr[.4 \leqslant \bar{X} \leqslant .6] = 2(.3413) = .6826$$

(d)
$$z = \frac{.3 - .5}{.1} = -2.00 \quad \text{and} \quad z = \frac{.7 - .5}{.1} = 2.00$$

$$\Pr[.3 \leqslant \bar{X} \leqslant .7] = 2(.4772) = .9544$$

PROBLEM 8-11 Consider operator reaction time to a warning signal that a chemical plant is experiencing significant drops in pressure. This variable is normally distributed with a mean of $\mu = 45$ seconds and a standard deviation of $\sigma = 8$ seconds. Find (*1*) the standard error of $\bar{X}$ and (*2*) the probability that $\bar{X}$ falls within $\mu \pm 1$ second when a random sample is taken of size

   (**a**) $n = 25$ (**b**) $n = 100$ (**c**) $n = 200$ (**d**) 500

Solution: This problem is similar to Problem 8-7, except that n rather than σ varies in computing the levels for $\sigma_{\bar{x}}$.

(a) (*1*) $\sigma_{\bar{x}} = 8/\sqrt{25} = 1.60$ $z = \pm 1/1.60 = \pm .63$

   (*2*) $\Pr[\bar{X} = \mu \pm 1] = 2(.2357) = .4714$

(b) (*1*) $\sigma_{\bar{x}} = 8/\sqrt{100} = .80$ $z = \pm 1/.80 = \pm 1.25$

   (*2*) $\Pr[\bar{X} = \mu \pm 1] = 2(.3944) = .7888$

(c) (*1*) $\sigma_{\bar{x}} = 8/\sqrt{200} = .566$ $z = \pm 1/.566 = \pm 1.77$

   (*2*) $\Pr[\bar{X} = \mu \pm 1] = 2(.4616) = .9232$

(d) (*1*) $\sigma_{\bar{x}} = 8/\sqrt{500} = .358$ $z = \pm 1/.358 = \pm 2.79$

   (*2*) $\Pr[\bar{X} = \mu \pm 1] = 2(.4974) = .9948$

PROBLEM 8-12 A cannery has automated filling equipment. To monitor the quantity of ingredients placed in cans, a random production sample is selected each hour, and the average weight $\bar{X}$ is determined. As long as the sample mean falls between 15.8 and 16.2 ounces, the operation continues; otherwise, the equipment is shut down and adjusted. Assuming that the true process mean μ is unknown and that the standard error of $\bar{X}$ is $\sigma_{\bar{x}} = .1$ ounce, determine the following probabilities.

   (**a**) The equipment is operating properly ($\mu = 16$ ounces), but it is adjusted anyway.
   (**b**) The equipment is overfilling ($\mu = 16.1$ ounces), but it isn't adjusted.
   (**c**) The equipment is underfilling ($\mu = 15.9$ ounces), and it is adjusted.

Solution: It will be quite helpful if you sketch a normal curve for each case and identify the applicable area. Note that each normal curve has a different center.

(a)
$$z = \frac{15.8 - 16}{.1} = -2.00 \quad \text{and} \quad z = \frac{16.2 - 16}{.1} = 2.00$$

$$\Pr[\bar{X} < 15.8 \text{ or } \bar{X} > 16.2] = 2(.5000 - .4772) = .0456$$

(b)
$$z = \frac{15.8 - 16.1}{.1} = -3.00 \quad \text{and} \quad z = \frac{16.2 - 16.1}{.1} = 1.00$$

$$\Pr[15.8 \leqslant \bar{X} \leqslant 16.2] = .49865 + .3413 = .83995$$

(c)
$$z = \frac{15.8 - 15.9}{.1} = -1.00 \quad \text{and} \quad z = \frac{16.2 - 15.9}{.1} = 3.00$$

$$\Pr[\bar{X} < 15.8 \text{ or } \bar{X} > 16.2] = (.5000 - .3413)$$
$$+ (.5000 - .49865) = .16005$$

PROBLEM 8-13 A telephone equipment manufacturer rejects any incoming shipment of switches in which the proportion of defectives in a sample of 25 switches tested exceeds .16. For each of the following shipments, use the normal approximation to estimate the probability for rejection.

	(a)	(b)	(c)	(d)
	$N = 200$	$N = 150$	$N = 250$	$N = 75$
	$\pi = .10$	$\pi = .12$	$\pi = .15$	$\pi = .18$

Solution: In each case you must first compute the standard error of P. Since the population sizes are small, use the finite population correction factor. It is given that $n = 25$, so since $.16 = 4/25 = r/n$, use $r = 4$. Since the probability is in the form $P > r/n$, check the equivalent form. It is $1 - \Pr[P \leqslant r/n]$, so you need make no changes in r/n when computing z.

(a)
$$\sigma_P = \sqrt{\frac{.10(.90)}{25}} \sqrt{\frac{200 - 25}{200 - 1}} = .0563 \qquad z = \frac{(4 + .5)/25 - .10}{.0563} = 1.42$$

$$\Pr[P > .16] = 1 - \Pr[P \leqslant 4/25] = 1 - (.5000 + .4222) = .0778$$

(b)
$$\sigma_P = \sqrt{\frac{.12(.88)}{25}} \sqrt{\frac{150 - 25}{150 - 1}} = .0595 \qquad z = \frac{(4 + .5)/25 - .12}{.0595} = 1.01$$

$$\Pr[P > .16] = 1 - \Pr[P \leqslant 4/25] = 1 - (.5000 + .3438) = .1562$$

(c)
$$\sigma_P = \sqrt{\frac{.15(.85)}{25}} \sqrt{\frac{250 - 25}{250 - 1}} = .0679 \qquad z = \frac{(4 + .5)/25 - .15}{.0679} = .44$$

$$\Pr[P > .16] = 1 - \Pr[P \leqslant 4/25] = 1 - (.5000 + .1700) = .3300$$

(d)
$$\sigma_P = \sqrt{\frac{.18(.82)}{25}} \sqrt{\frac{75 - 25}{75 - 1}} = .0632 \qquad z = \frac{(4 + .5)/25 - .18}{.0632} = 0$$

$$\Pr[P > .16] = 1 - \Pr[P \leqslant 4/25] = 1 - (.5000 - 0) = .5000$$

PROBLEM 8-14   A marketing researcher for Big Sky Enterprises believes that the proportion of persons favoring a new package design is $\pi = .6$. Suppose that a sample of $n = 100$ persons is selected at random from the entire market, which numbers in the millions. The sample proportion favoring the new design may be approximated by the normal distribution.

(a) Find the standard error of P.
(b) Assuming that the given parameter applies, determine the probability that 70% or more of the persons queried will favor the new package.
(c) Suppose that the parameter value is only $\pi = .57$.
  (1) Recompute the standard error of P.
  (2) Find the probability that 70% or more of the sample persons will favor the new design.

Solution: You may ignore the finite population correction factor in computing the standard error of P. Note that since the equivalent form of $\Pr[P \geqslant r/n]$ is $1 - \Pr[P \leqslant (r - 1)/n]$, you must compute the normal deviate using the value $(70 - 1)/100 = 69/100$ for r/n.

(a)
$$\sigma_P = \sqrt{\frac{.60(.40)}{100}} = .0490$$

(b)
$$z = \frac{(69 + .5)/100 - .60}{.0490} = 1.94$$

$$\Pr[P \geqslant .70] = 1 - \Pr[P \leqslant 69/100] = 1 - (.5000 + .4738) = .0262$$

(c) (1)
$$\sigma_P = \sqrt{\frac{.57(.43)}{100}} = .0495$$

(2)
$$z = \frac{(69 + .5)/100 - .57}{.0495} = 2.53$$

$$\Pr[P \geqslant .70] = 1 - \Pr[P \leqslant 69/100] = 1 - (.5000 + .4943) = .0057$$

PROBLEM 8-15   A buyer for Acme Brakes removes a random sample of 100 widgets from a shipment containing a total of 500 items. The true proportion of incorrectly sized widgets is unknown, although it is assumed that this quantity is .03. Determine the probabilities that the sample proportion of incorrectly sized widgets falls in the following ranges.

(a) $P \leqslant .05$ (b) $P \leqslant .02$ (c) $P > .04$ (d) $.02 \leqslant P \leqslant .03$

Solution: Be sure that you identify the proper matching area when making the normal approximation. You should apply the finite population correction factor in computing the standard error of P.

$$\sigma_P = \sqrt{\frac{.03(.97)}{100}} \sqrt{\frac{500 - 100}{500 - 1}} = .0153$$

(a) The probability is in the form $\Pr[P \leqslant r/n]$, so the form doesn't need to be changed.

$$z = \frac{(5 + .5)/100 - .03}{.0153} = 1.63$$

$$\Pr[P \leqslant .05] = \Pr[P \leqslant 5/100] = .5000 + .4484 = .9484$$

(b) Again, the form of the probability doesn't need to be changed.

$$z = \frac{(2 + .5)/100 - .03}{.0153} = -.33$$

$$\Pr[P \leqslant .02] = \Pr[P \leqslant 2/100] = .5000 - .1293 = .3707$$

(c) Since the probability is in the form $\Pr[P > r/n]$, you must use the equivalent form $1 - \Pr[P \leqslant r/n]$. Thus, you need to make no changes in r/n before computing z.

$$z = \frac{(4 + .5)/100 - .03}{.0153} = .98$$

$$\Pr[P > .04] = 1 - \Pr[P \leqslant 4/100] = 1 - (.5000 + .3365) = .1635$$

(d) Since the probability is in the form $\Pr[r_1/n \leqslant P \leqslant r_2/n]$, you must use the equivalent form $\Pr[P \leqslant r_2/n] - \Pr[P \leqslant (r_1 - 1)/n]$. Thus, you need to compute the z for $\Pr[P < .02]$ as $\Pr[P \leqslant (r_1 - 1)/n]$, or $\Pr[P \leqslant .01]$.

$$z = \frac{(3 + .5)/100 - .03}{.0153} = .33 \quad \text{and} \quad z = \frac{(1 + .5)/100 - .03}{.0153} = -.98$$

$$\Pr[.02 \leqslant P \leqslant .03] = \Pr[P \leqslant 3/100] - \Pr[P \leqslant 1/100]$$

$$= (.5000 + .1293) - (.5000 - .3365)$$

$$= .4658$$

PROBLEM 8-16   A production process is designed to produce only 10% defective items. Once each day, a sample of 100 items is chosen and the proportion of defectives P is determined. If this value lies below .15, production is continued. Otherwise, production is stopped for maintenance.

(a) Assuming that the process is operating as designed, determine the probability that operations will be continued.

(b) Suppose that the process is producing too many defectives, at the rate of 20% (but management doesn't know this). Find the probability that the process will be stopped for maintenance.

Solution: Again, it will help to sketch the normal curves and identify for each the required area. Whenever π changes, you must recompute the standard error of P. The population is of unlimited size, so you don't use the finite population correction factor.

(a) Here, $\pi = .10$. Production continues if $P < .15$. You must therefore use the equivalent form $\Pr[P \leqslant (r - 1)/n]$ in finding the probability. Thus, you need to change P to $(r - 1)/n$, or $(15 - 1)/100$, or $14/100$, to compute z.

$$\sigma_P = \sqrt{\frac{.10(.90)}{100}} = .03$$

$$z = \frac{(14 + .5)/100 - .10}{.03} = 1.50$$

$$\Pr[\text{continue}] = \Pr[P < .15] = \Pr[P \leqslant 14/100]$$

$$= .5000 + .4332 = .9332$$

(b) Here, $\pi = .20$. Production is stopped if $P \geqslant .15$. You must therefore use the equivalent form $1 - \Pr[P \leqslant (r-1)/n]$ in finding the probability. Again, use $(r-1)/n$, or 14/100, to compute z.

$$\sigma_P = \sqrt{\frac{.20(.80)}{100}} = .04$$

$$z = \frac{(14 + .5)/100 - .20}{.04} = -1.38$$

$$\Pr[\text{stop}] = \Pr[P \geqslant .15] = (1 - \Pr[P \leqslant 14/100]$$
$$= 1 - (.5000 - .4162) = .9162$$

PROBLEM 8-17 A quality control inspector checks a sample from each outgoing shipment of video display terminals. In one large shipment, 5% of the units are defective, though the inspector doesn't know this. She chooses a sample of 100 terminals to test. If 7% or more of the tested units are defective, she will hold the entire shipment for further testing. Find the probability that the inspector holds the shipment.

Solution: This problem is similar in form to Problem 8-16. Use $\pi = .05$, and ignore the finite population correction factor. Production is stopped if $P \geqslant .07$. You must therefore use the equivalent form $1 - \Pr[P \leqslant (r-1)/n]$ in finding the probability. Thus, you need to use $(r-1)/n$, or $(7-1)/100$, or 6/100, to compute z.

$$\sigma_P = \sqrt{\frac{.05(.95)}{100}} = .022$$

$$z = \frac{(6 + .5)/100 - .05}{.022} = .68$$

$$\Pr[\text{holds}] = \Pr[P \geqslant .07] = 1 - \Pr[P \leqslant 6/100]$$
$$= 1 - (.5000 + .2518) = .2482$$

PROBLEM 8-18 A robot that shapes metal needs overhauling if it is out of tolerance on 4.5% of the items processed, and it is operating satisfactorily if it is off on only .8% of its output.

A test is performed involving 50 sample items. If the sample proportion of out-of-tolerance items is greater than .02, the robot will be overhauled. Otherwise it will be allowed to continue to operate.

(a) What is the probability that a satisfactory robot will be overhauled unnecessarily?
(b) What is the probability that a robot in need of overhauling will be left in operation?

Solution: This problem follows the pattern of Problem 8-16. The population is of unlimited size, so ignore the finite population correction factor. Since $n = 50$, $r/n = .02 = 1/50$, so $r = 1$.
(a) Here, $\pi = .008$. The robot is overhauled if $P > .02$ so you must use the equivalent form $1 - \Pr[P \leqslant r/n]$. This requires no change in r/n when computing z.

$$\sigma_P = \sqrt{\frac{.008(.992)}{50}} = .0126$$

$$z = \frac{(1 + .5)/50 - .008}{.0126} = 1.75$$

$$\Pr[\text{overhauled}] = \Pr[P > .02] = 1 - \Pr[P \leqslant 1/50]$$
$$= 1 - (.5000 + .4599) = .0401$$

(b) Here, $\pi = .045$. The robot is left in operation if $P \leqslant .02$, so you don't need to work with an equivalent form.

$$\sigma_P = \sqrt{\frac{.045(.955)}{50}} = .0293$$

$$z = \frac{(1 + .5)/50 - .045}{.0293} = -.51$$

$$\Pr[\text{left in operation}] = \Pr[P \leqslant .02] = \Pr[P \leqslant 1/50]$$
$$= .5000 - .1950 = .3050$$

PROBLEM 8-19 The manufacturer of WeeTees is considering reformulating the product. The cereal currently has 30% of the total market. The value .30 is assumed to apply to the proportion of all persons in the market who will favor the reformulated product. The final decision for reformulating will be based on the results of a sample taste test involving 100 randomly chosen persons representing the entire market. If more than 25% of the sample likes the new formulation, it will be marketed.

(a) Suppose that the new product tastes so horrible that only 15% of the population likes it. Find the probability that the new formulation will be adopted.

(b) Suppose that the new WeeTees is so luscious that its market share would immediately jump to 40% if it is reformulated. Find the probability that it doesn't get adopted in spite of that.

Solution: This problem follows the pattern of Problem 8-16. The population is of unlimited size, so you ignore the finite population correction factor.

(a) Here, $\pi = .15$. The new cereal is adopted if $P > 25/100$, so you use the equivalent form $1 - \Pr[P \leqslant r/n]$. This requires no change in r/n when computing z.

$$\sigma_P = \sqrt{\frac{.15(.85)}{100}} = .036$$

$$z = \frac{(25 + .5)/100 - .15}{.036} = 2.92$$

$$\Pr[\text{adopt new}] = \Pr[P > .25] = 1 - \Pr[P \leqslant 25/100]$$
$$= 1 - (.5000 + .4982) = .0018$$

(b) Here $\pi = .40$. The new cereal won't be adopted if $P \leqslant 25/100$, so you don't need to use an equivalent form to find the probability.

$$\sigma_P = \sqrt{\frac{.40(.60)}{100}} = .049$$

$$z = \frac{(25 + .5)/100 - .40}{.049} = -2.96$$

$$\Pr[\text{not adopt new}] = \Pr[P \leqslant .25] = \Pr[P \leqslant 25/100]$$
$$= .5000 - .4985 = .0015$$

MIDTERM EXAMINATION

1. The following sample data were collected.

$$2 \quad 3 \quad 4 \quad 5 \quad 5 \quad 8 \quad 9 \quad 12$$

Determine the values for (a) the sample mean; (b) the sample variance; (c) the sample standard deviation; and (d) the sample median.

2. The following frequency distribution is for a group of car-battery lifetimes. For each interval determine (a) the relative frequency and (b) the cumulative relative frequency.

Class interval (months)	Frequency	(a) Relative frequency	(b) Cumulative relative frequency
25—under 30	38		
30—under 35	42		
35—under 40	12		
40—under 45	6		
45—under 50	2		
	100		

3. You have drawn a card from a fully shuffled deck of 52 ordinary playing cards. Find

(a) Pr[ace|red]
(b) Pr[ace of diamonds|red]
(c) Pr[diamond|red]
(d) Pr[face card|red]

4. A quality control inspector accepts only 5% of all bad items and rejects only 1% of all good items. Overall production quality is such that only 90% of items to be inspected later are good.

(a) Using the above percentages as probabilities for the next items inspected, find
  (1) Pr[accept|bad]   (2) Pr[reject|good]   (3) Pr[good]
(b) Construct the joint probability table.

5. Six of the ten employees of the Anchorage branch of XYZ Corporation are men. Suppose that two employees are successively selected at random without replacement.

(a) Find the probability that the two employees are of the same sex.
(b) Are the events "first person is a man" and "second person is a man" independent?

6. The following grade-point data apply for a group of students.

$$\text{Bob B (3)} \quad \text{Ed A (4)} \quad \text{Ann C (2)} \quad \text{Sue B (3)}$$

A random sample of two students is selected without replacement. Construct the sampling distribution for the sample mean grade points.

7. Sixty percent of the employees at a certain office are women. During the company picnic, there will be separate drawings for three separate prizes. Assuming that each person's name is represented exactly once in each drawing, find the probabilities that

(a) all prizes are won by women.
(b) men take all prizes.
(c) at least one prize is won by a man.
(d) women win more prizes than men.

8. A machine used to fill jars of instant coffee is shut down for adjustment whenever a mean of 25 sample jars is more than half an ounce under or over the intended mean of 32 ounces for a perfectly adjusted machine. The filling process has a standard deviation of 1 ounce per jar.

(a) What is the probability that the machine will be shut down when it is perfectly adjusted?

(b) What is the probability that the machine will be shut down when it overfills each jar by an average of 1 ounce?

ANSWERS TO MIDTERM EXAMINATION

1. (a) 6.0 (b) 11.43 (c) 3.38 (d) 5

2.

Class interval (months)	Frequency	**(a)** Relative frequency	**(b)** Cumulative relative frequency
25—under 30	38	.38	.38
30—under 35	42	.42	.80
35—under 40	12	.12	.92
40—under 45	6	.06	.98
45—under 50	2	.02	1.00
	100		

3. (a) 1/13 (b) 1/26 (c) 1/2 (d) 3/13

4. (a) (*1*) .05 (*2*) .01 (*3*) .90

(b)

Quality	Inspector action		Marginal probability
	Accept	Reject	
Good	.891	.009	.900
Bad	.005	.095	.100
Marginal probability	.896	.104	1.000

5. (a) .47 (b) No

6.

$\bar{x}$	$\Pr[\bar{X} = \bar{x}]$
2.50	1/3
3.00	1/3
3.50	1/3
	1

7. (a) .216 (b) .064 (c) .784 (d) .648

8. (a) .0124 (b) .9938

9 STATISTICAL ESTIMATION

THIS CHAPTER IS ABOUT

☑ **Estimators and Estimates**
☑ **Interval Estimates of the Mean**
☑ **Small Sample Statistics: Student *t* Distribution**
☑ **Interval Estimates of the Proportion**

Modern sampling investigations primarily involve **inferential statistics**, which generalizes about unknown populations from known sample results. The simplest form of inferential statistics is **estimation**, where a value computed from sample data represents the value of one or more population parameters.

9-1. Estimators and Estimates

Estimates of population parameters are ordinarily based on the observed level of their sample counterparts. Thus, μ is generally estimated by the computed value for $\bar{X}$, σ^2 by s^2, and π by P. The statistical measures themselves are **estimators**, which must be distinguished from specific numerical values or **estimates**.

A. Several criteria establish the suitability of an estimator.

The favored estimators have been chosen for their desirable properties. A suitable estimator falls into one or more of the following categories.

1. **Unbiased estimators:** A statistic is an **unbiased estimator** if its expected value equals the target parameter. This is a property shared by $\bar{X}$, s^2, and P:

$$E(\bar{X}) = \mu$$
$$E(s^2) = \sigma^2$$
$$E(P) = \pi$$

On the average, an unbiased estimator equals the parameter it is estimating.

2. **Consistent estimators:** A statistic whose precision and reliability improves as sample size is increased is a **consistent estimator**. The standard error of such a statistic becomes smaller as n becomes larger. You know that this property applies to $\bar{X}$ and P, since $\sigma_{\bar{X}} = \sigma/\sqrt{n}$ and $\sigma_P = \sqrt{\pi(1-\pi)/n}$ both decrease when the divisor n increases.

3. **Efficient estimators:** Any quantity providing greater precision and reliability than another statistic computed from a sample of the same size is a more **efficient estimator**. The more efficient estimator will have a smaller standard error. Mathematically, it can be shown that the sample mean is more efficient than the sample median. This feature makes $\bar{X}$ more desirable as an estimator of μ.

4. **Maximum likelihood estimators:** The most efficient estimator among all the unbiased ones is the **maximum likelihood estimator**. The sampling distribution of such an estimator approaches the normal distribution as the sample size becomes large. The sample mean is an example of a maximum likelihood estimator.

B. There are two types of estimates.

Statistical estimates take two basic forms.

1. **Point estimates:** You are probably most familiar with the **point estimate**. For example, you may recall such statements as the following:

   "The mean height of adult males is 5′9″."

   "The proportion of voters approving the President is .40."

   "Our car averages 35 miles per gallon in highway driving."

   To be statistically valid, each of the values in these statements must have been obtained in a sampling investigation where the respective findings gave the following computed values: $\bar{X} = 5′9″$, $P = .40$, and $\bar{X} = 35$ mpg.

2. **Interval estimates:** A sounder way to report findings is to use the **interval estimate**. This type of estimate places the unknown parameter between two limits. Consider the following examples:

   5′8″–5′10″ for the mean height μ of adult males

   .35–.45 for the proportion π of voters approving the President

   28.75–39.23 for the mean gasoline mileage μ

C. The interval estimate has important advantages.

An interval estimate acknowledges that the sampling procedure is prone to some error, so that any computed statistic may fall above or below its population parameter target.

One drawback to point estimates is that too often they are assumed to be precise and correct. Indeed, lay persons will often believe them to be the levels of the population parameters themselves. You should by now know better! Nevertheless, you will encounter occasions where a point estimate is the preferred form.

D. Interval estimates can be expressed in various formats.

There are several ways to symbolically represent the interval estimate of the mean. The one adopted in this book is an *inequality*. For example, the population mean height for a group of men would be reported in the form

$$5′8″ \leqslant \mu \leqslant 5′10″$$

Some books favor "strict" inequalities, using $<$ instead of $\leqslant$. Another method is to state the endpoints only—either in parentheses, (5′8″, 5′10″), or with a dash, 5′8″–5′10″.

It is often convenient to adopt the notation for measurement tolerances, really a more compact form of the inequality. This notation applies to most interval estimates, which are usually symmetrical around a point estimator midpoint. For example, the inequality $5′8″ \leqslant \mu \leqslant 5′10″$ can be represented equivalently as

$$\mu = 5′9″ \pm 1″$$

9-2. Interval Estimates of the Mean

Let's begin with making estimates of the population mean. In doing so you will become familiar with concepts useful in estimating any parameter.

A. Precision and credibility are important features of interval estimates.

There are two considerations in establishing the endpoints of an interval estimate. One is the *level of precision* obtained. The other involves the *credibility* of the estimate. You can improve each of these features at the expense of the other, but you can attain improvements in *both* precision and credibility only by increasing the quality of the sample itself.

EXAMPLE 9-1: CREDIBILITY VERSUS PRECISION—WHAT IS THE AVERAGE HEIGHT OF MARLBOROUGH MEN?

Suppose you are asked to construct an interval estimate of the mean height of adult males in Marlborough County. You would obviously agree that the following estimate is totally believable:

$$4′ \leqslant \mu \leqslant 8′$$

Indeed, almost any knowledgable person would accept it as true regardless of what (if any) sample evidence were obtained.

You could take a sample of size 1, measure that person, and from your finding report a very precise result, such as the following:

$$5'8.33'' \leqslant \mu \leqslant 5'8.34''$$

Although precise to one-hundredth of an inch, this result is not very likely to be true and would be believed by few people.

Although totally credible, the first interval is too wide to be of any practical use. A narrower, more precise interval would be mandatory. The second interval is very precise, but not credible. It is useless as well.

B. The interval estimate is referred to as a confidence interval.

You make the statistical estimate *after* collecting the sample data. The value of the sample mean $\bar{X}$ is at that time a known computed value. Probabilities no longer apply to $\bar{X}$. The population mean μ is still unknown, and it remains uncertain whether or not an interval centered on $\bar{X}$ will actually contain μ. In traditional statistics, no probability values are assigned to the possible levels for μ. Rather, it is common practice to instead assign a **confidence level** to the interval estimate that is obtained.

Confidence levels are expressed as percentages like 90%, 95%, or 99%. The confidence level indicates how often you will find a similarly obtained interval that does indeed contain the true value of the unknown population parameter within its limits. The interval itself is called a **confidence interval**.

You may use the following expression to construct a 95% confidence interval estimate of μ.

95% confidence interval estimate of the mean

$$\mu = \bar{X} \pm 1.96 \frac{s}{\sqrt{n}} \qquad \text{or} \qquad \bar{X} - 1.96 \frac{s}{\sqrt{n}} \leqslant \mu \leqslant \bar{X} + 1.96 \frac{s}{\sqrt{n}}$$

This expression applies when the population size is large in relation to n and when n itself is large. (These requirements are addressed later.)

To illustrate how you would construct such an interval estimate, consider one investigator's sampling study of supermarket operations. Using sample data collected with a stopwatch, she estimated the mean time that persons waited at the checkout stands. She observed $n = 100$ customers, and from their times spent in line she computed $\bar{X} = 12.35$ minutes and $s = 1.38$ minutes. Substituting these values into the expression for the confidence interval estimate, she obtained

$$\mu = 12.35 \pm 1.96 \frac{1.38}{\sqrt{100}} = 12.35 \pm .27 \text{ min.}$$

You can express this equivalently as

$$12.35 - .27 \leqslant \mu \leqslant 12.35 + .27 \text{ min.}$$

or

$$12.08 \leqslant \mu \leqslant 12.62 \text{ min.}$$

C. The confidence interval for the mean is related to the normal distribution.

The value 1.96 is related to the normal curve. The area between the center and a point lying $z = 1.96$ standard deviations above it is .4750 (see Table A in the Appendix). Twice this quantity is .9500, which indicates that for a normally distributed variable, 95% of the possible values will lie within 1.96 standard deviations above or below the mean.

In Chapter 8 you found that $\bar{X}$ tends to be a normally distributed random variable. Although the normal curve for $\bar{X}$ really only applies before the sample results are known, statisticians still use the normal curve in constructing and interpreting confidence intervals for the mean.

To properly interpret the confidence interval for the supermarket study, suppose the researcher conducts 100 similar experiments. Each hypothetical experiment involves the same number of stopwatch observations and results in somewhat different findings, with different values computed for $\bar{X}$ and s. When the researcher finds the confidence intervals from all of those hypothetical experiments, about 95% of the intervals will contain the true μ. But about 5% of the intervals will have endpoints falling totally to one side, above or below the true level for μ.

The statistician's dilemma is that there is no way to tell if the resulting interval is correct.

D. There are important considerations in constructing confidence intervals.

Statisticians have considerable leeway in setting the framework for their estimates.

1. **Choosing the level of confidence:** As an investigator, you will pick the level of confidence. You want your target audience to believe your results, and generally 90% is the lowest level encountered in practice. If you want to raise or lower the confidence level, it is only necessary to change the constant term. Since this constant corresponds to a particular area under the normal curve, it is a *normal deviate value* and will be denoted by the letter z. The following constants apply for the more common confidence levels.

Level of confidence	Applicable constant z
90%	1.64
95%	1.96
99%	2.57
99.9%	3.30

The greater the confidence level, the bigger will be the value of z, making the confidence interval wider.

EXAMPLE 9-2: ESTIMATING MEAN SALARY OF MARKETING GRADUATES

As a class research project, one student conducted a study of salaries of recent marketing graduates. He received completed financial questionnaires from 42 randomly chosen persons. After arranging the data, he computed $\bar{X} = \$17,300$ and $s = \$615$.

Desiring a high level of confidence, he constructed the following 99.9% confidence interval, replacing $z = 1.96$ by $z = 3.30$ in the confidence interval expression.

$$\mu = \$17,300 \pm 3.30 \frac{\$615}{\sqrt{42}} = \$17,300 \pm \$313$$

which can be expressed equivalently as

$$\$16,987 \leqslant \mu \leqslant \$17,613$$

A friend thought that the interval was too wide to be useful, since it overlapped with the interval she had found for management graduates. He therefore narrowed his estimate to an interval less than half as wide, achieved by using $z = 1.64$ instead:

$$\mu = \$17,300 \pm 1.64 \frac{\$615}{\sqrt{42}} = \$17,300 \pm \$156$$

or

$$\$17,144 \leqslant \mu \leqslant \$17,456$$

Although considerably tighter, the second estimate has only a 90% confidence level. It is less credible than the first.

---

2. **Picking the sample size:** You can resolve the conflict between precision and credibility by increasing the sample size. This results in a narrower confidence interval and thus

increases the precision of the estimate. As an illustration, suppose that in another store the supermarket observer collects $n = 250$ checkout waiting times, from which she computes $\bar{X} = 9.54$ minutes and $s = 1.27$ minutes. (Her new sample standard deviation is very close to the value found in her first investigation.) She obtains the following 95% confidence interval estimate of μ:

$$\mu = 9.54 \pm 1.96 \, \frac{1.27}{\sqrt{250}} = 9.54 \pm .16 \text{ minutes}$$

The second sample provides a precision of $\pm .16$ minute, considerably better than the $\pm .27$ achieved in the original investigation. Although partly due to a smaller s, the improved precision mainly results from the greater sample size.

3. **Balancing cost and estimate quality:** Of course, a bigger n requires more data collection time and resources. Only the investigator can decide if improved estimate quality is worth the added cost. Often, n is dictated by budgetary considerations, giving the analyst leeway only to trade precision against credibility.

E. The researcher must adjust for small population sizes.

By now you are familiar with treating the small population as a special case. When constructing confidence interval estimates of the mean, you must incorporate the finite population correction factor.

Confidence interval estimate of the mean (small population)

$$\mu = \bar{X} \pm z \, \frac{s}{\sqrt{n}} \sqrt{\frac{N - n}{N - 1}}$$

or

$$\bar{X} - z \, \frac{s}{\sqrt{n}} \sqrt{\frac{N - n}{N - 1}} \leqslant \mu \leqslant \bar{X} + z \, \frac{s}{\sqrt{n}} \sqrt{\frac{N - n}{N - 1}}$$

You ordinarily ignore the finite population correction factor whenever N is more than 10 times the sample size. In those cases, the confidence interval expression given earlier applies.

To illustrate, suppose you collect $n = 100$ 16-oz. cans at random from a shipment of 4 gross ($N = 576$). You find the mean content weight to be $\bar{X} = 16.1$ oz. with a standard deviation of $s = .2$ oz. To construct a 90% confidence interval estimate of the true mean content weight μ of the shipment, use $z = 1.64$. You get

$$\mu = 16.1 \pm 1.64 \, \frac{.2}{\sqrt{100}} \sqrt{\frac{576 - 100}{576 - 1}} = 16.1 \pm .03 \text{ oz.}$$

which reduces to

$$16.07 \leqslant \mu \leqslant 16.13 \text{ oz.}$$

9-3. Small Sample Statistics: Student t Distribution

Recall that the normal distribution ordinarily represents the sampling distribution of $\bar{X}$. The constant z used in constructing confidence intervals for the mean reflects that fact. But the normal approximation requires a given value for σ, which like μ is usually an *unknown* quantity. Ordinarily you have to use the computed s as a point estimate of σ.

An additional source of uncertainty is present when you must estimate both μ and σ. The normal distribution can work poorly when you use both $\bar{X}$ and s as estimators.

A. For small-sized samples, you should apply the Student t distribution instead of the normal distribution.

When the population standard deviation is unknown, you should use the following expression to establish statistical procedures.

Student *t* statistic

$$t = \frac{\bar{X} - \mu}{s/\sqrt{n}}$$

Before the data are collected, *t* is a random variable having the **Student *t* distribution**. Figure 9-1 shows the shape of the density curve for this distribution. Note the superficial resemblance to a normal curve.

Figure 9-1   The Student *t* Distribution.

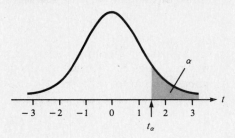

There are several distinct Student *t* distributions. Each of these is specified by a single parameter, the **number of degrees of freedom**.

- For applications involving *t*, the number of degrees of freedom equals $n - 1$.

Table B in the Appendix applies to the Student *t* distribution family. A portion of this table is reproduced here.

Degrees of freedom	Upper-tail area α		
	$\cdots$ .05	.025	.01 $\cdots$
$\vdots$		$\vdots$	
19	1.729	2.093	2.539
20	1.725	2.086	**2.528**
21	1.721	2.080	2.518
22	1.717	2.074	2.508
23	1.714	2.069	2.500
24	**1.711**	2.064	2.492
25	1.708	2.060	2.485
26	1.706	2.056	2.479
$\vdots$		$\vdots$	

A separate row is provided for each number of degrees of freedom. A column is provided for each of several common *upper-tail areas*. The symbol α (lowercase Greek *alpha*) represents any given upper-tail area. The entries in the body of the table are the **critical values**, denoted as t_α, corresponding to a particular α and a specific number of degrees of freedom. The area above t_α is equal to α.

When the number of degrees of freedom is 20 and the upper-tail area is $\alpha = .01$, you obtain the entry $t_{.01} = 2.528$ from the table. This tells you that from repeated sampling experiments, each involving *n* observations, only 1% of the samples will provide values of *t* that are greater than this critical value.

The Student *t* distribution tends to coincide with the normal distribution for large sample sizes.

- You will ordinarily use the Student *t* distribution only when *n* is less than 30. For larger sample sizes apply the normal distribution—even when σ remains unknown.

B. When the sample size is small, use critical values for *t* to construct confidence intervals for the mean.

A procedure similar to the one used when *n* is large applies for constructing confidence intervals from small-sized samples. The only difference is that you use a critical value for *t* instead of *z*. To compute a $100(1 - \alpha)\%$ confidence interval for μ, use the following expression.

Confidence interval estimate of the mean (small sample size)

$$\mu = \bar{X} \pm t_{\alpha/2} \frac{s}{\sqrt{n}} \quad \text{or} \quad \bar{X} - t_{\alpha/2} \frac{s}{\sqrt{n}} \leqslant \mu \leqslant \bar{X} + t_{\alpha/2} \frac{s}{\sqrt{n}}$$

Although the excluded area is α, half applies to the lower tail and half to the upper tail. The critical value is therefore $t_{\alpha/2}$.

- You ordinarily use this expression whenever n is less than 30. For larger sample sizes, replace $t_{\alpha/2}$ with the corresponding normal deviate z.

To illustrate the procedure, suppose that you want to estimate the mean number of back-ordered items of a particular product. Using a sample of $n = 25$ accounts, you find that $\bar{X} = 10.0$ and $s = 5.0$. The number of degrees of freedom is $n - 1 = 24$. You will construct a 90% or $100(1 - .10)\%$ confidence interval for μ. Using $\alpha = .10$, so that $\alpha/2 = .05$, the critical value is $t_{.05} = 1.711$. Substituting values into the expression for the confidence interval estimate, you have

$$\mu = 10.0 \pm 1.711 \frac{5.0}{\sqrt{25}} = 10.0 \pm 1.7$$

or

$$8.3 \leqslant \mu \leqslant 11.7$$

C. Small sample sizes are sometimes necessary.

You might wonder why statisticians even bother with small sample sizes. When there is a choice, they prefer to take samples much larger than 30. But sampling can be expensive, especially when lengthy tests involve human subjects. And sometimes rare events, such as accidents, are treated as sample evidence; in those cases the investigator has no control over the level of n.

EXAMPLE 9-3: FINDING THE MEAN AIR-SEARCH TIME

An FAA statistician estimated the mean time taken by search teams to locate downed aircraft. In one particular region there were $n = 10$ recent accidents for which data were available. Treating these data as a random sample from the population of all potential accident search time, she computed $\bar{X} = 7.8$ hours and $s = 5.9$ hours. She desired a 95% confidence level in estimating the unknown population mean. For $10 - 1 = 9$ degrees of freedom, Table B provides the critical value $t_{.025} = 2.262$. She determined the following 95% confidence interval estimate for μ:

$$\mu = 7.8 \pm 2.262 \frac{5.9}{\sqrt{10}} = 7.8 \pm 4.2 \text{ hrs.}$$

or

$$3.6 \leqslant \mu \leqslant 12.0 \text{ hrs.}$$

The statistician wasn't satisfied with the imprecision (width) of this interval estimate. But it was the best she could do, given the small sample size.

9-4. Interval Estimates of the Proportion

Estimation of the population proportion π follows the same pattern encountered with μ. Again, the procedure rests on the normal approximation.

A. The interval estimate is based on the observed sample proportion.

The following expression for the interval estimate uses the normal deviate z, which matches the desired level of confidence.

Confidence interval estimate of the proportion

$$\pi = P \pm z \sqrt{\frac{P(1 - P)}{n}} \quad \text{or} \quad P - z \sqrt{\frac{P(1 - P)}{n}} \leqslant \pi \leqslant P + z \sqrt{\frac{P(1 - P)}{n}}$$

Suppose that you want to estimate the true proportion of persons who regularly eat oatmeal for breakfast. You get a random collection of $n = 100$ responses. Out of these there are 23 positive responses, so that $P = 23/100 = .23$ is the sample proportion of persons eating that type of cereal. Using $z = 2.57$, you construct the following 99% confidence interval.

$$\pi = .23 \pm 2.57 \sqrt{\frac{.23(1 - .23)}{100}} = .23 \pm .11$$

which reduces to

$$.12 \leqslant \pi \leqslant .34$$

You don't know whether π actually falls between .12 and .34. Rather, you know that if you repeated the experiment many times, each time computing a new P, then about 99% of the intervals constructed in this fashion would contain the true π (the value that you can never know without taking a census of the population).

B. The procedure must be modified for small populations.

When the population is small (generally, whenever N is less than 10 times n), the finite population correction factor should be used.

Confidence interval estimate of the proportion (small population)

$$\pi = P \pm z \sqrt{\frac{P(1 - P)}{n}} \sqrt{\frac{N - n}{N - 1}}$$

SUMMARY

Estimation is the simplest form of inferential statistics, which uses known sample evidence to draw conclusions regarding unknown population characteristics. An *estimate* is a numerical value assigned to the unknown population parameter. In statistical investigations, the computed value of a sample statistic serves as the estimate. That statistic is referred to as the *estimator* of the unknown parameter.

There are several properties that are desirable for estimators. One is *unbiasedness*, so that the expected value of the estimator is equal to the parameter being estimated. A *consistent* estimator achieves improved reliability and precision as the sample size becomes larger. The more *efficient* of two estimators reaches the investigator's reliability and precision goals with the smaller sample size. *Maximum likelihood* estimators are the most efficient of the unbiased estimators.

Estimates take two forms. The *point estimate* is a single numerical quantity. Statisticians prefer the *interval estimate*, which acknowledges that some sampling error is unavoidable. The statistical art balances precision (interval width) against credibility while at the same time not devoting too many resources to collecting the sample data.

Interval estimates are qualified by a *confidence level,* a value stating how often the estimation procedure would provide a truthful solution if it were conducted over and over again with new samples. The estimate itself is called a *confidence interval*. A confidence interval estimate of the population mean is centered on the computed $\bar{X}$.

There are three main ways for finding the endpoints of a confidence interval for μ. When the sample size is large ($n \geqslant 30$), use a normal deviate value z:

$$\mu = \bar{X} \pm z \frac{s}{\sqrt{n}}$$

Apply the finite population correction factor for *populations* of small size N:

$$\mu = \bar{X} \pm z\,\frac{s}{\sqrt{n}}\sqrt{\frac{N-n}{N-1}}$$

For *samples* of small size n, use the critical value $t_{\alpha/2}$ for the *Student t distribution* instead of z.

$$\mu = \bar{X} \pm t_{\alpha/2}\,\frac{s}{\sqrt{n}}$$

The Student t distribution is characterized by a single parameter, the *number of degrees of freedom*. Its density function provides a bell-shaped curve resembling the normal curve. It applies to the random variable

$$t = \frac{\bar{X} - \mu}{s/\sqrt{n}}$$

which involves two uncertain quantities, $\bar{X}$ and s. The Student t allows us to make inferences about the mean when the population standard deviation σ is unknown. The normal curve for $\bar{X}$, on the other hand, is based on a stipulated value for σ. When the sample size is large, the normal and Student t distributions tend to coincide, and the normal curve is generally applied whenever $n \geqslant 30$.

The normal approximation also extends to constructing confidence intervals for the population proportion. These estimates take two forms, depending on whether the population size N is large or small.

$$\pi = P \pm z\sqrt{\frac{P(1-P)}{n}} \quad \text{or} \quad P \pm z\sqrt{\frac{P(1-P)}{n}}\sqrt{\frac{N-n}{N-1}}$$

RAISE YOUR GRADES

Can you explain...?

☑ the difference between precision and credibility
☑ what a 95% confidence level means
☑ why an interval estimate might be more desirable than a point estimate
☑ why unbiasedness is desirable in an estimator
☑ when the Student t distribution applies instead of the normal distribution

Do you know...?

☑ the difference between consistency and efficiency in estimators
☑ when to apply the finite population correction factor in constructing confidence intervals
☑ the statistician's dilemma in picking a confidence level
☑ why either absolute precision or total credibility—but not both—can nearly always be attained for an estimate
☑ an example where the interval estimate of one parameter is based partly on the point estimate of another parameter

RAPID REVIEW

1. A sample of $n = 100$ family incomes has a mean of $\bar{X} = \$10,000$ and a standard deviation of $s = \$1,000$. Which one of the following provides the 95% confidence interval estimate of the mean of this large population?   [Section 9-2B]

(a) $\$9,804 \leqslant \mu \leqslant \$10,196$ **(c)** $\$9,700 \leqslant \mu \leqslant \$10,300$
(b) $\$9,000 \leqslant \mu \leqslant \$11,000$ **(d)** $\$8,040 \leqslant \mu \leqslant \$11,960$

2. The 95% confidence interval estimate of the mean time taken to process a new insurance policy is $11 \leqslant \mu \leqslant 12$ days. Which one of the following statements is true?   [Section 9-2C]

   (a) Only 5% of all policies take less than 11 days or more than 12 days to process.
   (b) Only 5% of all policies take between 11 and 12 days to process.
   (c) About 95 out of every 100 intervals similarly constructed from samples of the same size will contain the true value of the mean.
   (d) The probability is .95 that μ lies between 11 and 12 days.

3. Which one of the following is true of an unbiased estimator?   [Section 9-1A]

   (a) It never misses its target.
   (b) It is impossible to obtain from any sample.
   (c) It is usually less efficient than a biased estimator.
   (d) It has an expected value that is equal to the parameter being estimated.

4. Which one of the following is true of a consistent estimator?   [Section 9-1A]

   (a) It will be more reliable when it is applied to large samples than when it is applied to small samples.
   (b) It has a standard error that becomes larger as n becomes larger.
   (c) It is impossible to obtain without a census.
   (d) It can never be unbiased.

5. Estimator A is more efficient than estimator B if which one of the following applies?   [Section 9-1A]

   (a) A is easier to calculate.
   (b) A has a smaller standard error.
   (c) A is both unbiased and consistent, and B is neither.
   (d) A will always lie closer to the parameter being estimated.

6. A sample of size n is collected from a population of unlimited size. Assuming that $\bar{X} = 100$ and $s = 6$, construct the 95% confidence interval estimate of μ that would apply for each of the following sample sizes.   [Section 9-2B]

   (a) 100   **(b)** 225   **(c)** 625   **(d)** 900

7. A sample of size 100 is collected from a population of unlimited size. Assuming that $\bar{X} = 100$ and $s = 6$, construct the confidence interval estimate of μ that would apply for each of the following confidence levels.   [Section 9-2B,D]

   (a) 90%   **(b)** 95%   **(c)** 99%   **(d)** 99.9%

8. A sample of size 100 is collected from a population of small size N. Assuming that $\bar{X} = 100$, construct the 95% confidence interval estimate of μ that would apply for each of the following cases.   [Section 9-2E]

(a)	**(b)**	**(c)**	**(d)**
$N = 250$	$N = 400$	$N = 500$	$N = 900$
$s = 10$	$s = 5$	$s = 2$	$s = 1$

9. A small-sized sample is collected from a population. Assuming that $\bar{X} = 25$ and $s = 2$, (*1*) determine the appropriate critical value for t necessary to construct a confidence interval estimate of μ at the stated level of confidence, and (*2*) find that interval.   [Section 9-3B]

(a)	**(b)**	**(c)**	**(d)**
$n = 10$	$n = 15$	$n = 20$	$n = 25$
95%	99%	90%	99.9%

10. A sample of size n is collected from a population of unlimited size. Construct the confidence interval estimate of π that would apply for each of the following cases.   [Section 9-4A]

(a)	(b)	(c)	(d)
$n = 25$	$n = 100$	$n = 400$	$n = 900$
$P = .10$	$P = .15$	$P = .20$	$P = .25$
90%	99%	95%	99.9%

Answers

1. (a)   **2. (c)**   **3. (d)**   **4. (a)**   **5. (b)**
6. (a) 100 ± 1.2 (98.8, 101.2)   **(c)** $100 \pm .5$ (99.5, 100.5)
   (b) $100 \pm .8$ (99.2, 100.8)   **(d)** $100 \pm .4$ (99.6, 100.4)
7. (a) 100 ± 1.0 (99.0, 101.0)   **(c)** 100 ± 1.5 (98.5, 101.5)
   (b) 100 ± 1.2 (98.8, 101.2)   **(d)** 100 ± 2.0 (98.0, 102.0)
8. (a) 100 ± 1.5 (98.5. 101.5)   **(c)** $100 \pm .4$ (99.6, 100.4)
   (b) $100 \pm .8$ (99.2, 100.8)   **(d)** $100 \pm .2$ (99.8, 100.2)
9. (a) (*1*) 2.262   (*2*) 25 ± 1.4 (23.6, 26.4)
   (b) (*1*) 2.977   (*2*) 25 ± 1.5 (23.5, 26.5)
   (c) (*1*) 1.729   (*2*) $25 \pm .8$ (24.2, 25.8)
   (d) (*1*) 3.745   (*2*) 25 ± 1.5 (23.5, 26.5)
10. (a) $.10 \pm .098$ (.002, .198)   **(c)** $.20 \pm .039$ (.161, .239)
   (b) $.15 \pm .092$ (.058, .242)   **(d)** $.25 \pm .048$ (.202, .298)

SOLVED PROBLEMS

PROBLEM 9-1   In estimating the mean time taken by a sheetrocker to nail one 8-foot sheet already in place, a sample of $n = 25$ observations were taken at random times. The worker was found to be nailing during just 5 of these observations.

(a) Make a point estimate of the proportion of all working time spent nailing.
(b) During the 200-minute span of time covering the observations, the sheetrocker hung 20 sheets. Make a point estimate of the mean time per sheet to do the nailing.

Solution:
(a) The simplest point estimate is the sample proportion, $p = 5/25 = .20$.
(b) Although the sample mean time $\bar{X}$ should provide a satisfactory point estimate, individual times weren't obtained. Instead, you can estimate the population mean using the sample proportion. Assuming that .20 is the proportion of time spent nailing, you can estimate the total nailing time during the 200 minutes to be

$$.20(200) = 40 \text{ min.}$$

If 40 minutes of nailing time encompasses 20 sheets, it follows that the mean time per sheet is

$$40/20 = 2 \text{ min.}$$

PROBLEM 9-2   A chemical engineer estimates the mean number of gallons of a key ingredient that are wasted in the manufacture of a ton of pesticide. He chooses a random sample of 100 tons and computes the results to be $\bar{X} = 5.4$ gallons and $s = .42$ gallons. Assuming an unlimited population size, construct a 95% confidence interval of the mean waste.

Solution: This confidence interval estimate of μ is based on a large sample size ($n > 30$), and the finite population correction factor may be ignored since the population is large. With 95% confidence, the normal deviate $z = 1.96$ applies. Thus,

$$\mu = 5.4 \pm 1.96 \frac{.42}{\sqrt{100}} = 5.4 \pm .08 \quad \text{or} \quad 5.32 \leqslant \mu \leqslant 5.48 \text{ gal.}$$

PROBLEM 9-3   The mean time to failure of a brand of batteries is estimated from a sample of 100 test items taken from a large population. Sample results provide $\bar{X} = 57.4$ hours and $s = 11.1$ hours. Construct a 99% confidence interval estimate of the population mean time to failure.

Solution: This confidence interval estimate of μ is based on a large sample size, and the finite population correction factor may be ignored. With 99% confidence, the normal deviate $z = 2.57$ applies. Thus,

$$\mu = 57.4 \pm 2.57 \frac{11.1}{\sqrt{100}} = 57.4 \pm 2.85 \quad \text{or} \quad 54.55 \leqslant \mu \leqslant 60.25 \text{ hrs.}$$

PROBLEM 9-4   A random sample of $n = 100$ package weights has been selected. Construct a 95% confidence interval estimate of the mean weight of the items in the entire population (which is large). The results show that $\bar{X} = 15.9$ ounces and $s = .5$ ounces.

Solution: This confidence interval estimate of μ is based on a large sample size, and the finite population correction factor may be ignored. With 95% confidence, the normal deviate $z = 1.96$ applies. Thus,

$$\mu = 15.9 \pm 1.96 \frac{.5}{\sqrt{100}} = 15.9 \pm .098 \quad \text{or} \quad 15.802 \leqslant \mu \leqslant 15.998 \text{ oz.}$$

PROBLEM 9-5   A student measures the heights of 35 men in her statistics class. She assumes that the data represent a random sample of all male students in her state. From the data she computes $\bar{X} = 70.2''$ and $s = 2.44''$. Construct a 95% confidence interval estimate of the population mean height.

Solution: This confidence interval estimate of μ is based on a large sample size, and the finite population correction factor may be ignored. With 95% confidence, the normal deviate $z = 1.96$ applies. Thus,

$$\mu = 70.2 \pm 1.96 \frac{2.44}{\sqrt{35}} = 70.2 \pm .81 \quad \text{or} \quad 69.39'' \leqslant \mu \leqslant 71.01''$$

PROBLEM 9-6   A large airline is estimating the mean distance traveled annually by its first-class business travelers. From a random sample of $n = 100$ it was determined that $\bar{X} = 76,400$ and $s = 5,250$ miles. Construct a 95% confidence interval estimate of the mean distance traveled.

Solution: This confidence interval estimate of μ is based on a large sample size, and the finite population correction factor may be ignored. With 95% confidence, the normal deviate $z = 1.96$ applies. Thus,

$$\mu = 76,400 \pm 1.96 \frac{5,250}{\sqrt{100}} = 76,400 \pm 1,029$$

or

$$75,371 \leqslant \mu \leqslant 77,429 \text{ mi.}$$

PROBLEM 9-7   You wish to estimate the mean contents in a shipment of 1,000 cans of asparagus. After weighing a sample of 200 cans you compute $\bar{X} = 15.9$ ounces and $s = .3$ ounces. Construct a 99% confidence interval estimate of the population mean.

Solution: This confidence interval estimate of μ is based on a large sample size. Since the population size is small ($N < 10n$), the finite population correction factor must be used. With 99% confidence, the normal deviate $z = 2.57$ applies. Thus,

$$\mu = 15.9 \pm 2.57 \frac{.3}{\sqrt{200}} \sqrt{\frac{1,000 - 200}{1,000 - 1}} = 15.9 \pm .049 \text{ oz.}$$

or

$$15.851 \leqslant \mu \leqslant 15.949 \text{ oz.}$$

PROBLEM 9-8   The following weights (in pounds) have been obtained for a random sample of men from a large population.

183	203	148
146	192	159
157	176	165

(a) Compute the sample mean and standard deviation.
(b) Construct a 95% confidence interval estimate of the population mean weight.

Solution:
(a) Compute the sample mean and standard deviation as follows:

X	$X - \bar{X}$	$(X - \bar{X})^2$
183	13.1	171.61
146	−23.9	571.21
157	−12.9	166.41
203	33.1	1,095.61
192	22.1	488.41
176	6.1	37.21
148	−21.9	479.61
159	−10.9	118.81
165	−4.9	24.01
1,529		3,152.89

$$\bar{X} = 1,529/9 = 169.9 \text{ lbs.} \qquad s = \sqrt{3,152.89/8} = 19.85 \text{ lbs}$$

(b) This confidence interval estimate of μ is based on a small sample size. With 95% confidence and $9 - 1 = 8$ degrees of freedom, the critical value is $t_{.025} = 2.306$. Thus,

$$\mu = 169.9 \pm 2.306 \frac{19.85}{\sqrt{9}} = 169.9 \pm 15.3 \text{ lbs.}$$

or

$$154.6 \leqslant \mu \leqslant 185.2 \text{ lbs.}$$

PROBLEM 9-9   The mean amount of gold consumed per batch in a plating operation is to be estimated. From a random sample of 15 batches, the following quantities (in ounces) were determined:

.25	.18	.24	.19	.20
.23	.27	.21	.23	.21
.19	.22	.20	.25	.25

(a) Compute the sample mean and standard deviation.
(b) Construct a 95% confidence interval estimate of the mean gold consumption.

Solution:
(a) Computing the sample mean and standard deviation as in Problem 9-8, you get

$$\bar{X} = .221 \text{ oz.} \qquad s = .0270 \text{ oz.}$$

(b) This confidence interval estimate of μ is based on a small sample size. With 95% confidence and $15 - 1 = 14$ degrees of freedom, the critical value is $t_{.025} = 2.145$. Thus,

$$\mu = .221 \pm 2.145 \frac{.0270}{\sqrt{15}} = .221 \pm .015 \text{ oz.}$$

or

$$.206 \leqslant \mu \leqslant .236 \text{ oz.}$$

PROBLEM 9-10   The following data pertain to the amount of time (in minutes) taken by a tax preparation service to complete client interviews.

8	12	26	10	23	21
16	22	18	17	36	9

You may assume these data are a representative sample of all client interview times.

(a) Compute the sample mean and standard deviation.
(b) Construct a 99% confidence interval estimate of the population mean interview time.

Solution:
(a) Computing the sample mean and standard deviation as in Problem 9-8, you get

$$\bar{X} = 18.17 \text{ minutes} \qquad s = 8.11 \text{ minutes}$$

(b) This confidence interval estimate of μ is based on a small sample size. With 99% confidence and $12 - 1 = 11$ degrees of freedom, the critical value is $t_{.005} = 3.106$. Thus,

$$\mu = 18.17 \pm 3.106 \frac{8.11}{\sqrt{12}} = 18.17 \pm 7.27 \text{ min.}$$

or

$$10.90 \leqslant \mu \leqslant 25.44 \text{ min.}$$

PROBLEM 9-11   The following rates of return were experienced by holding several common stocks for one year. You may assume that these data are a representative sample of a large population of historical rates of return.

5	−4	10	15	11	25	−5	17
−5	0	8	12	14	8	1	5

(a) Compute the sample mean and standard deviation.
(b) Construct a 95% confidence interval estimate of the population mean rate of return.

Solution:
(a) Computing the sample mean and standard deviation as in Problem 9-8, you get

$$\bar{X} = 7.31\% \qquad s = 8.52\%$$

(b) This confidence interval estimate of μ is based on a small sample size. With 95% confidence and $16 - 1 = 15$ degrees of freedom, the critical value is $t_{.025} = 2.131$. Thus,

$$\mu = 7.31 \pm 2.131 \frac{8.52}{\sqrt{16}} = 7.31 \pm 4.54\%$$

or

$$2.77\% \leqslant \mu \leqslant 11.85\%$$

PROBLEM 9-12   The proportion of voters in a large state approving a referendum is to be estimated. Construct a 95% confidence interval in each of the following cases for the true proportion of all voters approving.
(a) On July 1, 75 out of 130 persons sampled approved of the referendum.
(b) On October 15, 642 persons approved out of 1,056 polled.

Solution: In each of the following cases, you first compute the sample proportion. Since the population is large, you may ignore the finite population correction factor. Construct the confidence intervals for π based on the normal approximation, so that for 95% confidence, the normal deviate is $z = 1.96$.
(a) $P = 75/130 = .577$

$$\pi = .577 \pm 1.96 \sqrt{\frac{.577(.423)}{130}} = .577 \pm .085$$

or

$$.492 \leqslant \pi \leqslant .662$$

(b) $P = 642/1{,}056 = .608$

$$\pi = .608 \pm 1.96 \sqrt{\frac{.608(.392)}{1{,}056}} = .608 \pm .029$$

or

$$.579 \leqslant \pi \leqslant .637$$

PROBLEM 9-13 A lumber mill cuts redwood logs removed from a very large reforested area into boards of specified dimensions. The individual pieces of board are then sorted by grade. The proportion of boards that are of a high enough quality to be merchandised is to be estimated. A sample of 100 boards from various logs is taken for this purpose.

    (a) Suppose that the sample proportion of quality-grade boards is .5. Construct a 99% confidence interval estimate of the proportion of all lumber that will be cut and placed in this category.

    (b) Suppose that the sample proportion of quality-grade boards is .4. Construct a 95% confidence interval estimate of the proportion of all lumber that will be cut and placed in this category.

Solution: In each of these cases the population is large, so you may ignore the finite population correction factor. Construct the confidence intervals for π based on the normal approximation.
(a) For 99% confidence, $z = 2.57$.

$$\pi = .5 \pm 2.57 \sqrt{\frac{.5(.5)}{100}} = .5 \pm .13$$

or

$$.37 \leqslant \pi \leqslant .63$$

(b) For 95% confidence, $z = 1.96$.

$$\pi = .4 \pm 1.96 \sqrt{\frac{.4(.6)}{100}} = .4 \pm .10$$

or

$$.30 \leqslant \pi \leqslant .50$$

PROBLEM 9-14 An inspector found 34 overweight ball bearings in a sample of 200 taken at random from a batch containing 1,000 items. Construct a 99% confidence interval estimate of the proportion of overweight items in the entire batch.

Solution: The computed level of the sample proportion is

$$P = \frac{34}{200} = .17$$

Since the population size is small, you must use the finite population correction factor. Construct the 99% confidence interval for π based on the normal approximation, with $z = 2.57$.

$$\pi = .17 \pm 2.57 \sqrt{\frac{.17(.83)}{200}} \sqrt{\frac{1,000 - 200}{1,000 - 1}} = .17 \pm .061$$

or

$$.109 \leqslant \pi \leqslant .231$$

PROBLEM 9-15 The settings of a sheet-metal roller must be adjusted whenever the proportion π of overthick sheets is .015 or greater. The true level for π is unknown but is periodically estimated from samples of 100 sheets.

    (a) In one sample there were 4 overthick sheets. Construct the corresponding 95% confidence interval estimate of π.

    (b) Using the normal approximation, find the probability for getting as many or more thick sheets as in **(a)** when the true level for π is .01.

Solution:
(a) Since the population is unlimited, you may ignore the finite population correction factor. Construct the 95% confidence interval for π based on the normal approximation, with $z = 1.96$. The sample proportion is $P = 4/100 = .04$.

$$\pi = .04 \pm 1.96 \sqrt{\frac{.04(.96)}{100}} = .04 \pm .038$$

or

$$.002 \leqslant \pi \leqslant .078$$

(b) As you learned in Chapter 8, the first step in finding the probability of P is to find the normal deviate z of the proportion. Since you wish to find $\Pr[P \geqslant r/n]$, you must find the area under the normal curve by using the equivalent form $1 - \Pr[P \leqslant (r-1)/n]$, so that $P = (4-1)/100$ or $3/100$.

$$z = \frac{(3 + .5)/100 - .01}{\sqrt{.01(.99)/100}} = 2.51$$

The area corresponding to $z = 2.51$ is .4940, so that

$$\Pr[P \geqslant 4/100] = 1 - \Pr[P \leqslant 3/100]$$
$$= 1 - (.5000 + .4940) = .0060$$

10 STATISTICAL TESTING

THIS CHAPTER IS ABOUT

☑ **Basic Concepts: Hypothesis Testing with the Mean**
☑ **Standard Procedure for Testing the Mean—Large Sample Sizes**
☑ **Small Sample Test of the Mean**
☑ **Testing with the Proportion**

In addition to estimation, a second broad area of inferential statistics is **hypothesis testing**. This type of application is concerned with *decision making*, with the investigator using sample evidence to make the final choice. Hypothesis testing is a more dynamic statistical tool than passive estimation, which you know is mainly concerned with establishing a value for a population parameter.

10-1. Basic Concepts: Hypothesis Testing with the Mean

One type of hypothesis testing—applications involving the mean—is useful in making a variety of business decisions. A training director might use the mean performance rating of a sample group to determine whether or not to adopt a pilot indoctrination program. A food-processing manager could base her orders for corrective action on the mean level of a particular substance. And an auditor could use the mean transaction balance from a sample to trigger a more thorough verification.

A. Statistical tests involve two hypotheses.

Two fundamental assumptions or **hypotheses** underlie a statistical test. A **null hypothesis** places the unknown population mean at a certain level or within a prescribed range. A second hypothesis, the **alternative hypothesis**, presumes the opposite. It is convenient to use the symbol H_0 to denote the null hypothesis and H_1 for the alternative.

The following three cases will help you to understand these concepts. Each involves a decision focusing on a particular population.

Decision	Population	Null hypothesis (H_0)	Alternative hypothesis (H_1)
Accounting method	Price increases	$\mu \leqslant 5\%$ (moderate)	$\mu > 5\%$ (excessive)
Maintenance timing	Sugar sack content	$\mu \geqslant 10$ lbs. (satisfactory)	$\mu < 10$ lbs. (underweight)
Garment manufacturing	Clothing expenditure	$\mu = \$200$ (on target)	$\mu \neq \$200$ (off target)

The adjective "null" derives from early medical and biological applications where the assumption was ordinarily that a new method or procedure yielded "no change" over the existing one. As a practical matter, the null hypothesis should be tailor-made for the particular investigation. It is usually formulated so that the statistician can minimize the more serious of two possible types of incorrect action.

1. **Pivotal parameter level:** In each of the three cases just given, there is a **pivotal parameter level**, denoted as μ_0, which separates possible levels for μ into the two hypotheses. These are $\mu_0 = 5\%$, $\mu_0 = 10$ lbs, and $\mu_0 = \$200$. The pivotal population mean is ordinarily the largest or smallest level for μ that justifies a particular action.

2. **Composite and simple hypotheses:** A null hypothesis taking one of the following forms is called a **composite hypothesis**:

$$\mu \geqslant \mu_0 \qquad \mu \leqslant \mu_0$$

Should H_0 specify that μ be an exact value, in the form $\mu = \mu_0$, it is a **simple hypothesis**.

B. A decision rule establishes what action to take.

The possible actions in a statistical decision may be stated in terms of the null hypothesis:

$$\text{Accept } H_0 \qquad \text{or} \qquad \text{Reject } H_0$$

Each of these choices leads to a specific action, which is triggered by the computed level of a **test statistic**.

Note: Rejecting H_0 is the same as accepting the alternative hypothesis H_1.

In testing the mean, you would base the final decision on the level for the sample mean $\bar{X}$, which is the test statistic. The **decision rule** specifies one or more points of demarcation for $\bar{X}$, so that you take one action if $\bar{X}$ is too high or too low, with the opposite action otherwise. The following decision rules were chosen for the three cases being discussed. The appropriate actions for each decision rule are shown in parentheses. (Later on in this chapter you will learn how to compute the level of the test statistic.)

Accounting method
Accept H_0 if $\bar{X} \leqslant 6\%$ (and keep FIFO)
Reject H_0 if $\bar{X} > 6\%$ (and switch to LIFO)

Maintenance timing
Accept H_0 if $\bar{X} \geqslant 9.9$ lbs.   (and continue operations)
Reject H_0 if $\bar{X} < 9.9$ lbs.   (and do maintenance)

Garment manufacturing
Accept H_0 if $\$195 \leqslant \bar{X} \leqslant \$205$ (and use present plan)
Reject H_0 if $\bar{X} < \$195$ (and revise plan for lower expenditures)
      or if $\bar{X} > \$205$ (and revise plan for higher expenditures)

Note: You should specify your decision rules before collecting a sample.

1. **One-sided and two-sided tests:** The first of these decision rules rejects H_0 when $\bar{X}$ is large, and the second when $\bar{X}$ is small. Each is a **one-sided test**. The third test is a **two-sided test**, since unusually large or small levels for $\bar{X}$ will result in rejection of the null hypothesis.

2. **Critical value:** The level of the test statistic separating the two actions is called a **critical value**. For one-sided tests involving means, you can use the symbol $\bar{X}^*$ to denote the critical value. In the first two cases, you have $\bar{X}^* = 6\%$ and $\bar{X}^* = 9.9$ lbs. Two-sided tests have a pair of critical values, distinguished by a subscript 1 for the lower point and a subscript 2 for the higher one. Thus for the third test, $\bar{X}_1^* = \$195$ and $\bar{X}_2^* = \$205$.

C. Statisticians consider two error probabilities when selecting a decision rule.

Remember that you must make a decision even though the level of μ is uncertain. In establishing the decision rule, statisticians acknowledge two kinds of sampling error:

Type I error—to reject the null hypothesis when it is true
Type II error—to accept the null hypothesis when it is false

The following apply to the three cases in our illustration.

Decision	Type I error	Type II error
Accounting method	Switch to LIFO when price increases are moderate	Keep FIFO when price increases are excessive
Maintenance timing	Do maintenance when sugar sacks are satisfactory	Continue operations when sugar sacks are underweight
Garment manufacturing	Revise plan when expenditures are on target	Use present plan when expenditures are off target

Since you must base the final decision on sample evidence, there is no way to eliminate these errors. Therefore, you must conduct the investigation in such a way that you keep the incidence of the errors under control. Your decision rule should achieve an optimal balance between the probabilities for taking an incorrect action.

The following **error probabilities** apply to all hypothesis-testing situations.

$$\alpha = \Pr[\text{type I error}] = \Pr[\text{reject } H_0 \,|\, H_0 \text{ true}]$$
$$\beta = \Pr[\text{type II error}] = \Pr[\text{accept } H_0 \,|\, H_0 \text{ false}]$$

It is traditional to use α (lowercase Greek alpha) and β (lowercase Greek beta) to denote the respective error probabilities.

Figure 10-1 shows two sampling distributions for $\bar{X}$ that might be valid in the accounting method decision. (Remember, the true μ is unknown and could lie at any level.) The top normal curve applies when the null hypothesis is true and is centered at $\mu_0 = 5\%$. The bottom curve represents one possible circumstance under which the null hypothesis might be false. A guessed value of $\sigma = 3\%$ applies for the standard deviation of the price-increase population. A sample size of $n = 25$ products is used. The same standard deviation applies to both curves:

$$\sigma_{\bar{X}} = \frac{\sigma}{\sqrt{n}} = \frac{3}{\sqrt{25}} = .6\%$$

The following calculations determine the type I and II error probabilities. Each is represented by a tail area in the respective curve. Remember that $z = (\bar{X} - \mu)/\sigma_{\bar{X}}$.

$$z = \frac{6 - 5}{.6} = 1.67 \qquad\qquad z = \frac{6 - 6.5}{.6} = -.83$$

$$\alpha = \Pr[\bar{X} > 6\% \,|\, \mu = 5\%] \qquad \beta = \Pr[\bar{X} \leqslant 6\% \,|\, \mu = 6.5\%]$$
$$= .5000 - .4525 \qquad\qquad\quad = .5000 - .2967$$
$$= .0475 \qquad\qquad\qquad\quad = .2033$$

The values for α and β can differ from those given here, depending on several factors.

1. **Effect of sample size:** Recall that $\sigma_{\bar{X}}$ becomes smaller as n increases, so that the normal curves for $\bar{X}$ become taller and tighter. The tail areas above or below $\bar{X}^*$ will therefore be smaller as n becomes larger. Thus, *raising the sample size will reduce both α and β.* That of course requires devoting more resources to the collection of sample data.

2. **Centers of the normal curves:** The top curve in Figure 10-1 applies when H_0 is true. The null hypothesis states that $\mu \leqslant 5\%$ ($= \mu_0$). Any normal curve centered at a μ smaller than 5% satisfies the null hypothesis and provides a smaller tail area than the one centered at $\mu = 5\%$. (Look at Figure 10-1 and imagine the effect on the upper-tail area of the top curve beyond $\bar{X}^*$ when you move its center μ to the left.) Statisticians ordinarily compute α for the worst case, when $\mu = \mu_0$.

There are also lots of ways for H_0 to be false, and the bottom curve in Figure 10-1 represents just one case. A normal curve centered on a μ that is closer to the critical value $\bar{X}^*$ will have a greater lower-tail area extending from $\bar{X}^*$. That tail area will be smaller when μ is larger (the normal curve then being centered further to the right). For example, should the true mean increase in prices be $\mu = 6.75\%$, you can compute the corresponding type II error probability:

$$z = \frac{6 - 6.75}{.6} = -1.25$$

$$\beta = \Pr[\bar{X} \leqslant 6\% \,|\, \mu = 6.75\%] = .5000 - .3944 = .1056$$

This is smaller than before. There is no way to know which μ, if either of them, applies. Statisticians consider the various possibilities in establishing a suitable decision rule.

Figure 10-1   Accounting method decision ($n = 25$, $\sigma = 3\%$ assumed).

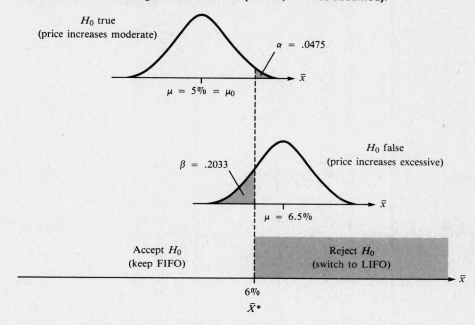

Accounting method decision ($n = 25$, $\sigma = 3\%$ assumed).

3. **The choice of the critical value:** The level chosen for $\bar{X}^*$ will affect both error probabilities. Look again at Figure 10-1 and imagine sliding $\bar{X}^*$ to the left while the curves remain fixed. The rejection region gets wider, making that action more likely. A larger α would apply, reflected by a greater upper-tail area in the top curve. That shift in $\bar{X}^*$ would reduce the probability β of accepting H_0, shown in the lower curve, giving it a smaller lower-tail area. The reverse holds if you shift $\bar{X}^*$ to the right. *By shifting the critical value of the test statistic, the value of α can be reduced at the expense of β, or vice versa.* The final choice of $\bar{X}^*$ should achieve an optimal balance between the two error probabilities.

D. Statistical tests may take various forms.

Whenever the type I error probability α corresponds to an upper-tail area, the statistical investigation is referred to as an **upper-tailed test**. Such a study involves a null hypothesis of the following form:

$$H_0: \mu \leqslant \mu_0$$

An example is the accounting method decision shown in Figure 10-1.

A **lower-tailed test** has a null hypothesis of the form

$$H_0: \mu \geqslant \mu_0$$

and you will find that its α corresponds to an area in the lower tail of the normal curve for $\bar{X}$.

The maintenance timing decision is an example of a lower-tailed test. Figure 10-2 shows two normal curves applicable to that case. A value of $\sigma = .5$ lb. is assumed for the population of sugar-sack content weights, and a sample of size $n = 100$ is used. The following standard deviation applies to the normal curves for $\bar{X}$:

$$\sigma_{\bar{X}} = \frac{\sigma}{\sqrt{n}} = \frac{.5}{\sqrt{100}} = .05 \text{ lb.}$$

Figure 10-2 Maintenance timing decision ($n = 100$, $\sigma = .5$ lb. assumed).

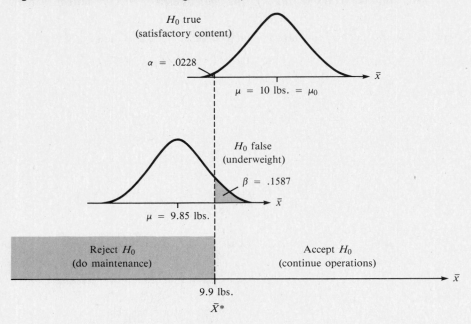

Maintenance timing decision ($n = 100$, $\sigma = .5$ lb. assumed).

The following calculations provide the applicable error probabilities. ($\mu = 9.85$ lbs. is used to illustrate one of the many ways for H_0 to be false.)

$$z = \frac{9.9 - 10}{.05} = -2.00 \qquad z = \frac{9.9 - 9.85}{.05} = 1.00$$

$$\alpha = \Pr[\bar{X} < 9.9 \,|\, \mu = 10] \qquad \beta = \Pr[\bar{X} \geqslant 9.9 \,|\, \mu = 9.85]$$
$$= .5000 - .4772 \qquad\qquad = .5000 - .3413$$
$$= .0228 \qquad\qquad\qquad = .1587$$

- For an *upper-tailed test*, the null hypothesis indicates that $\mu \leqslant \mu_0$ and $\bar{X}^*$ lies above μ_0. A large computed value for $\bar{X}$ will result in rejecting H_0, a small value in accepting H_0.
- For a *lower-tailed test*, the null hypothesis indicates that $\mu \geqslant \mu_0$ and $\bar{X}^*$ lies below μ_0. A small computed value for $\bar{X}$ will result in rejecting H_0, a large value in accepting H_0.

In two-sided tests, very large or very small computed levels for $\bar{X}$ cause rejection of the null hypothesis. This is illustrated in Figure 10-3 for the garment manufacturing decision. Under the null hypothesis, the normal curve for $\bar{X}$ is centered at $\mu_0 = \$200$. Notice that half of the type I error probability corresponds to each tail, since the type I error (rejecting a true null hypothesis) can happen in two ways.

The population standard deviation is assumed to be $\sigma = \$20$ per person, and a sample of $n = 25$ persons is used. The standard deviation for the normal distribution is

$$\sigma_{\bar{X}} = \frac{\sigma}{\sqrt{n}} = \frac{\$20}{\sqrt{25}} = \$4$$

Figure 10-3 Garment manufacturing decision ($n = 25$, $\sigma = \$25$ assumed).

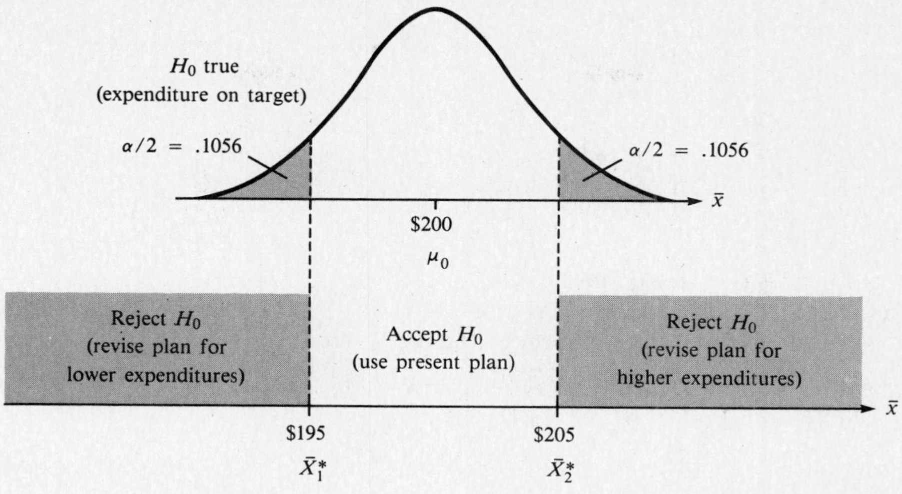

Garment manufacturing decision ($n = 25$, $\sigma = \$20$ assumed).

The probability for rejecting the null hypothesis because the sample mean is too large is as follows:

$$z = \frac{205 - 200}{4} = 1.25$$

$$\frac{\alpha}{2} = \Pr[\bar{X} > \$205 \,|\, \mu = \$200] = .5000 - .3944 = .1056$$

Since the same value applies for getting $\bar{X} < \$195$, the total type I error probability is twice this value:

$$\alpha = 2(.1056) = .2112$$

10-2. Standard Procedure for Testing the Mean—Large Sample Sizes

The ideal statistical decision rule gives the best balance between the type I and type II error probabilities, while at the same time the sample size n optimizes the expenditure of scarce resources.

But in practice, the sample size often doesn't meet this goal. Instead, the choice of n will ordinarily be dictated by budgetary limitations or n will be placed at some level deemed acceptable to the community. This leaves little leeway in balancing the α and β levels.

The standard practice is to identify the more serious of the two error types and designate it as the type I error (rejecting a true null hypothesis). H_0 is designated accordingly. The decision maker can then pick a decision rule that precisely meets a targeted level for α. But once α and n are fixed, the β probabilities for the less serious type II error can't be controlled at all.

A. There are five standard hypothesis-testing steps.

Regardless of application or statistical methodology, all hypothesis tests, with slight modification, involve the same basic steps.

STEP 1 Establish the null hypothesis: The null hypothesis for testing the mean will take one of the following forms:

$H_0: \mu \leqslant \mu_0$	$H_0: \mu \geqslant \mu_0$	$H_0: \mu = \mu_0$
upper-tailed test	lower-tailed test	two-sided test

You select H_0 in such a way that rejecting H_0 when it is true is the more serious error.

EXAMPLE 10-1: PRODUCERS, CONSUMERS, AND BLENDERS

A producer of lightbulbs must decide whether or not to ship a production batch to its regular customers or to scrap it and sell it as "seconds." The bulbs in any batch may be predominantly good ones with a long mean lifetime μ, or mainly bad ones with a short μ. Ideally, the regular customers would get nothing but good batches, and the bad bulbs would all be scrapped. But since the producer will decide a batch's disposition from sample data, there are two errors:

Some good batches will be scrapped.
Some bad batches will be shipped.

Producers tend (perhaps shortsightedly) to view the first error as the more serious one. The null hypothesis would then be that any particular batch is good, so that in terms of mean lifetime μ,

$$H_0: \mu \geq \mu_0$$

where μ_0 might be the advertised "minimum" lifetime.

The consumer of the lightbulbs can refuse or buy any particular shipment. This choice will be based on a sample inspection by the receiving department. The following two errors apply:

Some of the time a bad shipment will be bought.
Some of the time a good shipment will be refused.

Consumers are less concerned about inconveniencing suppliers than acquiring defective merchandise, so they judge the first error to be the more serious one. The null hypothesis is thus that the shipment is bad. In terms of mean lifetime,

$$H_0: \mu \leq \mu_0$$

where μ_0 might be a barely tolerable mean lifetime.

To achieve color consistency, a blender of Scotch whiskey wants to ensure a balance between the levels of dark and light whiskeys. The mixing process is designed so that any batch of barrels yields a mean color index of 100. When the true level for μ is lower, dark ingredients should be added; when it is higher, light additives should be included. Unfortunately, not all barrels can be opened, and μ can't be known. Some batches will be unnecessarily darkened, others improperly lightened. These errors are equally serious, and the simple null hypothesis of the following form applies:

$$H_0: \mu = \mu_0$$

The value $\mu_0 = 100$ would be appropriate here.

STEP 2 Select the test statistic: When you are testing means, the usual test statistic is $\bar{X}$. When the population standard deviation σ is unknown, an alternative procedure is to instead use the computed level of the normal deviate z.

Normal deviate test statistic

$$z = \frac{\bar{X} - \mu_0}{s/\sqrt{n}}$$

This quantity is approximately normally distributed and should be used only when n is large.

STEP 3 Establish the significance level and the acceptance and rejection regions for the decision rule: The probability α for the more serious type I error is referred to as the **significance level**. The investigator usually prescribes this in advance. Commonly used levels are $\alpha = .01$, $\alpha = .05$, and $\alpha = .10$.

The point separating the acceptance and rejection regions depends on the **critical normal deviate**, denoted as z_α. The area under the standard normal curve above z_α is equal to α. The values $z_{.01} = 2.33$, $z_{.05} = 1.64$, and $z_{.10} = 1.28$ apply.

The following expressions are used to find the critical value for $\bar{X}$.

Critical values for the sample mean (σ known)

Upper-tailed test:	$\bar{X}^* = \mu_0 + z_\alpha \sigma_{\bar{X}}$
Lower-tailed test:	$\bar{X}^* = \mu_0 - z_\alpha \sigma_{\bar{X}}$
Two-sided test:	$\bar{X}_1^* = \mu_0 - z_{\alpha/2} \sigma_{\bar{X}}$
	$\bar{X}_2^* = \mu_0 + z_{\alpha/2} \sigma_{\bar{X}}$

For two-sided tests, you split the significance level into two cases and use the critical normal deviate $z_{\alpha/2}$ to find the two critical values.

One of the following decision rules specifies the acceptance and rejection regions.

		Test statistic	
	Action	$\bar{X}$ is used	z is used
Upper-tailed test	Accept H_0	if $\bar{X} \leqslant \bar{X}^*$	if $z \leqslant z_\alpha$
	Reject H_0	if $\bar{X} > \bar{X}^*$	if $z > z_\alpha$
Lower-tailed test	Accept H_0	if $\bar{X} \geqslant \bar{X}^*$	if $z \geqslant -z_\alpha$
	Reject H_0	if $\bar{X} < \bar{X}^*$	if $z < -z_\alpha$
Two-sided test	Accept H_0	if $\bar{X}_1^* \leqslant \bar{X} \leqslant \bar{X}_2^*$	if $-z_{\alpha/2} \leqslant z \leqslant z_{\alpha/2}$
	Reject H_0	if $\bar{X} < \bar{X}_1^*$	if $z < -z_{\alpha/2}$
		or if $\bar{X} > \bar{X}_2^*$	or if $z > z_{\alpha/2}$

STEP 4 Collect the sample data and compute the value of the test statistic.

STEP 5 Make the decision.

B. Statistical testing is easy when done one step at a time.

The following examples illustrate the standard hypothesis-testing procedure for means. Consider first an upper-tailed test when σ is known.

EXAMPLE 10-2: FINE TUNING AN EMPLOYMENT SCREENING TEST

The Variety Galore Stores have redesigned their employment screening examination for sales clerk positions to eliminate sex bias. Management must decide whether to increase the new test's difficulty or to adopt it without further modification. The major uncertainty is the mean score μ to be achieved by the clerical applicant pool. If μ is as low or lower than the historical mean score of 80 points, the revised test is difficult enough. Should μ be higher, the new test is too easy. Since μ is unknown, there are two types of errors:

Using the new test without modification when it is too easy.
Increasing the difficulty when the test is hard enough.

The second outcome was judged least desirable, and the following null hypothesis applies:

$$H_0: \mu \leqslant 80 \qquad \text{(test is difficult enough)}$$

The pivotal value for the mean score is $\mu_0 = 80$.

Management will administer the new test to a random sample of $n = 100$ persons representing applicants for clerical positions. The mean score $\bar{X}$ achieved by this group will determine whether to accept or reject the null hypothesis. The historical standard deviation in individual scores of $\sigma = 7$ points is assumed to apply, so that the standard error of $\bar{X}$ is

$$\sigma_{\bar{X}} = \frac{\sigma}{\sqrt{n}} = \frac{7}{\sqrt{100}} = .7$$

The form of H_0 requires an upper-tailed test. Although a tiny significance level, such as $\alpha = .01$ would be ideal, that would be accompanied by unacceptably high chances of adopting the test with no changes when it is too easy. Management decides that a better balance will be achieved between the types I and II errors if they set the significance level at the higher level of $\alpha = .05$. Using $z_{.05} = 1.64$, the following critical value applies:

$$\bar{X}^* = 80 + 1.64(.7) = 81.15$$

This provides the following decision rule:

Accept H_0 if $\bar{X} \leqslant 81.15$ (use the test without modification)
Reject H_0 if $\bar{X} > 81.15$ (increase difficulty of the test)

Suppose that a mean of $\bar{X} = 75$ points is computed. The decision rule requires management to accept the null hypothesis and use the test without modification. If instead $\bar{X} = 83$ is computed for the sample mean, management would reject H_0 and increase the difficulty of the test.

The following example shows how you can lay out a lower-tailed test when the population standard deviation is unknown.

EXAMPLE 10-3: IS THERE ENOUGH SCOTCH TAPE?

A cellophane tape manufacturer has installed a new laser control to determine when a roll has reached the desired thickness. To exceed labeling requirements by an acceptable margin, the mean length μ of individual rolls must be at least 525 inches. Otherwise the control mechanism must be replaced.

The null hypothesis is that the control is working properly:

$$H_0: \mu \geqslant 525'' \; (=\mu_0)$$

The test is lower-tailed. The decision will be based on a random sample of $n = 50$ rolls, each of which will be measured for exact length. From those values $\bar{X}$ and s will be computed. No information is available regarding the population standard deviation, and σ remains unknown. Thus, $\bar{X}$ can't serve as the test statistic, since no critical value can be computed for it. The computed normal deviate z is used instead.

A significance level of $\alpha = .01$ is chosen. Using a critical normal deviate of $z_{.01} = 2.33$, the following rule applies:

Accept H_0 if $z \geqslant -2.33$ (continue to use present control)
Reject H_0 if $z < -2.33$ (replace control mechanism)

The first sample provides the following results:

$$\bar{X} = 530'' \qquad s = 11.3''$$

$$z = \frac{530 - 525}{11.3/\sqrt{50}} = 3.13$$

Since z falls in the acceptance region, the laser control should be kept in operation.

A later sample yields:

$$\bar{X} = 521'' \qquad s = 7.2''$$

$$z = \frac{521 - 525}{7.2/\sqrt{50}} = -3.93$$

Since this quantity falls in the rejection region, H_0 must be rejected and the control mechanism should be replaced.

The following example illustrates how you might apply a two-sided test. Here σ is known, and you must use the finite population correction factor.

EXAMPLE 10-4: ARE INGOTS OF PROPER WEIGHT?

A brass fixture manufacturer weighs all arriving shipments of copper ingots. The null hypothesis is that the mean weight is $\mu = 100$ lbs. for an entire shipment:

$$H_0: \mu = 100 \text{ lbs.}$$

The entire shipment can't be weighed all together because packaging materials aren't uniform. Individual sample ingots are weighed to spare expense. All ingots are weighed only if a shipment is believed to be underweight or overweight.

The sample mean $\bar{X}$ serves as the test statistic. The standard deviation in individual ingot weights has been historically established at $\sigma = 2$ lbs. Shipments usually contain $N = 800$ ingots, from which a sample of $n = 100$ is selected. The applicable standard error of $\bar{X}$ is

$$\sigma_{\bar{X}} = \frac{2}{\sqrt{100}} \sqrt{\frac{800 - 100}{800 - 1}} = .19 \text{ lb.}$$

The test is a two-sided one, with a pivotal mean value of $\mu_0 = 100$ lbs. Management has set the significance level at $\alpha = .05$. The type I error probability is represented by two tail areas of size $\alpha/2 = .025$. The critical normal deviate value is $z_{.025} = 1.96$, and the critical values for $\bar{X}$ are

$$\bar{X}_1^* = 100 - 1.96(.19) = 99.63 \text{ lbs.}$$
$$\bar{X}_2^* = 100 + 1.96(.19) = 100.37 \text{ lbs.}$$

The following decision rule applies.

Accept H_0 if $99.63 \leqslant \bar{X} \leqslant 100.37$ (don't weigh all ingots)
Reject H_0 if $\bar{X} < 99.63$ or if $\bar{X} > 100.37$ (weigh all ingots)

Should $\bar{X}$ turn out to be 100.12 lb, H_0 would be accepted. Values such as $\bar{X} = 99.5$ lbs. or $\bar{X} = 100.7$ lbs. would result in rejecting H_0.

10-3. Small Sample Test of the Mean

You have seen that the computed normal deviate z should serve as the test statistic in place of $\bar{X}$ when the population standard deviation σ is unknown. But recall from Chapter 9 that the extra source of uncertainty arising from using s as an estimator of σ makes the normal distribution a poor fit unless the sample size is large. When n is small, it is more appropriate to base the testing procedure on the Student t distribution.

The basic procedure is easily modified by using t in place of z. When the sample size is small (ordinarily, whenever $n < 30$), the following test statistic is used in evaluations involving the mean.

Student *t* test statistic
$$t = \frac{\bar{X} - \mu_0}{s/\sqrt{n}}$$

One-sided tests will be upper-tailed or lower-tailed and involve t_α as the critical value. Two-sided tests will use $t_{\alpha/2}$ analogously to $z_{\alpha/2}$. Once you have specified the significance level, you may read the critical value from Table B using $n - 1$ degrees of freedom.

The following three basic forms apply in testing the mean with small-sized samples.

Upper-tailed test ($H_0: \mu \leqslant \mu_0$): Accept H_0 if $t \leqslant t_\alpha$
  Reject H_0 if $t > t_\alpha$

Lower-tailed test ($H_0: \mu \geqslant \mu_0$): Accept H_0 if $t \geqslant -t_\alpha$
  Reject H_0 if $t < -t_\alpha$

Two-sided test ($H_0: \mu = \mu_0$): Accept H_0 if $-t_{\alpha/2} \leqslant t \leqslant t_{\alpha/2}$
  Reject H_0 if $t < -t_{\alpha/2}$ or if $t > t_{\alpha/2}$

EXAMPLE 10-5: HAS MANUAL DEXTERITY BEEN DROPPING?

Ace Assemblers is reviewing its employment screening procedures for detail work. Several new persons, none having prior experience, have been hired. They have all been given a manual dexterity test. An investigator wishes to test the null hypothesis that the mean test score μ of newly hired inexperienced persons will be just as high as that of the company's experienced workers, for which it has been established that the mean is 81, so that $H_0: \mu \geqslant 81$.

Only 15 inexperienced persons take the test. They achieve a mean score of $\bar{X} = 78.3$ with a standard deviation of $s = 5$. Should the null hypothesis be accepted or rejected at the .05 significance level?

The computed value for the test statistic is

$$t = \frac{78.3 - 81}{5/\sqrt{15}} = -2.091$$

The test is a lower-tailed one. Using $15 - 1 = 14$ degrees of freedom, Table B provides the critical value of $t_{.05} = 1.761$. Since the computed value falls below -1.761, H_0 must be rejected. It must be concluded that inexperienced persons don't have manual dexterity scores that are as high as those of experienced workers.

10-4. Testing with the Proportion

Hypothesis testing extends to decisions where the population proportion π is the key parameter. In those cases the sample proportion P ordinarily serves as the test statistic. You can readily adapt the procedures for testing means to testing proportions.

The following three basic forms apply in testing the proportion.

Upper-tailed test $(H_0: \pi \leqslant \pi_0)$:   Accept H_0 if $P \leqslant P^*$
                                                Reject H_0 if $P > P^*$

Lower-tailed test $(H_0: \pi \geqslant \pi_0)$:   Accept H_0 if $P \geqslant P^*$
                                                Reject H_0 if $P < P^*$

Two-sided test $(H_0: \pi = \pi_0)$:   Accept H_0 if $P_1^* \leqslant P \leqslant P_2^*$
                                                Reject H_0 if $P < P_1^*$ or if $P > P_2^*$

The normal approximation is ordinarily used to approximate the sampling distribution of P. In Chapter 8 you saw that the standard deviation of the normal curve is

$$\sigma_P = \sqrt{\frac{\pi(1 - \pi)}{n}}$$

In establishing critical values for P, you use the pivotal value π_0 as π. Once you have specified the significance level α, the following expressions apply.

Critical values of the proportion

Upper-tailed test: $P^* = \pi_0 - \dfrac{.5}{n} + z_\alpha \sqrt{\dfrac{\pi_0(1 - \pi_0)}{n}}$

Lower-tailed test: $P^* = \pi_0 + \dfrac{.5}{n} - z_\alpha \sqrt{\dfrac{\pi_0(1 - \pi_0)}{n}}$

Two-sided test: $P_1^* = \pi_0 + \dfrac{.5}{n} - z_{\alpha/2} \sqrt{\dfrac{\pi_0(1 - \pi_0)}{n}}$

                       $P_2^* = \pi_0 - \dfrac{.5}{n} + z_{\alpha/2} \sqrt{\dfrac{\pi_0(1 - \pi_0)}{n}}$

- For simplicity, some books drop the continuity correction terms involving $.5/n$.
- The finite population correction factor applies when N is less than 10 times n.

EXAMPLE 10-6: SHOULD A NEW PACKAGE DESIGN BE USED?

The Fruty Tooty product manager wishes to determine whether or not to change the package design for her cereal. She feels that it will be worth the bother only if more than 60% of nonusers prefer the new box to the old one. She most wants to avoid changing the box when the preference proportion π is smaller, so that her null hypothesis is

$$H_0: \pi \leqslant .60 \, (= \pi_0)$$

The manager selects a random sample of $n = 100$ persons who don't buy Fruty Tooty. She wants to protect herself at the 5% significance level against incorrectly rejecting the null hypothesis when it is true. She thus uses $\alpha = .05$, with a critical normal deviate of $z_{.05} = 1.64$. For this upper-tailed test the critical value for the sample proportion preferring the new box is

$$P^* = .60 - \frac{.5}{100} + 1.64 \sqrt{\frac{.60(1 - .60)}{100}} = .675$$

The manager's decision rule is as follows:

Accept H_0 if $P \leqslant .675$ (keep old box)
Reject H_0 if $P > .675$ (change to new box)

She finds that 73 sample respondents prefer the new box. Since her computed value $P = 73/100 = .73$ falls in the rejection region, she must reject the null hypothesis and change Fruty Tooty's package design.

SUMMARY

Because of its role in decision making, *hypothesis testing* is a more dynamic form of statistical inference than estimation. This chapter considers tests for the mean (μ) and the proportion (π). There are two possible actions, equivalent to accepting or rejecting a *null hypothesis* (H_0). While uncertain, the decision maker must make a choice as to whether or not the null hypothesis is true. The selected action is determined by applying a *decision rule* that specifies what to do for any computed level of the *test statistic*, $\bar{X}$ or P, or z or t. Before sample results are known, the test statistic is a random variable, and there is a chance that the decision will be incorrect—resulting in either a type I error (rejecting the null hypothesis when it is true) or a type II error (accepting the null hypothesis when it is false).

Statisticians consider the probabilities for these errors when setting a decision rule. These probabilities are as follows:

$$\alpha = \Pr[\text{type I error}] = \Pr[\text{reject } H_0 \,|\, H_0 \text{ true}]$$
$$\beta = \Pr[\text{type II error}] = \Pr[\text{accept } H_0 \,|\, H_0 \text{ false}]$$

You ordinarily designate H_0 so that the more undesirable outcome corresponds to the type I error.

You can always lower α by raising β, or vice versa. You do this by shifting the *critical value* of the test statistic so that accepting H_0 is more or less likely. You can reduce both error probabilities by increasing the sample size. However, n is often dictated by outside circumstances, and you will usually prescribe α to be a specific value, called the *significance level*. You should accept the contingency that substantial β probabilities might then apply for the less serious type II error.

The *pivotal parameter level* is denoted by μ_0 in testing the mean and by π_0 in testing the proportion. That value establishes the center of the sampling distribution for the test statistic, and this center is assumed to apply under the extreme case of the null hypothesis. Depending on the form of H_0, the procedure may be a *one-sided test* or a *two-sided test*. One-sided tests may be *upper-tailed* or *lower-tailed*. The following classifications apply:

Upper-tailed test	Lower-tailed test	Two-sided test
$\mu \leqslant \mu$	$\mu \geqslant \mu_0$	$\mu = \mu_0$
$\pi \leqslant \pi_0$	$\pi \geqslant \pi_0$	$\pi = \pi_0$

For an upper-tailed test the type I probability α corresponds to an area in the upper tail of the curve for the sampling distribution of the test statistic, and for a lower-tailed test it corresponds to an area in the lower tail. For a two-sided test, α is equal to the sum of the matching areas in both tails.

Using a targeted level for α, you establish the critical value of your test statistic before collecting the sample data. When you can specify all population parameters in advance, α sets the tabled value of the *critical normal deviate* z_α. The critical value $\bar{X}^*$ or P^* will lie z_α standard errors above the pivotal parameter level μ_0 or π_0 for an upper-tailed test, and an equal distance below it for a lower-tailed test. Two critical values apply for a two-sided test, one lying $z_{\alpha/2}$ standard errors below the pivotal parameter level and the other lying the same distance above.

In testing the mean, you may not know the population standard deviation σ. For those cases involving a large sample size, the computed level for the normal deviate z serves as the test statistic, with the critical value z_α or $z_{\alpha/2}$ being used to set the decision rule. For samples where $n < 30$, use the Student t statistic in place of z.

RAISE YOUR GRADES

Can you explain...?

☑ the difference between a type I error probability and a type II error probability
☑ the difference between testing and estimation
☑ the considerations in designating the null hypothesis
☑ why several β probabilities might be computed for a single decision rule
☑ why increasing the sample size should reduce both α and β

Do you know...?

☑ when a test is two-sided
☑ how to pick the appropriate test statistic
☑ when a test is upper-tailed or lower-tailed
☑ how to decide which test statistic to use in testing the mean
☑ why the type I error can't be eliminated

RAPID REVIEW

1. Either a type I or a type II error must occur. Is the statement true or false?   [Section 10-1C]

2. Find the critical value of the sample mean in testing the null hypothesis $\mu \leqslant 100$ when $\sigma = 10$ and $n = 100$. Use $\alpha = .05$.   [Section 10-2A]

3. Find the critical value of the sample mean in testing the null hypothesis $\mu \geqslant 10.5$ when $\sigma = .5$ and $n = 25$. Use $\alpha = .01$.   [Section 10-2A]

4. In testing the null hypothesis $\mu \leqslant 10\%$, the critical value of the sample mean is 10.5%. Determine for each of the following sample results whether H_0 should be accepted or rejected.   [Section 10-2A]

   (a) $\bar{X} = 11.1\%$ (b) $\bar{X} = 9.8\%$ (c) $\bar{X} = 10.4\%$ (d) $\bar{X} = 12.2\%$

5. In testing the null hypothesis $\mu = 900$ pounds per square inch (psi), the critical values of the sample mean are $\bar{X}_1^* = 875$ and $\bar{X}_2^* = 925$. Determine for each of the following sample results whether H_0 should be accepted or rejected.   [Section 10-2A]

   (a) $\bar{X} = 865$ psi   (b) $\bar{X} = 933$ psi   (c) $\bar{X} = 895$ psi   (d) $\bar{X} = 905$ psi

6. In testing the null hypothesis $\pi \leqslant .20$ regarding a population of large size, determine for each of the following cases the value of P^*.   [Section 10-4]

(a)	(b)	(c)	(d)
$\alpha = .05$	$\alpha = .01$	$\alpha = .025$	$\alpha = .05$
$n = 100$	$n = 25$	$n = 64$	$n = 225$

7. In testing the null hypothesis $\mu \geqslant \$25.00$, determine for each of the following cases (1) the value of z and (2) whether H_0 should be accepted or rejected at the $\alpha = .05$ significance level.   [Section 10-2A]

(a)	(b)	(c)	(d)
$\bar{X} = \$22.37$	$\bar{X} = \$23.55$	$\bar{X} = \$26.01$	$\bar{X} = \$24.88$
$s = \$5.15$	$s = \$4.19$	$s = \$7.75$	$s = \$6.50$
$n = 100$	$n = 50$	$n = 200$	$n = 150$

8. In testing the null hypothesis $\mu \leqslant 165$ lbs. at the $\alpha = .05$ significance level, determine for each of the following cases (1) the value of t_α, (2) the computed value for t, and (3) whether H_0 should be accepted or rejected at the $\alpha = .05$ significance level. [Section 10-3]

(a)	(b)	(c)	(d)
$\bar{X} = 169.2$	$\bar{X} = 173.4$	$\bar{X} = 170.6$	$\bar{X} = 167.3$
$s = 5$	$s = 4$	$s = 8$	$s = 6$
$n = 10$	$n = 25$	$n = 20$	$n = 15$

9. The following decision rule has been established for testing the mean under the null hypothesis $\mu \leqslant 100$.

$$\text{Accept } H_0 \text{ if } \bar{X} \leqslant 101.2$$
$$\text{Reject } H_0 \text{ if } \bar{X} > 101.2$$

   (a) Compute the type I error probability α assuming that $\mu = 100$, $\sigma = 5$, and $n = 100$.   [Section 10-1C]

(b) Compute the type II error probability β assuming that $\mu = 102$, $\sigma = 5$, and $n = 100$. [Section 10-1C]

10. The following decision rule has been established for testing the mean under the null hypothesis $\mu \geq \$27$.

$$\text{Accept } H_0 \text{ if } \bar{X} \geq \$26.00$$
$$\text{Reject } H_0 \text{ if } \bar{X} < \$26.00$$

Compute the type II error probability β for each of the possible levels of the population mean μ. Assume $\sigma = \$8.00$ and $n = 25$. [Section 10-1C]

　　(a) \$24.75　　(b) \$24.50　　(c) \$24.25　　(d) \$24.00

Answers
1. false　　**2.** 101.64　　**3.** 10.267
4. (a) Reject H_0.　(b) Accept H_0.　(c) Accept H_0.　(d) Reject H_0.
5. (a) Reject H_0.　(b) Reject H_0.　(c) Accept H_0.　(d) Accept H_0.
6. (a) .261　(b) .366　(c) .290　(d) .242
7. (a) (1) -5.11　(2) Reject H_0.　(c) (1) 1.84　(2) Accept H_0.
　　(b) (1) -2.45　(2) Reject H_0.　(d) (1) $-.23$　(2) Accept H_0.
8. (a) (1) 1.833　(2) 2.656　(3) Reject H_0.
　　(b) (1) 1.711　(2) 10.500　(3) Reject H_0.
　　(c) (1) 1.729　(2) 3.130　(3) Reject H_0.
　　(d) (1) 1.761　(2) 1.485　(3) Accept H_0.
9. (a) .0082　(b) .0548
10. (a) .2177　(b) .1736　(c) .1379　(d) .1056

SOLVED PROBLEMS

PROBLEM 10-1　Consider each hypothesis-testing situation. Then indicate for each of the four actions whether it is a correct decision, a type I error, or a type II error.

(a) H_0: New battery's lifetime is less than or equal to the old one's.
　　(1) Change to new when old lasts at least as long.
　　(2) Keep old when new lasts longer.
　　(3) Keep old when old lasts at least as long.
　　(4) Change to new when new lasts longer.
(b) H_0: Diodes are satisfactory.
　　(1) Reject satisfactory shipment.
　　(2) Accept satisfactory shipment.
　　(3) Reject unsatisfactory shipment.
　　(4) Accept unsatisfactory shipment.
(c) H_0: New plan is superior.
　　(1) Approve an inferior plan.
　　(2) Disapprove an inferior plan.
　　(3) Disapprove a superior plan.
　　(4) Approve a superior plan.

Solution: Classify each action as correct or as an error. The type I error is to reject the null hypothesis when it is true, while the type II error is to accept the null hypothesis when it is false.
(a) (1) type I error　　(3) correct
　　(2) type II error　　(4) correct
(b) (1) type I error　　(3) correct
　　(2) correct　　　　(4) type II error
(c) (1) type II error　　(3) type I error
　　(2) correct　　　　(4) correct

PROBLEM 10-2 You are asked to determine whether to accept or reject the null hypothesis that the mean processing time μ for special orders is less than or equal to 10 minutes. There will be a very large number of such orders processed, and you may assume that the standard deviation is 2 minutes per order (the same value that applies to regular orders). You will base your finding on a sample of $n = 100$ special orders timed.

   (a) Formulate the null and alternative hypotheses.

   (b) Suppose you wish to protect yourself with a probability of $\alpha = .01$ against rejecting the null hypothesis when it is true. Compute the critical value of the sample mean, and express the decision rule.

   (c) You collect the sample data. What action must you take (1) if $\bar{X} = 10.62$ min.? (2) if $\bar{X} = 10.47$ min.? (3) if $\bar{X} = 10.25$ min.?

Solution:
(a) The following apply:

$$H_0: \mu \leqslant 10 \text{ min.} (= \mu_0) \qquad H_1: \mu > 10 \text{ min.}$$

(b) The standard error of $\bar{X}$ is $\sigma_{\bar{x}} = \sigma/\sqrt{n} = 2/\sqrt{100} = .2$ min. The critical normal deviate is $z_{.01} = 2.33$. H_0 is oriented so that the test is upper-tailed. The critical value is

$$\bar{X}^* = 10 + 2.33(.2) = 10.47 \text{ min.}$$

The following decision rule applies:

$$\text{Accept } H_0 \text{ if } \bar{X} \leqslant 10.47 \text{ min.}$$
$$\text{Reject } H_0 \text{ if } \bar{X} > 10.47 \text{ min.}$$

(c) You will accept H_0 if the computed value is less than or equal to 10.47 min., and you will reject H_0 if the value is greater than 10.47 min. Thus,

   (1) Reject H_0.
   (2) Accept H_0. When the test statistic falls exactly on the critical value, you always accept.
   (3) Accept H_0.

PROBLEM 10-3 Your friend owns a retail store where she plans to give individual arriving customers a short verbal "commercial" message regarding the products for sale. Your friend asks you to determine if this will boost the mean sales transaction level μ, currently at $5.00. You may assume that the standard deviation per transaction is $1.00 and that the population is of unlimited size. You will monitor a random sample of $n = 200$ customers given this special treatment and determine the amount purchased by each.

   (a) Your friend will adopt a policy of giving messages if sample evidence indicates that sales will improve. She wants most to avoid adopting this policy when the mean sales transaction won't improve. Formulate the null and alternative hypotheses.

   (b) Suppose you wish to protect your friend with a probability of $\alpha = .05$ against rejecting the null hypothesis when it is true. Compute the critical value of the sample mean, and express the decision rule.

   (c) You collect the sample data. What action should you take (1) if $\bar{X} = \$5.37$? (2) if $\bar{X} = \$5.05$? (3) if $\bar{X} = \$4.97$? (4) if $\bar{X} = \$5.20$?

Solution:
(a) The null hypothesis is specified by the more serious error, which is to reject H_0 when it is true. Thus, the null hypothesis is

$$H_0: \mu \leqslant \$5.00 \qquad \text{(no improvement)}$$

The pivotal level for the population mean is $\mu_0 = \$5.00$. The alternative hypothesis is the opposite of the null hypothesis.

$$H_1: \mu > \$5.00 \quad \text{(an improvement)}$$

(b) The test is an upper-tailed one and the critical normal deviate is $z_{.05} = 1.64$. Using $\sigma_{\bar{x}} = \$1.00/\sqrt{200} = .071$, you find the following critical value for the sample mean:

$$\bar{X}^* = \$5.00 + 1.64(.071) = \$5.12$$

The decision rule is

> Accept H_0 if $\bar{X} \leqslant \$5.12$ (don't adopt policy)
> Reject H_0 if $\bar{X} > \$5.12$ (adopt policy)

(c) You will accept H_0 if the computed value is less than or equal to $5.12, and you will reject H_0 if the value is greater than $5.12. Thus,
  (1) Reject H_0.   *(2)* Accept H_0.   *(3)* Accept H_0.   *(4)* Reject H_0.

PROBLEM 10-4 A plant produces bearings with a specified 1-inch mean diameter. The standard deviation for all bearings produced is known to be .01 inch. A decision rule is to be established for determining when to correct for oversized or undersized items. This choice is based on a sample of 100 bearings, and the assumption is made that there is only an $\alpha = .01$ chance of taking corrective action when the production process is exactly meeting its mean target.

  (a) Formulate the null hypothesis.
  (b) What test statistic is appropriate?
  (c) Express the decision rule.
  (d) What action should be taken *(1)* if $\bar{X} = .993''$? *(2)* if $\bar{X} = 1.0023''$?

Solution:
(a) You may express the null hypothesis in terms of the mean bearing diameter μ as

$$H_0: \mu = 1''   \text{(process on target)}$$

Since the null hypothesis places the mean at an exact value, the test is a two-sided one.
(b) Since the standard deviation is given, you may use $\bar{X}$ as the test statistic.
(c) The population size is unlimited, so you ignore the finite population correction factor. Thus, the standard error of $\bar{X}$ is $\sigma_{\bar{X}} = .01''/\sqrt{100} = .001''$. Using the critical normal deviate value of $z_{\alpha/2} = z_{.005} = 2.57$, you get the following critical values:

$$\bar{X}_1^* = 1.0000 - 2.57(.001) = .9974''$$
$$\bar{X}_2^* = 1.0000 + 2.57(.001) = 1.0026''$$

The decision rule is

> Accept H_0 if $.9974'' \leqslant \bar{X} \leqslant 1.0026''$ (leave alone)
> Reject H_0 if $\bar{X} < .9974''$ (correct for undersizing)
>   or if $\bar{X} > 1.0026''$ (correct for oversizing)

(d) *(1)* Since .993'' falls below the lower critical value, you must reject H_0. Correction should be made for undersizing.
  (2) 1.0023'' falls between the critical values, inside the acceptance region, so you must accept H_0. The process should be left alone.

PROBLEM 10-5 The plant in Problem 10-4 will be manufacturing a bearing with a specified 1/2-inch diameter. The standard deviation in diameter is unknown, and corrective action will be taken based on a sample of 100 items measured.

  (a) Formulate the null hypothesis.
  (b) What test statistic is appropriate?
  (c) Express the decision rule.
  (d) What action should be taken *(1)* if $\bar{X} = .497''$ with $s = .0075''$? *(2)* if $\bar{X} = .508''$ with $s = .013''$?

Solution:
(a) You may express the null hypothesis in terms of the mean bearing diameter μ as

$$H_0: \mu = .5'' (= \mu_0)   \text{(process on target)}$$

Since the null hypothesis places the mean at an exact value, the test is a two-sided one.
(b) Since the standard deviation is unknown, you can't directly use $\bar{X}$ as the test statistic. However, the sample size is large, so you can use the normal deviate z instead.

(c) The critical normal deviate value is $z_{.005} = 2.57$. Thus, the decision rule is

> Accept H_0 if $-2.57 \leqslant z \leqslant 2.57$ (leave alone)
> Reject H_0 if $z < -2.57$ (correct for undersizing)
>   or if $z > 2.57$ (correct for oversizing)

(d) You must compute the normal deviate for each sample result.
   (1) $z = (.497 - .5)/(.0075/\sqrt{100}) = -4.00$. Since this falls below the lower critical value, you must reject H_0. Correction should be made for undersizing.
   (2) $z = (.508 - .5)/(.013/\sqrt{100}) = 6.15$. Since this falls above the upper critical value, you must reject H_0. Correction should be made for oversizing.

PROBLEM 10-6   As part of a class project, your statistics instructor asks you to weigh a sample of 100 items from a shipment of 500. You are testing the null hypothesis that the mean is greater than or equal to 10 lbs. You have been told that the standard deviation is $\sigma = .5$ lb. Accepting H_0 is the same as accepting the shipment.

   (a) Using a significance level of $\alpha = .05$, determine the critical value for the applicable test statistic and express the decision rule.
   (b) What action should you take (1) if $\bar{X} = 10.1$ lbs.? (2) if $\bar{X} = 9.95$ lbs.? (3) if $\bar{X} = 9.85$ lbs.?

Solution:
(a) Since the standard deviation is known, you may use the sample mean as the test statistic in testing the null hypothesis

$$H_0: \mu \geqslant 10 \text{ lbs.} (= \mu_0)$$

Since small values for $\bar{X}$ will tend to refute H_0, the test is a lower-tailed one. The population is small in relation to the sample size, so you must use the finite population correction factor in computing the standard error of $\bar{X}$.

$$\sigma_{\bar{X}} = \frac{.5}{\sqrt{100}} \sqrt{\frac{500 - 100}{500 - 1}} = .0448$$

Using $z_{.05} = 1.64$ as the critical normal deviate, you get the following critical value:

$$\bar{X}^* = 10 - 1.64(.0448) = 9.93 \text{ lbs.}$$

The decision rule is

> Accept H_0 if $\bar{X} \geqslant 9.93$ lbs.   (accept shipment)
> Reject H_0 if $\bar{X} < 9.93$ lbs.   (reject shipment)

(b) (1) Accept H_0 (and the shipment), since the computed value falls in the acceptance region.
   (2) Accept H_0 (and the shipment), since the computed value falls in the acceptance region.
   (3) Reject H_0 (and the shipment), since the computed value falls in the rejection region.

PROBLEM 10-7   A winery is evaluating a modified fermentation process that involves higher temperatures than its present method. Since the new procedure requires specially designed controls, it has been judged economic only if production batches ferment faster than the mean time of 30 hours under the present system. If that isn't supported by testing, the present process will be continued. The test will involve 50 pilot batches to be run under the modified procedure.

   (a) The more serious error is to adopt the modified process when it isn't actually the faster one. Express the null hypothesis in terms of the mean fermentation time μ.
   (b) The standard deviation in fermentation time is unknown. Assuming a significance level of $\alpha = .01$, express the decision rule.
   (c) The following results were obtained: $\bar{X} = 29.5$ hrs. and $s = 4.91$ hrs. What action should be taken?

Solution:
(a) The null hypothesis is specified by the more serious error, which is to reject H_0 when it is true. Thus, the null hypothesis is

$$H_0: \mu \geqslant 30 \text{ hrs.}   \text{(not faster)}$$

The pivotal level for the population mean is $\mu_0 = 30$ hrs. The test is a lower-tailed one.

(b) The normal deviate z serves as the test statistic, since the sample size is large enough and the population standard deviation is unknown. The critical normal deviate is $z_{.01} = 2.33$, and the decision rule is

Accept H_0 if $z \geqslant -2.33$ (retain present system)
Reject H_0 if $z < -2.33$ (adopt modified system)

(c) The sample results provide the following:

$$z = \frac{29.5 - 30}{4.91/\sqrt{50}} = -.72$$

Since this falls in the acceptance region, the null hypothesis must be accepted and the present system should be retained.

PROBLEM 10-8   The manufacturer of electronic timing devices is evaluating an experimental tuning stand as a possible substitute for the present manual method of calibration. The stand will be acquired only if it can calibrate the devices in a mean time μ of less than 15 minutes. A sample of 50 units is to be tested, and nothing is known regarding the population of calibration times.

   (a) Assuming a maximum chance of $\alpha = .01$ for acquiring the tuning stand when it takes 15 min. or longer to complete calibration, express the decision rule.
   (b) Test results provide a mean calibration time of 13.5 min. with a standard deviation of 3.4 min. What action should be taken?

Solution:
(a) The null hypothesis is $H_0: \mu \geqslant 15$ min., corresponding to a lower-tailed test. Since the population standard deviation isn't given, the sample mean can't be used directly as the test statistic. Because the sample size is large enough, the normal deviate z serves as the test statistic. For a critical value of $z_{.01} = 2.33$, the following decision rule applies:

Accept H_0 if $z \geqslant -2.33$ (retain present method of calibration)
Reject H_0 if $z < -2.33$ (adopt new tuning stand)

(b) The computed value of the test statistic is

$$z = \frac{13.5 - 15}{3.4/\sqrt{50}} = -3.12$$

which falls below -2.33. Therefore, H_0 must be rejected, and the new tuning stand should be adopted.

PROBLEM 10-9   A special paper has a desired thickness of .05 millimeter. If the mean value differs from this amount, the processing machinery requires adjustment. A sample of size $n = 100$ sheets has been selected, and $\bar{X} = .051$ mm. has been computed with $s = .002$ mm. At the $\alpha = .05$ significance level, should the machinery be adjusted or left alone?

Solution: The null hypothesis is $H_0: \mu = .05$ mm., corresponding to a two-sided test. Since the population standard deviation isn't given, the sample mean can't be used directly as the test statistic. Because the sample size is large enough, the normal deviate z serves as the test statistic. With a critical value of $z_{\alpha/2} = z_{.025} = 1.96$, the following decision rule applies:

Accept H_0 if $-1.96 \leqslant z \leqslant 1.96$ (leave machinery alone)
Reject H_0 if $z < -1.96$ or if $z > 1.96$ (adjust machinery)

The computed value of the test statistic is

$$z = \frac{.051 - .05}{.002/\sqrt{100}} = 5.00$$

which falls above 1.96. Therefore, you must reject H_0. The machinery should be adjusted.

PROBLEM 10-10   In packaging a soap powder, the desired weight is 5 pounds. If the true population mean value μ is above or below this amount, the machinery needs to be adjusted. Management has decided that unnecessary adjustments occur no more than 5% of the time.

Each day a random sample of 100 boxes is selected, and then, based on the sample mean weight, a decision is made whether to leave the equipment alone or to adjust it. Suppose that $\bar{X}$ is 5.1 lbs. and $s = .5$ lbs. What action should be taken?

Solution: The null hypothesis is H_0: $\mu = 5$ lbs., corresponding to a two-sided test. Since the population standard deviation is unknown, $\bar{X}$ can't be used directly as the test statistic. Because the sample size is large enough, the normal deviate z serves as the test statistic. Using a critical value of $z_{\alpha/2} = z_{.025} = 1.96$, you get the following decision rule:

Accept H_0 if $-1.96 \leqslant z \leqslant 1.96$ (leave equipment alone)
Reject H_0 if $z < -1.96$ or if $z > 1.96$ (adjust equipment)

The computed value of the normal deviate test statistic is

$$z = \frac{5.1 - 5}{.5/\sqrt{100}} = 2.00$$

which falls above 1.96. Therefore, you must reject the null hypothesis. The machinery should be adjusted.

PROBLEM 10-11   A company personnel manager is testing the physical aptitude of college graduates to determine whether or not they score higher than high-school graduates. If they do, the new test will be used in the future to screen college graduates, as well as nongraduates, applying for nonmanagement positions. The test is administered to a random sample of $n = 25$ persons. Management wants only an $\alpha = .05$ chance of incorrectly changing screening procedures when the actual mean aptitude test score is $\leqslant 86$, the historical mean for high-school graduates.

(a) Formulate the null hypothesis. Indicate which test statistic applies, and determine its critical value. Express the decision rule.
(b) Suppose the sample results are $\bar{X} = 88$ and $s = 10$. What action should the manager take?

Solution:
(a) The null hypothesis, expressed in terms of the mean aptitude test score, is H_0: $\mu \leqslant 86$. The test is upper-tailed. Since the population standard deviation is unknown and the sample size is small, the Student t statistic applies. For $25 - 1 = 24$ degrees of freedom, the critical value is $t_{.05} = 1.711$. The following decision rule applies:

Accept H_0 if $t \leqslant 1.711$ (keep present screening procedures)
Reject H_0 if $t > 1.711$ (change to new test)

(b) The computed value of the test statistic is

$$t = \frac{88 - 86}{10/\sqrt{25}} = 1.00$$

Since this falls below the critical value, the null hypothesis must be accepted. The manager should keep the present screening procedures.

PROBLEM 10-12   The product manager for Exonex wants to determine the time in which this experimental drug cures a skin disease. If management concludes that the drug yields a mean cure-time advantage over traditional treatment of more than 2 days, research will continue with the present formulation. Otherwise, a new formulation will be adopted for further testing. The drug will be administered to a sample of $n = 25$ persons and the cure-time advantage determined for each. The type I error probability has been set at $\alpha = .05$ for switching to a new formulation when the present one achieves the desired advantage.

(a) Formulate the null hypothesis. Indicate which test statistic applies, and determine its critical value. Express the decision rule.
(b) Suppose the sample results for the cure-time advantage are $\bar{X} = 1.6$ days and $s = .4$ day. What action should the manager take?

Solution:
(a) The null hypothesis, expressed in terms of the mean cure-time advantage, is H_0: $\mu \geqslant 2$ days. The test is lower-tailed. Since the population standard deviation is unknown and the sample size is small, the Student

t statistic applies. For $25 - 1 = 24$ degrees of freedom, the critical value is $t_{.05} = 1.711$. The following decision rule applies:

Accept H_0 if $t \geqslant -1.711$ (use present formulation)
Reject H_0 if $t < -1.711$ (use new formulation)

(b) The computed value of the test statistic is

$$t = \frac{1.6 - 2}{.4/\sqrt{25}} = -5.00$$

Since this falls below the critical value, the null hypothesis must be rejected. The manager should conduct future testing on the new formulation.

PROBLEM 10-13   A large accounting firm achieved the following percentage savings in audit time by using a new computer system for examining transactions.

80	10	37	26
45	29	44	5

(a) Compute the sample mean and standard deviation.
(b) At the $\alpha = .05$ significance level, can the firm conclude that the computer system will yield some level of savings in auditing time?

Solution:
(a) The following values apply:

$$\bar{X} = 34.5 \qquad s = 23.45$$

(b) In terms of the mean percentage time savings μ, the null hypothesis is that there will be no time saved by using the computer, so $H_0: \mu \leqslant 0$. The test is upper-tailed. Since the population standard deviation is unknown and the sample size is small, the Student t statistic applies. For $8 - 1 = 7$ degrees of freedom, the critical value is $t_{.05} = 1.895$. The following decision rule applies:

Accept H_0 if $t \leqslant 1.895$ (use present system)
Reject H_0 if $t > 1.895$ (use computer system)

The computed value of the test statistic is

$$t = \frac{34.5 - 0}{23.45/\sqrt{8}} = 4.161$$

Since this exceeds the critical value, the null hypothesis of no savings in auditing time must be rejected. The firm should conclude that the computer system will yield time savings.

PROBLEM 10-14   The following tire mileage data (in thousands of miles) were obtained for a new tread design.

62.3	44.4	49.2	63.3	47.6	60.1
37.4	55.8	57.5	58.3	56.2	54.3

(a) Compute the sample mean and standard deviation.
(b) At the $\alpha = .05$ significance level, should you accept or reject the null hypothesis that, on the average, tires with the new tread will last 50 thousand miles or more?

Solution:
(a) The following values apply:

$$\bar{X} = 53.87 \qquad s = 7.76$$

(b) In terms of mean tire mileage μ, the null hypothesis is $H_0: \mu \geqslant 50$. The test is lower-tailed. Since the population standard deviation is unknown and the sample size is small, the Student t statistic applies. For $12 - 1 = 11$ degrees of freedom, the critical value is $t_{.05} = 1.796$. The following decision rule applies:

Accept H_0 if $t \geqslant -1.796$ (new tread lasts 50 thousand miles or more)
Reject H_0 if $t < -1.796$ (new tread lasts less than 50 thousand miles)

The computed value of the test statistic is

$$t = \frac{53.87 - 50}{7.76/\sqrt{12}} = 1.728$$

Since this exceeds the critical value, you must accept the null hypothesis that the new tread will last at least 50 thousand miles.

PROBLEM 10-15 A presidential candidate is deciding whether or not to enter the New Hampshire primary. She orders a poll to determine if a substantial portion of the voters recognize her name. She will poll a sample of 100 voters and calculate the proportion that know her name. This is to be done in such a way that there will be only an $\alpha = .10$ chance of committing the type I error of skipping the New Hampshire primary when 70% or more of the voters actually recognize her.

(a) Formulate the null and alternative hypotheses.

(b) Compute the critical value of the sample proportion, and express the decision rule.

(c) Suppose that only $P = .50$ of the sampled voters know who she is. What action should she take?

Solution:

(a) The following hypotheses apply:

$$H_0: \pi \geqslant .70 \qquad H_1: \pi < .70$$

(b) The test is lower-tailed. For the critical normal deviate $z_{.10} = 1.28$, the following critical value applies:

$$P^* = .70 + \frac{.5}{100} - 1.28 \sqrt{\frac{.70(1 - .70)}{100}} = .646$$

(You ignore the finite population correction factor since the population size is large in relation to the sample size.) The candidate's decision rule is as follows:

Accept H_0 if $P \geqslant .646$ (enter New Hampshire primary)
Reject H_0 if $P < .646$ (skip New Hampshire)

(c) The value $P = .50$ falls in the rejection region. The candidate should skip New Hampshire.

PROBLEM 10-16 A telephone company policy is to add an information operator to the pool whenever sample data indicate that all operators are busy an excessive proportion of the time. A type I error probability of $\alpha = .05$ has been established for unncecessarily adding an operator when the pool is busy 50% of the time or less. A sample of $n = 20$ observations will be made at random times.

(a) The sample proportion of time busy will serve as the test statistic. Express the decision rule for deciding whether or not to add an operator.

(b) What action should be taken if all operators are busy during 65% of the sample observation times?

Solution:

(a) Expressed in terms of the proportion of time busy π, the null hypothesis is $H_0: \pi \leqslant .50$. The test is upper-tailed, and the critical normal deviate is $z_{.05} = 1.64$. The critical value of the sample proportion is

$$P^* = .50 - \frac{.5}{20} + 1.64 \sqrt{\frac{.50(1 - .50)}{20}} = .658$$

(You ignore the finite population correction factor, since the population is of unlimited size.) The decision rule is as follows:

Accept H_0 if $P \leqslant .658$ (don't add an operator)
Reject H_0 if $P > .658$ (add an operator)

(b) The sample proportion $P = .65$ falls in the acceptance region, and no operator should be added.

PROBLEM 10-17 A statistician is testing the null hypothesis that exactly half of all MBA's continue their formal education by taking courses within 10 years of graduation. Using a sample of 200 persons, he found that 111 had taken coursework since receiving their MBA. At the $\alpha = .05$ significance level, should the statistician accept or reject his null hypothesis?

Solution: The null hypothesis is that the proportion who continue their education is $\pi = .50$, exactly. The test is a two-sided one. For the critical normal deviate $z_{\alpha/2} = z_{.025} = 1.96$, the following critical values apply for the sample proportion:

$$P_1^* = .50 + \frac{.5}{200} - 1.96 \sqrt{\frac{.50(1 - .50)}{200}} = .433$$

$$P_2^* = .50 - \frac{.5}{200} + 1.96 \sqrt{\frac{.50(1 - .50)}{200}} = .567$$

(Again, you may ignore the finite population correction factor.) The decision rule is as follows:

Accept H_0 if $.433 \leqslant P \leqslant .567$ (conclude exactly half continue their education)
Reject H_0 if $P < .433$ or if $P > .567$ (conclude either more or less than half continue their education)

The computed value of the sample proportion is $P = 111/200 = .555$, which falls between the critical values, inside the acceptance region. The null hypothesis must therefore be accepted.

PROBLEM 10-18   A sample of $n = 100$ items will be selected at random from an incoming shipment of $N = 900$. The null hypothesis is that the proportion defective is at most .05. The sample proportion defective is .06. At the $\alpha = .05$ significance level, should the null hypothesis be accepted or rejected?

Solution: In terms of the proportion defective π, the null hypothesis is $H_0: \pi \leqslant .05$. The test is an upper-tailed one. For the critical normal deviate $z_{.05} = 1.64$, the following critical value applies for the sample proportion defective:

$$P^* = .05 - \frac{.5}{100} + 1.64 \sqrt{\frac{.05(1 - .05)}{100}} \sqrt{\frac{900 - 100}{900 - 1}} = .079$$

(You must use the finite population correction factor since the population size is less than 10 times the sample size.) The decision rule is as follows:

Accept H_0 if $P \leqslant .079$ (proportion defective is at most .05)
Reject H_0 if $P > .079$ (proportion defective is greater than .05)

Since the computed value $P = .06$ is less than .079, the null hypothesis must be accepted.

11 REGRESSION AND CORRELATION

THIS CHAPTER IS ABOUT

☑ **Regression Analysis**
☑ **Correlation Analysis**
☑ **Multiple Regression**

Now that you are familiar with estimation and testing, you are ready to learn about a third broad area of inferential statistics concerned with **association** between several variables, each representing a different population. Statistical association takes two important forms. You will first encounter **regression analysis**, which provides the tools to predict the level of one variable from the known value of one or more additional variables. Next you will learn about **correlation analysis**, which is concerned with the strength of the relationship between several variables.

Regression analysis is especially important in business applications of statistics where an unknown value needs to be predicted from the known levels for other variables. Correlation analysis can be helpful in searching for factors that might be useful in making future predictions.

11-1. Regression Analysis

When you know the relationship between two variables, it is an easy matter to determine the value of one of them given the level of the other.

A. The levels of two variables may be related by a straight line.

In computing interest due on a bank deposit earning 8% per annum, you can use the following expression to find the interest income I due from any given principal amount P held for one year:

$$I = .08P$$

The variable I is called the **dependent variable**, since its value is computed using a given level for P, the **independent variable**.

You can apply regression analysis to more complex circumstances, such as when the relationship between the two variables is itself unknown. It is conventional to use X to represent the independent variable and Y the dependent variable. Sample data are then used to establish an equation of the form

$$Y = a + bX$$

which plots on a graph as a straight line. Here, a and b represent the constant numbers of the equation. The first constant, a, is the height of the line where it cuts through the Y-axis; a is called the **Y-intercept**. The coefficient of X, b, indicates how much Y changes for each unit of X; it is called the **slope**.

B. A sample provides raw data that plot as a scatter diagram.

An illustration involving a duplicating facility will explain how regression analysis works. The **raw data** listed in the following table represent 20 sample observations for single-page jobs run on an offset press at the duplicating center. The table gives the number of copies X and the completion time Y for each job. Figure 11-1 provides a graph showing each set of values as a data point. Such a representation is called a **scatter diagram**.

Job i	Number of copies X	Completion time (in minutes) Y	Job i	Number of copies X	Completion time (in minutes) Y
1	150	2.9	11	500	4.2
2	310	3.9	12	200	3.4
3	450	3.9	13	50	.9
4	1,150	8.1	14	920	6.2
5	800	7.1	15	500	5.1
6	200	2.6	16	500	5.4
7	300	4.1	17	400	2.7
8	250	3.3	18	750	5.8
9	910	6.1	19	410	3.5
10	100	1.9	20	200	3.5

Figure 11-1

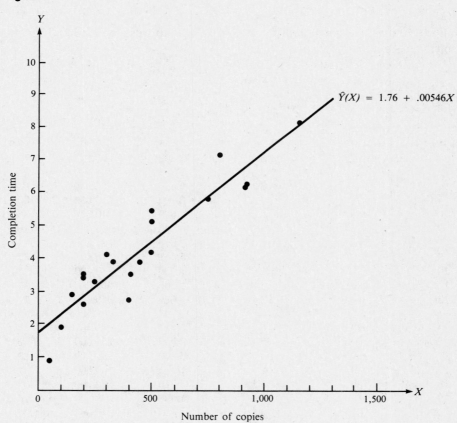

$\hat{Y}(X) = 1.76 + .00546X$

The sample data have been used to determine the **regression line** that provides the best fit. This regression line is superimposed on the scatter diagram in Figure 11-1. The mathematical expression for that line is the **estimated regression equation**. The equation can be used by the management of the duplicating center to predict how long it will take to run a job of any prescribed size.

The estimated regression equation may be expressed in general terms:

$$\hat{Y}(x) = a + bX$$

You compute Y-intercept a and slope b directly from the sample data. These values are therefore known as **estimated regression coefficients**.

C. The method of least squares finds the regression line that best fits the data.

The estimated regression coefficients describe a particular line. You position that regression line in such a way as to separate the data points from the line by the least possible total vertical distances, or **deviations**. You achieve this best fit by minimizing the squared deviations. The procedure is therefore called the **method of least squares**.

Mathematically, the following expressions provide the Y-intercept and slope meeting the least squares criterion.

Estimated regression coefficients

$$b = \frac{n\sum XY - (\sum X)(\sum Y)}{n\sum X^2 - (\sum X)^2}$$

$$a = \bar{Y} - b\bar{X}$$

- Compute the slope b first. You can only find the level for a after b is known.
- Some books use the following mathematically equivalent expression for the slope.

$$b = \frac{\sum XY - n\bar{X}\bar{Y}}{\sum X^2 - n\bar{X}^2}$$

To find a and b, you first compute the necessary value sums. The following calculations apply to the present illustration.

Job i	Number of copies X	Completion time (in minutes) Y	XY	X^2	Y^2
1	150	2.9	435	22,500	8.41
2	310	3.9	1,209	96,100	15.21
3	450	3.9	1,755	202,500	15.21
4	1,150	8.1	9,315	1,322,500	65.61
5	800	7.1	5,680	640,000	50.41
6	200	2.6	520	40,000	6.76
7	300	4.1	1,230	90,000	16.81
8	250	3.3	825	62,500	10.89
9	910	6.1	5,551	828,100	37.21
10	100	1.9	190	10,000	3.61
11	500	4.2	2,100	250,000	17.64
12	200	3.4	680	40,000	11.56
13	50	.9	45	2,500	.81
14	920	6.2	5,704	846,400	38.44
15	500	5.1	2,550	250,000	26.01
16	500	5.4	2,700	250,000	29.16
17	400	2.7	1,080	160,500	7.29
18	750	5.8	4,350	562,000	33.64
19	410	3.5	1,435	168,100	12.25
20	200	3.5	700	40,000	12.25
	9,050 $= \sum X$	84.6 $= \sum Y$	48,054 $= \sum XY$	5,883,700 $= \sum X^2$	419.18 $= \sum Y^2$

You now compute the slope by plugging in the appropriate sums and using $n = 20$ (the number of jobs):

$$b = \frac{20(48,054) - (9,050)(84.6)}{20(5,883,700) - (9,050)^2}$$

$$= .00546$$

The respective sample means are

$$\bar{X} = \frac{9{,}050}{20} = 452.5$$

$$\bar{Y} = \frac{84.6}{20} = 4.23$$

The Y-intercept is thus

$$a = 4.23 - .00546(452.5) = 1.76$$

and the estimated regression equation is

$$\hat{Y}(X) = 1.76 + .00546X$$

D. The estimated regression equation provides predicted values for Y.

The purpose of a regression equation is to make predictions of the dependent variable Y from the given value of the independent variable X. This is advantageous when the level of X is available now, while the actual value of Y can't be found until later.

Consider predicting how long it will take to duplicate a job of any specific size. To predict the time needed for an 850-page job, substitute $X = 850$ into the estimated regression equation just found:

$$\hat{Y}(850) = 1.76 + .00546(850) = 6.40 \text{ min.}$$

By plugging $X = 400$ into the regression equation, you can estimate that a 400-page job will take

$$\hat{Y}(400) = 1.76 + .00546(400) = 3.94 \text{ min.}$$

E. Regression predictions are subject to sampling error.

Of course, these values are merely statistical estimates of the duration of any job of the stated length. You may gauge the overall accuracy of the regression procedure by a statistic called the **standard error of the estimate**, $s_{Y \cdot X}$. This summarizes the degree of scatter about the regression line provided by the sample results. This statistic, which resembles the sample standard deviation, can be computed from

$$s_{Y \cdot X} = \sqrt{\frac{\sum [Y - \hat{Y}(X)]^2}{n - 2}}$$

Statisticians, however, prefer to use the following mathematically equivalent expression because it involves fewer computational steps.

Standard error of the estimate $$s_{Y \cdot X} = \sqrt{\frac{\sum Y^2 - a \sum Y - b \sum XY}{n - 2}}$$

You can see how to use this equation with the data and regression line for the duplicating jobs. Plugging in the respective values, you find the standard error of the estimate to be

$$s_{Y \cdot X} = \sqrt{\frac{419.18 - 1.76(84.6) - .00546(48{,}054)}{20 - 2}} = .663$$

The regression line "explains" some of the variability in Y that might otherwise go unaccounted for. The standard error of the estimate helps measure the impact of knowing the regression line. If it is assumed that nothing is known of X, the variability in Y can be summarized by the sample standard deviation:

$$s_Y = \sqrt{\frac{\sum Y^2 - n\bar{Y}^2}{n - 1}} = \sqrt{\frac{419.18 - 20(4.23)^2}{20 - 1}} = 1.80$$

Notice that the sample standard deviation is considerably larger than $s_{Y \cdot X}$. The regression line appears to explain much of the variability in Y.

11-2. Correlation Analysis

Often accompanying regression analysis is correlation analysis, which measures the strength of association between X and Y. The type of information provided by correlation analysis can be so useful that it is performed even when no regression line is sought and no predictions are required.

For example, a marketing researcher might need to identify only those factors, such as income and age, having a potential influence on the level of purchases of a product. Or an econometrician might use correlation analysis to identify which predictors, such as prime rates or stock prices, to include in a model of investment decision making.

A. The sample correlation coefficient measures the strength and direction of the relationship between X and Y.

The **sample correlation coefficient**, denoted by r, is a value expressing how strongly two variables relate to each other. Figure 11-2 shows two extreme cases. The graph in (a) shows how the sample observations of X and Y might be *uncorrelated*, with raw data scattered in no discernible pattern about the X-Y plane. For uncorrelated variables the value of the correlation coefficient r is 0. At the other extreme are *perfectly correlated* variables, shown in (b). Here the raw sample data points all fall on a straight line, and $r = 1$.

Figure 11-2

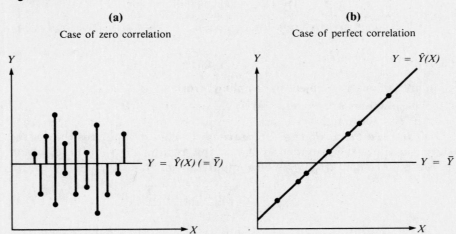

You can compute the sample correlation coefficient from the raw data using the following expression.

Sample correlation coefficient

$$r = \frac{\sum XY - (1/n)(\sum X)(\sum Y)}{\sqrt{[\sum X^2 - (1/n)(\sum X)^2][\sum Y^2 - (1/n)(\sum Y)^2]}}$$

This will always be a number falling between -1 and 1.

Figure 11-3 shows several examples of r. The sample correlation coefficient measures *linear* relationships only. The value of r is negative when the data are best fit by a downwardly sloping line (a line for which b is negative). The value of r becomes closer to 1 (or -1) when the data scatter more tightly about the line. Notice from the graph in (f) that r doesn't reflect any nonlinear relationship between X and Y.

Using the duplicating center data from before, you can compute r.

$$r = \frac{48,054 - (1/20)(9,050)(84.6)}{\sqrt{[5,883,700 - (1/20)(9,050)^2][419.18 - (1/20)(84.6)^2]}} = .933$$

This value suggests a relatively strong correlation between duplicating time Y and number of pages X.

Figure 11-3

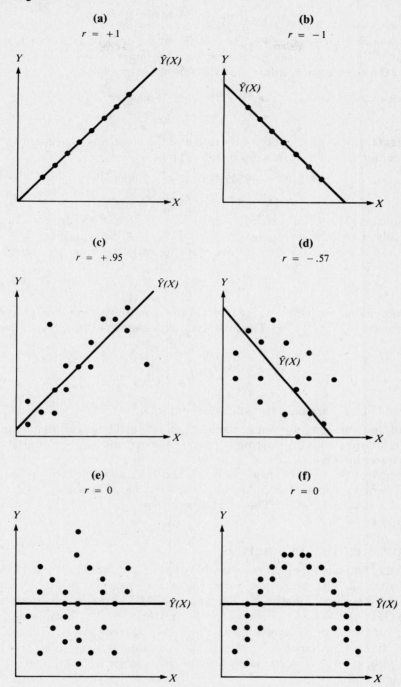

- Some books use equivalent expressions for the sample correlation coefficient. The following is common.

$$r = \frac{\sum XY - n\bar{X}\bar{Y}}{\sqrt{[\sum X^2 - n\bar{X}^2][\sum Y^2 - n\bar{Y}^2]}}$$

B. The sample coefficient of determination is commonly used to gauge the quality of a regression relationship.

The **sample coefficient of determination**, denoted by r^2, expresses the proportion of the variability in Y that the regression line explains:

$$r^2 = \frac{\text{Explained variability in } Y}{\text{Total variability in } Y}$$

This will always lie between 0 and 1. The coefficient of determination is the square of the correlation coefficient, but because it may be of primary interest, r^2 is often computed directly from the regression results using the following expression.

Sample coefficient of determination

$$r^2 = \frac{a\sum Y + b\sum XY - (1/n)(\sum Y)^2}{\sum Y^2 - (1/n)(\sum Y)^2}$$

To illustrate, consider again the raw data and the slope and Y-intercept values for the duplicating center jobs. The following result applies.

$$r^2 = \frac{1.76(84.6) + .00546(48,054) - (1/20)(84.6)^2}{419.18 - (1/20)(84.6)^2} = .87$$

This indicates that 87% of the variability in Y is explained by the regression line that relates duplicating time Y to number of pages X. Only 13% is left unexplained.

You could have reached this finding working directly from the sample correlation coefficient:

$$r^2 = (.933)^2 = .87$$

Other equivalent expressions may be used to compute r^2. You might have a book that uses $n\bar{Y}^2$ instead of $(1/n)^2(\sum Y)^2$. The following expression shows another useful relationship.

$$r^2 = 1 - \frac{s_{Y \cdot X}^2}{s_Y^2}\left(\frac{n-2}{n-1}\right)$$

C. The sample coefficients are only statistical estimators.

Keep in mind that you compute r or r^2 using *sample* data. These values may not accurately portray the true relationships existing between the corresponding *population* values. **The population correlation coefficient**, usually denoted as ρ (Greek lowercase *rho*), expresses the true strength of the relationship between X and Y. The sample correlation coefficient is only a statistical estimate of ρ. Likewise, there is a **population coefficient of determination** ρ^2, estimated by r^2. (The relationship between r and ρ is analogous to that between $\bar{X}$ and μ.)

11-3. Multiple Regression Analysis

When there is more than one independent variable or predictor, you may extend the techniques for regression analysis into **multiple regression analysis**. You should appreciate the advantages of using multiple predictors. For example, MBA admissions are generally based both on college GPA and GMAT scores, plus other criteria. Neither grades nor aptitude test scores would be totally suitable as the only major screening mechanism. Multiple independent variables are helpful in many business applications. For example, a manufacturer may predict a product's sales using several predictors, such as the unemployment rate, interest rates, and an index of consumer confidence.

A multiple regression equation makes greater use of existing information than its counterpart from **simple regression** (where there is only one independent variable).

A. The least squares procedure extends to multiple regression.

The simplest **estimated multiple regression equation** involves two independent variables, conveniently denoted as X_1 and X_2.

$$\hat{Y} = a + b_1 X_1 + b_2 X_2$$

when graphed in three dimensions, this equation provides the **estimated regression plane**. Figure 11-4 shows how such a graph would look. As before, a is the Y-intercept (the height at which the plane cuts through the Y axis). The values b_1 and b_2 are the **estimated partial**

regression coefficients; they play a role analogous to the slope of the two-dimensional regression line.

Figure 11-4

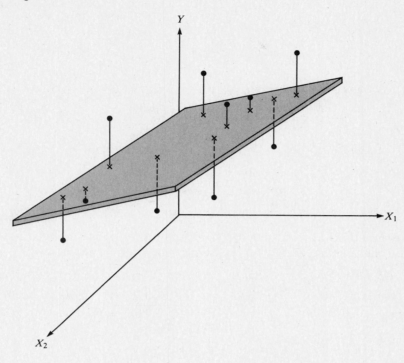

You find the levels of a, b_1, and b_2 by the method of least squares which, like before, minimizes the sum of the squared vertical deviations from each data point to the regression plane). You can achieve this by simultaneously solving the following system of three equations in three unknowns.

Normal equations

$$\sum Y = na + b_1\sum X_1 + b_2\sum X_2$$
$$\sum X_1 Y = a\sum X_1 + b_1\sum X_1^2 + b_2\sum X_1 X_2$$
$$\sum X_2 Y = a\sum X_2 + b_1\sum X_1 X_2 + b_2\sum X_2^2$$

To illustrate, consider the problem of estimating the total cost Y (in thousands of dollars) of a production batch of WeeTees, using quantity produced X_1 (in tons) and grain price index X_2 as the independent variables. The following sample data apply.

Sample i	Cost (in thousands of dollars) Y	Production quantity (in tons) X_1	Grain price index X_2
1	200	400	120
2	85	150	134
3	115	220	115
4	200	500	90
5	140	300	85
6	65	100	140
7	70	150	95
8	65	150	80
9	125	240	96
10	190	350	125

The procedure begins with the calculation of sums and sums of squares and products.

Y	X_1	X_2	X_1Y	X_2Y	X_1X_2	X_1^2	X_2^2	Y^2
200	400	120	80,000	24,000	48,000	160,000	14,400	40,000
85	150	134	12,750	11,390	20,100	22,500	17,956	7,225
115	220	115	25,300	13,225	25,300	48,400	13,225	13,225
200	500	90	100,000	18,000	45,000	250,000	8,100	40,000
140	300	85	42,000	11,900	25,500	90,000	7,225	19,600
65	100	140	6,500	9,100	14,000	10,000	19,600	4,225
70	150	95	10,500	6,650	14,250	22,500	9,025	4,900
65	150	80	9,750	5,200	12,000	22,500	6,400	4,225
125	240	96	30,000	12,000	23,040	57,600	9,216	15,625
190	350	125	66,500	23,750	43,750	122,500	15,625	36,100
1,255	2,560	1,080	383,300	135,215	270,940	806,000	120,772	185,125
$= \sum Y$	$= \sum X_1$	$= \sum X_2$	$= \sum X_1Y$	$= \sum X_2Y$	$= \sum X_1X_2$	$= \sum X_1^2$	$= \sum X_2^2$	$= \sum Y^2$

Placing the appropriate values in the normal equations, you get

$$1{,}255 = 10a + 2{,}560b_1 + 1{,}080b_2$$

$$383{,}300 = 2{,}560a + 806{,}000b_1 + 270{,}940b_2$$

$$135{,}215 = 1{,}080a + 270{,}940b_1 + 120{,}772b_2$$

To solve these normal equations, you must eliminate all but one of the unknowns. Start by combining the first two equations to eliminate a:

$$\left. \begin{array}{l} -256(1{,}255 = \quad 10a + \quad 2{,}560b_1 + \quad 1{,}080b_2) \\ 383{,}300 = 2{,}560a + 806{,}000b_1 + 270{,}940b_2 \end{array} \right\} \longrightarrow$$

$$\begin{array}{l} -321{,}280 = -2{,}560a - 655{,}360b_1 - 276{,}480b_2 \\ \underline{383{,}300 = \quad 2{,}560a + 806{,}000b_1 + 270{,}940b_2} \\ 62{,}020 = \qquad\quad 0a + 150{,}640b_1 - \quad 5{,}540b_2 \end{array}$$

Now combine the first and the third equations, again eliminating a:

$$\left. \begin{array}{l} -108(1{,}255 = \quad 10a + \quad 2{,}560b_1 + \quad 1{,}080b_2) \\ 135{,}215 = 1{,}080a + 270{,}940b_1 + 120{,}772b_2 \end{array} \right\} \longrightarrow$$

$$\begin{array}{l} -135{,}540 = -1{,}080a - 276{,}480b_1 - 116{,}640b_2 \\ \underline{135{,}215 = \quad 1{,}080a + 270{,}940b_1 + 120{,}772b_2} \\ -325 = \qquad\quad 0a - \quad 5{,}540b_1 + \quad 4{,}132b_2 \end{array}$$

By combining the two resulting equations and eliminating b_2, you will find the value of b_1.

$$\left. \begin{array}{l} 4{,}132(62{,}020 = 150{,}640b_1 - 5{,}540b_2) \\ 5{,}540(-325 = -5{,}540b_1 + 4{,}132b_2) \end{array} \right\} \longrightarrow$$

$$\begin{array}{l} 256{,}266{,}640 = \quad 622{,}444{,}480b_1 - 22{,}891{,}280b_2 \\ \underline{-1{,}800{,}500 = -30{,}691{,}600b_1 + 22{,}891{,}280b_2} \\ 254{,}466{,}140 = \quad 591{,}752{,}880b_1 + \qquad\qquad 0b_2 \\ \qquad\qquad\quad b_1 = .430 \end{array}$$

Substitute b_1 into either of the equations having two variables to find b_2.

$$62{,}020 = 150{,}640(.430) - 5{,}540b_2$$

$$62{,}020 = 64{,}775.2 - 5{,}540b_2$$

$$5{,}540b_2 = 2{,}755.2$$

$$b_2 = .497$$

Substitute b_1 and b_2 into one of the original equations with three variables to find a.

$$1{,}255 = 10a + 2{,}560(.430) + 1{,}080(.497)$$

$$1{,}255 = 10a + 1{,}100.80 + 536.76$$

$$1{,}255 = 10a + 1{,}637.56$$

$$-10a = 382.56$$

$$a = -38.3$$

Substituting the values you found for a, b_1, and b_2 into the estimated multiple regression equation, you get

$$\hat{Y} = -38.3 + .430X_1 + .497X_2$$

You can make predictions of the cost for WeeTees production runs from the estimated regression equation. Consider the following.

Tons	Price index	Predicted cost (in thousands of dollars)
$X_1 = 100$	$X_2 = 90$	$\hat{Y} = -38.3 + .430(100) = .497(90) = 49.4$
$X_1 = 150$	$X_2 = 110$	$\hat{Y} = -38.3 + .430(150) + .497(110) = 80.9$
$X_1 = 200$	$X_2 = 70$	$\hat{Y} = -38.3 + .430(200) + .497(70) = 82.5$

B. The standard error of the estimate measures the quality of the regression plane.

The quality of a multiple regression may be summarized by the **standard error of the estimate**. This quantity, which is analogous to its simple regression counterpart, is based on the squared vertical deviations about the regression plane.

Standard error of the estimate

$$S_{Y \cdot 12} = \sqrt{\frac{\sum Y^2 - a\sum Y - b_1 \sum X_1 Y - b_2 \sum X_2 Y}{n - 3}}$$

Substituting the values computed for the prediction of the cost of WeeTees production, you obtain the following:

$$S_{Y \cdot 12} = \sqrt{\frac{185{,}125 - (-38.3)(1{,}255) - .430(383{,}300) - .497(135{,}215)}{10 - 3}}$$

$$= 12.93$$

A satisfactory multiple regression plane should explain more of the variability in Y than would the simple regression for either of the independent variables. You can see that this is true for the following simple regression lines that have been fit to the WeeTees data.

Using X_1 only: $\qquad \hat{Y} = 20.1 + .412 X_1 \qquad (s_{Y \cdot X_1} = 16.16)$

Using X_2 only: $\qquad \hat{Y} = 134.0 - .079 X_2 \qquad (s_{Y \cdot X_2} = 58.73)$

Notice that the standard error for each simple regression line is greater than that for the multiple regression plane.

C. Multiple regression can involve more than two independent variables.

The number of independent predictor variables used in multiple regression can exceed two. The estimated multiple regression equation for three independent variables takes the form

$$\hat{Y} = a + b_1 X_1 + b_2 X_2 + b_3 X_3$$

For higher-dimensional multiple regressions, additional terms $b_k X_k$ are included as necessary. Such equations can't be shown on three-dimensional graphs. Nevertheless, statisticians retain the original geometrical terminology and refer to $\hat{Y}$ as the regression *hyperplane*.

You would ordinarily perform higher-dimensional multiple regression analysis with the assistance of a digital computer.

SUMMARY

Regression and correlation analyses are concerned with the *association* between two or more variables, each representing a separate quantitative population.

Regression analysis predicts the level of the *dependent variable Y* when only the value of the *independent variable X* is known. You compute the predicted Y by plugging a specific X into the *estimated regression equation*,

$$\hat{Y}(X) = a + bX$$

This is also called the *estimated regression line*, which you establish by the *method of least squares* from the sample raw data. The Y-intercept a and the slope b are the *regression coefficients*, found by the following equations:

$$b = \frac{n\sum XY - (\sum X)(\sum Y)}{n\sum X^2 - (\sum X)^2}$$

$$a = \bar{Y} - b\bar{X}$$

These values describe the regression line that best fits the raw data, which are often graphed on a *scatter diagram*.

The overall quality of the regression line is reflected by the *standard error of the estimate*,

$$S_{Y \cdot X} = \sqrt{\frac{\sum Y^2 - a\sum Y - b\sum XY}{n - 2}}$$

This quantity reflects the capacity of the regression line to "explain" some of the variability in values of Y. A satisfactory regression line will yield a value for $S_{Y \cdot X}$ that is considerably smaller than the sample standard deviation of Y, s_Y.

The *sample correlation coefficient*

$$r = \frac{\sum XY - (1/n)(\sum X)(\sum Y)}{\sqrt{[\sum X^2 - (1/n)(\sum X)^2][\sum Y^2 - (1/n)(\sum Y)^2]}}$$

measures the strength and direction of the relationship between X and Y. This value can help you determine when there exists a potentially useful linear relationship between two variables. *Perfect correlation* is approached as r becomes near to 1 or -1. X and Y are *uncorrelated* whenever $r = 0$. Often the correlation between X and Y is measured by the *sample coefficient of determination*, r^2. Although this value is equal to the square of the sample correlation coefficient, you might want to compute r^2 directly from the regression results and intermediate calculations:

$$r^2 = \frac{a\sum Y + b\sum XY - (1/n)(\sum Y)^2}{\sum Y^2 - (1/n)(\sum Y)^2}$$

The coefficient of determination expresses the proportion of the variability in Y that is explained by the regression line.

The theory underlying regression and correlation analyses assumes that X and Y may be related by a true regression line that can only be estimated by the sample results. Likewise, the true correlation coefficient ρ relating X and Y can only be estimated by r.

Multiple regression incorporates two or more independent predictor variables. The method of least squares provides an *estimated regression plane* (or hyperplane) described by an *estimated multiple regression equation* of the form

$$\hat{Y} = a + b_1 X_1 + b_2 X_2 + \cdots + b_k X_k$$

The quality of predictions reached using the higher dimensional regression plane is often greater than that obtainable from a *simple regression* involving a single independent variable. The Y-intercept a and *estimated partial regression coefficients* ($b_1, b_2, \ldots$) may be computed simultaneously solving a system of *normal equations*,

$$\sum Y = na + b_1\sum X_1 + b_2\sum X_2$$
$$\sum X_1 Y = a\sum X_1 + b_1\sum X_1^2 + b_2\sum X_1 X_2$$
$$\sum X_2 Y = a\sum X_2 + b_1\sum X_1 X_2 + b_2\sum X_2^2$$

formed from sums computed using the raw data. The accuracy of the multiple regression can be determined by the standard error of the estimate:

$$S_{Y \cdot 12} = \sqrt{\frac{\sum Y^2 - a\sum Y - b_1\sum X_1 Y - b_2\sum X_2 Y}{n - 3}}$$

A digital computer is ordinarily used for higher dimensional multiple regressions.

RAISE YOUR GRADES

Can you explain...?

☑ the difference between regression and correlation analyses
☑ the role played by the standard error of the estimate
☑ what the coefficient of determination expresses
☑ in what sense the method of least squares fits the best regression line to the raw data
☑ why some types of strong relationships between X and Y aren't acknowledged by the level of r

Do you know...?

☑ the difference between the Y-intercept and the slope
☑ what the standard error of the estimate measures
☑ how to make a prediction using an estimated regression equation
☑ how the slope of the regression line relates to the sign of r
☑ when it may be advantageous to perform a multiple regression analysis instead of a simple regression.

RAPID REVIEW

1. Use the regression line $\hat{Y}(X) = -5.0 + 3.4X$ to predict the level of Y corresponding to the stated level of X.   [Section 11-1D]
    (a) 10   **(b)** 55   **(c)** 17   **(d)** 30

2. Consider the following regression line.

$$\hat{Y}(X) = 35 - 10X$$

What is the sign of the sample correlation coefficient?   [Section 11-2A]

3. A correlation of coefficient $r = .95$ exists between X and Y. What is the sign of the slope b of the estimated regression line?   [Section 11-2A]

4. Find the predicted level of Y obtained from the following estimated regression plane $\hat{Y} = -12.5 + .24X_1 - 1.3X_2$ when $X_1 = 15$ and $X_2 = 40$?   [Section 11-3A]

5. Find the predicted level of Y obtained from the estimated regression hyperplane $\hat{Y} = 112.3 + 5.6X_1 + .40X_2 + .25X_3$ when $X_1 = -4.1$, $X_2 = 100.2$, and $X_3 = 88.5$. [Section 11-3C]

6. Which one of the following statements isn't supported by the regression relationship $\hat{Y}(X) = -6.0 + 4.1X$?   [Section 11-1]

    (a) A one-unit increase in X raises the predicted level of Y by 4.1.
    (b) When $X = 0$, the predicted level of Y is -6.0.
    (c) Since $a = -6.0$, a negative value applies for r.
    (d) When $X = 1$, the predicted level of Y is -1.9.

7. You have lost your scratch paper for a regression analysis. You remember that $a = 15$ and that $\hat{Y} = 100$ is the predicted value corresponding to $X = 5$. Find the corresponding value for the slope b.   [Section 11-1B]

8. You are told that $b = 11.1$, $\bar{X} = 3.5$, and $\bar{Y} = 10.0$. Find the Y-intercept a. [Section 11-1C]

9. Which one of the following statements is definitely true regarding the following multiple regression relationship?   [Section 11-3]

$$\hat{Y} = -10 + 1X_1 + .1X_2$$

(a) The correlation between Y and X_2 is .1.
(b) The Y-intercept is negative.
(c) The correlation between Y and X_1 is 1.
(d) As a predictor, X_1 is 10 times more important than X_2.

10. Which one of the following statements is false?   [Sections 11-1, 2, 3]

(a) Multiple regression is always better than simple regression, providing a sufficient number of sample data points are available.
(b) The method of least squares minimizes the collective *squared* vertical deviations of data points about the regression line.
(c) Normal equations are used to find the multiple regression coefficients.
(d) The coefficient of determination equals the square of the correlation coefficient.

Answers
1. (a) 29.0   (b) 182.0   (c) 52.8   (d) 97.0
2. negative   3. positive   4. −60.9   5. 151.5
6. (c)   7. 17   8. −28.85   9. (b)   10. (a)

SOLVED PROBLEMS

PROBLEM 11-1   On a piece of graph paper plot the following lines.

(a) $\hat{Y}(X) = 10 + 10X$ (b) $\hat{Y}(X) = 8 + 2X$ (c) $\hat{Y}(X) = 20 - 4X$

Solution: See Figure 11-5. In each case, begin by marking off the X and Y axes. Working with the equation form $\hat{Y}(X) = a + bX$, determine for each line the Y-intercept, a. This provides one point on the line. You plot the second point by fixing X at some arbitrary value and computing the corresponding $\hat{Y}(X)$. Draw a line connecting the two points. Using (a) as an example, the Y-intercept is 10. Fixing X at the value of 3, you get $\hat{Y}(X) = 40$. Draw a line connecting the points (0, 10) and (3, 40).

Figure 11-5

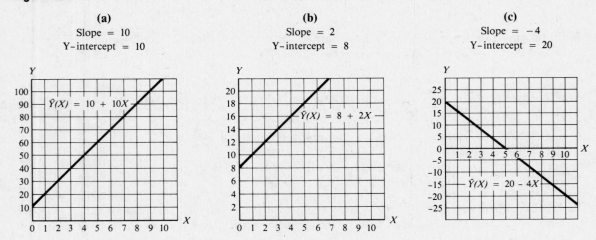

PROBLEM 11-2   The following data represent the years in practice and the annual income (in thousands of dollars) for a random sample of certified public accountants.

Years	Income	Years	Income
5	40	3	20
15	40	6	30
24	90	12	30
16	70	27	70
19	60	13	50

Treat income as the dependent variable.

(a) Plot these data as a scatter diagram.

(b) The following estimated regression lines have been recommended. Plot each on your graph.

(1) $\hat{Y}(X) = 0 + 1X$ (3) $\hat{Y}(X) = 100 - 3X$
(2) $\hat{Y}(X) = 40 + 0X$ (4) $\hat{Y}(X) = 20 + 2X$

(c) Which regression line appears to provide the best fit?

Solution:

(a) See Figure 11-6. First mark off the X and Y axes. Then position the data points on your graph in accordance with the coordinates given by the data: (5, 40), (15, 40), etc.

(b) See Figure 11-6, where each line has been plotted by determining the Y-intercept and by computing the $\hat{Y}(X)$ for some arbitrary value of X.

(c) Line (4) provides the best fit.

Figure 11-6

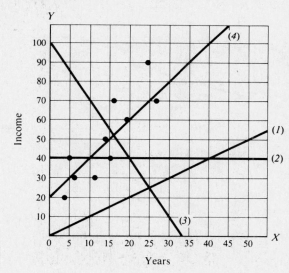

PROBLEM 11-3   An economist has established that personal income X may be used to predict personal consumption Y by the relationship

$$\hat{Y}(X) = -24.0 + .94X \qquad \text{(in billions of dollars)}$$

For each of the following levels of personal income, calculate the predicted value for personal consumption.

(a) $300 billion   (b) $500 billion   (c) $700 billion

Solution: You find the predicted value by plugging each value of X into the equation for the line.

(a) $\hat{Y}(300) = -24.0 + .94(300) = \$258$ billion

(b) $\hat{Y}(500) = -24.0 + .94(500) = \$446$ billion

(c) $\hat{Y}(700) = -24.0 + .94(700) = \$634$ billion

PROBLEM 11-4   The following data apply for the time required to inspect outgoing batches of a certain product for various percentages of defective items.

Percentage defective X	Inspection time (in minutes) Y	Percentage defective X	Inspection time (in minutes) Y
17	48	10	49
9	50	14	55
12	43	18	63
7	36	19	55
8	45	6	36

(a) Plot the scatter diagram for these data.

(b) Determine the estimated regression equation, and plot the estimated regression line on your graph.

(c) Compute (*1*) the sample standard deviation for inspection time and (*2*) the standard error of the estimate for inspection time.

Solution:

(a) See Figure 11-7.

Figure 11-7

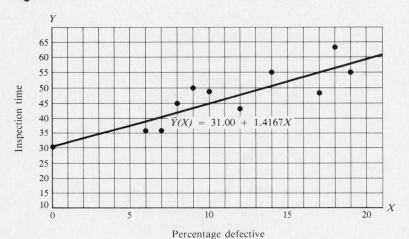

$$\hat{Y}(X) = 31.00 + 1.4167X$$

Percentage defective

(b) The following calculations provide the necesary values for computing the regression coefficients.

Observation	X	Y	XY	X^2	Y^2
1	17	48	816	289	2,304
2	9	50	450	81	2,500
3	12	43	516	144	1,849
4	7	36	252	49	1,296
5	8	45	360	64	2,025
6	10	49	490	100	2,401
7	14	55	770	196	3,025
8	18	63	1,134	324	3,969
9	19	55	1,045	361	3,025
10	6	36	216	36	1,296
	120	480	6,049	1,644	23,690
	$= \sum X$	$= \sum Y$	$= \sum XY$	$= \sum X^2$	$= \sum Y^2$

The sample means are

$$\bar{X} = \frac{120}{10} = 12.0 \qquad \bar{Y} = \frac{480}{10} = 48.0$$

Substituting these computed values into the expressions for b and a, you find the estimated regression coefficients:

$$b = \frac{10(6,049) - (120)(480)}{10(1,644) - (120)^2} = 1.4167$$

$$a = 48 - 1.4167(12) = 31.00$$

Thus the estimated regression equation is

$$\hat{Y}(X) = 31.00 + 1.4167X$$

This regression line is plotted on the graph in Figure 11-7.

(c) You plug the computed values from (b) into the respective equations to find the sample standard deviation and the standard error of the estimate.

(1) $\quad s_Y = \sqrt{\dfrac{23,690 - 10(48)^2}{10 - 1}} = 8.50$

(2) $\quad s_{Y \cdot X} = \sqrt{\dfrac{23,690 - 31.00(480) - 1.4167(6,049)}{10 - 2}} = 5.48$

PROBLEM 11-5 In using least squares regression to determine how the college GPA Y of a particular student relates to his or her high-school GPA X, you have computed the following from a random sample of 10 students.

$$\sum X = 33.0 \qquad \sum Y = 29.0 \qquad \sum XY = 97.74$$
$$\sum X^2 = 111.70 \qquad \sum Y^2 = 86.16$$

(a) Determine the estimated regression equation.
(b) Compare (1) the sample standard deviation for college GPA and (2) the standard error of the estimate for college GPA.

Solution:
(a) You first compute the estimated regression coefficients:

$$\bar{X} = \frac{33.0}{10} = 3.3 \qquad \bar{Y} = \frac{29.0}{10} = 2.9$$

$$b = \frac{10(97.74) - (33.0)(29.0)}{10(111.70) - (33.0)^2} = .7286$$

$$a = 2.9 - .7286(3.3) = .4956$$

The estimated regression equation is

$$\hat{Y}(X) = .4956 + .7286X$$

(b) (1) $\quad s_Y = \sqrt{\dfrac{86.16 - 10(2.9)^2}{10 - 1}} = .478$

(2) $\quad s_{Y \cdot X} = \sqrt{\dfrac{86.16 - .4956(29) - .7286(97.74)}{10 - 2}} = .268$

PROBLEM 11-6 The following sample results provide the number of arriving customers X per hour and the total hourly waiting time Y (in minutes).

X	Y	X	Y	X	Y
105	44	211	112	55	34
511	214	332	155	128	73
401	193	322	131	97	52
622	299	435	208	187	103
330	143	275	138	266	110

(a) Determine the estimated regression equation.
(b) Compute (*1*) the sample standard deviation for total waiting time and (*2*) the standard error of the estimate for total waiting time.

Solution:

(a)

X	Y	XY	X	Y
105	44	4,620	11,025	1,936
511	214	109,354	261,121	45,796
401	193	77,393	160,801	37,249
622	299	185,978	386,884	89,401
330	143	47,190	108,900	20,499
211	112	23,632	44,521	12,544
332	155	51,460	110,224	24,025
322	131	42,182	103,684	17,161
435	208	90,480	189,225	43,264
275	138	37,950	75,625	19,044
55	34	1,870	3,025	1,156
128	73	9,344	16,384	5,329
97	52	5,044	9,409	2,704
187	103	19,261	34,969	10,609
266	110	29,260	70,756	12,100
4,277	2,009	735,018	1,586,553	342,767
$= \sum X$	$= \sum Y$	$= \sum XY$	$= \sum X^2$	$= \sum Y^2$

$$\bar{X} = \frac{4,277}{15} = 285.133 \qquad \bar{Y} = \frac{2,009}{15} = 133.933$$

$$b = \frac{15(735,018) - (4,277)(2,009)}{15(1,586,553) - (4,277)^2} = .442$$

$$a = 133.933 - .442(285.133) = 7.904$$

Using these computed values, you find the estimated regression equation:

$$\hat{Y}(X) = 7.904 + .442X$$

(b) (*1*) $\quad s_Y = \sqrt{\dfrac{342,767 - 15(133.933)^2}{15 - 1}}$

$\qquad = 72.55$

(*2*) $\quad s_{Y \cdot X} = \sqrt{\dfrac{342,767 - 7.904(2,009) - .442(735,018)}{15 - 2}}$

$\qquad = 12.43$

PROBLEM 11-7   A cost accountant has obtained the following sample observations from an investigation involving the relationship between the weight of a production batch Y (in kilograms) and the volume of ingredient X (in liters).

X	Y	X	Y
14	68	22	95
23	105	5	31
9	40	12	72
17	79	6	45
10	81	16	93

(a) Determine the estimated regression equation.
(b) Compute (*1*) the sample standard deviation for batch weight and (*2*) the standard error of the estimate for batch weight.

Solution:

(a)

X	Y	XY	X^2	Y^2
14	68	952	196	4,624
23	105	2,415	529	11,025
9	40	360	81	1,600
17	79	1,343	289	6,241
10	81	810	100	6,561
22	95	2,090	484	9,025
5	31	155	25	961
12	72	864	144	5,184
6	45	270	36	2,025
16	93	1,488	256	8,649
$\overline{134}$	$\overline{709}$	$\overline{10,747}$	$\overline{2,140}$	$\overline{55,895}$
$=\sum X$	$=\sum Y$	$=\sum XY$	$=\sum X^2$	$=\sum Y^2$

$$\bar{X} = \frac{134}{10} = 13.4 \qquad \bar{Y} = \frac{709}{10} = 70.9$$

$$b = \frac{10(10,747) - (134)(709)}{10(2,140) - (134)^2} = 3.62$$

$$a = 70.9 - 3.62(13.4) = 22.4$$

Thus the estimated regression equation is

$$\hat{Y}(X) = 22.4 + 3.62X$$

(b) *(1)* $\quad s_Y = \sqrt{\dfrac{55,895 - 10(70.9)^2}{10 - 1}} = 25.00$

(2) $\quad s_{Y \cdot X} = \sqrt{\dfrac{55,895 - 22.4(709) - 3.62(10,747)}{10 - 2}} = 11.78$

PROBLEM 11-8 The following data relate annual household usage Y of a cleaning agent to the size X of the family.

Family size X	Bottles used Y	Family size X	Bottles used Y
5	2	4	2
8	3	5	3
7	4	5	2
3	2	6	4
2	1	7	5

Compute the sample correlation coefficient.

Solution: The following intermediate calculations are necessary as a first step.

X	Y	XY	X^2	Y^2
5	2	10	25	4
8	3	24	64	9
7	4	28	49	16
3	2	6	9	4
2	1	2	4	1
4	2	8	16	4
5	3	15	25	9
5	2	10	25	4
6	4	24	36	16
7	5	35	49	25
$\overline{52}$	$\overline{28}$	$\overline{162}$	$\overline{302}$	$\overline{92}$
$=\sum X$	$=\sum Y$	$=\sum XY$	$=\sum X^2$	$=\sum Y^2$

Substituting the appropriate values into the expression for r, you compute the sample correlation coefficient:

$$r = \frac{162 - (1/10)(52)(28)}{\sqrt{[302 - (1/10)(52)^2][92 - (1/10)(28)^2]}} = .791$$

PROBLEM 11-9 Refer to the data in Problem 11-6 for the number of arriving customers X and the total waiting time Y.

(a) Calculate the sample correlation coefficient directly from the given data.

(b) Using your earlier regression results, calculate the sample coefficient of determination. What percentage of the variation in waiting time does the estimated regression line explain?

Solution:

(a) $$r = \frac{735,018 - (1/15)(4,277)(2,009)}{\sqrt{[1,586,553 - (1/15)(4,277)^2][342,767 - (1/15)(2,009)^2]}} = .986$$

(b) $$r^2 = \frac{7.904(2,009) + .442(735,018) - (1/15)(2,009)^2}{342,767 - (1/15)(2,009)^2} = .9727$$

The estimated regression line explains 97.3% of the variation in waiting time.

PROBLEM 11-10 Refer to the data in Problem 11-7 for the volume of ingredients X and the weight of the production batch Y.

(a) Calculate the sample correlation coefficient directly from the given data.

(b) Using your earlier regression results, calculate the sample coefficient of determination. What percentage of the variation in the weight of the production batch does the estimated regression line explain?

Solution:

(a) $$r = \frac{10,747 - (1/10)(134)(709)}{\sqrt{[2,140 - (1/10)(134)^2][55,895 - (1/10)(709)^2]}} = .895$$

(b) $$r^2 = \frac{22.4(709) + 3.62(10,747) - (1/10)(709)^2}{55,895 - (1/10)(709)^2} = .8029$$

The estimated regression line explains 80.29% of the variation in the weight of the production batch.

PROBLEM 11-11 The following data have been obtained for the GPA Y and the number of outside activities X for a sample of 10 students.

Number of activities X	GPA Y	Number of activities X	GPA Y
10	3.9	3	2.8
0	3.1	4	3.3
5	3.4	5	2.6
2	2.8	4	2.5
0	1.9	3	3.2

(a) Find the estimated regression line for predicting a student's GPA from the number of his or her activities.

(b) Find (1) the sample standard deviation for GPA and (2) the standard error of the estimate for GPA.

(c) Compute (1) the sample coefficient of determination and (2) the sample correlation coefficient.

(d) What is the predicted GPA for a student having the following number of activities?
   (1) 5   (2) 2   (3) 4   (4) 10

Solution:

(a)

X	Y	XY	X^2	Y^2
10	3.9	39.0	100	15.21
0	3.1	0.0	0	9.61
5	3.4	17.0	25	11.56
2	2.8	5.6	4	7.84
0	1.9	0.0	0	3.61
3	2.8	8.4	9	7.84
4	3.3	13.2	16	10.89
5	2.6	13.0	25	6.76
4	2.5	10.0	16	6.25
3	3.2	9.6	9	10.24
36	29.5	115.8	204	89.81
$=\sum X$	$=\sum Y$	$=\sum XY$	$=\sum X^2$	$=\sum Y^2$

$$\bar{X} = \frac{36}{10} = 3.6 \qquad \bar{Y} = \frac{29.5}{10} = 2.95$$

$$b = \frac{10(115.8) - (36)(29.5)}{10(204) - (36)^2} = .129$$

$$a = 2.95 - .129(3.6) = 2.486$$

Using these calculations you compute the estimated regression line:

$$\hat{Y}(X) = 2.486 + .129X$$

(b) (1) $\quad s_Y = \sqrt{\dfrac{89.81 - 10(2.95)^2}{10 - 1}} = .556$

(2) $\quad s_{Y \cdot X} = \sqrt{\dfrac{89.81 - 2.486(29.5) - .129(115.8)}{10 - 2}} = .438$

(c) (1) $\quad r^2 = \dfrac{2.486(29.5) + .129(115.8) - (1/10)(29.5)^2}{89.81 - (1/10)(29.5)^2} = .449$

(2) $\quad r = \sqrt{.449} = .670$

(d) You find the predicted GPA for a given number of activities X by substituting the level of X into the estimated regression equation.

(1) $\quad \hat{Y}(5) = 2.486 + .129(5) = 3.13$
(2) $\quad \hat{Y}(2) = 2.486 + .129(2) = 2.74$
(3) $\quad \hat{Y}(4) = 2.486 + .129(4) = 3.00$
(4) $\quad \hat{Y}(10) = 2.486 + .129(10) = 3.78$

PROBLEM 11-12 Determine the predicted level of Y in each of the following situations.

(a) $\hat{Y} = 10 + 2X_1 + 3X_2$ given $X_1 = 5$ and $X_2 = 10$.
(b) $\hat{Y} = -20 + 4X_1 + 5X_2$ given $X_1 = 1$ and $X_2 = .5$.
(c) $\hat{Y} = 14.67 + .23X_1 - .58X_2$ given $X_1 = 55$ and $X_2 = 27$.

Solution: In each case, you find the predicted level of Y by plugging the given levels of X_1 and X_2 into the estimated multiple regression equation.
(a) $\hat{Y} = 10 + 2(5) + 3(10) = 50$
(b) $\hat{Y} = -20 + 4(1) + 5(.5) = -13.5$
(c) $\hat{Y} = 14.67 + .23(55) - .58(27) = 11.66$

PROBLEM 11-13 Solve the following system of simultaneous equations.

$$5 = 2a + 1b_1 - 5b_2$$
$$2 = 1a + 4b_1 + 2b_2$$
$$-1 = 2a + 2b_1 - 2b_2$$

Solution: Apply the "method of elimination" by combining the first two equations and eliminating a:

$$\begin{aligned} 5 &= 2a + 1b_1 - 5b_2 \\ -2(2 &= 1a + 4b_1 + 2b_2) \end{aligned} \Bigg\} \longrightarrow \begin{aligned} 5 &= 2a + 1b_1 - 5b_2 \\ -4 &= -2a - 8b_1 - 4b_2 \\ \hline 1 &= 0a - 7b_1 - 9b_2 \end{aligned}$$

Then do the same for the last two original equations:

$$\begin{aligned} 2 &= 1a + 4b_1 + 2b_2 \\ -.5(-1 &= 2a + 2b_1 - 2b_2) \end{aligned} \Bigg\} \longrightarrow \begin{aligned} 2.0 &= 1a + 4b_1 + 2b_2 \\ .5 &= -1a - 1b_1 + 1b_2 \\ \hline 2.5 &= 0a + 3b_1 + 3b_2 \end{aligned}$$

Drop $0a$ from both of the resulting equations, and solve them simultaneously by eliminating b_2:

$$\begin{aligned} 1 &= -7b_1 - 9b_2 \\ +3(2.5 &= 3b_1 + 3b_2) \end{aligned} \longrightarrow \begin{aligned} 1.0 &= -7b_1 - 9b_2 \\ 7.5 &= 9b_1 + 9b_2 \\ \hline 8.5 &= 2b_1 + 0b_2 \end{aligned}$$

You get

$$b_1 = \frac{8.5}{2} = 4.250$$

Plugging $b_1 = 4.250$ into the top equation of the last group, you find the value of b_2:

$$1 = -7(4.250) - 9b_2 \quad \text{or} \quad 9b_2 = -1 - 29.75 = -30.75$$

so that

$$b_2 = -\frac{30.75}{9} = -3.417$$

Plugging the values for b_1 and b_2 into the first original equation, you find the value for a:

$$5 = 2a + 1(4.250) - 5(-3.417) \quad \text{or} \quad 2a = 5 - 4.25 - 17.085 = -16.335$$

so that

$$a = -\frac{16.335}{2} = -8.17$$

PROBLEM 11-14 A real estate appraiser wishes to use the following sample data to establish a predictive relationship between the selling price of a home and the building and lot size.

Price (in thousands of dollars) Y	Building size (in hundreds of square feet) X_1	Lot size (in thousands of square feet) X_2
45	21	21
37	16	23
26	17	7
32	14	9
34	19	11
49	18	45
53	23	12
65	22	10
71	24	10
88	26	22

(a) Compute the sums for each of these and for the square and product terms.

(b) Express the normal equations, and solve them simultaneously to determine the estimated multiple regression coefficients. Then express the estimated multiple regression equation.

(c) Compute the standard error of the estimate for selling price.

Solution:

(a)

Y	X_1	X_2	X_1Y	X_2Y	X_1X_2	X_1^2	X_2^2	Y^2
45	21	21	945	945	441	441	441	2,025
37	16	23	592	851	368	256	529	1,369
26	17	7	442	182	119	289	49	676
32	14	9	448	288	126	196	81	1,024
34	19	11	646	374	209	361	121	1,156
49	18	45	882	2,205	810	324	2,025	2,401
53	23	12	1,219	636	276	529	144	2,809
65	22	10	1,430	650	220	484	100	4,225
71	24	10	1,704	710	240	576	100	5,041
88	26	22	2,288	1,936	572	676	484	7,744
500	200	170	10,596	8,777	3,381	4,132	4,074	28,470
$=\sum Y$	$=\sum X_1$	$=\sum X_2$	$=\sum X_1Y$	$=\sum X_2Y$	$=\sum X_1X_2$	$=\sum X_1^2$	$=\sum X_2^2$	$=\sum Y^2$

(b) The normal equations are as follows:

$$500 = 10a + 200b_1 + 170b_2$$
$$10{,}596 = 200a + 4{,}132b_1 + 3{,}381b_2$$
$$8{,}777 = 170a + 3{,}381b_1 + 4{,}074b_2$$

You solve these equations in the manner of Problem 11-12.

$$\left.\begin{array}{l} -20(500 = 10a + 200b_1 + 170b_2) \\ \underline{10{,}596 = 200a + 4{,}132b_1 + 3{,}381b_2} \end{array}\right\} \longrightarrow \begin{array}{l} -10{,}000 = -200a - 4{,}000b_1 - 3{,}400b_2 \\ \underline{10{,}596 = 200a + 4{,}132b_1 + 3{,}381b_2} \\ 596 = 0a + 132b_1 + {-19}b_2 \end{array}$$

$$\left.\begin{array}{l} 8.5(10{,}596 = 200a + 4{,}132b_1 + 3{,}381b_2) \\ \underline{-10(8{,}777 = 170a + 3{,}381b_1 + 4{,}074b_2)} \end{array}\right\} \longrightarrow \begin{array}{l} 90{,}066 = 1{,}700a + 35{,}122b_1 + 28{,}738.5b_2 \\ \underline{-87{,}770 = -1{,}700a - 33{,}810b_1 - 40{,}740.0b_2} \\ 2{,}296 = 0a + 1{,}312b_1 - 12{,}001.5b_2 \end{array}$$

Solve these two resulting equations for b_2.

$$\left.\begin{array}{l} 1{,}312(596 = 132b_1 - 19.0b_2) \\ \underline{-132(2{,}296 = 1{,}312b_1 - 12{,}001.5b_2)} \end{array}\right\} \longrightarrow \begin{array}{l} 781{,}952 = 173{,}184b_1 - 24{,}928b_2 \\ \underline{-303{,}072 = -173{,}184b_1 + 1{,}584{,}198b_2} \\ 478{,}880 = 0b_1 + 1{,}559{,}270b_2 \end{array}$$

$$b_2 = \frac{478{,}880}{1{,}559{,}270}$$

$$b_2 = .3071$$

Now find b_1 by plugging $b_2 = .3071$ into either of the equations with two variables:

$$596 = 132b_1 - 19(.3071)$$
$$596 = 132b_1 - 5.8349$$
$$132b_1 = 601.8349$$
$$b_1 = 4.5594$$

Finally, use one of the original equations with three variables, substituting in the values for b_1 and b_2, to find a.

$$500 = 10a + 200(4.5594) + 170(.3071)$$
$$500 = 10a + 911.88 + 52.207$$
$$500 = 10a + 964.087$$
$$-10a = 464.087$$
$$a = -46.4087$$

Thus, the estimated multiple regression equation is

$$\hat{Y} = -46.4087 + 4.5594X_1 + .3071X_2$$

(c) You find the standard error of the estimate by substituting the appropriate values into the expression for $S_{Y.12}$

$$S_{Y.12} = \sqrt{\frac{28{,}470 - (-46.4087)(500) - 4.5594(10{,}596) - .3071(8{,}777)}{10 - 3}}$$

$$= 9.765$$

PROBLEM 11-15   In finding the relationship between earnings Y and company net worth X_1 (both in thousands of dollars) and annual inventory turnover X_2, a statistician has taken a sample of $n = 100$ medium-sized retailers. He has obtained the following intermediate calculations:

$$\sum Y = 15{,}500 \qquad \sum X_1 = 2{,}500 \qquad \sum X_2 = 400$$
$$\sum X_1 Y = 388{,}000 \qquad \sum X_2 Y = 62{,}155 \qquad \sum X_1 X_2 = 10{,}377$$
$$\sum X_1^2 = 62{,}950 \qquad \sum X_2^2 = 1{,}700 \qquad \sum Y^2 = 2{,}413{,}000$$

(a) Find (1) the estimated multiple regression equation and (2) the standard error of the estimate of Y about the regression plane.

(b) Determine (1) the estimated regression line for predicting earnings using net worth alone and (2) the corresponding standard error of the estimate.

Solution:

(a) (1) The following normal equations apply:

$$15{,}500 = 100a + 2{,}500b_1 + 400b_2$$
$$388{,}000 = 2{,}500a + 62{,}950b_1 + 10{,}377b_2$$
$$62{,}155 = 400a + 10{,}377b_1 + 1{,}700b_2$$

Solve these equations simultaneously to find the estimated multiple regression coefficients.

$$\left. \begin{array}{l} -25(15{,}500 = 100a + 2{,}500b_1 + 400b_2) \\ 388{,}000 = 2{,}500a + 62{,}950b_1 + 10{,}377b_2 \end{array} \right\} \longrightarrow \begin{array}{l} -387{,}500 = -2{,}500a - 62{,}500b_1 - 10{,}000b_2 \\ 388{,}000 = 2{,}500a + 62{,}950b_1 + 10{,}377b_2 \\ \hline 500 = 0a + 450b_1 + 377b_2 \end{array}$$

$$\left. \begin{array}{l} -4(15{,}500 = 100a + 2{,}500b_1 + 400b_2) \\ 62{,}155 = 400a + 10{,}377b_1 + 1{,}700b_2 \end{array} \right\} \longrightarrow \begin{array}{l} -62{,}000 = -400a - 10{,}000b_1 - 1{,}600b_2 \\ 62{,}155 = 400a + 10{,}377b_1 + 1{,}700b_2 \\ \hline 155 = 0a + 377b_1 + 100b_2 \end{array}$$

Solve these two resulting equations for b_1.

$$\left. \begin{array}{l} -100(500 = 450b_1 + 377b_2) \\ 377(155 = 377b_1 + 100b_2) \end{array} \right\} \longrightarrow \begin{array}{l} -50{,}000 = -45{,}000b_1 - 37{,}700b_2 \\ 58{,}435 = 142{,}129b_1 + 37{,}700b_2. \\ \hline 8{,}435 = 97{,}129b_1 \\ b_1 = .0868 \end{array}$$

Substitute this value for b_1 into either of the equations with two variables to find b_2.

$$500 = 450(.0868) + 377b_2$$
$$500 = 39.06 + 377b_2$$
$$377b_2 = 460.94$$
$$b_2 = 1.2227$$

Solve for a by plugging the values for both b_1 and b_2 into one of the original equations in three variables.

$$15{,}500 = 100a + 2{,}500(.0868) + 400(1.2227)$$
$$15{,}500 = 100a + 217 + 489.08$$
$$15{,}500 = 100a + 706.08$$
$$100a = 14{,}793.92$$
$$a = 147.9392 \quad \text{or} \quad 147.94$$

The estimated multiple regression equation is

$$\hat{Y} = 147.94 + .0868X_1 + 1.2227X_2$$

(2)
$$S_{Y \cdot 12} = \sqrt{\frac{2{,}413{,}000 - 147.94(15{,}500) - .0868(388{,}000) - 1.2227(62{,}155)}{100 - 3}}$$

$$= 10.282$$

(b) (1) To find the simple estimated regression line for predicting earnings, let net worth (X_1) represent the single independent variable X.

$$b = \frac{100(388{,}000) - (2{,}500)(15{,}500)}{100(62{,}950) - (2{,}500)^2} = 1.1111$$

$$\bar{X} = \frac{2{,}500}{100} = 25 \qquad \bar{Y} = \frac{15{,}500}{100} = 155$$

$$a = 155 - 1.1111(25) = 127.22$$

The estimated regression line is

$$\hat{Y}(X_1) = 127.22 + 1.1111X_1$$

(2)
$$s_{Y \cdot X} = \sqrt{\frac{2{,}413{,}000 - 127.22(15{,}500) - 1.1111(388{,}000)}{100 - 2}}$$

$$= 10.093$$

PROBLEM 11-16 A systems programmer wishes to predict run times of payroll programs run on a particular software–hardware configuration. The following data resulted from 20 runs.

Run time (in minutes) Y	Required memory (in thousands of bytes) X_1	Amount of output (in thousands of lines) X_2	Amount of input (in thousands of lines) X_3
11.3	24	10	5
8.7	8	6	5
5.5	14	8	2
7.4	35	6	2
9.1	11	9	4
6.1	23	4	3
15.2	24	11	11
18.2	110	9	3
5.0	20	5	2
22.7	75	21	9
15.9	28	13	9
4.0	20	4	1
10.2	19	4	7
11.9	74	13	2
6.8	7	4	5
14.0	26	8	5
10.2	37	9	4
6.4	16	3	2
5.9	21	3	3
25.5	96	22	7

(a) Using required memory and amount of output as the independent variables and run time as the dependent variable, determine the equation for the estimated multiple regression equation.

(b) Using your regression plane from **(a)** compute the standard error of the estimate for run time.

Solution:

(a)

Y	X_1	X_2	X_1Y	X_2Y	X_1X_2	X_1^2	X_2^2	Y^2
11.3	24	10	271.2	113.0	240	576	100	127.69
8.7	8	6	69.6	52.2	48	64	36	75.69
5.5	14	8	77.0	44.0	112	196	64	30.25
7.4	35	6	259.0	44.4	210	1,225	36	54.76
9.1	11	9	100.1	81.9	99	121	81	82.81
6.1	23	4	140.3	24.4	92	529	16	37.21
15.2	24	11	364.8	167.2	264	576	121	231.04
18.2	110	9	2,002.0	163.8	990	12,100	81	331.24
5.0	20	5	100.0	25.0	100	400	25	25.00
22.7	75	21	1,702.5	476.7	1,575	5,625	441	515.29
15.9	28	13	445.2	206.7	364	784	169	252.81
4.0	20	4	80.0	16.0	80	400	16	16.00
10.2	19	4	193.8	40.8	76	361	16	104.04
11.9	74	13	880.6	154.7	962	5,476	169	141.61
6.8	7	4	47.6	27.2	28	49	16	46.24
14.0	26	8	364.0	112.0	208	676	64	196.00
10.2	37	9	377.4	91.8	333	1,369	81	104.04
6.4	16	3	102.4	19.2	48	256	9	40.96
5.9	21	3	123.9	17.7	63	441	9	34.81
25.5	96	22	2,448.0	561.0	2,112	9,216	484	650.25
220.0	688	172	10,149.4	2,439.7	8,004	40,440	2,034	3,097.74
$=\sum Y$	$=\sum X_1$	$=\sum X_2$	$=\sum X_1Y$	$=\sum X_2Y$	$=\sum X_1X_2$	$=\sum X_1^2$	$=\sum X_2^2$	$=\sum Y^2$

Using these totals, the following normal equations apply.

$$220.0 = 20a + 688b_1 + 172b_2$$
$$10,149.4 = 688a + 40,440b_1 + 8,004b_2$$
$$2,439.7 = 172a + 8,004b_1 + 2,034b_2$$

Solve these equations simultaneously to find the estimated multiple regression coefficients.

$$\left. \begin{array}{l} -43(220.0 = 20a + 688b_1 + 172b_2) \\ 5(2,439.7 = 172a + 8,004b_1 + 2,034b_2) \end{array} \right\} \longrightarrow \begin{array}{l} -9,460.0 = -860a - 29,584b_1 - 7,396b_2 \\ 12,198.5 = 860a + 40,020b_1 + 10,170b_2 \\ \hline 2,738.5 = 0a + 10,436b_1 + 2,774b_2 \end{array}$$

$$\left. \begin{array}{l} 10,149.4 = 688a + 40,440b_1 + 8,004b_2 \\ -4(2,439.7 = 172a + 8,004b_1 + 2,034b_2) \end{array} \right\} \longrightarrow \begin{array}{l} 10,149.4 = 688a + 40,440b_1 + 8,004b_2 \\ -9,758.8 = -688a - 32,016b_1 - 8,136b_2 \\ \hline 390.6 = 0a + 8,424b_1 - 132b_2 \end{array}$$

$$\left. \begin{array}{l} 132(2,738.5 = 10,436b_1 + 2,774b_2) \\ 2,774(390.6 = 8,424b_1 - 132b_2) \end{array} \right\} \longrightarrow \begin{array}{l} 361,482.0 = 1,377,552b_1 + 366,168b_2 \\ 1,083,524.4 = 23,368,176b_1 - 366,168b_2 \\ \hline 1,445,006.4 = 24,745,728b_1 + 0b_2 \\ b_1 = .0584 \end{array}$$

Substitute b_1 into either of the equations with two variables to find b_2.

$$390.6 = 8,424(.0584) - 132b_2$$
$$390.6 = 491.9616 - 132b_2$$
$$132b_2 = 101.3616$$
$$b_2 = .7679$$

Substitute b_1 and b_2 into one of the original equations with three variables to find a.

$$220.0 = 20a + 688(.0584) + 172(.7679)$$
$$220.0 = 20a + 40.1792 + 132.0788$$
$$220.0 = 20a + 172.258$$
$$-20a = -47.742$$
$$a = 2.3871$$

The estimated multiple regression equation is

$$\hat{Y} = 2.3871 + .0584X_1 + .7679X_2$$

(b) The standard error of the estimate for run time is

$$S_{Y \cdot 12} = \sqrt{\frac{3,097.74 - 2.3871(220.0) - .0584(10,149.4) - .7679(2,439.7)}{20 - 3}} = 2.502$$

PROBLEM 11-17 *Computer-assisted exercise.* Suppose that the real estate appraiser in Problem 11-14 also gathered data on the median neighborhood selling price, given below for the 10 homes in her sample. Treat this as her third independent variable X_3. (All data are in thousands of dollars.)

Price Y	Median X_3	Price Y	Median X_3
45	35	49	45
37	40	53	49
26	23	65	70
32	32	71	66
34	39	88	91

(a) You have been asked to run for her a higher dimensional multiple regression. Determine the estimated multiple regression equation.

(b) The standard error of the estimate for selling price using the regression hyperplane is $S_{Y \cdot 123} = 3.902$. Does it appear that including the additional independent variable sharpens the regression analysis?

Solution:
(a) You obtain the following estimated multiple regression equation from a computer run:

$$\hat{Y} = -16.545 + 1.5165X_1 + .1553X_2 + .6852X_3$$

(b) The standard error of the estimate for price found for the lower dimensional multiple regression in Problem 11-14 was $S_{Y \cdot 12} = 9.765$. $S_{Y \cdot 123}$ is considerably smaller. *Yes*, median selling price X_3 does dramatically sharpen the regression analysis.

PROBLEM 11-18 *Computer-assisted exercise.* A truck dispatcher wishes to predict how many driver hours it will take to deliver less-than-truckload shipments over any one of a number of routes. Using four independent variables, he has collected 20 sample observations:

Driver time (in hours) Y	Distance (in miles) X_1	Initial load (in tons) X_2	Deliveries X_3	Speed (mph) X_4
3.0	90	1.5	1	50
7.2	150	3.7	3	35
4.5	65	4.9	3	42
4.3	74	2.6	5	37
6.4	60	3.1	8	40
3.1	70	1.9	2	45
7.0	120	4.7	5	48
5.2	48	3.4	4	29
5.4	125	4.1	3	43
9.2	156	3.4	7	40
5.9	121	2.9	4	46
6.1	98	3.0	6	42
5.5	91	4.5	6	53
5.0	65	4.0	7	42
7.3	74	4.0	8	37
4.7	83	3.6	5	39
4.5	44	2.7	3	48
1.9	33	1.9	1	29
4.2	106	2.0	2	46
4.4	73	3.0	3	37

Find the estimated multiple regression equation.

Solution: You obtain the following equation from a computer run:

$$\hat{Y} = 1.5045 + .030X_1 + .250X_2 + .444X_3 - .038X_4$$

PROBLEM 11-19 *Computer-assisted exercise*. Refer to the data in Problem 11-16. Now include the amount of input as the third independent variable. Find the estimated multiple regression equation.

Solution: The following estimated multiple regression equation applies:

$$\hat{Y} = .3052 + .1039X_1 + .3171X_2 + .9654X_3$$

12 TIME-SERIES ANALYSIS

THIS CHAPTER IS ABOUT

☑ **The Basic Time-Series Model**
☑ **Analysis of Trend**
☑ **Forecasting Using Seasonal Indexes**
☑ **Cyclical and Irregular Fluctuation**
☑ **Exponential Smoothing**

Numerical values that are generated over time are referred to as **time series**. You are probably aware of many examples, such as successive closing prices of stocks, daily retail sales for a store, or a city's high temperatures on successive days. An important area of statistics uses time-series analysis to make forecasts and to plan for the future.

12-1. The Basic Time-Series Model

Time-series analysis is largely concerned with identifying the separate components of the actual data that were obtained. The following **multiplicative model** forms the basis for traditional time-series analysis.

$$Y_t = T_t \times C_t \times S_t \times I_t$$

For any time period, designated by the letter t, the actual data are represented by Y_t. The model assumes that Y_t equals the product of four components:

$$T_t = \text{Trend}$$
$$C_t = \text{Cyclical movement}$$
$$S_t = \text{Seasonal fluctuation}$$
$$I_t = \text{Irregular variations}$$

Figure 12-1 shows how these four components combine to generate the unit-sales time series of Speak E–Z Corporation. The fundamental building block is the **trend line**, T_t, which is either a straight line or a curve that relates series values to time. Note the trend line for Speak E–Z sales in graph (a). Trend represents the movement in values on a long-term basis—several years.

A second long-term component is **cyclical movement**, C_t, expressed as a percentage of trend. Cyclical movement results from the business cycle that coincides with recurring periods of economic expansion, stagnation, and contraction. When plotted, the cyclical time-series component might resemble the "sine wave" shown in (b).

The third component is the short-term **seasonal fluctuation**, S_t, which represents the predictable up-and-down pattern in values ordinarily associated with the seasons of the year. The model applies **seasonal indexes**, expressed as percentages, to the values obtained from the longer-term components. Graph (c) shows the regular "sawtooth" pattern typical of seasonal indexes.

The final component is also short term. It involves the **irregular variations**, I_t, which are nonrepeatable in nature and which occur without pattern and are thus explained in terms of random events. I_t values, also expressed as percentages, are applied to the value achieved by the three regular components. The assumed irregular-component percentages for Speak E–Z sales are provided in (d).

Figure 12-1   Construction of complete time series for speak E–Z's sales, using individual components.

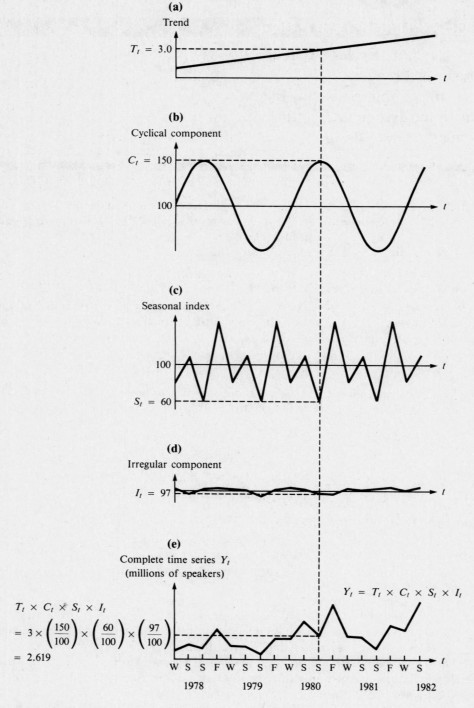

12-2. Analysis of Trend

The usual objective of time-series analysis is to identify and separate the various components. This ordinarily begins with an analysis of the trend. When the data are yearly values, you can find the trend line using regression techniques. When data are quarterly or monthly values, a **smoothed time series** is ordinarily obtained, isolating the longer term trend and cyclical components.

A. Linear regression fits a trend line to past data.

The most common representation of trend is a straight line. It is usually found by fitting a regression line to past data. The dependent variable Y comprises the original values for the time series. The independent variable X is the increment in time (years, quarters, or months), with zero designating the first period.

1. Equation for trend line: The following expression applies.

Regression equation for the trend line $\quad \hat{Y}(X) = a + bX$

You may want to refer back to Chapter 11 for a complete discussion of how to find the regression line. Recall that the method of least squares provides the slope b and Y-intercept a by the following equations.

Regression coefficients for the trend line
$$b = \frac{n\sum XY - (\sum X)(\sum Y)}{n\sum X^2 - (\sum X)^2} \qquad a = \bar{Y} - b\bar{X}$$

EXAMPLE 12-1: CIVILIAN EMPLOYMENT IN THE UNITED STATES

The following data apply to U.S. civilian employment from 1966 through 1975.

Year	X	Employment (in millions) Y	XY	X^2
1966	0	72.9	0	0
1967	1	74.4	74.4	1
1968	2	75.9	151.8	4
1969	3	77.9	233.7	9
1970	4	78.6	314.4	16
1971	5	79.1	395.5	25
1972	6	81.7	490.2	36
1973	7	84.4	590.8	49
1974	8	85.9	687.2	64
1975	9	84.8	763.2	81
	45	795.6	3,701.2	285
	$=\sum X$	$=\sum Y$	$=\sum XY$	$=\sum X^2$

The sample size is $n = 10$. From the data given in the table, you find the following means:

$$\bar{X} = \frac{45}{10} = 4.5 \qquad \bar{Y} = \frac{795.6}{10} = 79.56$$

You now compute the coefficients for the trend lines:

$$b = \frac{10(3,701.2) - 45(795.6)}{10(285) - (45)^2} = 1.47$$

$$a = 79.56 - 1.47(4.5) = 72.95$$

Thus, you express the trend line for civilian employment by the equation

$$\hat{Y}(X) = 72.95 + 1.47X \qquad \text{(in millions, with } X = 0 \text{ at 1966)}$$

Since 1966, U.S. civilian employment increased from an initial level of 72.95 million at a rate of 1.47 million per year through 1975. Figure 12-2 shows the trend line and actual time series.

Figure 12-2 Actual data and trend line for civilian employment in the United States.

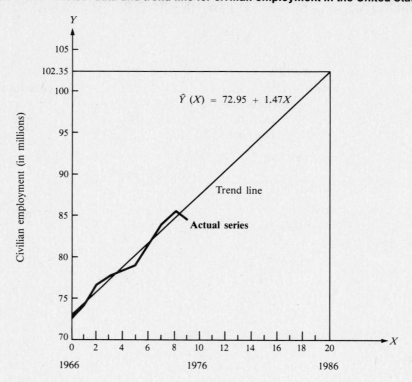

2. Making forecasts: You can make a forecast for 1986 employment using the regression line that was found in Example 12-1. Substituting $X = 1986 - 1966 = 20$, you obtain

$$\hat{Y}(20) = 72.95 + 1.47(20) = 102.35$$

This forecast is an **extrapolation**. Note that there is considerable danger in making forecasts, such as this one, so far beyond the range of actual data. (In actuality, civilian employment exceeded the forecast level several years earlier than 1986.)

B. The moving average isolates the trend and cyclical components.

When data involve periods less than a year long, such as quarters or months, you can remove the shorter-term seasonal and irregular time-series components. You accomplish this by computing for each period a **moving average**, either for four successive quarters or for twelve months.

The moving average smooths the seasonal and irregular variations out of the series, so that the resulting values represent trend and cyclical components only:

$$\text{Moving average} = T_t \times C_t$$

1. Using quarterly data: You begin by computing the sum of the first four successive values in the original time series. You then divide that total by 4, getting your first **four-quarter moving average**. That value represents one complete year. Repeat this process, dropping the initial quarter and adding the fifth, so that your second four-quarter average represents a full year. Continue the process until you have run out of new quarters.

The final step is to center the data by computing for each period the **centered moving average**. You accomplish this by averaging each successive pair of four-quarter averages.

The following example illustrates this procedure.

EXAMPLE 12-2: ICE CREAM SALES

The following time-series data apply for the sales of ice cream (in thousands of gallons) experienced by a dairy.

Quarter		Sales	Four quarter moving average	Centered moving average
1980	Winter	5,100		
	Spring	9,800		
			10,350	
	Summer	15,200		10,475
			10,600	
	Fall	11,300		10,913
			11,225	
1981	Winter	6,100		11,625
			12,025	
	Spring	12,300		12,263
			12,500	
	Summer	18,400		12,638
			12,775	
	Fall	13,200		13,000
			13,225	
1982	Winter	7,200		13,513
			13,800	
	Spring	14,100		14,000
			14,200	
	Summer	20,700		14,375
			14,550	
	Fall	14,800		14,850
			15,150	
1983	Winter	8,600		15,575
			16,000	
	Spring	16,500		16,213
			16,425	
	Summer	24,100		16,575
			16,725	
	Fall	16,500		17,088
			17,450	
1984	Winter	9,800		18,113
			18,775	
	Spring	19,400		18,988
			19,200	
	Summer	29,400		
	Fall	18,200		

You find the first four-quarter average by adding together the actual sales for the quarters of 1980 and dividing by 4:

$$\frac{5{,}100 + 9{,}800 + 15{,}200 + 11{,}300}{4} = 10{,}350$$

This value corresponds to that point in time when the Spring 1980 quarter ends and the Summer 1980 quarter begins—midnight, June 30, 1980.

The second four-quarter average is found by dropping sales for Winter 1980 and including the figure for Winter 1981:

$$\frac{9{,}800 + 15{,}200 + 11{,}300 + 6{,}100}{4} = 10{,}600$$

As before, this value applies to the point in time separating Summer 1980 from Fall 1980–midnight, September 30. Since the values apply between quarters, the column of four-quarter averages is positioned one-half line off the rest of the table.

The last column contains the centered moving averages. You find the first of these by averaging the first two four-quarter averages:

$$\frac{10{,}350 + 10{,}600}{2} = 10{,}475$$

This value applies to the midpoint of Summer 1980, coinciding in time with the original data.

You may use the centered moving averages to represent the combined trend and cyclical components for ice cream sales.

2. **Using monthly data:** When the original time series is given by months, you may amend the quarterly procedure for finding moving averages. You average a year's worth of successive monthly figures to provide **twelve-month moving averages**. You then average each successive pair of these to obtain the twelve-month centered moving average.

Note: Some books find the centered moving average by first computing four-quarter (or twelve-month) *totals*. You would then add successive pairs of totals and divide by 8 (or 24) to provide the centered moving averages.

12-3. Forecasting Using Seasonal Indexes

Seasonal influences are critical to the short-range planning of many businesses. You may isolate the seasonal time-series component when data are available for periods shorter than one year.

A. The moving average is used to isolate the seasonal and irregular components.

The time-series model indicates that you may find the seasonal and irregular components by dividing each value in the original series by the centered moving average:

$$\frac{Y_t}{\text{Centered moving average}} = \frac{T_t \times C_t \times S_t \times I_t}{T_t \times C_t} = S_t \times I_t$$

You can see that by dividing Y_t by the centered moving average, you are expressing the original data as a *percentage* of moving average.

B. The seasonal indexes are obtained from the medians of the percentages of moving averages.

You must remove the irregular component before you obtain a final set of seasonal indexes. You accomplish this by first finding for each season the *median* percentage of moving average for the applicable quarters. (Although the mean could be used instead for this purpose, the median is preferred because it is less affected by unusually large or small values.) You then make an adjustment so that the final indexes average to 100% for the entire year. The following example illustrates the procedure.

EXAMPLE 12-3: ICE CREAM SALES (CONTINUED)

The following table provides the original data as a percentage of moving average for the ice cream sales discussed in Example 12-2.

Quarter		Sales	Centered moving average	Original as percentage of moving average
1980	Winter	5,100		
	Spring	9,800		
	Summer	15,200	10,475	145.11
	Fall	11,300	10,913	103.55
1981	Winter	6,100	11,625	52.47
	Spring	12,300	12,263	100.30
	Summer	18,400	12,638	145.59
	Fall	13,200	13,000	101.54
1982	Winter	7,200	13,513	53.28
	Spring	14,100	14,000	100.71
	Summer	20,700	14,375	144.00
	Fall	14,800	14,850	99.66
1983	Winter	8,600	15,575	55.22
	Spring	16,500	16,213	101.77
	Summer	24,100	16,575	145.40
	Fall	16,500	17,088	96.56
1984	Winter	9,800	18,113	54.10
	Spring	19,400	18,988	102.17
	Summer	29,400		
	Fall	18,200		

You compute the first percentage of moving average, for Summer 1980, by dividing the original sales level of 15,200 by that quarter's centered moving average of 10,475. You then multiply the result by 100:

$$\frac{15,200}{10,475} \times 100 = 145.11$$

Sales for Summer 1980 were thus 145.11% of the trend and cyclical components.

After you have found all the percentages of moving averages, you arrange the percentages by year, as in the following table.

Year	Winter	Spring	Summer	Fall
1980			145.11	103.55
1981	52.47	100.30	145.59	101.54
1982	53.28	100.71	144.00	99.66
1983	55.22	101.77	145.40	96.56
1984	54.10	102.17		
Median	53.69	101.24	145.26	100.60

Sum of medians = 400.79

$$\text{Seasonal index} = \frac{400}{400.79} \times \text{median}$$

	53.58	101.04	144.97	100.40

There are four percentages for each quarter, and you find the median by averaging the middle-sized two. The sum of the medians is 400.79. To obtain indexes that sum to 400% (and that thus average to 100% throughout the year), you multiply each median by 400/400.79.

The seasonal indexes provide the S_t values for ice cream sales.

Note: For twelve-month data, the same procedure applies, except that the indexes should sum to 1,200%.

12-4. Cyclical and Irregular Fluctuation

Cyclical time-series movement isn't ordinarily built into long-range forecasts. Although C_t will oscillate up and down, much like S_t, it lacks the regularity of the seasonal component. You are familiar with the inaccuracies of the attempts of economic planners to forecast general economic conditions a few months in the future. Indeed, there may even be considerable controversy over identifying past cycles from actual time-series data. For these reasons, a true separation of the trend and cyclical components isn't ordinarily achieved with available statistical tools.

Since irregular fluctuations reflect no systematic influence, they aren't ordinarily computed and I_t isn't built into statistical forecasts based on time-series data.

12-5. Exponential Smoothing

A popular forecasting procedure is **exponential smoothing**, a process involving a built-in adjustment mechanism for regulating forecast values up or down in accordance with earlier errors. Exponential smoothing is similar in function to a thermostat.

A. The simplest model involves a single smoothing constant.

You can find next period's forecast from the current period's actual value and the earlier forecast value by the following expression.

Exponential smoothing function $\qquad F_{t+1} = \alpha Y_t + (1 - \alpha) F_t$

The subscript t represents the current time period, with F_{t+1} and F_t denoting the forecast values for the next and current periods, respectively; Y_t is the current actual value. The symbol α (lowercase Greek alpha) is the **smoothing constant**, a chosen value between 0 and 1.

As an illustration, consider the following data for the number of barrels sold by Blitz Beer.

Period t	Actual sales Y_t	Forecast sales F_t
1	4,890	—
2	4,910	4,890.0
3	4,970	4,894.0

Period t	Actual sales Y_t	Forecast sales F_t
4	5,010	4,909.2
5	5,060	4,929.4
6	5,100	4,955.5
7	5,050	4,984.4
8	5,170	4,997.5
9	5,180	5,032.0
10	5,240	5,061.6
11	5,220	5,097.3
12	5,280	5,121.8
13	5,330	5,153.5
14	5,380	5,188.8
15	5,440	5,227.0
16	5,460	5,269.6
17	5,520	5,307.7
18	5,490	5,350.2
19	5,550	5,378.1
20	5,600	5,412.5

Actual sales in period 10 where $Y_{10} = 5,240$ barrels, and $F_{10} = 5,061.6$ had been forecast for this period. Using a smoothing constant $\alpha = .20$, the forecast for period 11 sales is

$$F_{11} = .20(5,240) + (1 - .20)(5,061.6) = 5,097.3$$

In this illustration, the beginning forecast for period 2 was the actual level of sales for period 1. (After a few periods, the same F's will be obtained regardless of what value you use for the first forecast.) The smoothing constant may be revised over time and is usually established by trial and error.

Notice that the forecast values in this illustration are consistently smaller than the actual sales levels. You can expect such a lagging when there is a pronounced upward trend in actual data. You may expand the exponential smoothing procedure to correct for this.

B. Two-parameter exponential smoothing generally provides better forecasts.

To eliminate any lag in forecast values, you can explicitly account for trend by using a second smoothing constant. You will then employ three equations.

Two-parameter exponential smoothing equations

$$V_t = \alpha Y_t + (1 - \alpha)(V_{t-1} + b_{t-1}) \quad \text{(smooth the data)}$$
$$b_t = \gamma(V_t - V_{t-1}) + (1 - \gamma)b_{t-1} \quad \text{(smooth the trend)}$$
$$F_{t+1} = V_t + b_t \quad \text{(forecast)}$$

The symbol V_t represents the **smoothed value** for period t. The difference between the current and the prior smoothed values provides the current trend:

$$\text{Current trend} = V_t - V_{t-1}$$

The second equation contains the **trend-smoothing constant** γ (lowercase Greek gamma). You use that constant to obtain the **smoothed trend** denoted as b_t. The third equation provides the forecast.

The following table uses sales of Blitz Beer to illustrate the procedure.

Period t	Actual sales Y_t	Smoothed data V_t	Smoothed trend b_t	Forecast sales F_t
1	4,890	—	—	—
2	4,910	4,890	20.0	—
3	4,970	4,922	23.6	4,910.0
4	5,010	4,958	27.3	4,945.6
5	5,060	5,000	31.7	4,985.3
6	5,100	5,045	35.7	5,031.7
7	5,050	5,075	34.0	5,080.7
8	5,170	5,121	37.6	5,109.0
9	5,180	5,163	38.9	5,158.6

Period t	Actual sales Y_t	Smoothed data V_t	Smoothed trend b_t	Forecast sales F_t
10	5,240	5,210	41.3	5,201.9
11	5,220	5,245	39.4	5,251.3
12	5,280	5,283	39.0	5,284.4
13	5,330	5,324	39.6	5,322.0
14	5,380	5,367	40.6	5,363.6
15	5,440	5,414	42.5	5,407.6
16	5,460	5,457	42.7	5,456.5
17	5,520	5,504	44.0	5,499.7
18	5,490	5,536	40.4	5,548.0
19	5,550	5,571	38.8	5,576.4
20	5,600	5,608	38.3	5,609.8

The smoothing constants are $\alpha = .20$ and $\gamma = .30$. (The initial smoothed-data value of $V_2 = 4,890$ is the actual sales for period 1. The first smoothed-trend value of $b_2 = 20$ is the difference in actual sales for periods 1 and 2.) You can see how the sales for period 8 were forecast. First, you find the smoothed-data value for period 7:

$$V_7 = .20Y_7 + (1 - .20)(V_6 + b_6)$$
$$= .20(5,050) + .80(5,045 + 35.7)$$
$$= 5,075$$

Then you compute the smoothed-trend value for period 7:

$$b_7 = .30(V_7 - V_6) + (1 - .30)b_6$$
$$= .30(5,075 - 5,045) + .70(35.7)$$
$$= 34.0$$

This indicates that sales were increasing at a rate of 34.0 barrels per period at that time. You obtain the forecast for period 8 by adding the preceding period's smoothed-data and trend values:

$$F_8 = V_7 + b_7 = 5,075 + 34.0 = 5,109.0$$

SUMMARY

Numerical values generated over time are called *time series*. The basis for *time-series analysis* is the following *multiplicative model*:

$$Y_t = T_t \times C_t \times S_t \times I_t$$

This expresses the actual value Y for period t in terms of four components:

$$T_t = \text{Trend}$$
$$C_t = \text{Cyclical movement}$$
$$S_t = \text{Seasonal fluctuation}$$
$$I_t = \text{Irregular variations}$$

T_t is in the same units as Y_t, while C_t, S_t, and I_t are expressed as percentages.

You may isolate trend in two different ways. When using annual data, you express T_t as a *trend line*, with values computed from the *regression line*,

$$\hat{Y}(X) = a + bX$$

where X represents the successive time periods and $X = 0$ for the beginning period.

When the time series involves periods shorter than one year, such as quarters or months, you isolate the trend and cyclical components, $T_t \times C_t$, together by computing the *centered moving averages*.

You find the seasonal indexes S_t by first dividing each of the original data points by its centered moving average to get the *percentage of moving average*. This provides $S_t \times I_t$ values.

To eliminate I_t, you find the medians of these values. After adjustment so that each period within a year averages to 100%, the seasonal indexes S_t result.

The levels for the irregular time-series components, C_t and I_t, aren't ordinarily used in making forecasts.

A popular forecasting procedure is *exponential smoothing*. In its simplest form you employ a *smoothing constant* α, used to calculate a forecast value F_t:

$$F_{t+1} = \alpha Y_t + (1 - \alpha)F_t$$

Two-parameter forecasts are generally better. You achieve these by incorporating the *smoothed value* V_t and the *smoothed trend* b_t. This involves a second parameter, the *trend-smoothing constant* γ. You must evaluate three equations for each forecast:

$$V_t = \alpha Y_t + (1 - \alpha)(V_{t-1} + b_{t-1})$$
$$b_t = \gamma(V_t - V_{t-1}) + (1 - \gamma)b_{t-1}$$
$$F_{t+1} = V_t + b_t$$

RAISE YOUR GRADES

Can you explain ...?

☑ why time-series forecasts are extrapolations
☑ the role of moving averages in constructing seasonal indexes
☑ why the cyclical component isn't ordinarily used in making forecasts
☑ why two four-quarter moving averages need to be averaged to obtain the centered moving average
☑ why forecasts from single-parameter exponential smoothing "lag" the actual values

Do you know ...?

☑ the role of least squares regression in finding the trend line
☑ how to get the initial values for making forecasts using exponential smoothing
☑ how to separate S_t from I_t
☑ how to find a forecast value when you know the levels of the four components
☑ how to modify the procedures for quarterly data for use with monthly data

RAPID REVIEW

1. The four-quarter moving averages of the original time series results in which one of the following component products?   [Section 12-2B]

    (a) $C_t \times S_t$ (b) $T_t \times C_t$ (c) $T_t \times S_t$ (d) $S_t \times I_t$

2. Dividing the original time series by the centered moving averages to get the percentages of moving averages results in which one of the following component products?
[Section 12-3A]

    (a) $S_t \times I_t$ (b) $T_t \times C_t$ (c) $C_t \times S_t$ (d) $T_t \times S_t$

3. Dividing the original time series by trend results in which one of the following component products?   [Section 12-1]

    (a) $S_t \times I_t$ (b) $T_t \times C_t \times I_t$ (c) $C_t \times S_t$ (d) $C_t \times S_t \times I_t$

4. You find the centered moving average by dividing the sum of two successive four-quarter moving averages by which of the following?   [Section 12-2B]

    (a) 8   (b) 4   (c) 2   (d) S_t

5. A firm's sales trend for June 1984 is \$100,000. Actual sales were \$90,000, and $C_t = 100$ and $I_t = 90$. What is the value for S_t?   [Section 12-1]

    (a) 123.46   **(b)** 100   **(c)** 111.1   **(d)** 90

6. The basic time-series model states that a series of data may be expressed as the product of four factors: trend, cyclical, seasonal, and irregular. This statement is **(a)** true, **(b)** false.   [Section 12-1]

7. In calculating the centered moving averages for 1979 through 1984 data, there will be no moving averages for winter and spring of 1979 or for summer and fall of 1984. This statement is **(a)** true, **(b)** false.   [Section 12-3B]

8. The percentages of moving averages, calculated by dividing the original time-series data by their corresponding centered moving averages, contain no irregular component, because it has been previously removed by the moving averages. This statement is **(a)** true, **(b)** false.   [Section 12-3B]

9. Forecasting trend with a least squares regression line constructed from time-series data involves extrapolating beyond the range of observed independent variable values. This statement is **(a)** true, **(b)** false.   [Section 12-2A]

10. The basic time series assumes that the irregular component is normally distributed with a mean of 100. This statement is **(a)** true, **(b)** false.   [Section 12-1]

Answers

1. (b)   **2. (a)**   **3. (d)**   **4. (c)**   **5. (b)**
6. (a)   **7. (a)**   **8. (b)**   **9. (a)**   **10. (b)**

SOLVED PROBLEMS

PROBLEM 12-1   Use the multiplicative time-series model to determine the actual values for each of the following quarters.

t	T_t	C_t	S_t	I_t
Winter	2,000	80	120	105
Spring	2,200	90	100	100
Summer	2,400	100	70	98
Fall	2,600	110	110	95

Solution: Multiply the four terms together to get the actual values. In doing this, be sure to divide each value that is expressed as a percentage by 100 before multiplying.

$$\text{Winter:}\quad 2{,}000 \times \frac{80}{100} \times \frac{120}{100} \times \frac{105}{100} = 2{,}016$$

$$\text{Spring:}\quad 2{,}200 \times \frac{90}{100} \times \frac{100}{100} \times \frac{100}{100} = 1{,}980$$

$$\text{Summer:}\quad 2{,}400 \times \frac{100}{100} \times \frac{70}{100} \times \frac{98}{100} = 1{,}646$$

$$\text{Fall:}\quad 2{,}600 \times \frac{110}{100} \times \frac{110}{100} \times \frac{95}{100} = 2{,}989$$

PROBLEM 12-2   Find the missing values to complete the following quarterly data on sales by Bugoff Chemical Co.

Quarter	Trend	Cyclical (%)	Seasonal (%)	Irregular (%)	Sales
Winter	$100,000	110	50	100	
Spring	110,000	100	70		$ 76,460
Summer	120,000	90		96	124,416
Fall	130,000		160	100	197,600

Solution: The following missing values apply.

Winter: $Y_t = T_t \times C_t \times S_t \times I_t$

$$= \$100,000 \left(\frac{110}{100}\right)\left(\frac{50}{100}\right)\left(\frac{100}{100}\right) = \$55,000$$

Spring: $I_t = \dfrac{Y_t}{T_t \times C_t \times S_t}$

$$= \frac{\$76,460}{\$110,000(100/100)(70/100)} \times 100 = 99$$

Summer: $S_t = \dfrac{Y_t}{T_t \times C_t \times I_t}$

$$= \frac{\$124,416}{\$120,000(90/100)(96/100)} \times 100 = 120$$

Fall: $C_t = \dfrac{Y_t}{T_t \times S_t \times I_t}$

$$= \frac{\$197,600}{\$130,000(160/100)(100/100)} \times 100 = 95$$

PROBLEM 12-3   Find the missing values to complete the following quarterly data on sales by ChipMont Corp.

Quarter	Trend	Cyclical (%)	Seasonal (%)	Irregular (%)	Sales
Winter	$100,000	100		90	$ 99,000
Spring	200,000		80	100	168,000
Summer	300,000	110		110	
Fall	400,000	120	120		604,800

Solution: The following missing values apply. You find the seasonal index for Summer by using the fact that the S_t values must sum to 400.

Winter: $S_t = \dfrac{Y_t}{T_t \times C_t \times I_t}$

$$= \frac{\$99,000}{\$100,000(100/100)(90/100)} \times 100 = 110$$

Spring: $C_t = \dfrac{Y_t}{T_t \times S_t \times I_t}$

$$= \frac{\$168,000}{\$200,000(80/100)(100/100)} \times 100 = 105$$

Summer: $S_t = 400 - (110 + 80 + 120) = 90$

$Y_t = T_t \times C_t \times S_t \times I_t$

$$= \$300,000 \left(\frac{110}{100}\right)\left(\frac{90}{100}\right)\left(\frac{110}{100}\right) = \$326,700$$

Fall: $\qquad I_t = \dfrac{Y_t}{T_t \times C_t \times S_t}$

$$= \dfrac{\$604,800}{\$400,000(120/100)(120/100)} \times 100 = 105$$

PROBLEM 12-4 The trend equation for the demand for electricity by a particular city is

$$\hat{Y}(X) = 10,000 + 20X \text{ kilowatt-hours} \qquad (X = 0 \text{ in } 1973)$$

Find the demand trend level for

    (a) 1985   **(b)** 1975   **(c)** 1980   **(d)** 1990

Solution:

    (a) $X = 1985 - 1973 = 12$ $\hat{Y}(12) = 10,000 + 20(12) = 10,240$
    (b) $X = 1975 - 1973 = 2$ $\hat{Y}(2)\ \ = 10,000 + 20(2) = 10,040$
    (c) $X = 1980 - 1973 = 7$ $\hat{Y}(7)\ \ = 10,000 + 20(7) = 10,140$
    (d) $X = 1990 - 1973 = 17$ $\hat{Y}(17) = 10,000 + 20(17) = 10,340$

PROBLEM 12-5 A CPA firm achieved the following number of new accounts:

1975	300	1980	417
1976	321	1981	464
1977	342	1982	488
1978	383	1983	495
1979	406	1984	531

    (a) Determine the equation for the regression line using $X = 0$ in 1975.
    (b) Forecast the number of new clients established in the following years: (*1*) 1986, (*2*) 1991, (*3*) 1996.

Solution:
(a) You compute the regression line by using the regression procedure explained in Chapter 11. The X value is the increment in years, with 1975 assigned the value of $X = 0$.

Year	X	Y	XY	X^2
1975	0	300	0	0
1976	1	321	321	1
1977	2	342	684	4
1978	3	383	1,149	9
1979	4	406	1,624	16
1980	5	417	2,085	25
1981	6	464	2,784	36
1982	7	488	3,416	49
1983	8	495	3,960	64
1984	9	531	4,779	81
	45	4,147	20,802	285
	$=\sum X$	$=\sum Y$	$=\sum XY$	$=\sum X^2$

$$\bar{X} = \frac{45}{10} = 4.5 \qquad \bar{Y} = \frac{4,147}{10} = 414.7$$

$$b = \frac{10(20,802) - 45(4,147)}{10(285) - (45)^2} = 25.945$$

$$a = 414.7 - 25.945(4.5) = 297.95$$

Thus, the regression equation for the trend line is

$$\hat{Y}(X) = 297.95 + 25.945X \qquad (X = 0 \text{ at } 1975)$$

(b) (*1*) $X = 1986 - 1975 = 11$ $\hat{Y}(11) = 297.95 + 25.945(11) = 583.35$
    (*2*) $X = 1991 - 1975 = 16$ $\hat{Y}(16) = 297.95 + 25.945(16) = 713.07$
    (*3*) $X = 1996 - 1975 = 21$ $\hat{Y}(21) = 297.95 + 25.945(21) = 842.80$

PROBLEM 12-6   The following percentages of moving averages have been obtained for Speak E–Z sales of portable stereos.

Year	Winter	Spring	Summer	Fall
1979			25	149
1980	125	98	36	145
1981	115	95	31	157
1982	108	106	29	148
1983	123	107	30	152
1984	120	101		

Determine the seasonal indexes for each quarter.

Solution:

	Winter	Spring	Summer	Fall	Total
Median:	120	101	30	149	400
Seasonal index:	120	101	30	149	

PROBLEM 12-7   The number of transactions experienced by Beauty Boutiques (in thousands) are as follows:

1980 Winter	125	1983 Winter	150
Spring	57	Spring	62
Summer	108	Summer	125
Fall	127	Fall	158
1981 Winter	141	1984 Winter	157
Spring	55	Spring	67
Summer	119	Summer	133
Fall	149	Fall	180
1982 Winter	146		
Spring	59		
Summer	122		
Fall	161		

(a) Determine the four-quarter moving averages, centered moving averages, and percentages of moving averages.

(b) Determine the seasonal indexes for each quarter.

Solution:

(a) To find the first four-quarter moving average, you sum the four transactions for the 1980 quarters and divide by 4. You find the second moving average by dropping the winter 1980 transaction and instead adding in the one for winter 1981. Continue in this way until you have no new quarters to add in. Now find the centered moving averages by averaging each successive pair of four-quarter moving averages. Finally, divide each transaction by its centered moving average and multiply by 100 to find the percentages of moving averages.

		Transactions	Four-quarter moving average	Centered moving average	Original data as percentage of moving average
1980	Winter	125			
	Spring	57			
	Summer	108	104.25	106.250	101.647
	Fall	127	108.25	108.000	117.593
1981	Winter	141	107.75	109.125	129.210
	Spring	55	110.50	113.250	48.565
	Summer	119	116.00	116.625	102.036
	Fall	149	117.25	117.750	126.539
			118.25		

	Transactions	Four-quarter moving average	Centered moving average	Original data as percentage of moving average
1982 Winter	146		118.625	123.077
Spring	59	119.00	120.500	48.963
Summer	122	122.00	122.500	99.592
Fall	161	123.00	123.375	130.496
1983 Winter	150	123.75	124.125	120.846
Spring	62	124.50	124.125	49.950
Summer	125	123.75	124.625	100.301
Fall	158	125.50	126.125	125.273
1984 Winter	157	126.75	127.750	122.896
Spring	67	128.75	131.500	50.951
Summer	133	134.25		
Fall	180			

(b) You first arrange the percentages of moving averages by season. Then find the medians for each season, and obtain the seasonal indexes from these by adjusting so that the resulting values sum to 400. You make this adjustment by multiplying by 400 and then dividing by the median total.

Year	Winter	Spring	Summer	Fall	Total
1980			101.647	117.593	
1981	129.210	48.565	102.036	126.539	
1982	123.077	48.963	99.592	130.496	
1983	120.846	49.950	100.301	125.273	
1984	122.896	50.951			
Median	122.987	49.457	100.974	125.906	399.324
Seasonal index	123.2	49.5	101.1	126.1	

PROBLEM 12-8 Following are the seasonally adjusted quarterly sales data (in thousands of gallons) for Tuti-Fruti Yogurt. Use single-parameter exponential smoothing with $\alpha = .20$ to find the forecast sales levels.

Period	Sales	Period	Sales
1	2	9	12
2	3	10	14
3	5	11	15
4	7	12	17
5	6	13	18
6	8	14	22
7	9	15	24
8	10	16	27

Solution: Using $F_2 = Y_1 = 2$ as the beginning forecast value, you get the following for period 3:

$$F_3 = .20Y_2 + (1 - .20)F_2 = .20(3) + .80(2) = 2.20$$

and for period 4:

$$F_4 = .20Y_3 + (1 - .20)F_3 = .20(5) + .80(2.20) = 2.76$$

The following table lists the complete set of forecast values.

t	Y_t	F_t
1	2	
2	3	2
3	5	2.20
4	7	2.76
5	6	3.61
6	8	4.09
7	9	4.87
8	10	5.70

t	Y_t	F_t
9	12	6.56
10	14	7.65
11	15	8.92
12	17	10.14
13	18	11.51
14	22	12.81
15	24	14.65
16	27	16.52

PROBLEM 12-9 Use two-parameter exponential smoothing with $\alpha = .40$ and $\gamma = .10$ to forecast sales levels for the Tuti-Fruti Yogurt data given in Problem 12-8.

Solution: Using $V_2 = Y_1 = 2$ and $b_2 = Y_2 - Y_1 = 3 - 2 = 1$, you obtain the following values for period 3:

$$F_3 = V_2 + b_2 = 2 + 1 = 3$$
$$V_3 = .40Y_3 + (1 - .40)(V_2 + b_2)$$
$$= .40(5) + .60(2 + 1) = 3.80$$
$$b_3 = .10(V_3 - V_2) + (1 - .10)b_2$$
$$= .10(3.80 - 2) + .90(1) = 1.08$$

The forecast for period 4 is

$$F_4 = V_3 + b_3 = 3.80 + 1.08 = 4.88$$

The following table summarizes the results.

t	Y_t	V_t	b_t	F_t
1	2			
2	3	2	1	
3	5	3.80	1.08	3
4	7	5.73	1.17	4.88
5	6	6.54	1.13	6.90
6	8	7.80	1.14	7.67
7	9	8.96	1.14	8.94
8	10	10.06	1.14	10.10
9	12	11.52	1.17	11.20
10	14	13.21	1.22	12.69
11	15	14.66	1.24	14.43
12	17	16.34	1.28	15.90
13	18	17.77	1.30	17.62
14	22	20.24	1.42	19.07
15	24	22.60	1.51	21.66
16	27	25.27	1.63	24.11

PROBLEM 12-10 The quarterly sales data (in millions of dollars) for WearEver Brake Linings are as follows.

1980	Winter	8.5	1983	Winter	9.5
	Spring	10.4		Spring	11.7
	Summer	7.5		Summer	8.4
	Fall	11.8		Fall	12.9
1981	Winter	9.5	1984	Winter	10.9
	Spring	12.2		Spring	13.7
	Summer	8.8		Summer	10.1
	Fall	13.6		Fall	15.0
1982	Winter	10.4			
	Spring	13.5			
	Summer	9.7			
	Fall	13.1			

(a) Determine the four-quarter moving averages, centered moving averages, and percentages of moving averages.
(b) Find the seasonal indexes.
(c) Find the **deseasonalized** time-series data. This is accomplished by dividing the original data by the seasonal index and multiplying by 100.
(d) Using your deseasonalized data from (c), find the equation for the trend line in WearEver sales using least squares regression.

Solution:
(a) The computed averages appear in the following table.

		Sales Y_t	Four-quarter moving average	Centered moving average	Sales as percentage of moving average	Seasonal index S_t	Deseasonalized data
1980	Winter	8.5				90.4	9.4
	Spring	10.4	9.550			113.2	9.2
	Summer	7.5	9.800	9.675	77.52	78.7	9.5
	Fall	11.8	10.250	10.025	117.71	117.6	10.0
1981	Winter	9.5	10.575	10.413	91.23	90.4	10.5
	Spring	12.2	11.025	10.800	112.96	113.2	10.8
	Summer	8.8	11.250	11.138	79.01	78.7	11.2
	Fall	13.6	11.575	11.413	119.16	117.6	11.6
1982	Winter	10.4	11.800	11.688	88.98	90.4	11.5
	Spring	13.5	11.675	11.738	115.01	113.2	11.9
	Summer	9.7	11.450	11.563	83.89	78.7	12.3
	Fall	13.1	11.000	11.225	116.70	117.6	11.1
1983	Winter	9.5	10.675	10.838	87.65	90.4	10.5
	Spring	11.7	10.625	10.650	109.86	113.2	10.3
	Summer	8.4	10.975	10.800	77.78	78.7	10.7
	Fall	12.9	11.475	11.225	114.92	117.6	11.0
1984	Winter	10.9	11.900	11.688	93.26	90.4	12.1
	Spring	13.7	12.425	12.163	112.64	113.2	12.1
	Summer	10.1				78.7	12.8
	Fall	15.0				117.6	12.8

(b) Arranging the percentages of moving averages from the table, you obtain the following.

	Winter	Spring	Summer	Fall	Total
1980			77.52	117.71	
1981	91.23	112.96	79.01	119.16	
1982	88.98	115.01	83.89	116.70	
1983	87.65	109.86	77.78	114.92	
1984	93.26	112.64			
Median	90.11	112.80	78.40	117.21	398.52
Seasonal index	90.4	113.2	78.7	117.6	

Now transfer the seasonal indexes to the table in (a). The same four indexes apply to all the years.
(c) See the last column in the table.
(d) Using the deseasonalized values for Y, you get the following.

		X	Y	XY	X²
1980	Winter	0	9.4	0	0
	Spring	1	9.2	9.2	1
	Summer	2	9.5	19.0	4
	Fall	3	10.0	30.0	9
1981	Winter	4	10.5	42.0	16
	Spring	5	10.8	54.0	25
	Summer	6	11.2	67.2	36
	Fall	7	11.6	81.2	49
1982	Winter	8	11.5	92.0	64
	Spring	9	11.9	107.1	81
	Summer	10	12.3	123.0	100
	Fall	11	11.1	122.1	121

		X	Y	XY	X²
1983	Winter	12	10.5	126.0	144
	Spring	13	10.3	133.9	169
	Summer	14	10.7	149.8	196
	Fall	15	11.0	165.0	225
1984	Winter	16	12.1	193.6	256
	Spring	17	12.1	205.7	289
	Summer	18	12.8	230.4	324
	Fall	19	12.8	243.2	361
		190	221.3	2,194.4	2,470
		$= \sum X$	$= \sum Y$	$= \sum XY$	$= \sum X^2$

$$\bar{X} = \frac{190}{20} = 9.5 \qquad \bar{Y} = \frac{221.3}{20} = 11.065$$

$$b = \frac{20(2{,}194.4) - 190(221.3)}{20(2{,}470) - (190)^2} = .1384$$

$$a = 11.065 - .1384(9.5) = 9.750$$

$$\hat{Y}(X) = 9.750 + .1384X \qquad (X \text{ in quarters, } X = 0 \text{ for Winter 1980})$$

13 INDEX NUMBERS

THIS CHAPTER IS ABOUT

☑ **Aggregate Price Indexes**
☑ **Deflating Time Series**

Living in a world of inflation, you know the importance of measuring changes in prices. You should be familiar with the *U.S. Consumer Price Index* used in the United States as the main barometer of inflation. In this chapter you will learn the general concepts that underlie the construction and interpretation of such index numbers.

13-1. Aggregate Price Indexes

A numerical value that summarizes price levels is called a **price index**. Besides being barometers of inflation, price indexes allow us to adjust economic time-series values so that values from different periods may be meaningfully compared without distortions due to rising prices.

A detailed illustration will help you understand how to construct and interpret index numbers. The following table provides the prices for household utilities in a particular region.

Item	Price per unit				Quantity			
	1981	1982	1983	1984	1981	1982	1983	1984
Electricity	$ 3.94	$ 4.10	$ 4.18	$ 4.20	62	64	68	70
Gas	15.80	16.50	17.20	17.60	8.7	9.0	9.5	10.1
Water	.58	.60	.62	.64	296	297	298	300
Telephone	4.80	4.90	5.00	5.00	55	60	64	70

The electricity units are thousands of kilowatt-hours, and gas is expressed in hundreds of therms. The units for water are hundreds of cubic feet, while those for the telephone are given in terms of hundreds of message-units. The given quantities are the average annual household levels of usage assumed for the respective utility items.

A. The simplest price index involves no quantity weights.

Price indexes are ordinarily constructed for several items. To illustrate the procedure, the utility data just given will be used to establish a "utility" price index. The values obtained will be based on **price aggregates**, calculated by summing together the prices for all included items.

The simplest index is the **unweighted aggregate price index**. You construct it without using any quantity information.

Unweighted aggregate price index

$$I = \frac{\sum p_n}{\sum p_0} \times 100$$

The price level for any particular period is denoted by p. The subscript n refers to the time period. A subscript of zero applies to the **base period**, generally the first year in the index series.

You compute the unweighted aggregate price index for the utility data using the year 1981 as the base period. That designation is made more compactly as 1981 = 100.

The price aggregate for 1981 is

$$p_{81} = \$3.94 + 15.80 + .58 + 4.80 = \$25.12$$

For 1982, the price aggregate is

$$p_{82} = \$4.10 + 16.50 + .60 + 4.90 = \$26.10$$

From these values you can find the unweighted aggregate price index for 1982:

$$I = \frac{\sum p_{82}}{\sum p_{81}} \times 100 = \frac{\$26.10}{\$25.12} \times 100 = 103.9$$

This value tells you that utility prices for 1982 were 103.9% of their base period level. In other words, the unweighted aggregate price of utilities increased by 3.9% from 1981 to 1982.

B. Quantity weights eliminate distortion.

The units of measurement used for the included items will influence simple unweighted price aggregates. Different values would apply if water, for example, were priced per thousand liters instead of per hundred gallons. You can eliminate such distortions by using quantity weights, which you can apply in amounts that reflect the relative importance of the items.

The quantity weights are designated by the letter q. The product $p \times q$ represents the total value of the item, and it is unaffected by the particular units chosen. The more common price indexes involve weighted price aggregates of the form $\sum pq$.

You can compute **weighted aggregate price indexes** in two ways.

1. **Laspeyres index—base period quantity weights:** The easiest weighted price index to compute applies the quantity weights for the base period, q_0, to each period in the index-number series. The following expression summarizes the procedure.

Laspeyres index
$$I = \frac{\sum p_n q_0}{\sum p_0 q_0} \times 100$$

The numerator $\sum p_n q_0$ represents the weighted value of all the items purchased in time period n. The denominator $\sum p_0 q_0$ provides the weighted value of those items bought in the same quantities in the base period.

Using the earlier utility data, the following shows the Laspeyres index calculations for 1982, again with 1981 = 100.

Item	Price per unit 1981 p_{81}	Price per unit 1982 p_{82}	Quantity 1981 q_{81}	Value of items 1981 $p_{81}q_{81}$	Value of items 1982 $p_{82}q_{81}$
Electricity	$ 3.94	$ 4.10	62	$244.28	$254.20
Gas	15.80	16.50	8.7	137.46	143.55
Water	.58	.60	296	171.68	177.60
Telephone	4.80	4.90	55	264.00	269.50
				$817.42	$844.85

$$I = \frac{\sum p_{82} q_{81}}{\sum p_{81} q_{81}} \times 100 = \frac{\$844.85}{\$817.42} \times 100 = 103.4$$

Notice that the price level for 1982 is 103.4% that of the base year. (This is lower than the 103.9% computed earlier for 1982's unweighted aggregate price index.)

2. **Paasche index—new quantity weights for each period:** A disadvantage of the Laspeyres index is that it doesn't allow for shifts in quantities that may take place over time. These arise from changes in usage that are the inevitable result of the declining and rising relative importance of the various items. A second index—the Paasche

index—avoids that distortion through use of current period weights q_n in calculating the price aggregates.

Paasche index
$$I = \frac{\sum p_n q_n}{\sum p_0 q_n} \times 100$$

Notice that this index uses current quantities q_n with the base period prices in computing the denominator.

The Paasche index will provide different values than the Laspeyres index for the same circumstances. The following illustrates the procedure for the utility data.

| | Price per unit | | Quantity | Value of items | |
| | 1981 | 1982 | 1982 | 1981 | 1982 |
Item	p_{81}	p_{82}	q_{82}	$p_{81}q_{82}$	$p_{82}q_{82}$
Electricity	$ 3.94	$ 4.10	64	$252.16	$262.40
Gas	15.80	16.50	9.0	142.20	148.50
Water	.58	.60	297	172.26	178.20
Telephone	4.80	4.90	60	288.00	294.00
				$854.62	$883.10

$$I = \frac{\sum p_{82} q_{82}}{\sum p_{81} q_{82}} \times 100 = \frac{\$883.10}{\$854.62} \times 100 = 103.3$$

Thus 1982 prices were 103.3% of the base period level. (Although in this illustration the Paasche and Laspeyres indexes are nearly the same, the two indexes may diverge considerably after several time periods.)

13-2. Deflating Time Series

Meaningful economic comparisons of time-series values are difficult to make during periods of inflation. For example, in 1980 the U.S. Gross National Product (GNP) was $2,627.4 billion, while in 1979 it stood at $2,368.5 billion. Did economic activity really increase in 1980 by the 11% suggested by these two GNP levels?

Economists would say no. They would want you to compare "real" GNP values. You obtain such numbers by **deflating** the original time series by a price index, such as the special-purpose *Price Deflator Index*. The following table lists this index, with 1972 = 100, along with the GNP levels for the period 1963–1980.

Year	Price Deflator Index (1972 = 100)	U.S. GNP in current dollars (in billions)	Real GNP (in billions)
1963	71.59	$ 594.7	$ 830.7
1964	72.71	635.8	874.4
1965	74.32	688.1	925.9
1966	76.76	753.0	981.0
1967	79.02	796.3	1,007.7
1968	82.57	868.5	1,051.8
1969	86.72	935.5	1,078.8
1970	91.36	982.4	1,075.3
1971	96.02	1,063.4	1,107.5
1972	100.00	1,171.1	1,171.1
1973	105.80	1,306.6	1,235.0
1974	116.02	1,412.9	1,217.8
1975	127.15	1,528.7	1,202.3
1976	133.71	1,702.1	1,273.0
1977	141.70	1,899.5	1,340.5
1978	152.05	2,127.5	1,399.2
1979	165.50	2,368.5	1,431.1
1980	177.40	2,627.4	1,481.1

SOURCE: Economic Report of the President, 1980.

To deflate a time series, you divide each period in the original series by the corresponding index value. Thus, you find

$$\text{Real 1979 GNP} = \frac{\$2,368.5}{165.50} \times 100 = \$1,431.1 \text{ billion}$$

This GNP is in "1972 dollars." You also find

$$\text{Real 1980 GNP} = \frac{\$2,627.4}{177.40} \times 100 = \$1,481.1 \text{ billion}$$

The proper percentage increase in 1980 economic activity over that of the preceding year is thus

$$\frac{\$1,481.1}{\$1,431.1} \times 100 - 100 = 103.5 - 100 = 3.5$$

SUMMARY

Price indexes are useful in measuring inflation and in adjusting economic time-series data to eliminate the influence of rising prices. For this purpose you can use *price aggregates* by summing the prices of various items. The simplest price aggregate is the *unweighted aggregate price index*:

$$I = \frac{\sum p_n}{\sum p_0} \times 100$$

The subscript 0 represents the *base period*, while n denotes the current period.

This index may poorly reflect overall price levels because it will provide different values for different units of measurement. It also doesn't reflect the relative importance of an item. For this reason, quantity weights are generally applied in computing the price aggregates.

There are two common *weighted aggregate price indexes*. One of these is the *Laspeyres index*:

$$I = \frac{\sum p_n q_0}{\sum p_0 q_0} \times 100$$

Here you multiply prices for both the base period and the current period by the base period quantity q_0 to establish the item value.

A disadvantage of the Laspeyres index is that it doesn't reflect shifts in usage over time. A second index reflects changing usage and importance by applying instead current quantity weights. This is the *Paasche index*:

$$I = \frac{\sum p_n q_n}{\sum p_0 q_n} \times 100$$

In comparing time-series data from two different periods it is sometimes desirable to *deflate* the values. You may accomplish this by dividing the data points by a price index, such as the Price Deflator Index.

RAISE YOUR GRADES
Can you explain...?

☑ how to find the percentage increase in prices from one time period to another
☑ how a price index can measure inflation
☑ the difference between the Laspeyres and Paasche indexes
☑ why it might be desirable to deflate time-series data
☑ why quantity weights are desirable in measuring price changes

Do you know...?

☑ the difference between the unweighted aggregate price index and the Laspeyres index

☑ how to deflate a time series
☑ how to compute the Paasche index
☑ how to compute the Laspeyres index
☑ when to use base period quantities and when to use current quantities

RAPID REVIEW

1. The 1957–1959 base Consumer Price Index for 1969 was 127.7. This means that "what $1 bought in 1969, _____ could buy in the base period." [Section 13-1]

   (a) $.78   (b) $1.277   (c) $1   (d) $.87

2. For 1982, the price of product *A* was $1.50 and two million were sold. The same product sold for $2 in 1983, when three million were sold. For product *B*, the corresponding figures are $2.50 and two million for 1982, and $3 and four million for 1983. Using 1982 = 100, find the 1983 Laspeyres index for the two-product group. [Section 13-1B]

   (a) 124   (b) 133.33   (c) 150   (d) 125

3. Suppose that GNP is $2,000 billion. Using the current price index value of 125, what is the "real" GNP in terms of base period prices? [Section 13-2]

   (a) $1,500 billion   (c) $2,500 billion
   (b) $1,600 billion   (d) $2,000 billion

4. Suppose the 1970 price per pound of turkey was $.40 and 150 million pounds were consumed, and the 1971 price was $.30 and 100 million pounds were consumed. What is the 1971 Laspeyres index when 1970 = 100, for that single item? [Section 13-1B]

   (a) 133   (b) 200   (c) 75   (d) 150

5. The Laspeyres index is a weighted aggregate price index where the weights are based on [Section 13-1B]

   (a) current quantities
   (b) base period quantities
   (c) the ratio of current to base period prices
   (d) the ratio of base period to current prices

6. The Paasche index is a weighted aggregate price index where the weights are based on [Section 13-1B]

   (a) current quantities
   (b) base period quantities
   (c) the ratio of current to base period prices
   (d) the ratio of base period to current prices

7. If the value of a price index was 110.0 in 1981 and 115.5 in 1982 (1979 = 100), then the percentage price increase from 1981 to 1982 was [Section 13-2]

   (a) 15.5%   (b) 5.5%   (c) 5%   (d) 10%

8. The Laspeyres index is superior to the Paasche index in the sense that the former keeps up with the changing importance of items, whereas the Paasche index assigns the same weights as those of the base period. This statement is (a) true, (b) false. [Section 13-1B]

9. The unweighted aggregate price index doesn't use quantity data. This statement is (a) true, (b) false. [Section 13-1A]

10. A disadvantage of the Paasche index is that it uses base period quantity weights so that the changing importance of times isn't reflected. This statement is (a) true, (b) false. [Section 13-1B]

Answers
1. (a)   2. (d)   3. (b)   4. (c)   5. (b)
6. (a)   7. (c)   8. (b)   9. (a)   10. (h)

SOLVED PROBLEMS

PROBLEM 13-1   For the following price data, calculate the unweighted aggregate price indexes for sporting goods for 1983 and 1984, using 1982 = 100.

	1982	1983	1984
Skis	$210	$231	$252
Tents	300	270	300
Rifles	300	330	360
Golf clubs	450	540	540

Solution: First find the total of the prices in each column. These are the unweighted price aggregates:

	1982	1983	1984
Skis	$ 210	$ 231	$ 252
Tents	300	270	300
Rifles	300	330	360
Golf clubs	450	540	540
	$1,260	$1,371	$1,452

You find the index numbers by dividing the year's price aggregate by the base year price aggregate:

$$\underline{\qquad\qquad 1983 \qquad\qquad}$$

$$I = \frac{\sum p_{83}}{\sum p_{82}} \times 100$$

$$= \frac{\$1,371}{\$1,260} \times 100 = 108.8$$

$$\underline{\qquad\qquad 1984 \qquad\qquad}$$

$$I = \frac{\sum p_{84}}{\sum p_{82}} \times 100$$

$$= \frac{\$1,452}{\$1,260} \times 100 = 115.2$$

PROBLEM 13-2   Use the utility data given on page 247 to construct the unweighted aggregate price indexes for 1983 and 1984, using 1981 = 100.

Solution: This problem follows the pattern of Problem 13-1.

	1981	1983	1984
Electricity	$ 3.94	$ 4.18	$ 4.20
Gas	15.80	17.20	17.60
Water	.58	.62	.64
Telephone	4.80	5.00	5.00
	$25.12	$27.00	$27.44

Thus, the price indexes are

$$\underline{\qquad\qquad 1983 \qquad\qquad}$$

$$I = \frac{\sum p_{83}}{\sum p_{81}} \times 100$$

$$= \frac{\$27.00}{\$25.12} \times 100 = 107.5$$

$$\underline{\qquad\qquad 1984 \qquad\qquad}$$

$$I = \frac{\sum p_{84}}{\sum p_{81}} \times 100$$

$$= \frac{\$27.44}{\$25.12} \times 100 = 109.2$$

PROBLEM 13-3   Use the utility data given on page 247 to construct the Laspeyres indexes for 1983 and 1984, using 1981 = 100.

Solution: Applying base year quantity weights, find the weighted price aggregates for 1981, 1983, and 1984.

| | Price per unit | | | Quantity | Value of items | | |
| | 1981 | 1983 | 1984 | 1981 | 1981 | 1983 | 1984 |
Item	p_{81}	p_{83}	p_{84}	q_{81}	$p_{81}q_{81}$	$p_{83}q_{81}$	$p_{84}q_{81}$
Electricity	$ 3.94	$ 4.18	$ 4.20	62	$244.28	$259.16	$260.40
Gas	15.80	17.20	17.60	8.7	137.46	149.64	153.12
Water	.58	.62	.64	296	171.68	183.52	189.44
Telephone	4.80	5.00	5.00	55	264.00	275.00	275.00
					$817.42	$867.32	$877.96

You can now compute the index values.

1983

$$I = \frac{\sum p_{83}q_{81}}{\sum p_{81}q_{81}} \times 100$$

$$= \frac{\$867.32}{\$817.42} \times 100 = 106.1$$

1984

$$I = \frac{\sum p_{84}q_{81}}{\sum p_{81}q_{81}} \times 100$$

$$= \frac{\$877.96}{\$817.42} \times 100 = 107.4$$

PROBLEM 13-4 Use the utility data given on page 247 with 1981 = 100 to construct the Paasche indexes for (a) 1983, (b) 1984.

Solution:

(a) Apply the quantity weights for 1983 to compute the weighted price aggregates for 1981 and 1983.

| | Price per unit | | Quantity | Value of items | |
| | 1981 | 1983 | 1983 | 1981 | 1983 |
Item	p_{81}	p_{83}	q_{83}	$p_{81}q_{83}$	$p_{83}q_{83}$
Electricity	$ 3.94	$ 4.18	68	$267.92	$284.24
Gas	15.80	17.20	9.5	150.10	163.40
Water	.58	.62	298	172.84	184.76
Telephone	4.80	5.00	64	307.20	320.00
				$898.06	$952.40

The price index is

$$I = \frac{\sum p_{83}q_{83}}{\sum p_{81}q_{83}} \times 100 = \frac{\$952.40}{\$898.06} \times 100 = 106.1$$

(b) Apply 1984 quantity weights to compute the weighted price aggregates for 1981 and 1984.

| | Price per unit | | Quantity | Value of items | |
| | 1981 | 1984 | 1984 | 1981 | 1984 |
Item	p_{81}	p_{84}	q_{84}	$p_{81}q_{84}$	$p_{84}q_{84}$
Electricity	$ 3.94	$ 4.20	70	$275.80	$ 294.00
Gas	15.80	17.60	10.1	$159.58	$ 177.76
Water	.58	.64	300	174.00	192.00
Telephone	4.80	5.00	70	336.00	350.00
				$945.38	$1,013.76

The price index is

$$I = \frac{\sum p_{84} q_{84}}{\sum p_{81} q_{84}} \times 100 = \frac{\$1,013.76}{\$945.38} \times 100 = 107.2$$

PROBLEM 13-5 The following data apply to sporting goods.

	1982		1983		1984	
	Price	Quantity	Price	Quantity	Price	Quantity
Skis	$210	10 million	$231	10 million	$252	15 million
Tents	300	5	270	6	300	7
Rifles	300	5	330	5	360	5
Golf clubs	450	5	540	5	540	5

(a) Calculate the Laspeyres index for 1983 and 1984, using 1982 = 100.
(b) Using 1982 = 100, calculate the Paasche index for (1) 1983, (2) 1984.

Solution:
(a) Apply 1982 quantity weights to find the weighted price aggregates for 1982–1984.

	Price per unit			Quantity 1982	Value of items		
	1982	1983	1984		1982	1983	1984
Item	p_{82}	p_{83}	p_{84}	q_{82}	$p_{82} q_{82}$	$p_{83} q_{82}$	$p_{84} q_{82}$
Skis	$210	$231	$252	10	$2,100	$2,310	$2,520
Tents	300	270	300	5	1,500	1,350	1,500
Rifles	300	330	360	5	1,500	1,650	1,800
Golf clubs	450	540	540	5	2,250	2,700	2,700
					$7,350	$8,010	$8,520

The Laspeyres indexes are

1983	1984

$$I = \frac{\sum p_{83} q_{82}}{\sum p_{82} q_{82}} \times 100 \qquad I = \frac{\sum p_{84} q_{82}}{\sum p_{82} q_{82}} \times 100$$

$$= \frac{\$8,010}{\$7,350} \times 100 = 109.0 \qquad = \frac{\$8,520}{\$7,350} \times 100 = 115.9$$

(b) (1) Apply 1983 quantity weights to compute the weighted price aggregates for 1982 and 1983.

	Price per unit		Quantity 1983	Value of items	
	1982	1983		1982	1983
Item	p_{82}	p_{83}	q_{83}	$p_{82} q_{83}$	$p_{83} q_{83}$
Skis	$210	$231	10	$2,100	$2,310
Tents	300	270	6	1,800	1,620
Rifles	300	330	5	1,500	1,650
Golf clubs	450	540	5	2,250	2,700
				$7,650	$8,280

Thus the Paasche index for 1983 is

$$I = \frac{\sum p_{83} q_{83}}{\sum p_{82} q_{83}} \times 100 = \frac{\$8,280}{\$7,650} \times 100 = 108.2$$

(2) Apply 1984 quantity weights to compute the weighted price aggregates for 1982 and 1984.

Item	Price per unit 1982 p_{82}	Price per unit 1984 p_{84}	Quantity 1984 q_{84}	Value of items 1982 $p_{82}q_{84}$	Value of items 1984 $p_{84}q_{84}$
Skis	$210	$252	15	$3,150	$ 3,780
Tents	300	300	7	2,100	2,100
Rifles	300	360	5	1,500	1,800
Golf clubs	450	540	5	2,250	2,700
				$9,000	$10,380

Thus the Paasche index for 1984 is

$$I = \frac{\sum p_{84}q_{84}}{\sum p_{82}q_{84}} \times 100 = \frac{\$10,380}{\$\ 9,000} \times 100 = 115.3$$

PROBLEM 13-6 Deflate the following time-series data on average hourly wages for workers in a particular industry. The Consumer Price Index (CPI) values are based on 1967 = 100.

Year	Wages	CPI
1976	$15.30	170.5
1977	18.27	181.5
1978	20.20	195.4
1979	23.47	217.4
1980	25.10	247.7

Solution: Divide the wages for each year by that year's index number and multiply by 100:

Year	Wages	CPI	Real wages
1976	$15.30	170.5	100($15.30/170.5) = $ 8.97
1977	18.27	181.5	100($18.27/181.5) = 10.07
1978	20.20	195.4	100($20.20/195.4) = 10.34
1979	23.47	217.4	100($23.47/217.4) = 10.80
1980	25.10	247.7	100($25.10/247.7) = 10.13

14
TWO-SAMPLE INVESTIGATIONS

THIS CHAPTER IS ABOUT

☑ **Comparing Two Means Using Large Samples**
☑ **Comparing Two Means Using Small Samples**
☑ **Comparing Two Proportions**
☑ **Comparisons Using Nonparametric Statistics**

This chapter is concerned with controlled experiments where two populations are compared. Traditionally, the sample from one of these is referred to as the **control group**, and the sample from the second population is the **experimental group**. Evaluations with quantitative populations may be conducted using either two **independent** random samples or **matched pairs** involving partners from both groups.

Two-sample comparisons may involve either estimates or tests. A variety of procedures are available for each type of inference. In comparing population means, you base your procedure on either the normal or the Student t distribution, depending on the sample size. You ordinarily use the normal approximation when comparing qualitative populations in terms of proportions. It may be advantageous to employ **nonparametric statistics** when testing two quantitative populations.

14-1. Comparing Two Means Using Large Samples

When you are comparing two populations, you arbitrarily designate one population by the letter A and the second by B. You use these letters as subscripts in all expressions summarizing the procedures. Thus, you denote the respective population means as

$$\mu_A = \text{mean of population } A$$
$$\mu_B = \text{mean of population } B$$

Similarly, you represent the respective sample means by $\bar{X}_A$ and $\bar{X}_B$, the standard deviations by s_A and s_B, and the sample sizes by n_A and n_B.

A. The difference between means may be expressed in terms of a confidence interval estimate.

Just as you can estimate the mean of a single population by using the sample mean, you can estimate the difference $\mu_A - \mu_B$ from the computed value $\bar{X}_A - \bar{X}_B$. Alternatively, you might want to first match the sample units from each group, using as your estimator the mean value of the differences computed for each observation pair.

1. Independent samples: You ordinarily compute sample means separately when the investigation involves two independent samples. In those cases you find the confidence interval estimate of $\mu_A - \mu_B$ from the following expression.

Confidence interval estimate for difference in means using independent samples

$$\mu_A - \mu_B = \bar{X}_A - \bar{X}_B \pm z \sqrt{\frac{s_A^2}{n_A} + \frac{s_B^2}{n_B}}$$

EXAMPLE 14-1: MEASURING THE ADVANTAGE OF SHELF POSITION

A large greeting-card chain conducted an experiment to estimate the mean sales advantage due to favorable location of promotional cards. In group A stores the cards were interspersed within the regular line. In group B stores the same promotional cards were located in a separate special location. Sales of the promotional cards were recorded for two independent random samples. The following data apply:

$$
\begin{array}{ll}
n_A = 50 & n_B = 100 \\
\bar{X}_A = \$1{,}257 & \bar{X}_B = \$928 \\
s_A = \$152 & s_B = \$129
\end{array}
$$

Using $z = 1.96$, the following 95% confidence interval estimate applies to the difference in mean sales for all stores where promotional cards were displayed:

$$
\mu_A - \mu_B = 1{,}257 - 928 \pm 1.96 \sqrt{\frac{(152)^2}{50} + \frac{(129)^2}{100}}
$$

$$
= \$329 \pm 49
$$

or

$$
\$280 \leqslant \mu_A - \mu_B \leqslant \$378
$$

With 95% confidence, promotional card sales are on the average between \$280 and \$378 higher when interspersed with regular cards.

---

2. **Matched pairs:** You can estimate the difference in means another way by matching observations from each sample group into pairs. If X_{A_i} and X_{B_i} denote individual observed values, the difference for the ith pair is

$$
d_i = X_{A_i} - X_{B_i}
$$

Letting n represent the number of pairs, you can compute the mean and the standard deviation for this difference.

$$
\bar{d} = \frac{\sum d_i}{n} \qquad s_d = \sqrt{\frac{\sum d_i^2 - n\bar{d}^2}{n-1}}
$$

You then apply the following expression:

Confidence interval estimate for difference in means using matched pairs

$$
\mu_A - \mu_B = \bar{d} \pm z \frac{s_d}{\sqrt{n}}
$$

EXAMPLE 14-2: ORDERS FOR ENGRAVED INVITATIONS

A custom-printing company estimated the advantage of splitting its large catalog into two segments that are easier to handle. To accomplish this, the company conducted a sampling investigation involving group A retail stores, where the split catalog was displayed, and group B stores, where the large catalog was used. Stores from each group were paired according to historical sales, size, geographical location, and many other factors.

The following sales data were obtained.

Store	Sales		Difference	
i	X_{A_i}	X_{B_i}	d_i	d_i^2
1	\$ 1,052	\$ 987	\$ 65	4,225
2	4,226	3,929	297	88,209
3	2,550	2,743	−193	37,249
4	980	540	440	193,600
5	1,105	1,024	81	6,561

Store	Sales		Difference	
i	X_{A_i}	x_{B_i}	d_i	d_i^2
6	\$ 4,885	\$ 3,901	\$ 984	968,256
7	833	904	− 71	5,041
8	1,770	1,550	220	48,400
9	2,565	1,945	620	384,400
10	3,220	3,175	45	2,025
11	8,950	9,235	−285	81,225
12	5,025	4,810	215	46,225
13	2,714	2,705	9	81
14	922	741	181	32,761
15	4,455	3,693	762	580,644
16	2,500	3,100	−600	360,000
17	1,125	1,084	41	1,681
18	666	522	144	20,736
19	2,005	1,814	191	36,481
20	1,615	1,922	−307	94,249
21	2,050	1,975	75	5,625
22	550	375	175	30,625
23	840	525	315	99,225
24	2,250	2,170	80	6,400
25	1,777	1,523	254	64,516
26	1,627	1,552	75	5,625
27	902	822	80	6,400
28	1,220	1,110	110	12,100
29	4,250	4,527	−277	76,729
30	943	602	341	116,281
	\$69,572	\$65,505	\$4,067	3,415,575

The mean and standard deviation for the pair differences are

$$\bar{d} = \frac{4,067}{30} = \$135.57$$

$$s_d = \sqrt{\frac{3,415,575 - 30(135.57)^2}{30 - 1}} = \$314.27$$

Using $z = 1.96$, you find the following 95% confidence interval estimate for the difference in mean sales:

$$\mu_A - \mu_B = \$135.57 \pm 1.96 \frac{\$314.27}{\sqrt{30}}$$

$$= \$135.57 \pm 112.46$$

or

$$\$23.11 \leqslant \mu_A - \mu_B \leqslant \$248.03$$

It appears that splitting the catalog may result on the average in increased sales. But there is no way to be certain, since the true difference in means may not fall within the confidence interval.

B. Hypothesis tests are used to make decisions based on the difference in sample means.

The hypothesis testing procedures introduced in Chapter 10 extend to the difference in population means. Zero is the usual pivotal value for the $\mu_A - \mu_B$ difference, and you will usually encounter null hypotheses in one of the following forms:

$$H_0: \mu_A \leqslant \mu_B \quad \text{or} \quad H_0: \mu_A - \mu_B \leqslant 0 \qquad \text{(upper-tailed test)}$$
$$H_0: \mu_A \geqslant \mu_B \quad \text{or} \quad H_0: \mu_A - \mu_B \geqslant 0 \qquad \text{(lower-tailed test)}$$
$$H_0: \mu_A = \mu_0 \quad \text{or} \quad H_0: \mu_A - \mu_B = 0 \qquad \text{(two-sided test)}$$

The normal deviate z ordinarily serves as the test statistic in such tests.

1. **Independent samples:** When the two sample groups are selected independently, you use the following expression to establish the test statistic.

Normal deviate for independent samples
$$z = \frac{\bar{X}_A - \bar{X}_B}{\sqrt{\dfrac{s_A^2}{n_A} + \dfrac{s_B^2}{n_B}}}$$

EXAMPLE 14-3: DOES TELEPROCESSING SAVE TIME?

An oil company currently processes its bills from regional data centers. A sampling study will establish whether a new centralized teleprocessing system will speed the total time taken for bills to reach customers. One drawback of the new system is that the completed bills will travel greater distances through the mail.

The mean time needed for bills to be processed and received by customers under the new procedure (A) and under the present procedure (B) are denoted by μ_A and μ_B. The null hypothesis is

$$H_0: \mu_A \geqslant \mu_B \qquad \text{(New system is no faster.)}$$

An $\alpha = .05$ significance level is chosen, so that $z_{.05} = 1.64$. A large negative $\bar{X}_A - \bar{X}_B$ difference will refute the null hypothesis, and the test is lower-tailed. The following decision rule applies:

Accept H_0 if $z \geqslant -1.64$ (Keep present procedure.)
Reject H_0 if $z < -1.64$ (Switch to new procedure.)

The following sample data were obtained.

$$n_A = 500 \qquad n_B = 1,000$$
$$\bar{X}_A = 4.3 \text{ days} \qquad \bar{X}_B = 4.5 \text{ days}$$
$$s_A = 1.1 \text{ days} \qquad s_B = 1.3 \text{ days}$$

The computed value for the test statistic is

$$z = \frac{4.3 - 4.5}{\sqrt{\dfrac{(1.1)^2}{500} + \dfrac{(1.3)^2}{1,000}}} = -3.12$$

This z value falls in the rejection region, and the decision is therefore to switch to the new procedure.

---

2. **Matched pairs:** When the samples are matched into pairs, the following expression provides the test statistic.

Normal deviate for matched pairs
$$z = \frac{\bar{d}}{s_d / \sqrt{n}}$$

EXAMPLE 14-4: TIRE TREAD LIFETIME

A tire manufacturer will cancel the scheduled revision of its tire-tread template only if the new design exhibits significantly worse mileage than the present one. Letting A represent the present design and B the new one, the respective mean tire-tread lifetimes are μ_A and μ_B. The null hypothesis is

$$H_0: \mu_A \leqslant \mu_B \qquad \text{(New design is longer-lived.)}$$

A large positive $\bar{d}$ will refute this null hypothesis, and so the test is upper-tailed. A significance level of $\alpha = .01$ is chosen, so that the critical value is $z_{.01} = 2.33$. The decision rule is

Accept H_0 if $z \leqslant 2.33$ (Revise the template.)
Reject H_0 if $z > 2.33$ (Cancel the revision.)

A sample of 100 cars was driven with tires of the present design on one side and those of the new design on the other. After 30,000 miles of driving, an estimate was made for each car of the remaining lifetime for the two types of tires. Then the value for the revised tire was subtracted from that for the present tire. The following data apply:

$$\bar{d} = 76 \text{ mi.} \qquad s_d = 421 \text{ mi.}$$

The computed value for the test statistic is

$$z = \frac{76}{421/\sqrt{100}} = 1.81$$

Since this value doesn't exceed the critical value, H_0 is accepted, and the tire-tread template is revised.

C. The test for equality of means can be achieved using the confidence interval.

In a two-sided test with the null hypothesis $\mu_A = \mu_B$, you can base the decision on the interval estimate for $\mu_A - \mu_B$ constructed for a corresponding confidence level. If the interval contains zero within its limits, you must accept H_0. If the interval lies totally above or below zero, you should reject the null hypothesis.

To illustrate, consider the confidence interval constructed in Example 14-1 for the difference in mean sales of promotional cards under two alternative locations. You would reject the null hypothesis of equal mean sales at the .05 level because zero doesn't fall within the 95% confidence interval limits ($280, $378). Likewise, at the $\alpha = .05$ significance level the data in Example 14-2 would result in rejecting the null hypothesis of identical mean sales for the two catalog types; again, the 95% confidence interval ($23.11, $248.03) lies totally above zero.

14-2. Comparing Two Means Using Small Samples

By now you are familiar with the different procedures used for large sample sizes versus small ones. The small-sample procedures, ordinarily used only when the number of observations is less than 30, are based on the Student t distribution. That distribution's role is analogous to the role of the normal distribution, with t used instead of z.

The only computational differences arise with independent samples, where you pool the individual sample standard deviations rather than averaging them. This results in somewhat more complicated square root expressions.

A. Interval estimates are found using $t_{\alpha/2}$ in place of z.

1. Independent samples: The following expression applies in constructing the confidence interval estimate for $\mu_A - \mu_B$ when using independent samples of small size.

Confidence interval estimate for difference in means using small independent samples

$$\mu_A - \mu_B = \bar{X}_A - \bar{X}_B \pm t_{\alpha/2} \sqrt{\frac{(n_A - 1)s_A^2 + (n_B - 1)s_B^2}{n_A + n_B - 2}} \sqrt{\frac{1}{n_A} + \frac{1}{n_B}}$$

You read the critical value $t_{\alpha/2}$ from Table B in the Appendix for $n_A + n_B - 2$ degrees of freedom.

EXAMPLE 14-5: COST SAVINGS FROM AUTOMATED TELLERS

A large bank estimated the cost per transaction for customer cash withdrawals from checking accounts. The mean cost of human teller processing is μ_A, while that for automated teller processing is μ_B. Using the weekly costs per transaction from $n_A = 10$ branches and from $n_B = 15$ automated teller sites, the bank obtained the following data:

$$\bar{X}_A = \$.13 \qquad \bar{X}_B = \$.09$$
$$s_A = .021 \qquad s_B = .018$$

The following 90% confidence interval estimate for the difference in mean costs was found, with $t_{.05} = 1.714$ read from Table B for $10 + 15 - 2 = 23$ degrees of freedom.

$$\mu_A - \mu_B = \$.13 - .09 \pm 1.714 \sqrt{\frac{(10 - 1)(.021)^2 + (15 - 1)(.018)^2}{10 + 15 - 2}} \sqrt{\frac{1}{10} + \frac{1}{15}}$$

$$= \$.04 \pm .013$$

or

$$\$.027 \leqslant \mu_A - \mu_B \leqslant \$.053$$

This suggests that the mean cost savings for automated tellers may lie between three and five cents per transaction.

---

2. **Matched pairs:** The following expression applies in constructing the confidence interval estimate for $\mu_A - \mu_B$ when using a small number of sample matched pairs.

Confidence interval estimate for difference in means using a small number of matched pairs

$$\mu_A - \mu_B = \bar{d} \pm t_{\alpha/2} \frac{s_d}{\sqrt{n}}$$

You read the critical value $t_{\alpha/2}$ from Table B for $n - 1$ degrees of freedom.

EXAMPLE 14-6: TIME OF DAY AND MANUAL DEXTERITY

Production planners measured the drop-off in manual dexterity from midmorning to midafternoon by giving a sample of $n = 20$ workers a test in the morning and again in the afternoon. By pairing each person's morning score (A) with his or her afternoon score (B), the planners obtained the following results:

$$\bar{d} = 15.7 \qquad s_d = 2.3$$

They then constructed a 90% confidence interval estimate for the difference in mean manual dexterity scores. Using $t_{.05} = 1.729$ (read from Table B for $20 - 1 = 19$ degrees of freedom), they obtained the following:

$$\mu_A - \mu_B = 15.7 \pm 1.729 \frac{2.3}{\sqrt{20}}$$

$$= 15.7 \pm .89$$

or

$$14.81 \leqslant \mu_A - \mu_B \leqslant 16.59$$

They estimate that the mean drop-off in manual dexterity is about 15 points from morning to afternoon.

B. Statistical tests are performed using t in place of z.

1. **Independent samples:** When you are testing the difference in means using independent samples of small size, you use the following expression to compute the test statistic.

t Statistic for small independent samples

$$t = \frac{\bar{X}_A - \bar{X}_B}{\sqrt{\frac{(n_A - 1)s_A^2 + (n_B - 1)s_B^2}{n_A + n_B - 2}} \sqrt{\frac{1}{n_A} + \frac{1}{n_B}}}$$

You read the critical value that corresponds to the desired significance level from Table B using $n_A + n_B - 2$ as the number of degrees of freedom.

EXAMPLE 14-7: FORMULATING A SOAP

Laboratory researchers for a home products company are formulating a new soap. They plan to recommend version A if it is found to be significantly more effective than version B. The effectiveness of a soap is measured from wash tests by finding the mean percentage reduction in stain area. The following null hypothesis is tested:

$$H_0: \mu_A \leqslant \mu_B \qquad \text{(Version A isn't more effective.)}$$

Two independent sample washings are made, each involving $n_A = n_B = 10$ tubloads. An $\alpha = .01$ significance level is chosen for this upper-tailed test. For $10 + 10 - 2 = 18$ degrees of freedom, Table B provides the critical value $t_{.01} = 2.552$. The following decision rule applies:

$$\text{Accept } H_0 \text{ if } t \leqslant 2.552 \qquad \text{(Use version B.)}$$
$$\text{Reject } H_0 \text{ if } t > 2.552 \qquad \text{(Use version A.)}$$

The sample results provide

$$\bar{X}_A = 89.5\% \qquad \bar{X}_B = 81.2\%$$
$$s_A = 2.4\% \qquad s_B = 1.8\%$$

The computed value for the test statistic is

$$t = \frac{89.5 - 81.2}{\sqrt{\dfrac{(10-1)(2.4)^2 + (10-1)(1.8)^2}{10 + 10 - 2}} \sqrt{\dfrac{1}{10} + \dfrac{1}{10}}} = 8.749$$

Since this value exceeds the critical value, H_0 must be rejected and version A used.

---

2. **Matched pairs:** When you are testing the difference in means using a small number of matched sample pairs, you use the following expression to compute the test statistic.

t Statistic for matched pairs
$$t = \frac{\bar{d}}{s_d / \sqrt{n}}$$

You read the critical value that corresponds to the desired significance level from Table B using $n - 1$ as the number of degrees of freedom.

EXAMPLE 14-8: DOES METALLIC PAINT LAST LONGER THAN ACRYLIC PAINT?

You have been asked to test the null hypothesis that acrylic paint lasts at least as long as metallic paint. You will paint 15 metal plates on one side with acrylic paint (A) and on the other with metallic paint (B). In terms of the mean paint lifetimes, you are testing

$$H_0: \mu_A \geqslant \mu_B$$

You will deliver the plates to an environmental testing laboratory where they will be subjected to abuse until both paints are so worn that they must be replaced. The lab technicians will note the time until each paint is worn out.

You want to test at the $\alpha = .05$ significance level, using the critical value for $15 - 1 = 14$ degrees of freedom, so that $t_{.05} = 1.761$. After subtracting the survival time of the metallic paint from that of the acrylic, you will average the pair differences, compute their standard deviation, and find t. You will use the following decision rule:

$$\text{Accept } H_0 \text{ if } t \geqslant -1.761 \qquad \text{(Conclude acrylic paint lasts at least as long as metallic.)}$$
$$\text{Reject } H_0 \text{ if } t < -1.761 \qquad \text{(Conclude metallic paint outlasts acrylic.)}$$

Suppose you compute $\bar{d} = -1.4$ months with $s_d = 2$ months. You then have

$$t = \frac{-1.4}{2/\sqrt{15}} = -2.711$$

Since this value lies in the rejection region, you reject H_0 and conclude that metallic paint outlasts acrylic paint.

14-3. Comparing Two Proportions

You may need to compare two qualitative populations in terms of the respective proportions π_A and π_B. You may estimate each by their sample counterpart, P_A or P_B, computed from independent samples of size n_A and n_B. Although you may estimate the difference between the population proportions by $P_A - P_B$, you will ordinarily be interested in testing hypotheses regarding π_A and π_B. One of the following forms will apply.

$$H_0: \pi_A \leqslant \pi_B \quad \text{or} \quad H_0: \pi_A - \pi_B \leqslant 0 \qquad \text{(upper-tailed test)}$$
$$H_0: \pi_A \geqslant \pi_B \quad \text{or} \quad H_0: \pi_A - \pi_B \geqslant 0 \qquad \text{(lower-tailed test)}$$
$$H_0: \pi_A = \pi_B \quad \text{or} \quad H_0: \pi_A - \pi_B = 0 \qquad \text{(two-sided test)}$$

The statistical procedures for comparing proportions parallel those used in comparing means. This involves pooling the sample results to compute the **combined sample proportion**. The following expression applies.

Combined sample proportion
$$P_C = \frac{n_A P_A + n_B P_B}{n_A + n_B}$$

You use P_C in computing the normal deviate test statistic z.

Normal deviate for comparing two proportions

$$z = \frac{P_A - P_B}{\sqrt{P_C(1 - P_C)\left(\dfrac{1}{n_A} + \dfrac{1}{n_B}\right)}}$$

EXAMPLE 14-9: DOES HARD COPY REDUCE WORD-PROCESSING ERRORS?

In the rush to convert to word processing and direct composition, proofreading—once done at a less frenetic pace with hard copy (on paper)—is now done at the video display terminal. One newspaper publisher believes that restoring hard copy to the proofreading step might reduce the incidence of typographical errors. Not wanting to slow down procedures unnecessarily, he tests the null hypothesis that the proportion of errors is at least as high with hard copy (A) as it is without it (B). That is,

$$H_0: \pi_A \geqslant \pi_B$$

One sample of 100 text segments processed with hard copy was to be carefully inspected for typographical errors and the proportion P_A of lines having mistakes noted. A second sample of the same size without hard-copy processing was to be collected and P_B found. At the $\alpha = .01$ significance level, Table A provides the critical value of $z_{.01} = 2.33$. The following decision rule applies for this lower-tailed test:

Accept H_0 if $z \geqslant -2.33$ (Proofread directly from the video display terminal.)
Reject H_0 if $z < -2.33$ (Require all proofreading to be done from hard copy.)

The following results are obtained:

$$P_A = .03 \qquad P_B = .07$$

The combined sample proportion of errors is

$$P_C = \frac{100(.03) + 100(.07)}{100 + 100} = .05$$

The computed value of the test statistic is

$$z = \frac{.03 - .07}{\sqrt{.05(1 - .05)\left(\dfrac{1}{100} + \dfrac{1}{100}\right)}} = -1.30$$

This value falls in the acceptance region, and the publisher must accept the null hypothesis and continue to have proofreading done from the video display terminals.

14-4. Comparisons Using Nonparametric Statistics

The procedures for comparing means—the most common population parameters—fall into the broad category of **parametric statistics**. Those methods rest on several assumptions that may not always apply. You may prefer instead **nonparametric statistics**, which you may use to compare populations without the need for assumptions regarding population parameters.

A. The Wilcoxon rank-sum test may be used with independent random samples.

You may test various null hypotheses regarding the levels of population A values in relation to those of population B. Using the **Wilcoxon rank-sum test**, you can achieve this by first ranking all sample observations from lowest (starting with a 1) to highest. You then add the ranks from group A together to provide the **rank sum** W. From that quantity you compute the following test statistic.

Normal deviate for the Wilcoxon rank-sum test

$$z = \frac{W - \dfrac{n_A(n_A + n_B + 1)}{2}}{\sqrt{\dfrac{n_A n_B(n_A + n_B + 1)}{12}}}$$

- If two or more observations within the same group are equal in value, they receive successive ranks. If ties occur between two groups, you assign each observation the average rank of what would have been the successive ranks.

EXAMPLE 14-10: RATING TRAINING INSTRUCTORS

Bugoff Chemical Co. production workers are taking one-day training exercises. Samples of employees have been selected from those trained by two different instructors. Each subject was asked to rate the instructor in 20 categories numerically from 1 (terrible) to 5 (outstanding). Management wishes to test the null hypothesis that identical ratings apply to the two instructors.

The test is two-sided, so that at the $\alpha = .05$ significance level, the critical value of the test statistic is $z_{\alpha/2} = z_{.025} = 1.96$.

Accept H_0 if $-1.96 \leqslant z \leqslant 1.96$	(Conclude identical instructor ratings.)
Reject H_0 if $z < -1.96$	(Conclude lower ratings for A.)
or if $z > 1.96$	(Conclude lower ratings for B.)

The following data were obtained.

Instructor A		Instructor B	
Rating	Rank	Rating	Rank
67	7	82	16
83	17	85	18
67	8	82	15
64	4	72	10
60	3	77	13
55	1	69	9
58	2	79	14
75	12	66	6
65	5	74	11
		87	19
	$W = 59$	88	20
$n_A = 9$		$n_B = 11$	

The computed level for the test statistic is

$$z = \frac{59 - \dfrac{9(9 + 11 + 1)}{2}}{\sqrt{\dfrac{9(11)(9 + 11 + 1)}{12}}} = -2.70$$

Since this value falls in the lower rejection region, the null hypothesis must be rejected, and it must be concluded that instructor A receives lower ratings.

B. The Wilcoxon signed-rank test applies to matched-pairs testing.

A second Wilcoxon test is popular for testing with matched pairs. This is the **Wilcoxon signed-rank test**, which is based on the ranking of the absolute values of pair differences. This procedure involves the following steps:

1. Calculate the differences $d_i = X_{A_i} - X_{B_i}$.
2. Ignoring signs, rank the absolute values of the differences. Leave out any zero differences.
3. Calculate the rank sum V of the positive d's.

- In ranking the differences, ignore any ties within the positive or negative groupings, and use the average rank for each of the differences where ties occur between groupings.

The following expression provides the test statistic.

Normal deviate for the Wilcoxon signed-rank test

$$z = \frac{V - \dfrac{n(n + 1)}{4}}{\sqrt{\dfrac{n(n + 1)(2n + 1)}{24}}}$$

Here, n represents the number of pairs having nonzero differences.

To illustrate, consider again the data originally given in Example 14-2. There the difference in mean sales was estimated for two populations involving the catalog arrangement for engraved invitations. Suppose the printing company wants to test the null hypothesis that sales are the same under the two versions of the catalog:

$$\text{Population } A \text{ values} = \text{Population } B \text{ values}$$

The test is two-sided and the critical value of the normal deviate is $z_{.05/2} = z_{.025} = 1.96$. The following decision rule applies:

$$\text{Accept } H_0 \text{ if } -1.96 \leqslant z \leqslant 1.96 \qquad \text{(Sales are the same.)}$$
$$\text{Reject } H_0 \text{ if } z < -1.96 \qquad \text{(Sales are better with large catalog.)}$$
$$\text{or if } z > 1.96 \qquad \text{(Sales are better with split catalog.)}$$

The following data apply.

Store	Sales		Difference		Rank of absolute value
i	X_{A_i}	X_{B_i}	d_i	Sign	of differences
1	$1,052	$ 987	$ 65	+	4
2	4,226	3,929	297	+	22
3	2,550	2,743	−193	−	16
4	980	540	440	+	26
5	1,105	1,024	81	+	10
6	4,885	3,901	984	+	30
7	833	904	− 71	−	5
8	1,770	1,550	220	+	18
9	2,565	1,945	620	+	28
10	3,220	3,175	45	+	3

Store	Sales		Difference		Rank of absolute value
i	X_{A_i}	X_{B_i}	d_i	Sign	of differences
11	$8.950	$9,235	−285	−	21
12	5,025	4,810	215	+	17
13	2,714	2,705	9	+	1
14	922	741	181	+	14
15	4,455	3,693	762	+	29
16	2,500	3,100	−600	−	27
17	1,125	1,084	41	+	2
18	666	522	144	+	12
19	2,005	1,814	191	+	15
20	1,615	1,922	−307	−	23
21	2,050	1,975	75	+	7
22	550	375	175	+	13
23	840	525	315	+	24
24	2,250	2,170	80	+	8
25	1,777	1,523	254	+	19
26	1,627	1,552	75	+	6
27	902	822	80	+	9
28	1,220	1,110	110	+	11
29	4,250	4,527	−277	−	20
30	943	602	341	+	25

The following sum of positive ranks is obtained:

$$V = 1 + 2 + 3 + 4 + 6 + 7 + 8 + 9 + 10 + 11 + 12 + 13 + 14 + 15$$
$$+ 17 + 18 + 19 + 22 + 24 + 25 + 26 + 28 + 29 + 30$$
$$= 353$$

The following normal deviate applies.

$$z = \frac{353 - \dfrac{30(30 + 1)}{4}}{\sqrt{\dfrac{30(30 + 1)(60 + 1)}{24}}} = 2.48$$

This value is large enough to warrant rejecting the null hypothesis of identical means.

SUMMARY

Two-sample investigations typically involve comparisons of two means or two proportions. You can make a comparison by estimating the difference between the two population means or by conducting a hypothesis test to establish whether the mean or proportion for population A is significantly greater or smaller than that for population B.

For independently selected samples of large size, you establish the confidence interval estimate for the difference in means by

$$\mu_A - \mu_B = \bar{X}_A - \bar{X}_B \pm z \sqrt{\frac{s_A^2}{n_A} + \frac{s_B^2}{n_B}}$$

If you have ordered the observations into *matched pairs*, you compute the difference $d_i = X_{A_i} - X_{B_i}$ for each pair. You then find the mean difference $\bar{d}$ and the standard deviation s_d:

$$\bar{d} = \frac{\sum d_i}{n} \qquad s_d = \sqrt{\frac{\sum d_i^2 - n\bar{d}^2}{n - 1}}$$

Finally, you use $\bar{d}$ and s_d to compute an interval estimate of the difference in means:

$$\mu_A - \mu_B = \bar{d} + z \frac{s_d}{\sqrt{n}}$$

Testing procedures extend directly into the two-sample case. The normal deviate z is the usual test statistic. For independently selected samples of large size, you compute z from

$$z = \frac{\bar{X}_A - \bar{X}_B}{\sqrt{\dfrac{s_A^2}{n_A} + \dfrac{s_B^2}{n_B}}}$$

With matched pairs, the following expression applies:

$$z = \frac{\bar{d}}{s_d/\sqrt{n}}$$

When sample sizes are small, the Student t statistic replaces z. When constructing confidence interval estimates for the difference in means, you use the following expression for independent samples:

$$\mu_A - \mu_B = \bar{X}_A - \bar{X}_B \pm t_{\alpha/2} \sqrt{\frac{(n_A - 1)s_A^2 + (n_B - 1)s_B^2}{n_A + n_B - 2}} \sqrt{\frac{1}{n_A} + \frac{1}{n_B}}$$

In testing hypotheses for the difference in means, you compute the test statistic for independent samples from

$$t = \frac{\bar{X}_A - \bar{X}_B}{\sqrt{\dfrac{(n_A - 1)s_A^2 + (n_B - 1)s_B^2}{n_A + n_B - 2}} \sqrt{\dfrac{1}{n_A} + \dfrac{1}{n_B}}}$$

Except for t replacing z, the matched-pairs expression remains unchanged.

In testing for the difference in proportions, you pool the samples to compute the *combined sample proportion*:

$$P_C = \frac{n_A P_A + n_B P_B}{n_A + n_B}$$

The testing procedure employs the normal approximation, and you use P_C in computing the test statistic z:

$$z = \frac{P_A - P_B}{\sqrt{P_C(1 - P_C)\left(\dfrac{1}{n_A} + \dfrac{1}{n_B}\right)}}$$

All these procedures are *parametric* in that they focus on population means or proportions. As an alternative, *nonparametric statistics* provides testing procedures that are free from some often unrealistic assumptions required by those methods.

For tests involving independent samples you may use the *Wilcoxon rank-sum test*. You establish the test statistic by first ranking all observations, starting with the lowest value. In doing this you pool all the observations and assign ranks without regard to sample group. You then compute the sum W of the group A ranks. The following test statistic applies.

$$z = \frac{W - \dfrac{n_A(n_A + n_B + 1)}{2}}{\sqrt{\dfrac{n_A n_B(n_A + n_B + 1)}{12}}}$$

In the case of matched pairs, you use the *Wilcoxon signed-rank test*. This procedure is based on pair differences, which you rank according to absolute value (ignoring the signs and any zero differences). Then you compute the rank sum V for positive differences. You use the following test statistic.

$$z = \frac{V - \dfrac{n(n + 1)}{4}}{\sqrt{\dfrac{n(n + 1)(2n + 1)}{24}}}$$

RAISE YOUR GRADES

Can you explain ...?

☑ how to determine which population gets the A designation
☑ why observation pairing might be desirable
☑ why no nonparametric estimation procedure is needed
☑ how to determine whether a two-sample test is two-sided
☑ when independent sampling is appropriate

Do you know ...?

☑ how to compute the combined sample proportion
☑ how to assign ranks to observation values that are tied
☑ how the expressions for large-sample and small-sample investigations differ
☑ what distinguishes the two Wilcoxon rank sums
☑ which sample group is the experimental one and which is the control

RAPID REVIEW

1. In testing the null hypothesis $\mu_A \leqslant \mu_B$, the critical value of the normal deviate is $z_{.05} = 1.64$. The null hypothesis must be rejected for all but one of the following outcomes. For what result must you accept H_0?   [Section 14-1B]

    (a) $z = 2.03$ (b) $z = 3.41$ (c) $z = -1.68$ (d) $z = 1.75$

2. Confidence intervals at the 95% level were obtained for the results of four sampling studies. The null hypothesis $\mu_A = \mu_B$ was also tested at the 5% significance level. Which one of the following outcomes is valid?   [Section 14-1C]

    (a) $-3 \leqslant \mu_A - \mu_B \leqslant 2.5$; reject H_0
    (b) $1.8 \leqslant \mu_A - \mu_B \leqslant 2.9$; accept H_0
    (c) $2.5 \leqslant \mu_A - \mu_B \leqslant 3.7$; reject H_0
    (d) $-.9 \leqslant \mu_A - \mu_B \leqslant -.2$; accept H_0

3. Which one of the following decision rules would be appropriate for testing $H_0: \mu_A \geqslant \mu_B$?   [Section 14-1B]

    (a) Accept H_0 if $z \geqslant -1.4$, and reject H_0 if $z < -1.4$.
    (b) Accept H_0 if $z \geqslant .3$, and reject H_0 if $z < .3$.
    (c) Accept H_0 if $z \leqslant 1.5$, and reject H_0 if $z > 1.5$.
    (d) Accept H_0 if $z \leqslant -1.6$, and reject H_0 if $z > -1.6$.

4. Compute P_C when $P_A = .30$, $P_B = .40$, $n_A = 100$, and $n_B = 100$.   [Section 14-3]

5. For each of the following lower-tailed testing situations, determine the rank sum W for group A. Then compute z, and indicate whether you should accept or reject the null hypothesis that $\mu_A \geqslant \mu_B$ at the $\alpha = .05$ significance level.   [Section 14-4A]

    (a) A 8   6   5   10   12
         B 13   15   13   16   17

    (c) A 13   9   22   14   31
         B 4   16   19   45   27

    (b) A -10 -8 4   2   9
         B 10   11 -1 15   10

    (d) A 5   19   8   2   4
         B 3   6   6   6   18

6. For each of the following lower-tailed testing situations, determine the rank sum V for each matched-pair difference. Then compute z, and indicate whether you should accept or reject the null hypothesis that $\mu_A \geqslant \mu_B$ at the $\alpha = .05$ significance level.   [Section 14-4B].

(a)		(b)		(c)		(d)	
A	*B*	*A*	*B*	*A*	*B*	*A*	*B*
90	100	90	100	87	82	78	89
91	87	102	93	105	103	88	93
83	94	88	89	59	65	73	71
90	92	93	90	84	81	103	100
83	80	85	78	91	79	88	92
79	84	100	105	87	88	69	77
105	111	94	98	103	109	95	100
94	108	87	102	78	82	68	73
67	73	71	78	74	81	81	85
111	119	88	90	91	95	79	87

7. In testing the null hypothesis that an old drug has a cure rate at least as great as that of a new drug, which one of the following representations might apply?   [Section 14-1B]

(a) *A* represents new drug; $H_0: \pi_A \geqslant \pi_B$
(b) *B* represents old drug; $H_0: \pi_A \geqslant \pi_B$
(c) *A* represents old drug; $H_0: \pi_A \geqslant \pi_B$
(d) *B* represents new drug; $H_0: \pi_A \leqslant \pi_B$

8. The Wilcoxon rank-sum test can be   [Section 14-4]

(a) upper-tailed.
(b) lower-tailed.
(c) either of the above.
(d) none of the above.

9. Which of the following is true for tests involving ranks?   [Section 14-4]

(a) Ties always matter.
(b) Ties matter only when they occur between sample groups.
(c) Ties matter only when they occur within sample groups.
(d) Ties rarely happen.

10. Which of the following statements is false?   [Sections 14-1, 2, 3, 4]

(a) Matched-pairs testing may be employed regardless of the sample size.
(b) Two-sample tests must be two-sided as well.
(c) In all tests involving ranking, the lowest values receive the lowest ranks.
(d) The experimental group may correspond either to population *A* or to population *B*.

Answers

1. (c)   2. (c)   3. (a)   4. .35
5.   (a) $W = 15$ $z = -2.61$ reject
      (b) $W = 18$ $z = -1.98$ reject
      (c) $W = 25$ $z = -.52$ accept
      (d) $W = 26$ $z = -.31$ accept

6.   (a) $V = 5$ $z = -2.29$ reject
      (b) $V = 17.5$ $z = -1.02$ accept
      (c) $V = 21$ $z = -.66$ accept
      (d) $V = 3$ $z = -2.50$ reject

7. (c)   8. (c)   9. (b)   10. (b)

SOLVED PROBLEMS

PROBLEM 14-1   Two methods for fabricating a part are being considered. The following sample data pertain to completion times.

	Method A	Method B
	$n_A = 100$	$n_B = 200$
	$\bar{X}_A = 5.4$ min.	$\bar{X}_B = 5.1$ min.
	$s_A = 2.00$ min.	$s_B = 2.24$ min.

Construct a 95% confidence interval estimate of the difference in population mean completion times.

Solution: Using $z = 1.96$, you find the following:

$$\mu_A - \mu_B = 5.4 - 5.1 \pm 1.96 \sqrt{\frac{(2.00)^2}{100} + \frac{(2.24)^2}{200}}$$

$$= .3 \pm .50$$

or

$$-.20 \text{ min.} \leqslant \mu_A - \mu_B \leqslant .80 \text{ min.}$$

PROBLEM 14-2 In a sample test evaluation of assembly operations, two different sequences were considered. A sample of $n = 100$ workers were timed for batches of parts assembled under sequence A. The same workers were timed for another group of the same parts assembled under sequence B. The average time per part was found for each sequence and worker. Subtracting each worker's sequence B average time from that of sequence A, the mean difference was found to be .25 minute with a standard deviation of .75 minute. Construct a 95% confidence interval estimate of the difference in population mean assembly times.

Solution: Each worker's assembly times under sequence A and sequence B represent a matched pair, and you are given $\bar{d} = .25$ min. and $s_d = .75$ min. Using $z = 1.96$, you find the following:

$$\mu_A - \mu_B = .25 \pm 1.96 \frac{.75}{\sqrt{100}} = .25 \pm .15$$

or

$$.10 \text{ min.} \leqslant \mu_A - \mu_B \leqslant .40 \text{ min.}$$

PROBLEM 14-3 The following sample data have been collected independently for the transaction times (in seconds) of two computer teleprocessing monitors.

Monitor A				Monitor B			
12.7	13.4	14.5	11.7	9.8	10.4	12.6	13.7
10.6	11.4	12.2	13.7	12.3	11.7	12.1	10.8
14.1	13.3	12.6	12.2	12.6	11.9	10.1	9.9
11.3	12.5	12.3	13.7	12.3	12.1	11.6	10.8
15.1	13.7	12.5	14.4	13.1	11.5	10.9	11.4
12.5	13.3	13.3	14.5	10.2	10.4	12.7	12.6
12.5	13.3	13.5	12.5	11.2	11.7	12.4	13.1
10.7	10.5	12.4	11.9	11.0	12.0	13.1	12.0
12.0	13.5	14.1					

Construct a 99% confidence interval estimate for the difference in mean processing times for the two monitors.

Solution: First compute the sample means and standard deviations:

$$n_A = 35 \qquad n_B = 32$$
$$\bar{X}_A = 12.81 \text{ sec.} \qquad \bar{X}_B = 11.69 \text{ sec.}$$
$$s_A = 1.148 \text{ sec.} \qquad s_B = 1.035 \text{ sec.}$$

Now use these values and $z_{.005} = 2.57$ to construct the confidence interval.

$$\mu_A - \mu_B = 12.81 - 11.69 \pm 2.57 \sqrt{\frac{(1.148)^2}{35} + \frac{(1.035)^2}{32}} = 1.12 \pm .69$$

or

$$.43 \text{ sec.} \leqslant \mu_A - \mu_B \leqslant 1.81 \text{ sec.}$$

PROBLEM 14-4 The following grade-point data have been obtained from matched pairs taken randomly from two populations of university students. Group A consists of students who work less than 20 hours a week. Group B consists of full-time students who also hold full-time jobs.

A	B	A	B	A	B	A	B
3.65	3.71	2.84	2.75	3.22	3.15	3.61	3.40
3.25	2.96	2.86	2.91	3.11	2.95	3.55	3.35
3.33	3.17	3.55	3.51	4.00	3.86	3.74	3.55
2.54	2.27	2.85	2.62	3.45	3.28	3.61	3.48
3.44	3.42	3.65	3.51	3.12	2.88	3.05	3.12
3.14	3.02	3.67	3.50	3.24	3.18	3.15	2.91
3.29	3.17	3.64	3.52	3.78	3.42	3.20	2.95
2.65	2.90	2.85	2.69	3.53	3.37	3.15	3.11
3.22	2.84	3.55	3.65	3.52	3.44		

Construct a 95% confidence interval for the difference in mean GPA for all students in the respective populations.

Solution: You first find the difference d_i for each matched pair, and you then compute the means and standard deviations for those quantities:

$$n = 35 \qquad \bar{d} = .128 \qquad s_d = .1304$$

Using $z = 1.96$, you find

$$\mu_A - \mu_B = .128 \pm 1.96 \frac{.1304}{\sqrt{35}}$$

$$= .128 \pm .043$$

or

$$.085 \leqslant \mu_A - \mu_B \leqslant .171$$

PROBLEM 14-5 Two population means are to be compared using sample data. The null hypothesis is $H_0: \mu_A \geqslant \mu_B$. Using two independent samples of size 100, the following results have been obtained:

$$\bar{X}_A = 101.4 \qquad \bar{X}_B = 102.0$$
$$s_A = 3.7 \qquad s_B = 3.4$$

Use an $\alpha = .05$ significance level to test H_0.

Solution: The test is a lower-tailed one. The critical value of the normal deviate is $z_{.05} = 1.64$, and the following decision rule applies:

Accept H_0 if $z \geqslant -1.64$

Reject H_0 if $z < -1.64$

The computed value of the test statistic is

$$z = \frac{101.4 - 102.0}{\sqrt{\frac{(3.7)^2}{100} + \frac{(3.4)^2}{100}}} = -1.19$$

Since this is greater than the critical value, H_0 must be accepted.

PROBLEM 14-6 To evaluate two alternative assembly procedures, a production manager has gathered independent sample data from pilot runs of both. He wishes to protect himself from erroneously concluding that the procedures are equally fast, in terms of mean assembly times, at the $\alpha = .05$ significance level.

He has collected the following data:

$$n_A = 100 \qquad n_B = 100$$
$$\bar{X}_A = 10.8 \text{ min.} \qquad \bar{X}_B = 10.6 \text{ min.}$$
$$s_A = .21 \text{ min.} \qquad s_B = .19 \text{ min.}$$

What conclusion should the manager reach?

Solution: The test is two-sided, and the critical value of the normal deviate is $z_{.025} = 1.96$. The following decision rule applies:

Accept H_0 if $-1.96 \leqslant z \leqslant 1.96$ (Conclude procedures are equally fast.)

Reject H_0 if $z < -1.96$ (Conclude procedure A is faster.)

or if $z > 1.96$ (Conclude procedure B is faster.)

The following test statistic is computed:

$$z = \frac{10.8 - 10.6}{\sqrt{\dfrac{(.21)^2}{100} + \dfrac{(.19)^2}{100}}} = 7.06$$

Since this value exceeds the upper critical value of 1.96, the manager must reject H_0, and he should conclude that procedure A is the faster one.

PROBLEM 14-7 A statistician investigating the duration of a night's sleep for those who exercise regularly (A) and those who don't exercise (B) has obtained the following data:

$$n_A = 100 \qquad n_B = 100$$
$$\bar{X}_A = 7.5 \text{ hrs.} \qquad \bar{X}_B = 7.2 \text{ hrs.}$$
$$s_A = .5 \text{ hrs.} \qquad s_B = .6 \text{ hrs.}$$

(a) Construct a 95% confidence interval estimate for the difference in mean sleeping durations for the two populations.

(b) At a 5% significance level, should you accept or reject the null hypothesis that the mean sleeping time for those who exercise regularly is identical to that for those who don't exercise?

Solution:
(a) Using $z = 1.96$, you construct the following confidence interval:

$$\mu_A - \mu_B = 7.5 - 7.2 \pm 1.96 \sqrt{\frac{(.5)^2}{100} + \frac{(.6)^2}{100}}$$

$$= .3 \pm .15$$

or

$$.15 \text{ hrs.} \leqslant \mu_A - \mu_B \leqslant .45 \text{ hrs.}$$

(b) If $\mu_A = \mu_B$, then $\mu_A - \mu_B = 0$, and the interval estimate for the difference of these means should contain zero within its limits. Since the 95% confidence interval found in (a) doesn't contain zero, you may reject the null hypothesis of identical means at the .05 significance level.

PROBLEM 14-8 A ski equipment manufacturer compared two types of ski bindings. A total of 100 matched pairs of skiers participated in the study. Group A consisted of skiers with loosely adjusted bindings, group B skiers had tightly adjusted bindings. The number of accidents per hour of skiing was determined for each skier. The following results were obtained:

$$\bar{d} = .05 \qquad s_d = .01$$

(a) Construct a 95% confidence interval estimate for the difference in mean accident rates.

(b) At the 5% significance level, should the manufacturer accept or reject the null hypothesis that tightness of bindings makes no difference in the mean ski accident rate?

Solution:

(a) For $z = 1.96$, you construct the following confidence interval:

$$\mu_A - \mu_B = .05 \pm 1.96 \frac{.01}{\sqrt{100}} = .05 \pm .002$$

or

$$.048 \leqslant \mu_A - \mu_B \leqslant .052 \text{ accidents per hour}$$

(b) Since this interval doesn't include the difference $\mu_A - \mu_B = 0$, the manufacturer must reject the null hypothesis of identical means.

PROBLEM 14-9 Refer to the data for teleprocessing transaction times in Problem 14-3. Test the null hypothesis that monitor A involves times that are on the average less than or equal to those of monitor B. At the 1% significance level, should you accept or reject H_0?

Solution: The test is upper-tailed, and the critical value of the normal deviate is $z_{.01} = 2.33$. The following decision rule applies:

$$\text{Accept } H_0 \text{ if } z \leqslant 2.33 \qquad \text{(System } A \text{ is faster.)}$$
$$\text{Reject } H_0 \text{ if } z > 2.33 \qquad \text{(System } B \text{ is faster.)}$$

The computed value of the statistic is

$$z = \frac{12.81 - 11.69}{\sqrt{\frac{(1.148)^2}{35} + \frac{(1.035)^2}{32}}} = 4.20$$

Since this is greater than the critical value, you must reject the null hypothesis.

PROBLEM 14-10 Refer to the student GPA data in Problem 14-4. Test the null hypothesis that full-time job holders achieve grade-point averages at least as great as those of nonworking students. At the 1% significance level, should you accept or reject H_0?

Solution: This test is upper-tailed, and the critical value of the normal deviate is $z_{.01} = 2.33$. The following decision rule applies:

$$\text{Accept } H_0 \text{ if } z \leqslant 2.33 \qquad \text{(Working students have GPA's at least as great.)}$$
$$\text{Reject } H_0 \text{ if } z > 2.33 \qquad \text{(Working students have lower GPA's.)}$$

The computed value of the test statistic is

$$z = \frac{.128}{.1304/\sqrt{35}} = 5.81$$

Since this exceeds the critical value of 2.33, you must reject the null hypothesis.

PROBLEM 14-11 In comparing two population means using independent samples, you are testing the null hypothesis that $\mu_A \leqslant \mu_B$ at the $\alpha = .05$ significance level. You have obtained the following sample data:

$$n_A = 15 \qquad n_B = 10$$
$$\bar{X}_A = 6.58 \qquad \bar{X}_B = 6.39$$
$$s_A = .38 \qquad s_B = .60$$

Should you accept or reject the null hypothesis?

Solution: The test is upper-tailed, and you must use the Student t distribution since the sample size is less than 30. Using $15 + 10 - 2 = 23$ degrees of freedom, you obtain the critical value of $t_{.05} = 1.714$ from Table B. The following decision rule applies:

$$\text{Accept } H_0 \text{ if } t \leqslant 1.714$$
$$\text{Reject } H_0 \text{ if } t > 1.714$$

The computed value of the test statistic is

$$t = \frac{6.58 - 6.39}{\sqrt{\dfrac{(15 - 1)(.38)^2 + (10 - 1)(.60)^2}{15 + 10 - 2}} \sqrt{\dfrac{1}{15} + \dfrac{1}{10}}} = .973$$

Since this value lies in the acceptance region, you must accept the null hypothesis.

PROBLEM 14-12 A consumer testing service asks you to compare gas and electric ovens by baking one type of bread in each type of oven. The following baking times are obtained:

Gas	Electric
$n_A = 10$	$n_B = 12$
$\bar{X}_A = 2.1$ hrs.	$\bar{X}_B = 2.3$ hrs.
$s_A = .3$ hrs.	$s_B = .4$ hrs.

(a) Construct a 95% confidence interval estimate of the difference in mean baking times using the two oven types.

(b) At the $\alpha = .05$ significance level, should you accept or reject the null hypothesis of identical means?

Solution:

(a) For $10 + 12 - 2 = 20$ degrees of freedom, Table B provides $t_{.025} = 2.086$. You obtain the following confidence interval estimate.

$$\mu_A - \mu_B = 2.1 - 2.3 \pm 2.086 \sqrt{\frac{(10 - 1)(.3)^2 + (12 - 1)(.4)^2}{10 + 12 - 2}} \sqrt{\frac{1}{10} + \frac{1}{12}}$$

$$= -.2 \pm .32$$

or

$$-.52 \text{ hrs.} \leqslant \mu_A - \mu_B \leqslant .12 \text{ hrs.}$$

(b) Since the confidence interval found in (a) includes the difference $\mu_A - \mu_B = 0$, you must accept the null hypothesis of identical means.

PROBLEM 14-13 The following sample data represent the annual operating cost for two high-volume copiers.

Brand A			Brand B		
$12,366	$12,575	$13,589	$ 7,024	$11,115	$10,443
11,950	13,820	12,276	18,203	6,450	4,255
11,786	12,479	13,125	12,357	19,204	4,158
12,659			23,425	3,718	8,295
			6,225	4,870	9,146

(a) Compute the mean and standard deviation for each sample.

(b) Construct a 95% confidence interval estimate of the difference in mean costs for the two machine types.

(c) Machine B will be adopted if it is found to be significantly cheaper. The null hypothesis is that machine B is at least as expensive to operate as machine A. Using a 5% significance level, what action should be taken?

Solution:

(a) You should compute the following sample statistics:

$$n_A = 10 \qquad n_B = 15$$
$$\bar{X}_A = \$12,663 \qquad \bar{X}_B = \$9,926$$
$$s_A = \$664 \qquad s_B = \$6,044$$

(b) For $10 + 15 - 2 = 23$ degrees of freedom, Table B provides the critical value $t_{.025} = 2.069$. Using the computed statistics, you should obtain

$$\mu_A - \mu_B = \$12,663 - \$9,926 \pm 2.069 \sqrt{\frac{(10-1)(664)^2 + (15-1)(6,044)^2}{10 + 15 - 2}} \sqrt{\frac{1}{10} + \frac{1}{15}}$$

$$= \$2,737 \pm \$3,998$$

or

$$-\$1,261 \leqslant \mu_A - \mu_B \leqslant \$6,735$$

(c) You are testing the null hypothesis

$$H_0: \mu_A \leqslant \mu_B \qquad \text{(Machine } B \text{ is at least as expensive.)}$$

This is an upper-tailed test, and for 23 degrees of freedom the critical value is $t_{.05} = 1.714$. The following decision rule applies:

$$\text{Accept } H_0 \text{ if } t \leqslant 1.714$$

$$\text{Reject } H_0 \text{ if } t > 1.714$$

The computed value for the test statistic is

$$t = \frac{12,663 - 9,926}{\sqrt{\frac{9(664)^2 + 14(6,044)^2}{10 + 15 - 2}} \sqrt{\frac{1}{10} + \frac{1}{15}}} = 1.416$$

Since this falls below the critical value, the null hypothesis must be accepted, and machine A must be chosen.

PROBLEM 14-14 At the $\alpha = .01$ significance level, test the following null hypothesis:

$$H_0: \pi_A \geqslant \pi_B$$

You have taken samples of size $n_A = 100$ and $n_B = 25$, and you compute the sample proportions $P_A = .19$ and $P_B = .24$.

Solution: First compute the combined sample proportion:

$$P_C = \frac{100(.19) + 25(.24)}{100 + 25} = .20$$

This test is lower-tailed, and the critical value of the normal deviate is $z_{.01} = 2.33$. The following decision rule applies:

$$\text{Accept } H_0 \text{ if } z \geqslant -2.33$$

$$\text{Reject } H_0 \text{ if } z < -2.33$$

The computed value of the test statistic is

$$z = \frac{.19 - .24}{\sqrt{.20(1 - .20)\left(\frac{1}{100} + \frac{1}{25}\right)}} = -.56$$

Since this falls above the critical value, you must accept H_0.

PROBLEM 14-15 In determining how to allocate advertising expenditures, a marketing director wishes to test the null hypothesis that the proportion of persons in the North (A) that prefer WeeTees is at least as great as it is in the South (B). Using samples of 100 from each region, she tests at the $\alpha = .05$ significance level.

Suppose that 38 northern and 42 southern subjects are found to prefer WeeTees. What conclusion should the director reach?

Solution: The following sample results apply:

$$n_A = 100 \qquad n_B = 100$$

$$P_A = \frac{38}{100} \qquad P_B = \frac{42}{100}$$

The combined sample proportion is

$$P_C = \frac{100(.38) + 100(.42)}{100 + 100} = .40$$

This test is lower-tailed, and the critical value of the normal deviate is $z_{.05} = 1.64$. The following decision rule applies:

Accept H_0 if $z \geqslant -1.64$ (Conclude WeeTees preference at least as great in North.)

Reject H_0 if $z < -1.64$ (Conclude greater WeeTees preference in South.)

The computed value of the test statistic is

$$z = \frac{.38 - .42}{\sqrt{.40(1 - .40)\left(\dfrac{1}{100} + \dfrac{1}{100}\right)}} = -.58$$

Since this falls above the critical value, the director must accept H_0 and conclude that the WeeTees preference in the North is at least as great as it is in the South.

PROBLEM 14-16 You are asked to compare two chemical processes in terms of proportion of unsatisfactory batches yielded. You find that 100 sample batches from process A yielded 5% unsatisfactory, while the same number of runs made under process B yielded 7% unsatisfactory. At the $\alpha = .05$ significance level, should you accept or reject the null hypothesis of identical proportions unsatisfactory?

Solution: You have the following data:

$$n_A = 100 \quad\quad n_B = 100$$
$$P_A = .05 \quad\quad P_B = .07$$

The combined sample proportion is

$$P_C = \frac{100(.05) + 100(.07)}{100 + 100} = .06$$

This test is two-sided since you are testing $H_0\colon \mu_A = \mu_B$, and the critical value of the normal deviate is $z_{\alpha/2} = z_{.025} = 1.96$. You will accept H_0 if the computed value of the test statistic falls within ± 1.96. The computed value is

$$z = \frac{.05 - .07}{\sqrt{.06(1 - .06)\left(\dfrac{1}{100} + \dfrac{1}{100}\right)}} = -.60$$

which falls in the acceptance region. You must conclude that the two processes have identical proportions of unsatisfactory batches.

PROBLEM 14-17 In testing the null hypothesis that tire type B yields identical mileage to tire type A, two independent random samples of five sets of each tire type were selected and worn out on an endurance track. The following results and their rankings were obtained:

Brand	Mileage (per hour)	Rank	Brand	Mileage (per hour)	Rank
A	19.8	1	A	20.6	6
A	19.9	2	B	21.1	7
A	20.2	3	B	21.4	8
B	20.3	4	B	21.7	9
A	20.4	5	B	22.3	10

At the $\alpha = .05$ significance level, what conclusion should be reached?

Solution: The following rank sum applies to group A:

$$W = 1 + 2 + 3 + 5 + 6 = 17$$

The critical value for this two-sided test is $z_{.025} = 1.96$, and H_0: $\mu_A = \mu_B$ will be accepted if the test statistic falls within ± 1.96. The following computed level applies for the test statistic:

$$z = \frac{17 - \frac{5(5 + 5 + 1)}{2}}{\sqrt{\frac{5(5)(5 + 5 + 1)}{12}}} = -2.19$$

Since this lies below -1.96, H_0 must be rejected. It must be concluded that tire B lasts longer.

PROBLEM 14-18   At the 5% level of significance, use the Wilcoxon rank-sum test to evaluate the null hypothesis that brand A lightbulbs last at least as long as brand B lightbulbs. The following sample lifetimes apply.

Lifetime (in hours)

| Brand A | 586 | 691 | 656 | 617 | 730 | 603 | 661 | 700 | 684 | 681 |
| Brand B | 659 | 695 | 763 | 632 | 673 | 704 | 683 | 724 | 698 | 687 |

Solution: Sort the values in increasing sequence. The following data apply.

Lifetime	Rank	Brand	Lifetime	Rank	Brand
586	1	A	684	11	A
603	2	A	687	12	B
617	3	A	691	13	A
632	4	B	695	14	B
656	5	A	698	15	B
659	6	B	700	16	A
661	7	A	704	17	B
673	8	B	724	18	B
681	9	A	730	19	A
683	10	B	763	20	B

$$W = 1 + 2 + 3 + 5 + 7 + 9 + 11 + 13 + 16 + 19 = 86$$

The test is lower-tailed, and the critical value of the normal deviate is $z_{.05} = 1.64$. The following decision rule applies:

Accept H_0 if $z \geqslant -1.64$ (Brand A lightbulbs last at least as long.)

Reject H_0 if $z < -1.64$ (Brand B lightbulbs last longer.)

The computed value of the test statistic is

$$z = \frac{86 - \frac{10(10 + 10 + 1)}{2}}{\sqrt{\frac{10(10)(10 + 10 + 1)}{12}}} = -1.44$$

Since this exceeds the critical value, you must accept H_0, and you should conclude that brand A lightbulbs last at least as long as brand B lightbulbs.

PROBLEM 14-19   Two energy conservation methods are being evaluated to determine which provides the hotter water. The following data represent the temperatures, in degrees Fahrenheit, of independent samples of the water generated by the two methods.

Method A		Method B	
185	233	197	248
206	250	235	234
217	206	245	224
251	215	211	231
190	224	225	216
		245	258

Apply the Wilcoxon rank-sum test to evaluate the null hypothesis that the water generated by method A is at least as hot as that generated by method B. Use an $\alpha = .05$ significance level.

Solution: Arrange the data in order of increasing size, and assign ranks. Then compute the rank sum for the group A temperatures.

X_A	Rank	X_B	Rank
185	1	197	3
190	2	211	6
206	4	216	8
206	5	224	10.5
215	7	225	12
217	9	231	13
224	10.5	234	15
233	14	235	16
250	20	245	17
251	21	245	18
		248	19
		258	22

The sample sizes are

$$n_A = 10 \qquad n_B = 12$$

The test is lower-tailed and the critical value of the normal deviate is $z_{.05} = 1.64$. The following decision rule applies:

Accept H_0 if $z \geqslant -1.64$ (Method A generates water at least as hot.)

Reject H_0 if $z < -1.64$ (Method B generates hotter water.)

The computed value of the test statistic is

$$z = \frac{93.5 - \dfrac{10(10 + 12 + 1)}{2}}{\sqrt{\dfrac{10(12)(10 + 12 + 1)}{12}}} = -1.42$$

Since this value falls above the critical value, you must accept H_0 and conclude that method A water is at least as hot as that generated by method B.

PROBLEM 14-20   A financial analyst for a small bank must determine whether to recommend processing checks in house, replacing the present outside processor. That action will be taken if the analyst can show that the operating costs are significantly lower with in-house processing. The null hypothesis is that in-house processing would be at least as expensive as the present procedure. The following sample costs for check processing were obtained from a test where the same batches of checks were processed in both ways.

Pair	In-house (A)	Outside (B)
1	$.18	$.20
2	.17	.18
3	.23	.23
4	.19	.18
5	.21	.24
6	.23	.27
7	.19	.21
8	.22	.22
9	.19	.24
10	.20	.26

Using a significance level of .05, what action should the analyst recommend?

Solution: Each batch provides a matched pair, so you use the Wilcoxon signed-rank test. You begin by finding the following:

i	X_{A_i}	X_{B_i}	d_i	Sign	Rank of $|d_i|$
1	$.18	$.20	−.02	−	3
2	.17	.18	−.01	−	1.5
3	.23	.23	0.00	tie	—
4	.19	.18	.01	+	1.5
5	.21	.24	−.03	−	5
6	.23	.27	−.04	−	6
7	.19	.21	−.02	−	4
8	.22	.22	0.00	tie	—
9	.19	.24	−.05	−	7
10	.20	.26	−.06	−	8

For $n = 8$ nonzero pair differences, $V = 1.5$. The null hypothesis $H_0: \mu_A \geqslant \mu_B$ is refuted by small values of V or z, making the test a lower-tailed one. The critical value of the normal deviate is $z_{.05} = 1.64$. The following decision rule applies:

Accept H_0 if $z \geqslant -1.64$ (In-house processing is at least as expensive.)

Reject H_0 if $z < -1.64$ (Outside processing is more expensive.)

The computed value of the test statistic is

$$z = \frac{1.5 - \dfrac{8(8 + 1)}{4}}{\sqrt{\dfrac{8(8 + 1)(16 + 1)}{24}}} = -2.31$$

Since this lies below -1.64, the null hypothesis must be rejected. The analyst will recommend the in-house procedure.

PROBLEM 14-21 You are testing two methods for training. You have paired forty test subjects in terms of aptitude and experience. You train one member of each pair under method A, the partner under method B. You obtain the following scores by rating subsequent on-the-job performance.

Pair	A score	B score	Pair	A score	B score
1	87	85	11	62	77
2	55	73	12	67	43
3	62	62	13	77	75
4	51	68	14	71	67
5	48	53	15	58	42
6	66	39	16	58	81
7	53	56	17	61	66
8	24	38	18	51	33
9	91	83	19	80	75
10	63	60	20	44	55

Your null hypothesis is that method A scores are at least as high as those achieved by subjects who trained under method B. What conclusion will you reach at the 1% significance level?

Solution: First find the following data:

i	X_{A_i}	X_{B_i}	d_i	Sign	Rank of $|d_i|$
1	87	85	2	+	1
2	55	73	−18	−	15.5
3	62	62	0	tie	—
4	51	68	−17	−	14
5	48	53	−5	−	7
6	66	39	27	+	19
7	53	56	−3	−	3.5
8	24	38	−14	−	11
9	91	83	8	+	9

i	X_{A_i}	X_{B_i}	d_i	Sign	Rank of $|d_i|$
10	63	60	3	+	3.5
11	62	77	-15	$-$	12
12	67	43	24	+	18
13	77	75	2	+	2
14	71	67	4	+	5
15	58	42	16	+	13
16	58	81	-23	$-$	17
17	61	66	-5	$-$	7
18	51	33	18	+	15.5
19	80	75	5	+	7
20	44	55	-11	$-$	10

There are $n = 19$ nonzero pair differences. The rank sum of positive differences is

$$V = 1 + 19 + 9 + 3.5 + 18 + 2 + 5 + 13 + 15.5 + 7 = 93$$

The test is lower-tailed, and the critical value of the test statistic is $z_{.01} = 2.33$. The following decision rule applies:

Accept H_0 if $z \geqslant -2.33$ (Method A scores are at least as high.)

Reject H_0 if $z < -2.33$ (Method B scores are higher.)

You compute the following test statistic:

$$z = \frac{93 - \dfrac{19(19 + 1)}{4}}{\sqrt{\dfrac{19(19 + 1)(38 + 1)}{24}}} = -.08$$

Since this lies above the critical value, you must accept the null hypothesis. You must conclude that training-method A scores are at least as high as those of method B.

PROBLEM 14-22 You are evaluating a new food preservative compound. Ten sample batches have been prepared with the old preservative (A) and ten batches with the new formulation (B). Each A batch is matched with a B batch, and each pair is then sorted under a variety of environmental conditions. Following are the observed times until serious decomposition.

Pair	Shelf life (in days) Old preservative (A)	New preservative (B)
1	15.3	16.4
2	17.4	18.0
3	11.5	13.0
4	12.0	11.7
5	14.8	15.1
6	9.2	11.5
7	6.3	7.3
8	10.0	12.6
9	12.2	12.3
10	11.5	11.5

Test the null hypothesis that the old preservative lasts at least as long as the new one. Use $\alpha = .05$

Solution: This problem is similar to Problem 14-21.

i	X_{A_i}	X_{B_i}	d_i	Sign	Rank of $|d_i|$
1	15.3	16.4	-1.1	$-$	6
2	17.4	18.0	$-.6$	$-$	4
3	11.5	13.0	-1.5	$-$	7
4	12.0	11.7	.3	+	2.5

i	X_{A_i}	X_{B_i}	d_i	Sign	Rank of $|d_i|$
5	14.8	15.1	$-\,.3$	$-$	2.5
6	9.2	11.5	-2.3	$-$	8
7	6.3	7.3	-1.0	$-$	5
8	10.0	12.6	-2.6	$-$	9
9	12.2	12.3	$-\,.1$	$-$	1
10	11.5	11.5	0.0	tie	—

There are $n = 9$ nonzero pair differences, and the rank sum of positive differences is $V = 2.5$. The test is lower-tailed, and the critical value of the test statistic is $z_{.05} = 1.64$. The following decision rule applies:

Accept H_0 if $z \geqslant -1.64$ (Old preservative lasts at least as long.)

Reject H_0 if $z < -1.64$ (New preservative lasts longer.)

You compute the following test statistic:

$$z = \frac{2.5 - \dfrac{9(9+1)}{4}}{\sqrt{\dfrac{9(9+1)(18+1)}{24}}} = -2.37$$

Since this lies below the critical value, you must reject the null hypothesis and conclude that the new preservative is longer-lasting.

PROBLEM 14-23   The following product-rating data apply to two brands. Each observation pair represents an evaluation by a test subject who used both brands. (The higher the rating, the more favorable the evaluation.)

Subject	Brand A	Brand B	Subject	Brand A	Brand B
1	45	39	11	39	29
2	88	71	12	36	36
3	40	42	13	52	50
4	32	27	14	43	34
5	29	28	15	73	51
6	34	30	16	48	42
7	59	50	17	61	61
8	55	60	18	48	45
9	62	51	19	44	32
10	50	48	20	51	43

(a) Construct a 99% confidence interval estimate for the difference in mean ratings achieved by the two brands.

(b) Should the null hypothesis of identical means be accepted or rejected at the 1% significance level?

Solution:
(a) Here you are concerned with the means of the ratings, the sample size is less than 30, and the groups of ratings are matched into pairs. Therefore, you will make the confidence interval estimate using the t statistic and the expression for matched pairs. The following data apply.

i	X_{A_i}	X_{B_i}	d_i
1	45	39	6
2	88	71	17
3	40	42	$-\,2$
4	32	27	5
5	29	28	1
6	34	30	4
7	59	50	9
8	55	60	$-\,5$
9	62	51	11
10	50	48	2
11	39	29	10
12	36	36	0

i	X_{A_i}	X_{B_i}	d_i
13	52	50	2
14	43	34	9
15	73	51	22
16	48	42	6
17	61	61	0
18	48	45	3
19	44	32	12
20	51	43	8

The mean and standard deviation of the pair differences are

$$\bar{d} = 6.00 \qquad s_d = 6.505$$

For $20 - 1 = 19$ degrees of freedom, Table B provides the critical value $t_{.005} = 2.861$. You obtain the following 99% confidence interval estimate for the difference in mean ratings:

$$\mu_A - \mu_B = 6.00 \pm 2.861 \frac{6.505}{\sqrt{20}}$$

$$= 6.00 \pm 4.16$$

or

$$1.84 \leqslant \mu_A - \mu_B \leqslant 10.16$$

(b) Since the confidence interval doesn't contain $\mu_A - \mu_B = 0$, you must reject the null hypothesis of identical means.

PROBLEM 14-24 Perform the Wilcoxon signed-rank test with the data in Problem 14-23 to evaluate the null hypothesis that brand A yields ratings that are no greater than those of brand B. At the 5% significance level should you accept or reject H_0?

Solution: The following pair differences and ranks for the absolute values apply.

i	X_{A_i}	X_{B_i}	d_i	Sign	Rank of $|d_i|$
1	45	39	6	+	9
2	88	71	17	+	17
3	40	42	− 2	−	3
4	32	27	5	+	7.5
5	29	28	1	+	1
6	34	30	4	+	6
7	59	50	9	+	12
8	55	60	− 5	−	7.5
9	62	51	11	+	15
10	50	48	2	+	3
11	39	29	10	+	14
12	36	36	0	tie	—
13	52	50	2	+	3
14	43	34	9	+	13
15	73	51	22	+	18
16	48	42	6	+	10
17	61	61	0	tie	—
18	48	45	3	+	5
19	44	32	12	+	16
20	51	43	8	+	11

Altogether there are $n = 18$ nonzero pair differences. The sum of the ranks for positive differences is

$$V = 9 + 17 + 7.5 + 1 + 6 + 12 + 15 + 3 + 14 + 3 + 13 + 18 + 10 + 5 + 16 + 11 = 160.5$$

The test is upper-tailed, and the critical value of the test statistic is $z_{.05} = 1.64$. The following decision rule applies:

> Accept H_0 if $z \leqslant 1.64$ (Brand A ratings no greater.)
>
> Reject H_0 if $z > 1.64$ (Brand A ratings greater.)

The computed level for the test statistic is

$$z = \frac{160.5 - \dfrac{18(18 + 1)}{4}}{\sqrt{\dfrac{18(18 + 1)(36 + 1)}{24}}} = 3.27$$

Since this is greater than the critical value, you must reject the null hypothesis.

PROBLEM 14-25 You are using the following data to compare the grades achieved by nonworking students to those of working students.

Nonworking Students (*A*)				Working Students (*B*)			
GPA	SAT	GPA	SAT	GPA	SAT	GPA	SAT
3.3	655	3.2	712	3.1	588	2.7	578
3.9	722	3.5	690	3.8	716	3.7	695
2.9	623	2.8	575	3.1	627	3.2	634
3.3	710	3.8	690	3.5	713	3.9	730

Answer the following, assuming that you selected the samples independently.

(a) Construct a 95% confidence interval estimate for the difference in population mean GPA's for nonworking and working students.

(b) Apply the *t* test for the null hypothesis that nonworking students earn grades that are at least as high as those of working students. At the 5% significance level, should you accept or reject that hypothesis?

(c) Test the same null hypothesis using the Wilcoxon rank-sum test. What conclusion should you reach at the 5% significance level?

Solution:
(a) The following statistics apply:

$$n_A = 8 \qquad n_B = 8$$
$$\bar{X}_A = 3.338 \qquad \bar{X}_B = 3.375$$
$$s_A = .389 \qquad s_B = .417$$

The sample size is smaller than 30, so you use the *t* statistic. For $8 + 8 - 2 = 14$ degrees of freedom, you obtain from Table B the critical value of $t_{.025} = 2.145$. You construct the following confidence interval:

$$\mu_A - \mu_B = 3.338 - 3.375 \pm 2.145 \sqrt{\frac{7(.389)^2 + 7(.417)^2}{8 + 8 - 2}} \sqrt{\frac{1}{8} + \frac{1}{8}}$$

$$= -.037 \pm .432$$

or

$$-.469 \leqslant \mu_A - \mu_B \leqslant .395$$

(b) The test is lower-tailed, and the critical value of the test statistic is $t_{.05} = 1.761$. The following decision rule applies:

Accept H_0 if $z \geqslant -1.761$ (Grades of nonworking students are at least as high.)

Reject H_0 if $z < -1.761$ (Grades of working students are higher.)

The following test statistic applies:

$$t = \frac{3.338 - 3.375}{\sqrt{\dfrac{7(.389)^2 + 7(.417)^2}{8 + 8 - 2}} \sqrt{\dfrac{1}{8} + \dfrac{1}{8}}} = -.18$$

Since this exceeds the critical value, you must accept H_0.
(c) The following rank data apply:

X_A	Rank	X_B	Rank
3.3	8	3.1	5
3.9	15.5	3.8	13.5
2.9	3	3.1	4
3.3	9	3.5	10.5
3.2	6.5	2.7	1
3.5	10.5	3.7	12
2.8	2	3.2	6.5
3.8	13.5	3.9	15.5
	W = 68		

The sample sizes are

$$n_A = 8 \qquad n_B = 8$$

and the critical value is now $-z_{.05} = -1.64$. The computed value for the test statistic is

$$z = \frac{68 - \dfrac{8(8 + 8 + 1)}{2}}{\sqrt{\dfrac{8(8)(8 + 8 + 1)}{12}}} = 0$$

Since this exceeds the critical value, you must accept H_0.

PROBLEM 14-26   Consider the GPA data in Problem 14-25. Using SAT scores as the basis for assignment, match each nonworking student with a partner in the working group. Assuming that these were the matched pairs from the outset of the investigation, answer the following.

(a) Construct a 95% confidence interval estimate for the difference in population mean GPA's for nonworking and working students.
(b) Apply the t test for the null hypothesis that nonworking students earn grades that are at least as high as those of working students. At the 5% significance level, should you accept or reject that hypothesis?
(c) Test the same null hypothesis using the Wilcoxon signed-rank test. What conclusion should you reach at the 5% significance level?

Solution: The following data apply:

X_{A_i}	SAT	X_{B_i}	SAT	d_i	Sign	Rank of $\lvert d_i \rvert$
2.8	575	2.7	578	.1	+	1
2.9	623	3.1	588	−.2	−	4
3.3	655	3.1	627	.2	+	4
3.5	690	3.2	634	.3	+	6
3.8	690	3.7	695	.1	+	2
3.3	710	3.5	713	−.2	−	4
3.2	712	3.8	716	−.6	−	7
3.9	722	3.9	730	0.0	tie	—

(a) You find the following values:

$$n = 8 \qquad \bar{d} = -.0375 \qquad s_d = .2875$$

Since the sample size is smaller than 30, you use t as the test statistic. For $8 - 1 = 7$ degrees of freedom, the critical value from Table B is $t_{.025} = 2.365$. The confidence interval is

$$\mu_A - \mu_B = -.0375 \pm 2.365 \frac{.2875}{\sqrt{8}}$$

$$= -.0375 \pm .2404$$

or

$$-.2779 \leqslant \mu_A - \mu_B \leqslant .2029$$

(b) The test is lower-tailed, and the critical value of the test statistic is $t_{.05} = 1.895$. The following decision rule applies:

Accept H_0 if $t \geqslant -1.895$ (Grades of nonworking students are at least as high.)

Reject H_0 if $t < -1.895$ (Grades of working students are higher.)

The computed value for the test statistic is

$$t = \frac{-.0375}{.2875/\sqrt{8}} = -.369$$

Since this exceeds the critical value, you must accept the null hypothesis.

(c) For $n = 7$ nonzero pair differences, the sum of the ranks of positive differences is

$$V = 1 + 4 + 6 + 2 = 13$$

The critical value of the normal deviate is $-z_{.05} = -1.64$. The computed value of the test statistic is

$$z = \frac{13 - \dfrac{7(7 + 1)}{4}}{\sqrt{\dfrac{7(7 + 1)(14 + 1)}{24}}} = -.17$$

Since this exceeds the critical value, you must accept the null hypothesis.

15 CHI-SQUARE APPLICATIONS

THIS CHAPTER IS ABOUT

☑ **The Chi-Square Test for Independence**
☑ **Testing for the Equality of Several Proportions**
☑ **Estimating the Variance and Standard Deviation**
☑ **Testing the Variance**

So far in this book you have encountered statistical testing procedures based on two sampling distributions, the normal and the Student t. You will now encounter a third distribution, the chi-square, which is useful for testing a variety of conditions.

15-1. The Chi-Square Test for Independence

The most common statistical procedure involving the chi-square distribution is the test for independence of qualitative population variables.

A. Independence between qualitative variables is analogous to independence between events.

Recall from Chapter 4 that two events are *independent* whenever the probability of one of them is unaffected by the occurrence of the other. For example, consider the suit and denomination of a randomly selected playing card. The events "king" and "diamond" are independent, which is easy to establish from

$$\Pr[\text{king}\,|\,\text{diamond}] = \frac{1}{13} = \frac{4}{52} = \Pr[\text{king}]$$

One property of independent events is that you can find their joint probability by multiplying together their respective unconditional probabilities. Thus, you know that $\Pr[\text{king}] = 4/52$ and $\Pr[\text{diamond}] = 13/52 = 1/4$. It follows that

$$\Pr[\text{king } and \text{ diamond}] = \Pr[\text{king}] \times \Pr[\text{diamond}]$$

$$= \frac{4}{52} \times \frac{1}{4} = \frac{1}{52}$$

You may extend the concept of independence to qualitative variables. Two qualitative population variables A and B are **independent** if the proportion of the total population having any particular attribute of A remains the same for the part of the population having a particular attribute of B, no matter which attributes are considered.

EXAMPLE 15-1: DRIVER PREFERENCE AND TRAITS

One researcher tested the following variables pertaining to the characteristics of drivers and the car style they prefer.

Preferred body style	Driving traits
Sporty	Adventuresome
Conventional	Conservative
Utilitarian	Abusive

She found that drivers liking sporty cars are predominantly adventuresome but also heavily abusive and hardly conservative at all. Those preferring conventional or utilitarian cars are mainly conservative. She concluded that the two variables are *dependent*.

B. A contingency table conveniently summarizes sample data.

Suppose you wish to establish whether a student's business major is a variable that is independent of his or her area of employment. You will base your conclusion on a random sample of $n = 200$ responses. The following table summarizes the actual sample results.

Contingency Table—Actual Frequencies

Area of employment	Business major				Totals
	(1) Accounting	(2) Finance	(3) Marketing	(4) Management	
(1) Manufacturing	10	4	12	14	40
(2) Service	11	8	24	17	60
(3) Retailing	2	3	44	21	70
(4) Other	7	5	10	8	30
Totals	30	20	90	60	200

This is called a **contingency table**, since it shows the frequency for every combination of attributes—that is, for every possible "contingency." The entry in each cell is the **actual frequency** for the respective attribute pair. For easy reference, you can number each row and column, so that cell (i, j) refers to the frequency value in the ith row and the jth column. The frequencies are represented by the symbol f_{ij}.

C. You may establish independence or dependence by a statistical test.

You are testing the null hypothesis that business major and area of employment are independent variables. If H_0 is true, then the proportion of observations in any category should be the same regardless of what attribute applies for the other variable. It follows that each attribute pair has an **expected frequency** that you can compute from the following expression.

Expected frequencies
$$\hat{f}_{ij} = \frac{\text{Row } i \text{ total} \times \text{Column } j \text{ total}}{n}$$

The symbol $\hat{f}_{ij}$ denotes the expected frequency for cell (i, j). The following contingency table provides the expected frequencies for the present illustration.

Contingency Table—Expected Frequencies

Area of employment	Business major				Totals
	(1) Accounting	(2) Finance	(3) Marketing	(4) Management	
(1) Manufacturing	40 × 30/200 = 6	40 × 20/200 = 4	40 × 90/200 = 18	40 × 60/200 = 12	40
(2) Service	60 × 30/200 = 9	60 × 20/200 = 6	60 × 90/200 = 27	60 × 60/200 = 18	60
(3) Retailing	70 × 30/200 = 10.5	70 × 20/200 = 7	70 × 90/200 = 31.5	70 × 60/200 = 21	70
(4) Other	30 × 30/200 = 4.5	30 × 20/200 = 3	30 × 90/200 = 13.5	30 × 60/200 = 9	30
Totals	30	20	90	60	200

D. The test is based on the chi-square statistic.

You compute the test statistic from the actual and expected frequencies using the following expression.

Chi-square statistic
$$\chi^2 = \sum \frac{(f_{ij} - \hat{f}_{ij})^2}{\hat{f}_{ij}}$$

where the symbol χ is the lowercase Greek chi. The following table provides the χ^2 calculations for this illustration.

(i, j)	Actual frequency f_{ij}	Expected frequency $\hat{f}_{ij}$	$f_{ij} - \hat{f}_{ij}$	$(f_{ij} - \hat{f}_{ij})^2$	$\dfrac{(f_{ij} - \hat{f}_{ij})^2}{\hat{f}_{ij}}$
(1, 1)	10	6	4	16	2.667
(1, 2)	4	4	0	0	0.000
(1, 3)	12	18	−6	36	2.000
(1, 4)	14	12	2	4	.333
(2, 1)	11	9	2	4	.444
(2, 2)	8	6	2	4	.667
(2, 3)	24	27	−3	9	.333
(2, 4)	17	18	−1	1	.056
(3, 1)	2	10.5	−8.5	72.25	6.881
(3, 2)	3	7	−4	16	2.286
(3, 3)	44	31.5	12.5	156.25	4.960
(3, 4)	21	21	0	0	0.000
(4, 1)	7	4.5	2.5	6.25	1.389
(4, 2)	5	3	2	4	1.333
(4, 3)	10	13.5	−3.5	12.25	.907
(4, 4)	8	9	−1	1	.111
	200	200.0	0.0		$\chi^2 = 24.367$

The value $\chi^2 = 24.367$ will permit you to accept or reject the null hypothesis. Before you see how to do this, though, you should know about the sampling distribution for χ^2.

E. The chi-square distribution provides probabilities for levels of χ^2.

The **chi-square distribution** is similar to the Student t in that there is a separate distribution for each number of degrees of freedom. In testing for independence, the following rule applies.

Number of degrees of freedom $df = $ (Number of rows − 1)(Number of columns − 1)

In the present illustration, $df = (4 - 1)(4 - 1) = 9$.

Figure 15-1 shows the frequency curves for chi-square distributions when the degrees of freedom are 2, 4, 10, and 20. Table C in the Appendix provides upper-tail areas for the chi-square distribution. Using the symbol χ_α^2 to represent the level above which the upper-tail area is α, you have

$$\alpha = \Pr[\chi^2 \geqslant \chi_\alpha^2]$$

As with Table B for the Student t distribution, Table C provides a separate row for each df level indicating the critical values that correspond to the stated upper-tail area.

Figure 15-1   Various curves for the Chi-square distribution.

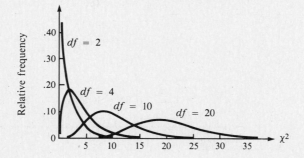

The curve for the chi-square distribution with 5 degrees of freedom is shown in Figure 15-2. To find the upper 5% value of χ^2, denoted by $\chi^2_{.05}$, you read Table C to find the entry in the row for 5 degrees of freedom and the column for the area $\bar{.05}$, obtaining $\chi^2_{.05} = 11.070$. Thus you have

$$.05 = \Pr[\chi^2 \geqslant 11.070]$$

You can also find the area above points lying in the lower portion of the curve: Thus, for an upper-tail area of .90, you obtain the value $\chi^2_{.90} = 1.610$ at 5 degrees of freedom (see Figure 15-2).

Figure 15-2   Chi-square curve for 5 degrees of freedom.

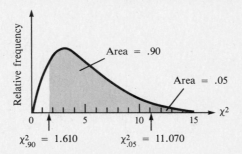

F.   The hypothesis test follows the same steps as the earlier procedures.

Figure 15-3 summarizes the test for the business major illustration. An $\alpha = .05$ significance level is assumed. Notice that the type I error probability is represented by an upper-tail area under the sampling distribution equal to .05. All tests of independence are upper-tailed. From Table C you read for $df = 9$ the critical value of $\chi^2_{.05} = 16.919$. Figure 15-3 shows the acceptance and rejection regions. Since you have already found the computed level to be $\chi^2 = 24.367$, you must reject H_0 and conclude that business major and area of employment are *not* independent.

Figure 15-3

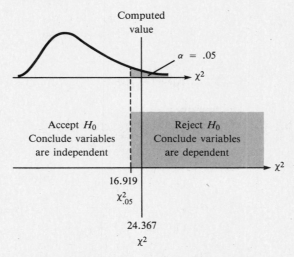

15-2.   Testing for the Equality of Several Proportions

You have already seen in Chapter 14 how to test for the equality of two proportions. When you need to evaluate three or more population proportions, you may extend that procedure, using the chi-square distribution. The following null hypothesis applies:

$$H_0: \pi_1 = \pi_2 = \cdots = \pi_k$$

You test this hypothesis using independent samples from the respective populations. As in Section 15-1, the actual frequencies are given, and from these you construct a contingency table for the expected frequencies. You then compute the chi-square test statistic. If $\chi^2 \leqslant \chi^2_\alpha$, you accept the null hypothesis of equality; if $\chi^2 > \chi^2_\alpha$, you reject it.

EXAMPLE 15-2: DO SUPPLIERS DIFFER IN QUALITY?

Ace Widgets has four suppliers of the main part of its product. Random samples of parts were selected from each vendor. The following results were obtained.

	1	2	3	4	Totals
		Supplier			
Number Satisfactory	84	91	135	112	422
Number defective	17	25	12	7	61
Number of parts	101	116	147	119	483
Proportion defective	$P_1 = .17$	$P_2 = .22$	$P_3 = .08$	$P_4 = .06$	

From these results, you can construct the following contingency table for the expected frequencies.

	Supplier				Totals
	1	2	3	4	
Number satisfactory	88.2	101.3	128.4	104.1	422
Number defective	12.8	14.7	18.6	14.9	61
Totals	101	116	147	119	483

The computed value of the test statistic is

$$\chi^2 = \frac{(84 - 88.2)^2}{88.2} + \frac{(91 - 101.3)^2}{101.3} + \cdots + \frac{(7 - 14.9)^2}{14.9}$$

$$= 17.328$$

The number of degrees of freedom is $df = (2 - 1)(4 - 1) = 3$. From Table C, you can see that you can reject H_0 at the $\alpha = .001$ level of significance, since the computed level of the test statistic exceeds $\chi^2_{.001} = 16.268$. You may therefore conclude that the suppliers do provide parts that differ in quality.

15-3. Estimating the Variance and Standard Deviation

You may estimate the population variance σ^2 or standard deviation σ by using the sample counterpart s^2 or s as the point estimator. You use the following expression to construct a $100(1 - \alpha)\%$ confidence interval estimate for σ^2.

Confidence interval estimate of the variance

$$\frac{(n - 1)s^2}{\chi^2_{\alpha/2}} \leqslant \sigma^2 \leqslant \frac{(n - 1)s^2}{\chi^2_{1 - \alpha/2}}$$

The critical chi-square values correspond to lower- and upper-tail areas of $\alpha/2$. You determine the two critical values from Table C in the Appendix, each using $df = n - 1$. You may find the corresponding confidence interval estimate for σ by taking the square root of the limits of the interval for σ^2.

EXAMPLE 15-3: THE VARIABILITY IN WAITING TIMES

You want to estimate the standard deviation in waiting time at a barbershop. For a random sample of $n = 25$ customers, you have computed the following values:

$$\bar{X} = 23.4 \text{ min.} \qquad s = 8.5 \text{ min.}$$

You want to construct a 90% confidence interval estimate of the variance σ^2 in waiting times. Using $\alpha/2 = .05$ and $1 - \alpha/2 = .95$, with $df = 25 - 1 = 24$, you find the critical values from

Table C:

$$\chi^2_{.05} = 36.415 \qquad \chi^2_{.95} = 13.848$$

The desired interval is thus

$$\frac{(25 - 1)(8.5)^2}{36.415} \leqslant \sigma^2 \leqslant \frac{(25 - 1)(8.5)^2}{13.848}$$

or

$$47.6 \leqslant \sigma^2 \leqslant 125.2$$

The units of this interval are in *square* minutes. By taking the square root of these limits, you obtain the 90% confidence interval estimate of the population standard deviation σ.

$$6.9 \, \text{min.} \leqslant \sigma \leqslant 11.2 \, \text{min.}$$

- Some books approximate the chi-square procedure, using the normal curve.

15-4. Testing the Variance

The hypothesis testing procedures for the mean and proportion extend to evaluations of the variance. The major difference is that χ^2 serves as the test statistic, with the chi-square distribution used to find the critical values. You use the following expression to compute χ^2.

Chi-square test statistic for the variance $\qquad \chi^2 = \frac{(n - 1)s^2}{\sigma_0^2}$

where σ_0^2 denotes the pivotal value of the variance.

For a stated significance level α, one of the following decision rules applies.

Upper-tailed test ($H_0: \sigma^2 \leqslant \sigma_0^2$)
  Accept H_0 if $\chi^2 \leqslant \chi^2_\alpha$ Reject H_0 if $\chi^2 > \chi^2_\alpha$

Lower-tailed test ($H_0: \sigma^2 \geqslant \sigma_0^2$)
  Accept H_0 if $\chi^2 \geqslant \chi^2_{1-\alpha}$ Reject H_0 if $\chi^2 < \chi^2_{1-\alpha}$

Two-sided test ($H_0: \sigma^2 = \sigma_0^2$)
  Accept H_0 if $\chi^2_{1-\alpha/2} \leqslant \chi^2 \leqslant \chi^2_{\alpha/2}$ Reject H_0 if $\chi^2 < \chi^2_{1-\alpha/2}$ or if $\chi^2 > \chi^2_{\alpha/2}$

EXAMPLE 15-4: VARIABILITY IN PORTFOLIO RATES OF RETURN

A financial analyst for Toro, Oso, and Toro tested the null hypothesis that her firm's clients experience rates of return on their stock investments that provide variability that is less than or equal to comparable portfolios in the investment community as a whole:

$$H_0: \sigma^2 \leqslant 100 \qquad (\text{i.e., } \sigma \leqslant 10\%)$$

She tested at the $\alpha = .01$ significance level.

The analyst obtained the following sample results for $n = 15$ client portfolios:

$$\bar{X} = 14.5\% \qquad s = 11.2\%$$

For $df = 15 - 1 = 14$, the critical chi-square value is $\chi^2_{.01} = 29.141$. For $\sigma_0^2 = 100$, the following decision rule applies for her upper-tailed test:

  Accept H_0 if $\chi^2 \leqslant 29.141$ (Conclude returns have less than or equal variability.)
  Reject H_0 if $\chi^2 > 29.141$ (Conclude returns have greater variability.)

The computed value of the test statistic is

$$\chi^2 = \frac{(15 - 1)(11.2)^2}{100} = 17.56$$

Since this falls in the acceptance region, the analyst concluded that the variability in her client's portfolios doesn't exceed that of the entire community.

SUMMARY

A large class of statistical procedures and applications makes use of the *chi-square distribution*. Like the Student *t*, there is a different distribution for each value of χ^2, depending on the *number of degrees of freedom* that applies for the particular test.

One important chi-square application involves testing two qualitative variables for independence. Two qualitative population variables *A* and *B* are *independent* if the proportion of the total population having any particular attribute of *A* remains the same for the part of the population having a particular attribute of *B*, no matter which attributes are considered.

You first arrange the actual sample data in a *contingency table* involving one row *i* for each attribute of the first variable and one column *j* for each attribute of the second. The cell entries in this matrix, f_{ij}, are the *actual frequencies* for the respective attribute pairs. You compute the corresponding *expected frequencies*, $\hat{f}_{ij}$, from the following:

$$\hat{f}_{ij} = \frac{\text{Row } i \text{ total} \times \text{Column } j \text{ total}}{n}$$

The sample size is *n*. Once you have found all $\hat{f}_{ij}$ values, you may arrange them in a second contingency table.

Matching the actual and expected frequencies from the respective cells, you use the following expression to establish the *chi-square test statistic*:

$$\chi^2 = \sum \frac{(f_{ij} - \hat{f}_{ij})^2}{\hat{f}_{ij}}$$

All tests of independence are upper-tailed, and for a significance level α there corresponds a critical value χ_α (found from Table C in the Appendix). You compute the number of degrees of freedom from

$$df = (\text{Number of rows} - 1) \times (\text{Number of columns} - 1)$$

If the computed value χ^2 exceeds χ^2_α, you must reject the null hypothesis of independence; otherwise you accept it.

An analogous procedure involves testing for the equality of several proportions. You compute the test statistic in exactly the same way, and you find the number of degrees of freedom and the critical value by an identical procedure.

You can use the chi-square distribution to make inferences regarding the population variance and standard deviation. You use the following expression to construct a $100(1 - \alpha)\%$ confidence interval estimate of σ^2:

$$\frac{(n-1)s^2}{\chi^2_{\alpha/2}} \leqslant \sigma^2 \leqslant \frac{(n-1)s^2}{\chi^2_{1-\alpha/2}}$$

The critical values correspond to lower- and upper-tail areas of size $\alpha/2$, and the number of degrees of freedom is $df = n - 1$. If you take the square root of the limits, you obtain the confidence interval estimate of the standard deviation.

If you desire to test the population variance, you compute the test statistic from the following expression:

$$\chi^2 = \frac{(n-1)s^2}{\sigma_0^2}$$

This test may be upper-tailed (with critical value χ^2_α), lower-tailed (with $\chi^2_{1-\alpha}$), or two-sided (with two critical values, $\chi^2_{1-\alpha/2}$ and $\chi^2_{\alpha/2}$).

RAISE YOUR GRADES

Can you explain . . . ?

☑ the similarities between independent events and independent population variables

☑ why the actual data display is called a "contingency table"
☑ why the chi-square distribution involves two separate critical values for constructing confidence intervals, while the Student t involves only one
☑ why the test for equality of proportions is conducted identically to the test for independence
☑ why a test for the variance might be desirable

Do you know ...?

☑ how to find the number of degrees of freedom that apply for each type of test
☑ how to determine the expected frequencies in testing for independence
☑ how to obtain a confidence interval for the standard deviation when you already have the interval for the variance
☑ how to tell whether a test for the variance is upper-tailed or lower-tailed
☑ when to accept and when to reject the null hypothesis of independence

RAPID REVIEW

1. Find the value of the chi-square statistic for which the stated upper-tail area holds, with the number of degrees of freedom given.   [Section 15-1E]

   (a) $\alpha = .01$ $df = 12$
   (b) $\alpha = .05$ $df = 20$
   (c) $\alpha = .10$ $df = 15$
   (d) $\alpha = .001$ $df = 16$

2. Following is a contingency table of actual sample frequencies.

| Area of employment | Business major | | | | Totals |
	(1) Accounting	(2) Finance	(3) Marketing	(4) Management	
(1) Manufacturing	5	14	14	17	50
(2) Service	17	2	27	14	60
(3) Retailing	12	13	24	11	60
(4) Other	5	7	8	10	30
Totals	39	36	73	52	200

Construct the contingency table for the expected frequencies under the null hypothesis of independence between business major and area of employment.   [Section 15-1C]

3. The following actual frequencies apply in a test for independence.

| Variable A | Variable B | | Totals |
	(1) B_1	(2) B_2	
(1) A_1	9	17	26
(2) A_2	11	13	24
Totals	20	30	50

Construct the contingency table for the expected frequencies.   [Section 15-1C]

4. Referring to the data in Problem 3 and your answer, compute the chi-square statistic for testing independence.   [Section 15-1D]

5. Referring to the data in Problem 3, how many degrees of freedom apply in testing for independence?   [Section 15-1E]

6. Refer to your answers to Problems 4 and 5. Should the null hypothesis that variables A and B are independent be accepted or rejected? Use $\alpha = .05$.   [Section 15-1F]

7. The number of degrees of freedom for a chi-square test of independence between brand preference (6 categories) and occupational status (10 categories) would be   [Section 15-1E]

(a) 60   (b) 16   (c) 45   (d) 2

8. For a sample of $n = 20$ responses, the sample standard deviation is $s = 5.0$. Using $\chi^2_{.05} = 30.144$ and $\chi^2_{.95} = 10.117$, construct a 90% confidence interval estimate for the population variance. [Section 15-3]

9. For a sample of $n = 25$ responses, the sample standard deviation is $s = 10.4$. Using $\chi^2_{.01} = 42.980$ and $\chi^2_{.99} = 10.856$, construct a 98% confidence interval estimate for the population standard deviation.   [Section 15-3]

10. In testing the null hypothesis that the population variance is no greater than 100, the sample standard deviation computed from $n = 25$ observations is $s = 5.9$. At the 5% significance level, should you accept or reject the null hypothesis?   [Section 15-4]

Answers
1. (a) 26.217   (b) 31.410   (c) 22.307   (d) 39.252
2.

Area of Employment	Business major				Totals
	(1) Accounting	*(2)* Finance	*(3)* Marketing	*(4)* Management	
(1) Manufacturing	9.75	9.00	18.25	13.00	50
(2) Service	11.70	10.80	21.90	15.60	60
(3) Retailing	11.70	10.80	21.90	15.60	60
(4) Other	5.85	5.40	10.95	7.80	30
Total	39	36	73	52	200

3.

Variable A	Variable B		Totals
	(1) B_1	*(2)* B_2	
(1) A_1	10.4	15.6	26
(2) A_2	9.6	14.4	24
Totals	20	30	50

4. .654   5. 1   6. accepted   7. (c)   8. $15.8 \leqslant \sigma^2 \leqslant 47.0$ 9. $7.8 \leqslant \sigma \leqslant 15.5$ 10. accept

SOLVED PROBLEMS

PROBLEM 15-1   Various random samples have been selected and the chi-square statistics have been computed for the following independence-testing situations. (*1*) Determine the applicable number of degrees of freedom. (*2*) Find the corresponding critical value for the stated significance level. (*3*) Indicate whether you should accept or reject the null hypothesis.

(**a**) Sex (male, female) versus attitude toward a product (preferred, not preferred). $\chi^2 = 3.54$ and $\alpha = .05$.
(**b**) College major (liberal arts, science, social science, professional) versus political affiliation (Democrat, Republican, other). $\chi^2 = 15.231$ and $\alpha = .010$.
(**c**) Number of bedrooms (1, 2, 3, 4 or more) versus family size (1, 2, 3, 4 or more). $\chi^2 = 15.018$ and $\alpha = .10$.
(**d**) Type of car (import, large domestic, small domestic) versus sexual attitude (repressive, permissive). $\chi^2 = 7.955$ and $\alpha = .01$.

Solution: In each case, determine the number of degrees of freedom from $df =$ (Number of rows $-$ 1)(Number of columns $-$ 1). Then look up the critical value for chi-square in Table C of the Appendix. Since all tests for independence are upper-tailed, you must reject H_0 if the computed value of the test statistic exceeds the critical value; otherwise, you should accept H_0.

(**a**) (*1*) $df = (2-1)(2-1) = 1$ (*2*) $\chi^2_{.05} = 3.841$ (*3*) accept
(**b**) (*1*) $df = (4-1)(3-1) = 6$ (*2*) $\chi^2_{.01} = 16.812$ (*3*) accept
(**c**) (*1*) $df = (4-1)(4-1) = 9$ (*2*) $\chi^2_{.10} = 14.684$ (*3*) reject
(**d**) (*1*) $df = (3-1)(2-1) = 2$ (*2*) $\chi^2_{.01} = 9.210$ (*3*) accept

PROBLEM 15-2 A marketing manager wants to determine if there are any significant differences between regions in terms of a new product's degree of acceptance. For a random sample of customers he obtained the following results.

Degree of Acceptance	Region				Totals
	(*1*) East	(*2*) Middle	(*3*) South	(*4*) West	
(*1*) Poor	22	35	0	5	62
(*2*) Moderate	84	55	8	24	171
(*3*) Strong	25	17	22	12	76
Totals	131	107	30	41	309

The null hypothesis is that region and degree of product acceptance by any given customer are independent.

(**a**) Determine the expected sample results.
(**b**) Calculate the chi-square statistic.
(**c**) How many degrees of freedom are associated with this test statistic?
(**d**) Assuming that the manager will tolerate a 1% chance of incorrectly concluding that degree of acceptance differs from region to region when this isn't so, find the critical value for the chi-square statistic. What conclusion should the manager reach?

Solution:
(**a**) Multiply the appropriate row and column totals and divide by the sample size to find the expected frequency for each cell.

Degree of acceptance	Region				Totals
	(*1*) East	(*2*) Middle	(*3*) South	(*4*) West	
(*1*) Poor	26.28	21.47	6.02	8.23	62.00
(*2*) Moderate	72.50	59.21	16.60	22.69	171.00
(*3*) Strong	32.22	26.32	7.38	10.08	76.00
Totals	131.00	107.00	30.00	41.00	309.00

(b)

Row i	Column j	f_{ij}	$\hat{f}_{ij}$	$f_{ij} - \hat{f}_{ij}$	$(f_{ij} - \hat{f}_{ij})^2/\hat{f}_{ij}$
1	1	22	26.28	− 4.28	.697
1	2	35	21.47	13.53	8.526
1	3	0	6.02	− 6.02	6.020
1	4	5	8.23	− 3.23	1.268
2	1	84	72.50	11.50	1.824
2	2	55	59.21	− 4.21	.299
2	3	8	16.60	− 8.60	4.455
2	4	24	22.69	1.31	.076
3	1	25	32.22	− 7.22	1.618
3	2	17	26.32	− 9.32	3.300
3	3	22	7.38	14.62	28.963
3	4	12	10.08	1.92	.366
		309	309.00	00.00	57.412 $= \chi^2$

(c) $df = (3 - 1)(4 - 1) = 6$

(d) From Table C, look up $\chi^2_{.01}$ for 6 degrees of freedom; the critical value is 16.812. Since the computed value exceeds this quantity, the manager should reject the null hypothesis of independence between region and degree of product acceptance.

PROBLEM 15-3 The manager in Problem 15-2 used the same sample group to determine if there was any significant difference between regions in response to a test ad. The following results were obtained.

Response	Region (1) East	(2) Middle	(3) South	(4) West	Totals
(1) Dislike	3	17	11	25	56
(2) Neutral	50	27	12	9	98
(3) Positive	44	35	3	7	89
(4) Enthusiastic	34	28	4	0	66
Totals	131	107	30	41	309

The null hypothesis is that customer response and region are independent.

(a) Determine the expected sample results.
(b) Calculate the chi-square statistic.
(c) How many degrees of freedom are associated with this test statistic?
(d) Assuming that the manager will tolerate only a 5% chance of incorrectly concluding that response to the test ad differs from region to region when this isn't so, find the critical value for the chi-square statistic. What conclusion should the manager reach?
(e) What would be your answer to (d) if the significance level were $\alpha = .01$?

Solution: Proceed as in Problem 15-2.

(a)

Response	Region (1) East	(2) Middle	(3) South	(4) West	Totals
(1) Dislike	23.74	19.39	5.44	7.43	56.00
(2) Neutral	41.55	33.94	9.51	13.00	98.00
(3) Positive	37.73	30.82	8.64	11.81	89.00
(4) Enthusiastic	27.98	22.85	6.41	8.76	66.00
Totals	131.00	107.00	30.00	41.00	309.00

(b)

Row i	Column j	f_{ij}	$\hat{f}_{ij}$	$f_{ij} - \hat{f}_{ij}$	$(f_{ij} - \hat{f}_{ij})^2 / \hat{f}_{ij}$
1	1	3	23.74	−20.74	18.119
1	2	17	19.39	− 2.39	.295
1	3	11	5.44	5.56	5.683
1	4	25	7.43	17.57	41.548
2	1	50	41.55	8.45	1.718
2	2	27	33.94	− 6.94	1.419
2	3	12	9.51	2.49	.652
2	4	9	13.00	− 4.00	1.231
3	1	44	37.73	6.27	1.042
3	2	35	30.82	4.18	.567
3	3	3	8.64	− 5.64	3.682
3	4	7	11.81	− 4.81	1.959
4	1	34	27.98	6.02	1.295
4	2	28	22.85	5.15	1.161
4	3	4	6.41	− 2.41	.906
4	4	0	8.76	− 8.76	8.760
		309	309.00	00.00	90.037 $= \chi^2$

(c) $df = (4 - 1)(4 - 1) = 9$

(d) From Table C look up $\chi^2_{.05}$ for 9 degrees of freedom; the critical value is 16.919. Since the computed value exceeds this amount, the manager should reject the null hypothesis that region and response to ad are independent.

(e) From Table C, $\chi^2_{.01} = 21.666$. As in **(d)**, the manager must still reject H_0.

PROBLEM 15-4 In testing the null hypothesis that the region where an accountant resides and that person's years of experience are independent, an investigator obtained the following sample results.

Residence	Years of experience			Totals
	(1) Less than 5	*(2)* Between 5 and 10	*(3)* More than 10	
(1) Northeast	24	76	15	115
(2) Southeast	17	51	9	77
(3) Southwest	32	38	5	75
(4) Pacific	16	55	6	77
Totals	89	220	35	344

At the 5% significance level, should the investigator accept or reject the null hypothesis?

Solution: First find the expected frequencies by multiplying together the respective row and column totals and dividing by the sample size.

Residence	Years of experience			Totals
	(1) Less than 5	*(2)* Between 5 and 10	*(3)* More than 10	
(1) Northeast	29.75	73.55	11.70	115.00
(2) Southeast	19.92	49.24	7.83	76.99
(3) Southwest	19.40	47.97	7.63	75.00
(4) Pacific	19.92	49.24	7.83	76.99
Totals	88.99	220.00	34.99	343.98

Then use the actual and expected frequencies to compute the level of the test statistic:

Row i	Column j	f_{ij}	$\hat{f}_{ij}$	$f_{ij} - \hat{f}_{ij}$	$(f_{ij} - \hat{f}_{ij})^2 / \hat{f}_{ij}$
1	1	24	29.75	− 5.75	1.111
1	2	76	73.55	2.45	.082
1	3	15	11.70	3.30	.931
2	1	17	19.92	2.92	.428
2	2	51	49.24	1.76	.063
2	3	9	7.83	1.17	.175
3	1	32	19.40	12.60	8.184
3	2	38	47.97	− 9.97	2.072
3	3	5	7.63	− 2.63	.907
4	1	16	19.92	− 3.92	.771
4	2	55	49.24	5.76	.674
4	3	6	7.83	− 1.83	.428
		344	343.98	00.02	$\chi^2 = 15.826$

The degrees of freedom are

$$df = (4 - 1)(3 - 1) = 6$$

From Table C you find that the critical value is $\chi^2_{.05} = 12.592$. Since the computed value falls above this, the investigator must reject the null hypothesis of independence.

PROBLEM 15-5 In testing the null hypothesis that a person's amount of driving and preferred car style are independent variables, a student received replies to her questionnaire from a random sample of drivers. The following summary applies.

Amount of driving	Preferred car style			Totals
	(1) Sporty	(2) Conventional	(3) Utility	
(1) Light	12	8	13	33
(2) Moderate	7	15	22	44
(3) Heavy	3	22	15	40
Totals	22	45	50	117

At the 1% significance level, should the student accept or reject H_0?

Solution: The expected frequencies are as follows.

Amount of Driving	Preferred car style			Totals
	(1) Sporty	(2) Conventional	(3) Utility	
(1) Light	6.21	12.69	14.10	33.00
(2) Moderate	8.27	16.92	18.80	43.99
(3) Heavy	7.52	15.38	17.09	39.99
Totals	22.00	44.99	49.99	116.98

The following calculations provide the test statistic.

Row i	Column j	f_{ij}	$\hat{f}_{ij}$	$f_{ij} - \hat{f}_{ij}$	$(f_{ij} - \hat{f}_{ij})^2 / \hat{f}_{ij}$
1	1	12	6.21	5.79	5.398
1	2	8	12.69	−4.69	1.733
1	3	13	14.10	−1.10	.086

Row i	Column j	f_{ij}	$\hat{f}_{ij}$	$f_{ij} - \hat{f}_{ij}$	$(f_{ij} - \hat{f}_{ij})^2/\hat{f}_{ij}$
2	1	7	8.27	-1.27	.195
2	2	15	16.92	-1.92	.218
2	3	22	18.80	3.20	.545
3	1	3	7.52	-4.52	2.717
3	2	22	15.38	6.62	2.849
3	3	15	17.09	-2.09	.256
		117	116.98	0.02	13.997 $= \chi^2$

The degrees of freedom are

$$df = (3 - 1)(3 - 1) = 4$$

From Table C the critical value is $\chi^2_{.01} = 13.277$. Since the computed value falls above the critical value, the student must reject the null hypothesis of independence.

PROBLEM 15-6 A cafeteria dietician wants to know if the time of day influences the tendency to consume coffee. The following data represent the beverage purchases for a random sample of cafeteria customers.

	(1) Early a.m.	(2) Late a.m.	(3) Early p.m.	(4) Late p.m.
(1) Number for coffee	3	5	8	11
(2) Number for other	52	48	51	47

The null hypothesis is that the proportions of coffee purchases throughout the day are identical. Using $\alpha = .05$, what conclusion should the dietician reach?

Solution: You must first determine the row and column totals for the given data, and then you can find the expected frequencies.

Beverage	Time of day				
	(1) Early a.m.	(2) Late a.m.	(3) Early p.m.	(4) Late p.m.	Totals
(1) Coffee	6.60	6.36	7.08	6.96	27.00
(2) Other	48.40	46.64	51.92	51.04	198.00
Totals	55.00	53.00	59.00	58.00	225.00

The following calculations provide the test statistic.

Row i	Column j	f_{ij}	$\hat{f}_{ij}$	$f_{ij} - \hat{f}_{ij}$	$(f_{ij} - \hat{f}_{ij})^2/\hat{f}_{ij}$
1	1	3	6.60	-3.60	1.964
1	2	5	6.36	-1.36	.291
1	3	8	7.08	.92	.120
1	4	11	6.96	4.04	2.345
2	1	52	48.40	3.60	.268
2	2	48	46.64	1.36	.040
2	3	51	51.92	$-.92$	.016
2	4	47	51.04	-4.04	.320
		225	225.00	0.00	5.364 $= \chi^2$

The number of degrees of freedom is

$$df = (2 - 1)(4 - 1) = 3$$

From Table C the critical value is $\chi^2_{.05} = 7.815$. Since the computed value falls below this value, the dietician must accept the null hypothesis of identical proportions of coffee purchases throughout the day.

PROBLEM 15-7 A printer wishes to determine if the proportion of lines typeset with errors is affected by the complexity of the text. The following sample data have been obtained.

	Complexity		
	(1) Low	(2) Medium	(3) High
(1) Number of lines with errors	42	28	29
(2) Number of lines correct	118	43	29

At the 1% significance level, should the printer conclude that the error rate is the same or different for all complexities?

Solution: The following expected frequencies apply.

Number of lines	Complexity			
	(1) Low	(2) Medium	(3) High	Totals
(1) With errors	54.81	24.32	19.87	99.00
(2) Correct	105.19	46.68	38.13	190.00
Totals	160.00	71.00	58.00	289.00

You compute the test statistic as follows.

Row i	Column j	f_{ij}	$\hat{f}_{ij}$	$f_{ij} - \hat{f}_{ij}$	$(\hat{f}_{ij} - \hat{f}_{ij})^2/\hat{f}_{ij}$
1	1	42	54.81	−12.81	2.994
1	2	28	24.32	3.68	.557
1	3	29	19.87	9.13	4.195
2	1	118	105.19	12.81	1.560
2	2	43	46.68	− 3.68	.290
2	3	29	38.13	− 9.13	2.186
		289	289.00	00.00	11.782 $= \chi^2$

The number of degrees of freedom is

$$df = (2 - 1)(3 - 1) = 2$$

From Table C the critical value is $\chi^2_{.01} = 9.210$. Since the computed value falls above this value, the printer must reject the null hypothesis of identical error rates.

PROBLEM 15-8 The following data have been obtained by a private aircraft manufacturer who wishes to establish important categories for plane owners.

Amount of Usage	Aircraft size			
	(1) Small	(2) Medium	(3) Large	Totals
(1) Low	34	19	12	65
(2) Moderate	24	28	5	57
(3) High	7	12	22	41
Totals	65	59	39	163

The manufacturer wishes to test the null hypothesis that amount of usage and aircraft size are independent. Using a 5% significance level, should he accept or reject the null hypothesis?

Solution: The following expected frequencies apply.

Amount of usage	Aircraft size			Totals
	(1) Small	(2) Medium	(3) Large	
(1) Low	25.92	23.53	15.55	65.00
(2) Moderate	22.73	20.63	13.64	57.00
(3) High	16.35	14.84	9.81	41.00
Totals	65.00	59.00	39.00	163.00

The following computations provide the test statistic.

Row i	Column j	f_{ij}	$\hat{f}_{ij}$	$f_{ij} - \hat{f}_{ij}$	$(f_{ij} - \hat{f}_{ij})^2/\hat{f}_{ij}$
1	1	34	25.92	8.08	2.519
1	2	19	23.53	− 4.53	.872
1	3	12	15.55	− 3.55	.810
2	1	24	22.73	1.27	.071
2	2	28	20.63	7.37	2.633
2	3	5	13.64	− 8.64	5.473
3	1	7	16.35	− 9.35	5.347
3	2	12	14.84	− 2.84	.544
3	3	22	9.81	12.19	15.147
		163	163.00	0.00	33.416 $= \chi^2$

The number of degrees of freedom is $df = (3 - 1)(3 - 1) = 4$. From Table C you find the critical value to be $\chi^2_{.05} = 9.488$. Since the computed value exceeds the critical value, the manufacturer must reject the null hypothesis of independence.

PROBLEM 15-9 An accountant is investigating the effectiveness of computer programs for preparing tax returns. She has collected the following data pertaining to the number of returns that require reprocessing.

Program type	Type of return				Totals
	(1) Short form	(2) Long form	(3) Multiple exhibits	(4) Corporate	
(1) Interactive	35	15	0	10	60
(2) Batched	40	10	10	15	75
Totals	75	25	10	25	135

She wishes to test the null hypothesis that type of program and type of return are independent variables. Using a 5% significance level, do these data indicate that she should accept or reject the null hypothesis?

Solution: The following expected frequencies apply.

Program type	Type of return				Totals
	(1) Short form	(2) Long form	(3) Multiple exhibits	(4) Corporate	
(1) Interactive	33.33	11.11	4.44	11.11	59.99
(2) Batched	41.67	13.89	5.56	13.89	75.01
Totals	75.00	25.00	10.00	25.00	135.00

You compute the test statistic as follows:

Row i	Column j	f_{ij}	$\hat{f}_{ij}$	$f_{ij} - \hat{f}_{ij}$	$(f_{ij} - \hat{f}_{ij})^2/\hat{f}_{ij}$
1	1	35	33.33	1.67	.084
1	2	15	11.11	3.89	1.362
1	3	0	4.44	−4.44	4.440
1	4	10	11.11	−1.11	.111
2	1	40	41.67	−1.67	.067
2	2	10	13.89	−3.89	1.089
2	3	10	5.56	4.44	3.546
2	4	15	13.89	1.11	.089
		135	135.00	0.00	10.788 $= \chi^2$

The number of degrees of freedom is

$$df = (2 - 1)(4 - 1) = 3$$

Table C provides the critical value $\chi^2_{.05} = 7.815$. Since the computed value exceeds the critical value, the accountant must reject the null hypothesis of independence.

PROBLEM 15-10   An auditor has taken random samples of 100 transactions from each of three branch offices. The proportions of errors found are .07 (branch 1), .13 (branch 2), and .09 (branch 3). At the 5% significance level, can the auditor conclude that the error rate differs among the branches?

Solution: The following table shows the actual frequencies for the data, with the expected frequencies given in parentheses.

	(1) Branch 1	(2) Branch 2	(3) Branch 3	Totals
(1) Number of errors	7 (9.67)	13 (9.67)	9 (9.67)	29 (29.01)
(2) Number correct	93 (90.33)	87 (90.33)	91 (90.33)	271 (270.99)
Totals	100	100	100	300

You now compute the level of the test statistic:

Row i	Column j	f_{ij}	$\hat{f}_{ij}$	$f_{ij} - \hat{f}_{ij}$	$(f_{ij} - \hat{f}_{ij})^2/\hat{f}_{ij}$
1	1	7	9.67	−2.67	.737
1	2	13	9.67	3.33	1.147
1	3	9	9.67	− .67	.046
2	1	93	90.33	2.67	.079
2	2	87	90.33	−3.33	.123
2	3	91	90.33	.67	.005
		300	300.00	0.00	2.137 $= \chi^2$

The number of degrees of freedom is $df = (2 - 1)(3 - 1) = 2$. Table C provides the critical value $\chi^2_{.05} = 5.991$. Since the computed value falls below the critical value, the auditor must accept the null hypothesis of equal proportions of errors among branches.

PROBLEM 15-11   Construct 90% confidence intervals for (1) the population variance and (2) the population standard deviation in each of the following cases:

$$\begin{array}{cc} \textbf{(a)} & \textbf{(b)} \\ s = 34.2 & s = .15 \\ n = 15 & n = 25 \end{array}$$

Solution:

(a) (*1*) Substitute the given values into the expression for the confidence interval. Here, $\alpha = .10$, since you are constructing a $100(1 - .10)\%$, or 90%, confidence interval. Since $\alpha/2 = .05$, you use $\chi^2_{.05} = 23.685$ and $\chi^2_{.95} = 6.571$, found from Table C for $15 - 1 = 14$ degrees of freedom.

$$\frac{14(34.2)^2}{23.685} \leqslant \sigma^2 \leqslant \frac{14(34.2)^2}{6.571}$$

or

$$691.36 \leqslant \sigma^2 \leqslant 2{,}492.00$$

(*2*) Taking the square root of the interval's limits, you obtain

$$26.294 \leqslant \sigma \leqslant 49.920$$

(b) (*1*) Substitute the given values into the expression for the confidence interval. Again, $\alpha = .10$, so you use $\chi^2_{.05} = 36.415$ and $\chi^2_{.95} = 13.848$, found from Table C for $25 - 1 = 24$ degrees of freedom.

$$\frac{24(.15)^2}{36.415} \leqslant \sigma^2 \leqslant \frac{24(.15)^2}{13.848}$$

or

$$.01483 \leqslant \sigma^2 \leqslant .03899$$

(*2*) Taking the square root of the interval's limits, you obtain

$$.122 \leqslant \sigma \leqslant .197$$

PROBLEM 15-12 The sample standard deviation for $n = 20$ observations was computed to be $s = 12.6$. Construct confidence interval estimates of the population standard deviation for each of the following levels of confidence:

    (a) 80%   **(b)** 90%   **(c)** 98%

Solution: In all cases the number of degrees of freedom is $20 - 1 = 19$.

(a) Here $\alpha = .20$, so $\alpha/2 = .10$. Read from Table C the critical values $\chi^2_{.10} = 27.204$ and $\chi^2_{.90} = 11.651$. The following applies.

$$\sqrt{\frac{19(12.6)^2}{27.204}} \leqslant \sigma \leqslant \sqrt{\frac{19(12.6)^2}{11.651}}$$

or

$$10.53 \leqslant \sigma \leqslant 16.09$$

(b) Here, $\alpha = .10$, so $\alpha/2 = .05$. Read from Table C the critical values $\chi^2_{.05} = 30.144$ and $\chi^2_{.95} = 10.117$. The following applies.

$$\sqrt{\frac{19(12.6)^2}{30.144}} \leqslant \sigma \leqslant \sqrt{\frac{19(12.6)^2}{10.117}}$$

or

$$10.00 \leqslant \sigma \leqslant 17.27$$

(c) Here, $\alpha = .02$, so $\alpha/2 = .01$. Read from Table C the critical values $\chi^2_{.01} = 36.191$ and $\chi^2_{.99} = 7.633$. The following applies.

$$\sqrt{\frac{19(12.6)^2}{36.191}} \leqslant \sigma \leqslant \sqrt{\frac{19(12.6)^2}{7.633}}$$

or

$$9.13 \leqslant \sigma \leqslant 19.88$$

PROBLEM 15-13 The following data apply to the transaction time (in seconds) for cashing checks at a particular bank.

25	18	24	19	20
23	27	21	23	21
19	22	20	25	25

Construct a 90% confidence interval estimate of the standard deviation in transaction time.

Solution: You compute the following sample statistics from the given data.

$$\bar{X} = 22.1 \qquad s = 2.7$$

The number of degrees of freedom is $df = 15 - 1 = 14$. Read from Table C the critical values $\chi^2_{.05} = 23.685$ and $\chi^2_{.95} = 6.571$. The following applies.

$$\sqrt{\frac{14(2.7)^2}{23.685}} \leqslant \sigma \leqslant \sqrt{\frac{14(2.7)^2}{6.571}}$$

or

$$2.1 \text{ sec.} \leqslant \sigma \leqslant 3.9 \text{ sec.}$$

PROBLEM 15-14   The following data apply to the drying time (in minutes) of a water-based paint.

8	12	26	10
16	22	18	17
23	21	36	9

Construct a 98% confidence interval estimate of the standard deviation in drying time.

Solution: You compute the following sample statistics from the given data.

$$\bar{X} = 18.17 \qquad s = 8.11$$

The number of degrees of freedom is $df = 12 - 1 = 11$. Read from Table C the critical values $\chi^2_{.01} = 24.725$ and $\chi^2_{.99} = 3.053$. The following applies.

$$\sqrt{\frac{11(8.11)^2}{24.725}} \leqslant \sigma \leqslant \sqrt{\frac{11(8.11)^2}{3.053}}$$

or

$$5.409 \text{ min.} \leqslant \sigma \leqslant 15.394 \text{ min.}$$

PROBLEM 15-15   The following sample data represent the actual transportation costs (in dollars) for moving a pallet of raw materials 500 miles.

105	110	108	97	99
104	112	103	98	105

Construct 90% confidence interval estimates of the following.

    (a) The variance in cost per pallet.
    (b) The standard deviation in cost per pallet.

Solution: You compute the following sample statistics from the given data.

$$\bar{X} = \$104.1 \qquad s = \$5.043$$

(a) For $df = 10 - 1 = 9$, Table C provides $\chi^2_{.05} = 16.919$ and $\chi^2_{.95} = 3.325$. The following confidence interval applies.

$$\frac{9(5.043)^2}{16.919} \leqslant \sigma^2 \leqslant \frac{9(5.043)^2}{3.325}$$

or

$$13.528 \leqslant \sigma^2 \leqslant 68.838$$

(b) Taking the square root of these limits, you obtain

$$\$3.68 \leqslant \sigma \leqslant \$8.30$$

PROBLEM 15-16 The following sample data were obtained for the percentage yields for a random sample of bonds.

11.2	18.5	8.7	12.4	13.5
9.9	12.9	15.4	12.6	16.7
10.2	10.5	14.4	17.7	15.5

Construct a 96% confidence interval estimate of the standard deviation in bond yield.

Solution: The sample statistics are

$$\bar{X} = 13.34 \qquad s = 2.9818$$

For $df = 15 - 1 = 14$, Table C provides $\chi^2_{.02} = 26.873$ and $\chi^2_{.98} = 5.368$. The following confidence interval applies:

$$\sqrt{\frac{14(2.9818)^2}{26.873}} \leqslant \sigma \leqslant \sqrt{\frac{14(2.9818)^2}{5.368}}$$

or

$$2.15\% \leqslant \sigma \leqslant 4.82\%$$

PROBLEM 15-17 Determine for each of the following whether you should accept or reject H_0. In each the sample size is $n = 25$.

(a)	(b)	(c)	(d)
$H_0: \sigma^2 \leqslant 100$	$H_0: \sigma^2 \geqslant 200$	$H_0: \sigma^2 = 150$	$H_0: \sigma^2 \leqslant 20$
$s^2 = 80$	$s^2 = 50$	$s^2 = 120$	$s^2 = 35$
$\alpha = .01$	$\alpha = .05$	$\alpha = .02$	$\alpha = .05$

Solution: In all cases the number of degrees of freedom is $df = 25 - 1 = 24$. You read the critical values from Table C.
(a) The computed value of the test statistic is

$$\chi^2 = \frac{24(80)}{100} = 19.20$$

This test is upper-tailed. The critical value is $\chi^2_\alpha = \chi^2_{.01} = 42.980$. You accept H_0 if $\chi^2 \leqslant 42.980$, and reject it otherwise. Since the computed value lies below the critical value, you must accept the null hypothesis.
(b) The computed value of the test statistic is

$$\chi^2 = \frac{24(50)}{200} = 6.0$$

This test is lower-tailed. The critical value is $\chi^2_{1-\alpha} = \chi^2_{.95} = 13.848$. You accept H_0 if $\chi^2 \geqslant 13.848$, and reject it otherwise. Since the computed value lies below the critical value, you must reject the null hypothesis.
(c) The computed value of the test statistic is

$$\chi^2 = \frac{24(120)}{150} = 19.20$$

This test is two-sided. The lower critical value is $\chi^2_{1-\alpha/2} = \chi^2_{1-.01} = \chi^2_{.99} = 10.856$, and the upper critical value is $\chi^2_{\alpha/2} = \chi^2_{.01} = 42.980$. You accept H_0 if $10.856 \leqslant \chi^2 \leqslant 42.980$, and you reject it otherwise. Since the computed value lies between these two limits, you must accept the null hypothesis.
(d) The computed value of the test statistic is

$$\chi^2 = \frac{24(35)}{20} = 42.00$$

This test is upper-tailed. The critical value is $\chi^2_{.05} = 36.415$. Since the computed value lies above the critical value, you must reject the null hypothesis.

PROBLEM 15-18 The setting time for a sample of $n = 25$ trials of a bonding agent has a sample mean of $\bar{X} = 24.7$ hours and a standard deviation of $s = 7.6$ hours. Using $\alpha = .10$, test the null hypothesis that $\sigma^2 = 25$.

Solution: The computed value of the test statistic is

$$\chi^2 = \frac{24(7.6)^2}{25} = 55.45$$

The number of degrees of freedom is $df = 25 - 1 = 24$. This test is two-sided. The critical values are $\chi^2_{1-\alpha/2} = \chi^2_{.95} = 13.848$ and $\chi^2_{\alpha/2} = \chi^2_{.05} = 36.415$, and you accept H_0 if χ^2 falls within these limits. Since the computed value lies above the upper critical value, you must reject the null hypothesis.

PROBLEM 15-19 A store manager wishes to test the null hypothesis that the variance in waiting time by customers at her supermarket is less than or equal to 25 minutes (squared). She logged a random sample of 30 customer waiting times and computed the sample variance to be 41.4. At the 5% significance level, should the manager accept or reject the null hypothesis?

Solution: The computed value of the test statistic is

$$\chi^2 = \frac{29(41.4)}{25} = 48.024$$

The number of degrees of freedom is $df = 30 - 1 = 29$. The null hypothesis is $H_0: \sigma^2 \leqslant 25$, and so this test is upper-tailed. The critical value is $\chi^2_\alpha = \chi^2_{.05} = 42.557$. You accept H_0 if $\chi^2 \leqslant 42.557$, and reject it otherwise. Since the computed value lies above the critical value, the manager must reject the null hypothesis.

PROBLEM 15-20 The following data were obtained for the amount of time (in days) it takes for a boxcar to travel between Gotham City and Metropolis.

.6	1.0	1.8	4.8	4.2
4.4	2.4	3.5	3.9	3.9
4.7	3.0	2.3	2.9	1.0

At the 5% significance level, test the null hypothesis that the standard deviation in travel time is less than or equal to .9 seconds ($\sigma_0^2 = .81$). Should you accept or reject H_0?

Solution: The sample statistics are

$$\bar{X} = 2.96 \qquad s = 1.40$$

The computed value of the test statistic is

$$\chi^2 = \frac{14(1.40)^2}{.81} = 33.877$$

The number of degrees of freedom is $df = 15 - 1 = 14$. The null hypothesis is $H_0: \sigma^2 \leqslant .81$, and so this test is upper-tailed. The critical value is $\chi^2_\alpha = \chi^2_{.05} = 23.685$. You accept H_0 if $\chi^2 \leqslant 23.685$, and reject it otherwise. Since the computed value lies above the critical value, you must reject the null hypothesis.

16 ANALYSIS OF VARIANCE

THIS CHAPTER IS ABOUT

☑ **Testing for the Equality of Several Means**
☑ **Two-Way Analysis of Variance**

Statistical procedures that compare three or more population means fall into a broad category called **analysis of variance**. (This terminology is somewhat misleading, since the focus is on *means*, not on variances.)

16-1. Testing for the Equality of Several Means

The null hypothesis in an analysis of variance is that the means are identical for three or more separate populations:

$$H_0: \mu_1 = \mu_2 = \mu_3 = \mu_4$$

Sample data collected from each population provide the basis for the decision to accept or reject H_0.

A. Sample data are organized in an experimental layout.

As an illustration of analysis of variance, suppose the marketing manager for a regional bakery wishes to determine if the shelf height of a product affects its supermarket sales. As a test, she selects a sample of ten stores. During each of four successive weeks, she shelves the donuts at a different height. She obtained the following unit sales data.

	Shelf height			
Observation	(1) Floor	(2) Lower	(3) Upper	(4) Top
1	28	30	31	29
2	26	29	29	27
3	29	30	33	30
4	30	30	33	31
5	28	28	29	27
6	31	32	33	32
7	26	29	28	27
8	32	32	32	32
9	25	28	27	27
10	29	30	32	30
Totals	284	298	307	292

$$\bar{\bar{X}} = \frac{284 + 298 + 307 + 292}{40} = 29.525$$

This table of sample data is the **experimental layout**. The **response variable** is the shelf height. For each level of treatment (shelf height), there is a separate population. To be tested is the null hypothesis that the treatment populations have identical mean responses (unit sales).

B. Various sample means are computed.

The first step in testing the null hypothesis is to summarize the sample data. You achieve this by computing the sample mean for each treatment or column.

**Sample mean
for the *j*th treatment column**

$$\bar{X}_j = \frac{\sum_i X_{ij}}{r}$$

Here the letter *j* denotes the particular treatment or column, with *i* denoting the row. The double subscripting makes it easy for you to place a particular response observation X_{ij}. For example X_{72} denotes the 7th observation in the 2nd treatment column. The number of rows in the experimental layout is represented by the letter *r*.

For the bakery experiment, the following sample means apply:

$$\bar{X}_1 = \frac{284}{10} = 28.4 \quad \text{(floor level)}$$

$$\bar{X}_2 = \frac{298}{10} = 29.8 \quad \text{(lower level)}$$

$$\bar{X}_3 = \frac{307}{10} = 30.7 \quad \text{(upper level)}$$

$$\bar{X}_4 = \frac{292}{10} = 29.2 \quad \text{(top level)}$$

A final mean value, the grand mean, relates to all observations collectively.

**Grand mean
for pooled sample results**

$$\bar{\bar{X}} = \frac{\sum_j \sum_i X_{ij}}{rc}$$

Here *c* denotes the number of columns in the experimental layout. The summation involves all observations. You first take the summation of the rows within each column, then you add the subtotals together. You divide the resulting sum by the combined sample size, *rc*. For the bakery experiment, the grand mean is

$$\bar{\bar{X}} = \frac{284 + 298 + 307 + 292}{10(4)} = 29.525$$

C. Variability is used to identify differences between sample groupings.

The analysis-of-variance procedure takes its name from the manner in which you identify differences between sample groupings. You find the basic building blocks by summing the squares of differences with respect to one of the sample means. Three sums of squares are important in the fundamental procedure: (1) The **treatments sum of squares** summarizes how the treatment columns differ; (2) the **error sum of squares** summarizes how individual values differ from each other within their treatment groups; and (3) the **total sum of squares** expresses the degree to which individual values differ from each other without regard to sample grouping. The following expressions apply.

Treatments sum of squares $$SST = r \sum_j (\bar{X}_j - \bar{\bar{X}})^2$$

The deviations in the *SST* are the differences between the respective sample treatment means and the grand mean. There is one term in this summation for each of the *c* treatments. You multiply the sum of the squared deviations by the number of observations *r*; this reflects the entire sample size of $r \times c$ observations. For the bakery experiment, the treatments sum of squares is

$$SST = 10[(28.4 - 29.525)^2 + (29.8 - 29.525)^2$$
$$+ (30.7 - 29.525)^2 + (29.2 - 29.525)^2]$$
$$= 10(1.265625 + .075625 + 1.380625 + .105625)$$
$$= 28.275$$

Error sum of squares
$$SSE = \sum_j \sum_i (X_{ij} - \bar{X}_j)^2$$

The SSE expresses the sum of the squared deviations formed by each observation with respect to its sample treatment mean. The following calculations apply to the bakery illustration:

i	$(X_{i1} - \bar{X}_1)^2$	$(X_{i2} - \bar{X}_2)^2$
1	$(28 - 28.4)^2 = $ .16	$(30 - 29.8)^2 = $ .04
2	$(26 - 28.4)^2 = $ 5.76	$(29 - 29.8)^2 = $ .64
3	$(29 - 28.4)^2 = $ .36	$(30 - 29.8)^2 = $ .04
4	$(30 - 28.4)^2 = $ 2.56	$(30 - 29.8)^2 = $ .04
5	$(28 - 28.4)^2 = $ .16	$(28 - 29.8)^2 = $ 3.24
6	$(31 - 28.4)^2 = $ 6.76	$(32 - 29.8)^2 = $ 4.84
7	$(26 - 28.4)^2 = $ 5.76	$(29 - 29.8)^2 = $ .64
8	$(32 - 28.4)^2 = $ 12.96	$(32 - 29.8)^2 = $ 4.84
9	$(25 - 28.4)^2 = $ 11.56	$(28 - 29.8)^2 = $ 3.24
10	$(29 - 28.4)^2 = $ .36	$(30 - 29.8)^2 = $ .04
	46.40	17.60

i	$(X_{i3} - \bar{X}_3)^2$	$(X_{i4} - \bar{X}_4)^2$
1	$(31 - 30.7)^2 = $ .09	$(29 - 29.2)^2 = $ .04
2	$(29 - 30.7)^2 = $ 2.89	$(27 - 29.2)^2 = $ 4.84
3	$(33 - 30.7)^2 = $ 5.29	$(30 - 29.2)^2 = $ .64
4	$(33 - 30.7)^2 = $ 5.29	$(31 - 29.2)^2 = $ 3.24
5	$(29 - 30.7)^2 = $ 2.89	$(27 - 29.2)^2 = $ 4.84
6	$(33 - 30.7)^2 = $ 5.29	$(32 - 29.2)^2 = $ 7.84
7	$(28 - 30.7)^2 = $ 7.29	$(27 - 29.2)^2 = $ 4.84
8	$(32 - 30.7)^2 = $ 1.69	$(32 - 29.2)^2 = $ 7.84
9	$(27 - 30.7)^2 = $ 13.69	$(27 - 29.2)^2 = $ 4.84
10	$(32 - 30.7)^2 = $ 1.69	$(30 - 29.2)^2 = $ .64
	46.10	39.60

$$SSE = 46.40 + 17.60 + 46.10 + 39.60 = 149.70$$

Total sum of squares
$$\text{Total } SS = \sum_j \sum_i (X_{ij} - \bar{\bar{X}})^2$$

You find this summation by adding together the squares of the differences between each individual value and the grand mean. With the bakery data, you can verify that

$$\text{Total } SS = (28 - 29.525)^2 + (30 - 29.525)^2 + \cdots + (30 - 29.525)^2 = 177.975$$

In the computation of sums of squares the following identity will prove useful:

$$\text{Total } SS = SST + SSE$$

For the bakery data, you have just seen that $SST = 28.275$ and $SSE = 149.700$, so that

$$\text{Total } SS = 28.275 + 149.700 = 177.975$$

D. The mean squares provide the basis for comparison.

The test statistic for evaluating H_0 is formed from two mean squares, each found by dividing the respective sum of squares by a constant. The **treatments mean square** expresses the amount of variation in responses that may be "explained" by the treatments, and the **error mean square** provides a summary of the amount of variation in the X_{ij}'s that can't be explained by the treatments. The following expressions apply.

Treatments mean square

$$MST = \frac{SST}{c - 1}$$

Error mean square

$$MSE = \frac{SSE}{(r - 1)c}$$

For the bakery shelf-height data,

$$MST = \frac{28.275}{4 - 1} = 9.425$$

$$MSE = \frac{149.70}{(10 - 1)4} = 4.158$$

- The treatments and error mean squares represent a series of computations similar to those used to find the sample variance s^2 from single-sample data. The mean squares are actually *sample variances*, which partly explains why this procedure is called *analysis of variance*.

If H_0 is to be rejected, MST should be quite a bit larger than MSE, so that most of the variation in the X_{ij}'s can be "explained" by (attributed to) the different treatment levels. You use the following test statistic to determine if MST is significantly larger than MSE.

Test statistic
for analysis of variance
$$F = \frac{\text{Variance explained by treatments}}{\text{Unexplained variance}} = \frac{MST}{MSE}$$

For the bakery experiment, the computed value is

$$F = \frac{9.425}{4.158} = 2.27$$

The F statistic has its own sampling distribution.

E. The *F* distribution provides critical values for the test.

You may evaluate the F statistic probabilistically by the **F distribution**, which is analogous to the Student t and chi-square distributions that you encountered in earlier chapters. Figure 16-1 shows a variety of frequency curves for the F distribution family. Each particular distribution is defined by *two* numbers for degrees of freedom, one for the *numerator* and another for the *denominator*. Critical values corresponding to upper-tail areas of $\alpha = .01$ or $\alpha = .05$ are provided in Table D of the Appendix. Use the following rule to determine the number of degrees of freedom parameters.

Number of degrees of freedom
Numerator: $c - 1$
Denominator: $(r - 1)c$

Figure 16-1   Various F distribution curves.

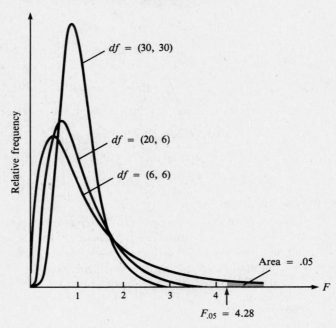

F. The ANOVA table provides a convenient summary of the sample results.

You can conveniently summarize the sample data for an analysis-of-variance investigation in an **ANOVA table**. The following ANOVA (ANalysis Of VAriance) table applies in the bakery experiment.

Variation	Degrees of freedom	Sum of squares	Mean square	F
Explained by treatments (between columns)	$c - 1 = 3$	$SST = 28.275$	$MST = 28.275/3$ $= 9.425$	$MST/MSE = 9.425/4.158$ $= 2.27$
Error or unexplained (within columns)	$(r - 1)c = 36$	$SSE = 149.700$	$MSE = 149.7/36$ $= 4.158$	
Totals	$rc - 1 = 39$	$SS = 177.975$		

Notice that the sum of the degrees of freedom numbers is $rc - 1$, the combined sample size minus one.

G. The computed value of *F* determines whether to accept or reject the null hypothesis.

All tests of the analysis-of-variance type are upper-tailed, since the null hypothesis of no treatment differences is refuted by large computed values for F. Figure 16-2 provides the decision rule for the bakery experiment. For an $\alpha = .05$ significance level, with $4 - 1 = 3$ degrees of freedom for the numerator and $(10 - 1)4 = 36$ for the denominator, Table D provides the critical value $F_{.05} = 2.86$. Since the computed F lies below the critical value, you must accept the null hypothesis of identical mean sales at the various shelf heights.

Figure 16-2

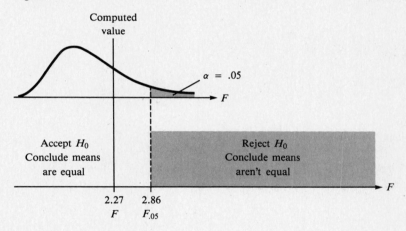

16-2. Two-Way Analysis of Variance

The analysis-of-variance approach extends to situations where two factors serve to explain variation in response. The procedure is referred to as a **two-way analysis of variance**. The second factor may be any identifiable influence other than the original treatment variable itself. When such a second contributing variable serves only to provide better experimental information, it is referred to as a **blocking variable**. For example, in the bakery experiment, store location might serve as the blocking variable, and some of the differences found for donut sales might be attributed to store site instead of shelf height.

A. The randomized block design is an efficient experimental procedure.

Each level of the blocking variable is referred to as a **block**, reflecting the history of agricultural experiments where separate parcels or blocks were used to compare crop treatments. The earlier bakery experiment can be expanded to illustrate this procedure. Applying the same sample data as before, the following experimental layout treats *store site* as the blocking variable. This arrangement is an example of a **randomized block design**.

Block i	Shelf height				Mean unit sales
	(1) Floor	*(2)* Lower	*(3)* Upper	*(4)* Top	
1	28	30	31	29	$\bar{X}_{1\cdot} = 29.50$
2	26	29	29	27	$\bar{X}_{2\cdot} = 27.75$
3	29	30	33	30	$\bar{X}_{3\cdot} = 30.50$
4	30	30	33	31	$\bar{X}_{4\cdot} = 31.00$
5	28	28	29	27	$\bar{X}_{5\cdot} = 28.00$
6	31	32	33	32	$\bar{X}_{6\cdot} = 32.00$
7	26	29	28	27	$\bar{X}_{7\cdot} = 27.50$
8	32	32	32	32	$\bar{X}_{8\cdot} = 32.00$
9	25	28	27	27	$\bar{X}_{9\cdot} = 26.75$
10	29	30	32	30	$\bar{X}_{10\cdot} = 30.25$
Mean unit sales	$\bar{X}_{\cdot 1} = 28.4$	$\bar{X}_{\cdot 2} = 29.8$	$\bar{X}_{\cdot 3} = 30.7$	$\bar{X}_{\cdot 4} = 29.2$	$\bar{\bar{X}} = 29.525$

B. The sample means are computed in the same way, with a new set for the rows.

In a two-way analysis of variance, you compute the sample means and sums of squares in the same way as before. Now, however, you compute an additional set of sample means for the blocks. Also, you measure the second source of variation by a new **blocks sum of squares** and a new **blocks mean square**.

The following expressions apply for the sample means. It is standard in two-way evaluations to include a dot subscript, thereby saving a position for the row or column.

Sample mean for the *i*th block row

$$\bar{X}_{i\cdot} = \frac{\sum_{j} X_{ij}}{c}$$

Notice that you make the summation using values in the *i*th row, including one entry from each column. The randomized block design in Section A gives the ten block sample means for the bakery experiment.

Sample mean for the *j*th treatment column

$$\bar{X}_{\cdot j} = \frac{\sum_{i} X_{ij}}{r}$$

You compute these means in exactly the same way as before; they remain unchanged for the bakery experiment.

Grand mean for pooled sample results

$$\bar{\bar{X}} = \frac{\sum_{j} \sum_{i} X_{ij}}{rc} = \frac{\sum_{i} \bar{X}_{i\cdot}}{r} = \frac{\sum_{j} \bar{X}_{\cdot j}}{c}$$

You may find the grand mean as before, by averaging all the individual values, or you may instead find it by averaging either the row or the column means. This value remains unchanged for the bakery experiment.

C. A new sum of squares applies for blocks.

The following expressions apply for the sums of squares.

Treatments sum of squares

$$SST = r \sum_{j} (\bar{X}_{\cdot j} - \bar{\bar{X}})^2$$

This expression reflects the dot notation and is essentially unchanged from before.

Blocks sum of squares

$$SSB = c\sum_i (\bar{X}_{i\cdot} - \bar{\bar{X}})^2$$

In computing the SSB, you first find the squares of the differences between each row mean and the grand mean. You then multiply the sum of these by the number of columns. With the bakery data, the following applies:

$$SSB = 4[(29.50 - 29.525)^2 + (27.75 - 29.525)^2 + \cdots + (30.25 - 29.525)^2]$$
$$= 132.725$$

It is convenient to compute the error sum of squares after you have obtained the SSB and the total SS. For this purpose, the following identity applies.

Error sum of squares

$$SSE = \text{Total } SS - SST - SSB$$

For the bakery experiment, the error sum of squares is

$$SSE = 177.975 - 28.275 - 132.725 = 16.975$$

The error sum of squares reflects the amount of variation in the X_{ij}'s that isn't explained by either the treatments or blocks variable. Notice that the SSE is considerably smaller than it was when applying a one-way evaluation on the same data.

D. The error mean square and ANOVA table change.

You compute the treatments mean square in the same way as before. Its value for the bakery experiment remains unchanged. The following applies for the error mean square.

Error mean square with two factors

$$MSE = \frac{SSE}{(r-1)(c-1)}$$

For the bakery experiment, you find

$$MSE = \frac{16.975}{(10-1)(4-1)} = .629$$

You compute the blocks mean square from the following.

Blocks mean square

$$MSB = \frac{SSB}{r-1}$$

For the bakery experiment,

$$MSB = \frac{132.725}{10-1} = 14.747$$

The following ANOVA table summarizes the sample results for the bakery experiment.

Variation	Degrees of freedom	Sum of squares	Mean square	F
Explained by treatments (between columns)	$c - 1 = 3$	$SST = 28.275$	$MST = 28.275/3$ $= 9.425$	MST/MSE $= 9.425/.629$ $= 14.98$
Explained by blocks (between rows)	$r - 1 = 9$	$SSB = 132.725$	$MSB = 132.725/9$ $= 14.747$	
Error or unexplained (within columns)	$(r-1)(c-1) = 27$	$SSE = 16.975$	$MSE = 16.975/27$ $= .629$	
Totals	$rc - 1 = 39$	$SS = 177.975$		

Notice that there is a third source of variation attributed to the blocks.

E. The test statistic is computed as before.

The F statistic for the two-way evaluation of the bakery experiment is

$$F = \frac{9.425}{.629} = 14.98$$

The F distribution provides the critical value, as before. The numbers for degrees of freedom, however, are *different*.

Number of degrees of freedom
Numerator: $c - 1$
Denominator: $(r - 1)(c - 1)$

For an $\alpha = .05$ significance level, with $4 - 1 = 3$ degrees of freedom for the numerator and $(10 - 1)(4 - 1) = 27$ for the denominator, Table D provides the critical value $F_{.05} = 2.96$. Since the computed F now falls above the critical value, you should reject the null hypothesis of identical mean sales at the various shelf heights. (Keep in mind that either the one-way test or the two-way test, but not both, may be applied in an actual situation. The same data are used here for both tests just to illustrate the procedure.)

SUMMARY

Analysis of variance compares several populations, each representing a level of the *treatment variable*. You are testing the null hypothesis that every *treatment* results in an identical mean for the *response variable*. Sample data are arranged in an *experimental layout*, forming a matrix. There are two ANOVA procedures. The *one-way analysis* uses a row to represent each sample observation and a separate column to represent each treatment. The *two-way analysis* involves a third factor, the *blocking variable*, which may serve to explain some of the variation in sample response.

The procedure will reject H_0 if the variation in response that is "explained" by or attributed to different treatments is significantly greater than the variation that is left unexplained. This is accomplished by an elaborate procedure leading to computation of the F statistic, which serves as the test statistic.

In the one-way analysis of variance, you compute for each column a *sample treatment mean*, which is summarized by the expression

$$\bar{X}_j = \frac{\sum_i X_{ij}}{r}$$

You also compute the *grand mean* using the pooled sample data:

$$\bar{\bar{X}} = \frac{\sum_j \sum_i X_{ij}}{rc}$$

Using these two means and the original data values, you compute the *treatments sum of squares*,

$$SST = r \sum_j (\bar{X}_j - \bar{\bar{X}})^2$$

and the *error sum of squares*,

$$SSE = \sum_j \sum_i (X_{ij} - \bar{X}_j)^2$$

Next you find the *total sum of squares*,

$$\text{Total } SS = \sum_j \sum_i (X_{ij} - \bar{\bar{X}})^2 = SST + SSE$$

To compute the test statistic, you first find the *treatments mean square* and the *error mean square*:

$$MST = \frac{SST}{c - 1} \qquad MSE = \frac{SSE}{(r - 1)c}$$

You can now compute

$$F = \frac{\text{Variance explained by treatments}}{\text{Unexplained variance}} = \frac{MST}{MSE}$$

You read critical F values from Table D in the Appendix. In reading that table you must first establish the *number of degrees of freedom*, a pair of values determined for the one-way analysis by the following rule:

$$\text{Numerator:} \quad c - 1$$
$$\text{Denominator:} \quad (r - 1)c$$

The tests are *upper-tailed*, so you reject the null hypothesis for computed levels of F exceeding the critical value.

You will find it convenient to arrange the computed information in an *ANOVA table*:

Variation	Degrees of freedom	Sum of squares	Mean square	F
Explained by treatments (between columns)	$c - 1$	SST	MST	MST/MSE
Error or unexplained (within columns)	$(r-1)c$	SSE	MSE	
Totals	$rc - 1$	SS		

A *two-way analysis of variance* involves a row in the experimental layout for each *block*, or level of the *blocking variable*. You need to find both row and column means. You compute each *sample block mean* from

$$\bar{X}_{i \cdot} = \frac{\sum\limits_{j} X_{ij}}{c}$$

and the sample treatment means from

$$\bar{X}_{\cdot j} = \frac{\sum\limits_{i} X_{ij}}{r}$$

You may find the grand mean in a variety of ways:

$$\bar{\bar{X}} = \frac{\sum\limits_{j}\sum\limits_{i} X_{ij}}{rc} = \frac{\sum\limits_{i} \bar{X}_{i \cdot}}{r} = \frac{\sum\limits_{j} \bar{X}_{\cdot j}}{c}$$

You compute the treatments sum of squares as before:

$$SST = r \sum_{j} (\bar{X}_{\cdot j} - \bar{\bar{X}})^2$$

The following expression provides the *blocks sum of squares*:

$$SSB = c \sum_{i} (\bar{X}_{i \cdot} - \bar{\bar{X}})^2$$

You compute the total sum of squares as before. It is easiest to use the following expression to compute the error sum of squares:

$$SSE = \text{Total } SS - SST - SSB$$

You find the treatments mean square as before, but you compute the error mean square differently:

$$MSE = \frac{SSE}{(r - 1)(c - 1)}$$

You can also compute the *blocks mean square,*

$$MSB = \frac{SSB}{r-1}.$$

although it isn't ordinarily used.

The following ANOVA table applies:

Variation	Degrees of freedom	Sum of squares	Mean square	F
Explained by treatments (between columns)	$c-1$	SST	MST	MST/MSE
Explained by blocks (between rows)	$r-1$	SSB	MSB	
Error or unexplained (within columns)	$(r-1)(c-1)$	SSE	MSE	
Totals	$rc-1$	SS		

The number of degrees of freedom for the denominator, the new divisor for *MSE*, is now $(r-1)(c-1)$.

RAISE YOUR GRADES

Can you explain...?

☑ why the term *analysis of variance* is used for a test involving means
☑ the difference between treatment and response
☑ the difference between treatment and block
☑ why the test for equality of several means is upper-tailed rather than two-sided
☑ when in testing for equality of several means you should use the *F* distribution rather than the Student *t* distribution

Do you know...?

☑ how to find the appropriate number of degrees of freedom for each analysis-of-variance test
☑ when you should accept it and when you should reject it
☑ whether *SST* measures variation between columns or between rows
☑ if you use *MSB* in computing *F*
☑ why inclusion of a blocking variable can reduce the amount of unexplained variation

RAPID REVIEW

1. From a one-way layout, the following sample means were obtained:

$$\bar{X}_1 = 100 \qquad \bar{X}_2 = 105 \qquad \bar{X}_3 = 110 \qquad \bar{\bar{X}} = 105$$

Each treatment group involves 10 observations. Compute *SST*.   [Section 16-1C]

2. In a one-way evaluation involving 5 rows and 4 columns, *SST* = 127.4 and *SSE* = 92.3. Compute *F*.   [Section 16-1D]

3. In a two-way evaluation, the total sum of squares is 512.1, the treatments sum of squares is 114.5, and the blocks sum of squares is 287.3. Determine the error sum of squares. [Section 16-2C]

4. An evaluation is made using a 10-block, 5-treatment layout. The following values apply: $SST = 37.4$, $SSB = 183.4$, $SSE = 24.3$. Compute F. [Sections 16-2D,E]

5. Determine the critical value in testing the equality of 3 means at the $\alpha = .05$ significance level when a random sample of 7 observations is made for each group,

    (a) assuming no blocking variable. [Section 16-1E]
    (b) assuming each group observation represents a different block. [Section 16-2E]

6. In a certain analysis of variance, the treatments mean square is 5.0 and the error mean square is 1.0. Which of the following equals the value of F? [Section 16-1D]

    (a) 5.0   (b) .2   (c) 1.0   (d) 4.0

7. In testing whether there is any difference between mean tire-tread lifetimes under various driving conditions, 3 samples of 5 similar cars are each driven under one of three conditions (city, highway, country). The tread wear is then determined for each car. What is the number of degrees of freedom (numerator, denominator) for the F test? [Section 16-1E]

    (a) $(3, 5)$ (b) $(15, 32)$ (c) $(2, 12)$ (d) $(12, 2)$

8. To test H_0 that the mean output of a synthetic chemical is identical under low-, medium-, and high-pressure settings, a chemical engineer has tested a different sample of five batches under each setting. The treatments sum of squares is 60,000, and the error sum of squares is 72,000. What is the value of the F statistic? [Section 16-1D]

    (a) .20   (b) 5.0   (c) .139   (d) 7.2

9. The F distribution [Section 16-2E]

    (a) is symmetrical.
    (b) is positively skewed.
    (c) exhibits only a one-tailed frequency curve.
    (d) is bimodal.

10. In its objective, analysis of variance is most similar to [Section 16-1]

    (a) a two-sided test of the population mean.
    (b) a two-sample test for the equality of two sample proportions.
    (c) a two-sample test for the equality of two population means.
    (d) a chi-square test for independence.

Answers
1. 500   2. 7.36   3. 110.3
4. 13.85   5. (a) 3.55 (b) 3.88
6. (a)   7. (c)   8. (b)   9. (b)   10. (c)

SOLVED PROBLEMS

PROBLEM 16-1 For each of the following situations, indicate the critical value F_α above which the stated tail area holds:

| | Degrees of Freedom | |
Area	Numerator	Denominator
(a) $\alpha = .01$	10	12
(b) $\alpha = .05$	10	10
(c) $\alpha = .05$	8	20
(d) $\alpha = .01$	12	10

Solution: Read the appropriate critical values from Table D.
(a) $F_{.01} = 4.30$ (b) $F_{.05} = 2.97$ (c) $F_{.05} = 2.45$ (d) $F_{.01} = 4.71$

PROBLEM 16-2 The effect of water dispersal on crop growth is being investigated. Five different plots have each been watered at three settings, and the results have been recorded. The null hypothesis of equal growth rate for each level of watering is to be tested at the $\alpha = .05$ significance level.

(a) Determine the critical value of the test statistic. For each of the following crops, indicate whether you should accept or reject H_0.
(b) For alfalfa the computed value is $F = 6.42$.
(c) For sugar beets the computed value is $F = 5.07$.
(d) For tomatoes the computed value is $F = 3.22$.

Solution:
(a) The degrees of freedom are $3 - 1 = 2$ for the numerator and $(5 - 1)3 = 12$ for the denominator. From Table D you find the critical value $F_{.05} = 3.88$.
(b) Since the computed value exceeds the critical value, reject H_0.
(c) Since the computed value exceeds the critical value, reject H_0.
(d) Since the computed value falls below the critical value, accept H_0.

PROBLEM 16-3 An experimenter investigated the impact of different temperature settings on the yield of a chemical process. She used four different settings with samples of five production runs each. She computed the following values:

$$SST = 390 \qquad SSE = 120$$

(a) Construct the ANOVA table.
(b) She tested her null hypothesis of identical mean yields using an $\alpha = .01$ significance level. Did she accept or reject H_0?

Solution:
(a) Here $r = 5$ and $c = 4$. The following ANOVA table applies.

Variation	Degrees of freedom	Sum of squares	Mean square	F
Treatments	$4 - 1 = 3$	$SST = 390$	$MST = 390/3$ $= 130$	$F = 130/7.5$ $= 17.33$
Error	$(5 - 1)4 = 16$	$SSE = 120$	$MSE = 120/16$ $= 7.5$	
Totals	$5(4) - 1 = 19$	$SS = 510$		

(b) For $df = 3$ for the numerator and $df = 16$ for the denominator, Table D provides the critical value $F_{.01} = 5.29$. Since the computed F exceeds this, the investigator rejected the null hypothesis.

PROBLEM 16-4 A security analyst obtained the following rates of return after exercising three stock-trading rules during five series of simulated trades.

	Trading Rule		
Series	*(1)* Buy and hold	*(2)* Sell on good news	*(3)* Buy on bad news
1	32%	17%	-5%
2	-11	23	8
3	14	15	2
4	9	7	12
5	16	13	10

The null hypothesis is that the trading rules provide identical mean rates of return.

(a) Find the critical value of the test statistic. Use $\alpha = .05$.

(b) Compute (*1*) the sample means, (*2*) the sums of squares, (*3*) the mean squares, and (*4*) the *F* statistic.

(c) Construct the ANOVA table.

(d) At the $\alpha = .05$ significance level, should the analyst accept or reject the null hypothesis of identical mean rates of return?

Solution:

(a) For $3 - 1 = 2$ degrees of freedom for the numerator and $(5 - 1)3 = 12$ degrees of freedom for the denominator, Table D provides the critical value $F_{.05} = 3.88$.

(b) (*1*) The following sample treatment means apply:

Series	Trading rule		
	(*1*) Buy and hold	(*2*) Sell on good news	(*3*) Buy on bad news
1	32%	17%	−5%
2	−11	23	8
3	14	15	2
4	9	7	12
5	16	13	10
	60	75	27
	$\bar{X}_1 = \dfrac{60}{5}$	$\bar{X}_2 = \dfrac{75}{5}$	$\bar{X}_3 = \dfrac{27}{5}$
	$= 12$	$= 15$	$= 5.4$

The grand mean is

$$\bar{\bar{X}} = \frac{60 + 75 + 27}{5(3)} = \frac{162}{15} = 10.8$$

(*2*) The treatments sum of squares is

$$SST = 5[(12 - 10.8)^2 + (15 - 10.8)^2 + (5.4 - 10.8)^2]$$
$$= 5(1.44 + 17.64 + 29.16)$$
$$= 241.2$$

You compute the error sum of squares as follows.

i	$(X_{i1} - \bar{X}_1)^2$	$(X_{i2} - \bar{X}_2)^2$	$(X_{i3} - \bar{X}_3)^2$
1	$(32 - 12)^2 = 400$	$(17 - 15)^2 = 4$	$(-5 - 5.4)^2 = 108.16$
2	$(-11 - 12)^2 = 529$	$(23 - 15)^2 = 64$	$(8 - 5.4)^2 = 6.76$
3	$(14 - 12)^2 = 4$	$(15 - 15)^2 = 0$	$(2 - 5.4)^2 = 11.56$
4	$(9 - 12)^2 = 9$	$(7 - 15)^2 = 64$	$(12 - 5.4)^2 = 43.56$
5	$(16 - 12)^2 = 16$	$(13 - 15)^2 = 4$	$(10 - 5.4)^2 = 21.16$
	958	136	191.20

$$SSE = 958 + 136 + 191.20 = 1,285.2$$

Although you can compute the total sum of squares by working with individual squares, once you have *SST* and *SSE* it is easier to use the following identity:

$$\text{Total } SS = SST + SSE = 241.2 + 1,285.2 = 1,526.4$$

(*3*) You compute the mean squares as follows:

$$MST = \frac{241.2}{3 - 1} = 120.6 \qquad MSE = \frac{1,285.2}{(5 - 1)3} = 107.1$$

(*4*) The test statistic is

$$F = \frac{MST}{MSE} = \frac{120.6}{107.1} = 1.13$$

(c) Arranging the computed results, you obtain the following ANOVA table.

Variation	Degrees of freedom	Sum of squares	Mean square	F
Treatments	2	241.2	120.6	1.13
Error	12	1,285.2	107.1	
Totals	14	1,526.4		

(d) Since the computed value for F falls below the critical value, the analyst should accept the null hypothesis of identical population mean rates of return.

PROBLEM 16-5   The manager of a telecommunications network is evaluating various strategies for routing calls. The following data represent the percentage of calls successfully completed during sample intervals of time.

Call-routing algorithm

Observation	(1) East-West	(2) North-South	(3) Central	(4) Random	(5) Shortest
1	90%	99%	95%	98%	87%
2	92	97	96	98	93
3	94	98	97	99	90
4	93	98	97	99	91
5	92	99	96	98	89

(a) Construct the ANOVA table.
(b) Find the critical value of the test statistic, and identify the acceptance and rejection regions. Use $\alpha = .01$.
(c) Should the manager accept or reject the null hypothesis of identical mean percentages of calls completed?

Solution:
(a) The following sample treatment means apply:

$$\bar{X}_1 = 92.2 \quad \bar{X}_2 = 98.2 \quad \bar{X}_3 = 96.2 \quad \bar{X}_4 = 98.4 \quad \bar{X}_5 = 90.0$$

The grand mean is $\bar{\bar{X}} = 95.0$. You compute the numbers of degrees of freedom, the sums of squares, the mean squares, and the F statistic as in Problem 16-4. The following ANOVA table applies.

Variation	Degrees of freedom	Sum of squares	Mean square	F
Treatments	4	280.40	70.10	39.38
Error	20	35.60	1.78	
Totals	24	316.00		

(b) Using $5 - 1 = 4$ degrees of freedom for the numerator and $(5 - 1)5 = 20$ degrees of freedom for the denominator, you find from Table D that the critical value is $F_{.01} = 4.43$. If the computed value is greater than 4.43, you reject H_0; otherwise you accept it.
(c) Since the computed value for F falls above the critical value, the manager should reject the null hypothesis of identical population mean percentages of calls completed.

PROBLEM 16-6   A marketing department chairman is evaluating various methods for presenting a basic course. A sample of 6 sections has been taught under each of three methods. The students obtained the following average class scores on a standardized examination.

Teaching method

Class	(1) Case study	(2) Project	(3) Lecture
1	78	77	83
2	85	86	91
3	64	71	75
4	77	75	78
5	81	80	82
6	75	77	80

What should the chairman conclude regarding the mean scores for all classes taught under the respective methods? Use $\alpha = .05$.

Solution: For $3 - 1 = 2$ degrees of freedom for the numerator and $(6 - 1)3 = 15$ degrees of freedom for the denominator, the critical value is $F_{.05} = 3.68$. The sample treatment means are

$$\bar{X}_1 = 76.67 \qquad \bar{X}_2 = 77.67 \qquad \bar{X}_3 = 81.50$$

and the grand mean is $\bar{\bar{X}} = 78.61$. Proceeding as in Problem 16-4, you obtain the following ANOVA table.

Variation	Degrees of freedom	Sum of squares	Mean square	F
Treatments	2	78.11	39.06	1.11
Error	15	530.17	35.34	
Totals	17	608.28		

Since the computed value for F falls below the critical value, the chairman should accept the null hypothesis that identical population mean scores result from the three methods.

Note: If you're working with numbers rounded off to two places, you will get slightly different answers when figuring the sums of squares. This won't affect the test.

PROBLEM 16-7 A chemical engineer is evaluating four methods for processing oil shale to obtain synthetic fuel. Using 9 random samples of raw material processed under each method, she obtained the following yields of usable liquid (in milliliters per ton):

Sample	Method A	Method B	Method C	Method D
1	-5	11	15	8
2	11	14	10	10
3	13	22	25	18
4	-5	0	2	1
5	25	35	40	28
6	21	24	28	27
7	11	15	19	17
8	33	30	28	32
9	105	224	328	276

(a) Can the engineer conclude that some methods for processing shale might be better than others? Use $\alpha = .01$.

(b) What factors other than processing method might explain variation in yield?

Solution:

(a) Using $4 - 1 = 3$ degrees of freedom for the numerator and $(9 - 1)4 = 32$ degrees of freedom for the denominator, the critical value is $F_{.01} = 4.46$. The sample treatment means are

$$\bar{X}_A = 23.22 \qquad \bar{X}_B = 41.67 \qquad \bar{X}_C = 55 \qquad \bar{X}_D = 46.33$$

and the grand mean is $\bar{\bar{X}} = 41.56$. The ANOVA table follows.

Variation	Degrees of freedom	Sum of squares	Mean square	F
Treatments	3	4,857.33	1,619.11	.27
Error	32	192,077.56	6,002.42	
Totals	35	196,934.89		

Since the computed value for F falls below the critical value, the engineer should accept the null hypothesis of identical population mean liquid yields obtained under the various processing methods. **(b)** Differences in type of shale is one factor that might explain variation in liquid yield.

PROBLEM 16-8 Refer to the information in Problem 16-6. Suppose that each row represents a different instructor, with the three class averages representing a separate class taught by that instructor using a different method. Treating instructor as the blocking variable, answer the following.

(a) Find the sample means.
(b) Determine (1) the sums of squares, (2) the mean squares, and (3) the F statistic.
(c) Construct the ANOVA table.
(d) Compare the value of SSE found for this problem to the one obtained in Problem 16-6. Does the blocking variable appear to reduce unexplained variation in average class score?
(e) At the $\alpha = .01$ significance level, should the chairman accept or reject the null hypothesis of identical mean examination scores under each teaching method?

Solution:
(a) The following sample means apply.

Instructor	Teaching method			Block mean
	(1) Case study	(2) Project	(3) Lecture	
1	78	77	83	$\bar{X}_{1.} = 79.33$
2	85	86	91	$\bar{X}_{2.} = 87.33$
3	64	71	75	$\bar{X}_{3.} = 70.00$
4	77	75	78	$\bar{X}_{4.} = 76.67$
5	81	80	82	$\bar{X}_{5.} = 81.00$
6	75	77	80	$\bar{X}_{6.} = 77.33$
Treatment mean	$\bar{X}_{.1} = 76.67$	$\bar{X}_{.2} = 77.67$	$\bar{X}_{.3} = 81.50$	$\bar{\bar{X}} = 78.611$

(b) (1) You compute the following sums of squares.

$$SST = 6[(76.67 - 78.611)^2 + (77.67 - 78.611)^2 + (81.50 - 78.611)^2]$$
$$= 78.11$$
$$SSB = 3[(79.33 - 78.611)^2 + (87.33 - 78.611)^2 + \cdots + (77.33 - 78.611)^2]$$
$$= 485.61$$
$$\text{Total } SS = (78 - 78.611)^2 + (77 - 78.611)^2 + \cdots + (80 - 78.611)^2$$
$$= 608.28$$
$$SSE = 608.28 - 78.11 - 485.61 = 44.56$$

(2) The applicable mean squares are

$$MST = \frac{78.11}{3 - 1} = 39.06 \qquad MSB = \frac{485.61}{6 - 1} = 97.12 \qquad MSE = \frac{44.56}{2(5)} = 4.46$$

(3) The value of the test statistic is

$$F = \frac{39.06}{4.46} = 8.76$$

(c) The following ANOVA table applies.

Variation	Degrees of freedom	Sum of squares	Mean square	F
Treatments	2	78.11	39.06	8.76
Blocks	5	485.61	97.12	
Error	10	44.56	4.46	
Totals	17	608.28		

(d) For the one-way analysis of variance, $SSE = 530.17$. For the two-way analysis of variance, $SSE = 44.56$, a dramatic reduction. Yes, the inclusion of the blocking variable does provide a promising reduction in unexplained variation.

(e) Using $3 - 1 = 2$ degrees of freedom for the numerator and $(6 - 1)(3 - 1) = 10$ degrees of freedom for the denominator, you read from Table D the critical value $F_{.01} = 7.56$. Since the computed value of $F = 8.76$ exceeds the critical value, the chairman must reject the null hypothesis of identical means.

PROBLEM 16-9   Refer to the information in Problem 16-7. Suppose that each row represents a different type of shale material, with the four yields representing a different portion of the same type of raw material. Using type of shale as the blocking variable, answer the following.

(a) Construct the ANOVA table.
(b) Compare the value of *SSE* found for this problem to the one obtained in Problem 16-7. Does the blocking variable appear to reduce unexplained variation in yield?
(c) At the $\alpha = .01$ significance level, should the engineer accept or reject the null hypothesis of identical mean yield under each processing method?

Solution:

(a) Compute the sample means as in Problem 16-7. The sample treatment means and the grand mean are the same as in Problem 16-7. The sample block means are as follows:

$$\bar{X}_{1.} = 7.25 \qquad \bar{X}_{4.} = -.50 \qquad \bar{X}_{7.} = 15.50$$
$$\bar{X}_{2.} = 11.25 \qquad \bar{X}_{5.} = 32.00 \qquad \bar{X}_{8.} = 30.75$$
$$\bar{X}_{3.} = 19.50 \qquad \bar{X}_{6.} = 25.00 \qquad \bar{X}_{9.} = 233.25$$

From these find the sums of squares and mean squares. Then compute F. The results appear in the following ANOVA table.

Variation	Degrees of freedom	Sum of squares	Mean square	F
Treatments	3	4,857.33	1,619.11	1.69
Blocks	8	169,032.89	21,129.11	
Error	24	23,044.67	960.19	
Totals	35	196,934.89		

(b) For the one-way analysis of variance, $SSE = 192,077.56$. For the two-way analysis of variance, $SSE = 23,044.67$, a dramatic reduction. Yes, the inclusion of the blocking variable does provide a promising reduction in unexplained variation.

(c) For $df = 3$ for the numerator and $df = 24$ for the denominator, Table D provides $F_{.01} = 4.72$. Since the computed value of $F = 1.69$ falls below the critical value, the engineer must accept the null hypothesis of identical means.

PROBLEM 16-10   A product manager for a cereal company wishes to evaluate several preservatives in terms of useful shelf life. He has obtained the following data (in months).

| | Bonding agent | | | |
Sample	(1)	(2)	(3)	(4)
1	5	6	5	7
2	6	8	7	6
3	5	9	7	5
4	5	9	7	5
5	6	8	7	6
6	5	9	8	7
7	7	8	6	6
8	5	9	7	7

(a) Construct the ANOVA table.

(b) Should the manager conclude that the mean shelf lives are different for the agents? Use $\alpha = .01$.

Solution:

(a) Compute the sample means as in Problem 16-4. The sample treatment means are

$$\bar{X}_1 = 5.5 \qquad \bar{X}_2 = 8.25 \qquad \bar{X}_3 = 6.75 \qquad \bar{X}_4 = 6.125$$

and the grand mean is $\bar{\bar{X}} = 6.66$. From these find the sums of squares and mean squares. Then compute F. The results appear in the following ANOVA table.

Variations	Degrees of freedom	Sum of squares	Mean square	F
Treatments	3	33.34	11.11	14.24
Error	28	21.88	.78	
Totals	31	55.22		

(b) For $4 - 1 = 3$ degrees of freedom for the numerator and $(8 - 1)4 = 28$ for the denominator, Table D provides the critical value $F_{.01} = 4.57$. Since the computed value of $F = 14.24$ exceeds the critical value, the manager must reject the null hypothesis of equal means.

PROBLEM 16-11 A financial analyst for a savings and loan is evaluating three rules for triggering changes in variable rate mortgages. Using randomly generated market interest-rate scenarios as the blocking variable, she obtained the following sample data from computer simulations.

| | Loan portfolio yield | | |
Scenario	(1) A	(2) B	(3) C
1	11.3	12.4	10.9
2	14.2	14.3	13.7
3	14.9	15.2	14.7
4	12.2	11.3	12.5

At the 5% significance level, what should the manager conclude regarding the mean yields?

Solution: Compute the sample means as in Problem 16-8. The sample treatment means are

$$\bar{X}_{.1} = 13.15 \qquad \bar{X}_{.2} = 13.30 \qquad \bar{X}_{.3} = 12.95$$

and the sample block means are

$$\bar{X}_{1.} = 11.53 \qquad \bar{X}_{2.} = 14.07 \qquad \bar{X}_{3.} = 14.93 \qquad \bar{X}_{4.} = 12$$

The grand mean is $\bar{X} = 13.13$. From these find the sums of squares and mean squares. Then compute F. The results appear in the following ANOVA table.

Variation	Degrees of freedom	Sum of squares	Mean square	F
Treatments (yield)	2	.247	.124	.36
Blocks (scenario)	3	23.867	7.956	
Error	6	2.073	.346	
Totals	11	26.187		

For $3 - 1 = 2$ degrees of freedom for the numerator and $(4 - 1)(3 - 1) = 6$ for the denominator, Table D provides the critical value $F_{.05} = 5.14$. Since the computed value of $F = .36$ falls below the critical value, the analyst must accept the null hypothesis of equal means.

FINAL EXAMINATION

1. A banana boat inspector accepts (A) 95% of all shipments inspected. Ultimately, 15% of all shipments prove to be bad (B), although he manages to reject (R) only 2% of the good (G) shipments. These percentages apply to any particular shipment. Consider probabilities for the next shipment inspected.

(a) Find the following probabilities.
    (1) $\Pr[A]$ (2) $\Pr[R]$ (3) $\Pr[B]$ (4) $\Pr[G]$ (5) $\Pr[R|G]$
(b) Use the multiplication law to find $\Pr[R \text{ and } G]$.
(c) Construct the joint probability table.
(d) Compute the following conditional probabilities.
    (1) $\Pr[A|B]$ (2) $\Pr[R|B]$ (3) $\Pr[B|R]$ (4) $\Pr[A|G]$

2. A machine used for filling containers of powdered cream substitute is shut down for adjustment whenever a mean of 100 sample jars is more than .5 ounce above or below the intended mean of 24 ounces for a perfectly adjusted machine. The filling process has a standard deviation of 2 ounces per jar.

(a) What is the probability that the machine will be shut down when it is perfectly adjusted?
(b) What is the probability that the machine will be shut down when it overfills each jar by an average of .4 ounce?

3. Construct a 95% confidence interval estimate of the mean income of MBA's. For a sample of 100 taken from a large population, the computed mean is $25,400 with standard deviation $2,100.

4. The following stopwatch measurements have been made for the waiting times (minutes) experienced by a random sample of customers at a fast food restaurant:

10	15	16	11	21	12
15	10	11	19	15	16

(a) Compute (1) the sample mean and (2) the sample standard deviation.
(b) Construct a 95% confidence interval estimate of the mean waiting time for all customers.

5. A personnel director plans to retain a new training program if she can accept the null hypothesis that scores on the follow-up achievement test have a mean greater than or equal to 75 points. Otherwise, she will drop the program. For a sample of 100 persons who took the program, the mean test score was 71.6 points with a standard deviation of 5.3 points. What action should she take, assuming a 5% significance level?

6. Ace Widgets will replace its present supplier of fluorescent tubes if the null hypothesis is rejected (at the 5% level of significance) that the mean lifetime for all tubes purchased is greater than or equal to 1,500 hours. Otherwise, the present source will be retained. A sample of tubes was tested, and the following lifetimes were obtained.

350	220	1,950	1,110	550	670	2,240
180	490	860	1,520	2,050	890	1,730

(a) Compute (1) the sample mean and (2) the sample standard deviation.
(b) What action should Ace take?

7. WeeTees plans to introduce a new cereal product if it can be concluded that the proportion of potential buyers exceeds .30. Otherwise, management will abandon the product. A sample of

100 persons is given a taste test, and 22 of them like WeeTees. Assuming a 5% significance level, what action should management take?

8. The following data apply to a sample of shoe store franchises.

Profit	Square Feet	Profit	Square Feet
15,200	890	9,300	750
106,200	2,250	40,300	1,500
−6,100	1,020	22,700	950
58,300	1,420	46,800	1,750
23,600	1,070	15,300	1,250

Find the estimated regression equation for predicting profit from square feet of retail space.

9. The following partial time series data apply to GizMo Corp. unit sales. Determine the missing values.

t	T_t	C_t	S_t	I_t	Y_t
Winter	2,000	80	120	105	
Spring		90	100	100	1,980
Summer	2,400		70	98	1,646
Fall	2,600	110		95	2,989

10. The following sample data apply to the test scores received by two groups of trainees.

Group A	Group B
75	62
81	72
63	64
74	81
82	71
	58
	63

(a) Use the Student t statistic to test the null hypothesis (at the 5% level of significance) that the population A mean score is less than or equal to the population B mean score.
(b) Repeat part (a) using instead the Wilcoxon rank-sum test.

ANSWERS TO FINAL EXAMINATION

1. (a) (*1*) .95   (*2*) .05   (*3*) .15   (*4*) .85   (*5*) .02
   (b) .017

   (c)

Quality	Action		Marginal probability
	Accept	Reject	
Good	.833	.017	.850
Bad	.117	.033	.150
Marginal probability	.950	.050	1.000

   (d) (*1*) .78   (*2*) .22   (*3*) .66   (*4*) .98
2. (a) .0124   (b) .3085
3. $\mu = \$25,400 \pm 411.60$
4. (a) (*1*) 14.25 min.   (*2*) 3.545 min.
   (b) $\mu = 14.25 \pm 2.25$
5. Drop the program.
6. (a) (*1*) 1,057.9   (*2*) 713.4
   (b) Replace present supplier.

7. Introduce the cereal.

8. $\hat{Y} = -47,459 + 62.74X$

9.

t	T_t	C_t	S_t	I_t	Y_t
Winter	2,000	80	120	105	2,016
Spring	2,200	90	100	100	1,980
Summer	2,400	100	70	98	1,646
Fall	2,600	110	110	95	2,989

10. **(a)** Accept H_0 **(b)** Accept H_0

SYMBOLIC GLOSSARY

A (1) An event or an event set
(2) Y intercept of the true regression line

A and B An event represented by the *intersection* of events A and B

A or B An event represented by the *union* of events A and B

a Y intercept for estimated regression equation used in:
(1) simple linear regression
(2) multiple regression

α(alpha)   (1) Tail area under curves for various distributions
(2) Probability of the type I error: rejecting H_0 when it is true
(3) Smoothing parameter for single-parameter exponential smoothing

B An event or an event set

b Slope of the estimated regression line

$b_1, b_2, \ldots$ Partial regression coefficients for the estimated multiple regression equation

b_t Smoothed trend value for period t; used in two-parameter exponential smoothing

β(beta)   Probability of the type II error: accepting H_0 when it is false

C Acceptance number

C_r^n Number of possible combinations of r items from a collection of size n, when order of selection is not counted

C_t Cyclical component of classical time series model

c Number of columns in analysis-of-variance layout

χ^2 Chi-square statistic

χ_α^2 Critical value for the chi-square statistic (random variable); represents the value exceeded α proportion of times (that is, with a probability of α) by χ^2 (values are found in Appendix C)

d_i Matched-pairs difference between two sample observations; used for comparing means of two populations

$\bar{d}$ Mean of matched-pairs differences d_i

e Base of natural logarithms

$E(X)$ Expected value of random variable X

F F statistic; used in analysis of variance

F_α Critical value for the F statistic (random variable); represents the value exceeded α proportion of the times (that is, with a probability of α) by F (values are found in Appendix D)

F_t Forecast value for period t; used in exponential smoothing

$f, \hat{f}$ Actual and expected class frequencies used in calculating the test statistic χ^2

$f(x)$ Function f at x; used to represent the height of the density curve (that is, $f(x)$ is the probability density function of the random variable X)

$f_1, f_2, f_3, \ldots$ Class frequencies for successive class intervals of a frequency distributions; used in calculating sample mean or standard deviation with grouped data

γ(gamma)   Smoothing parameter for trend in two-parameter exponential smoothing

H_0 Null hypothesis

H_1 Alternative hypothesis

I Value of an index number

I_t Irregular component of classical time series model

i Subscripts in a summation:

$$\sum_{i=1}^{n} X_i = X_1 + X_2 + \cdots + X_n$$

j Sometimes used to represent subscripts in a double summation:

$$\begin{aligned}\sum_{j=1}^{m}\sum_{i=1}^{n} X_{ij} =\ & (X_{11} + X_{21} + \cdots + X_{n1}) \\ & + (X_{12} + X_{22} + \cdots + X_{n2}) \\ & + (X_{1m} + X_{2m} + \cdots + X_{nm})\end{aligned}$$

MSB Mean square (between rows); used to calculate the F statistic in a two-factor analysis of variance when B represents the blocking variable

MSE Error mean square; used to calculate the F statistic:
(1) (within columns) for a one-factor analysis of variance
(2) (residual) for a two-factor analysis of variance

MST Mean square; used to calculate the F statistic (between columns): for the treatments in a one-factor analysis of variance

μ(mu)   Arithmetic mean of a population

μ_0 Value of the population mean assumed under the null hypothesis

$\mu_1, \mu_2, \mu_3, \ldots$ Means of populations; used in analysis of variance

μ_A, μ_B　Means of populations A and B, which are compared using two samples

N　Number of observations in population (population size)

n　(1) Number of observations in a sample (sample size)
(2) Number of trials in a Bernoulli process

$n!$　n factorial, or the product $n \times (n-1) \times (n-2) \times \cdots \times 2 \times 1$

n_A, n_B　Sample sizes for two-sample tests comparing the parameters of two populations A and B

P　Proportion of sample observations having a particular characteristic

$\Pr[A]$　Probability of event A

$\Pr[A|B]$　Conditional probability of event A given event B

$\Pr[A \text{ and } B]$　Probability of the intersection of events A and B; event occurs only when both A and B occur (also called the joint probability of A and B)

$\Pr[A \text{ or } B]$　Probability of the union of A and B; occurs when either A or B occurs, or when both A and B occur

$\Pr[X=x]$　Probability that the random variable X assumes one of several particular values

$\Pr[X \leq x]$　Cumulative probability that X assumes any value less than or equal to a particular value x

P^*　Critical value for P; used in one-sided hypothesis-testing procedure

P_A, P_B　Proportions of observations having a particular characteristic for samples from populations A and B

P_C　Combined sample proportion; used in two-sample inferences for comparing proportions of two populations

P_r^n　Number of permutations of r items taken from a collection of size n when different orders of selection are counted

P_n, P_0　Prices per unit of an item in year n and in base period 0; used in constructing index numbers

$\pi(\text{pi})$　(1) Proportion of a population having a particular characteristic
(2) Probability of a trial success in a Bernoulli process

π_0　Value of the population proportion assumed under the null hypothesis

$\pi_1, \pi_2, \pi_3, \ldots$　Values of population proportions in testing for equality of several population proportions

π_A, π_B　Proportions of populations A and B that are compared in two-sample hypothesis tests

q_n, q_0　Quantities of an item in year n and in base period 0; used in constructing index numbers

R　A random variable denoting the number of successes obtained from several trials of a Bernoulli process

r　(1) One of several possible values of the random variable R
(2) The sample correlation coefficient; expresses the strength and direction of the relationship between variables X and Y
(3) Number of rows in an analysis-of-variance layout

r^2　Sample coefficient of determination; represents the proportion of the variation in the dependent variable Y that can be explained by linear regression on the independent variable X

$\rho(\text{rho})$　Population correlation coefficient; estimated by r

ρ^2　Population coefficient of determination; estimated by r^2

S_t　Seasonal component of the classical time series model

$S_{Y \cdot 12}, S_{Y \cdot 123}$　Standard error of the estimate about the multiple regression plane

SSB　Sum of squares between rows for a two-factor analysis of variance when B represents the blocking variable

SSE　Error sum of squares:
(1) (within columns) for a one-factor analysis of variance
(2) (residual) for a two-factor or a three-factor analysis of variance

SST　Sum of squares (between columns) for the treatments in a one-factor analysis of variance

s　Sample standard deviation

s^2　Sample variance

s_A^2, s_B^2　Variances of samples from populations A and B; used in two-sample hypothesis tests

s_Y　Sample standard deviation of the dependent variable Y; used in correlation analysis

$s_{Y \cdot X}$　Standard error of the estimate about the regression line

s_d　Sample standard deviation of matched-pairs differences

$\sum$　Summation sign

σ(sigma) — Population standard deviation

σ^2 — Population variance

$\sigma(X)$ — Standard deviation of random variable X

$\sigma^2(X)$ — Variance of random variable X

σ_A^2, σ_B^2 — Variance of populations A and B compared by two-sample inferences

σ_P — Standard error (also called the standard deviation) of the sample proportion P

$\sigma_{\bar{X}}$ — Standard error of the sample mean $\bar{X}$

T_t — Trend component of classical time series model

Total SS — Total sum of squares; used in analysis-of-variance calculations

t — (1) Student t statistic and random variable of the Student t distribution
(2) A period of time in a time series model (appears in subscripts)

t_α — Critical value for the t statistic (random variable); represents that value exceeded α proportion of the times (that is, with a probability of α) by t (values are obtained from Appendix B)

V — Test statistic for the Wilcoxon signed-rank test for matched-pairs sampling; represents the sum of ranks for positive matched-pairs differences

V_t — Smoothed data value for period t: used in two-parameter exponential smoothing

W — Test statistic for the Wilcoxon two-sample, rank-sum test; represents the sum of the ranks of observations in the samples from population A

X — (1) An observation of a sample or a population elementary unit
(2) A random variable (many other letters are also used for this purpose)
(3) The independent variable in simple regression analysis

$\bar{X}$ — Sample mean

$\bar{\bar{X}}$ — Grand mean; used in calculating the F statistic for:
(1) one-factor analysis of variance
(2) two-factor analysis of variance

$X_1, X_2, X_3, \ldots$ — (1) Observations of elementary units in a sample or population; subscripts denote sequence positions

(2) Successive class interval midpoints; used in calculating the sample mean or standard deviation from grouped data
(3) Independent variables in multiple regression analysis

$\bar{X}_A, \bar{X}_B$ — Means of samples taken from populations A or B; used in two-sample hypothesis tests

X_{Ai}, X_{Bi} — Sample observations for elementary units in the ith matched pair taken from population A or B; used in two-sample inferences

X_i — Midpoint of ith class interval

$\bar{X}_{i\cdot}$ — Sample mean for the ith row in an analysis-of-variance layout; used in calculating the sum of squares for the second factor

$\bar{X}_j$ — Mean of the observations in the jth sample group; used in calculating the F statistic for one-factor analysis of variance

$\bar{X}_{\cdot j}$ — Sample mean for the jth column in an analysis-of-variance layout; used in calculating the sum of squares for the second factor

X_{ij} — Sample observation number i of the jth sample group; used in calculating the F statistic for analysis of variance

x — (1) Dummy variable for the random variable X (ordinarily, lower-case letters are used)
(2) Percentile value for the normal distribution

Y — Dependent variable in regression analysis

$\hat{Y}(X)$ — Represents values for the dependent variable Y calculated from the estimated regression line using specific levels for the independent variable X

Y_t — The total time series in the classical model

z — Normal deviate; measures the number of standard deviations separating a value from the mean

z_α — Value for the critical normal deviate corresponding to a tail area under the standard normal curve that is equal to α

APPENDIX A
Areas Under the Standard Normal Curve

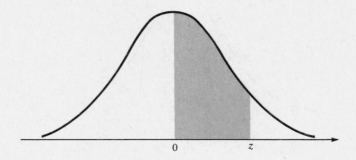

The following table provides the area between the mean and normal deviate value z.

Normal deviate z	.00	.01	.02	.03	.04	.05	.06	.07	.08	.09
0.0	.0000	.0040	.0080	.0120	.0160	.0199	.0239	.0279	.0319	.0359
0.1	.0398	.0438	.0478	.0517	.0557	.0596	.0636	.0675	.0714	.0753
0.2	.0793	.0832	.0871	.0910	.0948	.0987	.1026	.1064	.1103	.1141
0.3	.1179	.1217	.1255	.1293	.1331	.1368	.1406	.1443	.1480	.1517
0.4	.1554	.1591	.1628	.1664	.1700	.1736	.1772	.1808	.1844	.1879
0.5	.1915	.1950	.1985	.2019	.2054	.2088	.2123	.2157	.2190	.2224
0.6	.2257	.2291	.2324	.2357	.2389	.2422	.2454	.2486	.2518	.2549
0.7	.2580	.2612	.2642	.2673	.2704	.2734	.2764	.2794	.2823	.2852
0.8	.2881	.2910	.2939	.2967	.2995	.3023	.3051	.3078	.3106	.3133
0.9	.3159	.3186	.3212	.3238	.3264	.3289	.3315	.3340	.3365	.3389
1.0	.3413	.3438	.3461	.3485	.3508	.3531	.3554	.3577	.3599	.3621
1.1	.3643	.3665	.3686	.3708	.3729	.3749	.3770	.3790	.3810	.3830
1.2	.3849	.3869	.3888	.3907	.3925	.3944	.3962	.3980	.3997	.4015
1.3	.4032	.4049	.4066	.4082	.4099	.4115	.4131	.4147	.4162	.4177
1.4	.4192	.4207	.4222	.4236	.4251	.4265	.4279	.4292	.4306	.4319
1.5	.4332	.4345	.4357	.4370	.4382	.4394	.4406	.4418	.4429	.4441
1.6	.4452	.4463	.4474	.4484	.4495	.4505	.4515	.4525	.4535	.4545
1.7	.4554	.4564	.4573	.4582	.4591	.4599	.4608	.4616	.4625	.4633
1.8	.4641	.4649	.4656	.4664	.4671	.4678	.4686	.4693	.4699	.4706
1.9	.4713	.4719	.4726	.4732	.4738	.4744	.4750	.4756	.4761	.4767
2.0	.4772	.4778	.4783	.4788	.4793	.4798	.4803	.4808	.4812	.4817
2.1	.4821	.4826	.4830	.4834	.4838	.4842	.4846	.4850	.4854	.4857
2.2	.4861	.4864	.4868	.4871	.4875	.4878	.4881	.4884	.4887	.4890
2.3	.4893	.4896	.4898	.4901	.4904	.4906	.4909	.4911	.4913	.4916
2.4	.4918	.4920	.4922	.4925	.4927	.4929	.4931	.4932	.4934	.4936
2.5	.4938	.4940	.4941	.4943	.4945	.4946	.4948	.4949	.4951	.4952
2.6	.4953	.4955	.4956	.4957	.4959	.4960	.4961	.4962	.4963	.4964
2.7	.4965	.4966	.4967	.4968	.4969	.4970	.4971	.4972	.4973	.4974
2.8	.4974	.4975	.4976	.4977	.4977	.4978	.4979	.4979	.4980	.4981
2.9	.4981	.4982	.4982	.4983	.4984	.4984	.4985	.4985	.4986	.4986
3.0	.49865	.4987	.4987	.4988	.4988	.4989	.4989	.4989	.4990	.4990
4.0	.49997									

APPENDIX B
Student t Distribution

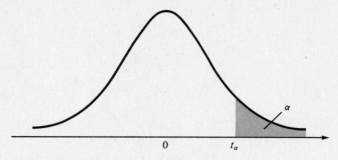

The following table provides the values of t_α that correspond to a given upper-tail area α and a specified number of degrees of freedom.

Degrees of freedom	Upper-tail area α									
	.4	.25	.1	.05	.025	.01	.005	.0025	.001	.0005
1	0.325	1.000	3.078	6.314	12.706	31.821	63.657	127.32	318.31	636.62
2	.289	.816	1.886	2.920	4.303	6.965	9.925	14.089	22.327	31.598
3	.277	.765	1.638	2.353	3.182	4.541	5.841	7.453	10.214	12.924
4	.271	.741	1.533	2.132	2.776	3.747	4.604	5.598	7.173	8.610
5	0.267	0.727	1.476	2.015	2.571	3.365	4.032	4.773	5.893	6.869
6	.265	.718	1.440	1.943	2.447	3.143	3.707	4.317	5.208	5.959
7	.263	.711	1.415	1.895	2.365	2.998	3.499	4.029	4.785	5.408
8	.262	.706	1.397	1.860	2.306	2.896	3.355	3.833	4.501	5.041
9	.261	.703	1.383	1.833	2.262	2.821	3.250	3.690	4.297	4.781
10	0.260	0.700	1.372	1.812	2.228	2.764	3.169	3.581	4.144	4.587
11	.260	.697	1.363	1.796	2.201	2.718	3.106	3.497	4.025	4.437
12	.259	.695	1.356	1.782	2.179	2.681	3.055	3.428	3.930	4.318
13	.259	.694	1.350	1.771	2.160	2.650	3.012	3.372	3.852	4.221
14	.258	.692	1.345	1.761	2.145	2.624	2.977	3.326	3.787	4.140
15	0.258	0.691	1.341	1.753	2.131	2.602	2.947	3.286	3.733	4.073
16	.258	.690	1.337	1.746	2.120	2.583	2.921	3.252	3.686	4.015
17	.257	.689	1.333	1.740	2.110	2.567	2.898	3.222	3.646	3.965
18	.257	.688	1.330	1.734	2.101	2.552	2.878	3.197	3.610	3.922
19	.257	.688	1.328	1.729	2.093	2.539	2.861	3.174	3.579	3.883
20	0.257	0.687	1.325	1.725	2.086	2.528	2.845	3.153	3.552	3.850
21	.257	.686	1.323	1.721	2.080	2.518	2.831	3.135	3.527	3.819
22	.256	.686	1.321	1.717	2.074	2.508	2.819	3.119	3.505	3.792
23	.256	.685	1.319	1.714	2.069	2.500	2.807	3.104	3.485	3.767
24	.256	.685	1.318	1.711	2.064	2.492	2.797	3.091	3.467	3.745
25	0.256	0.684	1.316	1.708	2.060	2.485	2.787	3.078	3.450	3.725
26	.256	.684	1.315	1.706	2.056	2.479	2.779	3.067	3.435	3.707
27	.256	.684	1.314	1.703	2.052	2.473	2.771	3.057	3.421	3.690
28	.256	.683	1.313	1.701	2.048	2.467	2.763	3.047	3.408	3.674
29	.256	.683	1.311	1.699	2.045	2.462	2.756	3.038	3.396	3.659
30	0.256	0.683	1.310	1.697	2.042	2.457	2.750	3.030	3.385	3.646
40	.255	.681	1.303	1.684	2.021	2.423	2.704	2.971	3.307	3.551
60	.254	.679	1.296	1.671	2.000	2.390	2.660	2.915	3.232	3.460
120	.254	.677	1.289	1.658	1.980	2.358	2.617	2.860	3.160	3.373
∞	.253	.674	1.282	1.645	1.960	2.326	2.576	2.807	3.090	3.291

Source: E. S. Pearson and H. O. Hartley, *Biometrika Tables for Statisticians*, Vol. I. London: Cambridge University Press, 1966. Partly derived from Table III of Fisher and Yates, *Statistical Tables for Biological, Agricultural and Medical Research*, published by Longman Group Ltd., London (previously published by Oliver & Boyd, Edinburgh, 1963). Reproduced with permission of the authors and publishers.

APPENDIX C
Chi-Square Distribution

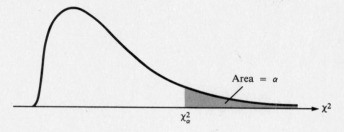

Area = α

χ^2_α χ^2

The following table provides the values of χ^2_α that correspond to a given upper-tail area α and a specified number of degrees of freedom.

Degrees of freedom	Upper-tail area α													
	.99	.98	.95	.90	.80	.70	.50	.30	.20	.10	.05	.02	.01	.001
1	.03157	.03628	.00393	.0158	.0642	.148	.455	1.074	1.642	2.706	3.841	5.412	6.635	10.827
2	.0201	.0404	.103	.211	.446	.713	1.386	2.408	3.219	4.605	5.991	7.824	9.210	13.815
3	.115	.185	.352	.584	1.005	1.424	2.366	3.665	4.642	6.251	7.815	9.837	11.345	16.268
4	.297	.429	.711	1.064	1.649	2.195	3.357	4.878	5.989	7.779	9.488	11.668	13.277	18.465
5	.554	.752	1.145	1.610	2.343	3.000	4.351	6.064	7.289	9.236	11.070	13.388	15.086	20.517
6	.872	1.134	1.635	2.204	3.070	3.828	5.348	7.231	8.558	10.645	12.592	15.033	16.812	22.457
7	1.239	1.564	2.167	2.833	3.822	4.671	6.346	8.383	9.803	12.017	14.067	16.622	18.475	24.322
8	1.646	2.032	2.733	3.490	4.594	5.527	7.344	9.524	11.030	13.362	15.507	18.168	20.090	26.125
9	2.088	2.532	3.325	4.168	5.380	6.393	8.343	10.656	12.242	14.684	16.919	19.679	21.666	27.877
10	2.558	3.059	3.940	4.865	6.179	7.267	9.342	11.781	13.442	15.987	18.307	21.161	23.209	29.588
11	3.053	3.609	4.575	5.578	6.989	8.148	10.341	12.899	14.631	17.275	19.675	22.618	24.725	31.264
12	3.571	4.178	5.226	6.304	7.807	9.034	11.340	14.011	15.812	18.549	21.026	24.054	26.217	32.909
13	4.107	4.765	5.892	7.042	8.634	9.926	12.340	15.119	16.985	19.812	22.362	25.472	27.688	34.528
14	4.660	5.368	6.571	7.790	9.467	10.821	13.339	16.222	18.151	21.064	23.685	26.873	29.141	36.123
15	5.229	5.985	7.261	8.547	10.307	11.721	14.339	17.322	19.311	22.307	24.996	28.259	30.578	37.697
16	5.812	6.614	7.962	9.312	11.152	12.624	15.338	18.418	20.465	23.542	26.296	29.633	32.000	39.252
17	6.408	7.255	8.672	10.085	12.002	13.531	16.338	19.511	21.615	24.769	27.587	30.995	33.409	40.790
18	7.015	7.906	9.390	10.865	12.857	14.440	17.338	20.601	22.760	25.989	28.869	32.346	34.805	42.312
19	7.633	8.567	10.117	11.651	13.716	15.352	18.338	21.689	23.900	27.204	30.144	33.687	36.191	43.820
20	8.260	9.237	10.851	12.443	14.578	16.266	19.337	22.775	25.038	28.412	31.410	35.020	37.566	45.315
21	8.897	9.915	11.591	13.240	15.445	17.182	20.337	23.858	26.171	29.615	32.671	36.343	38.932	46.797
22	9.542	10.600	12.338	14.041	16.314	18.101	21.337	24.939	27.301	30.813	33.924	37.659	40.289	48.268
23	10.196	11.293	13.091	14.848	17.187	19.021	22.337	26.018	28.429	32.007	35.172	38.968	41.638	49.728
24	10.856	11.992	13.848	15.659	18.062	19.943	23.337	27.096	29.553	33.196	36.415	40.270	42.980	51.179
25	11.524	12.697	14.611	16.473	18.940	20.867	24.337	28.172	30.675	34.382	37.652	41.566	44.314	52.620
26	12.198	13.409	15.379	17.292	19.820	21.792	25.336	29.246	31.795	35.563	38.885	42.856	45.642	54.052
27	12.879	14.125	16.151	18.114	20.703	22.719	26.336	30.319	32.912	36.741	40.113	44.140	46.963	55.476
28	13.565	14.847	16.928	18.939	21.588	23.647	27.336	31.391	34.027	37.916	41.337	45.419	48.278	56.893
29	14.256	15.574	17.708	19.768	22.475	24.577	28.336	32.461	35.139	39.087	42.557	46.693	49.588	58.302
30	14.953	16.306	18.493	20.599	23.364	25.508	29.336	33.530	36.250	40.256	43.773	47.962	50.892	59.703

Source: From Table IV of Fisher and Yates, *Statistical Tables for Biological, Agricultural and Medical Research*, published by Longman Group Ltd., London (previously published by Oliver & Boyd, Edinburgh, 1963). Reproduced with permission of the authors and publishers.

APPENDIX D
F Distribution

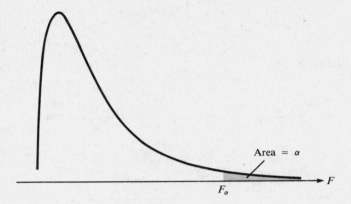

Area = α

F_α

F

The following table provides the values of F_z that correspond to a given upper-tail area α and a specified degrees of freedom pair. The values of $F_{.05}$ are in lightface type, while those for $F_{.01}$ are given in boldface type.

Degrees of freedom for denominator	\multicolumn{12}{c}{Degrees of freedom for numerator}
	1	2	3	4	5	6	7	8	9	10	11	12
1	161	200	216	225	230	234	237	239	241	242	243	244
	4,052	**4,999**	**5,403**	**5,625**	**5,764**	**5,859**	**5,928**	**5,981**	**6,022**	**6,056**	**6,082**	**6,106**
2	18.51	19.00	19.16	19.25	19.30	19.33	19.36	19.37	19.38	19.39	19.40	19.41
	98.49	**99.01**	**99.17**	**99.25**	**99.30**	**99.33**	**99.34**	**99.36**	**99.38**	**99.40**	**99.41**	**99.42**
3	10.13	9.55	9.28	9.12	9.01	8.94	8.88	8.84	8.81	8.78	8.76	8.74
	34.12	**30.81**	**29.46**	**28.71**	**28.24**	**27.91**	**27.67**	**27.49**	**27.34**	**27.23**	**27.13**	**27.05**
4	7.71	6.94	6.59	6.39	6.26	6.16	6.09	6.04	6.00	5.96	5.93	5.91
	21.20	**18.00**	**16.69**	**15.98**	**15.52**	**15.21**	**14.98**	**14.80**	**14.66**	**14.54**	**14.45**	**14.37**
5	6.61	5.79	5.41	5.19	5.05	4.95	4.88	4.82	4.78	4.74	4.70	4.68
	16.26	**13.27**	**12.06**	**11.39**	**10.97**	**10.67**	**10.45**	**10.27**	**10.15**	**10.05**	**9.96**	**9.89**
6	5.99	5.14	4.76	4.53	4.39	4.28	4.21	4.15	4.10	4.06	4.03	4.00
	13.74	**10.92**	**9.78**	**9.15**	**8.75**	**8.47**	**8.26**	**8.10**	**7.98**	**7.87**	**7.79**	**7.72**
7	5.59	4.74	4.35	4.12	3.97	3.87	3.79	3.73	3.68	3.63	3.60	3.57
	12.25	**9.55**	**8.45**	**7.85**	**7.46**	**7.19**	**7.00**	**6.84**	**6.71**	**6.62**	**6.54**	**6.47**
8	5.32	4.46	4.07	3.84	3.69	3.58	3.50	3.44	3.39	3.34	3.31	3.28
	11.26	**8.65**	**7.59**	**7.01**	**6.63**	**6.37**	**6.19**	**6.03**	**5.91**	**5.82**	**5.74**	**5.67**
9	5.12	4.26	3.86	3.63	3.48	3.37	3.29	3.23	3.18	3.13	3.10	3.07
	10.56	**8.02**	**6.99**	**6.42**	**6.06**	**5.80**	**5.62**	**5.47**	**5.35**	**5.26**	**5.18**	**5.11**
10	4.96	4.10	3.71	3.48	3.33	3.22	3.14	3.07	3.02	2.97	2.94	2.91
	10.04	**7.56**	**6.55**	**5.99**	**5.64**	**5.39**	**5.21**	**5.06**	**4.95**	**4.85**	**4.78**	**4.71**
11	4.84	3.98	3.59	3.36	3.20	3.09	3.01	2.95	2.90	2.86	2.82	2.79
	9.65	**7.20**	**6.22**	**5.67**	**5.32**	**5.07**	**4.88**	**4.74**	**4.63**	**4.54**	**4.46**	**4.40**
12	4.75	3.89	3.49	3.26	3.11	3.00	2.92	2.85	2.80	2.76	2.72	2.69
	9.33	**6.93**	**5.95**	**5.41**	**5.06**	**4.82**	**4.65**	**4.50**	**4.39**	**4.30**	**4.22**	**4.16**
13	4.67	3.80	3.41	3.18	3.02	2.92	2.84	2.77	2.72	2.67	2.63	2.60
	9.07	**6.70**	**5.74**	**5.20**	**4.86**	**4.62**	**4.44**	**4.30**	**4.19**	**4.10**	**4.02**	**3.96**
14	4.60	3.74	3.34	3.11	2.96	2.85	2.77	2.70	2.65	2.60	2.56	2.53
	8.86	**6.51**	**5.56**	**5.03**	**4.69**	**4.46**	**4.28**	**4.14**	**4.03**	**3.94**	**3.86**	**3.80**
15	4.54	3.68	3.29	3.06	2.90	2.79	2.70	2.64	2.59	2.55	2.51	2.48
	8.68	**6.36**	**5.42**	**4.89**	**4.56**	**4.32**	**4.14**	**4.00**	**3.89**	**3.80**	**3.73**	**3.67**
16	4.49	3.63	3.24	3.01	2.85	2.74	2.66	2.59	2.54	2.49	2.45	2.42
	8.53	**6.23**	**5.29**	**4.77**	**4.44**	**4.20**	**4.03**	**3.89**	**3.78**	**3.69**	**3.61**	**3.55**
17	4.45	3.59	3.20	2.96	2.81	2.70	2.62	2.55	2.50	2.45	2.41	2.38
	8.40	**6.11**	**5.18**	**4.67**	**4.34**	**4.10**	**3.93**	**3.79**	**3.68**	**3.59**	**3.52**	**3.45**

Appendix D (*continued*)

Degrees of freedom for denominator	Degrees of freedom for numerator											
	1	2	3	4	5	6	7	8	9	10	11	12
18	4.41	3.55	3.16	2.93	2.77	2.66	2.58	2.51	2.46	2.41	2.37	2.34
	8.28	**6.01**	**5.09**	**4.58**	**4.25**	**4.01**	**3.85**	**3.71**	**3.60**	**3.51**	**3.44**	**3.37**
19	4.38	3.52	3.13	2.90	2.74	2.63	2.55	2.48	2.43	2.38	2.34	2.31
	8.18	**5.93**	**5.01**	**4.50**	**4.17**	**3.94**	**3.77**	**3.63**	**3.52**	**3.43**	**3.36**	**3.30**
20	4.35	3.49	3.10	2.87	2.71	2.60	2.52	2.45	2.40	2.35	2.31	2.28
	8.10	**5.85**	**4.94**	**4.43**	**4.10**	**3.87**	**3.71**	**3.56**	**3.45**	**3.37**	**3.30**	**3.23**
21	4.32	3.47	3.07	2.84	2.68	2.57	2.49	2.42	2.37	2.32	2.28	2.25
	8.02	**5.78**	**4.87**	**4.37**	**4.04**	**3.81**	**3.65**	**3.51**	**3.40**	**3.31**	**3.24**	**3.17**
22	4.30	3.44	3.05	2.82	2.66	2.55	2.47	2.40	2.35	2.30	2.26	2.23
	7.94	**5.72**	**4.82**	**4.41**	**3.99**	**3.76**	**3.59**	**3.45**	**3.35**	**3.26**	**3.18**	**3.12**
23	4.28	3.42	3.03	2.80	2.64	2.53	2.45	2.38	2.32	2.28	2.24	2.20
	7.88	**5.66**	**4.76**	**4.26**	**3.94**	**3.71**	**3.54**	**3.41**	**3.30**	**3.21**	**3.14**	**3.07**
24	4.26	3.40	3.01	2.78	2.62	2.51	2.43	2.36	2.30	2.26	2.22	2.18
	7.82	**5.61**	**4.72**	**4.22**	**3.90**	**3.67**	**3.50**	**3.36**	**3.25**	**3.17**	**3.09**	**3.03**
25	4.24	3.38	2.99	2.76	2.60	2.49	2.41	2.34	2.28	2.24	2.20	2.16
	7.77	**5.57**	**4.68**	**4.18**	**3.86**	**3.63**	**3.46**	**3.32**	**3.21**	**3.13**	**3.05**	**2.99**
26	4.22	3.37	2.89	2.74	2.59	2.47	2.39	2.32	2.27	2.22	2.18	2.15
	7.72	**5.53**	**4.64**	**4.14**	**3.82**	**3.59**	**3.42**	**3.29**	**3.17**	**3.09**	**3.02**	**2.96**
27	4.21	3.35	2.96	2.73	2.57	2.46	2.37	2.30	2.25	2.20	2.16	2.13
	7.68	**5.49**	**4.60**	**4.11**	**3.79**	**3.56**	**3.39**	**3.26**	**3.14**	**3.06**	**2.98**	**2.93**
28	4.20	3.34	2.95	2.71	2.56	2.44	2.36	2.29	2.24	2.19	2.15	2.12
	7.64	**5.45**	**4.57**	**4.07**	**3.76**	**3.53**	**3.36**	**3.23**	**3.11**	**3.03**	**2.95**	**2.90**
29	4.18	3.33	2.93	2.70	2.54	2.43	2.35	2.28	2.22	2.18	2.14	2.10
	7.60	**5.52**	**4.54**	**4.04**	**3.73**	**3.50**	**3.33**	**3.20**	**3.08**	**3.00**	**2.92**	**2.87**
30	4.17	3.32	2.92	2.69	2.53	2.43	2.34	2.27	2.21	2.16	2.12	2.09
	7.56	**5.39**	**4.51**	**4.02**	**3.70**	**3.47**	**3.30**	**3.17**	**3.06**	**2.98**	**2.90**	**2.84**
32	4.15	3.30	2.90	2.67	2.51	2.40	2.32	2.25	2.19	2.14	2.10	2.07
	7.50	**5.34**	**4.46**	**3.97**	**3.66**	**3.42**	**3.25**	**3.12**	**3.01**	**2.94**	**2.86**	**2.80**
34	4.13	3.28	2.88	2.65	2.49	2.38	2.30	2.23	2.17	2.12	2.08	2.05
	7.44	**5.29**	**4.42**	**3.93**	**3.61**	**3.38**	**3.21**	**3.08**	**2.97**	**2.89**	**2.82**	**2.76**
36	4.11	3.26	2.86	2.63	2.48	2.36	2.28	2.21	2.15	2.10	2.06	2.03
	7.39	**5.25**	**4.38**	**3.89**	**3.58**	**3.35**	**3.18**	**3.04**	**2.94**	**2.86**	**2.78**	**2.72**
38	4.10	3.25	2.85	2.62	2.46	2.35	2.26	2.19	2.14	2.09	2.05	2.02
	7.35	**5.21**	**4.34**	**3.86**	**3.54**	**3.32**	**3.15**	**3.02**	**2.91**	**2.82**	**2.75**	**2.69**
40	4.08	3.23	2.84	2.61	2.45	2.34	2.25	2.18	2.12	2.08	2.04	2.00
	7.31	**5.18**	**4.31**	**3.83**	**3.51**	**3.29**	**3.12**	**2.99**	**2.88**	**2.80**	**2.73**	**2.66**

Source: Reprinted by permission from *Statistical Methods* by George W. Snedecor and William G. Cochran, 7th ed. © 1980 by Iowa State University Press, Ames, Iowa 50010.

INDEX

Actual frequency, 287
Addition law, general, 47
Addition law for mutually exclusive events, 46
Aggregate price indexes
unweighted, 247–248
weighted, 248–249
Alternative hypothesis, 180
Analysis of variance, 307–314
(*see also* ANOVA)
sums of squares, 308–309
test statistic, 309, 310
two-way, 311–314
ANOVA table, 310–311
Areas, normal curve, 140–144
finding, 141
Arithmetic mean, 24–25
Average, four-quarter, 233 (*see also* Mean)

Bayes' Theorem, 90, 91, 92
Bernoulli process, 121, 122, 148
binomial distribution, 129
Bias
prestige, 3
sampling, 3
Bias of nonresponse, 3
Bimodal distribution, 27
Binomial distribution, 121–124, 126–127, 128, 129
sampling distribution of the proportion, 128–129
Binomial formula, 121, 122, 123
Binomial probabilities, 121–129
Block, 311
Block design, randomized, 311
Blocking variable, 311
Blocks, treatments sum of squares, 312
Blocks mean square, 312, 313
Blocks sum of squares, 312, 313

Census, 2
Centered moving average, 232
Central limit theorem, 145, 148
Central tendency, measure of, 24–25
median and mode, 25–26
population distributions, 26–27
Certain event, 41
Chi-square, 286–289
distribution, 288, 289, 310
test for independence, 286–289
test statistic, 288, 289
for the variance, 291
Class frequency, 6
Class intervals, 5
Coefficient of determination, 207–208
Collectively exhaustive events, 44
union of, 45
Combinations, 88, 89
computing probabilities using, 89
Combined sample proportion, 263
Complementary events, 45
probabilities for, 47
Composite events, 39–40
Composite hypothesis, 181
Composite probability, 126–127

Compound event, joint event, 43
Compound events, 42–45
intersection of, 42–43
probabilities for, 46–48
joint probability for, 46
Conditional probability, 60, 63, 65
computing, 62
identity, 61
Conditional result probability, 91, 92
Confidence interval estimates (*see* Interval estimates)
Consistent estimator, 164
Contingency table, 287
Continuity correction, 148
Continuous random variables, 140
Control group, 5, 256
Controlled experiment, 5, 256
Convenience sample, 3
Correlation analysis, 202, 206–208
Correlation coefficient, sample, 206
Count-and-divide method, 40–41, 46, 60–61, 84
Critical normal deviate, 186, 187
Critical value, 181
Cumulative frequency, 8
Cumulative frequency distribution, 9
Cumulative probability, 126
Cumulative relative frequency, 8–9
Cyclical movement, 229
time-series model, 229–234

Data
grouped, 25
qualitative, 2
quantitative, 2
raw, 6, 202
statistical, 2
describing, 5–10
Data point, single, 2
Decision rules, 181–185
Deductive statistics, 2
Degrees of freedom, 310, 314
Dependent variable, 202
Descriptive statistics, 1–2
Deviation, 27–28
Deviations, regression line, 204
Distribution
bimodal, 27
binomial, 121–129
exponential, 10
hypergeometric, 129
negatively skewed, 10, 26
normal, 10, 138–149
positively skewed, 10, 26
sampling
of the mean, 108–110
of the grand mean, 145–147
of the proportion, 128–129
symmetrical, 26
uniform, 10
Dummy variable, 107

Efficient estimator, 164
Elementary events, 38, 41, 66

Elementary units, 2
Error mean square, ANOVA table, 313
Error probabilities, 181–183
Error sum of squares, 308, 309, 313
Estimated multiple regression equation, 208
Estimated partial regression coefficients, 208–209
Estimated regression coefficients, 204
Estimated regression equation, 203
values for *Y*, 205
Estimated regression plane, 208, 209
Estimates, 164
interval, 165
point, 165
Estimation, statistical, 164–171
Estimators, 164
Event relationships (*see also* Events)
collectively exhaustive events, 44, 45
complementary events, 45, 47
dependent events, 45
independent events, 45, 48, 63
intersection, 42
joint events, 43
mutually exclusive events, 43, 47
union, 42
Event, 38
certain, 41
given, 60
impossible, 40, 41
joint, 43
Event fork, 64
Events, 64
collectively exhaustive, 44–45
addition law and, 46
complementary, 45, 47
component, 42
composite, 39
compound, 42–45
dependent, 45, 63
elementary, 38, 41
independent, 45, 63
joint, 43
mutually exclusive, 43, 46–47
Event sets, 40
Expected frequency, 287
Expected value, 106–109
Experimental group, 5, 256
Experimental layout, 307–308
Exponential distribution, 10
Exponential smoothing, 235–237 (*see also* references for Smoothed, Smoothing)
Extrapolation, 232 (*see also* Forecast)

Factorials, 86, 87
F Distribution, 310
Family, 124
Finite population correction factor, 110, 129
Forecast, 231–232
Four-quarter moving average, 232, 233
Fractile, 30
Frequency
actual, 287
class, 6
expected, 287
long-run, 40

Frequency curve, 10
Frequency distribution, 6–10
  cumulative, 9
  cumulative relative, 8
  sample, 6
  population, 6
  of qualitative observations, 8
  relative, 8
Frequency polygon, 6

General addition law, 47
General multiplication law, 63, 66
Grand mean, 308, 312
Grouped data, 25

Histogram, 6
Hypergeometric distribution, 129
Hyperplane, multiple regression, 211
Hypothesis
  alternative, 180
  composite, 181
  null, 180–181
  simple, 181
Hypothesis testing, 180 (*see also* Test,
  Testing)
  difference in means, 258
  steps in, 185–187

Impossible event, 40, 41
Independence, chi-square test for, 286–289
Independent events, multiplication law
  for, 48
Independent random samples, 256
  and Wilcoxon rank-sum test, 264
Independent samples, 256, 259, 261
Independent sampling, 5
Independent variable, 202
Index numbers, 247–250
Inductive statistics, 2
Inferential statistics, 1–2, 164
Interquartile range, 31
Intersection, 42–43
  of mutually exclusive events, 43
  union and, 43
Interval estimates, 165
  of the mean, 165–168
  of the proportion, 170–171
Interval probability, 126–127
Intervals, class, 6
Irregular variations, time-series model, 229

Joint event, 43
Joint probability
  for compound events, 46
  for independent events, 48, 286
    multiplication law for, 48
Joint probability table, 62, 92, 93
Judgment sample, 3

Laspeyres index, 248, 249
Location, normal curve, 138
Long-run average, 107
Long-run frequency, 40

Lower tail, 143
Lower-tailed test, 183, 184, 186, 187,
  189, 190, 258, 263, 291

Matched pairs
  normal deviate for, 259
  two populations, 256
Matched-pairs sampling, 5
Maximum likelihood estimator, 164
Mean, 24–25
  arithmetic, 24–25
  computing, 24–25
  confidence interval estimate of the, 170
  grand, 308, 312
  interval estimates of the, 165–168
  normal curve of the, 138, 142–144
  population, 24
  sample, 24, 308, 312
  and standard deviation, 29
Means
  analysis of variance, 307–314
  comparing, 256–262
    confidence interval estimate, 256, 257
    small sample, 260, 263
Mean square
  blocks, 312, 313
  error, 309–310, 313
  treatments, 309–310
Measure of central tendency
  arithmetic mean, 24–25
  expected value, 106
  median, 25–26
  mode, 25–26
  population distributions, 26–27
Measures of variability, 27–30
Median, 25–26
  normal curve, 138
  as percentile, 30
  sample, 25
Method of least squares, 204, 209, 231
Midpoint, 25
Mode, 25–27
  sample, 26
Moving average, 232, 235
  centered, 232
  four-quarter, 232
  twelve-month, 233
Multiple regression, 208–211
  equation, estimated, 208
  higher dimensional, 211
  normal equations, 211
Multiplication law for independent events,
  48, 123
Multiplicative model (*see* Time-series
  analysis, basic model)
Mutually exclusive events, 43
  addition law for, 46

Negatively skewed distribution, 10, 26
Nonparametric statistics, 256, 264
Nonresponse, bias of, 3
Nonsampling error, 3
Normal approximation, 147–149
Normal curve, 138–145
  percentiles, 144

sampling distribution of the mean,
  145–147
  table, 141–144
Normal deviate, 140
  comparing two proportions, 263
  for independent samples, 259
  for matched pairs, 259
  of the proportion, 148
  of X, 146
  value, normal curve, 167
  for Wilcoxon rank-sum test, 264
  for Wilcoxon signed-rank test, 265
  z, 258
Normal distribution, 10
  confidence interval, 166–168
Normal equations, 209, 210
Null hypothesis, 180–181
  analysis of variance, 307
  establishing, 185

Objective probabilities, 41
Observation, 2
One-sided test, 181

Paasche index, 248–249
Pairs, matched, 257, 259–260
Parametric statistics, 264
Percentile, 30
Percentiles, normal population, 144
Permutations, 86–87, 88
Point estimate, 165
Population, 2
  finite, correction factor, 110
  large, 2
  parameters, 24
  partly inaccessible, 2–3
  qualitative, 2
  quantitative, 2
  size, 28
Population mean, 24
Population proportion, 30
Population variance, 28
Populations
  categorized, 10
  comparison of, 5
  independent random samples, 256
  matched pairs (samples), 256
  two-sample comparisons, 256–266
Positively skewed distribution, 10, 26
Posterior probability, 90–91, 92
Prestige bias, 3
Price indexes
  aggregate, 247–249
  deflating time series, 249–250
Principle of multiplication, 84
  factorial, 86
  permutation, 86, 87
  sequences, 86
Prior probability, 90, 92
Probabilities
  for compound events, 46–48
  computing using combinations, 88, 89
Probability, 2, 38–48, 60–66
  composite, 126–127
  for compound events, 46–48

conditional, 60, 63
   computing, 62
conditional result, 91, 92
count-and-divide method, 40–41, 46,
   60–61, 84
cumulative, 126
interval, 126–127
joint
   elementary events, 66
   independent events, 286
   multiplication law, 48
   table, 62
marginal, 62
objective, 41
posterior, 90–91, 92
principle of multiplication, 84
prior, 90, 92
subjective, 41
unconditional, 60–63
upper-tail, 127
Probability density function, 140
Probability distribution, 104–106
   of X, 108
Probability mass function, 105
Probability tree, 64–66
Proportion, 30
   combined sample, 263
   confidence interval estimate of, 171
   critical values of, 190
   normal deviate of, 148
   population, 170–171
   sampling distribution of, 147–149
   testing with, 190
Proportions, comparing
   two populations, 263–264
   three or more populations, 289

Qualitative observations, 8
Qualitative population, 2
Qualitative variables, 286
Qualitative data, class intervals, 5
Quantitative population, 2
Quartiles, 30–31
   interquartile range, 31

Random experiment, 38
Randomized block design, 311
Random numbers, 3–4
Random samples, 3–5
Random samples, independent, 256
   and Wilcoxon rank-sum test, 264
Random variable, 106–108
Range, 27
Raw data, 6, 202
Rank-sum, 264
Regression, 202–211
   linear, 231
   simple, 208
Regression analysis, 202–206
   linear, 231–232
   multiple, 208–211
Regression coefficients
   estimated, 204
   estimated partial, 208–209

Regression equation
   estimated, 203
   estimated multiple, 208
   trend line for, 231
   and values for Y, 205
Regression line, 203
Regression plane, estimated, 208, 209
Relative frequency, 8
Relative frequency distribution, 8
Response variable, 307

Sample, 2
   convenience, 3
   judgment, 3
   random, 3
   selecting, 3–5
Sample coefficient of determination, 207–208
Sample correlation coefficient, 206–207
Sample distribution of the mean,
   normal curve, 145–147
Sample distribution of the proportion,
   147–149
Sample frequency distribution, 6
Sample mean, 24, 308, 312
Sample median, 25
Sample mode, 26
Sample proportion P, 30, 128
Sample size, 25, 146–147
Sample space, 38
Sample statistic, 24
Sample variance, 28
Samples
   use of, 2–3
   disadvantage of using, 3
   random, 5
   types of, 3, 5
Sampling
   independent, 5
   matched pairs, 5
   reasons for, 2–3
   replacement, 129
   without replacement, 129
Sampling bias, 3, 5
Sampling distribution, 108–109, 145
Sampling error, 3
Scatter diagram, 203
Seasonal fluctuation, 229
Seasonal index, 234, 235
Sequences, 86
Significance level, 186
Simple hypothesis, 181
Simple random sample, 5
Simple regression, 208
Smoothed time series, 231
Smoothed trend, 236, 237
Smoothed value, 236
Smoothing constant, 235, 236, 237
Standard deviation, 28–30, 107
   estimating, 290–291
Standard error, 164
Standard error of P, 129, 148
Standard error of the estimate, 205, 211
Standard error of $\bar{X}$, 109–110, 145–146
Statistical data, 2
   describing, 5–10

Statistical measures, summary, 24–31
Statistical procedures, selecting, 5
Statistical testing, 180–190
Statistics
   deductive, 2
   definition of, 1
   descriptive, 1–2
   inductive, 2
   inferential, 1–2, 164
   meaning and role of, 1–2
   nonparametric, 256
   purpose and evaluation, 1–10
   types of, 1–2
Stratified sample, 5
Student t distribution, 168–170, 189, 260,
   288, 310
Subjective probability, 41 (*see* Prior
   probability)
Subset, 43
Sum of squares, 308–309
   blocks, 312, 313
   error, 309, 313
   total, 308, 309
   treatments, 308, 312
Summary measures, 24–31
Symmetrical distribution, 26
Systematic random sample, 5

t Statistic (*see* Student t distribution)
Tail area, 182
Test
   lower-tailed, 183, 184, 185, 186, 187, 189,
     190, 258, 263, 291
   two-sided, 181, 185, 186, 187, 189, 190, 258,
     263, 291
   upper-tailed, 183, 184, 185, 186, 187, 189,
     190, 258, 263, 289, 291, 311
Testing
   with the proportion, 190
   standard steps, 185, 186–187
   statistical, 180–190
Test of the mean
   large sample, 185–189
   small sample, 189
Test statistic, 181, 186, 187, 258, 309, 310, 314
Time series, 229
Time-series analysis, 229–237
   basic model, 229–230
   cyclical fluctuation, 235
   exponential smoothing, 235–237
   irregular fluctuation, 235
   seasonal indexes, 234–235
Total sum of squares, 308, 309
Treatments sum of squares, 308, 312
Trend analysis, 230–233
Trend line, 229, 230, 231
   equations, 231
Trend-smoothing constant, 236
Trial, 85
Twelve-month moving average, 233
Two-sided test, 181, 185, 186, 187, 189, 190,
   258, 263, 291
Two-way analysis of variance, 311–314
Type I error, 181, 183, 185
   probability for, 186, 289
Type II error, 181, 183, 185

Unbiased estimator, 164
Unconditional probability, 60, 63
Uniform distribution, 10
Union, 42
    of collectively exhaustive events, 45
    and intersection, 43
Unions, addition law, 46–47
Upper-tailed test, 183, 184, 185, 186, 187, 189,
    190, 258, 263, 289, 291, 311

Variability, measures of, 27–29
Variable
    dependent, 202
    independent, 202
    response, 307
Variables, continuous random, 140
Variance, 28, 107, 109
    estimating, 290
    population, 28

sample, 28
testing, 291

Weighted aggregate price indexes, 248
Weighted average, 106
Wilcoxon rank-sum test, 264–265
Wilcoxon signed-rank test, 265–266

5
G 6
H 7
I 8
J 9